Adaptive

THE **ADAPTIVE** **READING EXPERIENCE** DESIGNED TO TRANSFORM THE WAY STUDENTS READ

More students earn **A's** and **B's** when they use McGraw-Hill Education **Adaptive** products.

SmartBook®

Proven to help students improve grades and study more efficiently, SmartBook contains the same content within the print book, but actively tailors that content to the needs of the individual. SmartBook's adaptive technology provides precise, personalized instruction on what the student should do next, guiding the student to master and remember key concepts, targeting gaps in knowledge and offering customized feedback, and driving the student toward comprehension and retention of the subject matter. Available on tablets, SmartBook puts learning at the student's fingertips—anywhere, anytime.

Over **8 billion questions** have been answered, making McGraw-Hill Education products more intelligent, reliable, and precise.

www.mheducation.com

STUDENTS WANT

SMARTBOOK®

95% of students reported **SmartBook** to be a more effective way of reading material.

100% of students want to use the Practice Quiz feature available within **SmartBook** to help them study.

100% of students reported having reliable access to off-campus wifi.

90% of students say they would purchase **SmartBook** over print alone.

95% of students reported that **SmartBook** would impact their study skills in a positive way.

Mc Graw Hill Education

*Findings based on 2015 focus group results administered by McGraw-Hill Education

information systems 4e

Paige Baltzan
Daniels College of Business
University of Denver

McGraw Hill Education

information systems 4e

CHIEF PRODUCT OFFICER, SVP PRODUCTS & MARKETS **G. SCOTT VIRKLER**

DIRECTOR **SCOTT DAVIDSON**

SENIOR BRAND MANAGER **WYATT MORRIS**

PRODUCT DEVELOPER: **KEVIN WHITE**

DIGITAL DEVELOPMENT EDITOR II **KEVIN WHITE**

SENIOR MARKETING MANAGER **TIFFANY RUSSELL**

DIRECTOR, CONTENT PRODUCTION **TERRI SCHIESL**

CONTENT PROJECT MANAGER **RICK HECKER**

MEDIA PROJECT MANAGER **EVAN ROBERTS**

BUYER **LAURA FULER**

DESIGN **MATT DIAMOND**

CONTENT LICENSING SPECIALIST : **ANN MARIE JANNETTE;** *TEXT:* **SHANNON MANDERSCHEID**

COMPOSITOR **SPI GLOBAL**

PRINTER **LSC COMMUNICATIONS**

M: INFORMATION SYSTEMS, FOURTH EDITION

This book is printed on acid-free paper.

1 2 3 4 5 6 7 8 9 LMN 21 20 19 18 17

ISBN 978-1-259-81429-7
MHID 1-259-81429-7

Library of Congress Control Number: 2016956416

www.mhhe.com

brief contents

contents

information systems 4e

© Fry Design Ltd/Getty Images

coming up

BUSINESS DRIVEN MIS

Most companies today rely heavily on the use of management information systems (MIS) to run various aspects of their businesses. Whether they need to order and ship goods, interact with customers, or conduct other business functions, management information systems are often the underlying infrastructure performing the activities. Management information systems allow companies to remain competitive in today's fast-paced world and especially when conducting business on the Internet. Organizations must adapt to technological advances and innovations to keep pace with today's rapidly changing environment. Their competitors certainly will!

No matter how exciting technology is, successful companies do not use it simply for its own sake. Companies should have a solid business reason for implementing technology. Using a technological solution just because it is available is not a good business strategy.

The purpose of Module 1 is to raise your awareness of the vast opportunities made possible by the tight correlation between business and technology. Business strategies and processes should always drive your technology choices. Although awareness of an emerging technology can sometimes lead us in new strategic directions, the role of information systems, for the most part, is to support existing business strategies and processes. ■

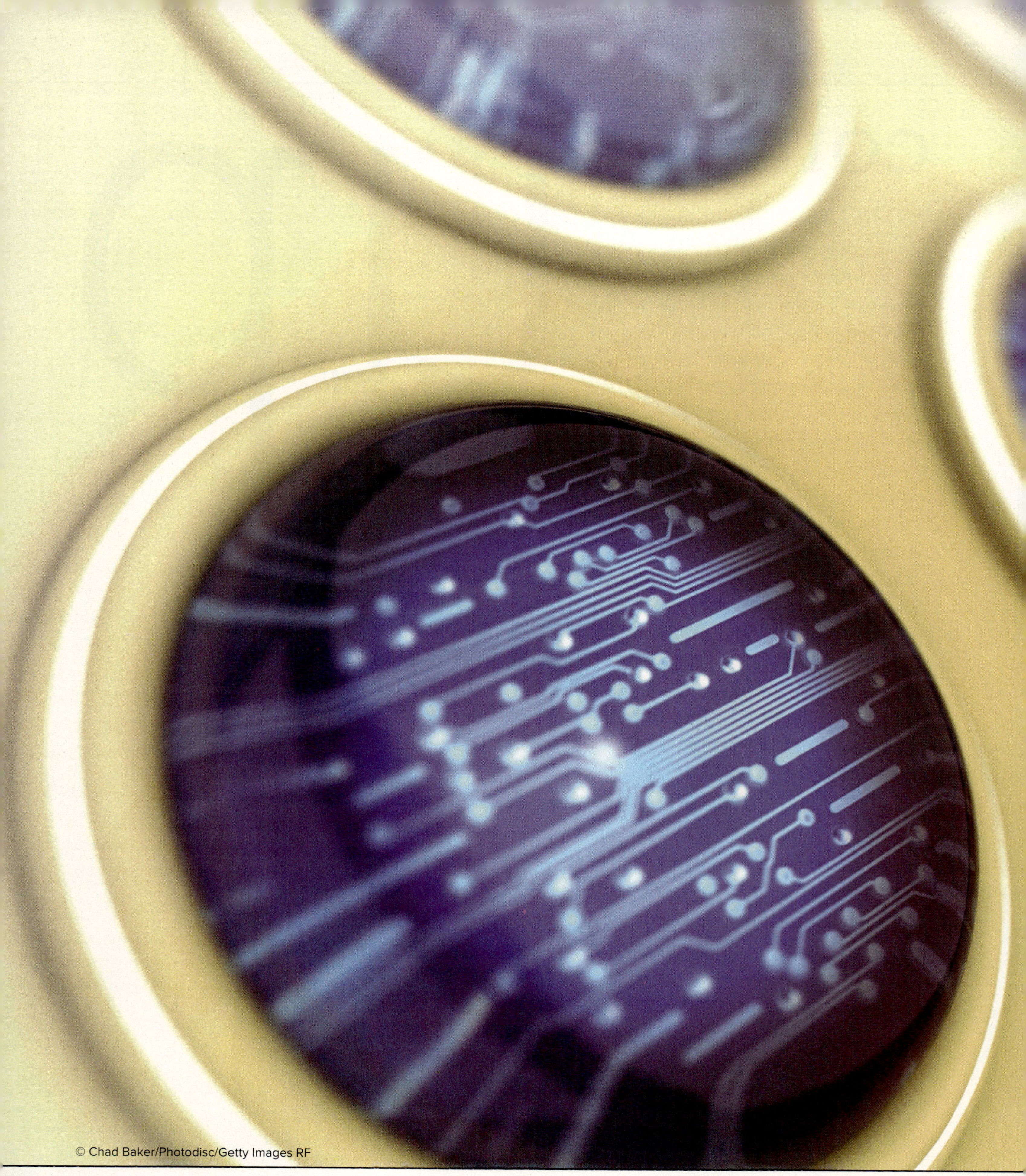

chapter one

management information systems: business driven MIS

what's in IT for me?

This chapter sets the stage for the textbook. It starts from ground zero by providing a clear description of what information is and how it fits into business operations, strategies, and systems. It provides an overview of how companies operate in competitive environments and why they must continually define and redefine their business strategies to create competitive advantages. Doing so allows them to survive and thrive. Information systems are key business enablers for successful operations in competitive environments.

You, as a business student, must understand the tight correlation between

continued on p. 6

CHAPTER OUTLINE

fact The confirmation or validation of an event or object.

information age The present time, during which infinite quantities of facts are widely available to anyone who can use a computer.

Internet of Things A world where interconnected, Internet-enabled devices or "things" can collect and share data without human intervention.

machine to machine (M2M) Devices that connect directly to other devices.

continued from p. 5

business and technology. You must first recognize information's role in daily business activities, and then understand how information supports and helps implement global business strategies and competitive advantages. After reading this chapter, you should have a solid understanding of business driven information systems and their role in managerial decision making and problem solving. ■

{SECTION 1.1} Business Driven MIS

LEARNING OUTCOMES

LO1.1 Describe the information age and the differences among data, information, business intelligence, and knowledge.

LO1.2 Identify the different departments in a company and why they must work together to achieve success.

LO1.3 Explain systems thinking and how management infor mation systems enable business communications.

COMPETING IN THE INFORMATION AGE LO1.1

Did you know that . . .

- The movie *Avatar* took more than four years to create and cost $450 million.
- Lady Gaga's real name is Stefani Joanne Angelina Germanotta.
- Customers pay $2.6 million for a 30-second advertising time slot during the Super Bowl.[1]

A **fact** is the confirmation or validation of an event or object. In the past, people primarily learned facts from books. Today, by simply pushing a button people can find out anything, from anywhere, at any time. We live in the **information age**, when infinite quantities of facts are widely available to anyone who can use a computer. The impact of information technology on the global business environment is equivalent to the printing press's impact on publishing and electricity's impact on productivity. College student startups were mostly unheard of before the information age. Now, it's not at all unusual to read about a business student starting a multimillion-dollar company from his or her dorm room. Think of Mark Zuckerberg, who started Facebook from his dorm, or Michael Dell (Dell Computers) and Bill Gates (Microsoft), who both founded their legendary companies as college students.

You may think only students well versed in advanced technology can compete in the information age. This is simply not true. Many business leaders have created exceptional opportunities by coupling the power of the information age with traditional business methods. Here are just a few examples:

- Amazon is not a technology company; its original business focus was to sell books, and it now sells nearly everything.
- Netflix is not a technology company; its primary business focus is to rent videos.
- Zappos is not a technology company; its primary business focus is to sell shoes, bags, clothing, and accessories.

Amazon's founder, Jeff Bezos, at first saw an opportunity to change the way people purchase books. Using the power of the information age to tailor offerings to each customer and speed the payment process, he in effect opened millions of tiny virtual bookstores, each with a vastly larger selection and far cheaper product than traditional bookstores. The success of his original business model led him to expand Amazon to carry many other types of products. The founders of Netflix and Zappos have done the same thing for videos and shoes. All these entrepreneurs were business professionals, not technology experts. However, they understood enough about the information age to apply it to a particular business, creating innovative companies that now lead entire industries.

Over 20 years ago a few professors at MIT began describing the **Internet of Things (IoT)**, a world where interconnected Internet-enabled devices or "things" have the ability to collect and share data without human intervention. Another term commonly associated with The Internet of Things is **machine-to-machine (M2M)**, which refers to devices that connect directly to other devices. With advanced technologies devices are connecting in ways not previously thought possible and researchers predict that over 50 billion IoT devices will be communicating by 2020. Kevin Ashton, cofounder and executive director of the Auto-ID Center at MIT, first mentioned the Internet of Things in a presentation he made to Procter & Gamble. Here's Ashton explanation of the Internet of Things:

"Today computers—and, therefore, the Internet—are almost wholly dependent on human beings for information. Nearly all

data Raw facts that describe the characteristics of an event or object.

structured data Data that has a defined length, type, and format and includes numbers, dates, or strings such as Customer Address.

machine-generated data Data created by a machine without human intervention.

human-generated data Data that humans, in interaction with computers, generate.

Living the DREAM

Sensors and Bears—A Perfect Match

Two London-based entrepreneurs are building an Internet of huggable things for sick children to make any hospital visit more like a trip to Disneyland. Teddy The Guardian captures heart rate, temperatures, and blood-oxygen levels when a child grabs it by the paw to give it a cuddle. All measurements are sent wirelessly to nurses and parents, mobile devices. The new cute, cuddly teddy bear is packed full of sensors designed to track children's vital signs and help quickly find out potential issues. Teddy The Guardian takes from 5 to 7 seconds to record measurements and is programmed to run five times per hour. Future versions of Teddy The Guardian will be interactive, using machine learning to find out the child's favorite song or bedtime story and then play the related content for a more soothing hospital visit. Big pharmaceutical companies in the United States have already placed over $500,000 in orders and plan to donate the bears to hospitals and clinics.

This is clearly a brilliant idea, and soon we will see Teddy The Guardian in many local hospitals and clinics. Can you identify any additional markets where Teddy The Guardian should focus? Can you think of any ethical issues related to huggable things? Can you think of any security issues related to huggable things?

of the roughly 50 petabytes (a petabyte is 1,024 terabytes) of data available on the Internet were first captured and created by human beings by typing, pressing a record button, taking a digital picture or scanning a bar code.

The problem is, people have limited time, attention and accuracy—all of which means they are not very good at capturing data about things in the real world. If we had computers that knew everything there was to know about things—using data they gathered without any help from us—we would be able to track and count everything and greatly reduce waste, loss and cost. We would know when things needed replacing, repairing or recalling and whether they were fresh or past their best."[2]

IoT is transforming our world into a living information system as we control our intelligent lighting from our smart phone to a daily health check from our smart toilet. Of course with all great technological advances come unexpected risks and you have to be prepared to encounter various security issues with IoT. Just imagine if your devices are hacked by someone who now has the ability to shut off your water, take control of your car, or unlock the doors of your home from thousands of miles away. We are just beginning to understand the security issues associated with IoT and M2M and you can be sure that sensitive data leakage from your IoT device is something you will most likely encounter in your life.

Students who understand business along with the power associated with the information age and IoT will create their own opportunities and perhaps even new industries. Realizing the value of obtaining real-time data from connected "things" will allow you to make more informed decisions, identify new opportunities, and analyze customer patterns to predict new behaviors. Our primary goal in this course is to arm you with the knowledge you need to compete in the information age. The core drivers of the information age include:

- Data
- Information
- Business intelligence
- Knowledge (see Figure 1.1)

LO1.1 Describe the information age and the differences among data, information, business intelligence, and knowledge.

Data

Data are raw facts that describe the characteristics of an event or object. Before the information age, managers manually collected and analyzed data, a time-consuming and complicated task without which they would have little insight into how to run their business. **Structured data** has a defined length, type, and format and includes numbers, dates, or strings such as Customer Address. Structured data is typically stored in a traditional system such as a relational database or spreadsheet and accounts for about 20 percent of the data that surrounds us. The sources of structured data include:

- **Machine-generated data** is created by a machine without human intervention. Machine-generated structured data includes sensor data, point-of-sale data, and web log data.
- **Human-generated data** is data that humans, in interaction with computers, generate. Human-generated structured data includes input data, click-stream data, or gaming data.

unstructured data Data that is not defined and does not follow a specified format and is typically free-form text such as emails, Twitter tweets, and text messages.

big data A collection of large, complex data sets, including structured and unstructured data, which cannot be analyzed using traditional database methods and tools.

snapshot A view of data at a particular moment in time.

Unstructured data is not defined and does not follow a specified format and is typically free-form text such as emails, Twitter tweets, and text messages. Unstructured data accounts for about 80 percent of the data that surrounds us. The sources of unstructured data include:

- Machine-generated unstructured data includes satellite images, scientific atmosphere data, and radar data.
- Human-generated unstructured data includes text messages, social media data, and emails.

Big data is a collection of large, complex data sets, including structured and unstructured data, which cannot be analyzed using traditional database methods and tools. Lacking data, managers often found themselves making business decisions about how many products to make, how much material to order, or how many employees to hire based on intuition or gut feelings. In the information age, successful managers compile, analyze, and comprehend massive amounts of data daily, which helps them make more successful business decisions.

A **snapshot** is a view of data at a particular moment in time. Figure 1.2 shows sales data for Tony's Wholesale Company, a fictitious business that supplies snacks to stores. The data highlight characteristics such as order date, customer, sales representative, product, quantity, and profit. The second line in Figure 1.2, for instance, shows that Roberta Cross sold 90 boxes of Ruffles to Walmart for $1,350, resulting in a profit of $450 (note that Profit = Sales - Costs). These data are useful for understanding individual sales; however, they do not provide us much insight into how Tony's business is performing as a whole. Tony needs to answer questions that will help him manage his day-to-day operations such as:

- Who are my best customers?
- Who are my least-profitable customers?
- What is my best-selling product?
- What is my slowest-selling product?
- Who is my strongest sales representative?
- Who is my weakest sales representative?

What Tony needs, in other words, is not data but *information.*

FIGURE 1.1 The Differences among Data, Information, Business Intelligence, and Knowledge

Data	Information	Business Intelligence	Knowledge
• Raw facts that describe the characteristics of an event or object	• Data converted into a meaningful and useful context	• Information collected from multiple sources that analyzes patterns, trends, and relationships for strategic decision making	• The skills, experience, and expertise, coupled with information and intelligence, that create a person's intellectual resources
• Order date • Amount sold • Customer number • Quantity ordered	• Best-selling product • Best customer • Worst-selling product • Worst customer	• Lowest sales per week compared with the economic interest rates • Best-selling product by month compared to sports season and city team wins and losses	• Choosing not to fire a sales representative who is underperforming knowing that person is experiencing family problems • Listing products that are about to expire first on the menu or creating them as a daily special to move the product

information Data converted into a meaningful and useful context.

report A document containing data organized in a table, matrix, or graphical format allowing users to easily comprehend and understand information.

static report A report created once based on data that does not change.

dynamic report A report that changes automatically during creation.

fyi

People in China and India Are Starving for Your Jobs[3]

"When I was growing up in Minneapolis, my parents always said, 'Tom, finish your dinner. There are people starving in China and India.' Today I tell my girls, 'Finish your homework, because people in China and India are starving for your jobs.' And in a flat world, they can have them, because there's no such thing as an American job anymore." Thomas Friedman.

In his book, *The World Is Flat,* Thomas Friedman describes the unplanned cascade of technological and social shifts that effectively leveled the economic world and "accidentally made Beijing, Bangalore, and Bethesda next-door neighbors." The video of Thomas Friedman's lecture at MIT discussing the flat world is available at http://mitworld.mit.edu/video/266. If you want to be prepared to compete in a flat world, you must watch this video and answer the following questions:

- Do you agree or disagree with Friedman's assessment that the world is flat?
- What are the potential impacts of a flat world for a student performing a job search?
- What can students do to prepare themselves for competing in a flat world?

© Terry Vine/Blend Images/Getty Images

FIGURE 1.2 Tony's Snack Company Data

Order Date	Customer	Sales Representative	Product	Qty	Unit Price	Total Sales	Unit Cost	Total Cost	Profit
4-Jan	Walmart	PJ Helgoth	Doritos	41	$24	$ 984	$18	$738	$246
4-Jan	Walmart	Roberta Cross	Ruffles	90	$15	$1,350	$10	$900	$450
5-Jan	Safeway	Craig Schultz	Ruffles	27	$15	$ 405	$10	$270	$135
6-Jan	Walmart	Roberta Cross	Ruffles	67	$15	$1,005	$10	$670	$335
7-Jan	7-Eleven	Craig Schultz	Pringles	79	$12	$ 948	$ 6	$474	$474
7-Jan	Walmart	Roberta Cross	Ruffles	52	$15	$ 780	$10	$520	$260
8-Jan	Kroger	Craig Schultz	Ruffles	39	$15	$ 585	$10	$390	$195
9-Jan	Walmart	Craig Schultz	Ruffles	66	$15	$ 990	$10	$660	$330
10-Jan	Target	Craig Schultz	Ruffles	40	$15	$ 600	$10	$400	$200
11-Jan	Walmart	Craig Schultz	Ruffles	71	$15	$1,065	$10	$710	$355

Information

Information is data converted into a meaningful and useful context. The simple difference between data and information is that computers or machines need data and humans need information. Data is a raw building block that has not been shaped, processed, or analyzed and frequently appears disorganized and unfriendly. Information gives meaning and context to analyzed data making it insightful for humans providing context and structure that is extremely valuable when making informed business decisions.

A **report** is a document containing data organized in a table, matrix, or graphical format allowing users to easily comprehend and understand information. Reports can cover a wide range of subjects or specific subject for a certain time period or event. A **static report** is created once based on data that does not change. Static reports can include a sales report from last year or salary report from five years ago. A **dynamic report** changes automatically during creation. Dynamic reports can include updating daily stock market prices or the calculation of available inventory.

Having the right information at the right moment in time can be worth a fortune. Having the wrong information at the right moment; or the right information at the wrong moment can be disastrous. The truth about information is that its value is only

variable A data characteristic that stands for a value that changes or varies over time.

business intelligence (BI) Information collected from multiple sources such as suppliers, customers, competitors, partners, and industries that analyze patterns, trends, and relationships for strategic decision making.

as good as the people who use it. People using the same information can make different decisions depending on how they interpret or analyze the information. Thus information has value only insofar as the people using it do as well.

Tony can analyze his sales data and turn them into information to answer all the above questions and understand how his business is operating. Figures 1.3 and 1.4, for instance, show us that Walmart is Roberta Cross's best customer, and that Ruffles is Tony's best product measured in terms of total sales. Armed with this information, Tony can identify and then address such issues as weak products and under-performing sales representatives.

A **variable** is a data characteristic that stands for a value that changes or varies over time. For example, in Tony's data, price and quantity ordered can vary. Changing variables allows managers to create hypothetical scenarios to study future possibilities. Tony may find it valuable to anticipate how sales or cost increases affect profitability. To estimate how a 20 percent increase in prices might improve profits, Tony simply changes the price variable for all orders, which automatically calculates the amount of new profits. To estimate how a 10 percent increase in costs hurts profits, Tony changes the cost variable for all orders, which automatically calculates the amount of lost profits. Manipulating variables is an important tool for any business.

Business Intelligence

Business intelligence (BI) is information collected from multiple sources such as suppliers, customers, competitors, partners, and industries that analyzes patterns, trends, and relationships for strategic decision making. BI manipulates

FIGURE 1.3 Tony's Data Sorted by Customer "Walmart" and Sales Representative "Roberta Cross"

Order Date	Customer	Sales Representative	Product	Quantity	Unit Price	Total Sales	Unit Cost	Total Cost	Profit
26-Apr	Walmart	Roberta Cross	Fritos	86	$ 19	$ 1,634	$ 17	$ 1,462	$ 172
29-Aug	Walmart	Roberta Cross	Fritos	76	$ 19	$ 1,444	$ 17	$ 1,292	$ 152
7-Sep	Walmart	Roberta Cross	Fritos	20	$ 19	$ 380	$ 17	$ 340	$ 40
22-Nov	Walmart	Roberta Cross	Fritos	39	$ 19	$ 741	$ 17	$ 663	$ 78
30-Dec	Walmart	Roberta Cross	Fritos	68	$ 19	$ 1,292	$ 17	$ 1,156	$ 136
7-Jul	Walmart	Roberta Cross	Pringles	79	$ 18	$ 1,422	$ 8	$ 632	$ 790
6-Aug	Walmart	Roberta Cross	Pringles	21	$ 12	$ 252	$ 6	$ 126	$ 126
2-Oct	Walmart	Roberta Cross	Pringles	60	$ 18	$ 1,080	$ 8	$ 480	$ 600
15-Nov	Walmart	Roberta Cross	Pringles	32	$ 12	$ 384	$ 6	$ 192	$ 192
21-Dec	Walmart	Roberta Cross	Pringles	92	$ 12	$ 1,104	$ 6	$ 552	$ 552
28-Feb	Walmart	Roberta Cross	Ruffles	67	$ 15	$ 1,005	$ 10	$ 670	$ 335
6-Mar	Walmart	Roberta Cross	Ruffles	8	$ 15	$ 120	$ 10	$ 80	$ 40
16-Mar	Walmart	Roberta Cross	Ruffles	68	$ 15	$ 1,020	$ 10	$ 680	$ 340
23-Apr	Walmart	Roberta Cross	Ruffles	34	$ 15	$ 510	$ 10	$ 340	$ 170
4-Aug	Walmart	Roberta Cross	Ruffles	40	$ 15	$ 600	$ 10	$ 400	$ 200
18-Aug	Walmart	Roberta Cross	Ruffles	93	$ 15	$ 1,395	$ 10	$ 930	$ 465
5-Sep	Walmart	Roberta Cross	Ruffles	41	$ 15	$ 615	$ 10	$ 410	$ 205
12-Sep	Walmart	Roberta Cross	Ruffles	8	$ 15	$ 120	$ 10	$ 80	$ 40
28-Oct	Walmart	Roberta Cross	Ruffles	50	$ 15	$ 750	$ 10	$ 500	$ 250
21-Nov	Walmart	Roberta Cross	Ruffles	79	$ 15	$ 1,185	$ 10	$ 790	$ 395
29-Jan	Walmart	Roberta Cross	Sun Chips	5	$ 22	$ 110	$ 18	$ 90	$ 20
12-Apr	Walmart	Roberta Cross	Sun Chips	85	$ 22	$ 1,870	$ 18	$ 1,530	$ 340
16-Jun	Walmart	Roberta Cross	Sun Chips	55	$ 22	$ 1,210	$ 18	$ 990	$ 220
				1,206	**$383**	**$20,243**	**$273**	**$14,385**	**$5,858**

Sorting the data reveals the information that Roberta Cross's total sales to Walmart were $20,243 resulting in a profit of $5,858. (Profit $5,858 = Sales $20,243 − Costs $14,385)

analytics The science of fact-based decision making.

predictive analytics Extracts information from data and uses it to predict future trends and identify behavioral patterns.

behavioral analytics Uses data about people's behaviors to understand intent and predict future actions.

knowledge Skills, experience, and expertise coupled with information and intelligence that creates a person's intellectual resources.

knowledge worker Individuals valued for their ability to interpret and analyze information.

FIGURE 1.4 Information Gained after Analyzing Tony's Data

Tony's Business Information	Name	Total Profit
Who is Tony's best customer by total sales?	Walmart	$ 560,789
Who is Tony's least-valuable customer by total sales?	Walgreens	$ 45,673
Who is Tony's best customer by profit?	7-Eleven	$ 324,550
Who is Tony's least-valuable customer by profit?	King Soopers	$ 23,908
What is Tony's best-selling product by total sales?	Ruffles	$ 232,500
What is Tony's weakest-selling product by total sales?	Pringles	$ 54,890
What is Tony's best-selling product by profit?	Tostitos	$ 13,050
What is Tony's weakest-selling product by profit?	Pringles	$ 23,000
Who is Tony's best sales representative by profit?	R. Cross	$1,230,980
Who is Tony's weakest sales representative by profit?	Craig Schultz	$ 98,980
What is the best sales representative's best-selling product by total profit?	Ruffles	$ 98,780
Who is the best sales representative's best customer by total profit?	Walmart	$ 345,900
What is the best sales representative's weakest-selling product by total profit?	Sun Chips	$ 45,600
Who is the best sales representative's weakest customer by total profit?	Krogers	$ 56,050

multiple variables and in some cases even hundreds of variables including such items as interest rates, weather conditions, and even gas prices. Tony could use BI to analyze internal data, such as company sales, along with external data about the environment such as competitors, finances, weather, holidays, and even sporting events. Both internal and external variables affect snack sales, and analyzing these variables will help Tony determine ordering levels and sales forecasts. For instance, BI can predict inventory requirements for Tony's business for the week before the Super Bowl if, say, the home team is playing, average temperature is above 80 degrees, and the stock market is performing well. This is BI at its finest, incorporating all types of internal and external variables to anticipate business performance.

Analytics is the science of fact-based decision making. A big part of business intelligence is called **predictive analytics**, which extracts information from data and uses it to predict future trends and identify behavioral patterns. Top managers use predictive analytics to define the future of the business, analyzing markets, industries, and economies to determine the strategic direction the company must follow to remain profitable. **Behavioral analytics** uses data about people's behaviors to understand intent and predict future actions. Tony will set the strategic direction for his firm, which might include introducing new flavors of potato chips or sports drinks as new product lines or schools and hospitals as new market segments based on both predictive and behavioral analytics.

Knowledge

Knowledge includes the skills, experience, and expertise, coupled with information and intelligence, that creates a person's intellectual resources. **Knowledge workers** are individuals valued for their ability to interpret and analyze information. Today's workers are commonly referred to as knowledge workers and they use BI along with personal experience to make decisions based on both information and intuition, a valuable resource for any company.

Imagine that Tony analyzes his data and finds his weakest sales representative for this period is Craig Schultz. If Tony considered only this information, he might conclude that firing Craig was a good business decision. However, because Tony has knowledge about how the company operates, he knows Craig has been out on medical leave for several weeks; hence, his sales numbers are low. Without this additional knowledge, Tony might have executed a bad business decision, delivered a negative message to the other employees, and sent his best sales representatives out to look for other jobs.

The key point in this scenario is that it is simply impossible to collect all the information about every situation, and yet without that, it can be easy to misunderstand the problem. Using data, information, business intelligence, *and* knowledge to make decisions and solve problems is the key to finding success in business. These core drivers of the information age are the building blocks of business systems. Figure 1.5 offers a few different examples of data through knowledge.

FIGURE 1.5
Transformation from Data to Knowledge

DATA: I have one item.

INFORMATION: The item I have is a product that has the most sales during the month of December.

BUSINESS INTELLIGENCE: The month of December this year is going to see interest rates rise by 10 percent and snow stores are expected to cause numerous problems throughout the East coast.

KNOWLEDGE: Given the unexpected financial issues caused by the storms and the interest rate hike we will offer a discount on purchase in November and December to ensure sales levels increase by 10 percent.

THE CHALLENGE: DEPARTMENTAL COMPANIES LO1.2

Companies are typically organized by department or functional area such as:

- **Accounting:** Records, measures, and reports monetary transactions.
- **Finance:** Deals with strategic financial issues including money, banking, credit, investments, and assets.
- **Human resources:** Maintains policies, plans, and procedures for the effective management of employees.
- **Marketing:** Supports sales by planning, pricing, and promoting goods or services.
- **Operations management:** Manages the process of converting or transforming or resources into goods or services.
- **Sales:** Performs the function of selling goods or services (see Figure 1.6).

Each department performs its own activities. Sales and marketing focus on moving goods or services into the hands of consumers; they maintain transactional data. Finance and accounting focus on managing the company's resources and maintain monetary data. Operations management focuses on manufacturing and maintains production data, while human resources focuses on hiring and training people and maintains employee data. Although each department has its own focus and data, none can work independently if the company is to operate as a whole. It is easy to see how a business decision made by one department can affect other departments. Marketing needs to analyze production and sales data to come up with product promotions and advertising strategies. Production needs to understand sales forecasts to determine the company's manufacturing needs. Sales needs to rely on information from operations to understand inventory, place orders, and forecast consumer demand. All departments need to understand the accounting and finance departments' information for budgeting. For the firm to be successful, all departments must work together as a single unit sharing common information and not operate independently or in a silo (see Figure 1.7).

LO1.2 Identify the different departments in a company and why they must work together to achieve success.

system A collection of parts that link to achieve a common purpose.

goods Material items or products that customers will buy to satisfy a want or need. Clothing, groceries, cell phones, and cars are all examples of goods that people buy to fulfill their needs.

service Tasks that customers will buy to satisfy a want or need.

FIGURE 1.6
Departments Working Independently

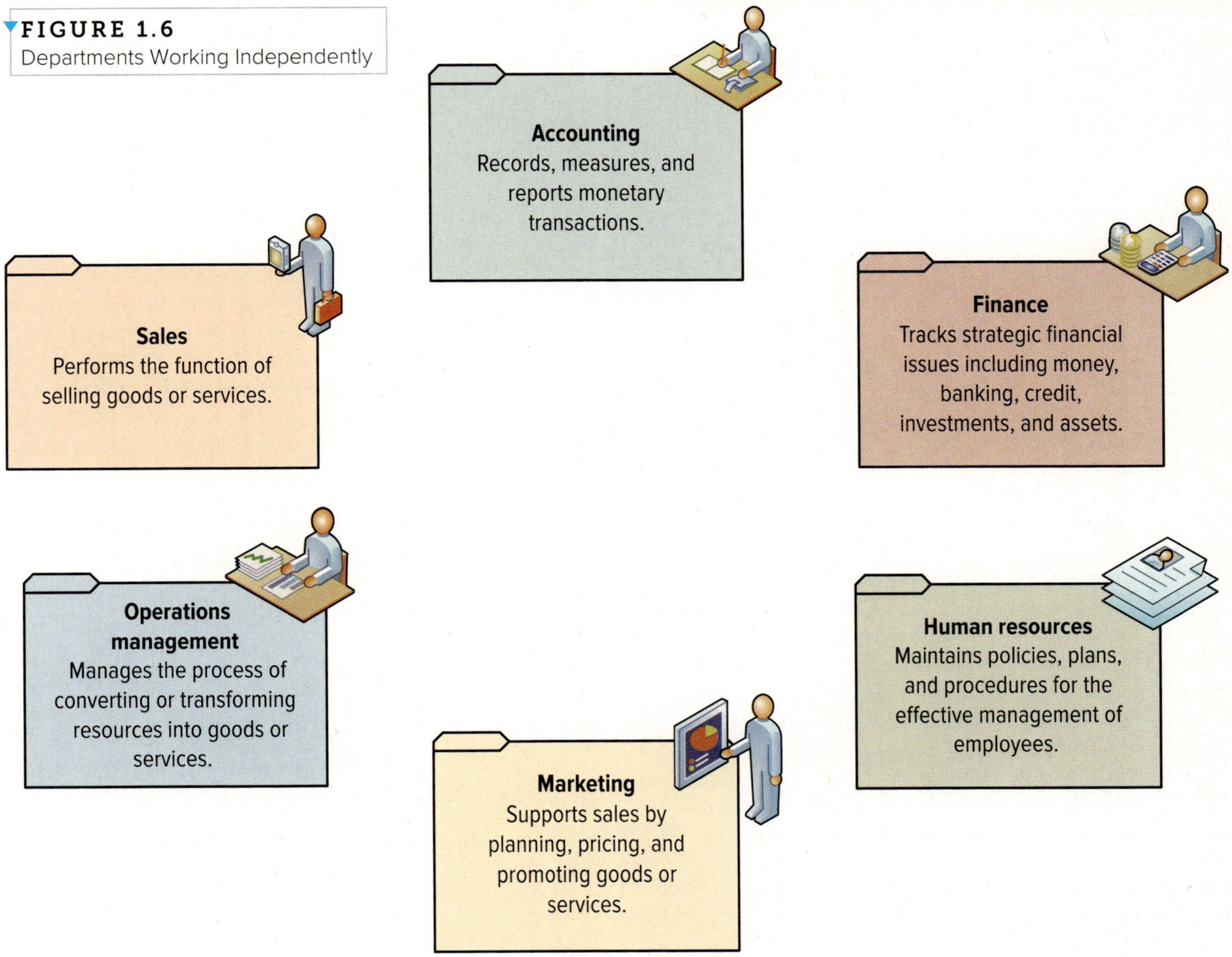

SYSTEMS THINKING AND MANAGEMENT INFORMATION SYSTEMS LO1.3

You probably recall the old story of three blind men attempting to describe an elephant. The first man, feeling the elephant's girth, said the elephant seemed very much like a wall. The second, feeling the elephant's trunk, declared the elephant was like a snake. The third man felt the elephant's tusks and said the elephant was like a tree or a cane. Companies that operate departmentally are seeing only one part of the elephant, a critical mistake that hinders successful operation.

Successful companies operate cross-functionally, integrating the operations of all departments. Systems are the primary enabler of cross-functional operations. A **system** is a collection of parts that link to achieve a common purpose. A car is a good example of a system, since removing a part, such as the steering wheel or accelerator, causes the entire system to stop working.

Before jumping into how systems work, it is important to have a solid understanding of the basic production process for goods and services. **Goods** are material items or products that customers will buy to satisfy a want or need. Clothing, groceries, cell phones, and cars are all examples of goods that people buy to fulfill their needs. **Services** are tasks performed by people that customers will buy to satisfy a want or need. Waiting tables, teaching, and cutting hair are all examples of services that people pay for to fulfill their needs (see Figure 1.8).

productivity The rate at which goods and services are produced based upon total output given total inputs.

production The process where a business takes raw materials and processes them or converts them into a finished product for its goods or services.

Production is the process where a business takes raw materials and processes them or converts them into a finished product for its goods or services. Just think about making a hamburger (see Figure 1.9). First, you must gather all of the *inputs* or raw materials such as the bun, patty, lettuce, tomato, and ketchup. Second, you *process* the raw materials, so in this example you would need to cook the patty, wash and chop the lettuce and tomato, and place all of the items in the bun. Finally, you would have your *output* or finished product—your hamburger! **Productivity** is the rate at which goods and services are produced based upon total output given total inputs. Given our previous example, if a business could produce the same hamburger with less expensive inputs or more hamburgers with the same inputs it would see a rise in productivity and possibly an increase in profits. Ensuring the input, process, and output of goods and services work across all of the departments of a company is where systems add tremendous value to overall business productivity.

FIGURE 1.7
Departments Working Together

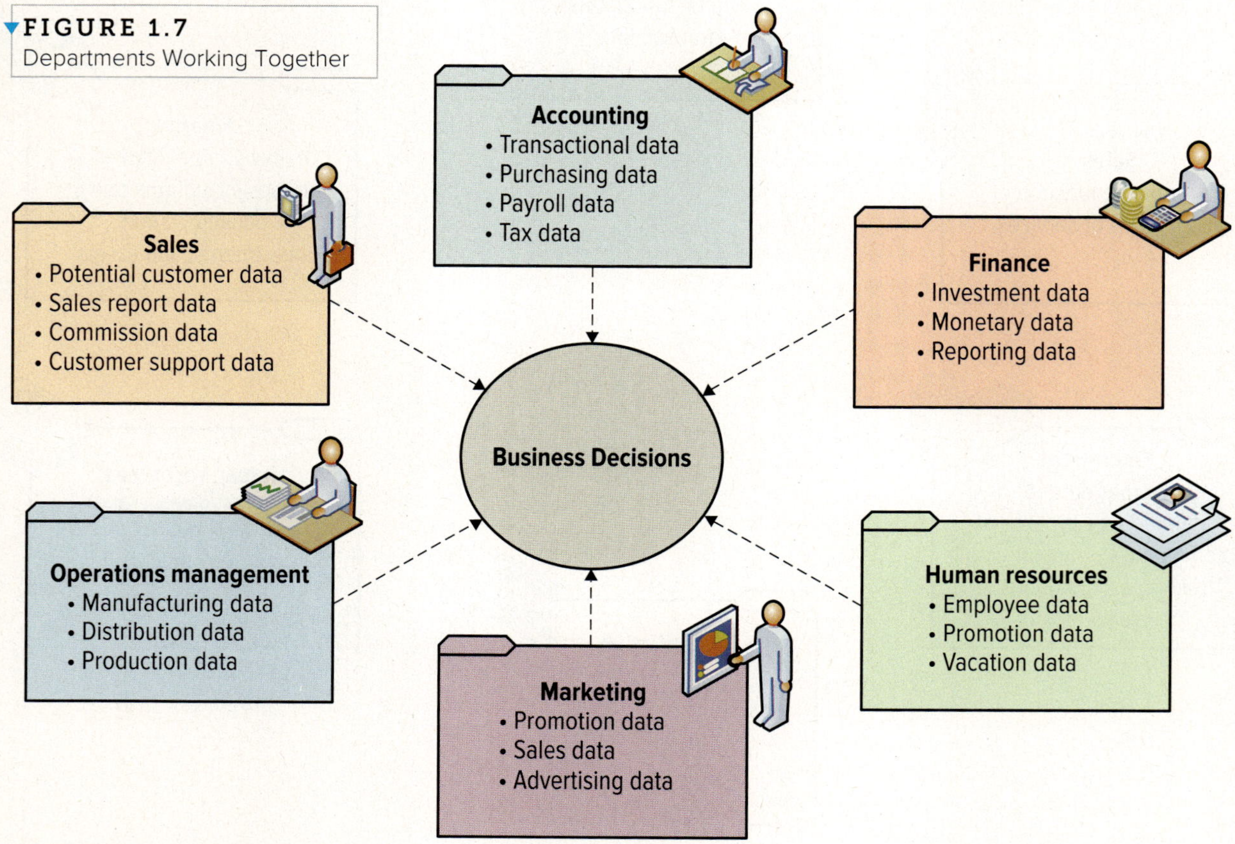

BUSTED The Interent of Things Is Wide Open—for Everyone!

IoT is transforming our world into a living information system as we control our intelligent lighting from our smart phone to a daily health check from our smart toilet. Of course, with all great technological advances come unexpected risks, and you have to be prepared to encounter various security issues with IoT. Just imagine if your devices are hacked by someone who now can shut off your water, take control of your car, or unlock the doors of your home from thousands of miles away. We are just beginning to understand the security issues associated with IoT and M2M, and you can be sure that sensitive data leakage from your IoT device is something you will most likely encounter in your life.[5]

In a group, identify a few IoT devices you are using today. These can include fitness trackers that report to your iPhone, sports equipment that provides immediate feedback to an app, or even smart vacuum cleaners. If you are not using any IoT devices today, brainstorm a few you might purchase in the future. How could a criminal or hacker use your IoT to steal your sensitive data? What potential problems or issues could you experience from these types of illegal data thefts? What might be some of the signs that someone had accessed your IoT data illegally? What could you do to protect the data in your device?

Systems Thinking

Systems thinking is a way of monitoring the entire system by viewing multiple inputs being processed or transformed to produce outputs while continuously gathering feedback on each part (see Figure 1.10). **Feedback** is information that returns to its original transmitter (input, transform, or output) and modifies the transmitter's actions. Feedback helps the system maintain stability. For example, a car's system continuously monitors the fuel level and turns on a warning light if the gas level is too low. Systems thinking provides an end-to-end view of how operations work together to create a product or service. Business students who understand systems thinking are valuable resources because they can implement solutions that consider the entire process, not just a single component.

Management information systems (MIS) is a business function, like accounting and human resources, which moves information about people, products, and processes across the company to facilitate decision making and problem solving. MIS incorporates systems thinking to help companies operate cross-functionally. For example, to fulfill product orders, an MIS for sales moves a single customer order across all functional areas including sales, order fulfillment, shipping, billing, and finally customer service. Although different functional areas handle different parts of the sale, thanks to MIS, to the customer the sale is one continuous process. If one part of the company is experiencing problems, however, then, like the car without a steering wheel, the entire system fails. If order fulfillment packages the wrong product, it will not matter that shipping, billing, and customer service did their jobs right, since the customer will not be satisfied when he or she opens the package.

MIS can be an important enabler of business success and innovation. This is not to say that MIS *equals* business success and innovation, or that MIS *represents* business success and innovation. MIS is a tool that is most valuable when it leverages the talents of people who know how to use and manage it effectively. To perform

systems thinking A way of monitoring the entire system by viewing multiple inputs being processed or transformed to produce outputs while continuously gathering feedback on each part.

feedback Information that returns to its original transmitter (input, transform, or output) and modifies the transmitter's actions.

management information systems A business function, like accounting and human resources, which moves information about people, products, and processes across the company to facilitate decision making and problem solving.

show me *the* MONEY

Who Really Won the 2014 Winter Olympics?

If you were watching the 2014 Winter Olympics, I bet you were excited to see your country and its amazing athletes compete. As you were following the Olympics day by day, you were probably checking different websites to see how your country ranked. And depending on the website you visited, you could get a very different answer to this seemingly easy question. On the NBC and ESPN networks, the United States ranked second, and on the official Sochie Olympic website, the United States ranked fourth. The simple question of who won the 2014 Winter Olympics changes significantly, depending on whom you asked.[4]

In a group, take a look at the following two charts and brainstorm the reasons each internationally recognized source has a different listing for the top five winners. What measurement is each chart using to determine the winner? Who do you believe is the winner? As a manager, what do you need to understand when reading or listening to business forecasts and reports?

Winter Olympics 2014 Medal Ranking According to NBC News

Rank	Country	Gold	Silver	Bronze	Total
1	Russian Fed.	13	11	9	33
2	United States	9	7	12	28
3	Norway	11	5	10	26
4	Canada	10	10	5	25
5	Netherlands	8	7	9	24

Winter Olympics 2014 Medal Ranking According to Official Sochie Olympic Website

Rank	Country	Gold	Silver	Bronze	Total
1	Russian Fed.	13	11	9	33
2	Norway	11	5	10	26
3	Canada	10	10	5	25
4	United States	9	7	12	28
5	Netherlands	8	7	9	24

the MIS function effectively, almost all companies, particularly large and medium-sized ones, have an internal MIS department, often called information technology (IT), information systems (IS), or management information systems (MIS). For the purpose of this text, we will refer to it as MIS.

MIS Department Roles and Responsibilities

Management information systems is a relatively new functional area, having been around formally in most organizations only for about 40 years. Job titles, roles, and responsibilities often differ dramatically from organization to organization. Nonetheless, clear trends are developing toward elevating some MIS positions within an organization to the strategic level.

Most organizations maintain positions such as chief executive officer (CEO), chief financial officer (CFO), and chief operations officer (COO) at the strategic level. Recently there are more MIS-related strategic positions such as chief information officer (CIO), chief data officer (CDO), chief technology officer (CTO), chief security officer (CSO), chief privacy officer (CPO), and chief knowledge officer (CKO). See Figure 1.11.

The **chief information officer (CIO)** is responsible for (1) overseeing all uses of information technology and (2) ensuring the strategic alignment of MIS with business goals and objectives. The CIO often reports directly to the CEO. CIOs must possess a solid and detailed understanding of every aspect of an organization coupled with tremendous insight into the capability of MIS. Broad functions of a CIO include:

1. *Manager*—ensure the delivery of all MIS projects, on time and within budget.
2. *Leader*—ensure the strategic vision of MIS is in line with the strategic vision of the organization.
3. *Communicator*—advocate and communicate the MIS strategy by building and maintaining strong executive relationships.

The **chief data officer (CDO)** is responsible for determining the types of information the enterprise will capture, retain, analyze, and share. The difference between the CIO and CDO is that the CIO is responsible for the *information systems* through which data is stored and processed, while the CDO is responsible for the *data,* regardless of the information system.

The **chief technology officer (CTO)** is responsible for ensuring the throughput, speed, accuracy, availability, and reliability

chief information officer (CIO) Responsible for (1) overseeing all uses of MIS and (2) ensuring that MIS strategically aligns with business goals and objectives.

chief data officer Responsible for determining the types of information the enterprise will capture, retain, analyze, and share.

chief technology officer (CTO) Responsible for ensuring the throughput, speed, accuracy, availability, and reliability of an organization's information technology.

FIGURE 1.8
Different Types of Goods and Services

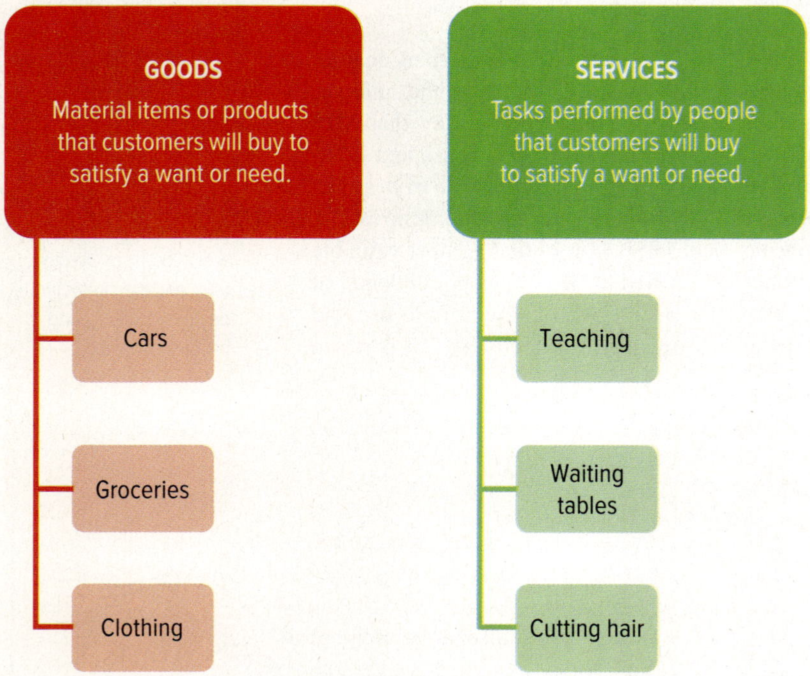

FIGURE 1.9
Input, Process, Output Example

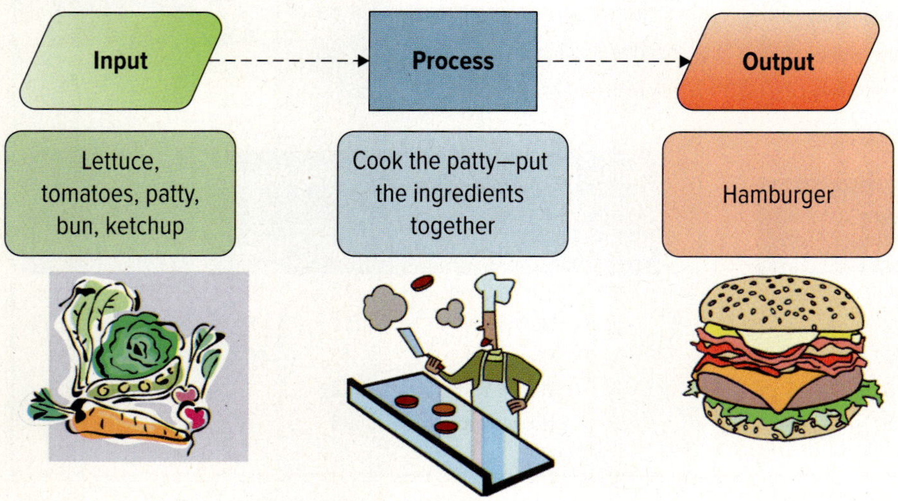

FIGURE 1.10 Overview of Systems Thinking

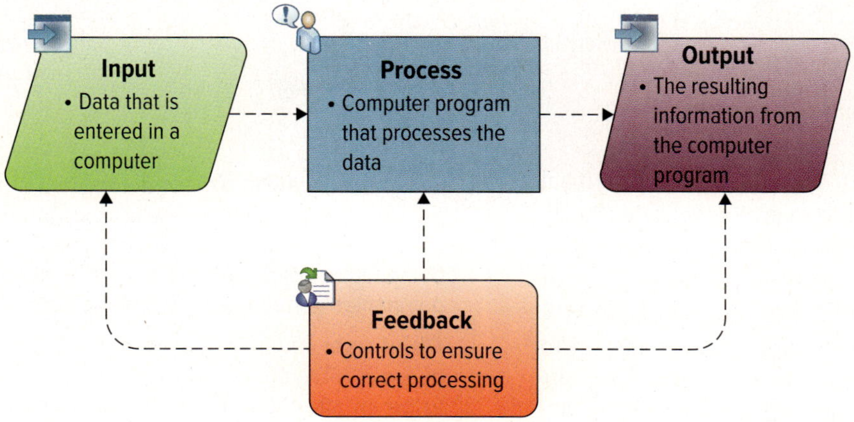

of an organization's information technology. CTOs are similar to CIOs, except that CIOs take on the additional responsibility for effectiveness of ensuring that MIS is aligned with the organization's strategic initiatives. CTOs have direct responsibility for ensuring the *efficiency* of MIS systems throughout the organization. Most CTOs possess well-rounded knowledge of all aspects of MIS, including hardware, software, and telecommunications.

The **chief security officer (CSO)** is responsible for ensuring the security of MIS systems and developing strategies and MIS safeguards against attacks from hackers and viruses. The role of a CSO has been elevated in recent years because of the number of attacks from hackers and viruses. Most CSOs possess detailed knowledge of networks and telecommunications because hackers and viruses usually find their way into MIS systems through networked computers.

The **chief privacy officer (CPO)** is responsible for ensuring the ethical and legal use of information within an organization. CPOs are the newest senior executive position in MIS. Recently, 150 of the *Fortune* 500 companies added the CPO position to their list of senior executives. Many CPOs are lawyers by training, enabling them to understand the often complex legal issues surrounding the use of information.

The **chief knowledge officer (CKO)** is responsible for collecting, maintaining, and distributing the organization's knowledge. The CKO designs programs and systems that make it easy for people to reuse knowledge. These systems create repositories of organizational documents, methodologies, tools, and practices, and they establish methods for filtering the information. The CKO must continuously encourage employee contributions to keep the systems up-to-date. The CKO can contribute directly to the organization's bottom line by reducing the learning curve for new employees or employees taking on new roles.

Danny Shaw was the first CKO at Children's Hospital in Boston. His initial task was to unite information from disparate systems to enable analysis of both the efficiency and effectiveness of the hospital's care. Shaw started by building a series of small, integrated information systems that quickly demonstrated value. He then gradually built on those successes, creating a knowledge-enabled organization one layer at a time. Shaw's information systems have enabled administrative and clinical operational analyses.

With the election of President Barack Obama comes the appointment of the first-ever national chief technology officer (CTO). The job description states that the first CTO must "ensure the safety of our networks and lead an interagency effort, working with chief technology and chief information officers of each of the federal agencies, to ensure that they use best-in-class technologies and share best practices." A federal-level CTO demonstrates the ongoing growth of technology positions outside corporate America. In the future expect to see many more technology positions in government and nonprofit organizations.

show me *the* MONEY

Is Technology Making Us Dumber or Smarter?

Choose a side and debate the following:

- **Side A** Living in the information age has made us smarter because we have a huge wealth of knowledge at our fingertips whenever or wherever we need it.
- **Side B** Living in the information age has caused people to become lazy and dumber because they are no longer building up their memory banks to solve problems; machines give them the answers they need to solve problems.

chief security officer (CSO) Responsible for ensuring the security of MIS systems and developing strategies and MIS safeguards against attacks from hackers and viruses.

chief privacy officer (CPO) Responsible for ensuring the ethical and legal use of information within a company.

chief knowledge officer (CKO) Responsible for collecting, maintaining, and distributing company knowledge.

chief intellectual property officer Manage and defend intellectual property, copyrights, and patents.

chief automation officer Determines if a person or business process can be replaced by a robot or software.

chief user experience officer Create the optimal relationship between user and technology.

MIS skills gap The difference between existing MIS workplace knowledge and the knowledge required to fulfill the business goals and strategies.

All the above MIS positions and responsibilities are critical to an organization's success. While many organizations may not have a different individual for each of these positions, they must have leaders taking responsibility for all these areas of concern. The individuals responsible for enterprisewide MIS and MIS-related issues must provide guidance and support to the organization's employees. According to *Fast Company* magazine a few executive levels you might see created over the next decade include:

- **Chief intellectual property officer** will manage and defend intellectual property, copyrights, and patents. The world of intellectual property law is vast and complicated as new innovations continually enter the market. Companies in the near future will need a core leadership team member who can not only wade through the dizzying sea of intellectual property laws and patents to ensure their own compliance, but also remain vigilant to protect their own company against infringement.
- **Chief automation officer** determines if a person or business process can be replaced by a robot or software. As we continue to automate jobs a member of the core leadership team of the future will be put in charge of identifying opportunities for companies to become more competitive through automation.
- **Chief user experience officer** will create the optimal relationship between user and technology. User experience used to be an afterthought for hardware and software designers. Now that bulky instruction manuals are largely (and thankfully) a thing of the past, technology companies need to ensure that their products are intuitive from the moment they are activated.

MIS skills gap is the difference between existing MIS workplace knowledge and the knowledge required to fulfill the business goals and strategies. Closing the MIS skills gap by aligning the current workforce with potential future business needs is a complicated proposition. Today, employers often

FIGURE 1.11
The Roles and Responsibilities of MIS

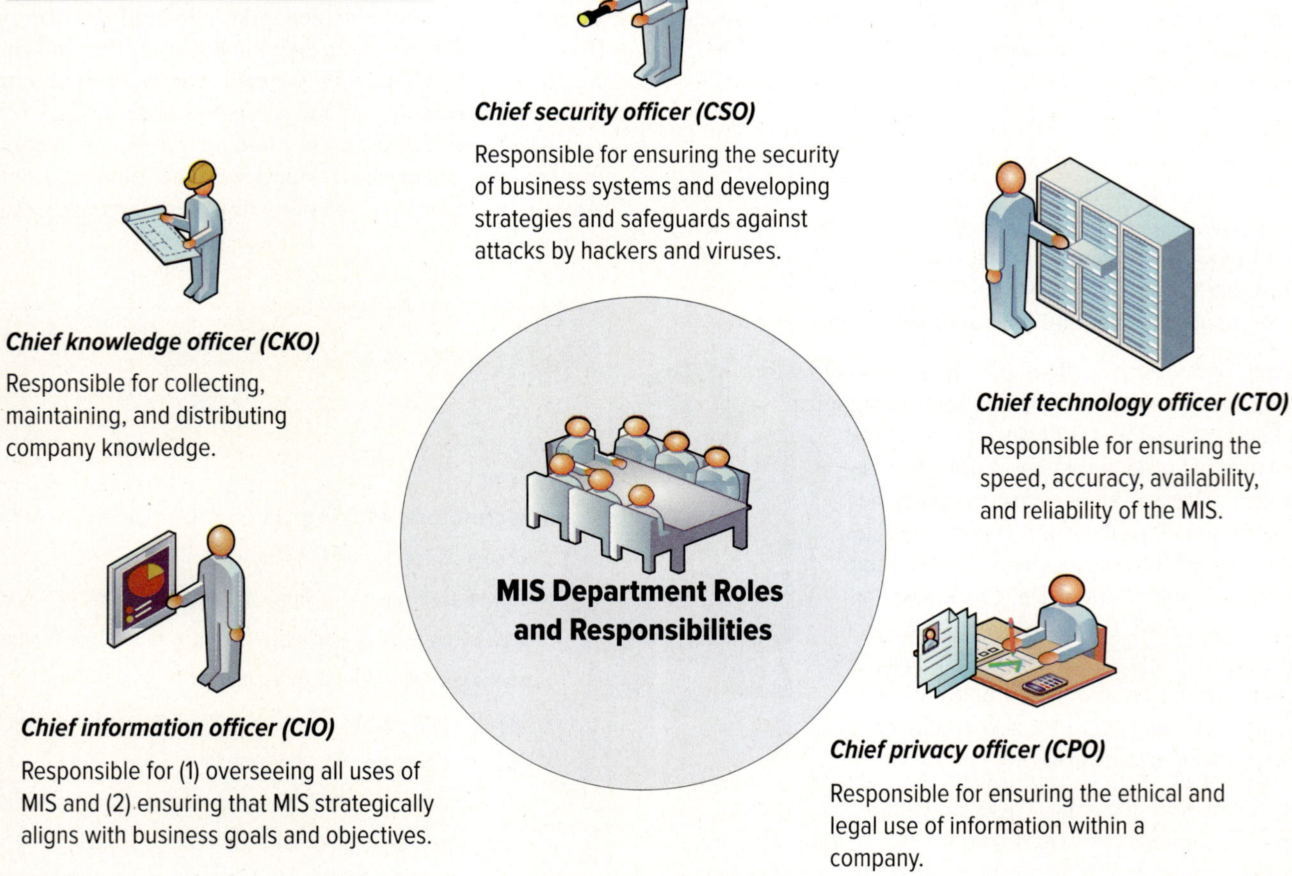

struggle to locate and retain qualified MIS talent, especially individuals with application development, information security, and data analysis skills.

Common approaches to closing an MIS skills gap include social recruiting, off-site training, mentoring services, and partnerships with universities. In many instances, an MIS job will remain unfilled for an extended period of time when an employer needs to hire someone who has a very specific set of skills. In recruiting lingo, such candidates are referred to as purple squirrels. Because squirrels in the real world are not often purple, the implication is that finding the perfect job candidate with exactly the right qualifications, education and salary expectations can be a daunting–if not impossible—task.

LO1.3 Explain systems thinking and how management information systems enable business communications.

{SECTION 1.2} Business Strategy

LEARNING OUTCOMES

LO1.4 Explain why competitive advantages are temporary along with the four key areas of a SWOT analysis.

LO1.5 Describe Porter's Five Forces Model and explain each of the five forces.

LO1.6 Compare Porter's three generic strategies.

LO1.7 Demonstrate how a company can add value by using Porter's value chain analysis.

business strategy A leadership plan that achieves a specific set of goals or objectives such as increasing sales, decreasing costs, entering new markets, or developing new products or services.

stakeholder A person or group that has an interest or concern in an organization.

IDENTIFYING COMPETITIVE ADVANTAGES LO1.4

Running a company today is similar to leading an army; the top manager or leader ensures all participants are heading in the right direction and completing their goals and objectives. Companies lacking leadership quickly implode as employees head in different directions attempting to achieve conflicting goals. To combat these challenges, leaders communicate and execute business strategies (from the Greek word *stratus* for army and *ago* for leading).

A **business strategy** is a leadership plan that achieves a specific set of goals or objectives such as increasing sales, decreasing costs, entering new markets, or developing new products or services. A **stakeholder** is a person or group that has an interest or concern in an organization. Stakeholders drive business strategies, and depending on the stakeholder's perspective, the business strategy can change. It is not uncommon to find stakeholders' business strategies have conflicting interests such as investors looking

Due Diligence //: Safekeeping Data

In the past few years, data collection rates have skyrocketed, and some estimate we have collected more data in the past four years than since the beginning of time. According to International Data Corporation, data collection amounts used to double every four years. With the massive growth of smart phones, tablets, and wearable technology devices, it seems as though data is being collected from everything, everywhere, all the time. It is estimated that data collection is doubling every two years, and soon it will double every six months. That is a lot of data! With the explosion of data collection, CTOs, CIOs, and CSOs are facing extremely difficult times as the threats to steal corporate sensitive data also growing exponentially. Hackers and criminals have recently stolen sensitive data from retail giant Target and even the Federal Reserve Bank.[6]

To operate, sensitive data has to flow outside an organization to partners, suppliers, community, government, and shareholders. List 10 types of sensitive data found in a common organization. Review the list of stakeholders; determine which types of sensitive data each has access to and whether you have any concerns about sharing this data. Do you have to worry about employees and sensitive data? How can using one of the four business strategies discussed in this section help you address your data leakage concerns?

© chrisdorney/Shutterstock

competitive advantage A feature of a product or service on which customers place a greater value than on similar offerings from competitors.

to increase profits by eliminating employee jobs. Figure 1.12 displays the different stakeholders found in an organization and their common business interests.

Good leaders also anticipate unexpected misfortunes, from strikes and economic recessions to natural disasters. Their business strategies build in buffers or slack, allowing the company the ability to ride out any storm and defend against competitive or environmental threats. Of course, updating business strategies is a continuous undertaking as internal and external environments rapidly change. Business strategies that match core company competencies to opportunities result in competitive advantages, a key to success!

A **competitive advantage** is a feature of a product or service on which customers place a greater value than they do on similar offerings from competitors. Competitive advantages provide the same product or service either at a lower price or with additional value that can fetch premium prices. Unfortunately, competitive advantages are typically temporary, because competitors often quickly seek ways to duplicate them. In turn, organizations must develop a strategy based on a new competitive advantage. Ways that companies duplicate competitive advantages include acquiring the new technology, copying the business operations, and hiring away key employees. The introduction of Apple's iPod and iTunes, a brilliant merger of technology, business, and entertainment, offers an excellent example.

In early 2000, Steve Jobs was fixated on developing video editing software when he suddenly realized that millions of people were using computers to listen to music, a new trend in the industry catapulted by illegal online services such as Napster. Jobs was worried that he was looking in the wrong direction and had missed the opportunity to jump on the online music bandwagon. He moved fast, however, and within four months he had developed the first version of iTunes for the Mac. Jobs' next challenge was to make a portable iTunes player that could hold thousands of songs and be completely transportable. Within nine months the iPod was born. With the combination of iTunes and iPod, Apple created a significant competitive advantage in the marketplace. Many firms began following Apple's lead by creating portable music players to compete with the iPod. In addition, Apple continues to create new and

FIGURE 1.12
Stakeholders' Interests

exciting products to gain competitive advantages, such as its iPad, a larger version of the iPod that functions more as a computer than a music player.[7]

When a company is the first to market with a competitive advantage, it gains a particular benefit, such as Apple did with its iPod. This **first-mover advantage** occurs when a company can significantly increase its market share by being first with a new competitive advantage. FedEx created a first-mover advantage by developing its customer self-service software, which allows people to request parcel pickups, print mailing slips, and track parcels online. Other parcel delivery companies quickly began creating their own online services. Today, customer self-service on the Internet is a standard feature of the parcel delivery business.

Competitive intelligence is the process of gathering information about the competitive environment, including competitors' plans, activities, and products, to improve a company's ability to succeed. It means understanding and learning as much as possible as soon as possible about what is occurring outside the company to remain competitive. Frito-Lay, a premier provider of snack foods such as Cracker Jacks and Cheetos, does not send its sales representatives into grocery stores just to stock shelves; they carry handheld computers and record the product offerings, inventory, and even product locations of competitors. Frito-Lay uses this information to gain competitive intelligence on everything from how well competing products are selling to the strategic placement of its own products. Managers use four common tools to analyze competitive intelligence and develop competitive advantages as displayed in Figure 1.13.

A **SWOT analysis** evaluates an organization's **s**trengths, **w**eaknesses, **o**pportunities, and **t**hreats to identify significant influences that work for or against business strategies (see Figure 1.14). Strengths and weaknesses originate inside an

first-mover advantage An advantage that occurs when a company can significantly increase its market share by being first to market with a competitive advantage.

competitive intelligence The process of gathering information about the competitive environment, including competitors' plans, activities, and products, to improve a company's ability to succeed.

SWOT analysis Evaluates an organization's strengths, weaknesses, opportunities, and threats to identify significant influences that work for or against business strategies.

What Happens on YouTube Stays on YouTube—FOREVER[8]

Are you looking for great career advice? Here it is: **Never** post anything on publicly accessible websites that you would not feel comfortable showing a recruiter or hiring manager. This includes inappropriate photos; negative comments about jobs, professors, or people; and binge drinking at a holiday party. Future employers will Google you!

The bad news: You have to continue to keep your cyber profile squeaky clean for the rest of your life. Companies can and will fire you for inappropriate website postings. One interesting story occurred when two employees created a private, password-protected group on Facebook where they would complain about their jobs, post derogatory comments about their managers, and highlight new top-secret product information. The managers, being computer savvy, obtained the password and immediately fired the two individuals after reviewing the site. Now one of the individuals is suing the former managers for invasion of privacy.

Do you agree that if you post something online it is open for the world to see? What do you consider is inappropriate material that you should never post to the web? What can you do to remove inappropriate material posted to the web by a friend that identifies you? How do efficiency and effectiveness enter into this scenario? What is the potential argument each of these sides might use in order to win the lawsuit?

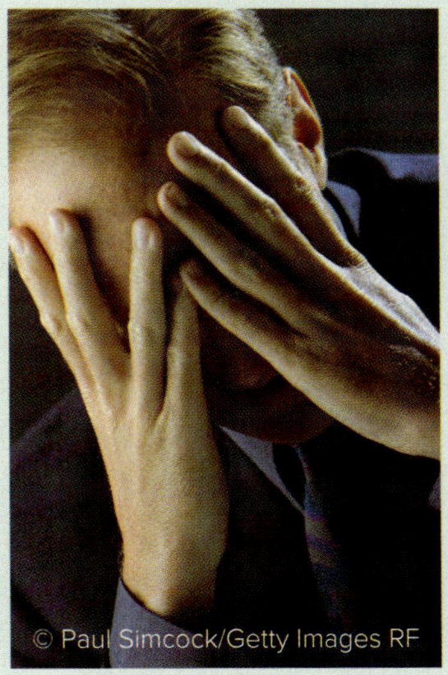

© Paul Simcock/Getty Images RF

Porter's Five Forces Model A model for analyzing the competitive forces within the environment in which a company operates, to assess the potential for profitability in an industry.

buyer power The ability of buyers to affect the price they must pay for an item.

organization, or internally. Opportunities and threats originate outside an organization, or externally and cannot always be anticipated or controlled.

- **Potential Internal Strengths (Helpful):** Identify all key strengths associated with the competitive advantage including cost advantages, new and/or innovative services, special expertise and/or experience, proven market leader, and improved marketing campaigns.
- **Potential Internal Weaknesses (Harmful):** Identify all key areas that require improvement. Weaknesses focus on the absence of certain strengths, including absence of an Internet marketing plan, damaged reputation, problem areas for service, and outdated technology employee issues.
- **Potential External Opportunities (Helpful):** Identify all significant trends along with how the organization can benefit from each, including new markets, additional customer groups, legal changes, innovative technologies, population changes, and competitor issues.
- **Potential External Threats (Harmful):** Identify all threats or risks detrimental to your organization, including new market entrants, substitute products, employee turnover, differentiating products, shrinking markets, adverse changes in regulations, and economic shifts.

FIGURE 1.13 Business Tools for Analyzing Business Strategies

FIGURE 1.14 Sample SWOT Analysis

LO1.4 Explain why competitive advantages are temporary along with the four key areas of a SWOT analysis.

THE FIVE FORCES MODEL—EVALUATING INDUSTRY ATTRACTIVENESS LO1.5

Michael Porter, a university professor at Harvard Business School, identified the following pressures that can hurt potential sales:

- Knowledgeable customers can force down prices by pitting rivals against each other.
- Influential suppliers can drive down profits by charging higher prices for supplies.
- Competition can steal customers.
- New market entrants can steal potential investment capital.
- Substitute products can steal customers.

Formally defined, **Porter's Five Forces Model** analyzes the competitive forces within the environment in which a company operates to assess the potential for profitability in an industry. Its purpose is to combat these competitive forces by identifying opportunities, competitive advantages, and competitive intelligence. If the forces are strong, they increase competition; if the forces are weak, they decrease competition. This section details each of the forces and its associated MIS business strategy (see Figure 1.15).[9]

LO1.5 Describe Porter's Five Forces Model and explain each of the five forces.

Buyer Power

Buyer power is the ability of buyers to affect the price they must pay for an item. Factors used to assess buyer power include number of customers,

show me *the* MONEY

SWOT Your Student

What is your dream job? Do you have the right skills and abilities to land the job of your dreams? If not, do you have a plan to acquire those sought-after skills and abilities? Do you have a personal career plan or strategy? Just like a business, you can perform a personal SWOT analysis to ensure your career plan will be successful. You want to know your strengths and recognize career opportunities while mitigating your weaknesses and any threats that can potentially derail your career plans. A key area where many people struggle is technology, and without the right technical skills, you might find you are not qualified for your dream job. One of the great benefits of this course is its ability to help you prepare for a career in business by understanding the key role technology plays in the different industries and functional areas. Regardless of your major, you will all use business driven information systems to complete the tasks and assignments associated with your career.

Perform a personal SWOT analysis for your career plan, based on your current skills, talents, and knowledge. Be sure to focus on your personal career goals, including the functional business area in which you want to work and the potential industry you are targeting, such as health care, telecommunications, retail, or travel.

PERSONAL CAREER SWOT ANALYSIS

After completing your personal SWOT analysis, take a look at the table of contents in this text and determine whether this course will eliminate any of your weaknesses or create new strengths. Determine whether you can find new opportunities or mitigate threats based on the material we cover over the next several weeks. For example, Chapter 9 covers project management in detail—a key skill for any business professional who must run a team. Learning how to assign and track work status will be a key tool for any new business professional. Where would you place this great skill in your SWOT analysis? Did it help eliminate any of your weaknesses? When you have finished this exercise, compare your SWOT with your peers to see what kind of competition you will encounter when you enter the workforce.

their sensitivity to price, size of orders, differences between competitors, and availability of substitute products. If buyer power is high, customers can force a company and its competitors to compete on price, which typically drives prices down.

One way to reduce buyer power is by manipulating **switching costs**, costs that make customers reluctant to switch to another product or service. Switching costs include financial as well as intangible values. The cost of switching doctors, for instance, includes the powerful intangible components of having to build relationships with the new doctor and nurses, as well as transferring all your medical history. With MIS, however, patients can store their medical records on DVDs or thumb drives, allowing easy transferability. The Internet also lets patients review websites for physician referrals, which takes some of the fear out of trying someone new.[10]

Companies can also reduce buyer power with **loyalty programs**, which reward customers based on their spending. The airline industry is famous for its frequent-flyer programs, for instance. Because of the rewards travelers receive (free airline tickets, upgrades, or hotel stays), they are more likely to be loyal to or give most of their business to a single company. Keeping track of the activities and accounts of many thousands or millions of customers covered by loyalty programs is not practical without large-scale business systems, however. Loyalty programs are thus a good example of using MIS to reduce buyer power.[11]

switching costs Costs that make customers reluctant to switch to another product or service.

loyalty program A program to reward customers based on spending.

supply chain All parties involved, directly or indirectly, in obtaining raw materials or a product.

supplier power One of Porter's five forces; measures the suppliers' ability to influence the prices they charge for supplies (including materials, labor, and services).

threat of substitute products or services One of Porter's five forces, high when there are many alternatives to a product or service and low when there are few alternatives from which to choose.

FIGURE 1.15 Porter's Five Forces Model

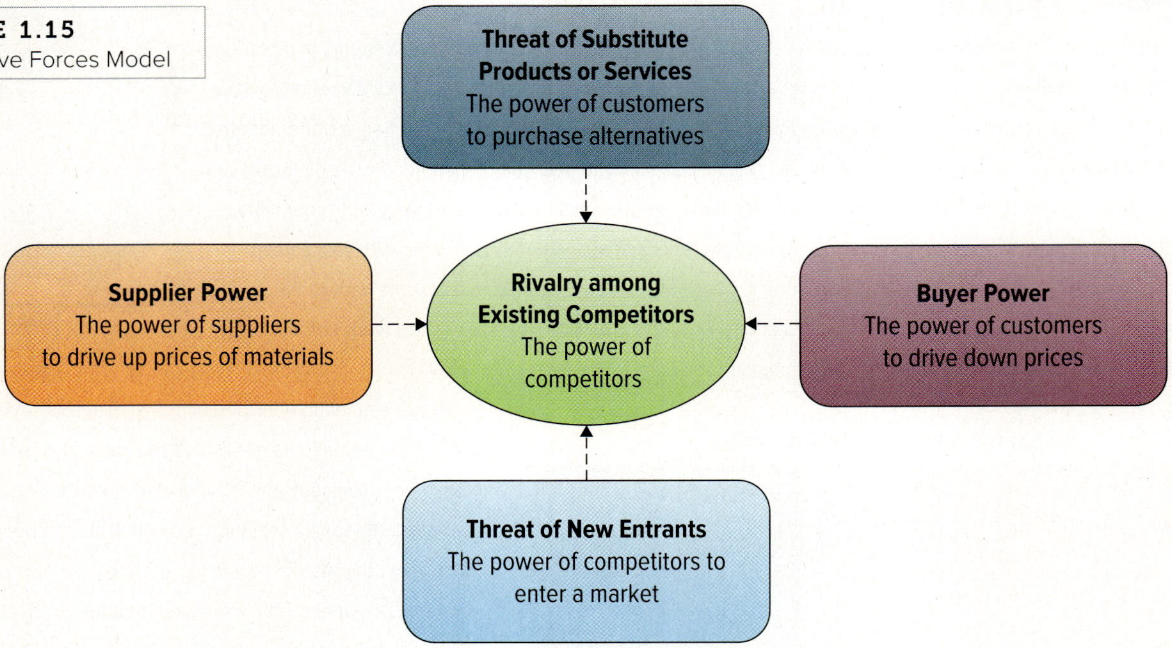

Supplier Power

A **supply chain** consists of all parties involved, directly or indirectly, in obtaining raw materials or a product. In a typical supply chain, a company will be both a supplier (to customers) and a customer (of other suppliers), as illustrated in Figure 1.16. **Supplier power** is the suppliers' ability to influence the prices they charge for supplies (including materials, labor, and services). Factors used to appraise supplier power include number of suppliers, size of suppliers, uniqueness of services, and availability of substitute products. If supplier power is high, the supplier can influence the industry by:

- Charging higher prices.
- Limiting quality or services.
- Shifting costs to industry participants.[12]

Typically, when a supplier raises prices, the buyers will pass on the increase to their customers by raising prices on the end product. When supplier power is high, buyers lose revenue because they cannot pass on the raw material price increase to their customers. Some powerful suppliers, such as pharmaceutical companies, can exert a threat over an entire industry when substitutes are limited and the product is critical to the buyers. Patients who need to purchase cancer-fighting drugs have no power over price and must pay whatever the drug company asks because there are few available alternatives.

FIGURE 1.16 Traditional Supply Chain

Using MIS to find alternative products is one way of decreasing supplier power. Cancer patients can now use the Internet to research alternative medications and practices, something that was next to impossible just a few decades ago. Buyers can also use MIS to form groups or collaborate with other buyers, increasing the size of the buyer group and reducing supplier power. For a hypothetical example, the collective group of 30,000 students from a university has far more power over price when purchasing laptops than a single student.[13]

Threat of Substitute Products or Services

The **threat of substitute products or services** is high when there are many alternatives to a product or service and

threat of new entrants One of Porter's five forces, high when it is easy for new competitors to enter a market and low when there are significant entry barriers to joining a market.

entry barrier A feature of a product or service that customers have come to expect and entering competitors must offer the same for survival.

rivalry among existing competitors One of Porter's five forces; high when competition is fierce in a market and low when competitors are more complacent.

product differentiation An advantage that occurs when a company develops unique differences in its products with the intent to influence demand.

low when there are few alternatives from which to choose. For example, travelers have numerous substitutes for airline transportation including automobiles, trains, and boats. Technology even makes videoconferencing and virtual meetings possible, eliminating the need for some business travel. Ideally, a company would like to be in a market in which there are few substitutes for the products or services it offers.

Polaroid had this unique competitive advantage for many years until it forgot to observe competitive intelligence. Then the firm went bankrupt when people began taking digital pictures with everything from video cameras to cell phones.

A company can reduce the threat of substitutes by offering additional value through wider product distribution. Soft-drink manufacturers distribute their products through vending machines, gas stations, and convenience stores, increasing the availability of soft drinks relative to other beverages. Companies can also offer various add-on services, making the substitute product less of a threat. For example, iPhones include capabilities for games, videos, and music, making a traditional cell phone less of a substitute.[14]

Threat of New Entrants

The **threat of new entrants** is high when it is easy for new competitors to enter a market and low when there are significant entry barriers to joining a market. An **entry barrier** is a feature of a product or service that customers have come to expect and entering competitors must offer the same for survival. For example, a new bank must offer its customers an array of MIS-enabled services, including ATMs, online bill paying, and online account monitoring. These are significant barriers to new firms entering the banking market. At one time, the first bank to offer such services gained a valuable first-mover advantage, but only temporarily, as other banking competitors developed their own MIS services.[15]

Rivalry among Existing Competitors

Rivalry among existing competitors is high when competition is fierce in a market and low when competitors are more complacent. Although competition is always more intense in some industries than in others, the overall trend is toward increased competition in almost every industry. The retail grocery industry is intensively competitive. Kroger, Safeway, and Albertsons in the United States compete in many different ways, essentially trying to beat or match each other on price. Most supermarket chains have implemented loyalty programs to provide customers special discounts while gathering valuable information about their purchasing habits. In the future, expect to see grocery stores using wireless technologies that track customer movements throughout the store to determine purchasing sequences.

Product differentiation occurs when a company develops unique differences in its products or services with the intent to influence demand. Companies can use differentiation to reduce rivalry. For example, while many companies sell books and videos on the Internet, Amazon differentiates itself by using customer profiling. When a customer visits Amazon.com repeatedly, Amazon begins to offer products tailored to that particular customer based on his or her profile. In this way, Amazon has reduced its rivals' power by offering its customers a differentiated service.

To review, the Five Forces Model helps managers set business strategy by identifying the competitive structure and economic environment of an industry. If the forces are strong, they increase competition; if the forces are weak, they decrease it (see Figure 1.17).[16]

Analyzing the Airline Industry

Let us bring Porter's five forces together to look at the competitive forces shaping an industry and highlight business

FIGURE 1.17 Strong and Weak Examples of Porter's Five Forces

	Weak Force: Decreases Competition or Few Competitors	Strong Force: Increases Competition or Lots of Competitors
Buyer Power	An international hotel chain purchasing milk	A single consumer purchasing milk
Supplier Power	A company that makes airline engines	A company that makes pencils
Threat of Substitute Products or Services	Cancer drugs from a pharmaceutical company	Coffee from McDonald's
Threat of New Entrants	A professional hockey team	A dog walking business
Rivalry among Existing Competitors	Department of Motor Vehicles	A coffee shop

Porter's three generic strategies Generic business strategies that are neither organization nor industry specific and can be applied to any business, product, or service.

strategies to help it remain competitive. Assume a shipping company is deciding whether to enter the commercial airline industry. If performed correctly, an analysis of the five forces should determine that this is a highly risky business strategy because all five forces are strong. It will thus be difficult to generate a profit.

- **Buyer power:** Buyer power is high because customers have many airlines to choose from and typically make purchases based on price, not carrier.
- **Supplier power:** Supplier power is high since there are limited plane and engine manufacturers to choose from, and unionized workforces (suppliers of labor) restrict airline profits.
- **Threat of substitute products or services:** The threat of substitute products is high from many transportation alternatives including automobiles, trains, and boats, and from transportation substitutes such as videoconferencing and virtual meetings.
- **Threat of new entrants:** The threat of new entrants is high because new airlines are continuously entering the market, including sky taxies offering low-cost on-demand air taxi service.
- **Rivalry among existing competitors:** Rivalry in the airline industry is high, and websites such as Travelocity and Priceline force them to compete on price (see Figure 1.18).[17]

THE THREE GENERIC STRATEGIES—CHOOSING A BUSINESS FOCUS LO1.6

Once top management has determined the relative attractiveness of an industry and decided to enter it, the firm must formulate a strategy for doing so. If our sample company decided to join the airline industry, it could compete as a low-cost, no-frills airline or as a luxury airline providing outstanding service and first-class comfort. Both options offer different ways of achieving competitive advantages in a crowded marketplace. The low-cost operator saves on expenses and passes the savings along to customers in the form of low prices. The luxury airline spends on high-end service and first-class comforts and passes the costs on to the customer in the form of high prices.

Porter's three generic strategies are generic business strategies that are neither organization nor industry specific and can be applied to any business, product, or service. These three generic business strategies for entering a new market are: (1) broad cost

FIGURE 1.18 Five Forces Model in the Airline Industry

	Strong (High) Force: Increases Competition or Lots of Competitors
Buyer Power	Many airlines for buyers to choose from forcing competition based on price.
Supplier Power	Limited number of plane and engine manufacturers to choose from along with unionized workers.
Threat of Substitute Products or Services	Many substitutes including cars, trains, and buses. Even substitutes to travel such as video conferencing and virtual meetings.
Threat of New Entrants	Many new airlines entering the market all the time including the latest sky taxis.
Rivalry among Existing Competitors	Intense competition—many rivals.

fyi Cool College Start-Ups

Not long ago, people would call college kids who started businesses quaint. Now they call them the boss. For almost a decade, *Inc.* magazine has been watching college start-ups and posting a list of the nation's top start-ups taking campuses by storm. Helped in part by low-cost technologies and an increased prevalence of entrepreneurship training at the university level, college students—and indeed those even younger—are making solid strides at founding companies. And they're not just launching local pizza shops and fashion boutiques. They are starting up businesses that could scale into much bigger companies and may already cater to a national audience.

Research *Inc.* magazine at www.inc.com and find the year's current Coolest College Startup listing. Choose one of the businesses and perform a Porter's Five Forces analysis. Be sure to highlight each force, including switching costs, product differentiation, and loyalty programs.

leadership, (2) broad differentiation, and (3) focused strategy. Broad strategies reach a large market segment, while focused strategies target a niche or unique market with either cost leadership or differentiation. Trying to be all things to all people is a recipe for disaster, since doing so makes it difficult to project a consistent image to the entire marketplace. For this reason, Porter suggests adopting only one of the three generic strategies illustrated in Figure 1.19.

Figure 1.20 applies the three strategies to real companies, demonstrating the relationships among strategies (cost leadership versus differentiation) and market segmentation (broad versus focused).

- **Broad market and low cost:** Walmart competes by offering a broad range of products at low prices. Its business strategy is to be the low-cost provider of goods for the cost-conscious consumer.
- **Broad market and high cost:** Neiman Marcus competes by offering a broad range of differentiated products at high prices. Its business strategy offers a variety of specialty and upscale products to affluent consumers.
- **Narrow market and low cost:** Payless competes by offering a specific product, shoes, at low prices. Its business strategy is to be the low-cost provider of shoes. Payless competes with Walmart, which also sells low-cost shoes, by offering a far bigger selection of sizes and styles.

show me *the* MONEY

Death of a Product

Porter's Five Forces Model is an essential framework for understanding industries and market forces. Choose one of the categories listed here and analyze what happened to the market using Porter's Five Forces:

- On-demand movies and blue-ray players.
- Digital camera and Polaroid camera.
- GPS device and a road atlas.
- Digital books and printed books.
- High-definition TV and radio.

- **Narrow market and high cost:** Tiffany & Co. competes by offering a differentiated product, jewelry, at high prices. Its business strategy allows it to be a high-cost provider of premier designer jewelry to affluent consumers.

LO1.6 Compare Porter's three generic strategies.

FIGURE 1.19
Porter's Three Generic Strategies

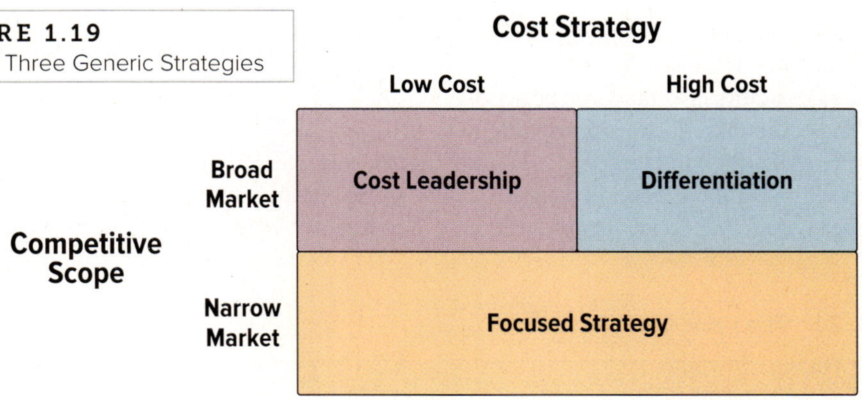

FIGURE 1.20
Examples of Porter's Three Generic Strategies

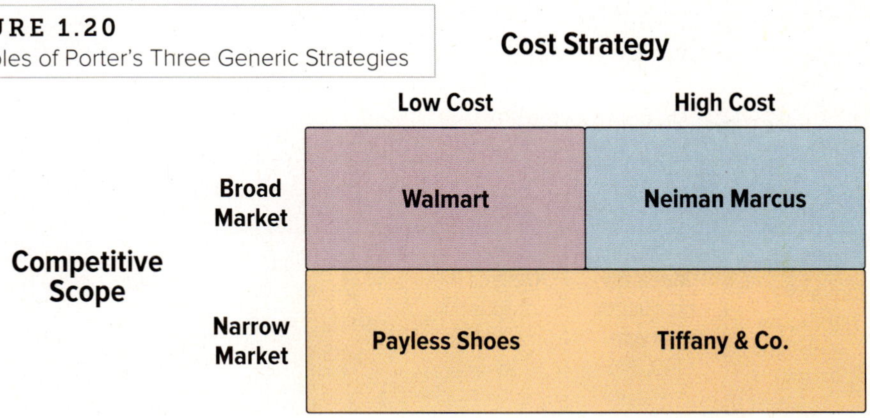

Living the DREAM

One Laptop per Child[18]

Nicholas Negroponte is the founder of the MIT Media Lab and has spent his career pushing the edge of the information revolution as an inventor, thinker, and angel investor. His latest project, One Laptop per Child, plans to build $100 laptops that he hopes to put in the hands of the millions of children in developing countries around the globe. The XO (the "$100 laptop") is a wireless Internet-enabled, pedal-powered computer costing roughly $100. What types of competitive advantages could children gain from Negroponte's $100 laptop? What types of issues could result from the $100 laptop? Which of Porter's three generic strategies is Negroponte following?

© Miguel Rojo/Getty Images

VALUE CHAIN ANALYSIS—EXECUTING BUSINESS STRATEGIES LO1.7

Firms make profits by taking raw inputs and applying a business process to turn them into a product or service that customers find valuable. A **business process** is a standardized set of activities that accomplish a specific task, such as processing a customer's order. Once a firm identifies the industry it wants to enter and the generic strategy it will focus on, it must then choose the business processes required to create its products or services. Of course, the firm will want to ensure the processes add value and create competitive advantages. To identify these competitive advantages, Michael Porter created **value chain analysis**, which views a firm as a series of business processes that each add value to the product or service.

Value chain analysis is a useful tool for determining how to create the greatest possible value for customers (see Figure 1.21). The goal of value chain analysis is to identify processes in which the firm can add value for the customer and create a competitive advantage for itself, with a cost advantage or product differentiation.

The *value chain* groups a firm's activities into two categories, primary value activities, and support value activities. **Primary value activities**, shown at the bottom of the value chain in

FIGURE 1.21 The Value Chain

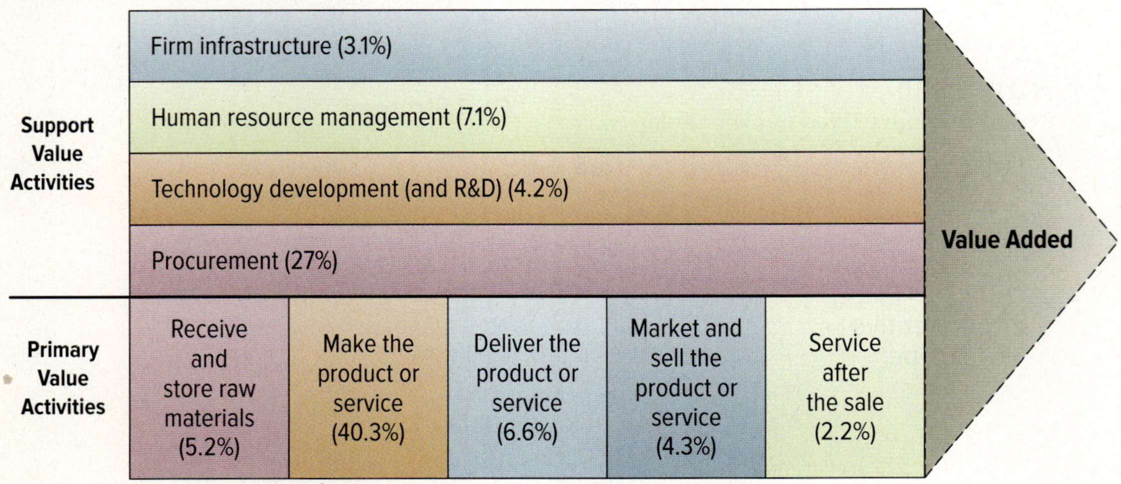

business process Standardized set of activities that accomplish a specific task.

value chain analysis Views a firm as a series of business processes that each add value to the product or service.

primary value activities Found at the bottom of the value chain, these include business processes that acquire raw materials and manufacture, deliver, market, sell, and provide after-sales services.

support value activities Found along the top of the value chain and includes business processes, such as firm infrastructure, human resource management, technology development, and procurement, that support the primary value activities.

BUSTED Listen to Spider-Man; He Knows What He's Talking About![20]

Spider-Man's infamous advice—"With great power comes great responsibility"—should be applied to every type of technology you encounter in business. Technology provides countless opportunities for businesses, but it can also lead to countless pitfalls and traps. A great example is how many companies profited from online trading and how many people lost their life savings in online trading scams. For example, Bernard Madoff, the owner of a high-profile New York investment company, was able to forge investment statements and allegedly spent almost $50 billion of his client's money. Craigslist allows anyone to become a provider of goods and services. Unfortunately, Craigslist does not describe exactly what types of goods and services are allowed. Adam Vitale was sentenced to two years in prison after he found running an online prostitution ring through Craigslist.

The IOT is generating massive amounts of data from millions of sensors. Research the Internet and find an example of unethical behavior with IOT data and share the examples with your peers. What can businesses to do to prevent IOT data from being used unethically?

© Ingram Publishing

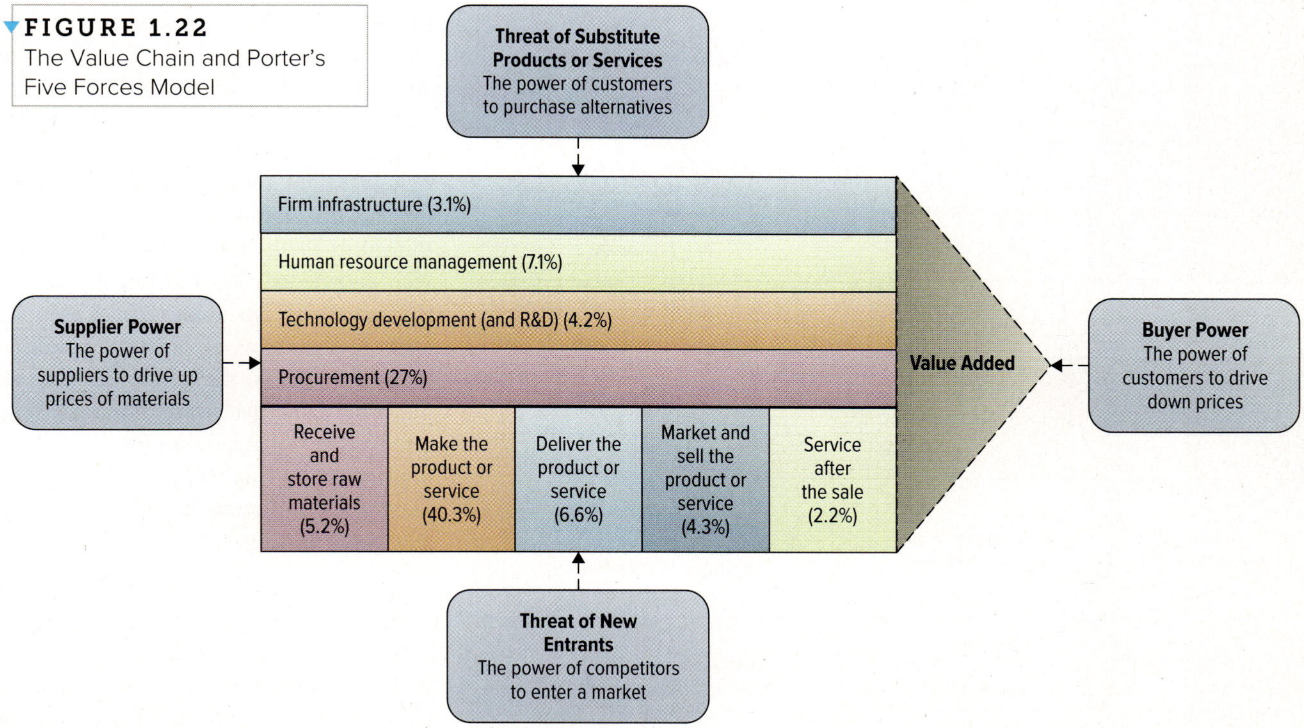

FIGURE 1.22
The Value Chain and Porter's Five Forces Model

FIGURE 1.23 Overview of Information Systems

MODULE 1: BUSINESS DRIVEN MIS

	Business Strategy	MIS Topics
Chapter 1: Management Information Systems	Understanding Business Driven MIS	Data Information Business Intelligence Knowledge Systems Thinking Porter's Business Strategies
Chapter 2: Decisions and Processes	Creating Value Driven Businesses	Transaction Processing Systems Decision Support Systems Executive Information Systems Artificial Intelligence Business Process Reengineering
Chapter 3: Ebusiness	Finding Electronic Business Value	eBusiness eBusiness Models Social Networking Knowledge Management Collaboration
Chapter 4: Ethics and Information Security	Identifying MIS Business Concerns	Information Security Policies Authentication and Authorization Prevention and Resistance Detection and Response

MODULE 2: TECHNICAL FOUNDATIONS OF MIS

	Business Strategy	MIS Topics
Chapter 5: Infrastructures	Deploying Organizational MIS	Grid Computing Cloud Computing Virtualization Sustainable MIS Infrastructures
Chapter 6: Data	Uncovering Business Intelligence	Database Data Management Systems Data Warehousing Data Mining
Chapter 7: Networks	Supporting Mobile Business	Business Networks Web 1.0, Web 2.0, Web 3.0 Mobile MIS Wireless MIS GPS, GIS, and LBS

MODULE 3: ENTERPRISE MIS

	Business Strategy	MIS Topics
Chapter 8: Enterprise Applications	Enhancing Business Communications	Customer Relationship Management Supply Chain Management Enterprise Resource Planning
Chapter 9: Systems Development and Project Management	Leading MIS Projects	MIS Development Methodologies Project Management Outsourcing

Figure 1.21, acquire raw materials and manufacture, deliver, market, sell, and provide after-sales services.

1. **Inbound logistics:** acquires raw materials and resources and distributes to manufacturing as required.
2. **Operations:** transforms raw materials or inputs into goods and services.
3. **Outbound logistics:** distributes goods and services to customers.
4. **Marketing and sales:** promotes, prices, and sells products to customers.
5. **Service:** provides customer support after the sale of goods and services.[19]

Support value activities, along the top of the value chain in Figure 1.21, include firm infrastructure, human resource management, technology development, and procurement. Not surprisingly, these support the primary value activities.

- **Firm infrastructure:** includes the company format or departmental structures, environment, and systems.
- **Human resource management:** provides employee training, hiring, and compensation.
- **Technology development:** applies MIS to processes to add value.
- **Procurement:** purchases inputs such as raw materials, resources, equipment, and supplies.

It is easy to understand how a typical manufacturing firm takes raw materials such as wood pulp and transforms it into paper. Adding value in this example might include using high-quality raw materials or offering next-day free shipping on any order. How, though, might a typical service firm take raw inputs such as time, knowledge, and MIS and transform them into valuable customer service knowledge? A hotel might use MIS to track customer reservations and then inform front-desk employees when a loyal customer is checking in so the employee can call the guest by name and offer additional services, gift baskets, or upgraded rooms. Examining the firm as a value chain allows managers to identify the important business processes that add value for customers and then find MIS solutions that support them.

When performing a value chain analysis, a firm could survey customers about the extent to which they believe each activity adds value to the product or service. This step generates responses the firm can measure, shown as percentages in Figure 1.22, to describe how each activity adds (or reduces) value. Then the competitive advantage decision for the firm is whether to (1) target high value-adding activities to further enhance their value, (2) target low value-adding activities to increase their value, or (3) perform some combination of the two.

MIS adds value to both primary and support value activities. One example of a primary value activity facilitated by MIS is the development of a marketing campaign management system that could target marketing campaigns more efficiently, thereby reducing marketing costs. The system would also help the firm better pinpoint target market needs, thereby increasing sales. One example of a support value activity facilitated by MIS is the development of a human resources system that could more efficiently reward employees based on performance. The system could also identify employees who are at risk of quitting, allowing managers' time to find additional challenges or opportunities that would help retain these employees and thus reduce turnover costs.

Value chain analysis is a highly useful tool that provides hard and fast numbers for evaluating the activities that add value to products and services. Managers can find additional value by analyzing and constructing the value chain in terms of Porter's Five Forces Model (see Figure 1.22). For example, if the goal is to decrease buyer power, a company can construct its value chain activity of "service after the sale" by offering high levels of customer service. This will increase customers' switching costs and reduce their power. Analyzing and constructing support value activities can help decrease the threat of new entrants. Analyzing and constructing primary value activities can help decrease the threat of substitute products or services.[21]

Revising Porter's three business strategies is critical. Firms must continually adapt to their competitive environments, which can cause business strategy to shift. In the remainder of this text we discuss how managers can formulate business strategies using MIS to create competitive advantages. Figure 1.23 gives an overview of the remaining chapters, along with the relevant business strategy and associated MIS topics. ■

LO1.7 Demonstrate how a company can add value by using Porter's value chain analysis.

View
Window

chapter two

decisions + processes: value driven business

what's in IT for me?

Working faster and smarter has become a necessity for companies. A firm's value chain is directly affected by how well it designs and coordinates its business processes. Business processes offer competitive advantages if they enable a firm to lower operating costs, differentiate, or compete in a niche market. They can also be huge burdens if they are outdated, which impedes operations, efficiency, and effectiveness. Thus, the ability of management information systems to improve business processes is a key advantage.

The goal of Chapter 2 is to provide an overview of specific MIS tools managers can use to support the strategies discussed in Chapter 1. After reading this

continued on p. 34

CHAPTER OUTLINE

SECTION 2.1 >>

Decision Support Systems

- Making Business Decisions
- Measuring Business Decisions
- Using MIS to Make Business Decisions
- Using AI to Make Business Decisions

SECTION 2.2 >>

Business Processes

- Managing Business Processes
- Business Process Modeling
- Using MIS to Improve Business Processes

operational level Employees develop, control, and maintain core business activities required to run the day-to-day operations.

structured decision Involves situations where established processes offer potential solutions.

continued from p. 33

chapter, you, the business student, should have detailed knowledge of the types of information systems that exist to support decision making and business process reengineering, which in turn can improve organization efficiency and effectiveness and help an organization create and maintain competitive advantages. ■

{SECTION 2.1} Decision Support Systems

LEARNING OUTCOMES

LO2.1 Explain the importance of decision making for managers at each of the three primary organization levels along with the associated decision characteristics.

LO2.2 Define critical success factors (CSFs) and key performance indicators (KPIs), and explain how managers use them to measure the success of MIS projects.

LO2.3 Classify the different operational support systems, managerial support systems, and strategic support systems, and explain how managers can use these systems to make decisions and gain competitive advantages.

LO2.4 Describe artificial intelligence, and identify its five main types.

MAKING BUSINESS DECISIONS LO2.1

Porter's strategies outlined in Chapter 1 suggest entering markets with a competitive advantage in either overall cost leadership, differentiation, or focus. To achieve these results, managers must be able to make decisions and forecast future business needs and requirements. The most important and most challenging question confronting managers today is how to lay the foundation for tomorrow's success while competing to win in today's business environment. A company will not have a future if it is not cultivating strategies for tomorrow. The goal of this section is to expand on Porter's Five Forces Model, three generic strategies, and value chain analysis to demonstrate how managers can learn the concepts and practices of business decision making to add value. It will also highlight how companies today are taking advantage of advanced MIS capable of generating significant competitive advantages across the value chain.

As we discussed in Chapter 1, decision making is one of the most important and challenging aspects of management. Decisions range from routine choices, such as how many items to order or how many people to hire, to unexpected ones such as what to do if a key employee suddenly quits or needed materials do not arrive. Today, with massive volumes of information available, managers are challenged to make highly complex decisions—some involving far more information than the human brain can comprehend—in increasingly shorter time frames. Figure 2.1 displays the three primary challenges managers face when making decisions.

LO2.1 Explain the importance of decision making for managers at each of the three primary organization levels along with the associated decision characteristics.

FIGURE 2.1 Managerial Decision-Making Challenges

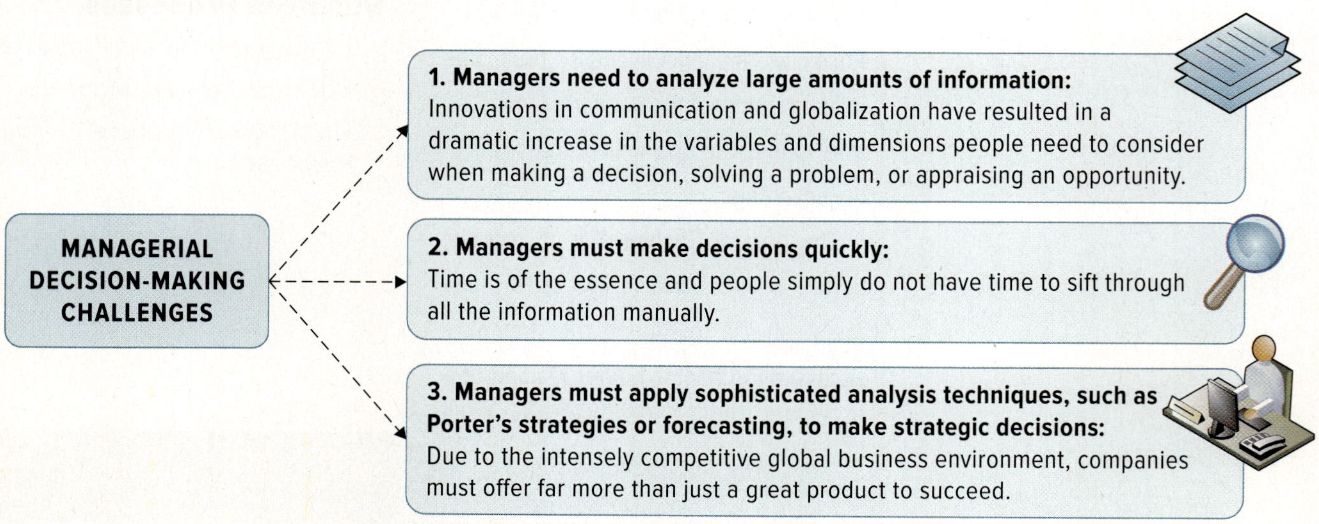

FIGURE 2.2 The Six-Step Decision-Making Process

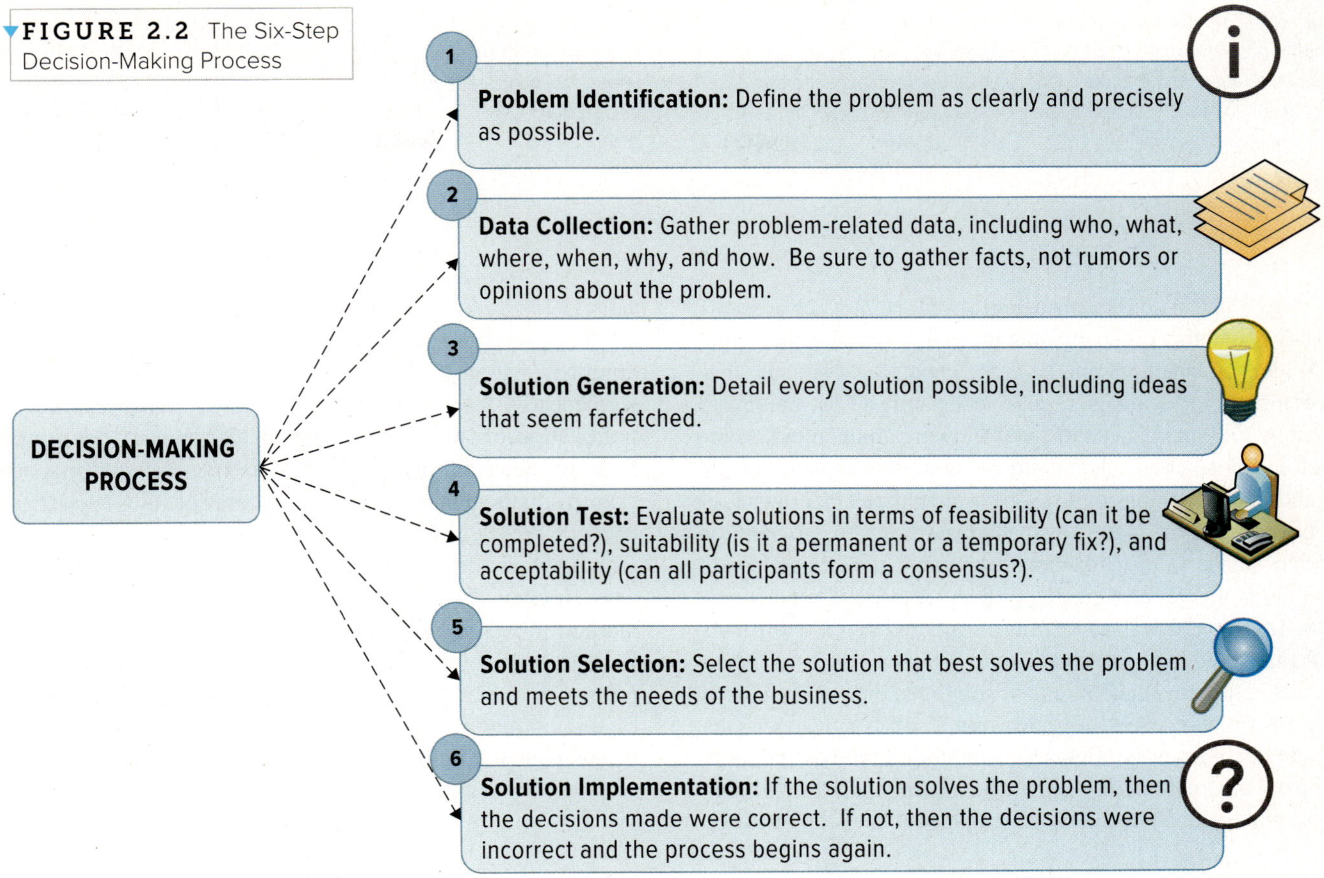

FIGURE 2.3 Common Company Structure

The Decision-Making Process

The process of making decisions plays a crucial role in communication and leadership for operational, managerial, and strategic projects. Analytics is the science of fact-based decision making. There are numerous academic decision-making models; Figure 2.2 presents just one example.[1]

Decision-Making Essentials

A few key concepts about organizational structure will help our discussion of MIS decision-making tools. The structure of a typical organization is similar to a pyramid, and the different levels require different types of information to assist in decision making, problem solving, and opportunity capturing (see Figure 2.3).

Operational At the **operational level**, employees develop, control, and maintain core business activities required to run the day-to-day operations. Operational decisions are considered **structured decisions**, which arise in situations where established processes offer potential solutions. Structured decisions are made frequently and are almost repetitive in nature; they affect short-term business strategies. Reordering inventory and creating the employee staffing and weekly production schedules are examples of routine structured decisions. Figure 2.4 highlights the essential elements required for operational decision making. All the elements in the figure should be familiar, except metrics, which are discussed in detail below.

managerial level Employees are continuously evaluating company operations to hone the firm's abilities to identify, adapt to, and leverage change.

semistructured decision Occurs in situations in which a few established processes help to evaluate potential solutions, but not enough to lead to a definite recommended decision.

strategic level Managers develop overall business strategies, goals, and objectives as part of the company's strategic plan.

unstructured decision Occurs in situations in which no procedures or rules exist to guide decision makers toward the correct choice.

Managerial At the **managerial level**, employees are continuously evaluating company operations to hone the firm's abilities to identify, adapt to, and leverage change. A company that has a competitive advantage needs to constantly adjust and revise its strategy to remain ahead of fast-following competitors. Managerial decisions cover short- and medium-range plans, schedules, and budgets along with policies, procedures, and business objectives for the firm. They also allocate resources and monitor the performance of organizational subunits, including departments, divisions, process teams, project teams, and other work groups. These types of decisions are considered **semistructured decisions**; they occur in situations in which a few established processes help to evaluate potential solutions, but not enough to lead to a definite recommended decision. For example, decisions about producing new products or changing employee benefits range from unstructured to semistructured. Figure 2.4 highlights the essential elements required for managerial decision making.

Strategic At the **strategic level**, managers develop overall business strategies, goals, and objectives as part of the company's strategic plan. They also monitor the strategic performance of the organization and its overall direction in the political, economic, and competitive business environment. Strategic decisions are highly **unstructured decisions**, occurring in situations in which no procedures or rules exist to guide decision makers toward the correct choice. They are infrequent, extremely important, and typically related to long-term business strategy. Examples include the decision to enter a new market or even a new industry over, say, the next three years. In these types of decisions, managers rely on many sources of information, along with personal knowledge, to find solutions. Figure 2.4 highlights the essential elements required for strategic decision making.

FIGURE 2.4 Overview of Decision Making

	Strategic Level	Managerial Level	Operational Level
Employee Types	• Senior management, presidents, leaders, executives	• Middle management, managers, directors	• Lower management, department managers, analysts, staff
Focus	• External, industry, cross company	• Internal, crossfunctional (sometimes external)	• Internal, functional
Time Frame	• Long term—yearly, multiyear	• Short term, daily, monthly, yearly	• Short term, day-to-day operations
Decision Types	• Unstructured, nonrecurring, one time	• Semistructured, ad hoc (unplanned) reporting	• Structured, recurring, repetitive
MIS Types	• Knowledge	• Business intelligence	• Information
Metrics	• Critical success factors focusing on effectiveness	• Key performance indicators focusing on efficiency, and critical success factors focusing on effectiveness	• Key performance indicators focusing on efficiency
Examples	• How will changes in employment levels over the next 3 years affect the company? • What industry trends are worth analyzing? • What new products and new markets does the company need to create competitive advantages? • How will a recession over the next year affect business? • What measures will the company need to prepare for due to new tax laws?	• Who are our best customers by region, by sales representative, by product? • What are the sales forecasts for next month? How do they compare to actual sales for last year? • What was the difference between expected sales and actual sales for each month? • What was the impact of last month's marketing campaign on sales? • What types of ad hoc or unplanned reports might the company require next month?	• How many employees are out sick? • What are next week's production requirements? • How much inventory is in the warehouse? • How many problems occurred when running payroll? • Which employees are on vacation next week? • How many products need to be made today?

project Temporary activity a company undertakes to create a unique product, service, or result.

metrics Measurements that evaluate results to determine whether a project is meeting its goals.

critical success factors (CSFs) Crucial steps companies perform to achieve their goals and objectives and implement their strategies.

key performance indicators (KPIs) Quantifiable metrics a company uses to evaluate progress towards critical success factors.

market share The proportion of the market that a firm captures.

MEASURING BUSINESS DECISIONS LO2.2

A **project** is a temporary activity a company undertakes to create a unique product, service, or result. For example, the construction of a new subway station is a project, as is a movie theater chain's adoption of a software program to allow online ticketing. Peter Drucker, a famous management writer, once said that if you cannot measure something, you cannot manage it. How do managers measure the progress of a complex business project?

Metrics are measurements that evaluate results to determine whether a project is meeting its goals. Two core metrics are critical success factors and key performance indicators. **Critical success factors (CSFs)** are the crucial steps companies perform to achieve their goals and objectives and implement their strategies (see Figure 2.5). **Key performance indicators (KPIs)** are the quantifiable metrics a company uses to evaluate progress toward critical success factors. KPIs are far more specific than CSFs.

It is important to understand the relationship between critical success factors and key performance indicators. CSFs are elements crucial for a business strategy's success. KPIs measure the progress of CSFs with quantifiable measurements, and one CSF can have several KPIs. Of course, both categories will vary by company and industry. Imagine *improve graduation rates* as a CSF for a college. The KPIs to measure this CSF can include:

- Average grades by course and gender.
- Student dropout rates by gender and major.
- Average graduation rate by gender and major.
- Time spent in tutoring by gender and major.

KPIs can focus on external and internal measurements. A common external KPI is **market share**, or the proportion of the market that a firm captures. We calculate it by dividing the firm's sales by the total market sales for the entire industry. Market share measures a firm's external performance relative to that of its competitors. For example, if a firm's total sales (revenues) are $2 million and sales for the entire industry are $10 million, the firm has captured 20 percent of the total market (2/10 = 20%) or a 20 percent market share.

FIGURE 2.5 CSF and KPI Metrics

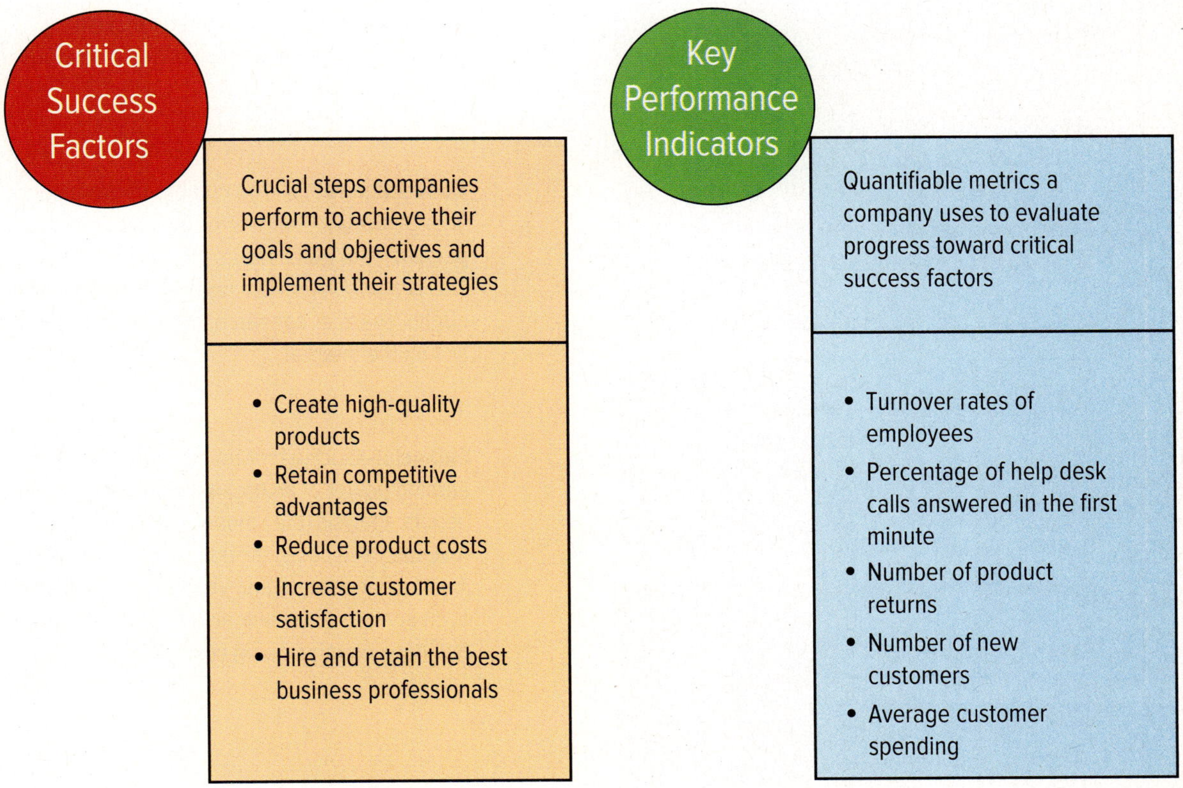

return on investment (ROI) Indicates the earning power of a project.

best practices The most successful solutions or problem-solving methods that have been developed by a specific organization or industry.

A common internal KPI is **return on investment (ROI)**, which indicates the earning power of a project. We measure it by dividing the profitability of a project by the costs. This sounds easy, and for many departments where the projects are tangible and self-contained it is; however, for projects that are intangible and cross departmental lines (such as MIS projects), ROI is challenging to measure. Imagine attempting to calculate the ROI of a fire extinguisher. If the fire extinguisher is never used, its ROI is low. If the fire extinguisher puts out a fire that could have destroyed the entire building, its ROI is astronomically high.

Creating KPIs to measure the success of an MIS project offers similar challenges. Think about a firm's email system. How could managers track departmental costs and profits associated with company email? Measuring by volume does not account for profitability, because one sales email could land a million-dollar deal while 300 others might not generate any revenue. Non-revenue-generating departments such as human resources and legal require email but will not be using it to generate profits. For this reason, many managers turn to higher-level metrics, such as efficiency and effectiveness, to measure MIS projects. **Best practices** are the most successful solutions or problem-solving methods that have been developed by a specific organization or industry. Measuring MIS projects helps determine the best practices for an industry.

LO2.2 Define critical success factors (CSFs) and key performance indicators (KPIs), and explain how managers use them to measure the success of MIS projects.

FIGURE 2.6 Common Types of Efficiency and Effectiveness Metrics

Efficiency Metrics

- **Throughput—**The amount of information that can travel through a system at any point in time.
- **Transaction speed—**The amount of time a system takes to perform a transaction.
- **System availability—**The number of hours a system is available for users.
- **Information accuracy—**The extent to which a system generates the correct results when executing the same transaction numerous times.
- **Response time—**The time it takes to respond to user interactions such as a mouse click.

Effectiveness Metrics

- **Usability—**The ease with which people perform transactions and/or find information.
- **Customer satisfaction—**Measured by satisfaction surveys, percentage of existing customers retained, and increases in revenue dollars per customer.
- **Conversion rates—**The number of customers an organization touches for the first time and persuades to purchase its products or services. This is a popular metric for evaluating the effectiveness of banner, pop-up, and pop-under ads on the Internet.
- **Financial—**Such as return on investment (the earning power of an organization's assets), cost-benefit analysis (the comparison of projected revenues and costs, including development, maintenance, fixed, and variable), and break-even analysis (the point at which constant revenues equal ongoing costs).

Efficiency and Effectiveness Metrics

Efficiency MIS metrics measure the performance of MIS itself, such as throughput, transaction speed, and system availability. **Effectiveness MIS metrics** measure the impact MIS has on business processes and activities, including customer satisfaction and customer conversion rates. Efficiency focuses on the extent to which a firm is using its resources in an optimal way, while effectiveness focuses on how well a firm is achieving its goals and objectives. Peter Drucker offers a helpful distinction between efficiency and effectiveness: Doing things right addresses efficiency—getting the most from each resource. Doing the right things addresses effectiveness—setting the right goals and objectives and ensuring they are accomplished. Figure 2.6 describes a few of the common types of efficiency and effectiveness MIS metrics. KPIs that measure MIS projects include both efficiency and effectiveness metrics. Of course, these metrics are not as concrete as market share or ROI, but they do offer valuable insight into project performance.[2]

Large increases in productivity typically result from increases in effectiveness, which focus on CSFs. Efficiency MIS metrics are far easier to measure, however, so most managers tend to focus on them, often incorrectly, to measure the success of MIS projects. Consider measuring the success of automated teller machines (ATMs). Thinking in terms of MIS efficiency metrics, a manager would measure the number of daily transactions, the average amount per transaction, and the average speed per transaction to determine the success of the ATM. Although these offer solid metrics on how well the system is performing, they miss many of the intangible or value-added benefits associated with ATM effectiveness. Effectiveness MIS metrics might measure how many new customers joined the bank due to its ATM locations or the ATMs' ease of use. They can also measure increases in customer satisfaction due to reduced ATM fees or additional ATM services such as the sale of stamps and movie tickets, significant time savers and value added features for customers. Being a great manager means taking the added viewpoint offered by effectiveness MIS metrics to analyze all benefits associated with an MIS project.

The Interrelationship Between Efficiency and Effectiveness MIS Metrics

Efficiency and effectiveness are definitely related. However, success in one area does not necessarily imply success in the other. Efficiency MIS metrics focus on the technology itself. While these efficiency MIS metrics are important to monitor, they do not always guarantee effectiveness. Effectiveness MIS metrics are determined according to an organization's goals, strategies, and objectives. Here, it becomes important to consider a company's CSFs, such as a broad cost leadership strategy (Walmart, for example), as well as KPIs such as increasing new customers by 10 percent or reducing new-product development cycle times to six months. In the private sector, eBay continuously benchmarks its MIS projects for efficiency and effectiveness. Maintaining constant website availability and optimal throughput performance are CSFs for eBay.

Figure 2.7 depicts the interrelationships between efficiency and effectiveness. Ideally, a firm wants to operate in the upper right-hand corner of the graph, realizing significant increases in both efficiency and effectiveness. However, operating in the upper left-hand corner (minimal effectiveness with increased efficiency) or the lower right-hand corner (significant effectiveness with minimal efficiency) may be in line with an organization's particular strategies. In general, operating in the lower left-hand

efficiency MIS metrics Measure the performance of MIS itself such as throughput, transaction speed, and system availability.

effectiveness MIS metrics Measure the impact MIS has on business processes and activities including customer satisfaction and customer conversion rates.

show me *the* MONEY

Is It Effective Or Is It Efficient?

Making business decisions is a key skill for all managers. Review the following list and, in a group, determine whether the question is focusing on efficiency, effectiveness, or both.

Business Decision	Efficiency	Effectiveness
What is the best route for dropping off products?		
Should we change suppliers?		
Should we reduce costs by buying lower-quality materials?		
Should we sell products to a younger market?		
Did we make our sales targets?		
What was the turnover rate of employees?		
What is the average customer spending?		
How many new customers purchased products?		
Did the amount of daily transactions increase?		
Is there a better way to restructure a store to increase sales?		

benchmark Baseline values the system seeks to attain.

benchmarking A process of continuously measuring system results, comparing those results to optimal system performance (benchmark values), and identifying steps and procedures to improve system performance.

model A simplified representation or abstraction of reality.

FIGURE 2.7
The Interrelationships Between Efficiency and Effectiveness

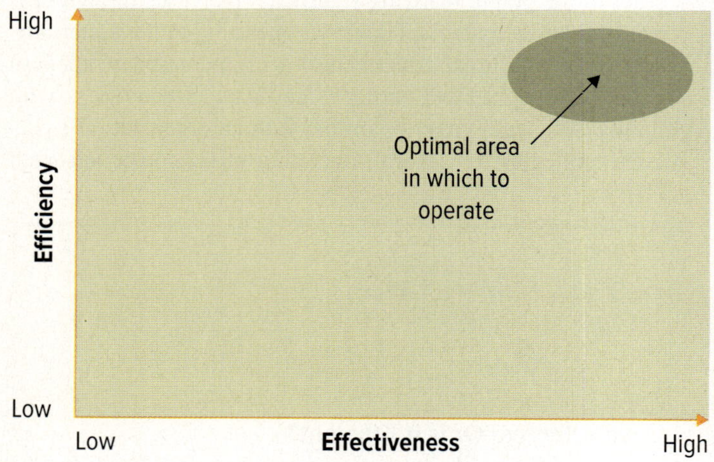

corner (minimal efficiency and minimal effectiveness) is not ideal for the operation of any organization.

Benchmarks Regardless of what process is measured, how it is measured, and whether it is performed for the sake of efficiency or effectiveness, managers must set **benchmarks**, or baseline values the system seeks to attain. **Benchmarking** is a process of continuously measuring system results, comparing those results to optimal system performance (benchmark values), and identifying steps and procedures to improve system performance. Benchmarks help assess how an MIS project performs over time. For instance, if a system held a benchmark for response time of 15 seconds, the manager would want to ensure response time continued to decrease until it reached that point. If response time suddenly increased to 1 minute, the manager would know the system was not functioning correctly and could start looking into potential problems. Continuously measuring MIS projects against benchmarks provides feedback so managers can control the system.

USING MIS TO MAKE BUSINESS DECISIONS LO2.3

Now that we've reviewed the essentials of decision making, we are ready to understand the powerful benefits associated with using MIS to support managers making decisions.

A **model** is a simplified representation or abstraction of reality. Models help managers calculate risks, understand uncertainty, change variables, and manipulate time to make decisions. MIS support systems rely on models for computational and analytical routines that mathematically express relationships among variables. For example, a spreadsheet program, such as Microsoft Office Excel, might contain models that calculate market share or ROI. MIS have the capability and functionality to express far more complex modeling relationships that provide information, business intelligence, and knowledge. Figure 2.8 highlights the three primary types of management information systems available to support decision making across the company levels.

LO2.3 Classify the different operational support systems, managerial support systems, and strategic support systems, and explain how managers can use these systems to make decisions and gain competitive advantages.

Due Diligence //: Get the Cow Out of The Ditch

Fortune magazine asked Anne Mulcahy, former Chairman and CEO of Xerox, what the best advice she had ever received in business was. She said it occurred at a breakfast meeting in Dallas, to which she had invited a group of business leaders. One of them, a plainspoken, self-made, streetwise guy, came up to Mulcahy and said:

When everything gets really complicated and you feel overwhelmed, think about it this way. You gotta do three things. First, get the cow out of the ditch. Second, find out how the cow got into the ditch. Third, make sure you do whatever it takes so the cow doesn't go into the ditch again.[3]

You are working for an international app developer that produces games. For months, you have been collecting metrics on usage by players from all over the world. You notice the metrics on the Asian and European players are falling sharply and sales are dropping. The United States and Canada metrics are still growing strongly, and sales are increasing. What can you do to get this cow out of the ditch?

transactional information Encompasses all of the information contained within a single business process or unit of work, and its primary purpose is to support the performing of daily operational or structured decisions.

online transaction processing (OLTP) The capturing of transaction and event information using technology to (1) process the information according to defined business rules, (2) store the information, and (3) update existing information to reflect the new information.

transaction processing system (TPS) The basic business system that serves the operational level (analysts) and assists in making structured decisions.

source document Describes the original transaction record along with details such as its date, purpose, and amount spent and includes cash receipts, canceled checks, invoices, customer refunds, employee time sheet, etc.

analytical information Encompasses all organizational information, and its primary purpose is to support the performing of managerial analysis or semistructured decisions.

FIGURE 2.8 Primary Types of MIS Systems for Decision Making

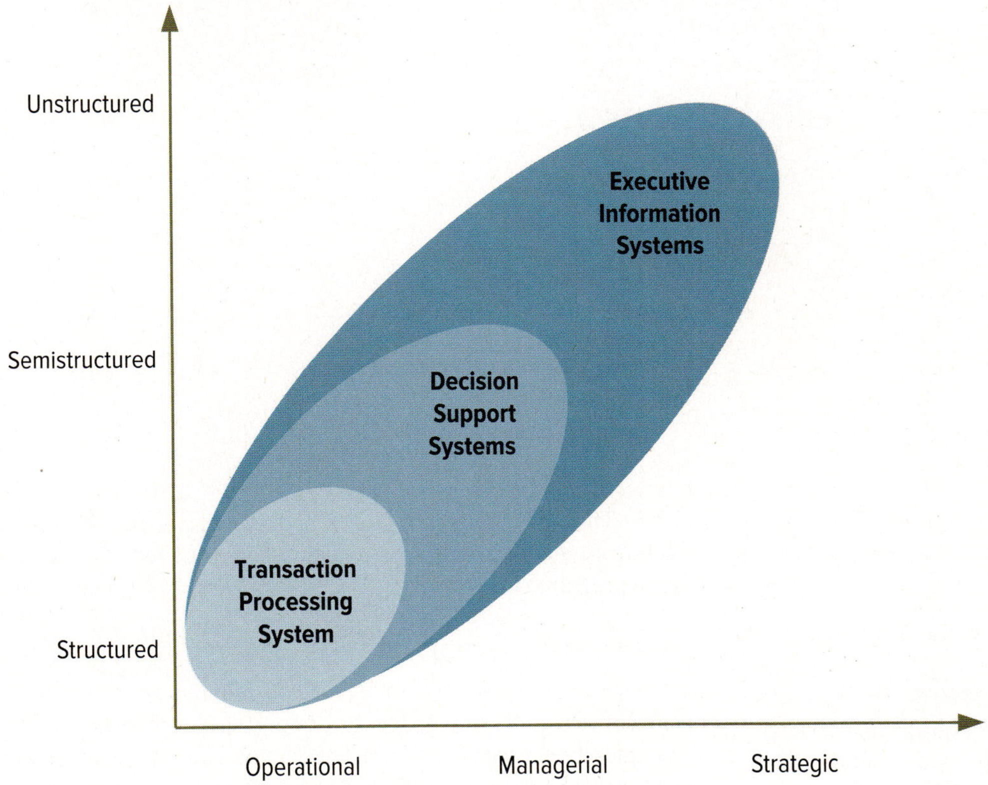

Operational Support Systems

Transactional information encompasses all the information contained within a single business process or unit of work, and its primary purpose is to support the performance of daily operational or structured decisions. Transactional information is created, for example, when customers are purchasing stocks, making an airline reservation, or withdrawing cash from an ATM. Managers use transactional information when making structured decisions at the operational level, such as when analyzing daily sales reports to determine how much inventory to carry.

Online transaction processing (OLTP) is the capture of transaction and event information using technology to (1) process the information according to defined business rules, (2) store the information, and (3) update existing information to reflect the new information. During OLTP, the organization must capture every detail of transactions and events. A **transaction processing system (TPS)** is the basic business system that serves the operational level (analysts) and assists in making structured decisions. The most common example of a TPS is an operational accounting system such as a payroll system or an order entry system.

Using systems thinking, we can see that the inputs for a TPS are **source documents**, which describes the original transaction record along with details such as its date, purpose, and amount spent and includes cash receipts, canceled checks, invoices, customer refunds, employee time sheet, etc. Source documents for a payroll system can include time sheets, wage rates, and employee benefit reports. Transformation includes common procedures such as creating, reading, updating, and deleting (commonly referred to as CRUD) employee records, along with calculating the payroll and summarizing benefits. The output includes cutting the paychecks and generating payroll reports. Figure 2.9 demonstrates the systems thinking view of a TPS.[4]

Managerial Support Systems

Analytical information encompasses all organizational information, and its primary purpose is to support the performance of managerial analysis or semistructured decisions. Analytical information includes transactional information along with other information such as market and industry information. Examples of analytical information are trends, sales, product statistics, and future growth projections. Managers use analytical

online analytical processing (OLAP) The manipulation of information to create business intelligence in support of strategic decision making.

decision support system (DSS) Model information using OLAP, which provides assistance in evaluating and choosing among different courses of action.

executive information system (EIS) A specialized DSS that supports senior-level executives and unstructured, long-term, nonroutine decisions requiring judgment, evaluation, and insight.

granularity Refers to the level of detail in the model or the decision-making process.

FIGURE 2.9 Systems Thinking Example of a TPS

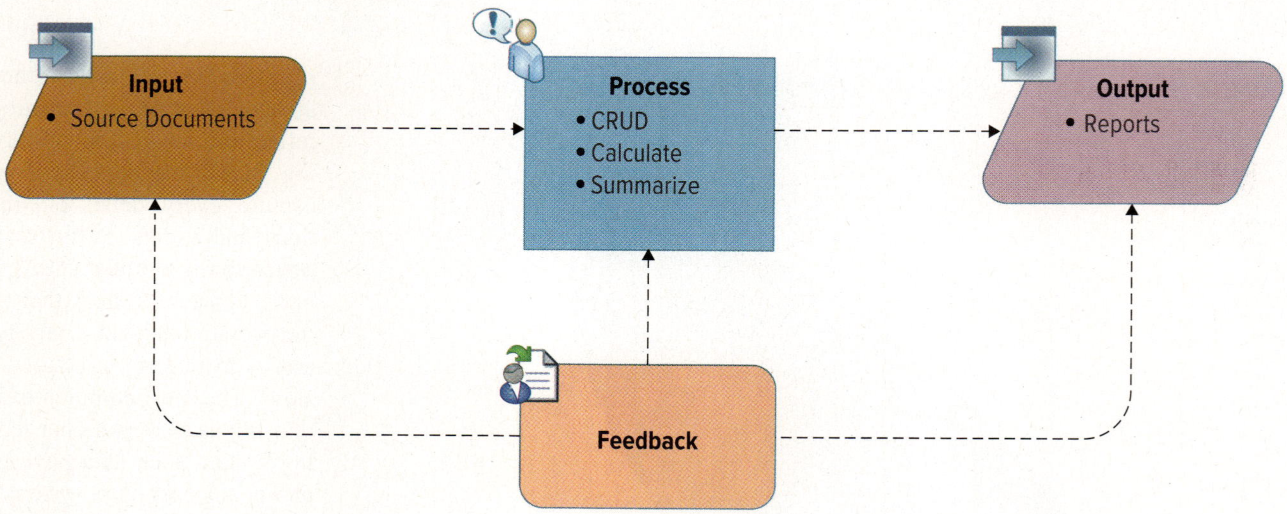

information when making important semistructured decisions, such as whether the organization should build a new manufacturing plant or hire additional sales reps.

Online analytical processing (OLAP) is the manipulation of information to create business intelligence in support of strategic decision making. **Decision support systems (DSSs)** model information using OLAP, which provides assistance in evaluating and choosing among different courses of action. DSSs enable high-level managers to examine and manipulate large amounts of detailed data from different internal and external sources. Analyzing complex relationships among thousands or even millions of data items to discover patterns, trends, and exception conditions is one of the key uses associated with a DSS. For example, doctors may enter symptoms into a decision support system so it can help diagnose and treat patients. Insurance companies also use a DSS to gauge the risk of providing insurance to drivers who have imperfect driving records. One company found that married women who are homeowners with one speeding ticket are rarely cited for speeding again. Armed with this business intelligence, the company achieved a cost advantage by lowering insurance rates to this specific group of customers. Figure 2.10 displays the common DSS analysis techniques.

Figure 2.11 shows the common systems view of a DSS. Figure 2.12 shows how TPSs supply transactional data to a DSS. The DSS then summarizes and aggregates the information from the different TPSs, which assist managers in making semistructured decisions.

Strategic Support Systems

Decision making at the strategic level requires both business intelligence and knowledge to support the uncertainty and complexity associated with business strategies. An **executive information system (EIS)** is a specialized DSS that supports senior-level executives and unstructured, long-term, nonroutine decisions requiring judgment, evaluation, and insight. These decisions do not have a right or wrong answer, only efficient and effective answers. Moving up through the organizational pyramid, managers deal less with the details ("finer" information) and more with meaningful aggregations of information ("coarser" information). **Granularity** refers to the level of detail in the model or the decision-making process. The greater the granularity, the deeper the level of detail or fineness of data (see Figure 2.13).

A DSS differs from an EIS in that an EIS requires data from external sources to support unstructured decisions (see Figure 2.14). This is not to say that DSSs never use data from external sources, but typically DSS semistructured decisions rely on internal data only.

visualization Produces graphical displays of patterns and complex relationships in large amounts of data.

digital dashboard Tracks KPIs and CSFs by compiling information from multiple sources and tailoring it to meet user needs.

artificial intelligence (AI) Simulates human thinking and behavior such as the ability to reason and learn.

intelligent system Various commercial applications of artificial intelligence.

FIGURE 2.10 Common DSS Analysis Techniques

WHAT-IF ANALYSIS

- ***What -if analysis*** checks the impact of a change in a variable or assumption on the model. For example, "What will happen to the supply chain if a hurricane in South Carolina reduces holding inventory from 30 percent to 10 percent?" A user would be able to observe and evaluate any changes that occurred to the values in the model, especially to a variable such as profits. Users repeat this analysis with different variables until they understand all the effects of various situations.

SENSITIVITY ANALYSIS

- ***Sensitivity analysis,*** a special case of what-if analysis, is the study of the impact on other variables when one variable is changed repeatedly. Sensitivity analysis is useful when users are uncertain about the assumptions made in estimating the value of certain key variables. For example, repeatedly changing revenue in small increments to determine its effects on other variables would help a manager understand the impact of various revenue levels on other decision factors.

GOAL SEEKING ANALYSIS

- ***Goal-seeking analysis*** finds the inputs necessary to achieve a goal such as a desired level of output. It is the reverse of what-if and sensitivity analysis. Instead of observing how changes in a variable affect other variables, goal-seeking analysis sets a target value (a goal) for a variable and then repeatedly changes other variables until the target value is achieved. For example, goal-seeking analysis could determine how many customers must purchase a new product to increase gross profits to $5 million.

OPTIMIZATION ANALYSIS

- ***Optimization analysis***, an extension of goal-seeking analysis, finds the optimum value for a target variable by repeatedly changing other variables, subject to specified constraints. By changing revenue and cost variables in an optimization analysis, managers can calculate the highest potential profits. Constraints on revenue and cost variables can be taken into consideration, such as limits on the amount of raw materials the company can afford to purchase and limits on employees available to meet production needs.

Visualization produces graphical displays of patterns and complex relationships in large amounts of data. Executive information systems use visualization to deliver specific key information to top managers at a glance, with little or no interaction with the system. A common tool that supports visualization is a **digital dashboard**, which tracks KPIs and CSFs by compiling information from multiple sources and tailoring it to meet user needs. Following is a list of potential features included in a dashboard designed for a manufacturing team:

- A hot list of key performance indicators, refreshed every 15 minutes.
- A running line graph of planned versus actual production for the past 24 hours.
- A table showing actual versus forecasted product prices and inventories.
- A list of outstanding alerts and their resolution status.
- A graph of stock market prices.

Digital dashboards, whether basic or comprehensive, deliver results quickly. As they become easier to use, more employees can perform their own analyses without inundating MIS staff with questions and requests for reports. Digital dashboards enable employees to move beyond reporting to using information to directly increase business performance. With them, employees can react to information as soon as it becomes available and make decisions, solve problems, and change strategies daily instead of monthly. Digital dashboards offer the analytical capabilities illustrated in Figure 2.15.

One thing to remember when making decisions is the old saying, "Garbage in, garbage out." If the transactional data used in the support system are wrong, then the managerial analysis will be wrong and the DSS will simply assist in making a wrong decision faster. Managers should also ask, "What is the DSS *not* telling me before I make my final decision?"

USING AI TO MAKE BUSINESS DECISIONS LO2.4

Executive information systems are starting to take advantage of artificial intelligence to facilitate unstructured strategic decision making. **Artificial intelligence (AI)** simulates human thinking and behavior, such as the ability to reason and learn. Its ultimate goal is to build a system that can mimic human intelligence.

Intelligent systems are various commercial applications of artificial intelligence. They include sensors, software, and devices that emulate and enhance human capabilities, learn

FIGURE 2.11 Systems Thinking Example of a DSS

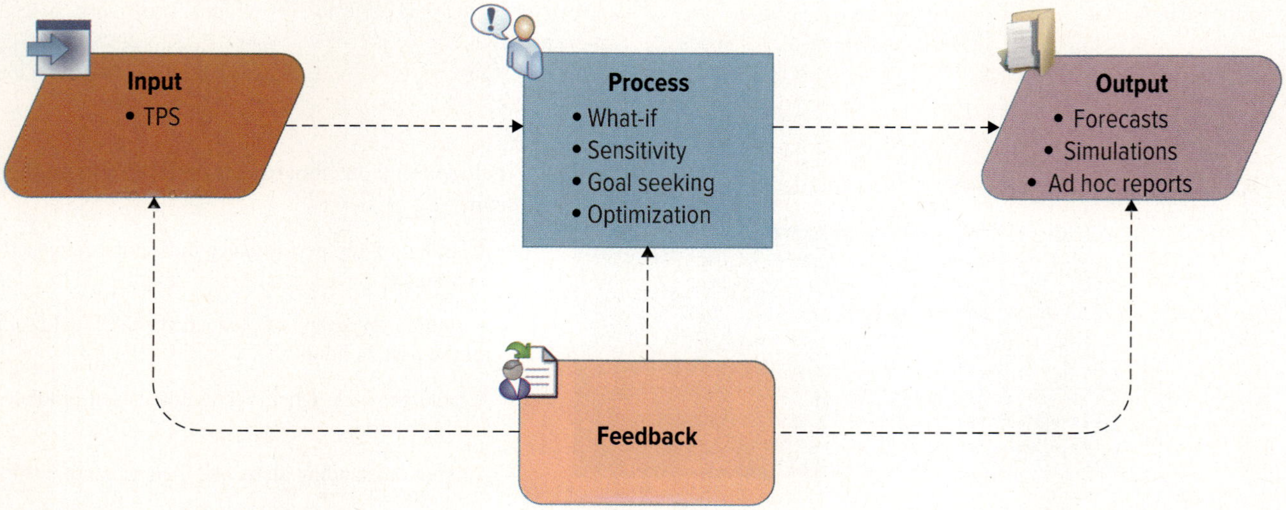

FIGURE 2.12 Interaction Between TPS and DSS to Support Semistructured Decisions

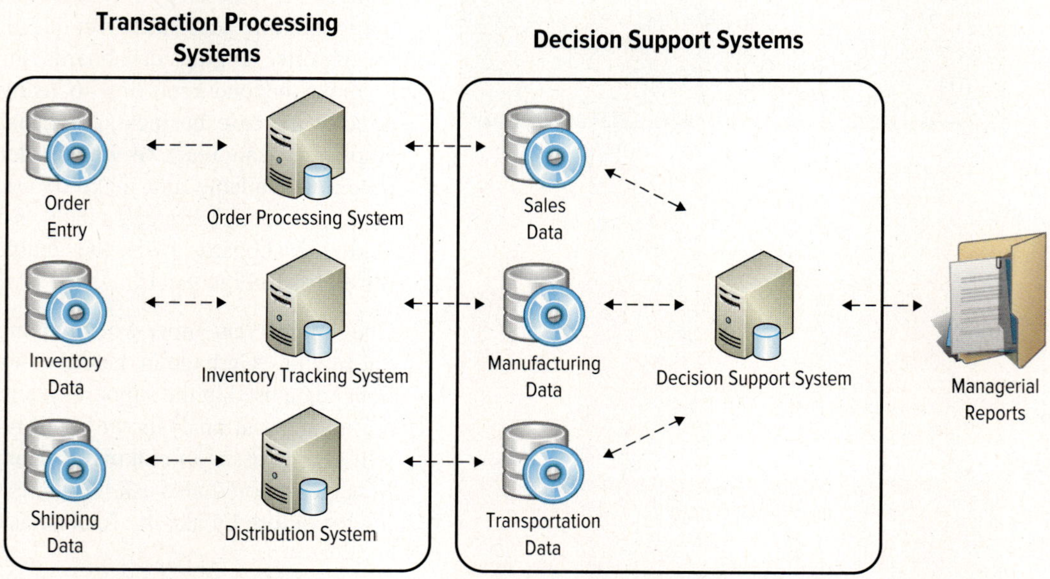

or understand from experience, make sense of ambiguous or contradictory information, and even use reasoning to solve problems and make decisions effectively. Intelligent systems perform such tasks as boosting productivity in factories by monitoring equipment and signaling when preventive maintenance is required. They are beginning to show up everywhere:

- At Manchester Airport in England, the Hefner AI Robot Cleaner alerts passengers to security and nonsmoking rules while it scrubs up to 65,600 square feet of floor per day. Laser scanners and ultrasonic detectors keep it from colliding with passengers.[7]
- Shell Oil's SmartPump keeps drivers in their cars on cold, wet winter days. It can service any automobile built after 1987 that has been fitted with a special gas cap and a windshield-mounted transponder that tells the robot where to insert the pump.
- Matsushita's courier robot navigates hospital hallways, delivering patient files, X-ray films, and medical supplies.
- The FireFighter AI Robot can extinguish flames at chemical plants and nuclear reactors with water, foam, powder, or inert gas. The robot puts distance between human operators and the fire.

AI systems increase the speed and consistency of decision making, solve problems with incomplete information, and resolve complicated issues that cannot be solved by conventional computing. There are many categories of AI systems; five of the most familiar are (1) expert systems, (2) neural networks, (3) genetic algorithms, (4) intelligent agents, and (5) virtual reality (see Figure 2.16).

LO2.4 Describe artificial intelligence, and identify its five main types.

Expert Systems

Expert systems are computerized advisory programs that imitate the reasoning processes of experts in solving difficult problems. Typically, they include a knowledge

expert system
Computerized advisory programs that imitate the reasoning processes of experts in solving difficult problems.

FIGURE 2.13 Information Levels Throughout an Organization

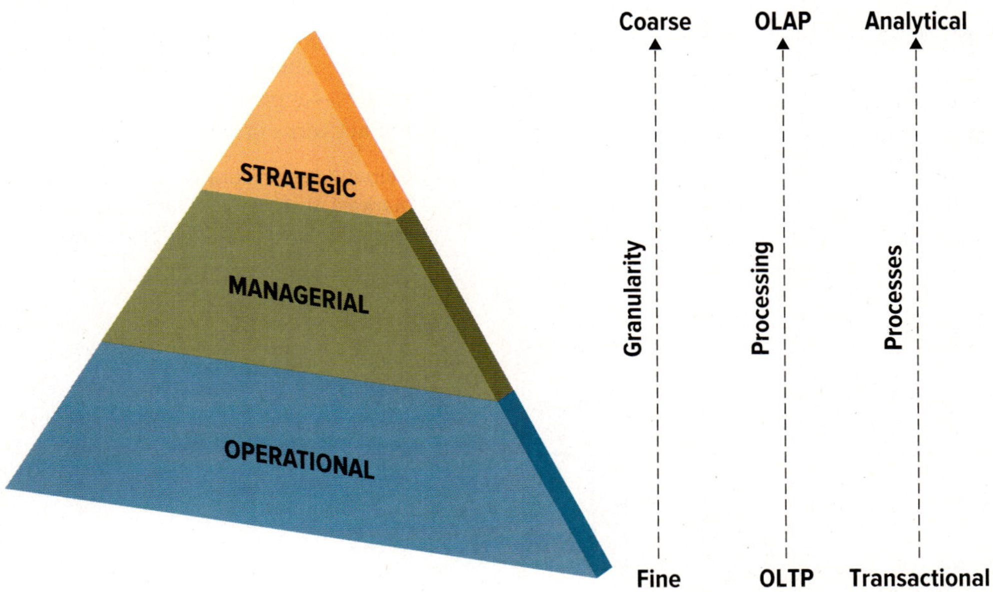

BUSTED The Criminal in the Cube Next Door[5]

What if the person sitting in the cube next to you was running a scam that cost your company $7 billion? An employee at a French bank allegedly used his inside knowledge of business processes to bypass the systems and make roughly $73 billion in bogus trades that cost the bank more than $7 billion to unwind.

Findings from the U.S. Secret Service and its examination of 23 incidents conducted by 26 insiders determined that 70 percent of the time, insiders took advantage of failures in business process rules and authorization mechanisms to steal from the company. Seventyeight percent of the time, insiders were authorized and active computer users, and a surprising 43 percent used their own username and passwords to commit their crime.

This is a daunting reminder that every employee has the potential to become a knowledgeable insider, and if they ever turned bad in a fraudulent, criminal, even destructive way, they could do tremendous damage to your company. You need to protect your company's assets, and many of your DSS and EIS systems contain the business intelligence your company needs to operate effectively. What types of sensitive information is housed in a company's TPS, DSS, and EIS? What issues could you encounter if one of your employees decided to steal the information housed in your DSS? How could you protect your EIS from unethical users? What would you do if you thought the person sharing your cube was a rogue insider?

neural network A category of AI that attempts to emulate the way the human brain works.

base containing various accumulated experience and a set of rules for applying the knowledge base to each particular situation. Expert systems are the most common form of AI in the business arena because they fill the gap when human experts are difficult to find or retain or are too expensive. The best-known systems play chess and assist in medical diagnosis.

Neural Networks

A **neural network**, also called an artificial neural network, is a category of AI that attempts to emulate the way the human brain works. Neural networks analyze large quantities of information to establish patterns and characteristics in situations where the logic or rules are unknown. Neural networks' many features include:

- Learning and adjusting to new circumstances on their own.
- Lending themselves to massive parallel processing.
- Functioning without complete or well-structured information.
- Coping with huge volumes of information with many dependent variables.
- Analyzing nonlinear relationships in information (they have been called fancy regression analysis systems).

The finance industry is a veteran in the use of neural network technology and has been relying on various forms for over two decades. It uses neural networks to review loan applications and create patterns or profiles of applications that fall into two categories—approved or denied. Here are some examples of neural networks in finance:

- Citibank uses neural networks to find opportunities in financial markets. By carefully examining historical stock market data with neural network software, Citibank financial managers learn of

FIGURE 2.14 Interaction Between a TPS and EIS

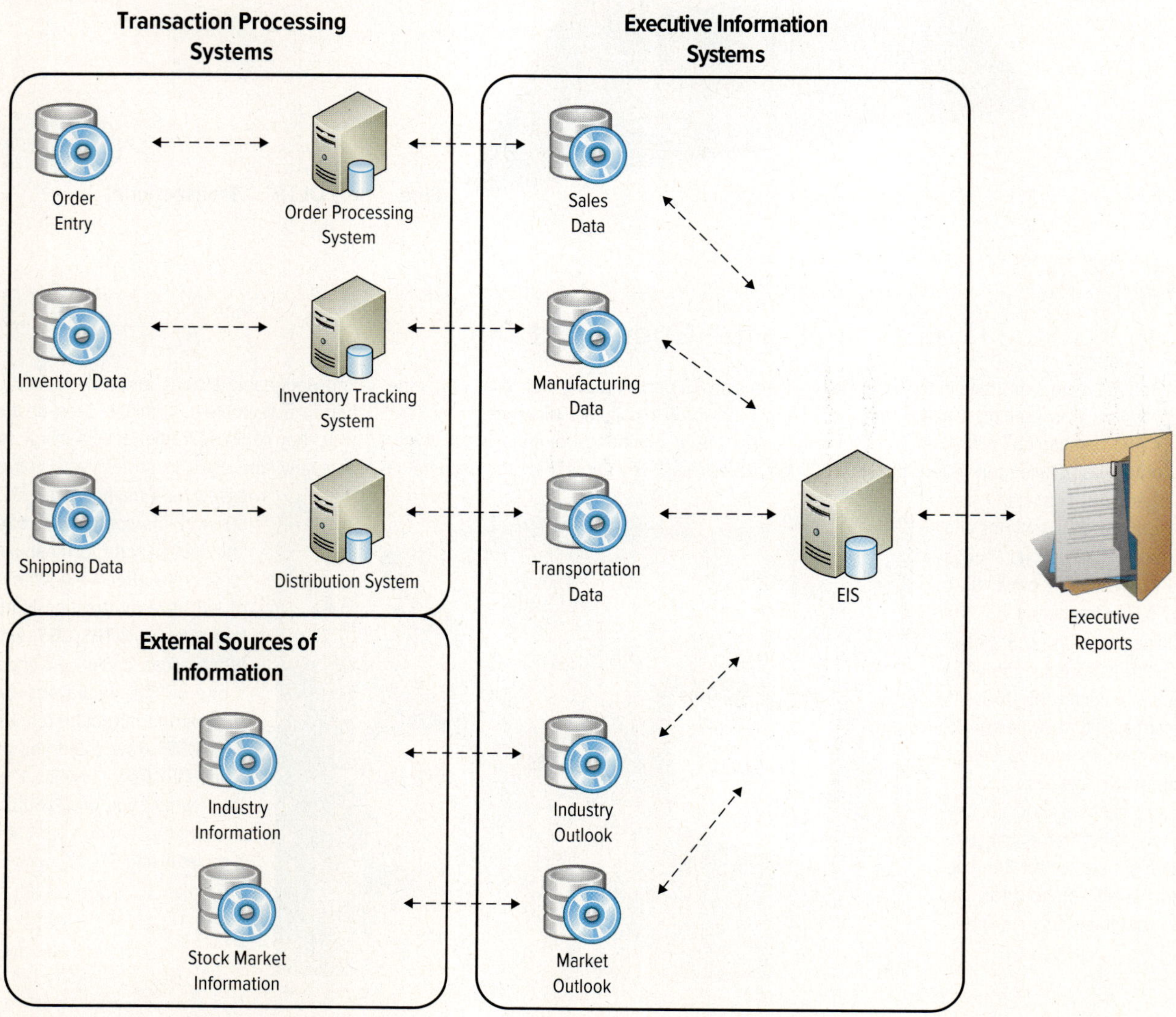

FIGURE 2.15 Digital Dashboard Analytical Capabilities

CONSOLIDATION

- ***Consolidation*** is the aggregation of data from simple roll-ups to complex groupings of interrelated information. For example, data for different sales representatives can then be rolled up to an office level, then a state level, then a regional sales level.

DRILL-DOWN

- ***Drill-down*** enables users to view details, and details of details, of information. This is the reverse of consolidation; a user can view regional sales data and then drill down all the way to each sales representative's data at each office. Drill-down capability lets managers view monthly, weekly, daily, or even hourly information.

Slice-and-Dice

- ***Slice-and-dice*** is the ability to look at information from different perspectives. One slice of information could display all product sales during a given promotion. Another slice could display a single product's sales for all promotions. Slicing and dicing is often performed along a time axis to analyze trends and find time-based patterns in the information.

Pivot

- ***Pivot*** (also known as rotation) rotates data to display alternative presentations of the data. For example, a Pivot can swap the rows and columns of a report to show the data in a different format.

interesting coincidences or small anomalies (called market inefficiencies). For example, it could be that whenever IBM stock goes up, so does Unisys stock, or that a U.S. Treasury note is selling for 1 cent less in Japan than in the United States. These snippets of information can make a big difference to Citibank's bottom line in a very competitive financial market.[9]

fuzzy logic A mathematical method of handling imprecise or subjective information.

- Visa, MasterCard, and many other credit card companies use a neural network to spot peculiarities in individual accounts and follow up by checking for fraud. MasterCard estimates neural networks save it $50 million annually.
- Insurance companies along with state compensation funds and other carriers use neural network software to identify fraud. The system searches for patterns in billing charges, laboratory tests, and frequency of office visits. A claim for which the diagnosis was a sprained ankle but treatment included an electrocardiogram would be flagged for the account manager.

Fuzzy logic is a mathematical method of handling imprecise or subjective information. The basic approach is to assign values between 0 and 1 to vague or ambiguous information. Zero represents information not included,

fyi

Got Junk? Get a Hunk![6]

Do you enjoy kidnapping your rival's team mascot or toilet-papering their frat houses? If so, you might find your ideal career at College Hunks Hauling Junk. The company launched in 2005 and hires college students and recent college grads to pick up junk. The founder, Nick Friedman, had a goal of capturing that friendly rivalry so often associated with college life and turn it into profits. When the company first launched, the haulers from Virginia found that their truck had been lathered in shaving cream and draped with a University of Maryland flag. The Virginia haulers retaliated and, soon after, dead fish were found coating the seats of the Maryland's truck. Friedman decided to use this energy as incentive instead of reprimanding the rather unorthodox behavior. "We wanted to harness that competitive, prankster enthusiasm and channel it for good," states Friedman.

Friedman made a bold move and decided that instead of tracking typical key performance metrics such as revenue, average job size, customer loyalty, etc., he would track volume of junk collected and amount of junk donated or recycled. The winning team gains such things as bragging rights and banners, modest monetary prizes, and "first table to eat" at the annual company meeting. Most employees check the dashboard daily to view their own and rivals' latest standings.

© Alistair Berg/Getty Images RF

Why do you think competition is helping College Hunks Hauling Junk exceed its revenue goals? If you were to build a team competition dashboard for your school or your work, what types of metrics would it track? What types of motivators would you use to ensure your team is always in the green? What types of external information would you want tracked in your dashboard? Could an unethical person use the information from your dashboard to hurt your team or your organization? What can you do to mitigate these risks?

genetic algorithm An artificial intelligence system that mimics the evolutionary, survival-of-the-fittest process to generate increasingly better solutions to a problem.

mutation The process within a genetic algorithm of randomly trying combinations and evaluating the success (or failure) of the outcome.

while 1 represents inclusion or membership. For example, fuzzy logic is used in washing machines that determine by themselves how much water to use or how long to wash (they continue washing until the water is clean). In accounting and finance, fuzzy logic allows people to analyze information with subjective financial values (intangibles such as goodwill) that are very important considerations in economic analysis. Fuzzy logic and neural networks are often combined to express complicated and subjective concepts in a form that makes it possible to simplify the problem and apply rules that are executed with a level of certainty.

Genetic Algorithms

A **genetic algorithm** is an artificial intelligence system that mimics the evolutionary, survival-of-the-fittest process to generate increasingly better solutions to a problem. A genetic algorithm is essentially an optimizing system: It finds the combination of inputs that gives the best outputs. **Mutation** is the process within a genetic algorithm of randomly trying combinations and evaluating the success (or failure) of the outcome.

Genetic algorithms are best suited to decision-making environments in which thousands, or perhaps millions, of solutions are possible. Genetic algorithms can find and evaluate solutions with many more possibilities, faster and more thoroughly than

FIGURE 2.16
Examples of Artificial Intelligence

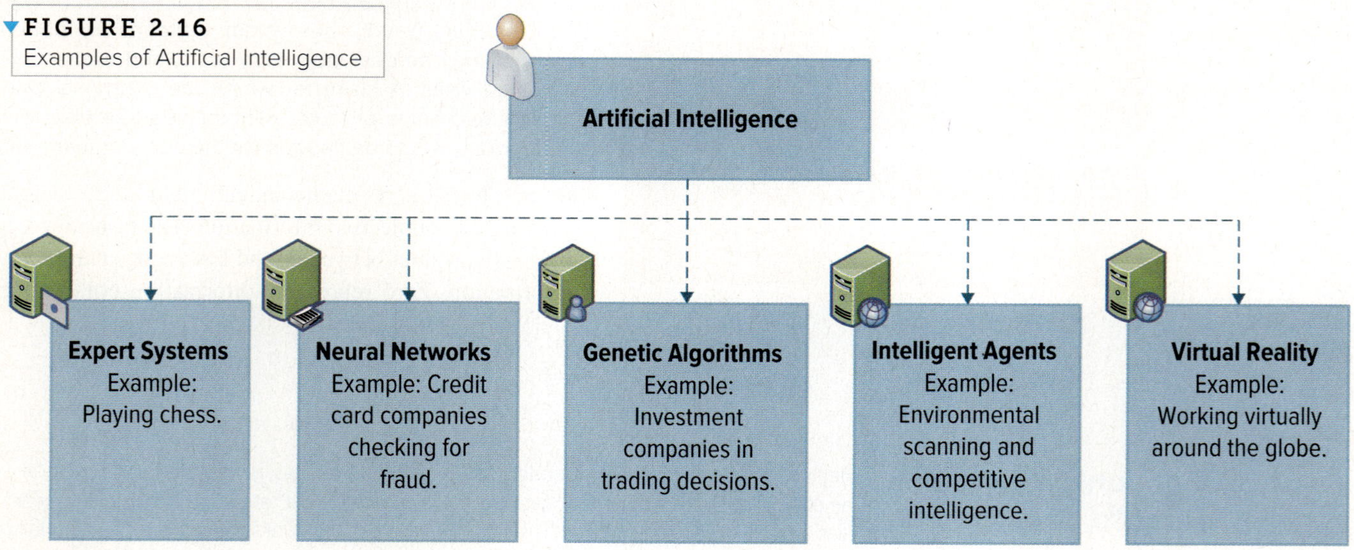

Living the DREAM

Track Your Life

With wearable technology, you can track your entire life. Nike's Fuelband and Jawbone's Up tracks all of your physical activity, caloric burn, and sleep patterns. You can track your driving patterns, tooth-brushing habits, and even laundry status. The question now becomes how to track all of your trackers.

A new company called Exist incorporates tracking devices with weather data, music choices, Netflix favorites, and Twitter activity all in one digital dashboard. Exist wants to understand every area of your life and provide correlation information between such things as your personal productivity and mood. As the different types of data expand, so will the breadth of correlations Exist can point out. For instance, do you tweet more when you are working at home? If so, does this increase productivity? Exist wants to track all of your trackers and analyze the information to help you become more efficient and more effective.[8]

Create a digital dashboard for tracking your life. Choose four areas you want to track and determine three ways you would measure each area. For example, if you track eating habits, you might want to measure calories and place unacceptable levels in red and acceptable levels in green. Once completed, determine whether you can find any correlations among the areas in your life.

intelligent agent A special-purpose knowledge-based information system that accomplishes specific tasks on behalf of its users.

shopping bot Software that will search several retailer websites and provide a comparison of each retailer's offerings including price and availability.

virtual reality A computer-simulated environment that can be a simulation of the real world or an imaginary world.

augmented reality The viewing of the physical world with computer-generated layers of information added to it.

a human. Organizations face decision-making environments for all types of problems that require optimization techniques, such as the following:

- Business executives use genetic algorithms to help them decide which combination of projects a firm should invest in, taking complicated tax considerations into account.
- Investment companies use genetic algorithms to help in trading decisions.
- Telecommunication companies use genetic algorithms to determine the optimal configuration of fiber-optic cable in a network that may include as many as 100,000 connection points. The genetic algorithm evaluates millions of cable configurations and selects the one that uses the least amount of cable.

show me the MONEY

If It Ain't Broke, Don't Fix It

Do you hate waiting in line at the grocery store? Do you find it frustrating when you go to the video store and cannot find the movie you wanted to rent? Do you get annoyed when the pizza delivery person brings you the wrong order? This is your chance to reengineer the annoying process that drives you crazy. Choose a problem you are currently experiencing, and reengineer the process to make it more efficient and effective. Be sure to provide an As-Is and To-Be business process model.

Intelligent Agents

An **intelligent agent** is a special-purpose knowledge-based information system that accomplishes specific tasks on behalf of its users. Intelligent agents usually have a graphical representation, such as "Sherlock Holmes" for an information search agent.

One of the simplest examples of an intelligent agent is a shopping bot. A **shopping bot** is software that will search several retailer websites and provide a comparison of each retailer's offerings including price and availability. Increasingly, intelligent agents handle the majority of a company's Internet buying and selling and complete such processes as finding products, bargaining over prices, and executing transactions. Intelligent agents also have the capability to handle all supply chain buying and selling.

Another application for intelligent agents is in environmental scanning and competitive intelligence. For instance, an intelligent agent can learn the types of competitor information users want to track, continuously scan the web for it, and alert users when a significant event occurs.

Multiagent Systems and Agent-Based Modeling What do cargo transport systems, book distribution centers, the video game market, and a flu epidemic have in common with an ant colony? They are all complex adaptive systems. By observing parts of Earth's ecosystem, like ant colonies, artificial intelligence scientists can use hardware and software models that incorporate insect characteristics and behavior to (1) learn how people-based systems behave, (2) predict how they will behave under a given set of circumstances, and (3) improve human systems to make them more efficient and effective. This process of learning from ecosystems and adapting their characteristics to human and organizational situations is called biomimicry.

In the past few years, AI research has made much progress in modeling complex organizations as a whole with the help of multiagent systems. In a multiagent system, groups of intelligent agents have the ability to work independently and to interact with each other. Agent-based modeling is a way of simulating human organizations using multiple intelligent agents, each of which follows a set of simple rules and can adapt to changing conditions.

Agent-based modeling systems are being used to model stock market fluctuations, predict the escape routes people seek in a burning building, estimate the effects of interest rates on consumers with different types of debt, and anticipate how changes in conditions will affect the supply chain, to name just a few.

Virtual Reality

Virtual reality is a computer-simulated environment that can be a simulation of the real world or an imaginary world. Virtual reality is a fast-growing area of artificial intelligence that had its origins in efforts to build more natural, realistic, multisensory human-computer interfaces. Virtual reality enables telepresence where users can be anywhere in the world and use virtual reality systems to work alone or together at a remote site. Typically, this involves using a virtual reality system to enhance the sight and touch of a human who is remotely manipulating equipment to accomplish a task. Examples range from virtual surgery, where surgeon and patient may be on opposite sides of the globe, to the remote use of equipment in hazardous environments such as chemical plants and nuclear reactors. **Augmented reality** is the viewing of the physical world with computer-generated layers of information added to it.

customer-facing process Results in a product or service that is received by an organization's external customer.

business-facing process Invisible to the external customer but essential to the effective management of the business; they include goal setting, day-to-day planning, giving performance feedback and rewards, and allocating resources.

Virtual Workforce At Microsoft's headquarters in Redmond, Washington, traffic congestion occurs daily for the 35,000 commuters. To alleviate the congestion Microsoft is offering its employees the ability to work virtually from home. Over 42 percent of IBM's 330,000 employees work virtually, saving over $100 million per year in real estate–related expenses. Working virtually offers several advantages such as fewer cars on the road, increases in worker productive, and decreased real estate expenses. Drawbacks include the fear among workers that they will jeopardize their careers by working from home, and some workers need a busy environment to stay productive. Virtual workers also tend to feel alone, secluded, and deprived of vital training and mentoring.

{SECTION 2.2} Business Processes

LEARNING OUTCOMES

LO2.5 Explain the value of business processes for a company, and differentiate between customer-facing and business-facing processes.

LO2.6 Demonstrate the value of business process modeling, and compare As-Is and To-Be models.

LO2.7 Differentiate among automation, streamlining, and reengineering.

MANAGING BUSINESS PROCESSES LO2.5

Most companies pride themselves on providing breakthrough products and services for customers. But if customers do not receive what they want quickly, accurately, and hassle-free, even fantastic offerings will not prevent a company from annoying customers and ultimately eroding its own financial performance. To avoid this pitfall and protect its competitive advantage, a company must continually evaluate all the business processes in its value chain. A business process is a standardized set of activities that accomplish a specific task, such as processing a customer's order. Business processes transform a set of inputs into a set of outputs—goods or services—for another person or process by using people and tools. Understanding business processes helps a manager envision how the entire company operates.

Improving the efficiency and effectiveness of its business processes will improve the firm's value chain. The goal of this section is to expand on Porter's value chain analysis by detailing the powerful value-adding relationships between business strategies and core business processes. Figure 2.17 illustrates several common business processes.

The processes outlined in Figure 2.17 reflect functional thinking. Some processes, such as a programming process, may be contained wholly within a single department. However, most, such as ordering a product, are cross-functional or cross-departmental processes and span the entire organization. The process of "order to delivery" focuses on the entire customer order process across functional departments (see Figure 2.18). Another example is "product realization," which includes not only the way a product is developed, but also the way it is marketed and serviced. Some other cross-functional business processes are taking a product from concept to market, acquiring customers, loan processing, providing post-sales service, claim processing, and reservation handling.

Customer-facing processes, also called front-office processes, result in a product or service received by an organization's external customer. They include fulfilling orders, communicating with customers, and sending out bills and marketing information. **Business-facing processes**, also called back office processes, are invisible to the external customer but essential to the effective management of the business; they include goal setting, day-to-day planning, giving performance feedback and rewards, and allocating resources. Figure 2.19 displays the different categories of customer-facing and business-facing processes along with an example of each.[11]

A company's strategic vision should provide guidance on which business processes are core, that is, which are directly linked to

fyi

Long-Distance Hugs

Haptic technology digitizes touch. CuteCircuit created the Hug shirt that you can hug and send the exact hug, including strength, pressure, distribution, and even heartbeat, to a long-distance friend who is wearing the partner to your Hug shirt. Ben Hui at Cambridge University is creating hand-squeezes that can be sent by mobile phones. You simply squeeze the phone and your friend feels it, in some form, at the other end. The value of these haptic devices is based on the idea that physical touch is an important element to all human interactions, and if you can transfer the physical touch, you can replicate the emotion. In a group, create a new business product that uses a haptic interface. Share your product idea with your peers.[10]

FIGURE 2.17 Sample Business Processes

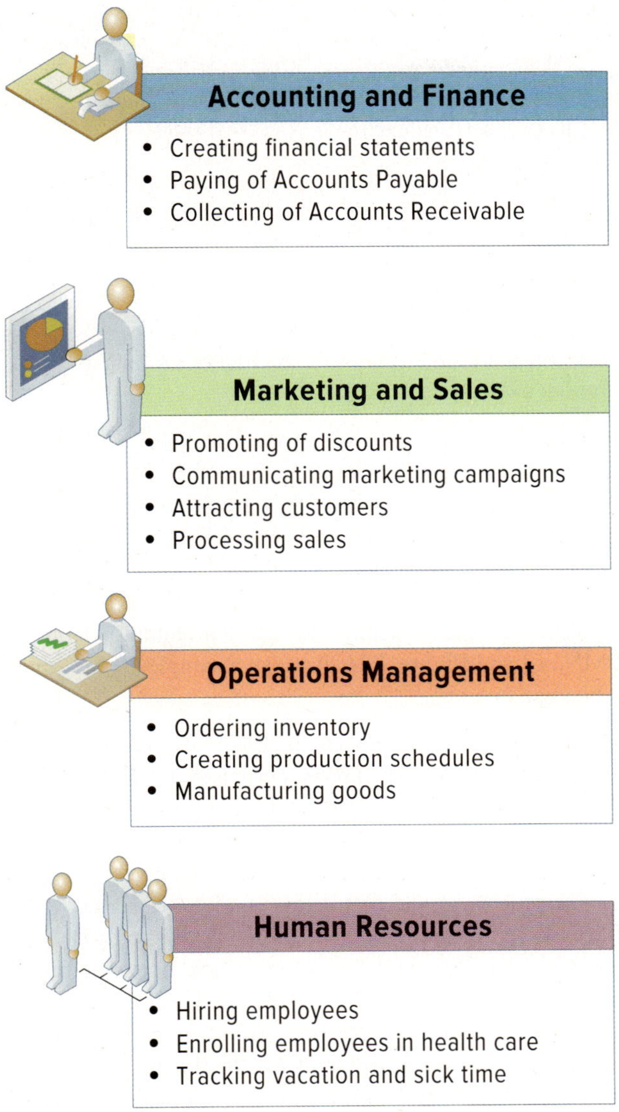

the firm's critical success factors. Mapping these core business processes to the value chain reveals where the processes touch the customers and affect their perceptions of value. This type of map conceptualizes the business as a value delivery system, allowing managers to ensure all core business processes are operating as efficiently and effectively as possible.

A **business process patent** is a patent that protects a specific set of procedures for conducting a particular business activity. A firm can create a value chain map of the entire industry to extend critical success factors and business process views beyond its boundaries. **Core processes** are business processes, such as manufacturing goods, selling products, and providing service, that make up the primary activities in a value chain.

A **static process** uses a systematic approach in an attempt to improve business effectiveness and efficiency. Managers constantly attempt to optimize static process. Examples of static processes include running payroll, calculating taxes, and creating financial statements. A **dynamic process** is continuously changing and provides business solutions to ever-changing business operations. As the business and its strategies change, so do the dynamic processes. Examples of dynamic processes include managing layoffs of employees, changing order levels based on currency rates, and canceling business travel due to extreme weather.

business process patent A patent that protects a specific set of procedures for conducting a particular business activity.

core process Business processes, such as manufacturing goods, selling products, and providing service that make up the primary activities in a value chain.

static process A systematic approach in an attempt to improve business effectiveness and efficiency.

dynamic process A continuously changing process that provides business solutions to ever-changing business operations.

FIGURE 2.18 Five Steps in the Order-to-Delivery Business Process

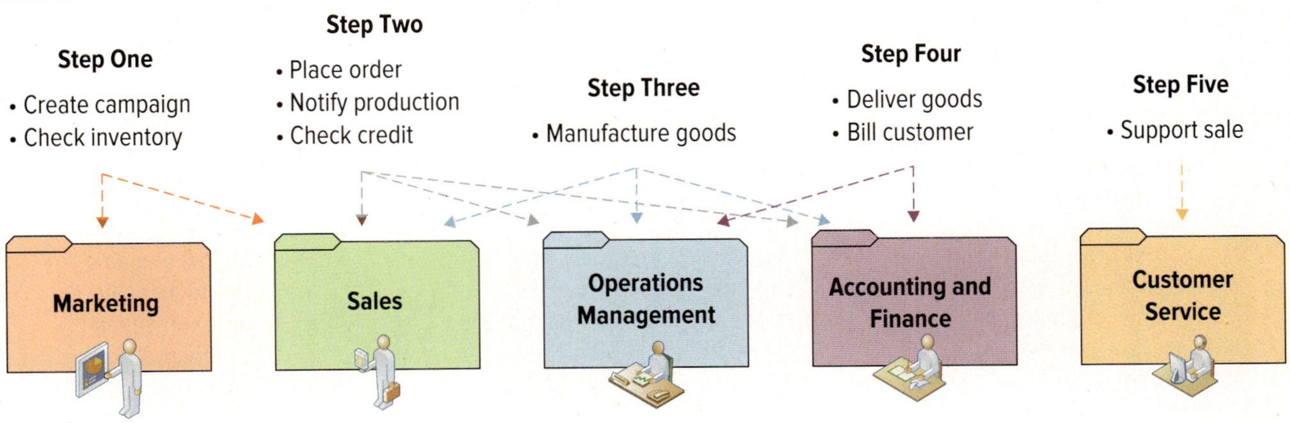

business process modeling (or mapping) The activity of creating a detailed flowchart or process map of a work process that shows its inputs, tasks, and activities in a structured sequence.

business process model A graphic description of a process, showing the sequence of process tasks, which is developed for a specific purpose and from a selected viewpoint.

business process model and notation (BPMN) A graphical notation that depicts the steps in a business process.

As-Is process model Represents the current state of the operation that has been mapped, without any specific improvements or changes to existing processes.

To-Be process model Shows the results of applying change improvement opportunities to the current (As-Is) process model.

Systems thinking offers a great story to help differentiate between static and dynamic processes. If you throw a rock in the air, you can predict where it will land. If you throw a bird in the air you can't predict where it will land. The bird, a living dynamic, system, will sense its environment and fly in any direction. The bird gathers and processes input and interacts with its environment. The rock is an example of a static process and the bird is an example of a dynamic process. Organizations have people and are characteristically dynamic, making it difficult to predict how the business will operate. Managers must anticipate creating and deploying both static and dynamic processes.

LO2.5 Explain the value of business processes for a company, and differentiate between customer-facing and business-facing processes.

BUSINESS PROCESS MODELING LO2.6

Business process modeling, or **mapping**, is the activity of creating a detailed flowchart or process map of a work process that shows its inputs, tasks, and activities in a structured sequence. A **business process model** is a graphic description of a process, showing the sequence of process tasks, which is developed for a specific purpose and from a selected viewpoint. A set of one or more process models details the many functions of a system or subject area with graphics and text, and its purpose is to:

- Expose process detail gradually and in a controlled manner.
- Encourage conciseness and accuracy in describing the process model.
- Focus attention on the process model interfaces.
- Provide a powerful process analysis and consistent design vocabulary. (See the end of the chapter for business process model examples.)[12]

Business Process Model and Notation (BPMN) is a graphical notation that depicts the steps in a business process. BPMN provides businesses with a graphical view of the end-to-end flow of their business processes. Diagramming business processes allows for easy communication and understanding of how core business processes are helping or hindering the business. Figure 2.20 displays the standard notation from www.BPMN.org and Figure 2.21 displays a sample BPMN diagram for hiring a taxi cab.[13]

Business process modeling usually begins with a functional process representation of the process problem, or an As-Is process model. **As-Is process models** represent the current state of the operation that has been mapped, without any specific improvements or changes to existing processes. The next step is to build a To-Be process model that displays how the process problem will be solved or implemented. **To-Be process models** show the results of applying change improvement opportunities to the current (As-Is) process model. This approach ensures that the process is fully and clearly understood before the details of a process solution are decided on. The To-Be process model shows how "the what" is to be realized. Figure 2.22 displays the As-Is and To-Be process models for ordering a hamburger.

As-Is and To-Be process models are both integral in business process reengineering projects because these diagrams are very powerful in visualizing the activities, processes, and data flow of an organization. Figure 2.23 illustrates an As-Is process model of the order-to-delivery process, using swim lanes

FIGURE 2.19 Customer-Facing, Industry-Specific, and Business-Facing Processes

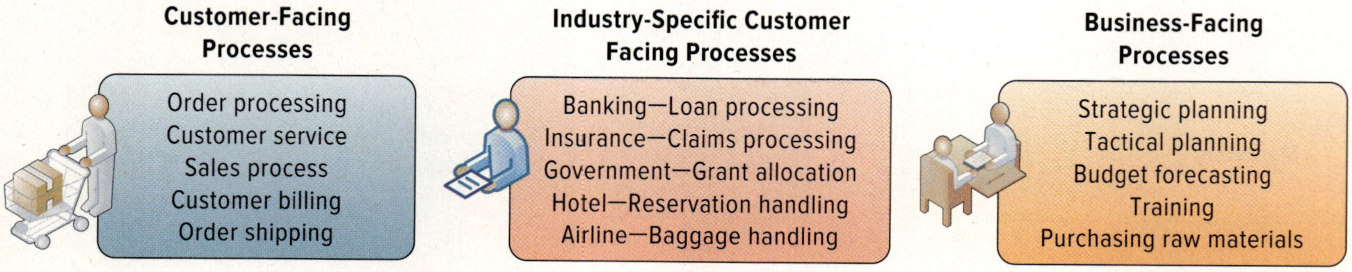

to represent the relevant departments. The **swim lane** layout arranges the steps of a business process into a set of rows depicting the various elements.

You need to be careful not to become inundated in excessive detail when creating an As-Is process model. The primary goal is to simplify, eliminate, and improve the To-Be processes. Process improvement efforts focus on defining the most efficient and effective process identifying all of the illogical, missing, or irrelevant processes.

Investigating business processes can help an organization find bottlenecks, remove redundant tasks, and recognize smooth-running processes. For example, a florist might have a key success factor of reducing delivery time. A florist that has an inefficient ordering process or a difficult distribution process will be unable to achieve this goal. Taking down inaccurate orders, recording incorrect addresses, or experiencing shipping delays can cause errors in the delivery process. Improving order entry, production, or scheduling processes can improve the delivery process.

Business processes should drive MIS choices and should be based on business strategies and goals (see Figure 2.24). Only after determining the most efficient and effective business process should an organization choose the MIS that supports that business process. Of course, this does not always happen, and managers may find themselves in the difficult position of changing a business process because the system cannot support the ideal solution (see Figure 2.24). Managers who make MIS choices and only then determine how their business processes should perform typically fail.

LO2.6 Demonstrate the value of business process modeling, and compare As-Is and To-Be models.

swim lane Layout arranges the steps of a business process into a set of rows depicting the various elements.

workflow Includes the tasks, activities, and responsibilities required to execute each step in a business process.

workflow control systems Monitor processes to ensure tasks, activities, and responsibilities are executed as specified.

USING MIS TO IMPROVE BUSINESS PROCESSES

LO2.7

Workflow includes the tasks, activities, and responsibilities required to execute each step in a business process. Understanding workflow, customers' expectations, and the competitive environment provides managers with the necessary ingredients to design and evaluate alternative business processes in order to maintain competitive advantages when internal or external circumstances change. **Workflow control systems** monitor processes to ensure tasks, activities, and responsibilities are executed as specified.

Alternative business processes should be effective (they deliver the intended results) and efficient (they consume the least amount of resources for the intended value). They should also be adaptable or flexible and support change as customers, market forces, and technology shift. Figure 2.25 shows the three primary types of business process change available to firms and the business areas in which they are most often effective. How does a company know whether it needs to undertake the giant step of changing core business processes? Three conditions indicate the time is right to initiate a business process change:

FIGURE 2.20 BPMN Notation

BUSINESS PROCESS MODEL AND NOTATION (BPMN)	
EVENT	***BPMN event*** is anything that happens during the course of a business process. An event is represented by a circle in a business process model. In Figure 2.21, the events include customer requests, time requests, or the end of the process.
ACTIVITY	***BPMN activity*** is a task in a business process. An activity is any work that is being performed in a process. An activity is represented by a rounded-corner rectangle in a business process model. In Figure 2.21, the activities include checking availability, picking up the customers, and confirming the booking.
GATEWAY	***BPMN gateway*** is used to control the flow of a process. Gateways handle the forking, merging, and joining of paths within a process. Gateways are represented by a diamond shape in a business process model. In Figure 2.21, the gateways include determining availability status or accepting/declining the request.
FLOW	***BPMN flows*** display the path in which the process flows. Flows are represented by arrows in a business process model. In Figure 2.21, the arrows show the path the customer takes through the taxi cab booking process.

FIGURE 2.21 BPMN Sample Diagram for Hiring a Taxi Cab

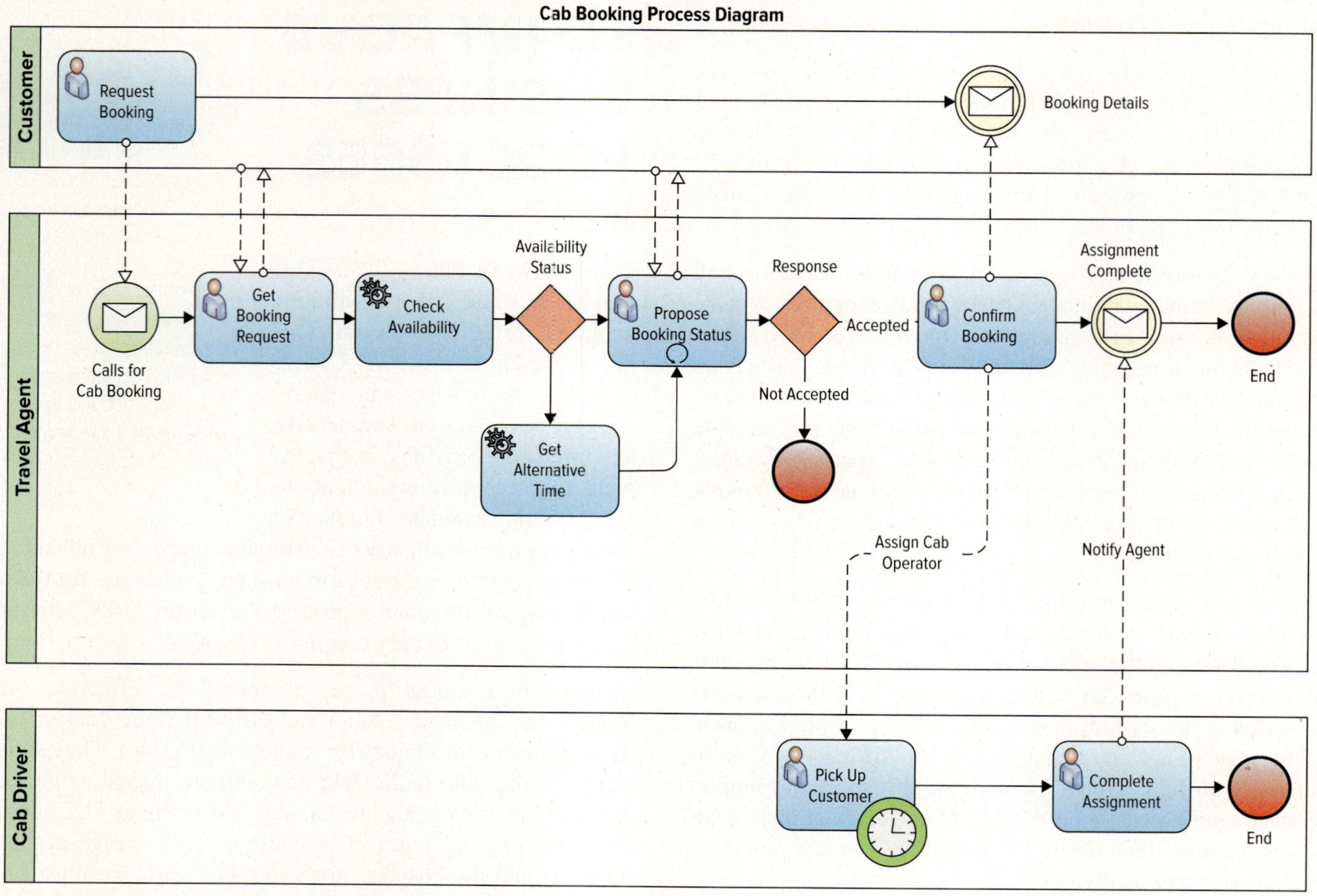

FIGURE 2.22
As-Is and To-Be Process Model for Ordering a Hamburger

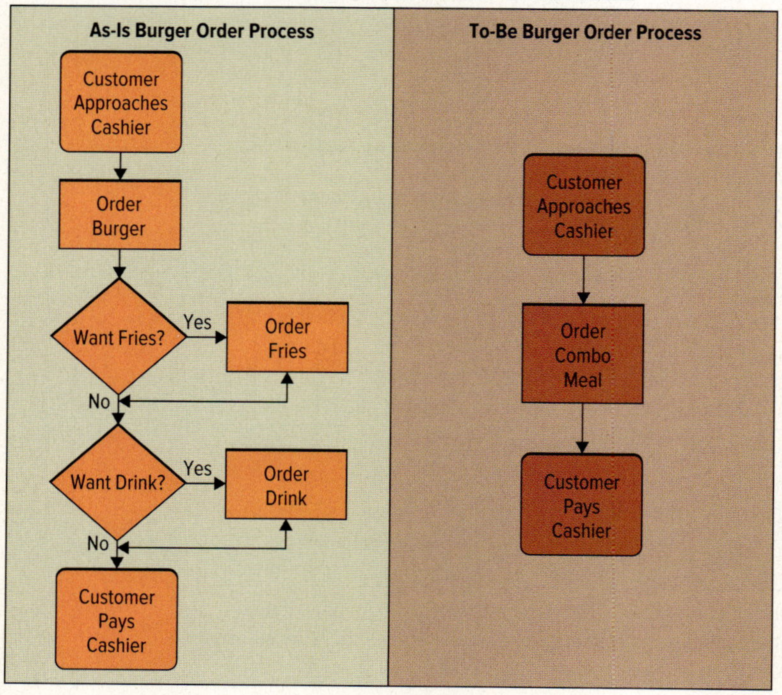

1. There has been a pronounced shift in the market the process was designed to serve.
2. The company is markedly below industry benchmarks on its core processes.
3. To regain competitive advantage, the company must leapfrog competition on key dimensions.[14]

LO2.7 Differentiate among business process improvements, streamlining, and reengineering.

Operational Business Processes—Automation

Operational business processes are static, routine, daily business processes such as stocking inventory, checking out customers, or daily opening and closing processes. Improving business processes is critical to staying competitive in today's electronic marketplace. Organizations must improve their business processes because customers are demanding better products and services; if customers do not receive what they want from one supplier, often they can simply click a mouse to find many other choices. **Business process improvement**

attempts to understand and measure the current process and make performance improvements accordingly. Figure 2.26 displays a typical business process improvement model.[15]

Early adopters of MIS recognized that they could enhance their value chain through automation, which reduces costs and increases the speed of performing activities. **Automation** is the process of computerizing manual tasks, making them more efficient and effective and dramatically lowering operational costs. Payroll offers an excellent example. Calculating and tracking payroll for 5,000 employees is a highly labor-intensive process requiring 30 full-time employees. Every two weeks accounting employees must gather everyone's hours worked, cross-check with wage rates, and then calculate the amount due, minus taxes and other withholding such as pension contributions and insurance premiums, to create the paychecks. They also track benefits, sick time, and vacation time. If the payroll process is automated, however, one employee can easily calculate payroll, track withholding and deductions, and create paychecks for 5,000 people in a few hours, since everything is performed by the system. Automation improves efficiency and effectiveness and reduces head count, lowering overall operational costs. Transaction processing systems (TPS) are primarily used to automate business processes.

Figure 2.27 illustrates the basic steps for business process improvement. Organizations begin by documenting what they currently do; then they establish a way to measure the process, follow the process, measure the performance, and finally identify improvement opportunities based on the collected information. The next step is to implement process improvements and measure the performance of the new improved process. The loop repeats over and over again as it is continuously improved.[16]

This method of improving business processes is effective for obtaining gradual, incremental improvement. However, several factors have accelerated the need to radically improve business processes. The most obvious is technology. New technologies (such as wireless Internet access) rapidly bring new capabilities to businesses, thereby raising the competitive bar and the need to improve business processes dramatically. For example, Amazon.com reinvented the supply chain for selling books online. After gaining from automation, companies began to look for new ways to use MIS to improve operations, and managers recognized the benefits of pairing MIS with business processes by streamlining. We look at this improvement method next.

Managerial Business Processes—Streamlining

Managerial business processes are semidynamic, semiroutine, monthly business processes such as resource allocation,

operational business processes Static, routine, daily business processes such as stocking inventory, checking out customers, or daily opening and closing processes.

business process improvement Attempts to understand and measure the current process and make performance improvements accordingly.

automation Involves computerizing manual tasks making them more efficient and effective and dramatically lowering operational costs.

FIGURE 2.23 As-Is Process Model for Order Fulfillment

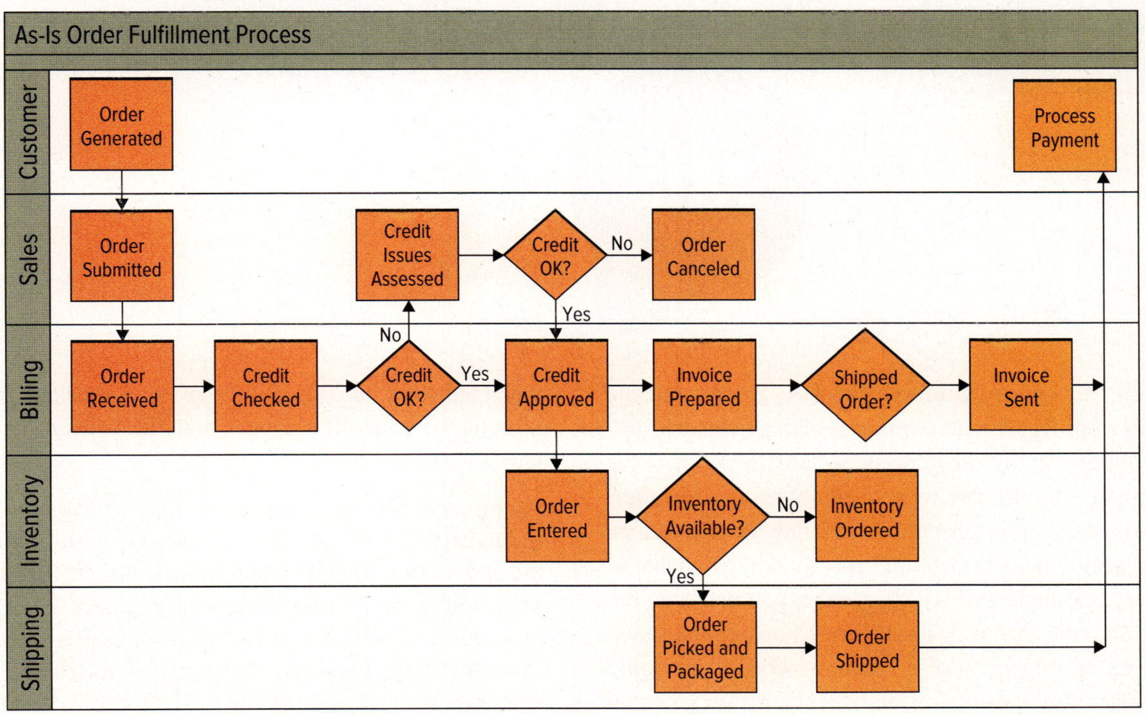

managerial business processes Semidynamic, semiroutine, monthly business processes such as resource allocation, sales strategy, or manufacturing process improvements.

streamlining Improves business process efficiencies simplifying or eliminating unnecessary steps.

bottleneck Occurs when resources reach full capacity and cannot handle any additional demands; they limit throughput and impede operations.

redundancy Occurs when a task or activity is unnecessarily repeated.

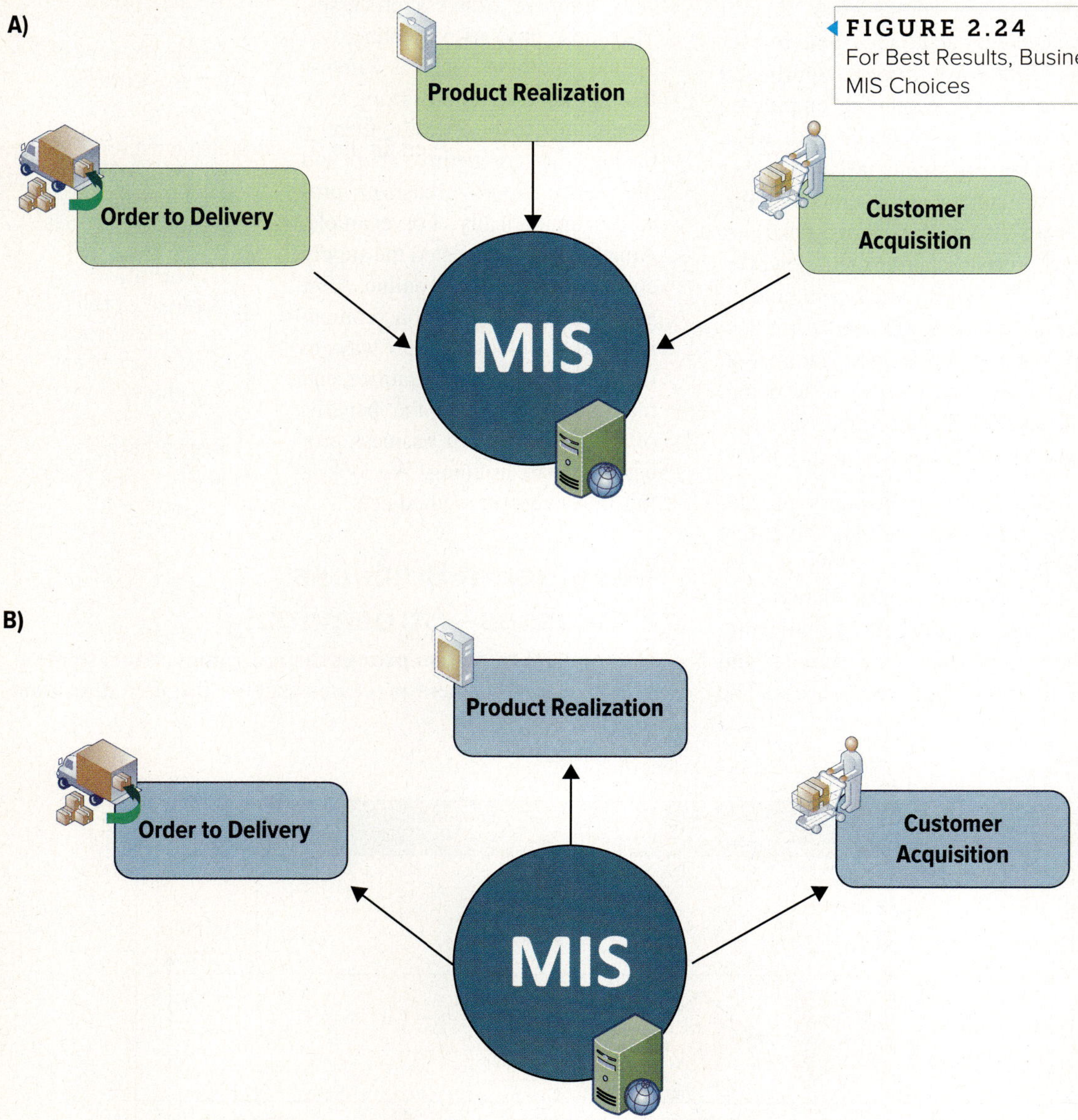

FIGURE 2.24
For Best Results, Business Processes Should Drive MIS Choices

sales strategy, or manufacturing process improvements. **Streamlining** improves business process efficiencies by simplifying or eliminating unnecessary steps. **Bottlenecks** occur when resources reach full capacity and cannot handle any additional demands; they limit throughput and impede operations. A computer working at its maximum capacity will be unable to handle increased demand and will become a bottleneck in the process. Streamlining removes bottlenecks, an important step if the efficiency and capacity of a business process are being increased. It also eliminates redundancy. **Redundancy** occurs when a task or activity is unnecessarily repeated, for example, if both the sales department and the accounting department check customer credit.

Automating a business process that contains bottlenecks or redundancies will magnify or amplify these problems if they are not corrected first. Here's an example based on a common source of tension in an organization. Increasing orders is a standard KPI for most marketing/sales departments. To meet this KPI, the sales department tends to say yes to any customer request, such as for rush or custom orders. Reducing

FIGURE 2.25 Primary Types of Business Process Change

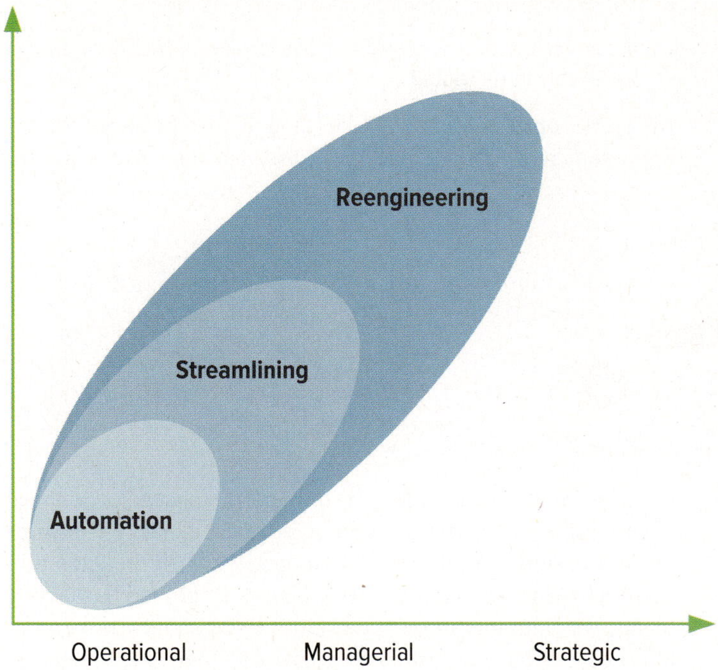

Strategic Business Processes—Reengineering

Strategic business processes are dynamic, nonroutine, long-term business processes such as financial planning, expansion strategies, and stakeholder interactions. The flat world is bringing more companies and more customers into the marketplace, greatly increasing competition. Wine wholesalers in the United States must now compete globally, for instance, because customers can just as easily order a bottle of wine from a winery in France as from them. Companies

cycle time The time required to process an order.

strategic business processes Dynamic, nonroutine, long-term business processes such as financial planning, expansion strategies, and stakeholder interactions.

FIGURE 2.26 Business Process Improvement Model

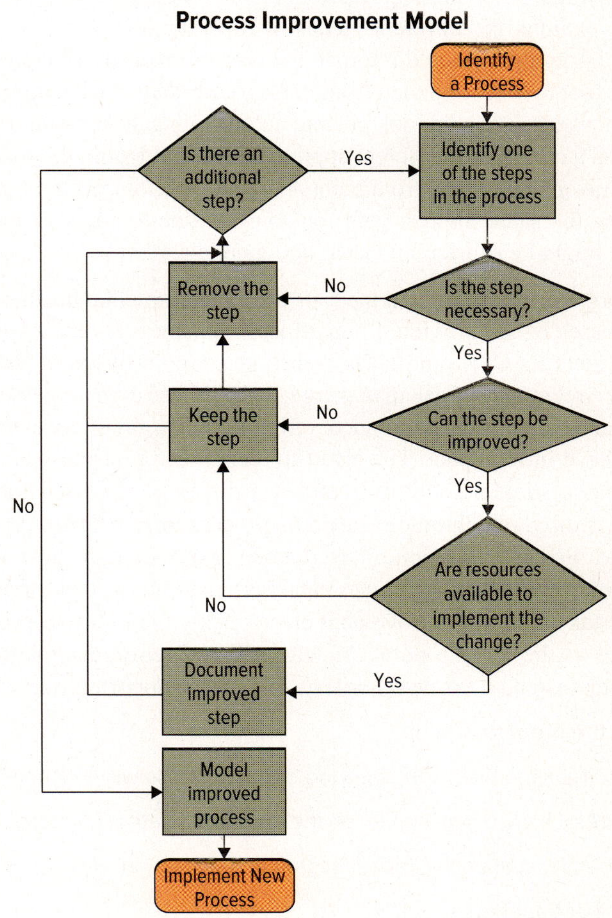

cycle time, the time required to process an order, is a common KPI for operations management. Rush and custom orders tend to create bottlenecks, causing operations to fall below its benchmarked cycle time. Removing these bottlenecks, however, can create master streamlined business processes that deliver both standard and custom orders reliably and profitably. The goal of streamlining is not only to automate but also to improve by monitoring, controlling, and changing the business process.

FedEx streamlined every business process to provide a CSF of speedy and reliable delivery of packages. It created one central hub in Memphis, Tennessee, that processed all its orders. It purchased its own planes to be sure it could achieve the desired level of service. FedEx combined MIS and traditional distribution and logistics processes to create a competitive advantage. FedEx soon identified another market segment of customers who cared a little less about speed and were willing to trade off early-morning delivery for delivery any time *within* the next day at a significantly lower price. The firm had to reevaluate its strategy and realign its business processes to capture this market segment. Had Federal Express focused only on improving its traditional delivery process to handle increased volume faster and more reliably, it could have missed an entire customer segment.[18]

FIGURE 2.27 Steps in Business Process Improvement

business process reengineering (BPR) The analysis and redesign of workflow within and between enterprises.

need breakthrough performance and business process changes just to stay in the game. As the rate of change increases, companies looking for rapid change and dramatic improvement are turning to **business process reengineering (BPR)**, the analysis and redesign of workflow within and between enterprises. Figure 2.28 highlights an analogy to process improvement by explaining the different means of traveling along the same route. A company could improve the way it travels by changing from foot to horse and then from horse to car. With a BPR mindset, however, it would look beyond automating and streamlining to find a completely different approach. It would ignore the road and travel by air to get from point A to point B. Companies often follow the same indirect path for doing business, not realizing there might be a different, faster, and more direct way.

FIGURE 2.28 Different Ways to Travel the Same Route

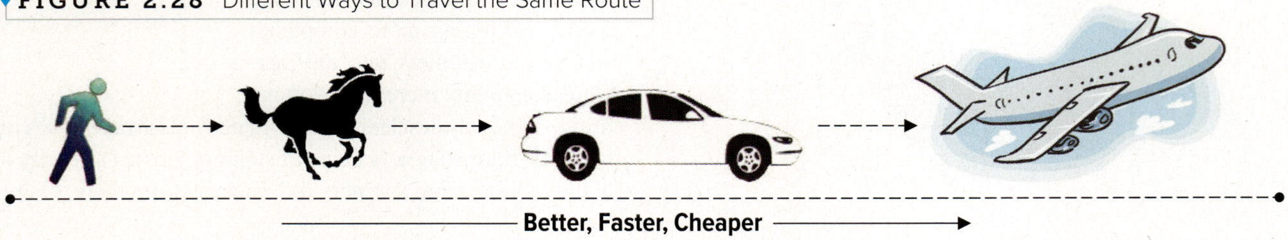

An organization can reengineer its cross-departmental business processes or an individual department's business processes to help meet its CSFs and KPIs. When selecting a business process to reengineer, wise managers focus on those core processes that are critical to performance, rather than marginal processes that have little impact. The effort to reengineer a business process as a strategic activity requires a different mind-set than that required in continuous business process improvement programs. Because companies have tended to overlook the powerful contribution that processes can make to strategy, they often undertake process improvement efforts using their current processes as the starting point. Managers focusing on reengineering can instead use several criteria to identify opportunities:

- Is the process broken?
- Is it feasible that reengineering of this process will succeed?
- Does it have a high impact on the agency's strategic direction?
- Does it significantly impact customer satisfaction?
- Is it antiquated?
- Does it fall far below best-in-class?
- Is it crucial for productivity improvement?
- Will savings from automation be clearly visible?
- Is the return on investment from implementation high and preferably immediate?

BPR relies on a different school of thought than business process improvement. *In the extreme,* BPR assumes the current process is irrelevant, does not work, or is broken and must be overhauled from scratch. Starting from such a clean slate enables business process designers to disassociate themselves from today's process and focus on a new process. It is as if they are projecting themselves into the future and asking: What should the process look like? What do customers want it to look like? What do other employees want it to look like? How do best-in-class companies do it? How can new technology facilitate the process?

Figure 2.29 displays the basic steps in a business process reengineering effort. It begins with defining the scope and objectives of the reengineering project and then takes the process designers through a learning process with customers, employees, competitors, and new technology. Given this knowledge base, the designers can create a plan of action based on the gap between current processes, technologies, and structures and their vision of the processes of the future. It is then top management's job to implement the chosen solution.[20]

System thinking plays a big role in BPR. Automation and streamlining operate departmentally, whereas BPR occurs at the systems level or company-wide level and the end-to-end view of a process.

Creating value for the customer is the leading reason for instituting BPR, and MIS often plays an important enabling role. Fundamentally new business processes enabled Progressive Insurance to slash its claims settlement time from 31 days to four hours, for instance. Typically, car insurance companies follow this standard claims resolution process: The customer gets into an accident, has the car towed, and finds a ride home. The customer then calls the insurance company to begin the claims process, which includes an evaluation of the damage, assignment of fault,

FIGURE 2.29 Business Process Reengineering Model

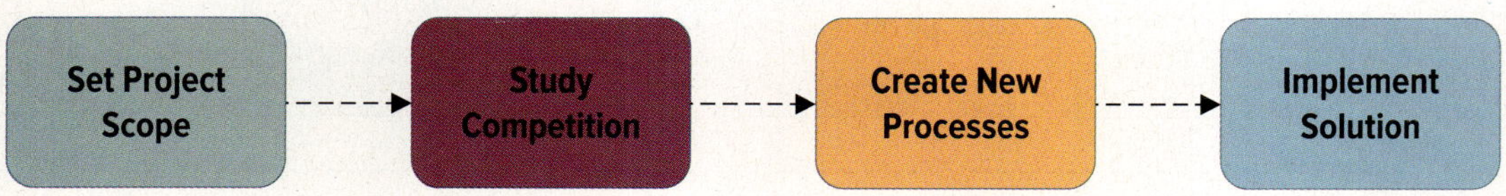

My Not To-Do List

You Accidently Sent Your Confidential Email to Your Significant Other to Your Grandmother—Ouch![17]

If someone at your work currently looked through your email, would they find anything unacceptable? There is a 99 percent chance that at some point you have been guilty of using your work email for personal use. Not only are you wasting company time and resources, but you are also putting yourself at serious risk of violating company policies. There is no doubt some of these mistakes are funny, like the embarrassing story of how a woman sent a racy email to her husband, only to have accidentally sent it to her boss instead. However, you stop laughing when you are fired because it was you who sent the unsuitable email!

You do not own your email; it is that simple. Your employer owns your email, and they have every right to read every single piece of email that you send or is sent to you. Some people argue that it is an invasion of privacy to read someone else's email, but it is not private when you are sitting in the company's office building, at the company's desk, using the company's computer equipment and email software. Technology is so advanced that your employer can flag anything with inappropriate language or keywords such as "résumé," "job search," or "confidential."

How do you prevent email blunders? It is a good idea to create a free Google Gmail account or a Hotmail account for your personal email. Also, before sending any email, ask yourself: If my boss was looking over my shoulder right now, would he or she approve? This is the true litmus test that can be applied to anything an employee does at work.

Now, here comes the hard part: What if you are working from home, using your own computer? Does the company still have a right to monitor your email? If you are using your own personal smartphone to work remotely and you receive the company's emails on your device, is it still company property? What do you think? What additional dilemmas do you see being created as innovative technologies continue to change the fundamental business process of how we work?

and an estimate of the cost of repairs, and which usually takes about a month (see Figure 2.30). Progressive Insurance's innovation was to offer a mobile claims process. When a customer has a car accident, he or she calls in the claim on the spot. The Progressive claims adjuster comes to the accident site, surveying the scene and taking digital photographs. The adjuster then offers the customer on-site payment, towing services, and a ride home. A true BPR effort does more for a company than simply improve a process by performing it better, faster, and cheaper. Progressive Insurance's BPR effort redefined best practices for an entire industry. Figure 2.31 through Figure 2.33 provide additional examples of business process modeling.[21]

show me the MONEY

Streamlining Your Email

The biggest problem with email is that it interferes with workflow. Many employees stop what they are working on and begin checking new email as soon as it arrives. If they do not have the time or capacity to answer it immediately, however, they leave it in the inbox, creating a bottleneck. This process continues all day, and eventually the inbox is overflowing with hundreds of emails, most of which require a response or action. Employees begin dreading email and feel stressed because their workflow process is off track, and they do not know which tasks need to be completed and when.

To streamline workflow, you can designate certain times for email processing (at the top of the hour or for 30 minutes at three set times a day, for example). Turning off email notification also ensures you are not interrupted during your workflow. When you do begin to check your emails, review them one at a time from top to bottom and deal with each one immediately. Reply, put a note on your to-do list, forward the email, or delete it. Now you are working far more efficiently and effectively, and you are less stressed because your inbox is empty.[19]

Choose a process in your life that is inefficient or ineffective and causing you stress. Using the principles of streamlining, remove the bottlenecks and reduce redundancies. Be sure to diagram the As-Is process and your newly created To-Be process.

FIGURE 2.30 Auto Insurance Claims Processes

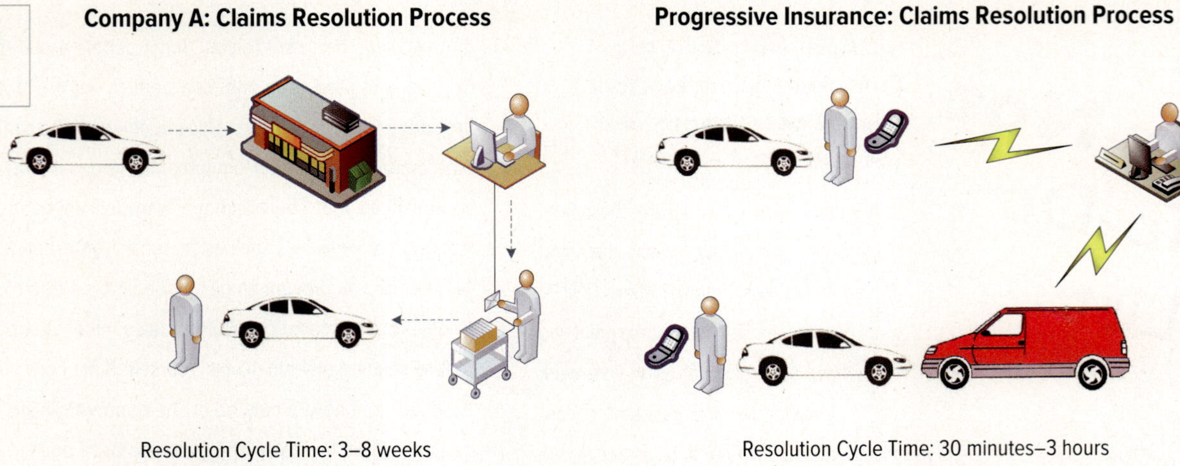

FIGURE 2.31 Online Sales Process Model

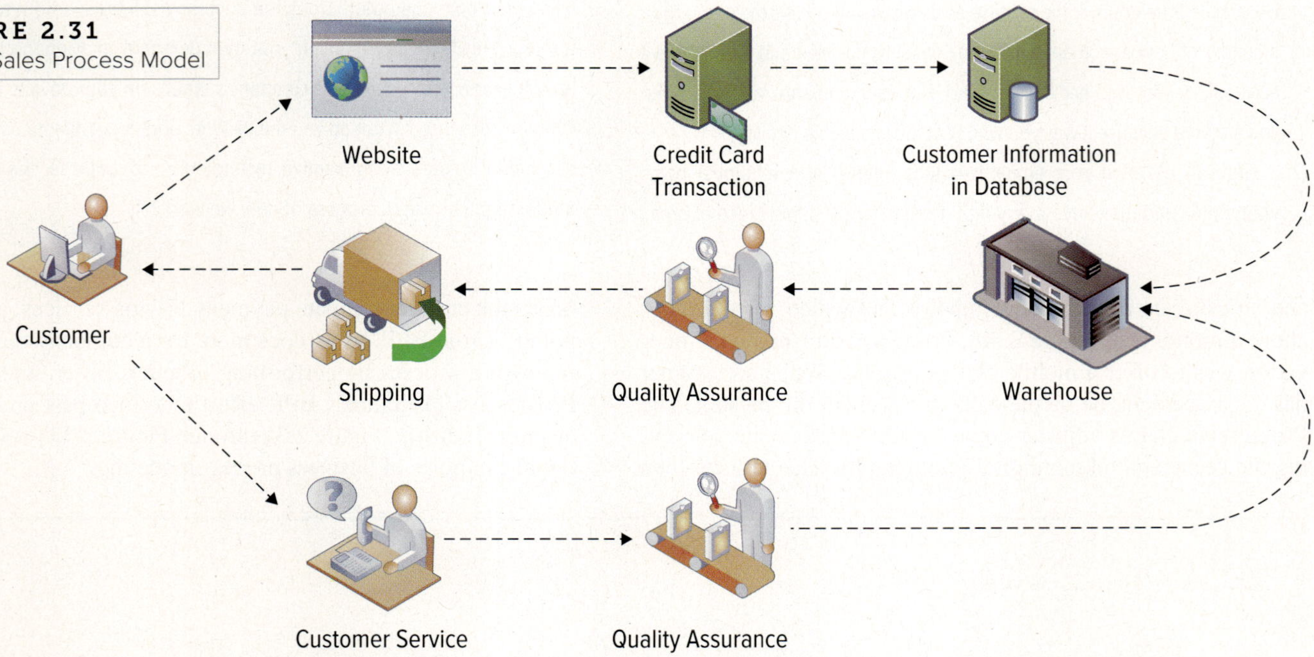

FIGURE 2.32 Online Banking Process Model

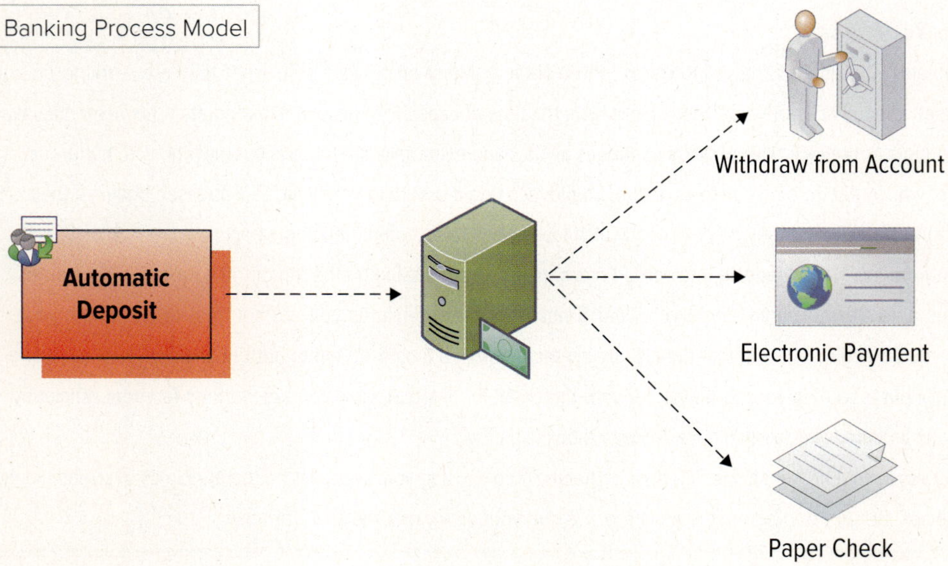

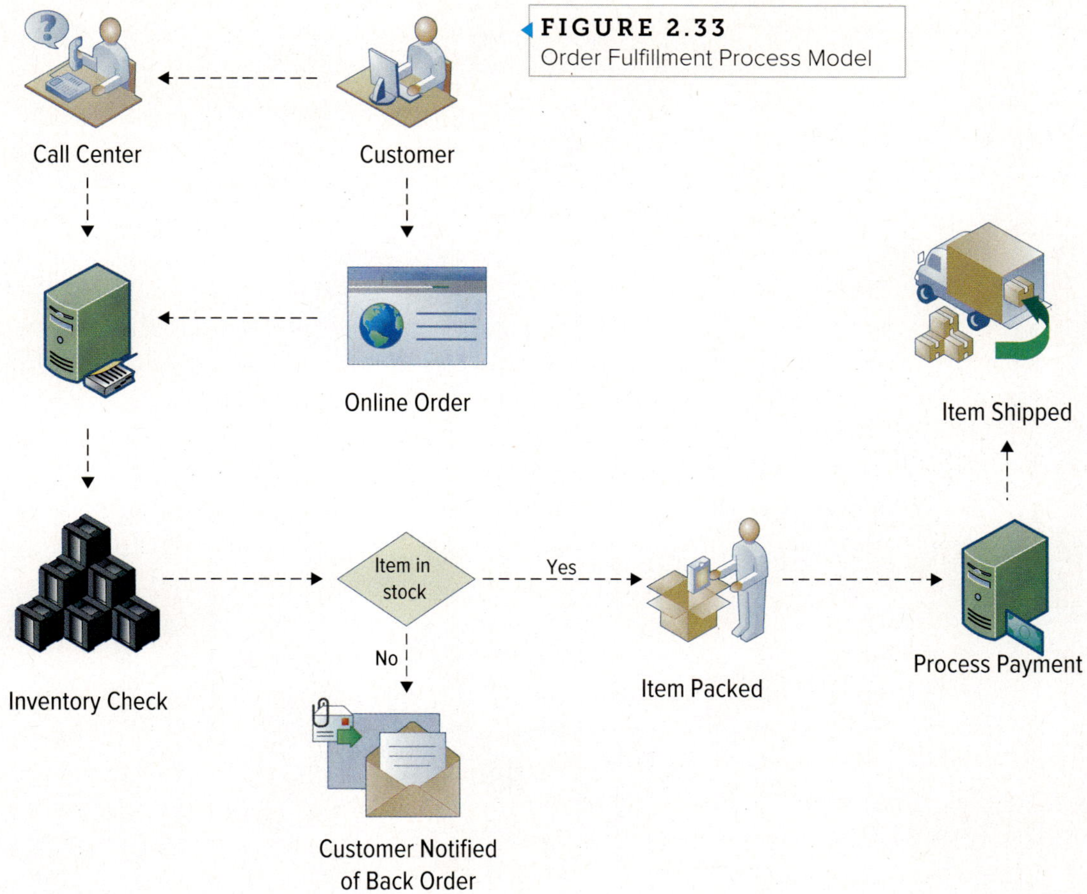

FIGURE 2.33
Order Fulfillment Process Model

0100 0111 0101 0010
VALID FROM
00/00
UNTIL END
00/00
DOT COM
www
01 0010
0100 0111 0101 0010
DOT COM

chapter three

ebusiness: electronic business value

what's in IT for me?

Internet and communication technologies have revolutionized the way business operates, improving upon traditional methods and even introducing new opportunities and ventures that were simply not possible before. More than just giving organizations another means of conducting transactions, online business provides the ability to develop and maintain customer relationships, supplier relationships, and even employee relationships between and within enterprises.

As future managers and organizational knowledge workers, you need to understand the benefits ebusiness can offer an organization and your career, the challenges that accompany web technologies and their impact on organizational communication and collaboration. You need to be aware of the strategies organizations can

continued on p. 64

CHAPTER OUTLINE

SECTION 3.1 >>

WEB 1.0: Ebusiness

- Disruptive Technologies
- Web 1.0 and the Catalyst for Ebusiness
- The Four Ebusiness Models
- Web 1.0: The Catalyst for Ebusiness
- Ebusiness Tools for Connecting and Communicating
- The Challenges of Ebusiness

SECTION 3.2 >>

WEB 2.0: Business 2.0

- Web 2.0: Advantages of Business 2.0
- Networking Communities with Business 2.0
- Business 2.0 Tools for Collaborating
- The Challenges of Business 2.0
- Web 3.0: Defining the Next Generation of Online Business Opportunities

continued from p. 63

use to deploy ebusiness and the methods of measuring ebusiness success. This chapter will give you this knowledge and help prepare you for success in tomorrow's electronic global marketplace. ■

{SECTION 3.1} Web 1.0: Ebusiness

LEARNING OUTCOMES

LO3.1 Compare disruptive and sustaining technologies, and explain how the Internet and WWW caused business disruption.

LO3.2 Describe ebusiness and its associated advantages.

LO3.3 Compare the four ebusiness models.

LO3.4 Describe the six ebusiness tools for connecting and communicating.

LO3.5 Identify the four challenges associated with ebusiness.

DISRUPTIVE TECHNOLOGIES LO3.1

Polaroid, founded in 1937, produced the first instant camera in the late 1940s. The Polaroid camera, whose pictures developed themselves, was one of the most exciting technological advances the photography industry had ever seen. The company eventually went public, becoming one of Wall Street's most prominent enterprises, with its stock trading above $60 per share in 1997. In 2002, the stock dropped to 8 cents and the company declared bankruptcy.[1]

How could a company such as Polaroid, which had innovative technology and a captive customer base, go bankrupt? Perhaps company executives failed to use Porter's Five Forces Model to analyze the threat of substitute products or services. If they had, would they have noticed the two threats—one-hour film processing and digital cameras—which eventually stole Polaroid's market share? Would they have understood that their customers, people who want instant access to their pictures, would be the first to try these alternatives? Could the company have found a way to compete with one-hour film processing and the digital camera to save Polaroid?

Many organizations face the same dilemma as Polaroid—what's best for the current business might not be what's best for it in the long term. Some observers of our business environment have an ominous vision of the future—digital Darwinism. **Digital Darwinism** implies that organizations that cannot adapt to the new demands placed on them for surviving in the information age are doomed to extinction.

LO3.1 Compare disruptive and sustaining technologies and explain how the Internet and WWW caused business disruption.

Disruptive versus Sustaining Technology

A **disruptive technology** is a new way of doing things that initially does not meet the needs of existing customers. Disruptive technologies tend to open new markets and destroy old ones. A **sustaining technology**, on the other hand, produces an improved product customers are eager to buy, such as a faster car or larger hard drive. Sustaining technologies tend to provide us with better, faster, and cheaper products in established markets. Incumbent companies most often lead sustaining technology to market, but they virtually never lead in markets opened by disruptive technologies. Figure 3.1 positions companies expecting future growth from new investments (disruptive technology) and companies expecting future growth from existing investments (sustaining technology).[2]

FIGURE 3.1 Disruptive and Sustaining Technologies

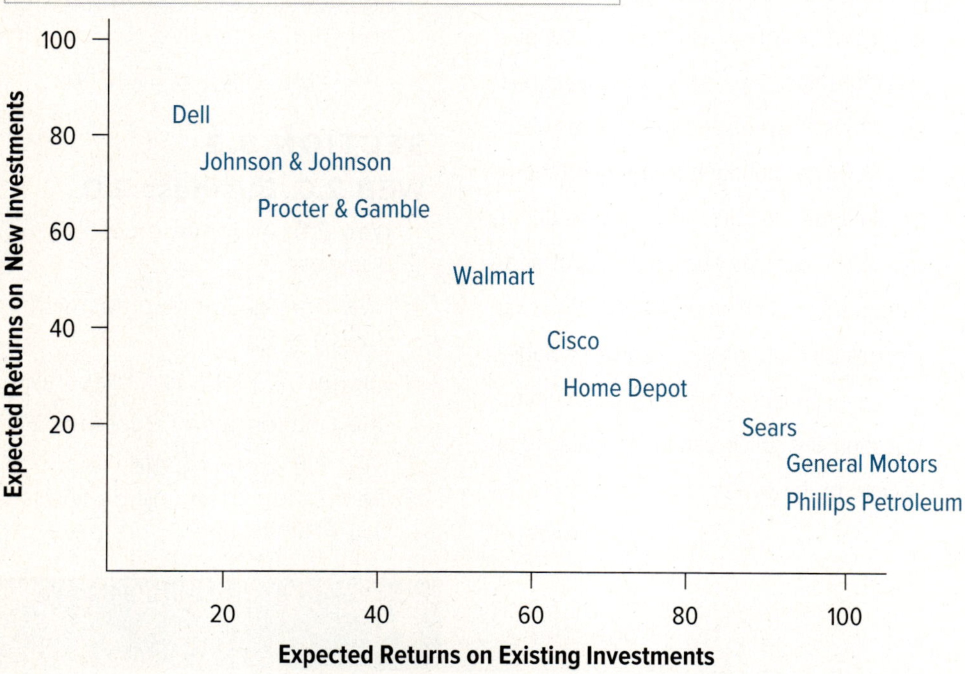

Disruptive technologies typically enter the low end of the marketplace and eventually evolve to displace high-end competitors and their reigning

digital Darwinism Implies that organizations that cannot adapt to the new demands placed on them for surviving in the information age are doomed to extinction.

disruptive technology A new way of doing things that initially does not meet the needs of existing customers.

sustaining technology Produces an improved product customers are eager to buy, such as a faster car or larger hard drive.

Internet A massive network that connects computers all over the world and allows them to communicate with one another.

technologies. Sony is a perfect example. Sony started as a tiny company that built portable, battery-powered transistor radios. The sound quality was poor, but customers were willing to overlook that for the convenience of portability. With the experience and revenue stream from the portables, Sony improved its technology to produce cheap, low-end transistor amplifiers that were suitable for home use and invested those revenues in improving the technology further, which produced still-better radios.[3]

The Innovator's Dilemma, a book by Clayton M. Christensen, discusses how established companies can take advantage of disruptive technologies without hindering existing relationships with customers, partners, and stakeholders. Xerox, IBM, Sears, and DEC all listened to existing customers, invested aggressively in technology, had their competitive antennae up, and still lost their market-dominant positions. They may have placed too much emphasis on satisfying customers' current needs, while neglecting new disruptive technology to meet customers' future needs and thus losing market share.

The Internet and World Wide Web—The Ultimate Business Disruptors

The **Internet** is a massive network that connects computers all over the world and allows them to communicate with one another. Computers connected via the Internet can send and receive information including text, graphics, voice, video, and software. Originally the Internet was essentially an emergency military communications system operated by the U.S. Department of Defense Advanced Research Project Agency (DARPA), which called the network ARPANET. No one foresaw the dramatic impact it would have on both business and personal communications. In time, all U.S. universities that had defense-related funding installed ARPANET computers, forming the first official Internet network. As users began to notice the value of electronic communications, the purpose of the network started shifting from a military pipeline to a communications tool for scientists.

The Internet and the World Wide Web are not synonymous. The WWW is just one part of the Internet, and its primary use is to correlate and disseminate information. The Internet includes the WWW and also other forms of communication systems such as email. Figure 3.2 lists the key terms associated with the WWW and Figure 3.3 lists the reasons for the massive growth of the WWW.[4]

WEB 1.0: THE CATALYST FOR EBUSINESS LO3.2

Web 1.0: The Catalyst for Ebusiness

As people began learning about the WWW and the Internet, they understood that it enabled a company to communicate with anyone, anywhere, at anytime, creating a new way to participate in business. The competitive advantages for first movers

Due Diligence //:

Unethical Disruption[5]

Did you know you can make a living naming things? Eli Altman has been naming things since he was six years old and has named more than 400 companies and brands while working for A Hundred Monkeys, a branding consulting company. Altman recently noticed an unfamiliar trend in the industry: nonsensical names such as Flickr, Socializr, Zoomr, Rowdii, Yuuguu, and Oooooc. Why are names like this becoming popular?

The reason is "domain squatting" or "cyber squatting," the practice of buying a domain to profit from a trademarked name. For example, if you wanted to start a business called Drink, chances are a domain squatter has already purchased drink.com and is just waiting for you to pay big bucks for the right to buy it. Domain squatting is illegal and outlawed under the 1999 Anticybersquatting Consumer Protection Act.

Do you agree that domain squatting should be illegal? Why or why not? If you were starting a business and someone were squatting on your domain, what would you do?

© Peter Scholey/Getty Images

FIGURE 3.2 Overview of the WWW

Term	Definition	Example
World Wide Web (WWW)	Provides access to Internet information through documents, including text, graphics, and audio and video files that use a special formatting language called Hypertext Markup Language.	Tim Berners-Lee, a British computer scientist, is considered the inventor of the WWW on March 12, 1989.
Hypertext markup language (HTML)	Publishes hypertext on the WWW, which allows users to move from one document to another simply by clicking a hot spot or link.	HTML uses tags such as <h1> and </h1> to structure text into headings, paragraphs, lists, hypertext links, and so on.
HTML 5	The current version of HTML delivers everything from animation to graphics and music to movies; it can also be used to build complicated web applications and works across platforms, including a PC, tablet, smartphone, or smart TV.	Includes new tags such as doctype, a simple way to tell the browser what type of document is being looked at. <!DOCTYPE html PUBLIC>
Hypertext transport protocol (HTTP)	The Internet protocol web browsers use to request and display web pages using universal resource locators (URLs).	To retrieve the file at the URL http://www.somehost.com/path/file.html
World Wide Web Consortium (W3C)	An international community that develops open standards to ensure the long-term growth of the Web (www.w3.org).	Tim Berners-Lee founded the W3C to act as a steward of web standards, which the organization has done for more than 15 years.
Web browser	Allows users to access the WWW.	Internet Explorer, Mozilla's Firefox, Google Chrome
Universal resource locator (URL)	The address of a file or resource on the web.	www.apple.com www.microsoft.com www.amazon.com
Domain name hosting (web hosting)	A service that allows the owner of a domain name to maintain a simple website and provide email capacity.	GoDaddy.com, 1&1.com, Web.com
Applet	A program that runs within another application such as a website.	The common "Hello World" applet types Hello World across the screen
Internet Corporation for Assigned Names and Numbers (ICANN)	A nonprofit organization that has assumed the responsibility for Internet Protocol (IP) address space allocation, protocol parameter assignment, domain name system management, and root server system management functions previously performed under U.S. government contract.	https://www.icann.org/ Individuals, industry, noncommercial, and government representatives discuss, debate, and develop policies about the technical coordination of the Internet's Domain Name System.

FIGURE 3.3 Reasons for Growth of the World Wide Web

The microcomputer revolution made it possible for an average person to own a computer.
Advancements in networking hardware, software, and media made it possible for business computers to be connected to larger networks at a minimal cost.
Browser software such as Microsoft's Internet Explorer and Netscape Navigator gave computer users an easy-to-use graphical interface to find, download, and display web pages.
The speed, convenience, and low cost of email have made it an incredibly popular tool for business and personal communications.
Basic web pages are easy to create and extremely flexible.

would be enormous, thus spurring the beginning of the Web 1.0 Internet boom. **Web 1.0 (or Business 1.0)** is a term to refer to the World Wide Web during its first few years of operation between 1991 and 2003. **Ecommerce** is the buying and selling of goods and services over the Internet. Ecommerce refers only to online transactions. **Ebusiness** includes ecommerce along with all activities related to internal and external business operations such as servicing customer accounts, collaborating with partners, and exchanging real-time information. During Web 1.0, entrepreneurs began creating the first forms of ebusiness.

Ebusiness opened up a new marketplace for any company willing to move its business operations online. A **paradigm shift** occurs when a new radical form of business enters the market that reshapes the way companies and organizations behave. Ebusiness

Web 1.0 (or Business 1.0) Refers to the World Wide Web during its first few years of operation between 1991 and 2003.

ecommerce The buying and selling of goods and services over the Internet.

ebusiness Includes ecommerce along with all activities related to internal and external business operations such as servicing customer accounts, collaborating with partners, and exchanging real-time information.

paradigm shift Occurs when a new radical form of business enters the market that reshapes the way companies and organizations behave.

information richness Refers to the depth and breadth of details contained in a piece of textual, graphic, audio, or video information.

information reach Measures the number of people a firm can communicate with all over the world.

created a paradigm shift, transforming entire industries and changing enterprisewide business processes that fundamentally rewrote traditional business rules. Deciding not to make the shift to ebusiness proved fatal for many companies (see Figure 3.4 for an overview of industries revamped by the disruption of ebusiness).[6]

Both individuals and organizations have embraced ebusiness to enhance productivity, maximize convenience, and improve communications. Companies today need to deploy a comprehensive ebusiness strategy, and business students need to understand its advantages, outlined in Figure 3.5. Let's look at each.

LO3.2 Describe ebusiness and its associated advantages.

Expanding Global Reach

Easy access to real-time information is a primary benefit of ebusiness. **Information richness** refers to the depth and breadth of details contained in a piece of textual, graphic, audio, or video information. **Information reach** measures the number of people a firm can communicate with all over the world. Buyers need information richness to make informed purchases, and sellers need information reach to properly market and differentiate themselves from the competition.

Ebusinesses operate 24 hours a day, 7 days a week. This availability directly reduces transaction costs, since consumers no longer have to spend a lot of time researching purchases or traveling great distances to make them. The faster delivery cycle for online sales helps strengthen customer relationships, improving customer satisfaction and ultimately sales.

A firm's website can be the focal point of a cost-effective communications and marketing strategy. Promoting products online allows the company to precisely target its customers whether they are local or around the globe. A physical location is restricted by size and limited to those customers who can get there, while an online store has a global marketplace with customers and information seekers already waiting in line.

FIGURE 3.4 Ebusiness Disruption of Traditional Industries

Industry	Business Changes Due to Technology
Auto	AutoTrader.com is the world's largest used-car marketplace, listing millions of cars from both private owners and dealers. AutoTrader.com actually helps to increase used-car dealer's business as it drives millions of qualified leads (potential used-car buyers) to participating automotive dealers and private sellers.
Publishing	With the Internet, anyone can publish online content. Traditionally, publishers screened many authors and manuscripts and selected those that had the best chances of succeeding. Lulu.com turned this model around by providing self-publishing along with print-on-demand capabilities.
Education and Training	Continuing medical education is costly, and just keeping up-to-date with advances often requires taking training courses and traveling to conferences. Now continuing education in many fields is moving online, and by 2016 over 50 percent of doctors will be building their skills through online learning. Companies such as Cisco save millions by moving training to the Internet.
Entertainment	The music industry was hit hard by ebusiness, and online music traders such as iTunes average billions of annual downloads. Unable to compete with online music, the majority of record stores closed. The next big entertainment industry to feel the effects of ebusiness will be the multibillion-dollar movie business. Video rental stores are closing their doors as they fail to compete with online streaming and home rental delivery companies such as Netflix.
Financial Services	Nearly every public efinance company makes money, with online mortgage service Lending Tree leading the pack. Processing online mortgage applications is over 50 percent cheaper for customers.
Retail	Forrester Research predicts ebusiness retail sales will grow at a 10 percent annual growth rate through 2014. It forecasts U.S. online retail sales will be nearly $250 billion, up from $155 billion in 2009. Online retail sales were recently up 11 percent, compared to 2.5 percent for all retail sales.
Travel	Travel site Expedia.com is now the biggest leisure-travel agency, with higher profit margins than even American Express. The majority of travel agencies closed as a direct result of ebusiness.

mass customization The ability of an organization to tailor its products or services to the customers' specifications.

personalization Occurs when a company knows enough about a customer's likes and dislikes that it can fashion offers more likely to appeal to that person, say by tailoring its website to individuals or groups based on profile information, demographics, or prior transactions.

long tail Referring to the tail of a typical sales curve.

intermediaries Agents, software, or businesses that provide a trading infrastructure to bring buyers and sellers together.

disintermediation Occurs when a business sells direct to the customer online and cuts out the intermediary.

FIGURE 3.5 Ebusiness Advantages

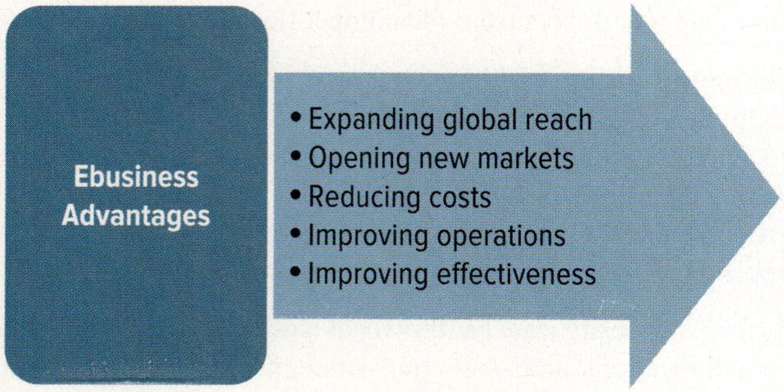

Opening New Markets

Ebusiness is perfect for increasing niche-product sales. **Mass customization** is the ability of an organization to tailor its products or services to the customers' specifications. For example, customers can order M&M's in special colors or with customized sayings such as "Marry Me." **Personalization** occurs when a company knows enough about a customer's likes and dislikes that it can fashion offers more likely to appeal to that person, say by tailoring its website to individuals or groups based on profile information, demographics, or prior transactions. Amazon uses personalization to create a unique portal for each of its customers.

Reducing Costs

Chris Anderson, editor-in-chief of *Wired* magazine, describes niche-market ebusiness strategies as capturing the **long tail**, referring to the tail of a typical sales curve. This strategy demonstrates how niche products can have viable and profitable business models when selling via ebusiness. In traditional sales models, a store is limited by shelf space when selecting products to sell. For this reason, store owners typically purchase products that will be wanted or needed by masses, and the store is stocked with broad products as there is not room on the shelf for niche products that only a few customers might purchase. Ebusinesses such as Amazon and eBay eliminated the shelf-space dilemma and were able to offer infinite products.

Netflix offers an excellent example of the long tail. Let's assume that an average Blockbuster store maintains 3,000 movies in its inventory, whereas Netflix, without physical shelf limitations, can maintain 100,000 movies in its inventory. Looking at sales data, the majority of Blockbuster's revenue comes from new releases that are rented daily, whereas older selections are rented only a few times a month and don't repay the cost of keeping them in stock. Thus Blockbuster's sales tail ends at title 3,000 (see Figure 3.6). However, Netflix, with no physical limitations, can extend its tail beyond 100,000 (and with streaming video perhaps 200,000). By extending its tail, Netflix increases sales, even if a title is rented only a few times.[7]

Intermediaries are agents, software, or businesses that provide a trading infrastructure to bring buyers and sellers together. The introduction of ebusiness brought about **disintermediation**, which occurs when a business sells directly to the customer online and cuts out the intermediary (see Figure 3.7). This business strategy lets the company shorten the order process and add value with reduced costs or a more responsive and efficient service. The disintermediation of the travel agent occurred as people began to book their own vacations online, often at a

FIGURE 3.6 The Long Tail

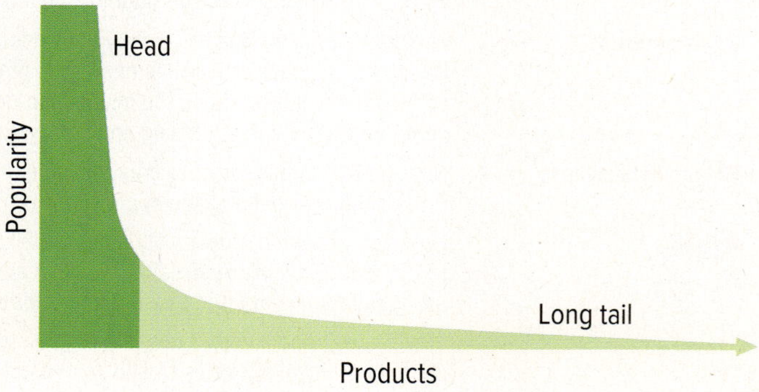

cheaper rate. At Lulu.com, anyone can publish and sell print-on-demand books, online music, and custom calendars, making the publisher obsolete.[8]

In **reintermediation**, steps are *added* to the value chain as new players find ways to add value to the business process. Levi Strauss originally thought it was a good business strategy to limit all online sales to its own website. A few years later, the company realized it could gain a far larger market share by allowing all retailers to sell its products directly to customers. As ebusiness matures it has become evident that to serve certain markets in volume, some reintermediation may be desirable. **Cybermediation** refers to the creation of new kinds of intermediaries that simply could not have existed before the advent of ebusiness, including comparison-shopping sites such as Kelkoo and bank account aggregation services such as Citibank.[9]

Operational benefits of ebusiness include business processes that require less time and human effort or can be eliminated. Compare the cost of sending out 100 direct mailings (paper, postage, labor) to the cost of a bulk email campaign. Think about the cost of renting a physical location and operating phone lines versus the cost of maintaining an online site. Switching to an ebusiness model can eliminate many traditional costs associated with communicating by substituting systems, such as Live Help, that let customers chat live with support or sales staff.

Online air travel reservations cost less than those booked over the telephone. Online ordering also offers the possibility of merging a sales order system with order fulfillment and delivery so customers can check the progress of their orders at all times. Ebusinesses can also inexpensively attract new customers with innovative marketing and retain present customers with improved service and support.

One of the most exciting benefits of ebusiness is its low start-up costs. Today, anyone can start an ebusiness with just a website and a great product or service. Even a dog-walking operation can benefit from being an ebusiness.

Improving Effectiveness

Just putting up a simple website does not create an ebusiness. Ebusiness websites must create buzz, be innovative, add value, and provide useful information. In short, they must build a sense of community and collaboration.

MIS measures of efficiency, such as the amount of traffic on a site, don't tell the whole story. They do not necessarily indicate large sales volumes, for instance. Many websites with lots of traffic have minimal sales. The best way to measure ebusiness success is to use *effectiveness* MIS metrics, such as the revenue generated by web traffic, number of new customers acquired by web traffic, and reductions in customer service calls resulting from web traffic.

Interactivity measures advertising effectiveness by counting visitor interactions with the target ad, including time spent viewing the ad, number of pages viewed, and number of repeat visits to the advertisement. Interactivity measures are a giant step forward for advertisers, since traditional advertising methods—newspapers, magazines, radio, and television—provide few ways to track effectiveness. Figure 3.8 displays the ebusiness marketing initiatives allowing companies to expand their reach while measuring effectiveness.[11]

The ultimate outcome of any advertisement is a purchase. Organizations use metrics to tie revenue amounts

reintermediation Steps are added to the value chain as new players find ways to add value to the business process.

cybermediation Refers to the creation of new kinds of intermediaries that simply could not have existed before the advent of ebusiness.

interactivity Measures advertising effectiveness by counting visitor interactions with the target ad, including time spent viewing the ad, number of pages viewed, and number of repeat visits to the advertisement.

clickstream data Exact pattern of a consumer's navigation through a site.

FIGURE 3.7 Business Value of Disintermediation

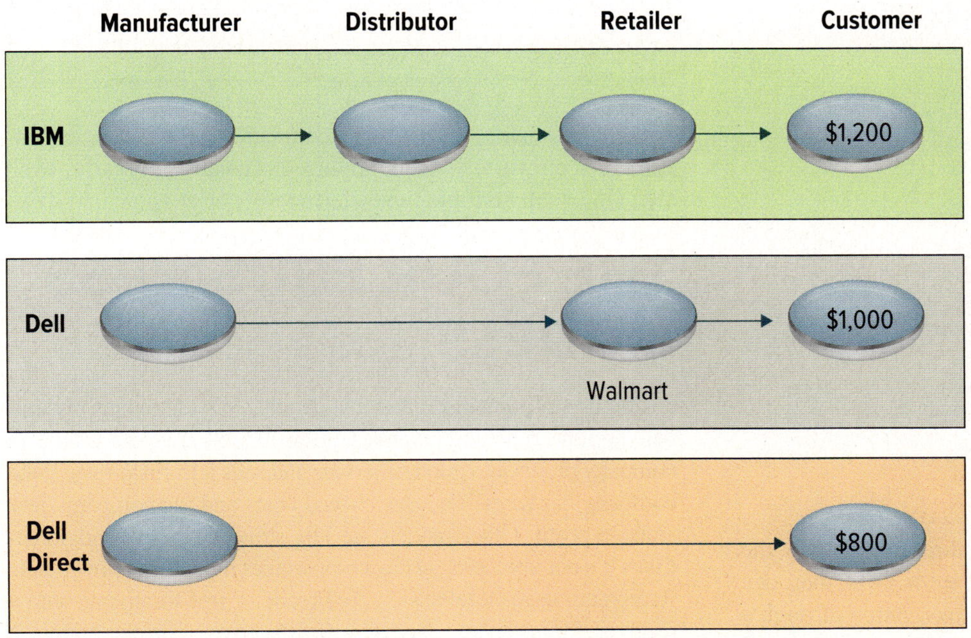

The more intermediaries that are cut from the distribution chain, the lower the product price. When Dell decided to sell its PCs through Walmart many were surprised, because Dell's direct-to-customer sales model was the competitive advantage that had kept Dell the market leader for years.

FIGURE 3.8 Marketing Received Tremendous Benefits from Ebusiness

Marketing via Ebusiness
An **associate (affiliate) program allows** a business to generate commissions or referral fees when a customer visiting its website clicks on a link to another merchant's website. For example, if a customer to a company website clicks on a banner ad to another vendor's website, the company will receive a referral fee or commission when the customer performs the desired action, typically making a purchase or completing a form.
A **banner ad** is a box running across a website that advertises the products and services of another business, usually another ebusiness. The banner generally contains a link to the advertiser's website. Advertisers can track how often customers click on a banner ad resulting in a click-through to their website. Often the cost of the banner ad depends on the number of customers who click on the banner ad. Web-based advertising services can track the number of times users click the banner, generating statistics that enable advertisers to judge whether the advertising fees are worth paying. Banner ads are like living, breathing classified ads. Tracking the number of banner ad clicks is an excellent way to understand the effectiveness of the ad on the website.
A **click-through** is a count of the number of people who visit one site and click on an advertisement that takes them to the site of the advertiser. Tracking effectiveness based on click-throughs guarantees exposure to target ads; however, it does not guarantee that the visitor liked the ad, spent any substantial time viewing the ad, or was satisfied with the information contained in the ad.
A **cookie** is a small file deposited on a hard drive by a website containing information about customers and their browsing activities. Cookies allow websites to record the comings and goings of customers, usually without their knowledge or consent.
A **pop-up ad** is a small web page containing an advertisement that appears outside of the current website loaded in the browser. A pop-under ad is a form of a pop-up ad that users do not see until they close the current web browser screen.
Viral marketing is a technique that induces websites or users to pass on a marketing message to other websites or users, creating exponential growth in the message's visibility and effect. One example of successful viral marketing is Hotmail, which promotes its service and its own advertisers' messages in every user's email notes. Viral marketing encourages users of a product or service supplied by an ebusiness to encourage friends to join. Viral marketing is a word-of-mouth type advertising program.

show me the MONEY

Nasty-Gal: 8 Years Old and Worth $100 Million

Sophia Amoruso is the founder and CEO of Nasty Gal, an 8-year-old online fashion retail company worth over $100 million. Nasty Gal sells new and vintage clothing, accessories, and shoes online. Founder Sophia Amoruso started the company on eBay, selling one-of-a-kind vintage pieces that she sourced, styled, photographed, and shipped herself. The following is excerpted from her new book, *#GIRLBOSS.*

"I never started a business. I started an eBay store, and ended up with a business. I never would have done it had I known it was going to become this big. I was 22 and, like most 22-year-olds, I was looking for a way to pay my rent and buy my Starbucks chai. Had someone shown me the future of where Nasty Gal would be in 2014, I would have gasped in revulsion, thinking, 'Oh, no, that is way too much work.'

There are different kinds of entrepreneurs. There are the ones who start a business because they're educated and choose to, and the ones who do it because it is really the only option. I definitely fall into the latter category."[10]

The Internet is a great place to start a business! If Sophia Amoruso started her business in a traditional store, would she have found success? List the advantages Sophia Amoruso gained by selling her items on eBay. If you could start a business on eBay, what would it be and how would you use ebusiness to your advantage?

and number of new customers created directly back to the websites or banner ads. Through **clickstream data** they can observe the exact pattern of a consumer's navigation through a site. Figure 3.9 displays different types of clickstream metrics, and Figure 3.10 provides definitions of common metrics based on clickstream data. To interpret such data properly, managers try to benchmark against other companies. For instance, consumers seem to visit their preferred websites regularly, even checking back multiple times during a given session.

THE FOUR EBUSINESS MODELS LO3.3

A **business model** is a plan that details how a company creates, delivers, and generates revenues. Some models are quite simple: A company produces a good or service and sells it to customers. If the company is successful, sales exceed costs and the company generates a profit. Other models are less straightforward, and sometimes it's not immediately clear who makes money and how much. Radio and network television are broadcast free to anyone with a receiver, for instance; advertisers pay the costs of programming.

The majority of online business activities consist of the exchange of products and services either between businesses or

business model A plan that details how a company creates, delivers, and generates revenues.

ebusiness model A plan that details how a company creates, delivers, and generates revenues on the Internet.

dot-com The original term for a company operating on the Internet.

business-to-business (B2B) Applies to businesses buying from and selling to each other over the Internet.

business-to-consumer (B2C) Applies to any business that sells its products or services directly to consumers online.

eshop (estore or etailer) An online version of a retail store where customers can shop at any hour.

FIGURE 3.9 Clickstream Data Metrics

Types of Clickstream Data Metrics
The number of page views (i.e., the number of times a particular page has been presented to a visitor).
The pattern of websites visited, including most frequent exit page and most frequent prior website.
Length of stay on the website.
Dates and times of visits.
Number of registrations filled out per 100 visitors.
Number of abandoned registrations.
Demographics of registered visitors.
Number of customers with shopping carts.
Number of abandoned shopping carts.

FIGURE 3.10 Website Metrics

METRICS MEASURING WEBSITE SUCCESS	
Website Visit Metrics	
Stickiness (visit duration time)	The length of time a visitor spends on a website.
Raw visit depth (total web pages exposure per session)	The total number of pages a visitor is exposed to during a single visit to a website.
Visit depth (total unique web pages exposure per session)	The total number of unique pages a visitor is exposed to during a single visit to a website.
Website Visitor Metrics	
Unidentified visitor	A visitor is an individual who visits a website. An "unidentified visitor" means that no information about that visitor is available.
Unique visitor	A unique visitor is one who can be recognized and counted only once within a given period of time.
Identified visitor	An ID is available that allows a user to be tracked across multiple visits to a website.
Website Hit Metrics	
Hits	When visitors reach a website, their computer sends a request to the site's computer server to begin displaying pages. Each element of a requested page is recorded by the website's server log file as a "hit."

between businesses and consumers. An **ebusiness model** is a plan that details how a company creates, delivers, and generates revenues on the Internet. **Dot-com** was the original term for a company operating on the Internet. Ebusiness models fall into one of four categories: (1) business-to-business, (2) business-to-consumer, (3) consumer-to-business, and (4) consumer-to-consumer (see Figure 3.11).

LO3.3 Compare the four ebusiness models.

Business-to-Business (B2B)

Business-to-business (B2B) applies to businesses buying from and selling to each other over the Internet. Examples include medical billing service, software sales and licensing, and virtual assistant businesses. B2B relationships represent 80 percent of all online business and are more complex with greater security needs than the other types. B2B examples include Oracle and SAP.

Electronic marketplaces, or emarketplaces, are interactive business communities providing a central market where multiple buyers and sellers can engage in ebusiness activities. By tightening and automating the relationship between the two parties, they create structures for conducting commercial exchange, consolidating supply chains, and creating new sales channels.

Business-to-Consumer (B2C)

Business-to-consumer (B2C) applies to any business that sells its products or services directly to consumers online. Carfax offers car buyers detailed histories of used vehicles for a fee. An **eshop**, sometimes referred to as an *estore* or *etailer,* is an online version of a retail store where customers can shop at any hour. It can be an extension of an existing store such as The Gap or operate only online such as Amazon.com. There are three ways to operate as a B2C: brick-and-mortar, click-and-mortar, and pure play (see Figure 3.12).

consumer-to-business (C2B) Applies to any consumer who sells a product or service to a business on the Internet.

consumer-to-consumer (C2C) Applies to customers offering goods and services to each other on the Internet.

Consumer-to-Business (C2B)

Consumer-to-business (C2B) applies to any consumer who sells a product or service to a business on the Internet. One example is customers of Priceline.com, who set their own prices for items such as airline tickets or hotel rooms and wait for a seller to decide whether to supply them. The demand for C2B ebusiness will increase over the next few years due to customers' desire for greater convenience and lower prices.

Consumer-to-Consumer (C2C)

Consumer-to-consumer (C2C) applies to customers offering goods and services to each other on the Internet. A good example of a C2C is an auction where buyers and sellers solicit consecutive bids from each other and prices are determined dynamically. Craigslist and eBay are two examples of successful C2C websites, linking like-minded buyers with sellers. Other types of online auctions include forward auctions where sellers market to many buyers and the highest bid wins, and reverse auctions where buyers select goods and services from the seller with the lowest bid.

Ebusiness Forms and Revenue-Generating Strategies

As more and more companies began jumping on the ebusiness bandwagon new forms of ebusiness began to emerge

FIGURE 3.11 Ebusiness Models

Ebusiness Term	Definition
Business-to-business (B2B)	Applies to businesses buying from and selling to each other over the Internet.
Business-to-consumer (B2C)	Applies to any business that sells its products or services to consumers over the Internet.
Consumer-to-business (C2B)	Applies to any consumer that sells a product or service to a business over the Internet.
Consumer-to-consumer (C2C)	Applies to sites primarily offering goods and services to assist consumers interacting with each other over the Internet.

	Business	Consumer
Business	B2B	B2C
Consumer	C2B	C2C

FIGURE 3.12 Forms of Business-to-Consumer Operations

Brick-and-Mortar Business
A business that operates in a physical store without an Internet presence.
Example: T.J. Maxx

Click-and-Mortar Business
A business that operates in a physical store and on the Internet.
Example: Barnes & Noble

Pure-Play (Virtual) Business
A business that operates on the Internet only without a physical store.
Example: Google

adwords Keywords that advertisers choose to pay for and appear as sponsored links on the Google results pages.

search engine Website software that finds other pages based on keyword matching.

search engine ranking Evaluates variables that search engines use to determine where a URL appears on the list of search results.

search engine optimization (SEO) Combines art along with science to determine how to make URLs more attractive to search engines, resulting in higher search engine ranking.

FIGURE 3.13 Ebusiness Forms

Form	Description	Examples
Content providers	Generate revenues by providing digital content such as news, music, photos, or videos.	Netflix.com, iTunes.com, CNN.com
Infomediaries	Provide specialized information on behalf of producers of goods and services and their potential customers	Edmunds.com, BizRate.com, Bloomberg.com, Zillow.com
Online marketplaces	Bring together buyers and sellers of products and services.	Amazon.com, eBay.com, Priceline.com
Portals	Operate central website for users to access specialized content and other services.	Google.com, Yahoo.com, MSN.com
Service providers	Provide services such as photo sharing, video sharing, online backup and storage.	Flickr.com, Mapquest.com, YouTube.com
Transaction brokers	Process online sales transactions.	Etrade.com, Charlesschwab.com, Fidelity.com

(see Figure 3.13). Many of the new forms of ebusiness went to market without clear strategies on how they were going to generate revenue. Google is an excellent example of an ebusiness that did not figure out a way to generate profits until many years after its launch.

Google is an excellent example of an ebusiness that did not figure out a way to generate profits until many years after its launch. Google's primary line of business is its search engine; however, the company does not generate revenue from people using its site to search the Internet. It generates revenue from the marketers and advertisers that pay to place their ads on the site. **Adwords** are keywords that advertisers choose to pay for and appear as sponsored links on the Google results pages.

About 200 million times each day, people from all over the world access Google to perform searches. Adwords, a part of the Google site, allows advertisers to bid on common search terms. The advertisers simply enter in the keywords they want to bid on and the maximum amounts they want to pay per click per day. Google then determines a price and a search ranking for those keywords based on how much other advertisers are willing to pay for the same terms. Pricing for keywords can range from 5 cents to $10 a click. Paid search is the ultimate in targeted advertising because consumers type in exactly what they want. A general search term such as *tropical vacation* costs less than a more specific term such as *Hawaiian vacation.* Whoever bids the most for a term appears in a sponsored advertisement link either at the top or along the side of the search-results page.[12]

A **search engine** is website software that finds other pages based on keyword matching similar to Google. **Search engine ranking** evaluates variables that search engines use to determine where a URL appears on the list of search results. **Search engine optimization (SEO)** combines art along with science to determine how to make URLs more attractive to search engines resulting in higher search engine ranking. The better the SEO, the higher the ranking for a website in the list of

Living the DREAM

Crazy over Access[13]

You are all familiar with Craigslist, but are you familiar with the Craigslist Foundation that takes on social causes? www.craigslistfoundation.org hosts information ranging from nonprofit boot camps to nonprofit support resources. Craigslist Foundation views its role as a community catalyst, providing and highlighting events and online resources that provide nonprofit leaders with the knowledge, resources, and visibility they need to find success for their organizations.

Review the Craigslist Foundation website and the nonprofit boot camp online. Create a new online social program using the resources found on the site.

pay-per-click
Generates revenue each time a user clicks on a link to a retailer's website.

pay-per-call
Generates revenue each time users click on a link that takes them directly to an online agent waiting for a call.

pay-per-conversion
Generates revenue each time a website visitor is converted to a customer.

search engine results. SEO is critical because most people only view the first few pages of a search result. After that a person is more inclined to begin a new search than review pages and pages of search results. Websites can generate revenue through:

- **Pay-per-click**: generates revenue each time a user clicks on a link to a retailer's website.
- **Pay-per-call**: generates revenue each time a user clicks on a link that takes the user directly to an online agent waiting for a call.
- **Pay-per-conversion**: generates revenue each time a website visitor is converted to a customer.

Ebusinesses must have a revenue model, or a model for making money. For instance, will it accept advertising, or sell subscriptions or licensing rights? Figure 3.14 lists the different benefits and challenges of various ebusiness revenue models.[14]

FIGURE 3.14 Ebusiness Revenue Models

Ebusiness Revenue Model	Benefits	Challenges
Advertising fees	■ Well-targeted advertisements can be perceived as value-added content by trading participants. ■ Easy to implement.	■ Limited revenue potential. ■ Overdone or poorly targeted advertisements can be disturbing elements on the website.
License fees	■ Creates incentives to do many transactions. ■ Customization and back-end integration lead to lock-in of participants.	■ Up-front fee is a barrier to entry for participants. ■ Price differentiation is complicated.
Subscription fees	■ Creates incentives to do transactions. ■ Price can be differentiated. ■ Possibility to build additional revenue from new user groups.	■ Fixed fee is a barrier to entry for participants.
Transaction fees	■ Can be directly tied to savings (both process and price savings). ■ Important revenue source when high level of liquidity (transaction volume) is reached.	■ If process savings are not completely visible, use of the system is discouraged (incentive to move transactions offline). ■ Transaction fees likely to decrease with time.
Value-added services fees	■ Service offering can be differentiated. ■ Price can be differentiated. ■ Possibility to build additional revenue from established and new user groups (third parties).	■ Cumbersome process for customers to continually evaluate new services.

EBUSINESS TOOLS FOR CONNECTING AND COMMUNICATING LO3.4

As firms began to move online, more MIS tools were created to support ebusiness processes and requirements. The tools supporting and driving ebusiness are highlighted in Figure 3.15 and covered below in detail.

LO3.4 Describe the six ebusiness tools for connecting and communicating.

Email

Email, short for electronic mail, is the exchange of digital messages over the Internet. No longer do business professionals have to wait for the mail to receive important documents as email single-handedly increased the speed of business by allowing the transfer of documents with the same speed as the telephone. Its chief business advantage is the ability to inform and communicate with many people simultaneously, immediately,

Internet service provider (ISP) A company that provides access to the Internet for a monthly fee.

real-time communication Occurs when a system updates information at the same rate it receives it.

instant messaging (sometimes called IM or IMing) A service that enables "instant" or real-time communication between people.

podcasting Converts an audio broadcast to a digital music player.

video-conference Allows people at two or more locations to interact via two-way video and audio transmissions simultaneously as well as share documents, data, computer displays, and whiteboards.

and with ease. There are no time or place constraints, and users can check, send, and view emails whenever they require.

An **Internet service provider (ISP)** is a company that provides access to the Internet for a monthly fee. Major ISPs in the United States include AOL, AT&T, Comcast, Earthlink, and Netzero, as well as thousands of local ISPs including regional telephone companies.

Instant Messaging

Real-time communication occurs when a system updates information at the same rate it receives it. Email was a great advancement over traditional communication methods such as the U.S. mail, but it did not operate in real time. **Instant messaging (IMing)** is a service that enables instant or real-time communication between people. Businesses immediately saw what they could do:

- Answer simple questions quickly and easily.
- Resolve questions or problems immediately.
- Transmit messages as fast as naturally flowing conversation.
- Easily hold simultaneous IM sessions with multiple people.
- Eliminate long-distance phone charges.
- Quickly identify which employees are at their computers.

FIGURE 3.15 Ebusiness Tools

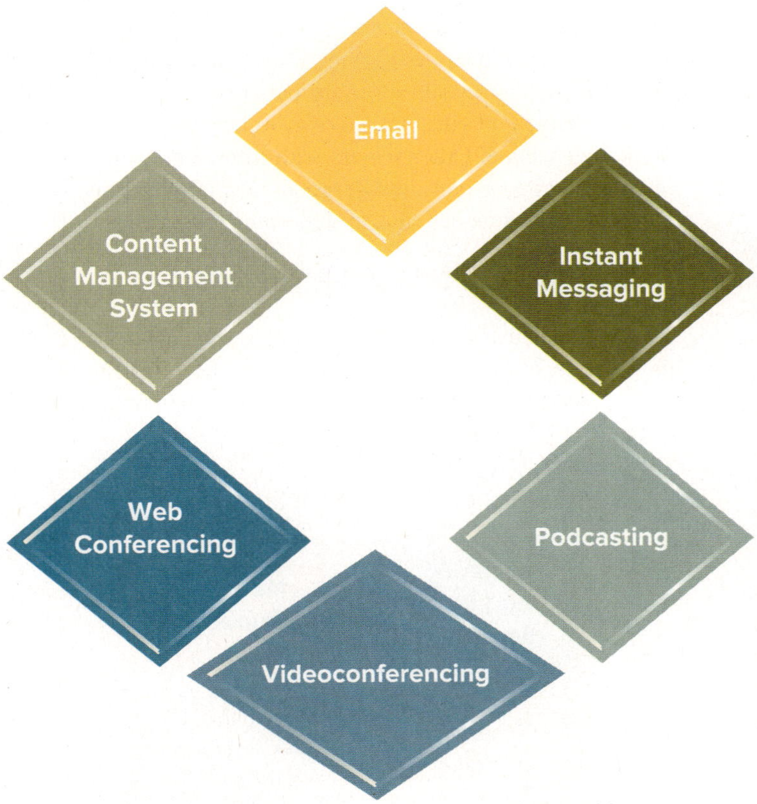

Podcasting

Podcasting converts an audio broadcast to a digital music player. Podcasts can increase marketing reach and build customer loyalty. Companies use podcasts as marketing communication channels discussing everything from corporate strategies to detailed product overviews. The senior executive team can share weekly or monthly podcasts featuring important issues or expert briefings on new technical or marketing developments.

Videoconferencing

A **videoconference** allows people at two or more locations to interact via two-way video and audio transmissions simultaneously as well as share documents, data, computer displays, and whiteboards. Point-to-point videoconferences connect two people, and multipoint conferences connect more than two people at multiple locations.

Videoconferences can increase productivity because users participate without leaving their offices. It can improve communication and relationships, because participants see each other's facial expressions and body language, both important aspects of communication that are lost with a basic telephone call or email. It also reduces travel expenses, a big win for firms facing economic challenges. Of course, nothing can replace meeting someone face-to-face and shaking hands, but videoconferencing offers a viable and cost-effective alternative.

web conferencing (webinar) Blends videoconferencing with document-sharing and allows the user to deliver a presentation over the web to a group of geographically dispersed participants.

web conferencing (webinar) Blends videoconferencing with document-sharing and allows the user to deliver a presentation over the web to a group of geographically dispersed participants.

content management system (CMS) Helps companies manage the creation, storage, editing, and publication of their website content.

taxonomy The scientific classification of organisms into groups based on similarities of structure or origin.

information architecture The set of ideas about how all information in a given context should be organized.

Web Conferencing

Web conferencing, or a **webinar**, blends videoconferencing with document sharing and allows the user to deliver a presentation over the web to a group of geographically dispersed participants. Regardless of the type of hardware or software the attendees are running, every participant can see what is on anyone else's screen. Schools use web conferencing tools such as Illuminate Live to deliver lectures to students, and businesses use tools such as WebEx to demonstrate products. Web conferencing is not quite like being there, but professionals can accomplish more sitting at their desks than in an airport waiting to make travel connections.

Content Management Systems

In the fourth century BC Aristotle catalogued the natural world according to a systematic organization, and the ancient library at Alexandria was reportedly organized by subject, connecting like information with like. Today **content management systems (CMS)** help companies manage the creation, storage, editing, and publication of their website content. CMSs are user-friendly; most include web-based publishing, search, navigation, and indexing to organize information; and they let users with little or no technical expertise make website changes.

A search is typically carried out by entering a keyword or phrase (query) into a text field and clicking a button or a hyperlink. Navigation facilitates movement from one web page to another. Content management systems play a crucial role in getting site visitors to view more than just the home page. If navigation choices are unclear, visitors may hit the "Back" button on their first (and final) visit to a website. One rule of thumb to remember is that each time a user has to click to find search information, there is a 50 percent chance the user will leave the website instead. A key principle of good website design, therefore, is to keep the number of clicks to a minimum.

Taxonomy is the scientific classification of organisms into groups based on similarities of structure or origin. Taxonomies are also used for indexing the content on the website into categories and subcategories of topics. For example, car is a subtype of vehicle. Every car is a vehicle, but not every vehicle is a car; some vehicles are vans, buses, and trucks. Taxonomy terms are arranged so that narrower/more specific/"child" terms fall under broader/more generic/"parent" terms. **Information architecture** is the set of ideas about how all information in a given context should be organized. Many companies hire information architects to create their website taxonomies. A well-planned taxonomy ensures search and navigation are easy and user-friendly. If the taxonomy is confusing, the site will soon fail.

THE CHALLENGES OF EBUSINESS LO3.5

Although the benefits of ebusiness are enticing, developing, deploying, and managing ebusiness systems are not always easy. Figure 3.16 lists the challenges facing ebusiness.[15]

LO3.5 Identify the four challenges associated with ebusiness.

Identifying Limited Market Segments

The main challenge of ebusiness is the lack of growth in some sectors due to product or service limitations. The online food sector has not grown in sales, in part because food products are perishable and consumers prefer to buy them at the supermarket as needed. Other sectors with limited ebusiness appeal include fragile or consumable goods and highly sensitive or confidential businesses such as government agencies.

Managing Consumer Trust

Trust in the ebusiness exchange deserves special attention. The physical separation of buyer and seller, the physical separation of buyer and merchandise, and customer perceptions about

FIGURE 3.16
Challenges Facing Ebusiness

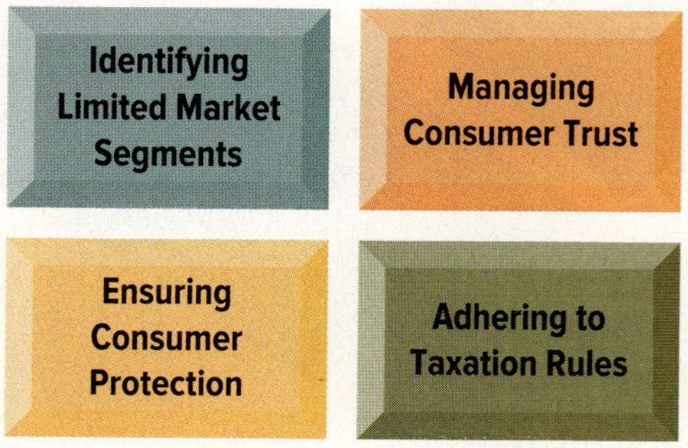

BUSTED Virtual Abandonment

Approximately 35 percent of online shopping carts are abandoned prior to checkout. Abandoned shopping carts relates directly to lost revenues for a business. It is like a customer walking out of the store leaving their cart full of chosen items. Businesses need to focus on why the customers are virtually walking out of their stores. The problem typically lies in the checkout process and can be fixed by the following:

- Make sure the checkout button is easy to find.
- Make sure personal information is safe and the website's security is visible.
- Streamline the checkout process so the customer has as few clicks as possible.
- Do not ask shoppers to create an account prior to checkout, but you can ask them to create an account after checkout.
- Ensure your return policy is visible.

Have you ever abandoned a virtual shopping cart? In a group, visit a website that you or your peers have recently abandoned and review the checkout process. Was it difficult, cumbersome, or lacking security? Then visit Amazon.com and review its checkout process and determine whether Amazon is meeting the preceding recommendations.

the risk of doing business online provide unique challenges. Internet marketers must develop a trustworthy relationship to make that initial sale and generate customer loyalty. A few ways to build trust when working online include being accessible and available to communicate in person with your customers; using customers' testimonials that link to your client website or to provide their contact information; and accepting legitimate forms of payment such as credit cards.

Ensuring Consumer Protection

An organization that wants to dominate with superior customer service as a competitive advantage must not only serve but also protect its customers, guarding them against unsolicited goods and communication, illegal or harmful goods, insufficient information about goods and suppliers, invasion of privacy and misuse of personal information, and online fraud. System security, however, must not make ebusiness websites inflexible or difficult to use.

Adhering to Taxation Rules

Many believe that U.S. tax policy should provide a level playing field for traditional retail businesses, mail-order companies, and online merchants. Yet the Internet marketplace remains mostly free of traditional forms of sales tax, partly because ecommerce law is vaguely defined and differs from state to state. For now, companies that operate online must obey a patchwork of rules about which customers are subject to sales tax on their purchases and which are not.

SECTION 3.2
Web 2.0: Business 2.0

LEARNING OUTCOMES

LO3.6 Explain Web 2.0, and identify its four characteristics.

LO3.7 Explain how Business 2.0 is helping communities network and collaborate.

LO3.8 Describe the three Business 2.0 tools for collaborating.

LO3.9 Explain the three challenges associated with Business 2.0.

LO3.10 Describe Web 3.0 and the next generation of online business.

WEB 2.0: ADVANTAGES OF BUSINESS 2.0 LO3.6

In the mid-1990s the stock market reached an all-time high as companies took advantage of ebusiness and Web 1.0, and many believed the Internet was the wave of the future. When new online businesses began failing to meet earning expectations, however, the bubble burst. Some then believed the ebusiness boom was over, but they could not have been more wrong.

Web 2.0 (or **Business 2.0**) is the next generation of Internet use—a more mature, distinctive communications platform characterized by new qualities such as collaboration, sharing, and free. Business 2.0 encourages user participation and the formation of communities that contribute to the content. In Business 2.0, technical skills are no longer required to use and publish information to the World Wide Web, eliminating entry barriers for online business.

Traditional companies tended to view technology as a tool required to perform a process or activity, and employees picked up information by walking through the office or hanging out around the water cooler. Business 2.0 technologies provide a virtual environment that, for many new employees, is just as vibrant and important as the physical environment. Figure 3.17 highlights the common characteristics of Web 2.0.[16]

LO3.6 Explain Web 2.0 and identify its four characteristics.

Web 2.0 (or Business 2.0) The next generation of Internet use—a more mature, distinctive communications platform characterized by new qualities such as collaboration, sharing, and free.

open system Consists of nonproprietary hardware and software based on publicly known standards that allows third parties to create add-on products to plug into or interoperate with the system.

source code Contains instructions written by a programmer specifying the actions to be performed by computer software.

closed source Any proprietary software licensed under exclusive legal right of the copyright holder.

open source Refers to any software whose source code is made available free for any third party to review and modify.

user-contributed content (also referred to as user-generated content) Content created and updated by many users for many users.

FIGURE 3.17 Four Characteristics of Web 2.0

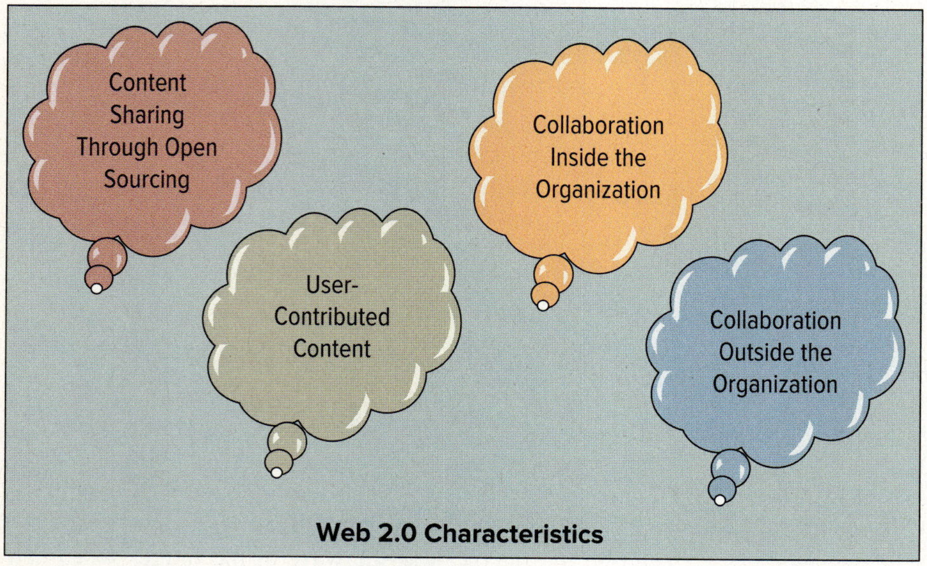

Content Sharing through Open Sourcing

An **open system** consists of nonproprietary hardware and software based on publicly known standards that allows third parties to create add-on products to plug into or interoperate with the system. Thousands of hardware devices and software applications created and sold by third-party vendors interoperate with computers, such as iPods, drawing software, and mice.

Source code contains instructions written by a programmer specifying the actions to be performed by computer software. **Closed source** is any proprietary software licensed under exclusive legal right of the copyright holder. **Open source** refers to any software whose source code is made available free (not on a fee or licensing basis as in ebusiness) for any third party to review and modify. Business 2.0 is capitalizing on open source software. Mozilla, for example, offers its Firefox web browser and Thunderbird email software free. Mozilla believes the Internet is a public resource that must remain open and accessible to all; it continuously develops free products by bringing together thousands of dedicated volunteers from around the world. Mozilla's Firefox now holds over 20 percent of the browser market and is quickly becoming a threat to Microsoft's Internet Explorer. How do open source software companies generate revenues? Many people are still awaiting an answer to this very important question.[17]

User-Contributed Content

Ebusiness was characterized by a few companies or users posting content for the masses. Business 2.0 is characterized by the masses posting content for the masses. **User-contributed content** (or **user-generated content**) is created and updated by many users for many users. Websites such as Flickr, Wikipedia, and YouTube, for example, move control of online media from the hands of leaders to the hands of users. Netflix and Amazon both use user-generated content to drive their recommendation tools, and websites such as Yelp use customer reviews to express opinions on products and services. Companies are embracing user-generated content to help with everything from marketing to product development and quality assurance.

Native advertising is an online marketing concept in which the advertiser attempts to gain attention by providing content in the context of the user's experience in terms of its content, format, style, or placement. One of the most popular forms of user-generated content is a **reputation system**, where buyers post feedback on sellers. EBay buyers voluntarily comment on the quality of service, their satisfaction with the item traded, and promptness of shipping. Sellers comment about prompt payment from buyers or respond to comments left by the buyer. Companies ranging from Amazon to restaurants are using reputation systems to improve quality and enhance customer satisfaction.

native advertising An online marketing concept in which the advertiser attempts to gain attention by providing content in the context of the user's experience in terms of its content, format, style, or placement.

reputation system Where buyers post feedback on sellers.

collaboration system A set of tools that supports the work of teams or groups by facilitating the sharing and flow of information.

collective intelligence Collaborating and tapping into the core knowledge of all employees, partners, and customers.

knowledge management (KM) Involves capturing, classifying, evaluating, retrieving, and sharing information assets in a way that provides context for effective decisions and actions.

knowledge management system (KMS) Supports the capturing, organization, and dissemination of knowledge (i.e., know-how) throughout an organization.

Collaboration Inside the Organization

A **collaboration system** is a set of tools that supports the work of teams or groups by facilitating the sharing and flow of information. Business 2.0's collaborative mind-set generates more information faster from a wider audience. **Collective intelligence** is collaborating and tapping into the core knowledge of all employees, partners, and customers. Knowledge can be a real competitive advantage for an organization. The most common form of collective intelligence found inside the organization is **knowledge management (KM)**, which involves capturing, classifying, evaluating, retrieving, and sharing information assets in a way that provides context for effective decisions and actions. The primary objective of knowledge management is to be sure that a company's knowledge of facts, sources of information, and solutions are readily available to all employees whenever it is needed. A **knowledge management system (KMS)** supports the capturing, organization, and dissemination of knowledge (i.e., know-how) throughout an organization. KMS can distribute an organization's knowledge base by interconnecting people and digitally gathering their expertise.

A great example of a knowledge worker is a golf caddie. Golf caddies give advice such as, "The rain makes the third hole play 10 yards shorter." If a golf caddie is good and gives accurate advice it can lead to big tips. Collaborating with other golf caddies can provide bigger tips for all. How can knowledge management make this happen? Caddies could be rewarded for sharing course knowledge by receiving prizes for sharing knowledge. The course manager could compile all of the tips and publish a course notebook for distribution to all caddies. The goal of a knowledge management system is that everyone wins. Here the caddies make bigger tips and golfers improve their play by benefiting from the collaborative experiences of the caddies, and the course owners win as business increases.

KM has assumed greater urgency in American business over the past few years as millions of

show me the MONEY

Analyzing Websites

Wishes is a nonprofit company that specializes in selling items online that are donated by celebrities, such as clothing, jewelry, purses, and many other forms of memorabilia. The profits from Wishes are used to support initiatives at children's hospitals around the country. There have been many volunteers helping at Wishes, which has been great for the company but not so great for the company's online presence. The company now has four different websites created by four different volunteers, and the only information you can find on the success of the four websites follows:

Website	Classic	Contemporary	New Age	Traditional
Traffic analysis	5,000 hits/day	200 hits/day	10,000 hits/day	1,000 hits/day
Stickiness (average)	20 min.	1 hr.	20 min.	50 min.
Number of abandoned shopping carts	400/day	0/day	5,000/day	200/day
Number of unique visitors	2,000/day	100/day	8,000/day	200/day
Number of identified visitors	3,000/day	100/day	2,000/day	800/day
Average revenue per sale	$1,000	$ 1,000	$50	$1,300

You have been hired to run Wishes, and your first action item is to choose one website to continue running the business. The other three websites will be removed. Analyze the metrics described in the table and determine which site you want to use as you move the business forward.

explicit knowledge Consists of anything that can be documented, archived, and codified, often with the help of MIS.

tacit knowledge The knowledge contained in people's heads.

crowdsourcing Refers to the wisdom of the crowd.

crowdfunding Sources capital for a project by raising many small amounts from a large number of individuals, typically via the Internet.

asynchronous communication Communication such as email in which the message and the response do not occur at the same time.

synchronous communication Communications that occur at the same time such as IM or chat.

baby boomers prepare to retire. When they punch out for the last time, the knowledge they gleaned about their jobs, companies, and industries during their long careers will walk out with them—unless companies take measures to retain their insights.

Explicit and Tacit Knowledge Not all information is valuable. Individuals must determine what information qualifies as intellectual and knowledge-based assets. In general, intellectual and knowledge-based assets fall into one of two categories: explicit or tacit. As a rule, **explicit knowledge** consists of anything that can be documented, archived, and codified, often with the help of MIS. Examples of explicit knowledge are assets such as patents, trademarks, business plans, marketing research, and customer lists. **Tacit knowledge** is the knowledge contained in people's heads. The challenge inherent in tacit knowledge is figuring out how to recognize, generate, share, and manage knowledge that resides in people's heads. While information technology in the form of email, instant messaging, and related technologies can help facilitate the dissemination of tacit knowledge, identifying it in the first place can be a major obstacle.

Collaboration Outside the Organization

The most common form of collective intelligence found outside the organization is **crowdsourcing**, which refers to the wisdom of the crowd. The idea that collective intelligence is greater than the sum of its individual parts has been around for a long time (see Figure 3.18). With Business 2.0 the ability to efficiently tap into its power is emerging. For many years organizations believed that good ideas came from the top. CEOs collaborated only with the heads of sales and marketing, the quality assurance expert, or the road warrior salesman. The organization chart governed who should work with whom and how far up the chain of command a suggestion or idea would travel. With Business 2.0 this belief is being challenged, as firms capitalize on crowdsourcing by opening up a task or problem to a wider group to find better or cheaper results from outside the box.

Crowdfunding sources capital for a project by raising many small amounts from a large number of individuals, typically via the Internet. With Business 2.0, people can be continuously connected, a driving force behind collaboration. Traditional ebusiness communications were limited to face-to-face conversations and one-way technologies that used **asynchronous communications**, or communication such as email in which the message and the response do not occur at the same time. Business 2.0 brought **synchronous communication**, or communications that occur at the same time such as IM or chat. Ask a group of college students when they last spoke to their parents. For most the answer is less than hour ago, as opposed to the traditional response of a few days ago. In business, too, continuous connections are now expected in today's collaborative world.

NETWORKING COMMUNITIES WITH BUSINESS 2.0 LO3.7

Social media refers to websites that rely on user participation and user-contributed content, such as Facebook and YouTube. A **social network** is an application that connects people by matching profile information. Providing individuals with the ability to network is by far one of the greatest advantages of Business 2.0.

FIGURE 3.18 Crowdsourcing: The Crowd Is Smarter Than the Individual

© Punchstock/Digital Vision RF

social media Refers to websites that rely on user participation and user-contributed content.

social network An application that connects people by matching profile information.

social networking The practice of expanding your business and/or social contacts by constructing a personal network.

social networking analysis (SNA) Maps group contacts identifying who knows each other and who works together.

social graphs Represent the interconnection of relationships in a social network.

Social Not Working[18]

There are a number of stories of new employees who spend so much time on social networking sites that they don't have time to perform their jobs, resulting in their termination. Here are a few tips on what you should *not* be doing with your social networking sites.

- Do not work on your personal social networking sites while at work.
- Be careful not to accidentally reply to multiple recipients on messages.
- Be sure to post a professional profile picture. Do not use shots of your children or your pets or your fraternity.
- Be careful to set up all of the security and privacy features in your profile.
- Do not ever address politics or religion.
- Never continually post something every 5 minutes or spam friends with messages. Every time you make a move on Facebook, other people know, and you don't want to become annoying.

Facebook, LinkedIn, and Twitter seem to be everywhere, and it is not only new employees who are finding the sites difficult to use in a work environment. The question companies are asking is how to tap the social networking trend as a business opportunity, rather than simply a way to connect. Face-to-face networking enables employees to share ideas, information, and resources, but can social networking achieve the same goals? Sites such as LinkedIn are helpful in connecting with people you want to meet for professional purposes, and Twitter and Facebook can be helpful when trying to notify a group of people about a product promotion or event, but how can a business integrate social networking into its core processes and add real value to the bottom line?

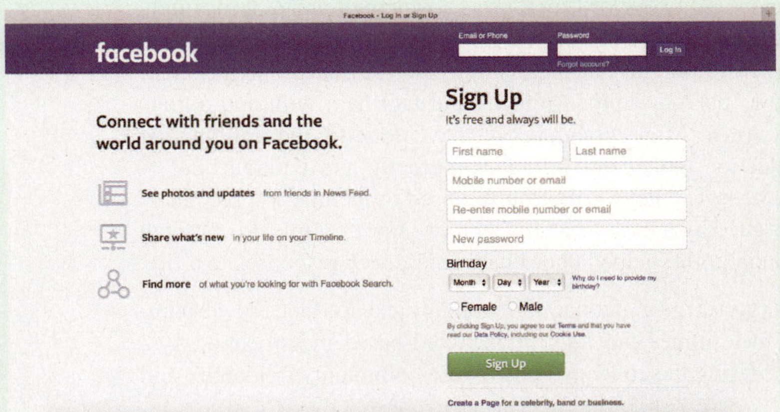

Source: Facebook.com

Social networking is the practice of expanding your business and/or social contacts by constructing a personal network (see Figure 3.19). Social networking sites provide two basic functions. The first is the ability to create and maintain a profile that serves as an online identity within the environment. The second is the ability to create connections between other people within the network. **Social networking analysis (SNA)** maps group contacts (personal and professional) identifying who knows each other and who works together. In a company it can provide a vision of how employees work together. It can also identify key experts with specific knowledge such as how to solve a complicated programming problem or launch a new product.

Business 2.0 simplifies access to information and improves the ability to share it. Instead of spending $1,000 and two days at a conference to meet professional peers, business people can now use social networks such as LinkedIn to meet new contacts for recruiting, prospecting, and identifying experts on a topic. With executive members from all the *Fortune* 500 companies, LinkedIn has become one of the more useful recruiting tools on the web.

Social graphs represent the interconnection of relationships in a social network. Social networking sites can be especially useful to employers trying to find job candidates with unique or highly specialized skill sets that may be harder to locate in larger communities. Many employers also search social networking sites to find "dirt" and character references for potential employees. Keep in mind that what you post on the Internet stays on the Internet.[19]

tag Specific keywords or phrases incorporated into website content for means of classification or taxonomy.

social tagging Describes the collaborative activity of marking shared online content with keywords or tags as a way to organize it for future navigation, filtering, or search.

hashtag A keyword or phrase used to identify a topic and is preceded by a hash or pound sign (#).

folksonomy Similar to taxonomy except that crowdsourcing determines the tags or keyword-based classification system.

website bookmark A locally stored URL or the address of a file or Internet page saved as a shortcut.

social bookmarking Allows users to share, organize, search, and manage bookmarks.

LO3.7 Explain how Business 2.0 is helping communities network and collaborate.

Social Tagging

Tags are specific keywords or phrases incorporated into website content for means of classification or taxonomy. An item can have one or more tags associated with it, to allow for multiple browseable paths through the items, and tags can be changed with minimal effort (see Figure 3.20). **Social tagging** describes the collaborative activity of marking shared online content with keywords or tags as a way to organize it for future navigation, filtering, or search. The entire user community is invited to tag, and thus essentially defines, the content. Flickr allows users to upload images and tag them with appropriate keywords. After enough people have done so, the resulting tag collection will identify images correctly and without bias. A **hashtag** is a keyword or phrase used to identify a topic and is preceded by a hash or pound sign (#). For example, the hashtag #sandiegofire helped coordinate emergency responses to a fire.

Folksonomy is similar to taxonomy except that crowdsourcing determines the tags or keyword-based classification system. Using the collective power of a community to identify and classify content significantly lowers content categorization costs, because there is no complicated nomenclature to learn. Users simply create and apply tags as they wish. For example, while cell phone manufacturers often refer to their products as mobile devices, the folksonomy could include mobile phone, wireless phone, smartphone, iPhone, and so on. All these keywords, if searched, should take a user to the same site. Folksonomies reveal what people truly call things (see Figure 3.21). They have been a point of discussion on the web because the whole point of having a website is for your customers to find it. The majority of websites are found through search terms that match the content.

A **website bookmark** is a locally stored URL or the address of a file or Internet page saved as a shortcut. **Social bookmarking**

FIGURE 3.19 Social Network Example

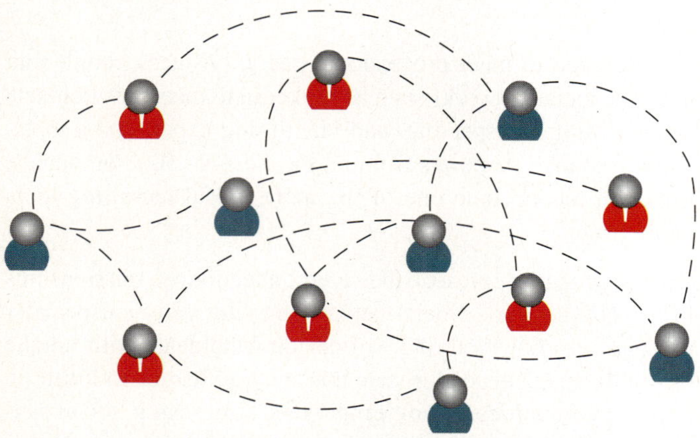

Source: Daniel Nations, "What Is Social Bookmarking,"About.com: Web Trends,http://webtrends.about.com/od/socialbookmarking101/p/aboutsocialtags.htm, accessed April 2013.

FIGURE 3.20 Social Tagging Occurs When Many Individuals Categorize Content

© Radius Images / Alamy Stock Photo

allows users to share, organize, search, and manage bookmarks. Del.icio.us, a website dedicated to social bookmarking, provides users with a place to store, categorize, annotate, and share favorites. StumbleUpon is another popular social bookmarking website that allows users to locate interesting websites based on their favorite subjects. The more you use the service, the more the system "learns" about your interests and the better it can show you websites that interest you. StumbleUpon represents a new social networking model in which content finds the users instead of the other way around. StumbleUpon is all about the users and the content they enjoy.

FIGURE 3.21 Folksonomy Example: The User-Generated Names for Cellular Phones

© Fotosearch/Getty Images RF

My Not To-Do List

Viral Foxes and Devil Babies

Viral marketing can be a company's greatest success or its worst nightmare. Here are a few popular examples:

- "What Does the Fox Say?" The video created by a pair of Norwegian variety show brothers displays people dressed up as animals dancing around in the woods singing a catchy song. The video received over 400 million views on YouTube and skyrocketed the band Ylvis to virtual stardom.
- The video of a robotic devil baby left in an unattended stroller in the middle of the street in Manhattan attracted over 50 million views in a month. The creators of the devil baby video, Thinkmodo, was creating buzz for the 20th Century Fox movie it was promoting, *Devil's Due.*
- Domino's Pizza employees posted a video showing them making sandwiches with unsanitary ingredients. The video went viral and ended with the arrest of the employees and an apology from the CEO.

Research the web and find an example of a viral video that helped a business achieve success and one that caused a business to fail. Do you think it is important for a business to try to manage its online reputation actively? What can a company do if a negative video goes viral, such as the one concerning Domino's Pizza?

Due Diligence//:

Anti-Social Networking[20]

Before the Internet, angry customers could write letters or make phone calls, but their individual power to find satisfaction or bring about change was relative weak. Now, disgruntled consumers can create a website or upload a video bashing a product or service, and their efforts can be instantly seen by millions of people. Though many companies monitor the Internet and try to respond to such postings quickly, power has clearly shifted to the consumer. Create an argument for or against the following statement: "Social networking has given power to the consumer that benefits society and creates socially responsible corporations."

© Jetta Productions/Getty Images

blog, or web log An online journal that allows users to post their own comments, graphics, and video.

selfie A self-photograph placed on a social media website.

microblogging The practice of sending brief posts (140 to 200 characters) to a personal blog, either publicly or to a private group of subscribers who can read the posts as IMs or as text messages.

real simple syndication (RSS) A web format used to publish frequently updated works, such as blogs, news headlines, audio, and video in a standardized format.

wiki A type of collaborative web page that allows users to add, remove, and change content, which can be easily organized and reorganized as required.

BUSINESS 2.0 TOOLS FOR COLLABORATING LO3.8

Social networking and collaborating are leading businesses in new directions, and Figure 3.22 provides an overview of the tools that harness the "power of the people," allowing users to share ideas, discuss business problems, and collaborate on solutions.

LO3.8 Describe the three Business 2.0 tools for collaborating.

Blogs

A **blog**, or **Web log**, is an online journal that allows users to post their own comments, graphics, and video. Unlike traditional HTML web pages, blog websites let writers communicate—and reader's respond—on a regular basis through a simple yet customizable interface that does not require any programming. A **selfie** is a self-photograph placed on a social media website.

From a business perspective, blogs are no different from marketing channels such as video, print, audio, or presentations. They all deliver results of varying kinds. Consider Sun Microsystem's Jonathan Schwartz and GM's Bob Lutz, who use their blogs for marketing, sharing ideas, gathering feedback, press response, and image shaping. Starbucks has developed a blog called My Starbucks Idea, allowing customers to share ideas, tell Starbucks what they think of other people's ideas, and join discussions. Blogs are an ideal mechanism for many businesses since they can focus on topic areas more easily than traditional media, with no limits on page size, word count, or publication deadline.

FIGURE 3.22 Business 2.0 Communication and Collaboration Tools

BLOG	WIKI	MASHUP
• An online journal that allows users to post their own comments, graphics, and videos	• Collaborative website that allows users to add, remove, and change content	• Content from more than one source to create a new product or service
• Popular business examples include Sweet Leaf Tea, Stoneyfield Farm, Nuts about Southwest, Disney Parks	• Popular business examples include Wikipedia, National Institute of Health, Intelopedia, LexisNexis, Wiki for Higher Education	• Examples include Zillow, Infopedia, Trendsmap, SongDNA, ThisWeKnow

Microblogs

Microblogging is the practice of sending brief posts (140 to 200 characters) to a personal blog, either publicly or to a private group of subscribers who can read the posts as IMs or as text messages. The main advantage of microblogging is that posts can be submitted by a variety of means, such as instant messaging, email, or the web. By far the most popular microblogging tool is Twitter, which allows users to send microblog entries called tweets to anyone who has registered to "follow" them. Senders can restrict delivery to people they want to follow them or, by default, allow open access. Microblogging is covered in detail in Chapter 7.

Real Simple Syndication (RSS)

Real Simple Syndication (RSS) is a web format used to publish frequently updated works, such as blogs, news headlines, audio, and video, in a standardized format. An RSS document or feed includes full or summarized text, plus other information such as publication date and authorship. News websites, blogs, and podcasts use RSS, constantly feeding news to consumers instead of having them search for it. In addition to facilitating syndication, RSS allows a website's frequent readers to track updates on the site.

Wikis

A **wiki** (the word is Hawaiian for quick) is a type of collaborative web page that allows users to add, remove, and change content, which can be easily organized and reorganized as required. While blogs have largely drawn on the creative and personal goals of individual authors, wikis are based on open collaboration with anybody and everybody. Wikipedia, the open encyclopedia that launched in 2001, has become one of the 10 most popular web destinations, reaching an estimated 217 million unique visitors a month.

A wiki user can generally alter the original content of any article, while the blog user can only add information in the form of comments. Large wikis, such as Wikipedia, protect the quality and accuracy of their information by assigning users roles such as reader, editor, administrator, patroller, policy maker, subject matter expert, content maintainer, software developer, and system operator. Access to some important or sensitive Wikipedia material is limited to users in these authorized roles.

The **network effect** describes how products in a network increase in value to users as the number of users increases. The more users and content managers on a wiki, the greater the network effect because more users attract more contributors, whose work attracts more users, and so on. For example, Wikipedia becomes more valuable to users as the number of its contributors increases.

Wikis internal to firms can be vital tools for collecting and disseminating knowledge throughout an organization, across geographic distances, and between functional business areas. For example, what U.S. employees call a "sale" may be called "an order booked" in the United Kingdom, an "order scheduled" in Germany, and an "order produced" in France. The corporate wiki can answer any questions about a business process or definition. Companies are also using wikis for documentation, reporting, project management, online dictionaries, and discussion groups. Of course, the more employees who use the corporate wiki, the greater the network effect and valued added for the company.

Mashups

A **mashup** is a website or web application that uses content from more than one source to create a completely new product or service. The term is typically used in the context of music; putting Jay-Z lyrics over a Radiohead song makes something old new. The web version of a mashup allows users to mix map data, photos, video, news feeds, blog entries, and so on to create content with a new purpose. Content used in mashups is typically sourced from an **application programming interface (API)**, which is a set of routines, protocols, and tools for building software applications. A programmer then puts these building blocks together.

Most operating environments, such as Microsoft Windows, provide an API so that programmers can write applications consistent with them. Many people experimenting with mashups are using Microsoft, Google, eBay, Amazon, Flickr, and Yahoo APIs, leading to the creation of mashup editors. **Mashup editors** are WYSIWYG, or What You See Is What You Get tools. They provide a visual interface

network effect Describes how products in a network increase in value to users as the number of users increases.

mashup A website or web application that uses content from more than one source to create a completely new product or service.

application programming interface (API) A set of routines, protocols, and tools for building software applications.

mashup editor WYSIWYGs or What You See Is What You Get tools.

fyi

Don't You Just Love Mötley Crüe?[21]

© UpperCut Images/Glow Images

Eurpac, an employee-owned company, performs business in several industries from tobacco to video games. Mike Skinner, CIO of Eurpac, asks the following questions every single time he meets with his staff:

- Where are resources invested?
- What progress have we made?
- What's our next goal?

By cultivating a corporate culture focused on innovation and technology, his creative team developed the platform for Artist2Market, a website where performing artists can record, develop, and distribute their work, a unique alternative to the traditional music label infrastructure. The goal of Artist2Market is to give the artist complete creative control of their project, maximize their exposure to their fan base, and minimize their project costs. The idea for Artist2Market was developed out of a chance meeting between Mötley Crüe drummer Tommy Lee and A2M General Manager Paul Ignasinski. Tommy Lee was interested in producing and distributing a record without having to rely on a major label. Ignasinski went back to Michigan and developed the concept that is now known as Artist2Market.

Artist2Market is an excellent example of how you can use the power of the Internet to fundamentally change entire industries. Takelessons.com is also highly profitable as it connects music students with instructors. One of the easiest ways to create a new online business is to create a mashup. Using your knowledge of mashups, create a new website that would have the ability to completely transform an industry such as Artist2Market did with the recording industry.

Living the DREAM

Kiva Collaboration

Kiva's mission is to connect people through lending for the sake of alleviating poverty. Kiva is a micro-lending online nonprofit organization that enables individuals to lend directly to entrepreneurs throughout the world. If you want to participate in Kiva you simply browse the website (www.kiva.org) and choose an entrepreneur that interests you, make a loan, then track your entrepreneur for the next 6 to 12 months while he or she builds the business and makes the funds to repay the loan. When the loan is up you can relend the money to someone else who is in need.[23]

Kiva is an excellent example of blending ethics and information technology. How is Kiva operating differently than traditional nonprofits? What are the risks associated with investing in Kiva? When you invest in Kiva you run three primary risks: entrepreneur risk, local field partner risk, and country risk. Analyze each of these risks for potential unethical issues that might arise when donating to Kiva.

to build a mashup, often allowing the user to drag and drop data points into a web application. An ezine is a magazine published only in electronic form on a computer network. Flipboard is a social-network aggregation, magazine-format application software for multiple devices that collects content from social media and other websites, presents it in magazine format, and allows users to flip thorough the content from social media and other websites, presents it in magazine format, and allows users to flip through the content.

Whoever thought technology could help sell bananas? Dole Organic now places three-digit farm codes on each banana and creates a mashup using Google Earth and its banana database. Socially and environmentally conscious buyers can plug the numbers into Dole's website and look at a bio of the farm where the bananas were raised. The site tells the story of the farm and its surrounding community, lists its organic certifications, posts some photos, and offers a link to satellite images of the farm in Google Earth. Customers can personally monitor the production and treatment of their fruit from the tree to the grocer. The process assures customers that their bananas have been raised to proper organic standards on an environmentally friendly, holistically minded plantation.[22]

THE CHALLENGES OF BUSINESS 2.0 LO3.9

As much as Business 2.0 has positively changed the global landscape of business, a few challenges remain in open source software, user-contributed content systems, and collaboration systems, all highlighted in Figure 3.23. We'll briefly describe each one.

LO3.9 Explain the three challenges associated with Business 2.0.

FIGURE 3.23 Challenges of Business 2.0

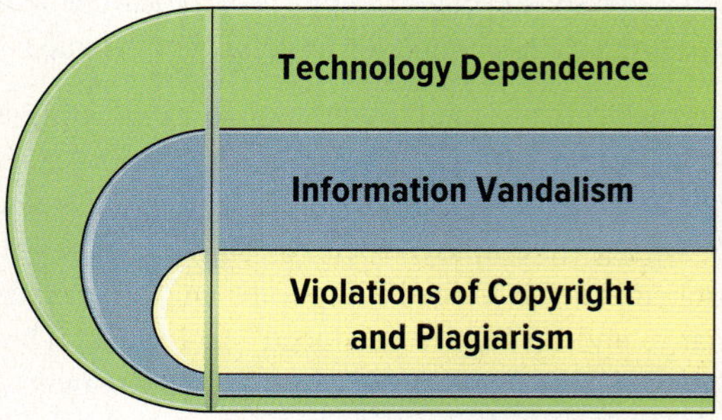

Technology Dependence

Many people today expect to be continuously connected, and their dependence on technology glues them to their web connections for everything from web conferencing for a university class or work project to making plans with friends for dinner. If a connection is down, how will they function? How long can people go without checking email, text messaging, or listening to free music on Pandora or watching on-demand television? As society becomes more technology-dependent, outages hold the potential to cause ever-greater havoc for people, businesses, and educational institutions.

Information Vandalism

Open source and sharing are both major advantages of Business 2.0, and ironically they are major challenges as well. Allowing anyone to edit anything opens the door for individuals to purposely damage, destroy, or vandalize website content. One of the most famous examples of wiki vandalism occurred when a false biography entry read that John Seigenthaler Sr. was assistant to Attorney General Robert F. Kennedy in the early 1960s and was thought to have been directly involved in the assassinations of both Kennedy and his brother, President John F. Kennedy. Seigenthaler did work as an assistant to Robert Kennedy, but he was never involved in the assassinations. Wiki vandalism is a hot issue and for this reason wiki software can now store all versions of a web page, tracking updates and changes and ensuring the site can be restored to its original form if the site is vandalized. It can also color-code the background ensuring the user understands which areas have been validated and which areas have not. The real trick to wiki

fyi Using Hashtags

If you have ever seen a word with a # before it in Facebook or Twitter, you have seen a hashtag. A hashtag is a keyword or phrase used to identify a topic and is preceded by a hash or pound sign (#). Hashtags provide an online audience to expand business exposure and directly engage with customers. Customers can type any search keyword in a social media site with a hashtag before the word and the search results will show all related posts. Hashtags can be used to reference promotions, observe market trends, and even provide links to helpful tips.

When you understand hashtags, you can use them to find business ideas and research potential employers. Pick a company you would like to work for and see whether you can find any related hashtags including what they are tweeting and posting. See whether you can find any information on partners and competitors. Which hashtags generate discussion or offer business insights? Check Twitter's and Facebook's trending topics and see whether there are any issues or insights on your career area.

software is to determine which statements are true and which are false, a huge issue when considering how easy and frequently wiki software is updated and changed.[24]

Violations of Copyright and Plagiarism

Online collaboration makes plagiarism as easy as clicking a mouse. Unfortunately a great deal of copyrighted material tends to find its way to blogs and wikis where many times blame cannot be traced to a single person. Clearly stated copyright and plagiarism policies are a must for all corporate blogs and wikis. These topics are discussed in detail in Chapter 4.

WEB 3.0: DEFINING THE NEXT GENERATION OF ONLINE BUSINESS OPPORTUNITIES LO3.10

While Web 1.0 refers to static text-based information websites and Web 2.0 is about user-contributed content, Web 3.0 is based on "intelligent" web applications using natural language processing, machine-based learning and reasoning, and intelligent applications. Web 3.0 is the next step in the evolution of the Internet and web applications. Business leaders who explore its opportunities will be the first to market with competitive advantages.

Web 3.0 offers a way for people to describe information such that computers can start to understand the relationships among concepts and topics. To demonstrate the power of Web 3.0, let's look at a few sample relationships, such as Adam Sandler is a comedian, Lady Gaga is a singer, and Hannah is friends with Sophie. These are all examples of descriptions that can be added to web pages allowing computers to learn about relationships while displaying the information to humans. With this kind of information in place, there will be a far richer interaction between people and machines with Web 3.0.

Applying this type of advanced relationship knowledge to a company can create new opportunities. After all, businesses run on information. Where Web 2.0 brings people closer together with information using machines, Web 3.0 brings *machines* closer together using *information.* These new relationships unite people, machines, and information so a business can be smarter, quicker, more agile, and more successful.

One goal of Web 3.0 is to tailor online searches and requests specifically to users' preferences and needs. For example, instead of making multiple searches, the user might type a complex sentence or two in a Web 3.0 browser, such as "I want to

BUSTED Connectivity Break-Down

When you are considering connectivity services for your business, you need to take continuous access and connectivity seriously. What if one of your employees is about to close a huge multimillion-dollar deal and loses the Internet connection, jeopardizing the deal? What if a disgruntled employee decides to post your business's collective intelligence on an open-source blog or wiki? What if your patient scheduling software crashes and you have no idea which patients are scheduled to which operating rooms with which doctors? These are far worse scenarios than a teenage boy not gaining access to his email or Facebook page. What management and technical challenges do you foresee as people and businesses become increasingly dependent on connectivity? What can managers do to meet these challenges and prevent problems?

semantic web A component of Web 3.0 that describes things in a way that computers can understand.

egovernment Involves the use of strategies and technologies to transform government(s) by improving the delivery of services and enhancing the quality of interaction between the citizen-consumer within all branches of government.

see a funny movie and then eat at a good Mexican restaurant. What are my options?" The Web 3.0 browser will analyze the request, search the web for all possible answers, organize the results, and present them to the user.

Tim Berners-Lee, one of the founders of the World Wide Web, has described the **semantic web** as a component of Web 3.0 that describes things in a way that computers can understand. The semantic web is not about links between web pages; rather it describes the relationships between *things* (such as A is a part of B and Y is a member of Z) and the properties of things (size, weight, age, price). If information about music, cars, concert tickets, and so on is stored in a way that describes the information and associated resource files, semantic web applications can collect information from many different sources, combine it, and present it to users in a meaningful way. Although Web 3.0 is still a bit speculative, some topics and features are certain to be included in it, such as:

- Integration of legacy devices: the ability to use current devices such as iPhones, laptops, and so on as credit cards, tickets, and reservations tools.
- Intelligent applications: the use of agents, machine learning, and semantic web concepts to complete intelligent tasks for users.
- Open ID: the provision of an online identity that can be easily carried to a variety of devices (cell phones, PCs) allowing for easy authentication across different websites.
- Open technologies: the design of websites and other software so they can be easily integrated and work together.
- A worldwide database: the ability for databases to be distributed and accessed from anywhere.[25]

LO3.10 Describe Web 3.0 and the next generation of online business.

Egovernment: The Government Moves Online

Recent business models that have arisen to enable organizations to take advantage of the Internet and create value are within egovernment. **Egovernment** involves the use of strategies and technologies to transform government(s) by improving the delivery of services and enhancing the quality of interaction between the citizen-consumer within all branches of government.

One example of an egovernment portal, First-Gov.gov, the official U.S. gateway to all government information, is the catalyst for a growing electronic government. Its powerful search engine and ever-growing collection of topical and customer-focused links connect users to millions of web pages, from the federal government, to local and tribal governments, to foreign nations around the world. Figure 3.24 highlights specific egovernment models.

FIGURE 3.24 Extended Ebusiness Models

	Business	Consumer	Government
Business	B2B conisint.com	B2C dell.com	B2G lockheedmartin.com
Consumer	C2B priceline.com	C2C ebay.com	C2G egov.com
Government	G2B export.gov	G2C medicare.gov	G2G disasterhelp.gov

Mbusiness: Supporting Anywhere Business

Internet-enabled mobile devices are quickly outnumbering personal computers. **Mobile business** (or **mbusiness**, **mcommerce**) is the ability to purchase goods and services through a wireless Internet-enabled device. The emerging technology behind mbusiness is a mobile device equipped with a web-ready micro-browser that can perform the following services:

- Mobile entertainment—downloads for music, videos, games, voting, ring tones, as well as text-based messaging services.
- Mobile sales/marketing—advertising, campaigns, discounts, promotions, and coupons.
- Mobile banking—manage accounts, pay bills, receive alerts, and transfer funds.
- Mobile ticketing—purchase tickets for entertainment, transportation, and parking including the ability to automatically feed parking meters.
- Mobile payments—pay for goods and services including instore purchases, home delivery, vending machines, taxis, gas, and so on.

mobile business (or mbusiness, mcommerce) The ability to purchase goods and services through a wireless Internet-enabled device.

Organizations face changes more extensive and far reaching in their implications than anything since the modern industrial revolution occurred in the early 1900s. Technology is a primary force driving these changes. Organizations that want to survive must recognize the immense power of technology, carry out required organizational changes in the face of it, and learn to operate in an entirely different way.

scanning
matching

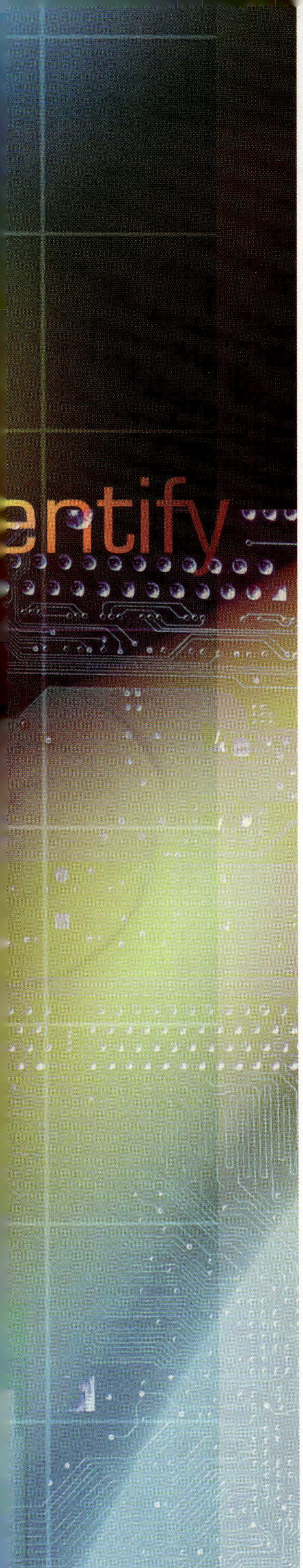

chapter four

ethics + information security: MIS business concerns

what's in IT for me?

This chapter concerns itself with protecting information from potential misuse. Organizations must ensure they collect, capture, store, and use information in an ethical manner. This means any type of information they collect and utilize, including about customers, partners, and employees. Companies must ensure that personal information collected about someone remains private. This is not just a nice thing to do. The law requires it. Perhaps more important, information must be kept physically secure to prevent access and possible dissemination and use by unauthorized sources.

continued on p. 92

CHAPTER OUTLINE

copyright The legal protection afforded an expression of an idea, such as a song, book, or video game.

intellectual property Intangible creative work that is embodied in physical form and includes copyrights, trademarks, and patents.

patent An exclusive right to make, use, and sell an invention granted by a government to the inventor.

ethics The principles and standards that guide our behavior toward other people.

privacy The right to be left alone when you want to be, to have control over your personal possessions, and not to be observed without your consent.

confidentiality The assurance that messages and information remain available only to those authorized to view them.

continued on p. 91

You, the business student, must understand ethics and security because they are the top concerns voiced by customers today. The way they are handled directly influences a customer's likelihood of embracing electronic technologies and conducting business over the web–and thus the company's bottom line. You can find evidence in recent news reports about how the stock price of organizations falls dramatically when information privacy and security breaches are made known. Further, organizations face potential litigation if they fail to meet their ethical, privacy, and security obligations in the handling of information. ■

{SECTION 4.1} Ethics

LEARNING OUTCOMES

LO4.1 Explain the ethical issues in the use of information technology.

LO4.2 Identify the six epolicies organizations should implement to protect themselves.

INFORMATION ETHICS LO4.1

Ethics and security are two fundamental building blocks for all organizations. In recent years, enormous business scandals along with 9/11 have shed new light on the meaning of ethics and security. When the behavior of a few individuals can destroy billion-dollar organizations, the value of ethics and security should be evident.

Copyright is the legal protection afforded an expression of an idea, such as a song, book, or video game. **Intellectual property** is intangible creative work that is embodied in physical form and includes copyrights, trademarks, and patents. A **patent** is an exclusive right to make, use, and sell an invention and is granted by a government to the inventor. As it becomes easier for people to copy everything from words and data to music and video, the ethical issues surrounding copyright infringement and the violation of intellectual property rights are consuming the ebusiness world. Technology poses new challenges for our **ethics**—the principles and standards that guide our behavior toward other people.

The protection of customers' privacy is one of the largest, and murkiest, ethical issues facing organizations today. **Privacy** is the right to be left alone when you want to be, to have control over your personal possessions, and not to be observed without your consent. Privacy is related to **confidentiality**, which is the assurance that messages and information remain available only to those authorized to view them. Each time employees make a decision about a privacy issue, the outcome could sink the company.

Trust among companies, customers, partners, and suppliers is the support structure of ebusiness. Privacy is one of its main ingredients. Consumers' concerns that their privacy will be violated because of their interactions on the web continue to be one of the primary barriers to the growth of ebusiness.

Information ethics govern the ethical and moral issues arising from the development and use of information technologies, as well as the creation, collection, duplication, distribution, and processing of information itself (with or without the aid of computer technologies). Ethical dilemmas in this area usually arise not as simple, clear-cut situations but as clashes among competing goals, responsibilities, and loyalties. Inevitably, there will be more than one socially acceptable or "correct" decision. The two primary areas concerning software include pirated software and counterfeit software. **Pirated software** is the unauthorized use, duplication, distribution, or sale of copyrighted software. **Counterfeit software** is software that is manufactured to look like the real thing and sold as such. **Digital rights management** is a technological solution that allows publishers to control their digital media to discourage, limit, or prevent illegal copying and distribution. Figure 4.1 contains examples of ethically questionable or unacceptable uses of information technology.[1]

Unfortunately, few hard and fast rules exist for always determining what is ethical. Many people can either justify or condemn the actions in Figure 4.1, for example. Knowing the law

information ethics Govern the ethical and moral issues arising from the development and use of information technologies, as well as the creation, collection, duplication, distribution, and processing of information itself (with or without the aid of computer technologies).

pirated software The unauthorized use, duplication, distribution, or sale of copyrighted software.

counterfeit software Software that is manufactured to look like the real thing and sold as such.

digital rights management A technological solution that allows publishers to control their digital media to discourage, limit, or prevent illegal copying and distribution.

FIGURE 4.1 Ethically Questionable or Unacceptable Information Technology Use

Individuals copy, use, and distribute software.

Employees search organizational databases for sensitive corporate and personal information.

Organizations collect, buy, and use information without checking the validity or accuracy of the information.

Individuals create and spread viruses that cause trouble for those using and maintaining IT systems.

Individuals hack into computer systems to steal proprietary information.

Employees destroy or steal proprietary organization information such as schematics, sketches, customer lists, and reports.

is important but that knowledge will not always help, because what is legal might not always be ethical, and what might be ethical is not always legal. For example, Joe Reidenberg received an offer for AT&T cell phone service. AT&T used Equifax, a credit reporting agency, to identify potential customers such as Joe Reidenberg. Overall, this seemed like a good business opportunity between Equifax and AT&T wireless. Unfortunately, the Fair Credit Reporting Act (FCRA) forbids repurposing credit information except when the information is used for "a firm offer of credit or insurance." In other words, the only product that can be sold based on credit information is credit. A representative for Equifax stated, "As long as AT&T Wireless (or any company for that matter) is offering the cell phone service on a credit basis, such as allowing the use of the service before the consumer has to pay, it is in compliance with the FCRA." However, the question remains—is it ethical?[2]

Figure 4.2 shows the four quadrants where ethical and legal behaviors intersect. The goal for most businesses is to make decisions within quadrant I that are both legal and ethical. There are times when a business will find itself in the position of making a decision in quadrant III, such as hiring child labor in foreign countries, or in quadrant II where a business might pay a foreigner who is in the process of getting her immigration status approved because the company is in the process of hiring the person. A business should never find itself operating in quadrant IV. Ethics are critical to operating a successful business today.

LO4.1 Explain the ethical issues in the use of information technology.

FIGURE 4.2 Acting Ethically and Acting Legally Are Not Always the Same Thing

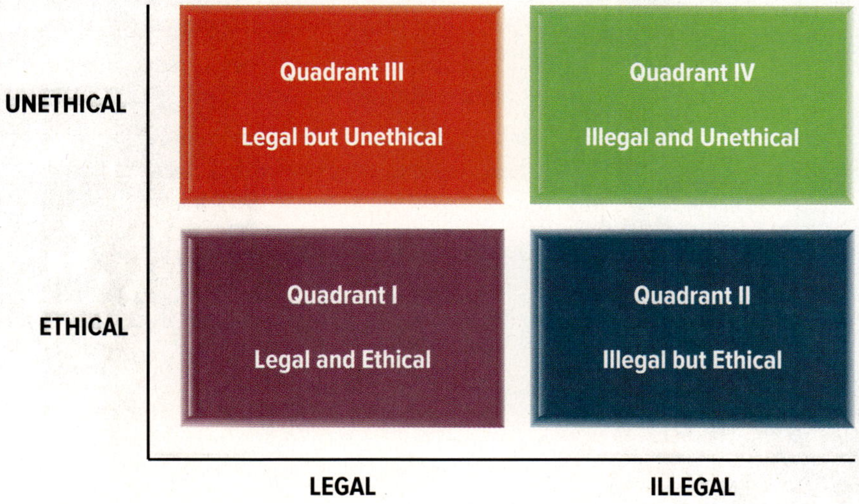

Information Does Not Have Ethics; People Do

Information itself has no ethics. It does not care how it is used. It will not stop itself from spamming customers, sharing itself if it is sensitive or personal, or revealing details to third parties. Information cannot delete or preserve itself. Therefore, it falls to those who own the information to develop ethical guidelines about how to manage it.

A few years ago the ideas of information management, governance, and compliance were relatively obscure. Today, these concepts are a must for virtually every company, both domestic and global, primarily due to the role digital information plays in corporate legal proceedings or litigation. Frequently, digital information serves as key evidence in legal proceedings and it is

BUSTED Information - Does It Have Ethics?

A high school principal decided it was a good idea to hold a confidential conversation about teachers, salaries, and student test scores on his cellular phone in a local Starbucks. Not realizing that one of the students' parents was sitting next to him, the principal accidentally divulged sensitive information about his employees and students. The irate parent soon notified the school board about the principal's inappropriate behavior and a committee was formed to decide how to handle the situation.

With the new wave of collaboration tools, electronic business, and the Internet, employees are finding themselves working outside the office and beyond traditional office hours. Advantages associated with remote workers include increased productivity, decreased expenses, and boosts in morale as employees are given greater flexibility to choose their work location and hours. Unfortunately, disadvantages associated with workers working remotely include new forms of ethical challenges and information security risks.

In a group, discuss the following statement: Information does not have any ethics. If you were elected to the committee to investigate the principal's inappropriate Starbucks phone conversation, what types of questions would you want answered? What type of punishment, if any, would you enforce on the principal? What types of policies would you implement across the school district to ensure that this scenario is never repeated? Be sure to highlight how workers working remotely affect business along with any potential ethical challenges and information security issues.

far easier to search, organize, and filter than paper documents. Digital information is also extremely difficult to destroy, especially if it is on a corporate network or sent via email. In fact, the only reliable way to truly obliterate digital information is to destroy the hard drives where the file was stored. **Ediscovery** (or **electronic discovery**) refers to the ability of a company to identify, search, gather, seize, or export digital information in responding to a litigation, audit, investigation, or information inquiry. As the importance of ediscovery grows, so does information governance and information compliance. The **Child Online Protection Act (COPA)** was passed to protect minors from accessing inappropriate material on the Internet. Figure 4.3 displays the ethical guidelines for information management.[4]

FIGURE 4.3
Ethical Guidelines for Information Management

Information Secrecy
The category of computer security that addresses the protection of data from unauthorized disclosure and confirmation of data source authenticity

Information Governance
A method or system of government for information management or control

Information Management
Examines the organizational resource of information and regulates its definitions, uses, value, and distribution, ensuring that it has the types of data/information required to function and grow effectively

Information Compliance
The act of conforming, acquiescing, or yielding information

Information Property
An ethical issue that focuses on who owns information about individuals and how information can be sold and exchanged

ediscovery (or electronic discovery) Refers to the ability of a company to identify, search, gather, seize, or export digital information in responding to a litigation, audit, investigation, or information inquiry.

Child Online Protection Act (COPA) A law that protects minors from accessing inappropriate material on the Internet.

epolicies Policies and procedures that address information management along with the ethical use of computers and the Internet in the business environment.

cyberbulling Threats, negative remarks, or defamatory comments transmitted via the Internet or posted on a website.

My Not To-Do List

Do You Really Want to Risk It?[4]

Ethics. It's just one tiny word, but it has monumental impact on every area of business. From the magazines, blogs, and newspapers you read to the courses you take, you will encounter ethics because it is a hot topic in today's electronic world. Technology has provided so many incredible opportunities, but it has also provided those same opportunities to unethical people. Discuss the ethical issues surrounding each of the following situations (yes, these are true stories):

- A student stands up the first day of class before the professor arrives and announces that his fraternity scans textbooks and that he has the textbook for this course on his thumb drive, which he will gladly sell for $20. Several students pay on the spot and upload the scanned textbook to their PCs. One student takes down the student information and contacts the publisher about the incident.
- A senior manager is asked to monitor his employee's email because there is a rumor that the employee is looking for another job.
- A vice president of sales asks her employee to burn all of the customer data onto an external hard drive because she made a deal to provide customer information to a strategic partner.
- A senior manager is asked to monitor his employee's email to discover if she is sexually harassing another employee.
- An employee is looking at the shared network drive and discovers his boss's entire hard drive, including his email backup, has been copied to the network and is visible to all.
- An employee is accidentally copied on an email that lists the targets for the next round of layoffs.

DEVELOPING INFORMATION MANAGEMENT POLICIES LO4.2

Treating sensitive corporate information as a valuable resource is good management. Building a corporate culture based on ethical principles that employees can understand and implement is responsible management. Organizations should develop written policies establishing employee guidelines, employee procedures, and organizational rules for information. These policies set employee expectations about the organization's practices and standards and protect the organization from misuse of computer systems and IT resources. If an organization's employees use computers at work, the organization should, at a minimum, implement epolicies. **Epolicies** are policies and procedures that address information management along with the ethical use of computers and the Internet in the business environment. Figure 4.4 displays the epolicies a firm should implement to set employee expectations.

LO4.2 Identify the six epolicies organizations should implement to protect themselves.

Ethical Computer Use Policy

In a case that illustrates the perils of online betting, a leading Internet poker site reported that a hacker exploited a security flaw to gain an insurmountable edge in high-stakes, no-limit Texas hold-'em tournaments—the ability to see his opponents' hole cards. The cheater, whose illegitimate winnings were estimated at between $400,000 and $700,000 by one victim, was an employee of AbsolutePoker.com and hacked the system to show that it could be done. Regardless of what business a company operates—even one that many view as unethical—the company must protect itself from unethical employee behavior.[6] **Cyberbulling** includes threats, negative remarks, or defamatory

threat An act or object that poses a danger to assets.

click-fraud The abuse of pay-per-click, pay-per-call, and pay-per-conversion revenue models by repeatedly clicking on a link to increase charges or costs for the advertiser.

competitive click-fraud A computer crime where a competitor or disgruntled employee increases a company's search advertising costs by repeatedly clicking on the advertiser's link.

ethical computer use policy Contains general principles to guide computer user behavior.

bring your own device (BYOD) policy Allows employees to use their personal mobile devices and computers to access enterprise data and applications.

information privacy policy Contains general principles regarding information privacy.

FIGURE 4.4 Overview of Epolicies

comments transmitted via the Internet or posted on the website. A **threat** is an act or object that poses a danger to assets. **Click-fraud** is the abuse of pay-per-click, pay-per-call, and pay-per-conversion revenue models by repeatedly clicking on a link to increase charges or costs for the advertiser. **Competitive click-fraud** is a computer crime where a competitor or disgruntled employee increases a company's search advertising costs by repeatedly clicking on the advertiser's link. Cyberbullying and click-fraud are just a few examples of the many types of unethical computer use found today.

One essential step in creating an ethical corporate culture is establishing an ethical computer use policy. An **ethical computer use policy** contains general principles to guide computer user behavior. For example, it might explicitly state that users should refrain from playing computer games during working hours. This policy ensures the users know how to behave at work and the organization has a published standard to deal with infractions. For example, after appropriate warnings, the company may terminate an employee who spends significant amounts of time playing computer games at work.

Organizations can legitimately vary in how they expect employees to use computers, but in any approach to controlling such use, the overriding principle should be informed consent. The users should be *informed* of the rules and, by agreeing to use the system on that basis, *consent* to abide by them.

Managers should make a conscientious effort to ensure all users are aware of the policy through formal training and other means. If an organization were to have only one epolicy, it should be an ethical computer use policy because that is the starting point and the umbrella for any other policies the organization might establish.

Part of an ethical computer use policy can include a BYOD policy. A **bring your own device (BYOD) policy** allows employees to use their personal mobile devices and computers to access enterprise data and applications. BYOD policies offer four basic options, including:

- Unlimited access for personal devices.
- Access *only* to nonsensitive systems and data.
- Access, but with IT control over personal devices, apps, and stored data.
- Access, but preventing local storage of data on personal devices.

Information Privacy Policy

An organization that wants to protect its information should develop an **information privacy policy**, which contains general principles regarding information privacy. Visa created Inovant to handle all its information systems, including its coveted customer information, which details how people are spending their money, in which stores, on which days, and even at what time of day. Just imagine what a sales and marketing department could do if it gained access to this information. For this reason, Inovant bans the use of Visa's customer information for anything outside its intended purpose—billing. Innovant's privacy specialists developed a strict credit card information privacy policy, which it follows.

Now Inovant is being asked if it can guarantee that unethical use of credit card information will never occur. In a large majority of cases, the unethical use of information happens not through the malicious scheming of a rogue marketer, but rather unintentionally. For instance, information is collected and stored for some purpose, such as record keeping or billing. Then, a sales or marketing professional figures out another way to use it internally, share it with partners, or sell it to a trusted third party. The information is "unintentionally" used for new purposes. The classic example of this type of unintentional information reuse is the Social Security number, which started simply as a way to identify government retirement benefits and then was used as a sort of universal personal ID, found on everything from drivers' licenses to savings accounts.

fair information practices A general term for a set of standards governing the collection and use of personal data and addressing issues of privacy and accuracy.

acceptable use policy (AUP) A policy that a user must agree to follow to be provided access to corporate email, information systems, and the Internet.

nonrepudiation A contractual stipulation to ensure that ebusiness participants do not deny (repudiate) their online actions.

Internet use policy Contains general principles to guide the proper use of the Internet.

Due Diligence //:
The Right To Be Forgotten

The European Commissioner for Justice, Fundamental Rights, and Citizenship, Viviane Reding, announced the European Commission's proposal to create a sweeping new privacy right—the right to be forgotten, allowing individuals to request to have all content that violates their privacy removed. The right to be forgotten addresses an urgent problem in the digital age: the great difficulty of escaping your past on the Internet now that every photo, status update, and tweet lives forever in the cloud. To comply with the European Court of Justice's decision, Google created a new online form by which individuals can request search providers to remove links that violate their online privacy. In the first month, Google received more than 50,000 submissions from people asking the company to remove links. Many people in the United States believe that the right to be forgotten conflicts with the right to free speech. Do people who want to erase their past deserve a second chance? Do you agree or disagree?[5]

Fair information practices is a general term for a set of standards governing the collection and use of personal data and addressing issues of privacy and accuracy. Different organizations and countries have their own terms for these concerns. The United Kingdom terms it "Data Protection," and the European Union calls it "Personal Data Privacy"; the Organisation for Economic Co-operation and Development (OECD) has written *Guidelines on the Protection of Privacy and Transborder Flows of Personal Data,* which can be found at www.oecd.org/unitedstates.

Acceptable Use Policy

An **acceptable use policy (AUP)** requires a user to agree to follow it to be provided access to corporate email, information systems, and the Internet. **Nonrepudiation** is a contractual stipulation to ensure that ebusiness participants do not deny (repudiate) their online actions. A nonrepudiation clause is typically contained in an acceptable use policy. Many businesses and educational facilities require employees or students to sign an acceptable use policy before gaining network access. When signing up with an email provider, each customer is typically presented with an AUP, which states the user agrees to adhere to certain stipulations. Users agree to the following in a typical acceptable use policy:

- Not using the service as part of violating any law.
- Not attempting to break the security of any computer network or user.
- Not posting commercial messages to groups without prior permission.
- Not performing any nonrepudiation.

Some organizations go so far as to create a unique information management policy focusing solely on Internet use. An **Internet use policy** contains general principles to guide the proper use of the Internet. Because of the large amounts of computing resources that Internet users can expend, it is essential that such use be legitimate. In addition, the Internet contains numerous materials that some believe are offensive, making

show me *the* MONEY

15 Million Identity Theft Victims

Identity theft has quickly become the most common, expensive, and pervasive crime in the United States. The identities of more than 15 million U.S. citizens are stolen each year, with financial losses exceeding $50 billion. This means that the identities of almost 10 percent of U.S. adults will be stolen this year, with losses of around $4,000 each, not to mention the 100 million U.S. citizens whose personal data will be compromised due to data breaches on corporate and government databases.

The growth of organized crime can be attributed to the massive amounts of data collection along with the increased cleverness of professional identity thieves. Starting with individually tailored phishing and vishing scams, increasingly successful corporate and government databases hackings, and intricate networks of botnets that hijack millions of computers without a trace, we must wake up to this ever-increasing threat to all Americans.[6]

You have the responsibility to protect yourself from data theft. In a group, visit the Federal Trade Commission's Consumer Information Identity Theft website at http://www.consumer.ftc.gov/features/feature-0014-identity-theft and review what you can do today to protect your identity and how you can ensure that your personal information is safe.

cybervandalism The electronic defacing of an existing website.

typosquatting A problem that occurs when someone registers purposely misspelled variations of well-known domain names.

website name stealing The theft of a website's name that occurs when someone, posing as a site's administrator, changes the ownership of the domain name assigned to the website to another website owner.

Internet censorship Government attempts to control Internet traffic, thus preventing some material from being viewed by a country's citizens.

email privacy policy Details the extent to which email messages may be read by others.

regulation in the workplace a requirement. **Cybervandalism** is the electronic defacing of an existing website. **Typosquatting** is a problem that occurs when someone registers purposely misspelled variations of well-known domain names. These variants sometimes lure consumers who make typographical errors when entering a URL. **Website name stealing** is the theft of a website's name that occurs when someone, posing as a site's administrator, changes the ownership of the domain name assigned to the website to another website owner. These are all examples of unacceptable Internet use. **Internet censorship** is government attempts to control Internet traffic, thus preventing some material from being viewed by a country's citizens. Generally, an Internet use policy:

- Describes the Internet services available to users.
- Defines the organization's position on the purpose of Internet access and what restrictions, if any, are placed on that access.
- Describes user responsibility for citing sources, properly handling offensive material, and protecting the organization's good name.
- States the ramifications if the policy is violated.

Email Privacy Policy

An **email privacy policy** details the extent to which email messages may be read by others. Email is so pervasive in organizations that it requires its own specific policy. Most working professionals use email as their preferred means of corporate communications. While email and instant messaging are common business communication tools, there are risks associated with using them. For instance, a sent email is stored on at least three or four computers (see Figure 4.5). Simply deleting an email from one computer does not delete it from the others. Companies can mitigate many of the risks of using electronic messaging systems by implementing and adhering to an email privacy policy.

One major problem with email is the user's expectations of privacy. To a large extent, this expectation is based on the false assumption that email privacy protection exists somehow analogous to that of U.S. first-class mail. Generally, the organization that owns the email system can operate the system as openly or as privately as it wishes. Surveys indicate that the majority of large firms regularly read and analyze employees' email looking for confidential data leaks such as unannounced financial results or the sharing of trade secrets that result in the violation of an email privacy policy and eventual termination of the employee. That means that if the organization wants to read everyone's email, it can do so. Basically, using work email for anything other than work is not a good idea. A typical email privacy policy:

- Defines legitimate email users and explains what happens to accounts after a person leaves the organization.
- Explains backup procedure so users will know that at some point, even if a message is deleted from their computer, it is still stored by the company.
- Describes the legitimate grounds for reading email and the process required before such action is performed.
- Discourages sending junk email or spam to anyone who does not want to receive it.

FIGURE 4.5 Email Is Stored on Multiple Computers

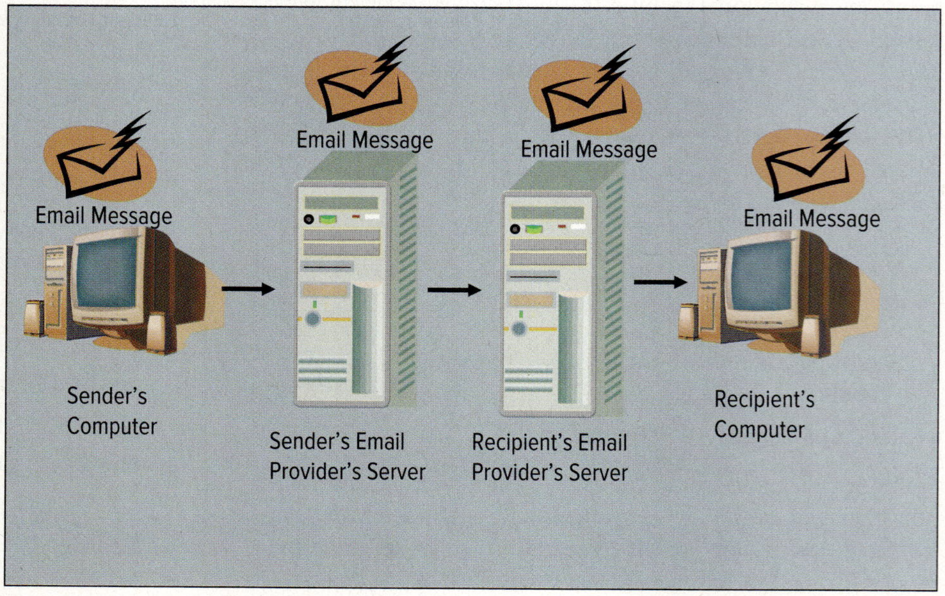

mail bomb Sends a massive amount of email to a specific person or system that can cause that user's server to stop functioning.

spam Unsolicited email.

anti-spam policy Simply states that email users will not send unsolicited emails (or spam).

opt out Customer specifically chooses to deny permission of receiving emails.

opt in A user can *opt in* to receive emails by choosing to allow permissions to incoming emails.

teergrubing Anti-spamming approach where the receiving computer launches a return attack against the spammer, sending email messages back to the computer that originated the suspected spam.

social media policy Outlines the corporate guidelines or principles governing employee online communications.

fyi Monitoring Employees

Every organization has the right to monitor its employees. Organizations usually inform their employees when workplace monitoring is occurring, especially regarding organizational assets such as networks, email, and Internet access. Employees traditionally offer their consent to be monitored and should not have any expectations of privacy when using organizational assets.

Do you agree or disagree that organizations have an obligation to notify employees about the extent of workplace monitoring, such as how long employees are using the Internet and which websites they are visiting? Do you agree or disagree that organizations have the right to read all employees' email sent or received on an organizational computer, including personal Gmail accounts?

- Prohibits attempting to mail bomb a site. A **mail bomb** sends a massive amount of email to a specific person or system that can cause that user's server to stop functioning.
- Informs users that the organization has no control over email once it has been transmitted outside the organization.

Spam is unsolicited email. It plagues employees at all levels within an organization, from receptionist to CEO, and clogs email systems and siphons MIS resources away from legitimate business projects. An **anti-spam policy** simply states that email users will not send unsolicited emails (or spam). It is difficult to write anti-spam policies, laws, or software because there is no such thing as a universal litmus test for spam. One person's spam is another person's newsletter. End users have to decide what spam is, because it can vary widely not just from one company to the next, but from one person to the next. A user can **opt out** of receiving emails by choosing to deny permission to incoming emails. A user can **opt in** to receive emails by choosing to allow permissions to incoming emails. **Teergrubing** is an anti-spamming approach where the receiving computer launches a return attack against the spammer, sending email messages back to the computer that originated the suspected spam.

Social Media Policy

Did you see the YouTube video showing two Domino's Pizza employees violating health codes while preparing food by passing gas on sandwiches? Millions of people did and the company took notice when disgusted customers began posting negative comments all over Twitter. Not having a Twitter account, corporate executives at Domino's did not know about the damaging tweets until it was too late. The use of social media can contribute many benefits to an organization, and implemented correctly it can become a huge opportunity for employees to build brands. But there are also tremendous risks as a few employees representing an entire company can cause tremendous brand damage. Defining a set of guidelines implemented in a social media policy can help mitigate that risk. Companies can protect themselves by implementing a **social media policy** outlining the corporate guidelines or principles governing employee online communications. Having a single social media policy might not be enough to ensure the company's online reputation is protected. Additional, more specific, social media policies a company might choose to implement include:[7]

- Employee online communication policy detailing brand communication.
- Employee blog and personal blog policies.
- Employee social network and personal social network policies.
- Employee Twitter, corporate Twitter, and personal Twitter policies.
- Employee LinkedIn policy.
- Employee Facebook usage and brand usage policy.
- Corporate YouTube policy.

social media monitoring The process of monitoring and responding to what is being said about a company, individual, product, or brand.

social media manager A person within the organization who is trusted to monitor, contribute, filter, and guide the social media presence of a company, individual, product, or brand.

physical security Tangible protection such as alarms, guards, fireproof doors, fences, and vaults.

workplace MIS monitoring Tracks people's activities by such measures as number of keystrokes, error rate, and number of transactions processed.

employee monitoring policy States explicitly how, when, and where the company monitors its employees.

Social media monitoring is the process of monitoring and responding to what is being said about a company, individual, product, or brand. Social media monitoring typically falls to the **social media manager**, a person within the organization who is trusted to monitor, contribute, filter, and guide the social media presence of a company, individual, product, or brand. Organizations must protect their online reputations and continuously monitor blogs, message boards, social networking sites, and media sharing sites. However, monitoring the hundreds of social media sites can quickly become overwhelming. To combat these issues, a number of companies specialize in online social media monitoring; for example, Trackur.com creates digital dashboards that allow executives to view at a glance the date published, source, title, and summary of every item tracked. The dashboard not only highlights what's being said but also the influence of the particular person, blog, or social media site.

Workplace Monitoring Policy

Increasingly, employee monitoring is not a choice; it is a risk-management obligation. Michael Soden, CEO of the Bank of Ireland, issued a mandate stating that company employees could not surf illicit websites with company equipment. Next, he hired Hewlett-Packard to run the MIS department and illicit websites were discovered on Soden's own computer, forcing Soden to resign. Monitoring employees is one of the biggest challenges CIOs face when developing information management policies.[8]

Physical security is tangible protection such as alarms, guards, fireproof doors, fences, and vaults. New technologies make it possible for employers to monitor many aspects of their employees' jobs, especially on telephones, computer terminals, through electronic and voice mail, and when employees are using the Internet. Such monitoring is virtually unregulated. Therefore, unless company policy specifically states otherwise (and even this is not assured), your employer may listen, watch, and read most of your workplace communications. **Workplace MIS monitoring** tracks people's activities by such measures as number of keystrokes, error rate, and number of transactions processed (see Figure 4.6 for an overview). The best path for an organization planning to engage in employee monitoring is open communication including an **employee monitoring policy** stating explicitly how, when, and where the company monitors its employees. Several common stipulations an organization can follow when creating an employee monitoring policy include:

- Be as specific as possible stating when and what (email, IM, Internet, network activity, etc.) will be monitored.
- Expressly communicate that the company reserves the right to monitor all employees.
- State the consequences of violating the policy.
- Always enforce the policy the same for everyone.

Many employees use their company's high-speed Internet access to shop, browse, and surf the web. Most managers do

FIGURE 4.6 Internet Monitoring Technologies

Common Internet Monitoring Technologies	
Key logger, or key trapper, software	A program that records every keystroke and mouse click.
Hardware key logger	A hardware device that captures keystrokes on their journey from the keyboard to the motherboard.
Cookie	A small file deposited on a hard drive by a website containing information about customers and their web activities. Cookies allow websites to record the comings and goings of customers, usually without their knowledge or consent.
Adware	Software that generates ads that install themselves on a computer when a person downloads some other program from the Internet.
Spyware (sneakware or stealthware)	Software that comes hidden in free downloadable software and tracks online movements, mines the information stored on a computer, or uses a computer's CPU and storage for some task the user knows nothing about.
Web log	Consists of one line of information for every visitor to a website and is usually stored on a web server.
Clickstream	Records information about a customer during a web surfing session such as what websites were visited, how long the visit was, what ads were viewed, and what was purchased.

BUSTED I'm Being Fired for Smoking, but I Was at Home and It Was Saturday[9]

If on the weekend you like to smoke and eat fast food, you need to be careful, not because it is bad for you but because it just might get you fired. Corporations are starting to implement policies against smoking and obesity and are testing their employees for tobacco use and high-blood pressure. If the tests are positive, the employee can face fines or even dismissal. At Weyco Inc., four employees were fired for refusing to take a test to determine whether they smoke cigarettes. Weyco Inc. adopted a policy that mandates that employees who smoke will be fired, even if the smoking happens after business hours or at home. Howard Weyers, Weyco founder, believes the anti-smoking policies were designed to protect the firm from high health care costs. "I don't want to pay for the results of smoking," states Weyers.

© Stockbyte/Getty Images RF

Minority and pregnant women are protected by law from discrimination in the workplace. Unfortunately, if you have a few bad habits, you are on your own. How would you feel if you were fired because you were smoking on the weekend? Do you agree that unhealthy habits warrant disciplinary actions? If companies are allowed to implement policies against smoking and obesity, what unhealthy habit might be next? To date, there have not been any policies on the consumption of alcohol outside of work. Do you agree that overeating and smoking are worse than a drinking habit?

not want their employees conducting personal business during working hours, and they implement a Big Brother approach to employee monitoring. Many management gurus advocate that organizations whose corporate cultures are based on trust are more successful than those whose corporate cultures are based on mistrust. Before an organization implements monitoring technology, it should ask itself, "What does this say about how we feel about our employees?" If the organization really does not trust its employees, then perhaps it should find new ones. If an organization does trust its employees, then it might want to treat them accordingly. An organization that follows its employees' every keystroke might be unwittingly undermining the relationships with its employees, and it might find the effects of employee monitoring are often worse than lost productivity from employee web surfing.

{SECTION 4.2} Information Security

LEARNING OUTCOMES

LO4.3 Describe the relationships and differences between hackers and viruses.

LO4.4 Describe the relationship between information security policies and an information security plan.

LO4.5 Provide an example of each of the three primary information security areas: (1) authentication and authorization, (2) prevention and resistance, and (3) detection and response.

PROTECTING INTELLECTUAL ASSETS LO4.3

To accurately reflect the crucial interdependence between MIS and business processes, we should update the old business axiom "Time is money" to say "Uptime is money." **Downtime** refers to a period of time when a system is unavailable. Unplanned downtime can strike at any time for any number of reasons, from tornadoes to sink overflows to network failures to power outages (see Figure 4.7). Although natural disasters may appear to be the most devastating causes of MIS outages, they are hardly the most frequent or most expensive. Figure 4.8 demonstrates that the costs of downtime are not only associated with lost revenues, but also with financial performance, damage to reputations, and even travel or legal expenses. A few questions managers should ask when determining the cost of downtime are:[10]

- How many transactions can the company afford to lose without significantly harming business?
- Does the company depend upon one or more mission-critical applications to conduct business?
- How much revenue will the company lose for every hour a critical application is unavailable?
- What is the productivity cost associated with each hour of downtime?
- How will collaborative business processes with partners, suppliers, and customers be affected by an unexpected IT outage?

downtime Refers to a period of time when a system is unavailable.

information security A broad term encompassing the protection of information from accidental or intentional misuse by persons inside or outside an organization.

- What is the total cost of lost productivity and lost revenue during unplanned downtime?

The reliability and resilience of IT systems have never been more essential for success as businesses cope with the forces of globalization, 24/7 operations, government and trade regulations, global recession, and overextended IT budgets and resources. Any unexpected downtime in today's business environment has the potential to cause both short- and long-term costs with far-reaching consequences.

Information security is a broad term encompassing the protection of information from accidental or intentional misuse by persons inside or outside an organization. Information security is the primary tool an organization can use to combat the threats

FIGURE 4.7 Sources of Unplanned Downtime

Sources of Unplanned Downtime		
Bomb threat	Frozen pipe	Snowstorm
Burst pipe	Hacker	Sprinkler malfunction
Chemical spill	Hail	Static electricity
Construction	Hurricane	Strike
Corrupted data	Ice storm	Terrorism
Earthquake	Insects	Theft
Electrical short	Lightning	Tornado
Epidemic	Network failure	Train derailment
Equipment failure	Plane crash	Smoke damage
Evacuation	Power outage	Vandalism
Explosion	Power surge	Vehicle crash
Fire	Rodents	Virus
Flood	Sabotage	Water damage (various)
Fraud	Shredded data	Wind

FIGURE 4.8 The Cost of Downtime

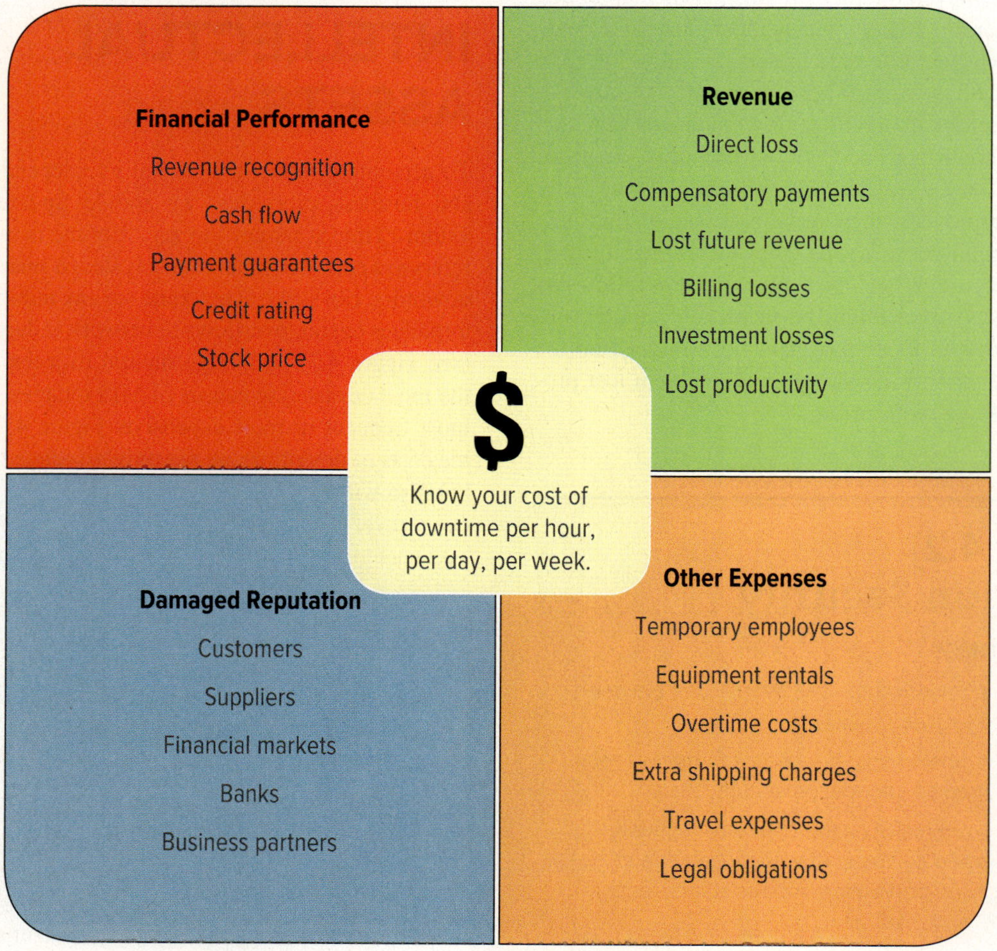

hackers Experts in technology who use their knowledge to break into computers and computer networks, either for profit or motivated by the challenge.

drive-by hacking A computer attack where an attacker accesses a wireless computer network, intercepts data, uses network services, and/or sends attack instructions without entering the office or organization that owns the network.

virus Software written with malicious intent to cause annoyance or damage.

worm Spreads itself not only from file to file but also from computer to computer.

associated with downtime. Understanding how to secure information systems is critical to keeping downtime to a minimum and uptime to a maximum. Hackers and viruses are two of the hottest issues currently facing information security.

LO4.3 Describe the relationships and differences between hackers and viruses.

Security Threats Caused by Hackers and Viruses

Hackers are experts in technology who use their knowledge to break into computers and computer networks, either for profit or just motivated by the challenge. Smoking is not just bad for a person's health; it seems it is also bad for company security as hackers regularly use smoking entrances to gain building access. Once inside they pose as employees from the MIS department and either ask for permission to use an employee's computer to access the corporate network, or find a conference room where they simply plug-in their own laptop. **Drive-by hacking** is a computer attack where an attacker accesses a wireless computer network, intercepts data, uses network services, and/or sends attack instructions without entering the office or organization that owns the network. Figure 4.9 lists the various types of hackers for organizations to be aware of, and Figure 4.10 shows how a virus is spread.

One of the most common forms of computer vulnerabilities is a virus. A **virus** is software written with malicious intent to cause annoyance or damage. Some hackers create and leave viruses causing massive computer damage. A **worm** spreads itself not only from file to file but also from computer to computer. The primary difference between a virus and a worm is that a virus must attach to something, such as an executable file, to spread. Worms do not need to attach to anything to spread and can tunnel themselves into computers. Figure 4.11 provides an overview of the most common types of viruses.

FIGURE 4.10 How Computer Viruses Spread

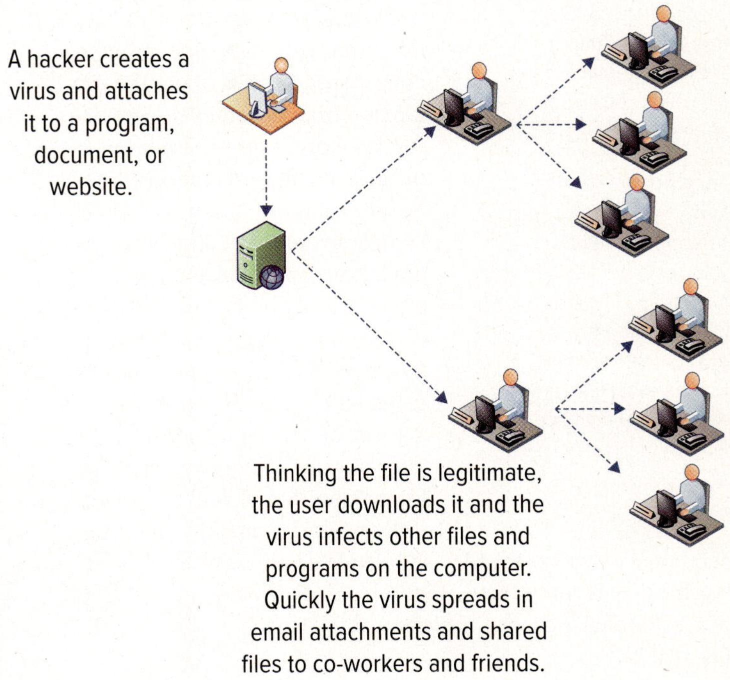

FIGURE 4.9 Types of Hackers

Common Types of Hackers
• **Black-hat hackers** break into other people's computer systems and may just look around or may steal and destroy information.
• **Crackers** have criminal intent when hacking.
• **Cyberterrorists** seek to cause harm to people or to destroy critical systems or information and use the Internet as a weapon of mass destruction.
• **Hactivists** have philosophical and political reasons for breaking into systems and will often deface the website as a protest.
• **Script kiddies or script bunnies** find hacking code on the Internet and click-and-point their way into systems to cause damage or spread viruses.
• **White-hat hackers** work at the request of the system owners to find system vulnerabilities and plug the holes.

adware Software, while purporting to serve some useful function and often fulfilling that function, also allows Internet advertisers to display advertisements without the consent of the computer user.

spyware A special class of adware that collects data about the user and transmits it over the Internet without the user's knowledge or permission.

ransomware A form of malicious software that infects your computer and asks for money. Simplelocker is a new ransomware program that encrypts your personal files and demands payment for the files' decryption keys.

Two additional computer vulnerabilities include adware and spyware. **Adware** is software that, while purporting to serve some useful function and often fulfilling that function, also allows Internet advertisers to display advertisements without the consent of the computer user. **Spyware** is a special class of adware that collects data about the user and transmits it over the Internet without the user's knowledge or permission. Spyware programs collect specific data about the user, ranging from general demographics such as name, address, and browsing habits to credit card numbers, Social Security numbers, and user names and passwords. Not all adware programs are spyware and used correctly it can generate revenue for a company allowing users to receive free products. Spyware is a clear threat to privacy. **Ransomware** is a form of malicious software that infects your computer and asks for money. Simplelocker is a new ransomware program that encrypts your personal files and demands payment for the files' decryption keys. Figure 4.12 displays a few additional weapons hackers use for launching attacks.[11]

Organizational information is intellectual capital. Just as organizations protect their tangible assets—keeping their money in an insured bank or providing a safe working environment for employees—they must also protect their intellectual capital, everything from patents to transactional and analytical information. With security breaches and viruses on the rise and computer hackers everywhere, an organization must put in place strong security measures to survive.

show me the MONEY

Beyond Passwords

The password, a combination of a user name and personal code, has been the primary way to secure systems since computers first hit the market in the 1980s. Of course, in the 1980s, users had only one password to maintain and remember, and chances are they still probably had to write it down. Today, users have dozens of user names and passwords they have to remember to multiple systems and websites—it is simply no longer sustainable! A few companies are creating new forms of identification, hoping to eliminate the password problem.

- Bionym is developing the Nymi, a wristband with two electrodes that reads your heart's unique electrocardiogram signal and can unlock all your devices.
- Clef is developing the Clef Wave, a free app that generates a unique image on your smart phone that you can point at your webcam, which reads the image and unlocks your websites. The image cannot be stolen because it only stays on your screen for a few seconds. More than 300 websites have enabled the Clef Wave service.
- Illiri is developing an app that emits a unique sound on your smart phone that can be used to unlock other devices, process payments, and access websites. The sound lasts for 10 seconds and can be heard within 1 foot of your device.

In a group, evaluate the three preceding technologies and determine which one you would choose to implement at your school.

FIGURE 4.11 Common Forms of Viruses

Backdoor programs open a way into the network for future attacks.

Denial-of-service attack (DoS) floods a website with so many requests for service that it slows down or crashes the site.

Distributed denial-of-service attack (DDoS) attacks from multiple computers that flood a website with so many requests for service that it slows down or crashes. A common type is the Ping of Death, in which thousands of computers try to access a website at the same time, overloading it and shutting it down.

Polymorphic viruses and worms change their form as they propagate.

Trojan-horse virus hides inside other software, usually as an attachment or a downloadable file.

Worm spreads itself, not only from file to file, but also from computer to computer. The primary difference between a virus and a worm is that a virus must attach to something, such as an executable file, to spread. Worms do not need to attach to anything to spread and can tunnel themselves into computers.

insiders Legitimate users who purposely or accidentally misuse their access to the environment and cause some kind of business-affecting incident.

social engineering Hackers use their social skills to trick people into revealing access credentials or other valuable information.

dumpster diving Looking through people's trash, another way hackers obtain information.

pretexting A form of social engineering in which one individual lies to obtain confidential data about another individual.

information security policies Identify the rules required to maintain information security, such as requiring users to log off before leaving for lunch or meetings, never sharing passwords with anyone, and changing passwords every 30 days.

information security plan Details how an organization will implement the information security policies.

FIGURE 4.12 Hacker Weapons

Elevation of privilege is a process by which a user misleads a system into granting unauthorized rights, usually for the purpose of compromising or destroying the system. For example, an attacker might log onto a network by using a guest account and then exploit a weakness in the software that lets the attacker change the guest privileges to administrative privileges.

Hoaxes attack computer systems by transmitting a virus hoax, with a real virus attached. By masking the attack in a seemingly legitimate message, unsuspecting users more readily distribute the message and send the attack on to their co-workers and friends, infecting many users along the way.

Malicious code includes a variety of threats such as viruses, worms, and Trojan horses.

Packet tampering consists of altering the contents of packets as they travel over the Internet or altering data on computer disks after penetrating a network. For example, an attacker might place a tap on a network line to intercept packets as they leave the computer. The attacker could eavesdrop or alter the information as it leaves the network.

A sniffer is a program or device that can monitor data traveling over a network. Sniffers can show all the data being transmitted over a network, including passwords and sensitive information. Sniffers tend to be a favorite weapon in the hacker's arsenal.

Spoofing is the forging of the return address on an email so that the message appears to come from someone other than the actual sender. This is not a virus but rather a way by which virus authors conceal their identities as they send out viruses.

Splogs (spam blogs) are fake blogs created solely to raise the search engine rank of affiliated websites. Even blogs that are legitimate are plagued by spam, with spammers taking advantage of the Comment feature of most blogs to comments with links to spam sites.

Spyware is software that comes hidden in free downloadable software and tracks online movements, mines the information stored on a computer, or uses a computer's CPU and storage for some task the user knows nothing about.

THE FIRST LINE OF DEFENSE—PEOPLE LO4.4

Organizations today are able to mine valuable information such as the identity of the top 20 percent of their customers, who usually produce 80 percent of revenues. Most organizations view this type of information as intellectual capital and implement security measures to prevent it from walking out the door or falling into the wrong hands. At the same time, they must enable employees, customers, and partners to access needed information electronically. Organizations address security risks through two lines of defense; the first is people, the second technology.

Surprisingly, the biggest problem is people as the majority of information security breaches result from people misusing organizational information. **Insiders** are legitimate users who purposely or accidentally misuse their access to the environment and cause some kind of business-affecting incident. For example, many individuals freely give up their passwords or write them on sticky notes next to their computers, leaving the door wide open for hackers. Through **social engineering**, hackers use their social skills to trick people into revealing access credentials or other valuable information. **Dumpster diving**, or looking through people's trash, is another way hackers obtain information. **Pretexting** is a form of social engineering in which one individual lies to obtain confidential data about another individual.

Information security policies identify the rules required to maintain information security, such as requiring users to log off before leaving for lunch or meetings, never sharing passwords with anyone, and changing passwords every 30 days. An **information security plan** details how an organization will implement the information security policies. The best way a company can safeguard itself from people is by implementing and communicating its information security plan. This becomes even more important with Web 2.0 and as the use of mobile devices, remote workforce, and contractors is growing. A few details managers should consider surrounding people and information security policies include defining the best practices for:[12]

destructive agents Malicious agents designed by spammers and other Internet attackers to farm email addresses off websites or deposit spyware on machines.

identity theft The forging of someone's identity for the purpose of fraud.

information secrecy The category of computer security that addresses the protection of data from unauthorized disclosure and confirmation of data source authenticity.

phishing A technique to gain personal information for the purpose of identity theft, usually by means of fraudulent emails that look as though they came from legitimate sources.

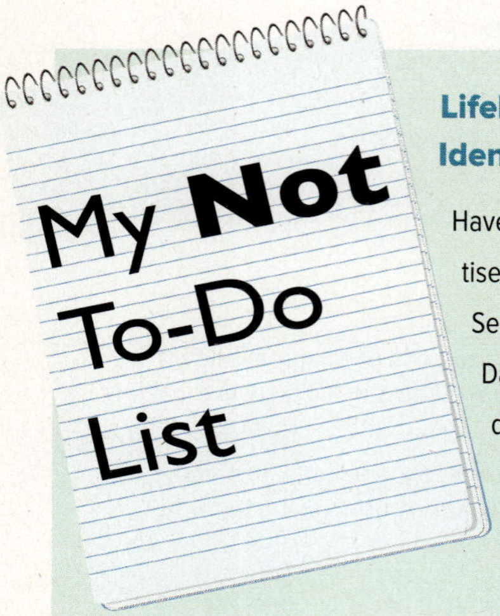

Lifelock: Keeping Your Identity Safe

Have you ever seen a LifeLock advertisement? If so, you know the Social Security number of LifeLock CEO Todd Davis because he posts it in all ads daring hackers to try to steal his identity. Davis has been a victim of identity theft at least 13 times. The first theft occurred when someone used his identity to secure a $500 loan from a check-cashing company. Davis discovered the crime only after the company called his wife's cell phone to recover the unpaid debt.[13]

If you were starting an identity theft prevention company, do you think it would be a good idea to post your Social Security number in advertisements? Why or why not? What do you think happened that caused Davis's identity to be stolen? What types of information security measures should LifeLock implement to ensure that Davis's Social Security number is not stolen again? If you were LifeLock's CEO, what type of marketing campaign would you launch next?

- Applications allowed to be placed on the corporate network, especially various file sharing applications (Kazaz), IM software, and entertainment or freeware created by unknown sources (iPhone applications).
- Corporate computer equipment used for personal reason on personal networks.
- Password creation and maintenance including minimum password length, characters to be included while choosing passwords, and frequency for password changes.
- Personal computer equipment allowed to connect to the corporate network.
- Virus protection including how often the system should be scanned and how frequently the software should be updated. This could also include if downloading attachments is allowed and practices for safe downloading from trusted and untrustworthy sources.

LO4.4 Describe the relationship between information security policies and an information security plan.

THE SECOND LINE OF DEFENSE—TECHNOLOGY LO4.5

Once an organization has protected its intellectual capital by arming its people with a detailed information security plan, it can begin to focus on deploying technology to help combat attackers. **Destructive agents** are malicious agents designed by spammers and other Internet attackers to farm email addresses off websites or deposit spyware on machines. Figure 4.13 displays the three areas where technology can aid in the defense against attacks.

LO4.5 Provide an example of each of the three primary information security areas: (1) authentication and authorization, (2) prevention and resistance, and (3) detection and response.

People: Authentication and Authorization

Identity theft is the forging of someone's identity for the purpose of fraud. The fraud is often financial, because thieves apply for and use credit cards or loans in the victim's name. Two means of stealing an identity are phishing and pharming. **Information secrecy** is the category of computer security that addresses the protection of data from unauthorized disclosure and confirmation of data source authenticity. **Phishing** is a technique to gain personal information for the purpose of identity theft, usually by means of fraudulent emails that look as though they came from legitimate businesses. The messages appear to be genuine, with official-looking formats and logos, and typically ask for verification of important information such as passwords and account numbers, ostensibly for accounting or auditing purposes. Since the emails look

phishing expedition A masquerading attack that combines spam with spoofing.

spear phishing A phishing expedition in which the emails are carefully designed to target a particular person or organization.

vishing (or voice phishing) A phone scam that attempts to defraud people by asking them to call a bogus telephone number to "confirm" their account information.

pharming Reroutes requests for legitimate websites to false websites.

zombie A program that secretly takes over another computer for the purpose of launching attacks on other computers.

zombie farm A group of computers on which a hacker has planted zombie programs.

pharming attack Uses a zombie farm, often by an organized crime association, to launch a massive phishing attack.

authentication A method for confirming users' identities.

authorization The process of providing a user with permission including access levels and abilities such as file access, hours of access, and amount of allocated storage space.

password String of alphanumeric characters used to authenticate a user and provide access to a system.

FIGURE 4.13 Three Areas of Information Security

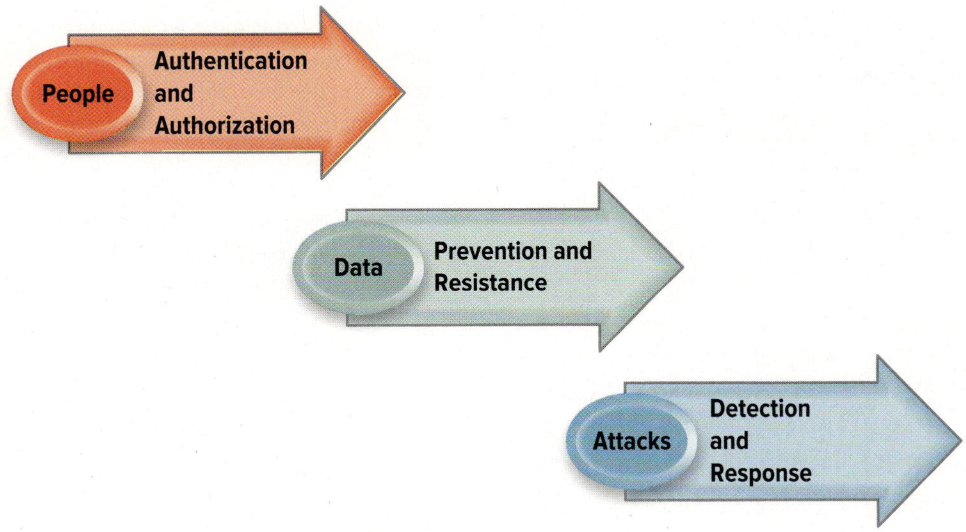

authentic, up to one in five recipients responds with the information and subsequently becomes a victim of identity theft and other fraud. Figure 4.14 displays a phishing scam attempting to gain information for Skyline Bank; you should never click on emails asking you to verify your identity as companies will never contact you directly asking for your username or password.[15] **phishing expedition** is a masquerading attack that combines spam with spoofing. The perpetrator sends millions of spam emails that appear to be from a respectable company. The emails contain a link to a website that is designed to look exactly like the company's website. The victim is encouraged to enter his or her username, password, and sometimes credit card information. **Spear phishing** is a phishing expedition in which the emails are carefully designed to target a particular person or organization. **Vishing (or voice phishing)** is a phone scam that attempts to defraud people by asking them to call a bogus telephone number to "confirm" their account information.

Pharming reroutes requests for legitimate websites to false websites. For example, if you were to type in the URL to your bank, pharming could redirect to a fake site that collects your information. A **zombie** is a program that secretly takes over another computer for the purpose of launching attacks on other computers. Zombie attacks are almost impossible to trace back to the attacker. A **zombie farm** is a group of computers on which a hacker has planted zombie programs. A **pharming attack** uses a zombie farm, often by an organized crime association, to launch a massive phishing attack.

Authentication and authorization technologies can prevent identity theft, phishing, and pharming scams. **Authentication** is a method for confirming users' identities. Once a system determines the authentication of a user, it can then determine the access privileges (or authorization) for that user. **Authorization** is the process of providing a user with permission including access levels and abilities such as file access, hours of access, and amount of allocated storage space. Authentication and authorization techniques fall into three categories; the most secure procedures combine all three:

1. Something the user knows, such as a user ID and password.
2. Something the user has, such as a smart card or token.
3. Something that is part of the user, such as a fingerprint or voice signature.

Something the User Knows Such as a User ID and Password

A **password** is string of alphanumeric characters used to authenticate a user and provide access to a system. The first type of authentication, using something the user knows, is the most common way to identify individual users and typically consists of a unique user ID and password. However, this is actually one of the most *ineffective* ways for determining authentication because passwords are not secure.

tokens Small electronic devices that change user passwords automatically.

smart card A device about the size of a credit card, containing embedded technologies that can store information and small amounts of software to perform some limited processing.

biometrics The identification of a user based on a physical characteristic, such as a fingerprint, iris, face, voice, or handwriting.

voiceprint A set of measurable characteristics of a human voice that uniquely identifies an individual.

single-factor authentication The traditional security process, which requires a username and password.

FIGURE 4.14 Skyline Bank Phishing Scam

FROM	SkyLine Bank customerservice@skylinebank.com
SUBJECT	Your Account Verification

SKYLINE BANK "Your Local Banking Experts"

Dear Customer,

As your premier local banking choice, we take our commitment to your account security very seriously. To that end, we are communicating with you to inform you that due to an internal error, we are at this time, unable to confirm your account data. It is of the utmost importance that you reply to this email in a timely fashion to avoid any interruption of service on your account.

To avoid suspension of your account, please click the link below to verify your account details. We apologize for this inconvenience.

Click Here

Thank you,
SkyLine Bank Corp.
Online Banking Division

All it typically takes to crack one is enough time. More than 50 percent of help-desk calls are password related, which can cost an organization significant money, and a social engineer can coax a password from almost anybody.

Something the User Has Such as a Smart Card or Token

The second type of authentication, using something the user has, offers a much more effective way to identify individuals than a user ID and password. Tokens and smart cards are two of the primary forms of this type of authentication. **Tokens** are small electronic devices that change user passwords automatically. The user enters his or her user ID and token-displayed password to gain access to the network. A **smart card** is a device about the size of a credit card, containing embedded technologies that can store information and small amounts of software to perform some limited processing. Smart cards can act as identification instruments, a form of digital cash, or a data storage device with the ability to store an entire medical record.

Something That Is Part of the User Such as a Fingerprint or Voice Signature

The third kind of authentication, something that is part of the user, is by far the best and most effective way to manage authentication. **Biometrics** (narrowly defined) is the identification of a user based on a physical characteristic, such as a fingerprint, iris, face, voice, or handwriting. A **voiceprint** is a set of measurable characteristics of a human voice that uniquely identifies an individual. These characteristics, which are based on the physical configuration of a speaker's mouth and throat, can be expressed as a mathematical formula. Unfortunately, biometric authentication such as voiceprints can be costly and intrusive.

Single-factor authentication is the traditional security process, which requires a username and password. **Two-factor authentication** requires the user to provide two means of authentication, what the user knows (password) and what the user has (security token). **Multifactor authentication** requires more than two means of authentication such as what the user knows (password), what the user has (security token), and what the user is (biometric verification). The goal of multifactor authentication

two-factor authentication Requires the user to provide two means of authentication, what the user knows (password) and what the user has (security token).

multifactor authentication Requires more than two means of authentication such as what the user knows (password),

privilege escalation A network intrusion attack that takes advantage of programming errors or design flaws to grant the attacker elevated access to the network and its associated data and applications.

vertical privilege escalation Attackers grant themselves a higher access level such as administrator, allowing the attacker to perform illegal actions such as running unauthorized code or deleting data.

horizontal privilege escalation Attackers grant themselves the same access levels they already have but assume the identity of another user.

time bombs Computer viruses that wait for a specific date before executing instructions.

Due Diligence //:

Doodling Passwords[14]

As our online world continues to explode, people are finding the number of usernames and passwords they need to remember growing exponentially. For this reason, many users will assign the same password for every logon, choose easy-to-remember names and dates, or simply write down their passwords on sticky notes and attach them to their computers. Great for the person who needs to remember 72 different passwords, but not so great for system security.

© Brand X Pictures/Jupiterimages

Of course, the obvious answer is to deploy biometrics across the board, but once you start reviewing the costs associated with biometrics, you quickly realize that this is not feasible. What is coming to the rescue to help with the password nightmare we have created? The doodle. Background Draw-a-Secret (BDAS) is a new program created by scientists at Newcastle University in England. BDAS begins by recording the number of strokes it takes a user to draw a doodle. When the user wants to gain access to the system, he simply redraws the doodle on a touchpad and it is matched against the stored prototype. If the doodle matches, the user is granted access. Doodles are even described as being far more anonymous, therefore offering greater security, than biometrics.

You are probably thinking that you'll end up right back in the same position having to remember all 72 of your password doodles.

The good news is that, with doodle passwords, you don't have to remember a thing. The doodle password can be displayed to the user, and they simply have to redraw it since the system analyzes how the user draws or the user's unique hand strokes, not the actual doodle (similar to handwriting recognition technologies).

If you were going to deploy doodle passwords in your organization, what issues and concerns do you think might occur? Do you agree that doodles are easier to remember than text passwords? Do you agree that doodles offer the most effective way to manage authentication, even greater than biometrics? What types of unethical issues do you think you might encounter with doodle passwords?

is to make it difficult for an unauthorized person to gain access to a system because, if one security level is broken, the attacker will still have to break through additional levels.

Data: Prevention and Resistance

A **privilege escalation** is a network intrusion attack that takes advantage of programming errors or design flaws to grant the attacker elevated access to the network and its associated data and applications. There are two kinds of privilege escalation:

- **Vertical privilege escalation** Attackers grant themselves a higher access level such as administrator, allowing the attacker to perform illegal actions such as running unauthorized code or deleting data.
- **Horizontal privilege escalation** Attackers grant themselves the same access levels they already have but assume the identity of another user. For example, someone gaining access to another person's online banking account would constitute horizontal privilege escalation.

Prevention and resistance technologies stop intruders from accessing and reading data by means of content filtering, encryption, and firewalls. **Time bombs** are computer viruses that wait for a specific date before executing their instructions. **Content filtering** occurs when organizations use software that filters content, such as emails, to prevent the accidental or malicious transmission of unauthorized information. Organizations can use content filtering technologies to filter email and prevent emails containing sensitive information from transmitting, whether the transmission was malicious or accidental. It can also filter emails and prevent any suspicious files from transmitting such as potential virus-infected files. Email content filtering can also filter for spam, a form of unsolicited email.

Encryption scrambles information into an alternative form that requires a key or password to decrypt. If there were a security breach and the stolen information were encrypted, the thief would be unable to read it. Encryption can switch the order of characters, replace characters with other characters, insert or

content filtering Occurs when organizations use software that filters content, such as emails, to prevent the accidental or malicious transmission of unauthorized information.

encryption Scrambles information into an alternative form that requires a key or password to decrypt.

decrypt Decodes information and is the opposite of encrypted.

cryptography The science that studies encryption, which is the hiding of messages so that only the sender and receiver can read them.

advanced encryption standard (AES) Introduced by the National Institute of Standards and Technology (NIST), AES is an encryption standard designed to keep government information secure.

public key encryption (PKE) Uses two keys: a public key that everyone can have and a private key for only the recipient.

certificate authority A trusted third party, such as VeriSign, that validates user identities by means of digital certificates.

digital certificate A data file that identifies individuals or organizations online and is comparable to a digital signature.

remove characters, or use a mathematical formula to convert the information into a code. Companies that transmit sensitive customer information over the Internet, such as credit card numbers, frequently use encryption. To **decrypt** information is to decode it and is the opposite of encrypt. **Cryptography** is the science that studies encryption, which is the hiding of messages so that only the sender and receiver can read them. The National Institute of Standards and Technology (NIST) introduced an **advanced encryption standard (AES)** designed to keep government information secure.

Some encryption technologies use multiple keys. **Public key encryption (PKE)** uses two keys: a public key that everyone can have and a private key for only the recipient (see Figure 4.15). The organization provides the public key to all customers, whether end consumers or other businesses, who use that key to encrypt their information and send it via the Internet. When it arrives at its destination, the organization uses the private key to unscramble it.

Public keys are becoming popular to use for authentication techniques consisting of digital objects in which a trusted third party confirms correlation between the user and the public key. A **certificate authority** is a trusted third party, such as VeriSign, that validates user identities by means of digital certificates. A **digital certificate** is a data file that identifies individuals or organizations online and is comparable to a digital signature.

A **firewall** is hardware and/or software that guard a private network by analyzing incoming and outgoing information for the correct markings. If they are missing, the firewall prevents the information from entering the network. Firewalls can even detect computers communicating with the Internet without approval. As Figure 4.16 illustrates, organizations typically place a firewall between a server and the Internet. Think of a firewall as a gatekeeper that protects computer networks from intrusion by providing a filter and safe transfer points for access to and from the Internet and other networks. It screens all network traffic for proper passwords or other security codes and allows only authorized transmissions in and out of the network.

show me the MONEY

Hackers Love Phish, and I Don't Mean the Band

Phishing is a technique used to gain personal information for the purpose of identity theft, usually by means of fraudulent email. Phishers will pretend to be your favorite website or social networking friend to see if you will fall for the bait and send them your personal information. In other words, the keys to your online identity kingdom. Review each of the following and see if you would end up as Phish bait.

1. Which of the following are real websites and which are phishing scams?
   a. www.books-google.com
   b. www.amazom.com
   c. www.hotmail.com.profile.php.id.371233.cn
   d. www.gmaill.com
2. True or False: HTTPS represents a fraudulent site and the S stands for Scam.
3. Which of the following are the best ways to determine if a website is legitimate?
   a. Cut-and-paste the URL into a browser to see if it works
   b. Review the site to see if it has an information privacy policy
   c. Type in your username and the wrong password to see if the site accepts it
   d. Check the email for typos
4. True or False: The IRS sends emails informing individuals what they need to do to collect their economic stimulus refund.

firewall Hardware and/or software that guard a private network by analyzing incoming and outgoing information for the correct markings.

antivirus software Scans and searches hard drives to prevent, detect, and remove known viruses, adware, and spyware.

cyberwar An organized attempt by a country's military to disrupt or destroy information and communication systems for another country.

cyberterrorism The use of computer and networking technologies against persons or property to intimidate or coerce governments, individuals, or any segment of society to attain political, religious, or ideological goals.

intrusion detection software (IDS) Features full-time monitoring tools that search for patterns in network traffic to identify intruders.

FIGURE 4.15 Public Key Encryption (PKE)

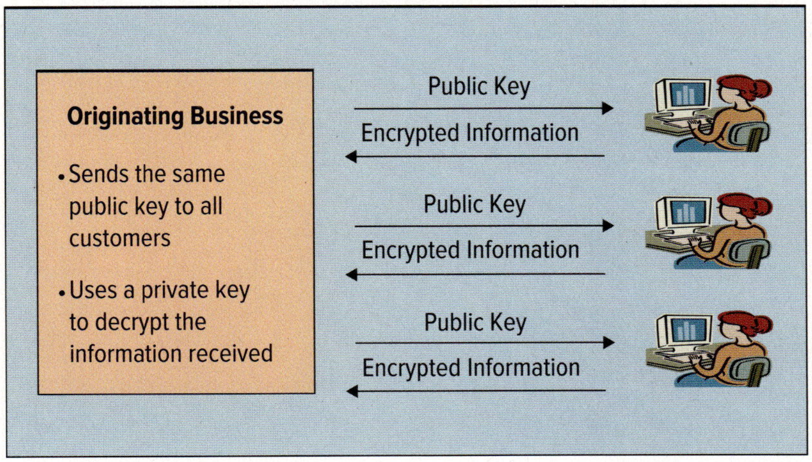

Firewalls do not guarantee complete protection, and users should enlist additional security technologies such as antivirus software and antispyware software. **Antivirus software** scans and searches hard drives to prevent, detect, and remove known viruses, adware, and spyware. Antivirus software must be frequently updated to protect against newly created viruses.

Attack: Detection and Response

Cyberwar is an organized attempt by a country's military to disrupt or destroy information and communication systems for another country. **Cyberterrorism** is the use of computer and networking technologies against persons or property to intimidate or coerce governments, individuals, or any segment of society to attain political, religious, or ideological goals. With so many intruders planning computer attacks, it is critical that all computer systems are protected. The presence of an intruder can be detected by watching for suspicious network events such as bad passwords, the removal of highly classified data files, or unauthorized user attempts. **Intrusion detection software (IDS)** features full-time monitoring tools that search for patterns in network traffic to identify intruders. IDS protects against suspicious network traffic and attempts to access files and data. If a suspicious event or unauthorized traffic is identified, the IDS will generate an alarm and can even be customized to shut down a particularly sensitive part of a network. After identifying an attack, an MIS department can implement response tactics to mitigate the damage. Response tactics outline procedures such as how long a system under attack will remain plugged in and connected to the corporate network, when to shut down a compromised system, and how quickly a backup system will be up and running.

Guaranteeing the safety of organization information is achieved by implementing the two lines of defense: people and technology. To protect information through people, firms should develop information security policies and plans that provide employees with specific precautions they should take in creating, working with, and transmitting the organization's information assets. Technology-based lines of defense fall into three categories: authentication and authorization; prevention and resistance; and detection and response.

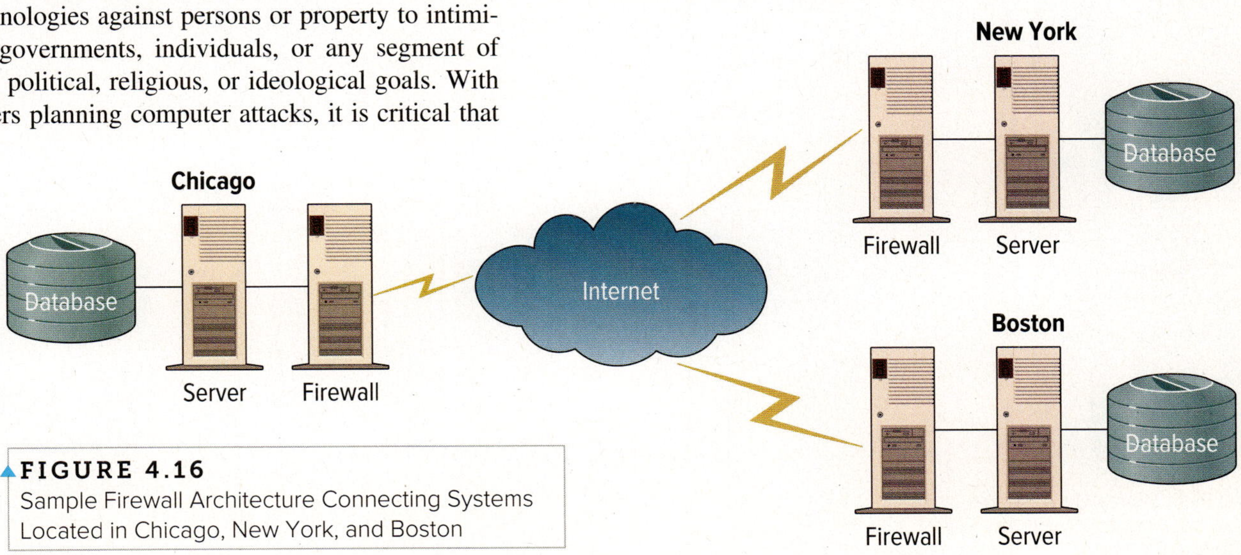

FIGURE 4.16 Sample Firewall Architecture Connecting Systems Located in Chicago, New York, and Boston

© Ryan McVay/Getty Images

coming up

Module 2 concentrates on the technical foundations of MIS. The power of MIS comes from its ability to carry, house, and support information. And information is power to an organization. This module highlights this point and raises awareness of the significance of information to organizational success. Understanding how the MIS infrastructure supports business operations, how business professionals access and analyze information to make business decisions, and how wireless and mobile technologies can make information continuously and instantaneously available are important for strategically managing any company, large or small. Thus, these are the primary learning outcomes of Module 2.

The module begins by reviewing the role of MIS in supporting business growth, operations, and performance. We quickly turn to the need for MIS to be sustainable given today's focus on being "green," and then dive into databases, data warehousing, networking, and wireless technologies—all fundamental components of MIS infrastructures. A theme throughout the module is the need to leverage and yet safeguard the use of information as key to the survival of any company. Information must be protected from misuse and harm, especially with the continued use, development, and exploitation of the Internet and the web. ■

TECHNICAL FOUNDATIONS OF MIS

© Colin Anderson/Getty Images

chapter five

infrastructures: sustainable technologies

what's in IT for me?

Why do you, as a business student, need to understand the underlying technology of any company? Most people think "that technical stuff" is something they will never personally encounter and for that reason do not need to know anything about MIS infrastructures. Well, those people will be challenged in the business world. When your database fails and you lose all of your sales history, you will personally feel the impact when you are unable to receive your bonus. When your computer crashes and you lose all of your confidential information, not to mention your emails, calendars, and messages, then you will understand why

continued on p. 118

CHAPTER OUTLINE

MIS infrastructure Includes the plans for how a firm will build, deploy, use, and share its data, processes, and MIS assets.

hardware Consists of the physical devices associated with a computer system.

software The set of instructions the hardware executes to carry out specific tasks.

network A communications system created by linking two or more devices and establishing a standard methodology in which they can communicate.

client A computer designed to request information from a server.

continued from p. 117

everyone needs to learn about MIS infrastructures. You never want to leave the critical task of backing up your data to your MIS department. You want to personally ensure that your information is not only backed up, but also safeguarded and recoverable. For these reasons, business professionals in the 21st century need to acquire a base-level appreciation of what MIS can and cannot do for their company. Understanding how MIS supports growth, operations, profitability, and most recently sustainability, is crucial whether one is new to the workforce or a seasoned *Fortune* 500 employee. One of the primary goals of this chapter is to create a more level playing field between you as a business professional and the MIS specialists with whom you will work. After reading it you should have many of the skills you need to assist in analyzing current and even some future MIS infrastructures; in recommending needed changes in processes; and in evaluating alternatives that support a company's growth, operations, and profits. ■

{SECTION 5.1} MIS Infrastructures

LEARNING OUTCOMES

LO5.1 Explain MIS infrastructure and its three primary types.

LO5.2 Identify the three primary areas associated with an information MIS infrastructure.

LO5.3 Describe the characteristics of an agile MIS infrastructure.

THE BUSINESS BENEFITS OF A SOLID MIS INFRASTRUCTURE LO5.1

Management information systems have played a significant role in business strategies, affected business decisions and processes, and even changed the way companies operate. What is the foundation supporting all of these systems that enable business growth, operations, and profits? What supports the volume and complexity of today's user and application requirements? What protects systems from failures and crashes? It is the **MIS infrastructure**, which includes the plans for how a firm will build, deploy, use, and share its data, processes, and MIS assets. A solid MIS infrastructure can reduce costs, improve productivity, optimize business operations, generate growth, and increase profitability.

Briefly defined, **hardware** consists of the physical devices associated with a computer system, and **software** is the set of instructions the hardware executes to carry out specific tasks. In today's business environment, most hardware and software is run via a network. A **network** is a communications system created by linking two or more devices and establishing a standard methodology in which they can communicate. As more companies need to share more information, the network takes on greater importance in the infrastructure. Most companies use a specific form of network infrastructure called a client and server network. A **client** is a computer designed to request information from a server. A **server** is a computer dedicated to providing information in response to requests. A good way to understand this is when someone uses a web browser (this would be the client) to access a website (this would be a server that would respond with the web page being requested by the client). Anyone not familiar with the basics of hardware, software, or networks should review Appendix A, "Hardware and Software," and Appendix B, "Networks and Telecommunications," for more information.

In the physical world, a detailed blueprint would show how public utilities, such as water, electricity, and gas support the foundation of a building. MIS infrastructure is similar as it shows in detail how the hardware, software, and network connectivity support the firm's processes. Every company, regardless of size, relies on some form of MIS infrastructure, whether it is a few personal computers networked together sharing an Excel file or a large multinational company with thousands of employees interconnected around the world.

An MIS infrastructure is dynamic; it continually changes as the business needs change. Each time a new form of Internet-enabled device, such as an iPhone or BlackBerry, is created and made available to the public, a firm's MIS infrastructure must be revised to support the device. This moves beyond just innovations in hardware to include new types of software and network connectivity. An **enterprise architect** is a person grounded in technology, fluent in business, and able to provide the important bridge between MIS and the business.

server A computer dedicated to providing information in response to requests.

enterprise architect A person grounded in technology, fluent in business, and able to provide the important bridge between MIS and the business.

information MIS infrastructure Identifies where and how important information, such as customer records, is maintained and secured.

agile MIS infrastructure Includes the hardware, software, and telecommunications equipment that, when combined, provides the underlying foundation to support the organization's goals.

sustainable MIS infrastructure Identifies ways that a company can grow in terms of computing resources while simultaneously becoming less dependent on hardware and energy consumption.

FIGURE 5.1 MIS Infrastructure

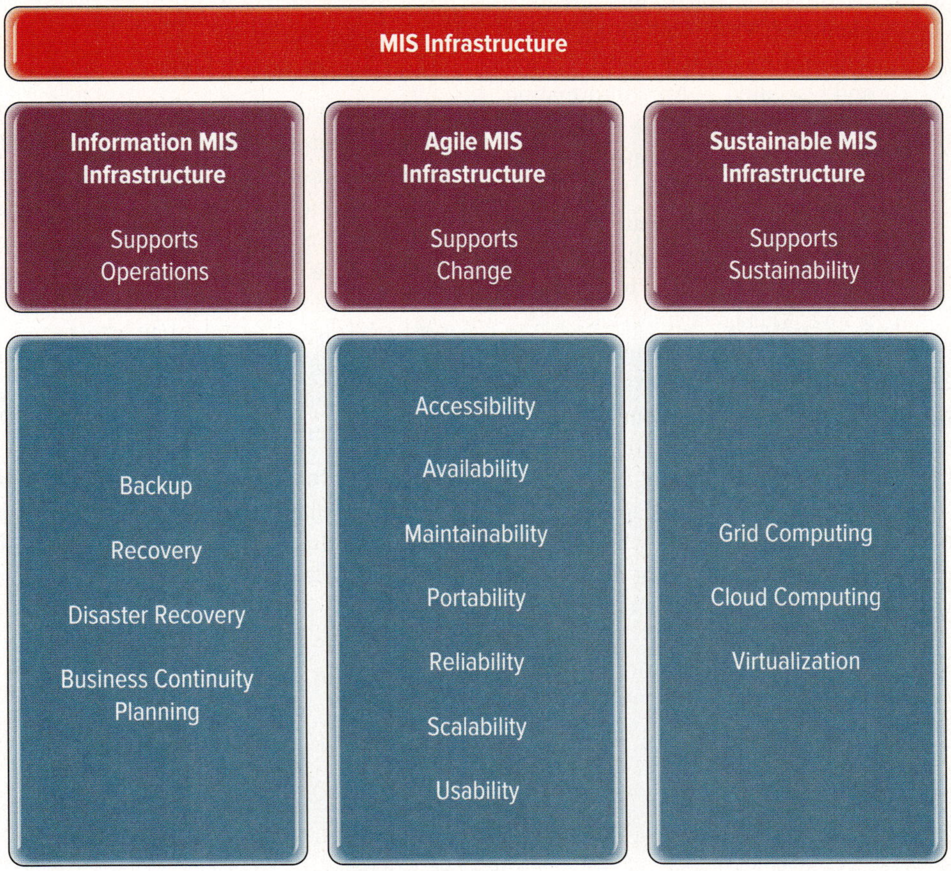

Firms employ enterprise architects to help manage change and dynamically update MIS infrastructure. Figure 5.1 displays the three primary areas where enterprise architects focus when maintaining a firm's MIS infrastructure.

- **Supporting operations: Information MIS infrastructure** identifies where and how important information, such as customer records, is maintained and secured.
- **Supporting change: Agile MIS Infrastructure** includes the hardware, software, and telecommunications equipment that, when combined, provides the underlying foundation to support the organization's goals.
- **Supporting the environment: Sustainable MIS infrastructure** identifies ways that a company can grow in terms of computing resources while simultaneously becoming less dependent on hardware and energy consumption.

LO5.1 Explain MIS infrastructure and its three primary types.

SUPPORTING OPERATIONS: INFORMATION MIS INFRASTRUCTURE LO5.2

Imagine taking a quick trip to the printer on the other side of the room, and when you turn around you find that your laptop has been stolen. How painful would you find this experience? What types of information would you lose? How much time

backup An exact copy of a system's information.

recovery The ability to get a system up and running in the event of a system crash or failure that includes restoring the information backup.

fault tolerance A general concept that a system has the ability to respond to unexpected failures or system crashes as the backup system immediately and automatically takes over with no loss of service.

would it take you to recover all of that information? A few things you might lose include music, movies, emails, assignments, saved passwords, not to mention that all-important 40-page paper that took you more than a month to complete. If this sounds painful then you want to pay particular attention to this section and learn how to eliminate this pain.

An information MIS infrastructure identifies where and how important information is maintained and secured. An information infrastructure supports day-to-day business operations and plans for emergencies such as power outages, floods, earthquakes, malicious attacks via the Internet, theft, and security breaches to name just a few. Managers must take every precaution to make sure their systems are operational and protected around the clock every day of the year. Losing a laptop or experiencing bad weather in one part of the country simply cannot take down systems required to operate core business processes. In the past, someone stealing company information would have to carry out boxes upon boxes of paper. Today, as data storage technologies grow in capabilities while shrinking in size, a person can simply walk out the front door of the building with the company's data files stored on a thumb drive or external hard drive. Today's managers must act responsibly to protect one of their most valued assets, information. To support continuous business operations, an information infrastructure provides three primary elements:

- Backup and recovery plan.
- Disaster recovery plan.
- Business continuity plan (see Figure 5.2).

LO5.2 Identify the three primary areas associated with an information MIS infrastructure.

Backup and Recovery Plan

Each year businesses lose time and money because of system crashes and failures. One way to minimize the damage of a system crash is to have a backup and recovery strategy in place. A **backup** is an exact copy of a system's information. **Recovery** is the ability to get a system up and running in the event of a system crash or failure that includes restoring the information backup. Many different types of backup and recovery media are available, including maintaining an identical replica or redundant of the storage server, external hard drives, thumb drives, and even DVDs. The primary differences between them are speed and cost.

Fault tolerance is the ability for a system to respond to unexpected failures or system crashes as the backup system immediately and automatically takes over with no loss of service. For example, fault tolerance enables a business to support continuous business operations if there is a power failure or

FIGURE 5.2 Areas of Support Provided by Information Infrastructure

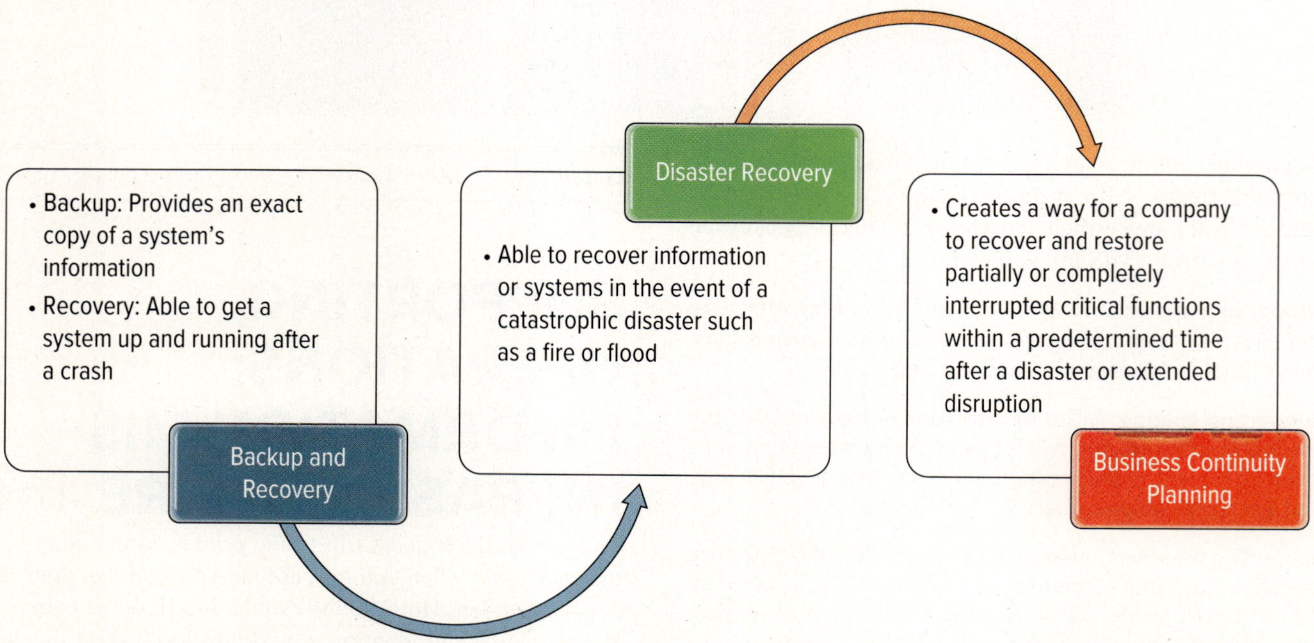

flood. Fault tolerance is an expensive form of backup, and only mission-critical applications and operations use it. **Failover**, a specific type of fault tolerance, occurs when a redundant storage server offers an exact replica of the real-time data, and if the primary server crashes, the users are automatically directed to the secondary server or backup server. This is a high-speed and high-cost method of backup and recovery. **Failback** occurs when the primary machine recovers and resumes operations, taking over from the secondary server.

Using DVDs or thumb drives to store your data offers a low-speed and low-cost backup method. It is a good business practice to back up data at least once a week using a low-cost method. This will alleviate the pain of having your laptop stolen or your system crash as you will still have access to your data, and it will only be a few days old.

Deciding how often to back up information and what media to use is a critical decision. Companies should choose a backup and recovery strategy in line with their goals and operational needs. If the company deals with large volumes of critical information, it will require daily, perhaps hourly, backups to storage servers. If it relies on small amounts of noncritical information, then it might require only weekly backups to external hard drives or thumb drives. A company that backs up on a weekly basis is taking the risk that, if a system crash occurs, it could lose a week's worth of work. If this risk is acceptable, a weekly backup strategy will work. If it is unacceptable, the company needs more frequent backup.

failover A specific type of fault tolerance, occurs when a redundant storage server offers an exact replica of the real-time data, and if the primary server crashes the users are automatically directed to the secondary server or backup server.

failback Occurs when the primary machine recovers and resumes operations, taking over from the secondary server.

Disaster Recovery Plan

Disasters such as power outages, fires, floods, hurricanes, and even malicious activities such as hackers and viruses strike companies every day. Disasters can have the following effects on companies and their business operations.

Due Diligence //: I Don't Have a Temperature, but I'm Positive I Have a Virus[1]

There is nothing worse than finishing your paper at 4 a.m. and finding out that your computer has a virus and you just lost your entire document. Well, there might be one thing that is worse. You submit your final paper, which is worth 50 percent of your grade, and then you head off to Florida for spring break. You return to find that you failed the course and you frantically check email to find out what happened. In your email is a message from your professor informing you that your paper was corrupt and couldn't be opened and that you had 24 hours to resend the file, which, of course, you missed because you were lying on the beach.

There is an entrepreneur in every bunch, and good business-people can take lemons and make lemonade. One such savvy individual saw lemonade in the corrupted file issue and launched Corrupted-Files.com, which sells students (for only $3.95) intentionally corrupted files. Why would anyone want to purchase a corrupted file? According to the website, the reasons are obvious.

"Step 1: After purchasing a file, rename the file, e.g., Mike_FinalPaper. Step 2: Email the file to your professor along with your 'here's my assignment' e-mail. Step 3: It will take your professor several hours if not days to notice your file is 'unfortunately' corrupted. Use the time this website just bought you wisely and finish that paper!!! This download includes a 2, 5, 10, 20, 30 and 40 page corrupted Word file. Use the appropriate file size to match each assignment. Who's to say your 10-page paper didn't get corrupted? Exactly! No one can! It's the perfect excuse to buy yourself extra time and not hand in a garbage paper. Cheating is not the answer to procrastination!—Corrupted-Files.com is! Keep this site a secret!"

When discussing service-oriented architectures, there are three primary components, services, interoperability, and loose coupling. What is the service in Corrupted-Files.com? Does it matter if a student is using a Mac or a PC when submitting the corrupted file, and how does this relate to interoperability?

© J.R.Bale/Alamy RF

disaster recovery plan A detailed process for recovering information or a system in the event of a catastrophic disaster.

hot site A separate and fully equipped facility where the company can move immediately after a disaster and resume business.

cold site A separate facility that does not have any computer equipment but is a place where employees can move after a disaster.

warm site A separate facility with computer equipment that requires installation and configuration.

disaster recovery cost curve Charts (1) the cost to the company of the unavailability of information and technology and (2) the cost to the company of recovering from a disaster over time.

- **Disrupting communications:** Most companies depend on voice and data communications for daily operational needs. Widespread communications outages, from either direct damage to the infrastructure or sudden spikes in usage related to an outside disaster, can be as devastating to some firms as shutting down the whole business.
- **Damaging physical infrastructures:** Fire and flood can directly damage buildings, equipment, and systems, making structures unsafe and systems unusable. Law enforcement officers and firefighters may prohibit business professionals from entering a building, thereby restricting access to retrieve documents or equipment.
- **Halting transportation:** Disasters such as floods and hurricanes can have a deep effect on transportation. Disruption to major highways, roads, bridges, railroads, and airports can prevent business professionals from reporting to work or going home, slow the delivery of supplies, and stop the shipment of products.
- **Blocking utilities:** Public utilities, such as the supply of electric power, water, and natural gas, can be interrupted for hours or days even in incidents that cause no direct damage to the physical infrastructure. Buildings are often uninhabitable and systems unable to function without public utilities.

These effects can devastate companies by causing them to cease operations for hours, days, or longer and risk losing customers whom they cannot then supply. Therefore, to combat these disasters a company can create a **disaster recovery plan**, which is a detailed process for recovering information or a system in the event of a catastrophic disaster. This plan includes such factors as which files and systems need to have backups and their corresponding frequency and methods along with the strategic location of the storage in a separate physical site that is geographically dispersed. A company might strategically maintain operations in New York and San Francisco, ensuring that a natural disaster would not impact both locations. A disaster recovery plan also foresees the possibility that not only the computer equipment but also the building where employees work may be destroyed. A **hot site** is a separate and fully equipped facility where the company can move immediately after a disaster and resume business. A **cold site** is a separate facility that does not have any computer equipment but is a place where employees can move after a disaster. A **warm site** is a separate facility with computer equipment that requires installation and configuration. Figure 5.3 outlines these resources that support disaster recovery.

A disaster recovery plan usually has a disaster recovery cost curve to support it. A **disaster recovery cost curve** charts (1) the cost to the company of the unavailability of information and technology and (2) the cost to the company of recovering from a disaster over time. Figure 5.4 displays a disaster recovery cost curve and shows that the best recovery plan in terms of cost and time is where the two lines intersect. Creating such a curve is no small task. Managers must consider the cost of losing information and technology within each department or functional area, and across the whole company. During the first few hours of a disaster, those costs may be low, but they rise over time. With those costs in hand, a company must then determine the costs of recovery. Figure 5.5 displays TechTarget's disaster recovery strategies for business.

FIGURE 5.3 Sites to Support Disaster Recovery

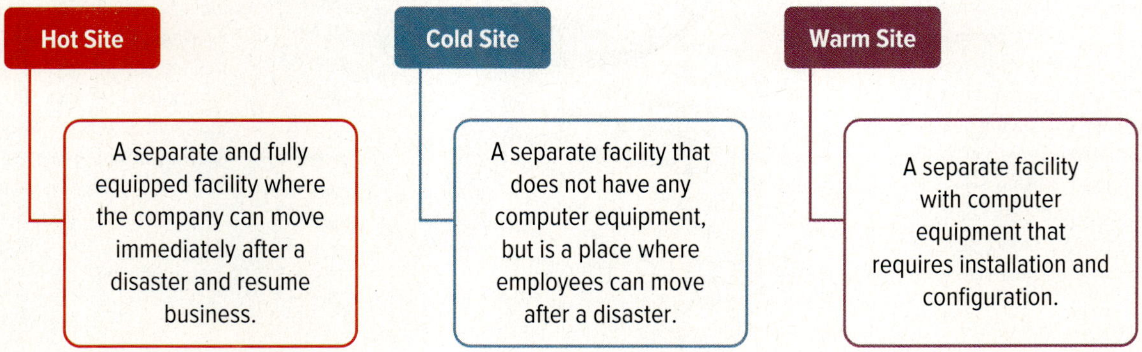

On April 18, 1906, San Francisco was rocked by an earthquake that destroyed large sections of the city and claimed the lives of more than 3,000 inhabitants. More than a century later, a rebuilt and more durable San Francisco serves as a central location for major MIS corporations as well as a major world financial center. Managers of these corporations are well aware of the potential disasters that exist along the San Andreas Fault and actively update their business continuity plans anticipating such issues as earthquakes and floods. The Union Bank of California is located in the heart of downtown San Francisco and maintains a highly detailed and well-developed business continuity plan. The company employs hundreds of business professionals scattered around the world that coordinate plans for addressing the potential loss of a facility, business professionals, or critical systems so that the company can continue to operate if a disaster happens. Its disaster recovery plan includes hot sites where staff can walk in and start working exactly as if they were in their normal location. It would be a matter of minutes, not hours, for the Union Bank of California to be up and running again in the event of a disaster.[3]

FIGURE 5.4 Disaster Recovery Cost Curve

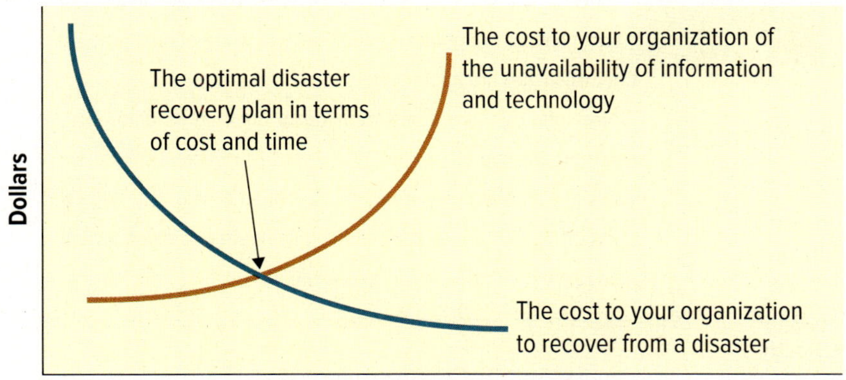

Business Continuity Plan

An **emergency** is a sudden, unexpected event requiring immediate action due to potential threat to health and safety, the environment, or property. **Emergency preparedness** ensures a company is ready to respond to an emergency in an organized, timely, and effective manner. Natural disasters and terrorist attacks are on the minds of business professionals who take safeguarding their information assets seriously. Disaster recovery plans typically focus on systems and data, ignoring cross-functional and intraorganizational business processes that can be destroyed during an emergency. For this reason many companies are turning to a more comprehensive and all-encompassing emergency preparedness plan known as **business continuity planning (BCP)**, which details how a company recovers and restores critical business operations and systems after a disaster or extended disruption. BCP includes such factors as identifying critical systems, business processes, departments, and the maximum amount of time the business can continue to operate without functioning systems (see Figure 5.6). BCP contains disaster recovery plans along with many additional plans, including prioritizing business impact analysis, emergency notification plans, and technology recovery strategies.

emergency A sudden, unexpected event requiring immediate action due to potential threat to health and safety, the environment, or property.

emergency preparedness Ensures a company is ready to respond to an emergency in an organized, timely, and effective manner.

business continuity planning (BCP) Details how a company recovers and restores critical business operations and systems after a disaster or extended disruption.

FIGURE 5.5 TechTarget's Disaster Recovery Strategies

DISASTER RECOVERY STRATEGIES	
1. Activate backup and recovery facilities in secondary company data center; transfer production to that site	Assumes the secondary data center has sufficient resources, e.g., storage capacity, server hardware to accommodate additional processing requirements
2. Activate recovery resources in a cloud-based service; failover critical systems to that site and resume operations	Ensure that your contract for this service has the ability to flex as your needs dictate; ensure that security of your data can be maintained
3. Activate backup systems and data at a hot site; transfer operations to that site	Be sure you know what resources you have available at the hot site, what the declaration rules and fees are, and what your options are if multiple declarations are occurring at the same time
4. Replace damaged equipment with spare components	As much as possible, have available spare systems, circuit boards, and power supplies; backup disks with system software; and hard and soft copies of critical documentation
5. Recover virtual machines at an alternate site; assumes VMs have been updated to be current with production VMs	Create VM clones at an alternate site, keep them updated, and if needed they can quickly become production VMs
6. Activate alternate network routes and re-route data and voice traffic away from the failed network service	Ensure that network infrastructures have diverse routing of local access channels as well as diverse routing of high-capacity circuits [2]

business impact analysis A process that identifies all critical business functions and the effect that a specific disaster may have upon them.

emergency notification service An infrastructure built for notifying people in the event of an emergency.

Business Impact Analysis

A **business impact analysis** identifies all critical business functions and the effect that a specific disaster may have upon them. A business impact analysis is primarily used to ensure a company has made the right decisions about the order of recovery priorities and strategies. For example, should the accounting department have its systems up and running before the sales and marketing departments? Will email be the first system for recovery to ensure employees can communicate with each other and outside stakeholders such as customers, suppliers, and partners? The business impact analysis is a key part of BCP as it details the order in which functional areas should be restored, ensuring the most critical are focused on first.

Emergency Notification Services

A business continuity plan typically includes an **emergency notification service**, that is, an infrastructure built for notifying people in the event of an emergency. Radio stations' occasional tests of the national Emergency Alert System are an example of a very large-scale emergency notification system. A firm will implement an emergency notification service to warn employees of unexpected events and provide them with instructions about how to handle the situation. Emergency notification services can be deployed through the firm's own infrastructure, supplied by an outside service provider on company premises, or hosted remotely by an outside service provider. All three methods provide notification using a variety of methods such as email, voice notification to a cell phone, and text messaging. The notifications can be sent to all the devices selected, providing multiple means in which to get critical information to those who need it.

show me *the* MONEY

Recovering from Disaster

Backup and recovery are essential for any computer system. How painful would it be if someone stole your laptop right now? How much critical information would you lose? How many hours would it take you to re-create your data? Perhaps that will motivate you to implement a backup procedure. How many of you have a disaster recovery plan? Disaster recovery is needed when your best friend dumps a grande latte on your computer or you accidentally wash your thumb drive.

Disaster recovery plans are crucial for any business, and you should ensure that your company has everything it needs to continue operations if there is ever a disaster, such as 9/11. You need to decide which disasters are worth worrying about and which ones probably will never occur. For example, if you live in Colorado, chances are good you don't have to worry about hurricanes, but avalanches are another story.

How often does a company need to back up its data? Where should the backup be stored? What types of disasters should companies in your state prepare for in case of an emergency? Why is it important to test the backup? What could happen to a company if it failed to create a disaster recovery plan?

Technology Recovery Strategies Companies create massive amounts of data vital to their survival and continued operations. A **technology failure** occurs when the ability of a company to operate is impaired because of a hardware,

FIGURE 5.6 TechTarget's Business Continuity Strategies

BUSINESS CONTINUITY STRATEGIES	
1. Evacuate existing building and relocate to a prearranged alternate work area	Assumes the alternate site is ready for occupancy, or can be made ready quickly, based on recovery time objectives; ensure that transportation is available
2. Work from home	Ensure that staff have broadband and Internet access at home; ensure that there are sufficient network access points to accommodate the increase in usage
3. Move selected staff to a hot site.	Assumes a hot site program is in place and that space is available at the site for staff
4. Move alternate staff into leadership roles in the absence of key leaders; ensure that they have been cross-trained	Succession planning is a key strategy in business continuity; it ensures that loss of a senior manager or someone with special expertise can be replaced with minimal disruption to the business
5. Move staff into local or nearby hotels and set up temporary work space	Make sure this kind of arrangement is set up with hotels in advance, especially in case of an incident that disrupts many other businesses in the same area
6. Relocate staff to another company office	Organizations with multiple offices that have access to the company network as well as work space can be leveraged to temporarily house employees [4]

technology failure Occurs when the ability of a company to operate is impaired because of a hardware, software, or data outage.

incident Unplanned interruption of a service.

incident record Contains all of the details of an incident.

incident management The process responsible for managing how incidents are identified and corrected.

technology recovery strategies Focus specifically on prioritizing the order for restoring hardware, software, and data across the organization that best meets business recovery requirements.

software, or data outage. Technology failures can destroy large amounts of vital data, often causing **incidents**, unplanned interruption of a service. An **incident record** contains all of the details of an incident. **Incident management** is the process responsible for managing how incidents are identified and corrected. **Technology recovery strategies** focus specifically on prioritizing the order for restoring hardware, software, and data across the organization that best meets business recovery requirements. A technology recovery strategy details the order of importance for recovering hardware, software, data centers, and networking (or connectivity). If one of these four vital components is not functioning, the entire system will be unavailable, shutting down cross-functional business processes such as order management and payroll. Figure 5.7 displays the key areas a company should focus on when developing technology recovery strategies.

FIGURE 5.7 Key Areas of Technology Recovery Strategies

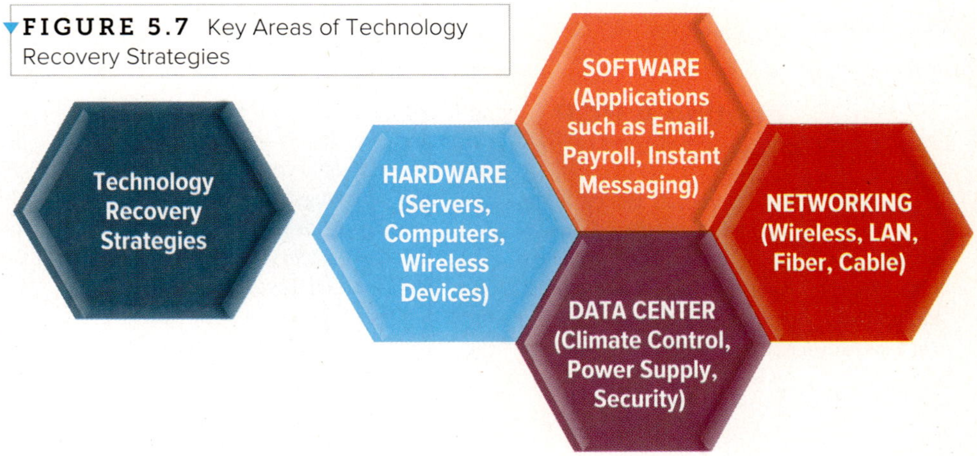

Due Diligence //:

Zombies Attack the University of Florida[5]

Backup and recovery are essential for any computer system. Hopefully, most of you have a backup of your data. If you have not, let me ask you a question: How painful would it be if someone stole your laptop right now? How much critical information would you lose? How many hours would it take you to re-create your data? Perhaps that will motivate you to implement a backup procedure. Now, how many of you have a disaster recovery plan? I'd be surprised if any of you have disaster recovery plans for your personal computers. Disaster recovery occurs when your best friend decides to dump a grande latte on your computer or your roommate accidentally washes your thumb drive.

Disaster recovery plans are crucial for any business, and you should ensure that your company has everything it needs to continue operations if there is ever a disaster, such as 9/11. Now, you need to decide which disasters are worth worrying about and which ones are probably never going to occur. For example, if you live in Colorado, chances are good you don't have to worry about hurricanes, but avalanches are another story. There are a few companies that take disaster recovery too far, such as the University of Florida that lists the disaster recovery plans for a zombie apocalypse on its disaster recovery website. Yes, you read that correctly. The zombie apocalypse disaster recovery exercise details how the school could respond to an outbreak of the undead, along with plans for dealing with hurricanes and pandemics. I guess you can never be too prepared to deal with the unexpected!

© Ian McDonnell/Getty Images RF

How often does a company need to back up its data? Where should the backup be stored? What types of disasters should companies in your state prepare for in case of an emergency? Why is it important to test the backup? What could happen to a company if it failed to back up its data and applications?

accessibility Refers to the varying levels that define what a user can access, view, or perform when operating a system.

administrator access Unrestricted access to the entire system.

web accessibility Means that people with disabilities—including visual, auditory, physical, speech, cognitive, and neurological disabilities—can use the web.

web accessibility initiative (WAI) Brings together people from industry, disability organizations, government, and research labs from around the world to develop guidelines and resources to help make the web accessible to people with disabilities, including auditory, cognitive, neurological, physical, speech, and visual disabilities.

fyi

Creating A BCP Plan

Business disruption costs money. In the event of a disaster or emergency, you will not only lose revenue, you will also incur additional expenses. If you are expecting your insurance to cover your losses, be careful—there are many losses your insurance will not cover such as lost sales, lost business intelligence, and lost customers. To mitigate the risks of a catastrophe, you will want to create a detailed business continuity plan. A business continuity plan (BCP) is not only a good idea but also one of the least expensive plans a company can develop. A BCP will detail how employees will contact each other and continue to keep operations functioning in the event of a disaster or emergency such as a fire or flood. Regrettably, many companies never take the time to develop such a plan until it is too late.

Research the web for sample BCP plans for a small business or a start-up. In a group, create a BCP for a start-up of your choice. Be sure to think of such things as data storage, data access, transaction processing, employee safety, and customer communications.

SUPPORTING CHANGE: AGILE MIS INFRASTRUCTURE LO5.3

Agile MIS infrastructure includes the hardware, software, and telecommunications equipment that, when combined, provides the underlying foundation to support the organization's goals. If a company grows by 50 percent in a single year, its infrastructure and systems must be able to handle a 50 percent growth rate. If they cannot, they can severely hinder the company's ability not only to grow but also to function.

The future of a company depends on its ability to meet its partners, suppliers, and customers any time of the day in any geographic location. Imagine owning an ebusiness and everyone on the Internet is tweeting and collaborating about how great your business idea is and how successful your company is going to be. Suddenly, you have 5 million global customers interested in your website. Unfortunately, you did not anticipate this many customers so quickly, and the system crashes. Users typing in your URL find a blank message stating the website is unavailable and to try back soon. Or even worse, they can get to your website but it takes three minutes to reload each time they click on a button. The buzz soon dies about your business idea as some innovative web-savvy fast follower quickly copies your idea and creates a website that can handle the massive number of customers. The characteristics of agile MIS infrastructures can help ensure your systems can meet and perform under any unexpected or unplanned changes. Figure 5.8 lists the seven abilities of an agile infrastructure.

LO5.3 Describe the characteristics of an agile MIS infrastructure.

Accessibility

Accessibility refers to the varying levels that define what a user can access, view, or perform when operating a system. Imagine the people at your college accessing the main student information system. Each person that accesses the system will have different needs and requirements; for example, a payroll employee will need to access vacation information and salary information, or a student will need to access course information and billing information. Each system user is provided with an access level that details which parts of the system the user can and cannot access and what the user can do when in the system. For example, you would not want your students to be able to view payroll information or professor's personal information; also, some users can only view information and are not allowed to create or delete information. Top-level MIS employees require **administrator access**, or unrestricted access to the entire system. Administrator access can perform functions such as resetting passwords, deleting accounts, and shutting down entire systems.

Tim Berners-Lee, W3C director and inventor of the World Wide Web, stated, "the power of the web is in its universality. Access by everyone regardless of disability is an essential aspect." **Web accessibility** means that people with disabilities, including visual, auditory, physical, speech, cognitive, and neurological disabilities, can use the web. The **web accessibility initiative (WAI)** brings together people from industry, disability organizations, government, and research labs from around the world to develop guidelines and resources to help make the web accessible to people with disabilities, including auditory, cognitive, neurological, physical, speech, and visual disabilities. The goal of WAI is to allow people to access the full potential of the web, enabling people with disabilities to participate equally. For example, Apple includes screen magnification and VoiceOver on its iPhone, iPad, and iPod, which allows the blind and visually impaired to use the devices.

Availability

In a 24/7/365 ebusiness environment, business professionals need to use their systems whenever they want from wherever they want. **Availability** refers to the time frames when the system is operational. A system is called **unavailable** when it is not operating and cannot be used. **High availability** occurs when a system is continuously operational at all times. Availability is typically measured relative to "100 percent operational" or "never failing." A widely held but difficult-to-achieve standard of availability for a system is known as "five 9s" (99.999 percent) availability. Some companies have systems available around the clock to support ebusiness operations, global customers, and online suppliers.

Sometimes systems must be taken down for maintenance, upgrades, and fixes, which are completed during downtime. One challenge with availability is determining when to schedule system downtime if the system is expected to operate continuously. Performing maintenance during the evening might seem like a great idea, but evening in one city is morning somewhere else in the world, and business professionals scattered around the globe may not be able to perform specific job functions if the systems they need are unavailable. This is where companies deploy failover systems so they can take the primary system down for maintenance and activate the secondary system to ensure continuous operations.

Maintainability

Companies must watch today's needs, as well as tomorrow's, when designing and building systems that support agile infrastructures. Systems must be flexible enough to meet all types of company changes, environmental changes, and business

FIGURE 5.8 Agile MIS Infrastructure Characteristics

Characteristic	Description
Accessibility	• Varying levels allow system users to access, view, or perform operational functions.
Availability	• The system is operational during different time frames.
Maintainability	• The system quickly transforms to support environmental changes.
Portability	• The system is available to operate on different devices or software platforms.
Reliability	• The system functions correctly and provides accurate information.
Scalability	• The system can "scale up" or adapt to the increased demands of growth.
Usability	• The system is easy to learn and efficient and satisfying to use.

availability Refers to the time frames when the system is operational.

unavailable When a system is not operating or cannot be used.

high availability Occurs when a system is continuously operational at all times.

maintainability (or flexibility) Refers to how quickly a system can transform to support environmental changes.

portability Refers to the ability of an application to operate on different devices or software platforms, such as different operating systems.

reliability (or accuracy) Ensures a system is functioning correctly and providing accurate information.

vulnerability A system weakness that can be exploited by a threat; for example, a password that is never changed or a system left on while an employee goes to lunch.

changes. **Maintainability (or flexibility)** refers to how quickly a system can transform to support environmental changes. Maintainability helps to measure how quickly and effectively a system can be changed or repaired after a failure. For example, when starting a small business you might not consider that you will have global customers, a common mistake. When building your systems, you might not design them to handle multiple currencies and different languages, which might make sense if the company is not currently performing international business. Unfortunately, when the first international order arrives, which happens easily with ebusiness, the system will be unable to handle the request because it does not have the flexibility to be easily reconfigured for a new language or currency. When the company does start growing and operating overseas, the system will need to be redeveloped, which is not an easy or cheap task, to handle multiple currencies and different languages.

Building and deploying flexible systems allow easy updates, changes, and reconfigurations for unexpected business or environmental changes. Just think what might have happened if Facebook had to overhaul its entire system to handle multiple languages. Another social networking business could easily have stepped in and become the provider of choice. That certainly would not be efficient or effective for business operations.

Portability

Portability refers to the ability of an application to operate on different devices or software platforms, such as different operating systems. Apple's iTunes is readily available to users of Mac computers and also users of PC computers, smartphones, iPods, iPhones, iPads, and so on. It is also a portable application. Because Apple insists on compatibility across its products, both software and hardware, Apple can easily add to its product, device, and service offerings without sacrificing portability. Many software developers are creating programs that are portable to all three devices—the iPhone, iPod, and iPad—which increases their target market and, they hope, their revenue.

Reliability

Reliability (or accuracy) ensures a system is functioning correctly and providing accurate information. Inaccuracy can occur for many reasons, from the incorrect entry of information to the corruption of information during transmissions. Many argue that the information contained in Wikipedia is unreliable. Because the Wikipedia entries can be edited by any user, there are examples of rogue users inaccurately updating information. Many users skip over Google search findings that correlate to Wikipedia for this reason. Housing unreliable information on a website can put a company at risk of losing customers, placing inaccurate supplier orders, or even making unreliable business decisions. A **vulnerability** is a system weakness, such as a password that is never changed or a system left on while an employee goes to lunch, that can be exploited by a threat. Reliable systems ensure that vulnerabilities are kept at a minimum to reduce risk.

show me *the* MONEY

Ranking the -ilities

Agile MIS infrastructure includes the hardware, software, and telecommunications equipment that, when combined, provide the underlying foundation to support the organization's goals. As an organization changes, its systems must be able to change to support its operations. If an organization grows by 50 percent in a single year, its systems must be able to handle a 50 percent growth rate. Systems that cannot adapt to organizational changes can severely hinder the organization's ability to operate. The future of an organization depends on its ability to meet its partners and customers on their terms, at their pace, any time of the day, in any geographic location.

Evaluate the agile MIS infrastructure for your school. Review the list of agile MIS infrastructure characteristics and rank them in order of their impact on your school's success. Use a rating system of 1 to 7, where 1 indicates the biggest impact and 7 indicates the least impact.

Agile MIS Infrastructure Qualities	Business Impact
Accessibility	
Availability	
Maintainability	
Portability	
Reliability	
Scalability	
Usability	

scalability Describes how well a system can scale up or adapt to the increased demands of growth.

performance Measures how quickly a system performs a process or transaction.

capacity Represents the maximum throughput a system can deliver; for example, the capacity of a hard drive represents the size or volume.

capacity planning Determines future environmental infrastructure requirements to ensure high-quality system performance.

usability The degree to which a system is easy to learn and efficient and satisfying to use.

serviceability How quickly a third party or vendor can change a system to ensure it meets user needs and the terms of any contracts, including agreed levels of reliability, maintainability or availability.

Scalability

Estimating company growth is a challenging task, in part because growth can occur in a number of different forms—the firm can acquire new customers, new product lines, or new markets. **Scalability** describes how well a system can scale up, or adapt to the increased demands of growth. If a company grows faster than anticipated, it might experience a variety of problems, from running out of storage space to taking more time to complete transactions. Anticipating expected, and unexpected, growth is key to building scalable systems that can support that development.

Performance measures how quickly a system performs a process or transaction. Performance is a key component of scalability as systems that can't scale suffer from performance issues. Just imagine your college's content management system suddenly taking five minutes to return a page after a button is pushed. Now imagine if this occurs during your midterm exam and you miss the two-hour deadline because the system is so slow. Performance issues experienced by firms can have disastrous business impacts causing loss of customers, loss of suppliers, and even loss of help-desk employees. Most users will wait only a few seconds for a website to return a request before growing frustrated and either calling the support desk or giving up and moving on to another website.

Capacity represents the maximum throughput a system can deliver; for example, the capacity of a hard drive represents its size or volume. **Capacity planning** determines future environmental infrastructure requirements to ensure high-quality system performance. If a company purchases connectivity software that is outdated or too slow to meet demand, its employees will waste a great deal of time waiting for systems to respond to user requests. It is cheaper for a company to design and implement agile infrastructure that envisions growth requirements than to update all the equipment after the system is already operational. If a company with 100 workers merges with another company and suddenly there are 400 people using the system, performance time could suffer. Planning for increases in capacity can ensure systems perform as expected. Waiting for a system to respond to requests is not productive.

Web 2.0 is a big driver for capacity planning to ensure agile infrastructures can meet the business's operational needs. Delivering videos over the Internet requires enough bandwidth to satisfy millions of users during peak periods such as Friday and Saturday evenings. Video transmissions over the Internet cannot tolerate packet loss (blocks of data loss), and allowing one additional user to access the system could degrade the video quality for every user.

Usability

Usability is the degree to which a system is easy to learn and efficient and satisfying to use. Providing hints, tips, shortcuts, and instructions for any system, regardless of its ease of use, is recommended. Apple understood the importance of usability when it designed the first iPod. One of the iPod's initial attractions was the usability of the click wheel. One simple and efficient button operates the iPod, making it usable for all ages. And to ensure ease of use, Apple also made the corresponding iTunes software intuitive and easy to use. **Serviceability** is how quickly a third party can change a system to ensure it meets user needs and the terms of any contracts, including agreed levels of reliability, maintainability, or availability. When using a system from a third party, it is important to ensure the right level of serviceability for all users, including remote employees.

{SECTION 5.2} Building Sustainable MIS Infrastructures

LEARNING OUTCOMES

LO5.4 Identify the environmental impacts associated with MIS.

LO5.5 Explain the three components of a sustainable MIS infrastructure along with their business benefits.

Moore's Law Refers to the computer chip performance per dollar doubling every 18 months.

sustainable, or "green," MIS Describes the production, management, use, and disposal of technology in a way that minimizes damage to the environment.

corporate social responsibility Companies' acknowledged responsibility to society.

clean computing A subset of sustainable MIS, refers to the environmentally responsible use, manufacture, and disposal of technology products and computer equipment.

green personal computer (green PC) Built using environment-friendly materials and designed to save energy.

MIS AND THE ENVIRONMENT LO5.4

The general trend in MIS is toward smaller, faster, and cheaper devices. Gordon Moore, co-founder of Intel, the world's largest producer of computer chips or microprocessors, observed in 1965 that continued advances in technological innovation made it possible to reduce the size of a computer chip (the brains of a computer, or even a cell phone now) while doubling its capacity every two years. His prediction that this trend would continue has come to be known as **Moore's Law**, which refers to the computer chip performance per dollar doubles every 18 months. Although Moore originally assumed a two-year period, many sources today refer to the 18-month figure.

Moore's Law is great for many companies because they can acquire large amounts of MIS equipment for cheaper and cheaper costs. As ebusinesses continue to grow, companies equip their employees with multiple forms of electronic devices ranging from laptops to cell phones to iPads. This is great for supporting a connected corporation, but significant unintended side effects include our dependence on fossil fuels and increased need for safe disposal of outdated computing equipment. Concern about these side effects has led many companies to turn to an ecological practice known as sustainable MIS. **Sustainable, or green, MIS** describes the production, management, use, and disposal of technology in a way that minimizes damage to the environment. Sustainable MIS is a critical part of **corporate social responsibility**, that is, companies' acknowledged responsibility to society. **Clean computing**, a subset of sustainable MIS, refers to the environmentally responsible use, manufacture, and disposal of technology products and computer equipment. Although sustainable MIS refers to the environmental impact of computing as a whole, clean computing is specifically focused on the production of environmental waste. A **green personal computer (green PC)** is built using environment-friendly materials and designed to save energy. Building sustainable MIS infrastructures is a core initiative and critical success factor for socially responsible corporations. Figure 5.9 displays the three primary side effects of businesses' expanded use of technology.

LO5.4 Identify the environmental impacts associated with MIS.

Increased Electronic Waste

Moore's Law has made technological devices smaller, cheaper, and faster, allowing more people from all income levels to purchase computing equipment. This increased demand is causing

FIGURE 5.9 Three Pressures Driving Sustainable MIS Infrastructures

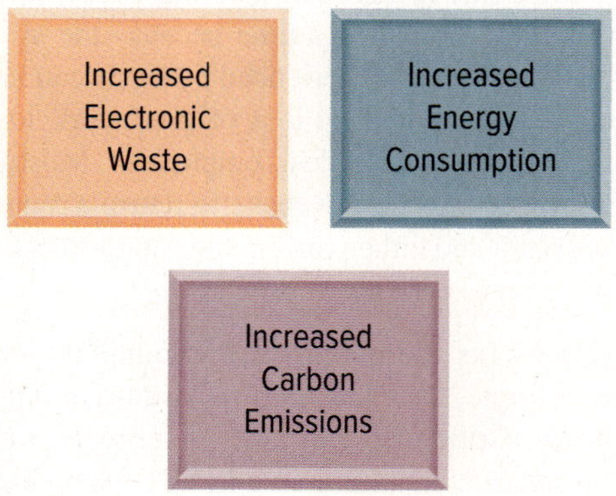

Due Diligence //: Laptop? Notebook? Netbook? Tablet?

Thanks to Moore's Law, computing devices are getting smaller, cheaper, and faster every year, allowing innovative companies to create new devices that are smaller and more powerful than current devices. Just look at desktop, laptop, notebook, and tablet computers. These are all different devices allowing users to connect and compute around the globe. Moore's Law has been accurate about computing power roughly doubling every 18 months. Do you agree or disagree that Moore's Law will continue to apply for the next 20 years? Why or why not?

Living the DREAM

Solving The Ewaste Problem

The United States disposes of more than 384 million units of ewaste yearly and currently recycles less than 20 percent, according to the Electronics TakeBack Coalition. The remaining 80 percent is burned or dumped in landfills, leaking toxic substances such as mercury, lead, cadmium, arsenic, and beryllium into the environment. Reports predict that ewaste will weigh as much as 200 Empire State Buildings by 2017. **S**olving **t**he **E**waste **P**roblem (**StEP**) Initiative is a group represented by the United Nations organizations, governments, and science organizations, and their mission is to ensure safe and responsible ewaste disposal. StEP predicts ewaste will grow by a third in the next five years with the United States and China being the biggest contributors. Until recently, comprehensive data on global ewaste has been hard to collect because the definition of ewaste differs among countries. For example, the United States only includes consumer electronics such as TVs and computers, whereas Europe includes everything that has a battery or power cord in the ewaste category.[6]

© Alan Thornton/Getty Images

The growth of ewaste is an opportunity for entrepreneurs. Research the web and find examples of schools around the country that are responsibly tackling the ewaste problem. In a group, create a plan for implementing an ewaste recycling program at your school.

numerous environmental issues. **Ewaste** refers to discarded, obsolete, or broken electronic devices. Ewaste includes CDs, DVDs, thumb drives, printer cartridges, cell phones, iPods, external hard drives, TVs, VCRs, DVD players, microwaves, and so on. Some say one human year is equivalent to seven years of technological advancements. A personal computer has a life expectancy of only three to five years and a cell phone is less than two years. An **upcycle** reuses or refurbishes ewaste and creates a new product.

Sustainable MIS disposal refers to the safe disposal of MIS assets at the end of their life cycle. It ensures that ewaste does not end up in landfills causing environmental issues. A single computer contains more than 700 chemicals; some are toxic, such as mercury, lead, and cadmium. If a computer ends up in a landfill, the toxic substances it contains can leach into our land, water, and air. Recycling costs from $15 to $50 for a monitor or computer. Many companies, including public schools and universities, simply can't afford the recycling costs.[7]

Ewaste also occurs when unused equipment stored in attics, basements, and storage facilities never reaches a recycling center. Retrieving the silver, gold, and other valuable metals from these devices is more efficient and less environmentally harmful than removing it from its natural environment.

Currently, less than 20 percent of ewaste in the United States is recycled; however, even recycling does not guarantee the

fyi

Ewaste and the Environment

By some estimates, there may be as many as 1 billion surplus or obsolete computers and monitors in the world. Consider California, where 6,000 computers become surplus every day. If not disposed of properly, this enormous ewaste stream, which can contain more than 1,000 toxic substances, is harmful to human beings and the environment. Beryllium is found in computer motherboards, chromium in floppy disks, lead in batteries and computer monitors, and mercury in alkaline batteries. One of the most toxic chemicals known is cadmium, found in many old laptops and computer chips.

In poorer countries, where the United States and Europe export some of their ewaste, the full impact of the environmental damage is quickly being realized. These areas have little use for obsolete electronic equipment so local recyclers resell some parts and burn the rest in illegal dumps, often near residential areas, releasing toxic and carcinogenic substances into the air, land, and water.[9]

Have you ever participated in ewaste? What can you do to ensure that you are safely disposing of electronic equipment including batteries? What can governments do to encourage companies to dispose of ewaste safely? What can be done to protect poorer countries from receiving ewaste? Create a list of the ways you can safely dispose of cell phones, computers, printers, ink cartridges, MP3 players, and batteries. What could you do to inform citizens of the issues associated with ewaste and educate them on safe disposal practices?

ewaste Refers to discarded, obsolete, or broken electronic devices.

upcycle Reuses or refurbishes ewaste and creates a new product.

sustainable MIS disposal Refers to the safe disposal of MIS assets at the end of their life cycle.

energy consumption The amount of energy consumed by business processes and systems.

carbon emissions Includes the carbon dioxide and carbon monoxide in the atmosphere, produced by business processes and systems.

Living the DREAM

Smart Cities[8]

Smart cities are being created around the globe with the use of advanced technology coupled with strong government. Smart cities use mobility, construction, energy, transportation, and the latest green technology in new and innovative ways to help the environment. A few examples include:

- San Francisco's California Academy of Sciences building sports a living roof and is one of the most sustainable structures in the world. Its 2.5-acre "living roof" features local plants and a glass canopy of photovoltaic cells that produces energy for the building.
- Stockholm uses sensors, software, and computer networks to monitor traffic during peak periods.
- Shanghai boasts the world's first low-pollution magnetic railway that transports passengers at more than 100 mph.
- Massachusetts plans to install 300 wind turbines in its towns and cities.
- San Francisco's smart trash provides incentives and a go-green attitude to induce San Franciscans to recycle 72 percent of their refuse. SF Recycling & Disposal sorts glass, plastic, and paper products at Pier 96 and presses the materials into compact cubes.

What types of programs are being deployed in your city to green the environment? What types of programs are being deployed around your school to help green the environment? Devise a new program using technology that your school could implement to help green the environment.

© Rob Crandall/Alamy

equipment is disposed of safely. While some recyclers process the material ethically, others ship it to countries such as China and India, where environmental enforcement is weak. This action poses its own global environmental problems.

Increased Energy Consumption

Energy consumption is the amount of energy consumed by business processes and systems. Huge increases in technology use have greatly amplified energy consumption. The energy consumed by a computer is estimated to produce as much as 10 percent of the amount of carbon dioxide produced by an automobile. Computer servers in the United States account for about 1 percent of the total energy needs of the country. Put in perspective, this is roughly equivalent to the energy consumption of Mississippi.

Computers consume energy even when they are not being used. For convenience and to allow for automatic updates and backup, the majority of computer equipment is never completely shut down. It draws energy 24 hours a day.

Increased Carbon Emissions

The major human-generated greenhouse gases, such as carbon emissions from energy use, are very likely responsible for the increases in climatic temperature over the past half a century. Additional temperature increases are projected over the next hundred years, with serious consequences for Earth's environment, if **carbon emissions**, including the carbon dioxide and carbon monoxide produced by business processes and systems, are not reduced.

In the United States, coal provides more than 50 percent of electrical power. When left on continuously, a single desktop computer and monitor can consume at least 100 watts of power per hour. To generate that much energy 24 hours a day for a year would require approximately 714 pounds of coal. When that coal is burned, it releases on average 5 pounds of sulfur dioxide, 5 pounds of nitrogen oxides, and 1,852 pounds (that is almost a ton) of carbon dioxide.[10]

SUPPORTING THE ENVIRONMENT: SUSTAINABLE MIS INFRASTRUCTURE LO5.5

Combating ewaste, energy consumption, and carbon emissions requires a firm to focus on creating sustainable MIS infrastructures. A sustainable MIS infrastructure identifies ways that a company can grow in terms of computing resources while simultaneously becoming less dependent on hardware and energy consumption. The components of a sustainable MIS infrastructure are displayed in Figure 5.10.

LO5.5 Explain the three components of a sustainable MIS infrastructure along with their business benefits.

Grid Computing

When a light is turned on, the power grid delivers exactly what is needed, instantly. Computers and networks can now work that way using grid computing. **Grid computing** is a collection of computers, often geographically dispersed, that are coordinated to solve a common problem. With grid computing a problem is broken into pieces and distributed to many machines, allowing faster processing than could occur with a single system (see Figure 5.11). Computers typically use less than 25 percent of their processing power, leaving more than 75 percent available for other tasks. Innovatively, grid computing takes advantage of this unused processing power by linking thousands of individual computers around the world to create a "virtual supercomputer" that can process intensive tasks. Grid computing makes better use of MIS resources, allowing greater scalability as systems can easily grow to handle peaks and valleys in demand, become more cost efficient, and solve problems that would be impossible to tackle with a single computer (see Figures 5.12 and Figure 5.13).[12]

grid computing A collection of computers, often geographically dispersed, that are coordinated to solve a common problem.

The uses of grid computing are numerous, including the creative environment of animated movies. DreamWorks Animation used grid computing to complete many of its hit films including *Antz, Shrek, Madagascar,* and *How to Train Your Dragon.* The third *Shrek* film required more than 20 million computer hours to make (compared to 5 million for the first *Shrek* and 10 million for the second). At peak production times, DreamWorks dedicated more than 4,000 computers to its *Shrek* grid, allowing it to complete scenes in days and hours instead of months. With the increased grid computing power, the DreamWork's animators were able to add more realistic movement to water, fire, and magic scenes (see Figure 5.14). With grid computing a company can work faster or more efficiently, providing a potential competitive advantage and additional cost savings.[13]

show me the MONEY

How Big is Your Carbon Footprint?

Inevitably, in going about our daily lives—commuting, sheltering our families, eating—each of us contributes to the greenhouse gas emissions that are causing climate change. Yet, there are many things each of us, as individuals, can do to reduce our carbon emissions. The choices we make in our homes, our travel, the food we eat, and what we buy and throw away all influence our carbon footprint and can help ensure a stable climate for future generations.[11]

The Nature Conservancy's carbon footprint calculator measures your impact on our climate. Its carbon footprint calculator estimates how many tons of carbon dioxide and other greenhouse gases your choices create each year. Visit the Nature Conservancy's carbon footprint calculator to determine your carbon footprint and what you can do to reduce your emissions (http://www.nature.org/greenliving/carboncalculator/).

smart grid Delivers electricity using two-way digital technology.

virtualization Creates multiple "virtual" machines on a single computing device.

storage virtualization Combines multiple network storage devices so they appear to be a single storage device.

network virtualization Combines networks by splitting the available bandwidth into independent channels that can be assigned in real time to a specific device.

server virtualization Combines the physical resources, such as servers, processors, and operating systems, from the applications.

FIGURE 5.10 Sustainable MIS Infrastructure Components

GRID COMPUTING	VIRTUALIZATION	CLOUD COMPUTING
• A collection of computers, often geographically dispersed, that are coordinated to solve a common problem	• Creates multiple virtual machines on a single computing device	• Stores, manages, and processes data and applications over the Internet rather than on a personal computer or server

Solving the Energy Issue with Smart Grids A **smart grid** delivers electricity using two-way digital technology. It is meant to solve the problem of the world's outdated electrical grid, making it more efficient and reliable by adding the ability to remotely monitor, analyze, and control the transmission of power. The current U.S. power grid is said to have outlived its life expectancy by as much as 30 years. Smart grids provide users with real-time usage monitoring, allowing them to choose off-peak times for noncritical or less urgent applications or processes. Residents of Boulder, Colorado, can monitor their use of electricity and control appliances remotely due to the city's large-scale smart grid system. Xcel Energy has installed 21,000 smart grid meters since the $100 million program started several years ago. Energy use by early adopters is down as much as 45 percent.[14]

Virtualized Computing

Most computers and even servers typically run only one operating system, such as Windows or Mac OS, and only one application. When a company invests in a large system such as inventory management, it dedicates a single server to house the system. This ensures the system has enough capacity to run during peak times and to scale to meet demand. Also, many systems have specific hardware requirements along with detailed software requirements, making it difficult to find two systems with the same requirements that could share the same machine. Through the use of virtualization, computers can run multiple operating systems along with multiple software applications—all at the same time. **Virtualization** creates multiple "virtual" machines on a single computing device. A good analogy is a computer printer. In the past you had to purchase a fax machine, copy machine, answering machine, and computer printer separately. This was expensive, required enough energy to run four separate machines, not to mention created additional amounts of ewaste. Today, you can buy a virtualized computer printer that functions as a fax machine, answering machine, and copy machine all on one physical machine, thereby reducing costs, power requirements, and ewaste. Virtualization is essentially a form of consolidation that can benefit sustainable MIS infrastructures in a variety of ways, for example:

- By increasing availability of applications that can give a higher level of performance depending on the hardware used.
- By increasing energy efficiency by requiring less hardware to run multiple systems or applications.
- By increasing hardware usability by running multiple operating systems on a single computer.

Originally, computers were designed to run a single application on a single operating system. This left most computers vastly underutilized (as mentioned earlier, 75 percent of most computing power is available for other tasks). Virtualization allows multiple virtual computers to exist on a single machine, which allows it to share its resources, such as memory and hard disk space, to run different applications and even different operating systems. Mac computers have the ability to run both the Apple

FIGURE 5.11 Virtual Organizations Using Grid Computing.

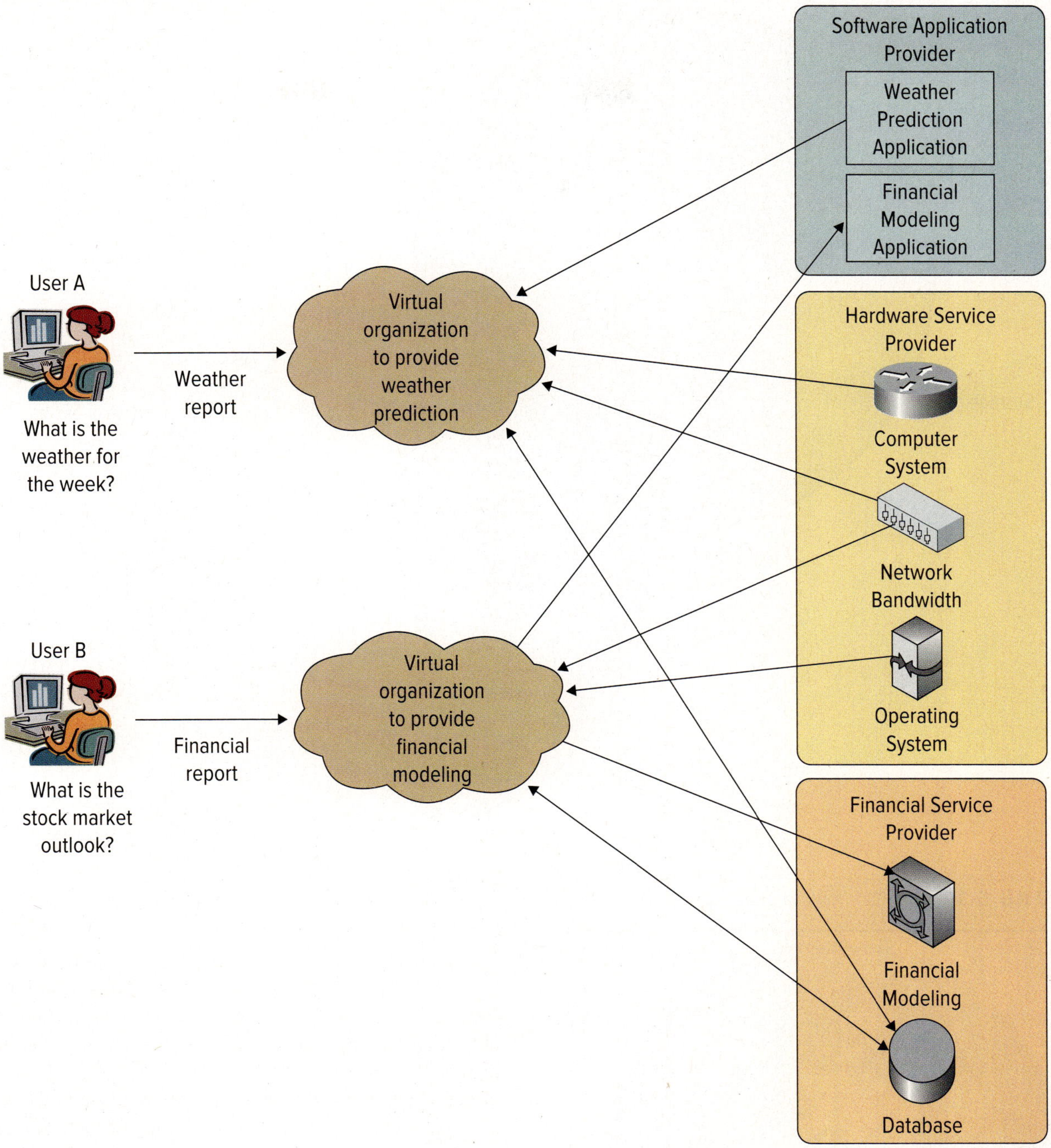

operating system and the Windows PC operating system, with the use of virtualization software (see Figure 5.15). Unfortunately, virtualization, at least at the moment, is not available for a PC to run Mac software. There are three basic categories of virtualization:

- **Storage virtualization** combines multiple network storage devices so they appear to be a single storage device.
- **Network virtualization** combines networks by splitting the available bandwidth into independent channels that can be assigned in real time to a specific device.
- **Server virtualization** combines the physical resources, such as servers, processors, and operating systems, from the applications. (This is the most common form and typically when you hear the term virtualization, you can assume server virtualization.)

Virtualization is also one of the easiest and quickest ways to achieve a sustainable MIS infrastructure because it reduces power consumption and requires less equipment that needs to be manufactured, maintained, and later disposed of safely. Managers no longer have to assign servers, storage, or network

FIGURE 5.12 Grid Computer Network.

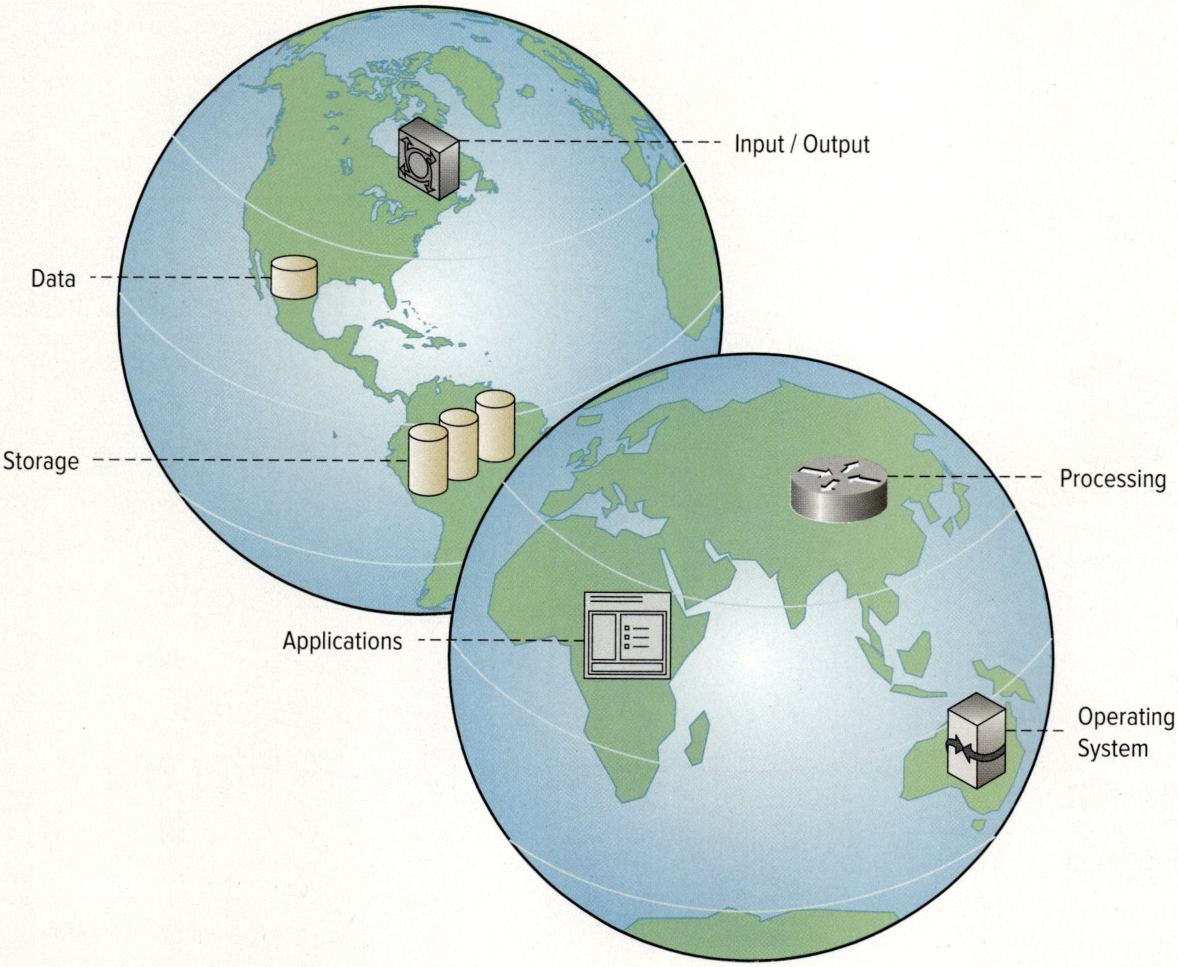

FIGURE 5.13 Grid Computing Example

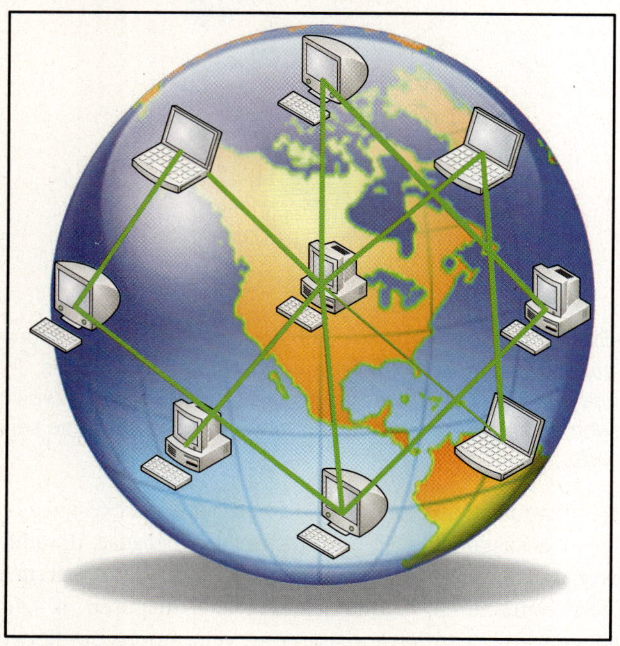

capacity permanently to single applications. Instead, they can assign the hardware resources when and where they are needed, achieving the availability, flexibility, and scalability a company needs to thrive and grow. Also, by virtually separating the operating system and applications from the hardware, if there is a disaster or hardware failure, it is easy to port the virtual machine to a new physical machine allowing a company to recovery quickly from disasters. One of the primary uses of virtualization is for performing backup, recovery, and disaster recovery. Using virtual servers or a virtualization service provider, such as Google, Microsoft, or Amazon, to host disaster recovery is more sustainable than a single company incurring the expense of having redundant physical systems. Also, these providers' data centers are built to withstand natural disasters and are typically located far away from big cities (see Figure 5.16).

System virtualization is the ability to present the resources of a single computer as if it is a collection of separate computers ("virtual machines"), each with its own virtual CPUs, network interfaces, storage, and operating system.

FIGURE 5.14 Making *Shrek 2* with Grid Computing

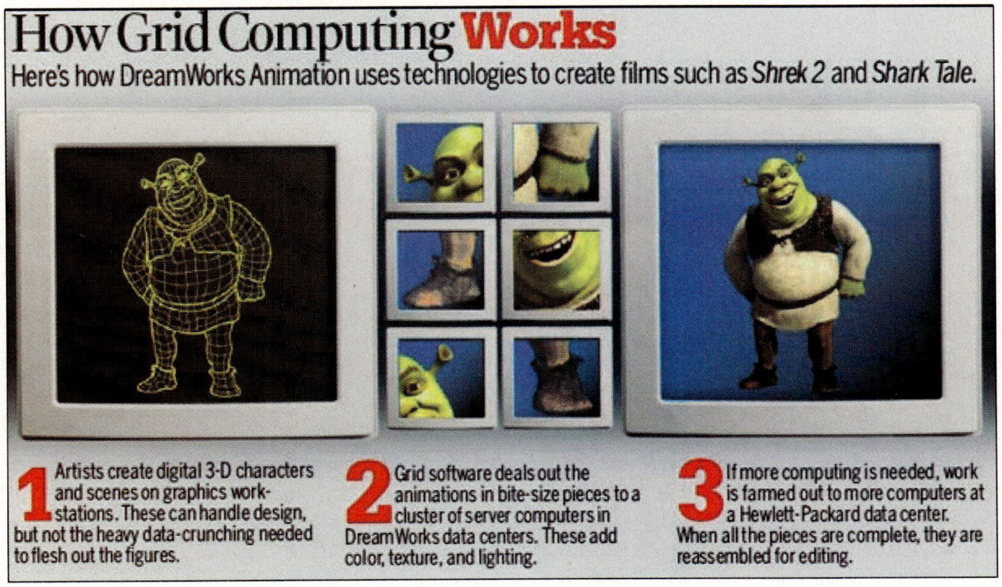

Reproduced with permission of Bloomberg Businessweek Magazine

system virtualization The ability to present the resources of a single computer as if it is a collection of separate computers ("virtual machines"), each with its own virtual CPUs, network interfaces, storage, and operating system.

data center A facility used to house management information systems and associated components, such as telecommunications and storage systems.

FIGURE 5.15 Virtualization Allows an Apple Macintosh Computer to Run OS X and Windows

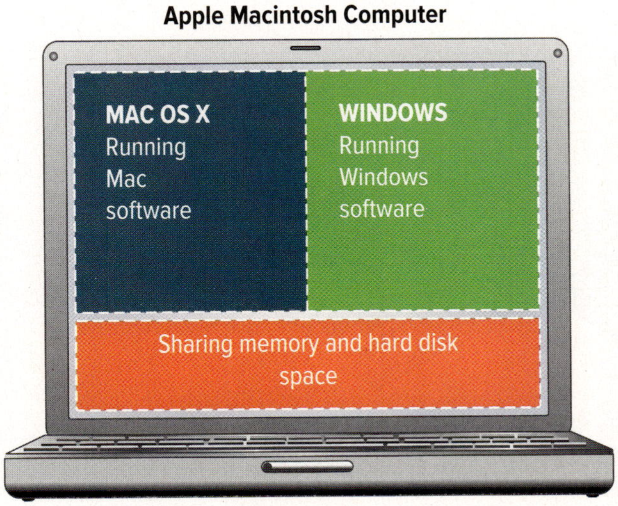

Virtual machine technology was first implemented on mainframes in the 1960s to allow the expensive systems to be partitioned into separate domains and used more efficiently by more users and applications. As standard PC servers became more powerful in the past decade, virtualization has been brought to the desktop and notebook processors to provide the same benefits.

Virtual machines appear both to the user within the system and the world outside as separate computers, each with its own network identity, user authorization and authentication capabilities, operating system version and configuration, applications, and data. The hardware is consistent across all virtual machines: While the number or size of them may differ, devices are used that allow virtual machines to be portable, independent of the actual hardware type on the underlying systems. Figure 5.17 shows an overview of what a system virtualization framework looks like.

Virtual Data Centers A **data center** is a facility used to house management information systems and associated components, such as telecommunications and storage systems. Data centers, sometimes referred to as server farms, consume power and require cooling and floor space while working to support business growth without disrupting normal business operations and the quality of service. The amount of data a data center stores has grown exponentially over the years as our reliance on information increases. Backups, graphics, documents, presentations, photos, audio and video files all contribute to the ever-expanding information footprint that requires storage. One of the most effective ways to limit the power consumption and cooling requirements of a data center is to consolidate parts of the physical infrastructure, particularly by reducing the number of physical servers through virtualization. For this reason, virtualization is having a profound impact on data centers as the sheer number of servers a company requires to operate decreases, thereby boosting growth and performance while reducing environmental impact, as shown in Figure 5.18. Google, Microsoft, Amazon, and Yahoo! have all created data centers along the Columbia River in the northwestern United States. In this area, each company can benefit from affordable land, high-speed Internet access, plentiful water for cooling, and even more important, inexpensive electricity. These factors are critical to today's large-scale data centers, whose sheer size

FIGURE 5.16 Virtualization Architecture

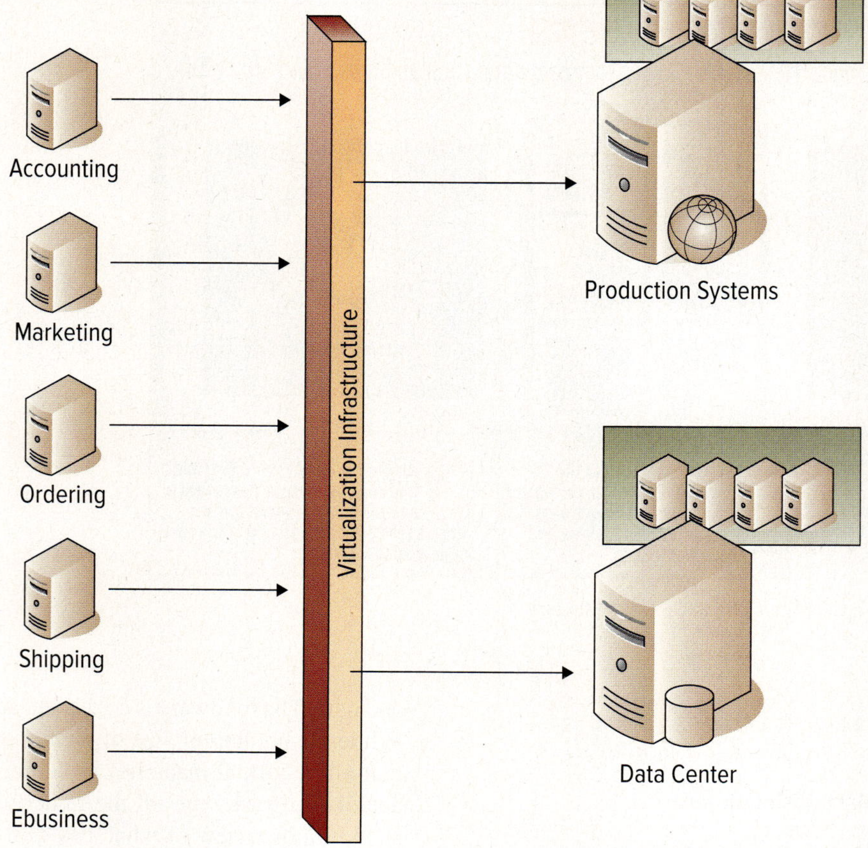

FIGURE 5.17 System Virtualization

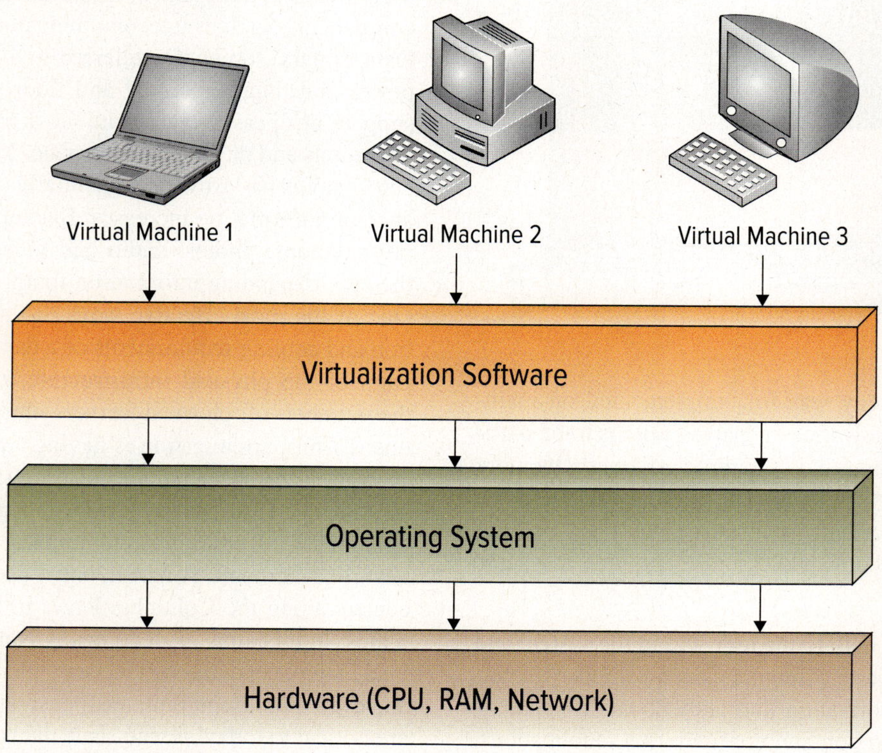

and power needs far surpass those of the previous generation. Microsoft's data center in Quincy, Washington, is larger than 10 football fields and is powered entirely by hydroelectricity, power generated from flowing water rather than from the burning of coal or other fossil fuel.[15]

If we take a holistic and integrated approach to overall company growth, the benefits of integrating information MIS infrastructures, environmental MIS infrastructures, and sustainable MIS infrastructures become obvious. For example, a company could easily create a backup of its software and important information in one or more geographically dispersed locations using cloud computing. This would be far cheaper than building its own hot and cold sites in different areas of the country. In the case of a security breach, failover can be deployed as a virtual machine in one location of the cloud can be shut down as another virtual machine in a different location on the cloud comes online.

Cloud Computing

Imagine a cyclical business that specializes in Halloween decorations and how its sales trends and orders vary depending on the time of year. The majority of sales occur in September and October, and the remaining 10 months have relatively small sales and small system usage. The company does not want to invest in massive expensive servers that sit idle 10 months of the year just to meet its capacity spikes in September and October. The perfect solution for this company is cloud computing, which makes it easier to gain access to the computing power that was once reserved for large corporations. Small to medium-size companies no longer have to make big capital investments to access the same powerful systems that large companies run.

cloud computing Stores, manages, and processes data and applications over the Internet rather than on a personal computer or server.

According to the National Institute of Standards and Technology (NIST) **cloud computing** is a model for enabling ubiquitous, convenient, on-demand network access to a shared pool of configurable computing resources (e.g., networks, servers, storage, applications, and services) that can be rapidly provisioned and released with minimal management effort or service provider interaction. Cloud computing offers new ways to store, access, process, and analyze information and connect people and resources from any location in the world where an Internet connection is available.

FIGURE 5.18 Ways for Data Centers to Become Sustainable

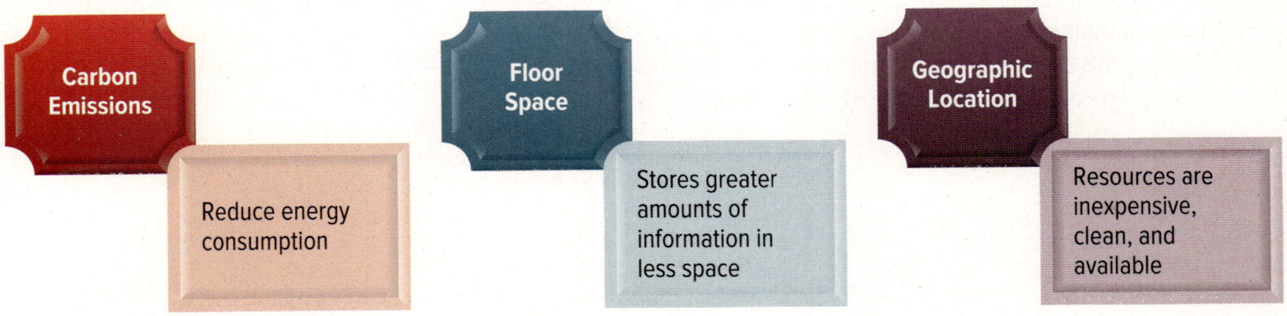

fyi Virtualization for Your Cell Phone

Virtualization is a difficult concept to understand. The formal definition is a framework dividing the resources of a computer into multiple execution environments. OK, let's try that again in English. Imagine you have three cell phones, one for the company you work for, one for a company you are starting on the side, and one for personal calls. For the most part, the phones are idle and they seldom ever ring at the same time. Because the phones are idle the majority of the time, you notice that it's a waste of time and resources to support idle time, especially when you are paying for cell service on each phone. You decide to use virtualization to help your situation.

What this would do is essentially put three virtual cell phones on one device. The individual services and application for each phone would be independently stored on the one device. From the device's perspective, it sees three separate virtual phones. This saves time and money in expenses and maintenance. You could even use virtualization to turn your cell phone into a scanner. Just visit ScanR.com; for just $5 a month you can use the camera on your phone to scan documents. Take a photo of any document, business card, or whiteboard and upload it to ScanR's website, and in minutes it is returned to you in a digital file. Could be helpful if your friend has to miss class and you want to save your professor's notes.

Virtualization is a hot topic these days as more and more businesses focus on social responsibility and attempt to find ways to reduce their carbon footprints. What are the potential environmental impacts of virtualization? What are the business advantages of virtualization? What risks are associated with virtualization?

multi-tenancy A single instance of a system serves multiple customers.

single-tenancy Each customer or tenant must purchase and maintain an individual system.

cloud fabric The software that makes the benefits of cloud computing possible, such as multi-tenancy.

cloud fabric controller An individual who monitors and provisions cloud resources similar to a server administrator at an individual company.

As shown in Figure 5.19, users connect to the cloud from their personal computers or portable devices using a client, such as a web browser. To these individual users, the cloud appears as their personal application, device, or document. It is like storing all of your software and documents "in the cloud," and all you need is a device to access the cloud. No more hard drives, software, or processing power—that is all located in the cloud, transparent to the users. Users are not physically bound to a single computer or network; they can access their programs and documents from wherever they are, whenever they need to. Just think of having your hard drive located in the sky and you can access your information and programs using any device from wherever you are. The best part is that even if your machine crashes, is lost, or is stolen, the information hosted in the cloud is safe and always available. (See Figure 5.20 for cloud providers and Figure 5.21 for cloud computing advantages.)

Multi-tenancy in the cloud means that a single instance of a system serves multiple customers. In the cloud, each customer is called a tenant and multiple tenants can access the same system. Multi-tenancy helps to reduce operational costs associated with implementing large systems as the costs are dispersed across many tenants as opposed to **single-tenancy**, in which each customer or tenant must purchase and maintain an individual system. With a multi-tenancy cloud approach, the service provider only has one place to update its system. With a single-tenancy cloud approach, the service provider would have to update its system in every company where the software was running. The **cloud fabric** is the software that makes possible the benefits of cloud computing, such as multi-tenancy. A **cloud fabric controller** is an individual who monitors and provisions cloud resources, similar to a server administrator at an individual company. Cloud fabric controllers provision resources, balance loads, manage servers, update systems, and ensure all environments are available and operating correctly. Cloud fabric is the primary reason cloud computing promotes all of the seven abilities, allowing a business to make its data and applications accessible, available, maintainable, portable, reliable, scalable, and usable. Figure 5.22 displays the top business cloud applications.

The cloud offers a company higher availability, greater reliability, and improved accessibility—all with affordable high-speed access. For flexibility, scalability, and cost efficiency, cloud computing is quickly becoming a viable option for companies

FIGURE 5.19 Cloud Computing Example

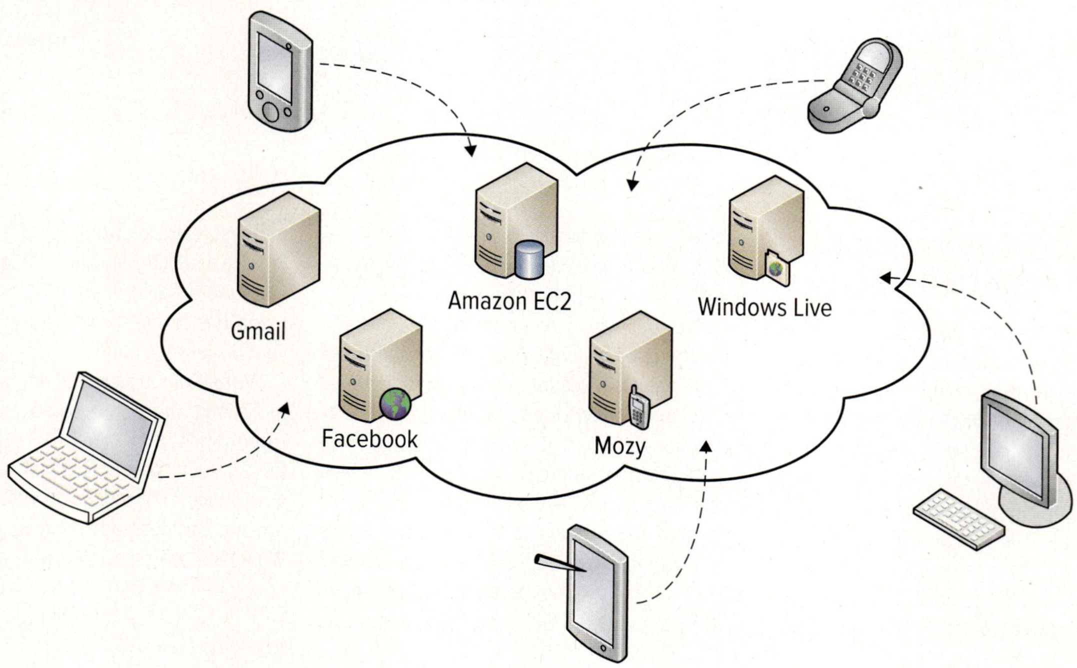

FIGURE 5.20 Overview of Cloud Providers

Provider	Cloud Provider
Amazon **Cloud Drive, Cloud Player, Amazon Prime**	Amazon Kindle Fire is sold at a loss to push various types of media through Amazon Prime and Cloud Player where users can stream videos and music.
Apple **iCloud, iWork, iBooks, iTunes**	iCloud brings together iPhones, iPads, and Mac to synchronize data across Apple devices. iWork helps users collaborate.
Google **Google Apps, Google Drive, Gmail, Google Calendar**	Google offers a number of cloud services, including Google apps, Gmail, and Google Drive to store data.
Micrsoft **Office 365, OneDrive, OneNote, Exchange**	OneDrive and Office 365 offer ways to collaborate and share data, photos, emails, and documents.

FIGURE 5.21 Cloud Computing Advantages

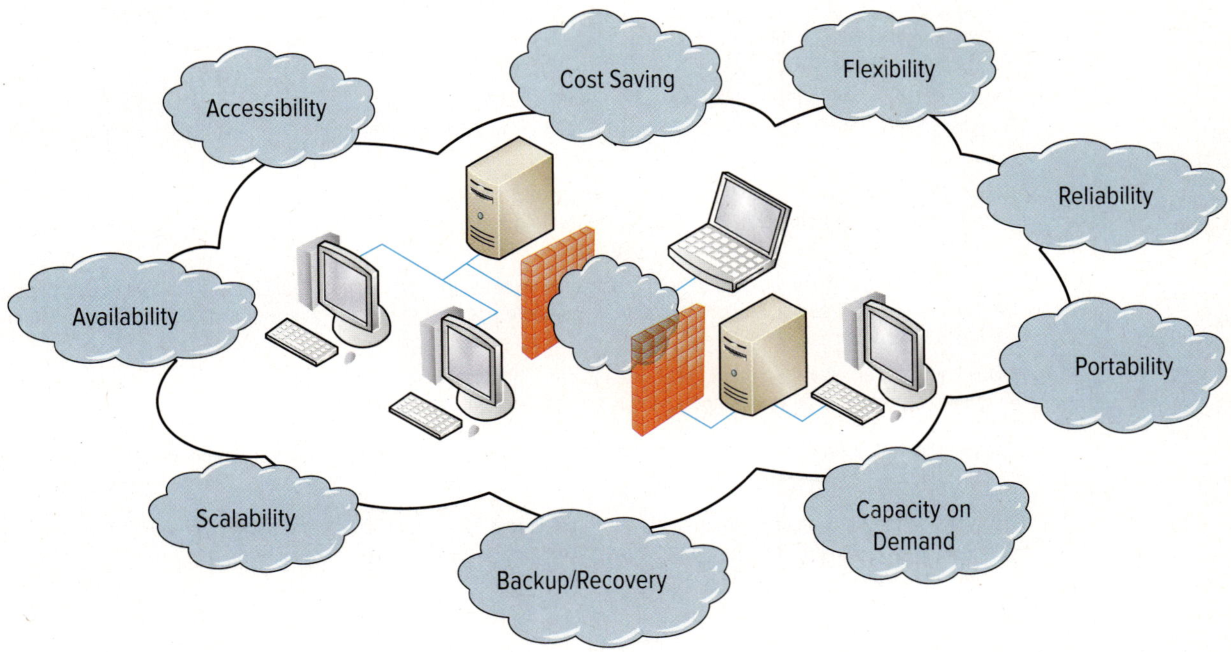

of all sizes. With the cloud, you could simply purchase a single license for software such as Microsoft Office or Outlook at a far discounted rate and not worry about the hassle of installing and upgrading the software on your computer. No more worries that you don't have enough memory to run a new program because the hardware is provided in the cloud, along with the software. You simply pay to access the program. Think of this the same way you do your telephone service. You simply pay to access a vendor's service, and you do not have to pay for the equipment required to carry the call around the globe. You also don't have to worry about scalability because the system automatically handles peak loads, which can be spread out among the systems in the cloud. Figure 5.23 displays the characteristics of cloud computing.

Because additional cloud resources are always available, companies no longer have to purchase systems for infrequent computing tasks that need intense processing power, such as preparing tax returns during tax season or increased sales transactions during certain holiday seasons. If a company needs more processing power, it is always there in the cloud—and available on a cost-efficient basis. Heroku is the leading cloud platform for building and deploying social and mobile customer applications. Built on open standards, Heroku supports multiple open frameworks, languages, and databases.

With cloud computing, individuals or businesses pay only for the services they need, when they need them, and where, much as we use and pay for electricity. In the past, a company would have to pay millions of dollars for the hardware, software, and networking equipment required to implement a large system such as payroll or sales management. A cloud computing user can simply access the cloud and request a single license to a

FIGURE 5.22 Top Cloud-Based Business Applications

CLOUD APPLICATIONS	
Box box.com	Box.com is like a file folder that all your gadgets and devices can access. You simply drag a file into Box, and you can instantly access it from anywhere.
Chatter.com! Chatter.com	Chatter is essentially an in-house social network. It allows your employees to share files, collaborate easily on projects, and pose questions to the whole company, which cuts down on meeting times, decreases the number of emails sent, and increases how quickly employees can gather information.
Evernote evernote.com	Evernote makes organizing notes simple. It organizes online all the sticky notes, scribbled-on notepads, and random pictures that you would have cluttering up your desk. It can even recognize writing in images, so if you take a picture of a whiteboard full of notes, you can find that image by searching for one of the phrases in it.
Google Apps Google.com	Google Apps pretty much eliminates the need for many computer programs. You can create and save text documents, spreadsheets, slide shows and more on Google Docs, and several people can work on one file simultaneously. Google Calendar makes creating and sharing calendars easy, and event reminders can be emailed to invitees. Gmail for Business gives companies personalized email accounts that are easy to set up and amend and that have the flexibility and storage space of Gmail.
MailChimp mailchimp.com	MailChimp is an email publishing platform that allows businesses of all sizes to design and send their email campaigns. Measuring the success of your email campaigns is really easy because the software integrates with Google Analytics for tracking purposes.
Moo uk.moo.com	Moo offers a design and printing service for business cards, postcards, and minicards. Users can customize existing Moo designs, upload their own designs, or import their own images from their Etsy, Facebook, Flickr, Picasa, or SmugMug account.
Mozy mozy.co.uk	Mozy is an online backup service that continuously backs up the files on your computer or server. It gives small businesses the space to back up all their computer and server files for a very reasonable price, so owners know their files are retrievable, even during a data loss crisis.
Outright outright.com	Outright is a cloud finance app that helps small businesses with their business accounting. It allows you to track income/expenses, tax obligations, and profits/losses in real time. Ideal for small companies or just entrepreneurs looking to get a hold on their finances.
Quickbooks quickbooks.intuit.co.uk	Quickbooks is an online accounting service and can help with all accounting needs, including monitoring cash flow, creating reports, and setting budgets, and is accessible from anywhere in the world.
Skype skype.com	Skype turns your computer into a phone; you can call or chat (with or without video) to other Skype users for free.
Toggl toggl.com	Toggl is a time-tracking application. It allows you to create tasks and projects and assign a certain amount of time to each project. It also logs how long tasks take to complete and how much time you have left to spend in a project.

FIGURE 5.23 Benefits of Cloud Computing

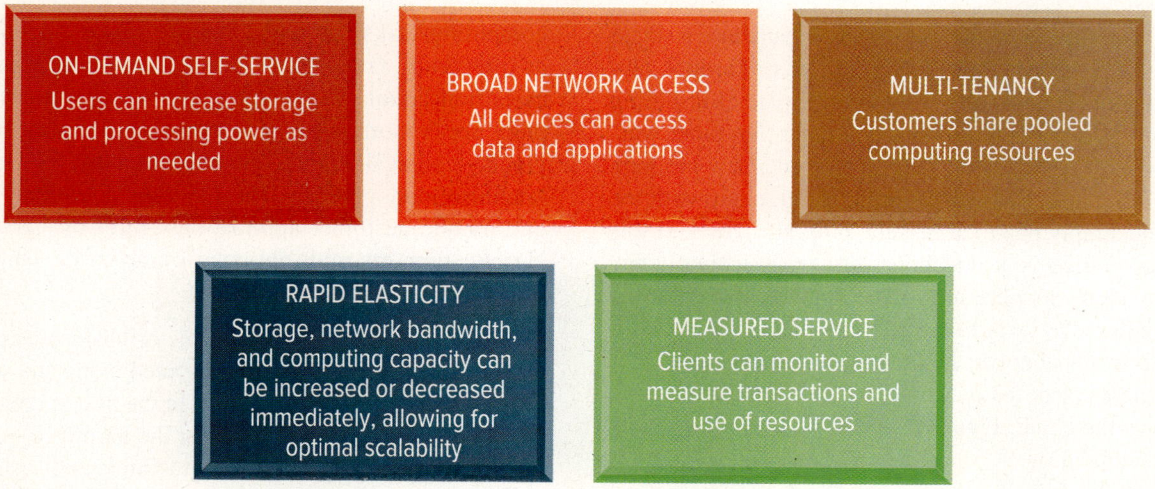

payroll application. The user does not have to incur any hardware, software, or networking expenses. As the business grows and the user requires more employees to have access to the system, the business simply purchases additional licenses. Rather than running software on a local computer or server, companies can now reach to the cloud to combine software applications, data storage, and considerable computing power.

Regardless of which cloud model a business chooses, it can select from four different cloud computing environments—public, private, community, and hybrid (see Figure 5.24).

Public Cloud **Public cloud** promotes massive, global, and industrywide applications offered to the general public. In a public cloud, customers are never required to provision, manage, upgrade, or replace hardware or software. Pricing is utility-style and customers pay only for the resources they use. Public clouds are the type used by service providers to offer free or paid-for services to the general public. They are open, but often with standard restrictions requiring passwords. A few great examples of public cloud computing include Amazon Web Services (AWS), Windows Azure, and Google Cloud Connect.

Private Cloud **Private cloud** serves only one customer or organization and can be located on the customer's premises or off the customer's premises. A private cloud is the optimal solution for an organization such as the government that has high data security concerns and values information privacy. Private clouds are far more expensive than public clouds because costs are not shared across multiple customers. Private clouds are mostly used by firms and groups who need to keep data secure. The main downside is that they still require significant investment of time and money to set them up.

public cloud Promotes massive, global, industrywide applications offered to the general public.

private cloud Serves only one customer or organization and can be located on the customers' premises or off the customer's premises.

BUSTED Hack Attack[13]

A few years ago, it would have been difficult to pull off a hacker attack like the one that took down Twitter. A sophisticated hacker would have needed either the technical savvy to hijack thousands of computers simultaneously or tens of thousands of dollars to pay someone else to do it. Not today. The tools for taking down websites like Twitter, Amazon, or Facebook are getting so cheap and easy to use that the average Joe could easily wreak havoc on any website.

In the Twitter attack, hackers were trying to silence a single blogger who criticized the Russian government, Georgy Jakhaia, who is known online as Cyxymu. The hackers launched a denial-of-service attack, in which thousands of computers try to communicate with the target website at the same time so the site's computers are overwhelmed and can't handle legitimate requests. In what appears to be collateral damage, the hackers took down the entire Twitter service and hobbled the blogging sites LiveJournal and Facebook, where Jakhaia also posted.

How does it work? Criminal groups and hackers have infected tens of millions of computers around the world with viruses that allow them to control the machines to launch attacks or send spam. These networks of zombie computers, called "botnets," are then rented out on a per-machine and per-day basis through websites that make executing a denial-of-service attack almost as easy as getting a book from Amazon. No password cracking or software coding is necessary. And it is almost as cheap. A few years ago the cost of renting out 10,000 machines would have been between $2,000 and $5,000. Today you can rent 10,000 machines—enough to take down Twitter—for a mere $200.

© Yvan Dube/Getty Images RF

With all that you have read in this chapter, highlight the steps an organization can take to protect itself from hacker attacks. Explain how a denial-of-service attack works and why it is illegal. Would using a service-oriented architecture protect a company from a denial-of-service attack? If you were using virtualization, how could you protect your computers from a denial-of-service attack?

community cloud Serves a specific community with common business models, security requirements, and compliance considerations.

hybrid cloud Includes two or more private, public, or community clouds, but each cloud remains separate and is only linked by technology that enables data and application portability.

Community Cloud **Community cloud** serves a specific community with common business models, security requirements, and compliance considerations. Community clouds are emerging in highly regulated industries such as financial services and pharmaceutical companies. Community clouds are private, but spread over a variety of groups within one organization. Different sections of the cloud can be set up specifically for each department or group.

Hybrid Cloud **Hybrid cloud** includes two or more private, public, or community clouds, but each cloud remains separate and is only linked by technology that enables data and application portability. For example, a company might use a private cloud for critical applications that maintain sensitive data and a public cloud for nonsensitive data applications. The usage of both private and public clouds together is an example of a hybrid cloud. Hybrid clouds offer services even if connectivity faults occur and are often used to provide backup to critical online services. **Cloud bursting** is when a company uses its own computing infrastructure for normal usage and accesses the cloud when it needs to scale for peak load requirements, ensuring a sudden spike in usage does not result in poor performance or system crashes.

Deploying an MIS infrastructure in the cloud forever changes the way an organization's MIS systems are developed, deployed, maintained, and managed. Moving to the cloud is a fundamental shift from moving from a physical world to a logical world, making irrelevant the notion of which individual server applications or data reside on. As a result, organizations and MIS departments need to change the way they view systems and the new opportunities to find competitive advantages.

FIGURE 5.24 Cloud Computing Environments

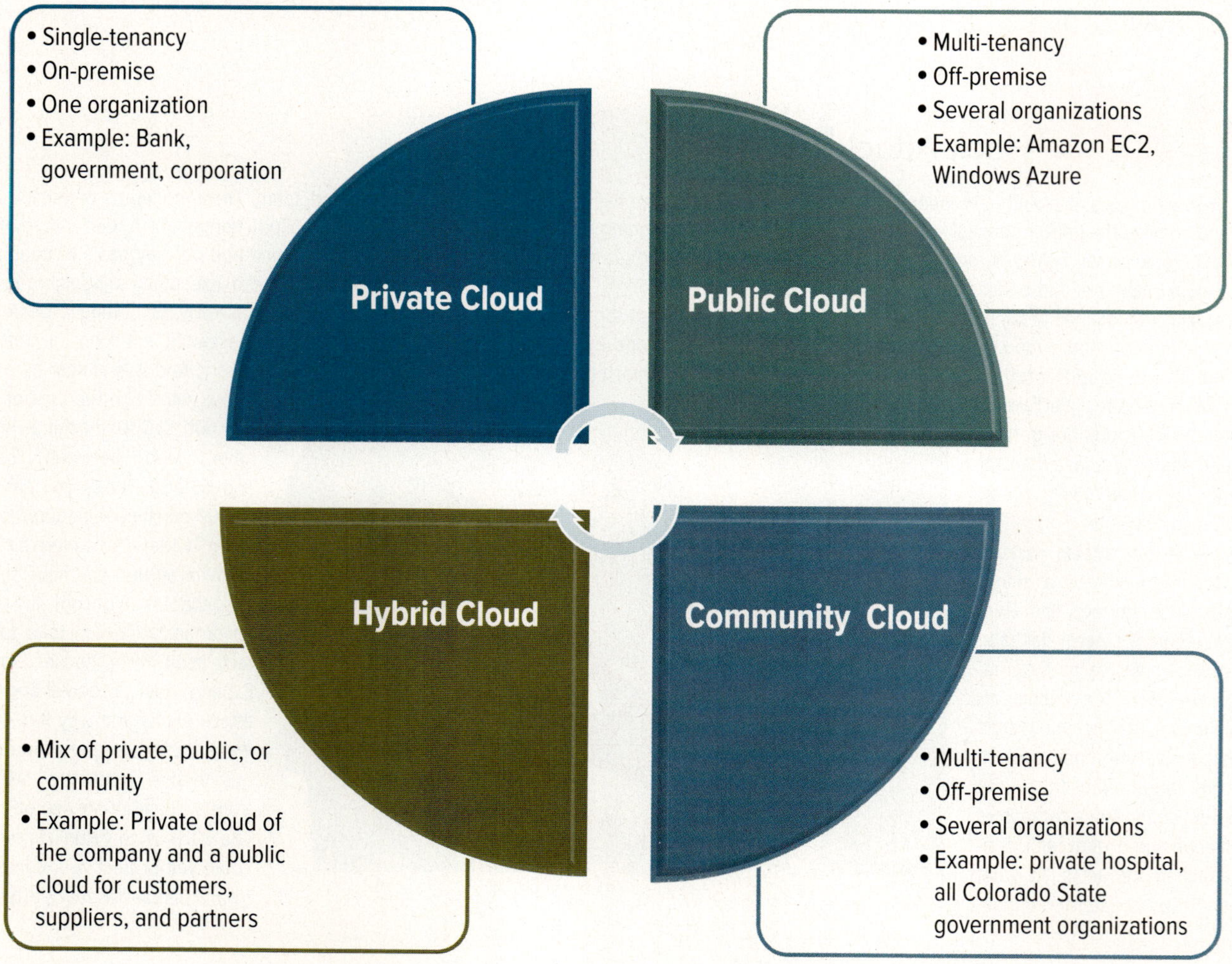

cloud bursting When a company uses its own computing infrastructure for normal usage and accesses the cloud when it needs to scale for high/peak load requirements, ensuring a sudden spike in usage does not result in poor performance or system crashes.

utility computing Offers a pay-per-use revenue model similar to a metered service such as gas or electricity.

Infrastructure as a Service (IaaS) The delivery of computer hardware capability, including the use of servers, networking, and storage, as a service.

dynamic scaling Means that the MIS infrastructure can be automatically scaled up or down based on needed requirements.

disaster recovery as a service (DRaaS) Offers backup services that use cloud resources to protect applications and data from disruption caused by disaster.

Utility Computing

Utility computing offers a pay-per-use revenue model similar to a metered service such as gas or electricity. Many cloud computing service providers use utility computing cloud infrastructures, which are detailed in Figure 5.25.

Infrastructure as a Service (IaaS)

Infrastructure as a Service (IaaS) delivers hardware networking capabilities, including the use of servers, networking, and storage, over the cloud using a pay-per-use revenue model. With IaaS, the customer rents the hardware and provides its own custom applications or programs. IaaS customers save money by not having to spend a large amount of capital purchasing expensive servers, which is a great business advantage considering some servers cost more than $100,000. The service is typically paid for on a usage basis, much like a basic utility service such as electricity or gas. IaaS offers a cost-effective solution for companies that need their computing resources to grow and shrink as business demand changes. This is known as **dynamic scaling**, which means the MIS infrastructure can be automatically scaled up or down based on requirements. **Disaster Recovery as a Service (DRaaS)** offers backup services that use cloud resources to protect applications and data from disruption caused by disaster. It gives an organization a total system backup that allows for business continuity in the event of system failure. DRaaS is typically part of a disaster recovery plan or business continuity plan.

Currently the most popular IaaS operation is Amazon's Elastic Compute Cloud, generally known as Amazon EC2, or simply EC2. EC2 provides a web interface through which customers can load and run their own applications on Amazon's computers. Customers control their own operating environment, so they can create, run, and stop services as needed, which is why Amazon describes EC2 as *elastic*. IaaS is a perfect fit for companies with research-intensive projects that need to process large amounts of information at irregular intervals, such as

FIGURE 5.25 Cloud Service Delivery Models

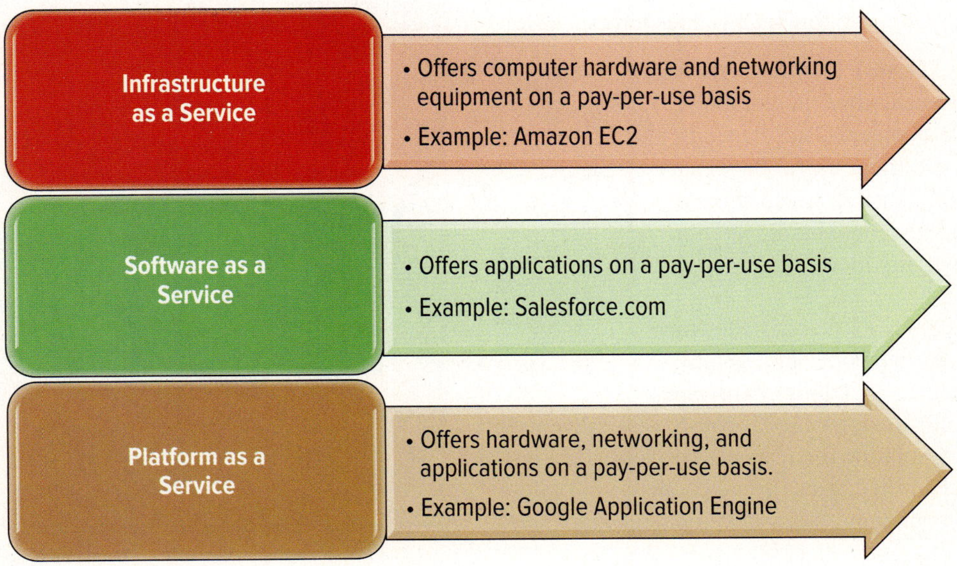

Software as a Service (SaaS) Delivers applications over the cloud using a pay-per-use revenue model.

Data as a Service (DaaS) Facilitates the accessibility of business-critical data in a timely, secure, and affordable manner.

Platform as a Service (PaaS) Supports the deployment of entire systems including hardware, networking, and applications using a pay-per-use revenue model.

Big Data as a Service (BDaaS) Offers a cloud-based Big Data service to help organizations analyze massive amounts of data to solve business dilemmas.

those in the scientific or medical fields. Cloud computing services offer these companies considerable cost savings because they can perform testing and analysis at levels that are not possible without access to additional and very costly computing infrastructure.

Software as a Service (SaaS)

Software as a Service (SaaS) delivers applications over the cloud using a pay-per-use revenue model. Before its introduction, companies often spent huge amounts of money implementing and customizing specialized applications to satisfy their business requirements. Many of these applications were difficult to implement, expensive to maintain, and challenging to use. Usability was one of the biggest drivers for creating interest in and success for cloud computing service providers.

SaaS offers a number of advantages; the most obvious is tremendous cost savings. The software is priced on a per-use basis with no up-front costs, so companies get the immediate benefit of reducing capital expenditures. They also get the added benefits of scalability and flexibility to test new software on a rental basis.

Salesforce.com is one of the most popular SaaS providers. It built and delivered a sales automation application, suitable for the typical salesperson, that automates functions such as tracking sales leads and prospects and forecasting. Tapping the power of SaaS can provide access to a large-scale, secure infrastructure, along with any needed support, which is especially valuable for a start-up or small company with few financial resources.

Data as a Service (DaaS) facilitates the accessibility of business-critical data in a timely, secure, and affordable manner. DaaS depends on the principle that specified, useful data can be supplied to users on demand, irrespective of any organizational or geographical separation between consumers and providers.

Platform as a Service (PaaS)

Platform as a Service (PaaS) supports the deployment of entire systems, including hardware, networking, and applications, using a pay-per-use revenue model. PaaS is a perfect solution for a business because it passes on to the service provider the headache and challenges of buying, managing, and maintaining web development software. With PaaS the development, deployment, management, and maintenance is based entirely in the cloud and performed by the PaaS provider, allowing the company to focus resources on its core initiatives. Every aspect of development, including the software needed to create it and the hardware to run it, lives

show me *the* MONEY

Upcycle Your Old PC

Imagine walking into your friend's home and seeing her computer with live fish swimming around inside it. Upon taking a second look, you realize she has upcycled her old Mac into an innovative macquarium. Some young entrepreneurs are making a fortune by upcycling old Mac desktops as fish tanks. An upcycle reuses or refurbishes ewaste and creates a new product. With the growing problem of ewaste, one alternative is to upcycle your old technology by creating innovative household products or personal accessories. Take a look at one of the devices you are currently using to see whether you can create an upcycled product. Here are a few great ideas to get you started:

- Keyboard magnets
- Computer aquariums
- Mac mailboxes
- Keyboard calendars
- Floppy disk pencil holders
- Circuit board key rings
- RAM key chains
- Circuit earrings
- Cable bracelets
- Motherboard clocks
- Mouse belt buckles

in the cloud. PaaS helps companies minimize operational costs and increase productivity by providing all the following without up-front investment:

- Increased security.
- Access to information anywhere and anytime.
- Centralized information management.
- Easy collaboration with partners, suppliers, and customers.
- Increased speed to market with significantly less cost.

One of the most popular PaaS services is Google's Application Engine, which builds and deploys web applications for a company. Google's Application Engine is easy to build, easy to maintain, and easy to scale as a company's web-based application needs grow. Google's Application Engine is free and offers a standard storage limit and enough processing power and network usage to support a web application serving about 5 million page views a month. When a customer scales beyond these initial limits, it can pay a fee to increase capacity and performance. This can turn into some huge costs savings for a small business that does not have enough initial capital to buy expensive hardware and software for its web applications. Just think, a two-person company can access the same computing resources as Google. That makes good business sense. Regardless of which cloud model a business chooses, it can select from four cloud computing environments—public, private, community, and hybrid.

Combining infrastructure as a service, platform as a service, and data as a service we arrive at Big Data as a Service. **Big Data as a Service (BDaaS)** offers a cloud-based Big Data service to help organizations analyze massive amounts of data to solve business dilemmas. BDaaS is a somewhat nebulous term often used to describe a wide variety of outsourcing of various Big Data functions to the cloud. This can range from the supply of data, to the supply of analytical tools with which to interrogate the data (often through a web dashboard or control panel) to carrying out the actual analysis and providing reports. Some BDaaS providers also include consulting and advisory services within their BDaaS packages.

Market
(daily)

chapter SIX

data: business intelligence

what's in IT for me?

This chapter introduces the concepts of information and data and their relative importance to business professionals and firms. It distinguishes between data stored in transactional databases and powerful business intelligence gleaned from data warehouses. Students who understand how to access, manipulate, summarize, sort, and analyze data to support decision making find success. Information has power, and understanding that power will help you compete in the global marketplace. This chapter will provide you with an overview of database fundamentals and the characteristics associated with high-quality information. It will also explain how the

continued on p. 148

CHAPTER OUTLINE

SECTION 6.1 >>

Data, Information, and Databases

- The Business Benefits of High-Quality Information
- Storing Information Using a Relational Database Management System
- Using a Relational Database for Business Advantages
- Driving Websites with Data

SECTION 6.2 >>

Business Intelligence

- Data Warehouses
- Business Intelligence
- The Power of Big Data
- Data Mining
- Data Analytics

information granularity The extent of detail within the information (fine and detailed or coarse and abstract).

continued from p. 147

various bits of data stored across multiple, operational databases can be transformed in a centralized repository of summarized information in a data warehouse, which can be used for discovering business intelligence.

You, as a business student, need to understand the differences between transactional data and summarized information and the different types of questions you could use a transactional database to answer versus a data warehouse. You need to be aware of the complexity of storing data in databases and the level of effort required to transform operational data into meaningful, summarized information. You need to realize the power of information and the competitive advantage a data warehouse brings an organization in terms of facilitating business intelligence. Armed with the power of information, business students will make smart, informed, and datasupported managerial decisions. ■

{SECTION 6.1} Data, Information, and Databases

LEARNING OUTCOMES

LO6.1 Explain the four primary traits that determine the value of information.

LO6.2 Describe a database, a database management system, and the relational database model.

LO6.3 Identify the business advantages of a relational database.

LO6.4 Explain the business benefits of a data-driven website.

THE BUSINESS BENEFITS OF HIGH-QUALITY INFORMATION LO6.1

Information is powerful. Information can tell an organization how its current operations are performing and help it estimate and strategize about how future operations might perform. The ability to understand, digest, analyze, and filter information is key to growth and success for any professional in any industry. Remember that new perspectives and opportunities can open up when you have the right data that you can turn into information and ultimately business intelligence.

Information is everywhere in an organization. Managers in sales, marketing, human resources, and management need information to run their departments and make daily decisions. When addressing a significant business issue, employees must be able to obtain and analyze all the relevant information so they can make the best decision possible. Information comes at different levels, formats, and granularities. **Information granularity** refers to the extent of detail within the information (fine and detailed or coarse and abstract). Employees must be able to correlate the different levels, formats, and granularities of information when making decisions. For example, a company might be collecting information from various suppliers to make needed decisions, only to find that the information is in different levels, formats, and granularities. One supplier might send detailed information in a spreadsheet, while another supplier might send summary information in a Word document, and still another might send a collection of information from emails. Employees will need to compare these different types of information for what they commonly reveal to make strategic decisions. Figure 6.1 displays the various levels, formats, and granularities of organizational information.

Successfully collecting, compiling, sorting, and finally analyzing information from multiple levels, in varied formats, and exhibiting different granularities can provide tremendous insight into how an organization is performing. Exciting and unexpected results can include potential new markets, new ways of reaching customers, and even new methods of doing business. After understanding the different levels, formats, and granularities of information, managers next want to look at the four primary traits that help determine the value of information (see Figure 6.2).

LO6.1 Explain the four primary traits that determine the value of information.

Information Type: Transactional and Analytical

As discussed previously in the text, the two primary types of information are transactional and analytical. Transactional information encompasses all of the information contained within a single business process or unit of work, and its primary purpose is to support daily operational tasks. Organizations need to capture and store transactional information to perform operational tasks and repetitive decisions such as analyzing daily sales reports and production schedules to

FIGURE 6.1 Levels, Formats, and Granularities of Organizational Information

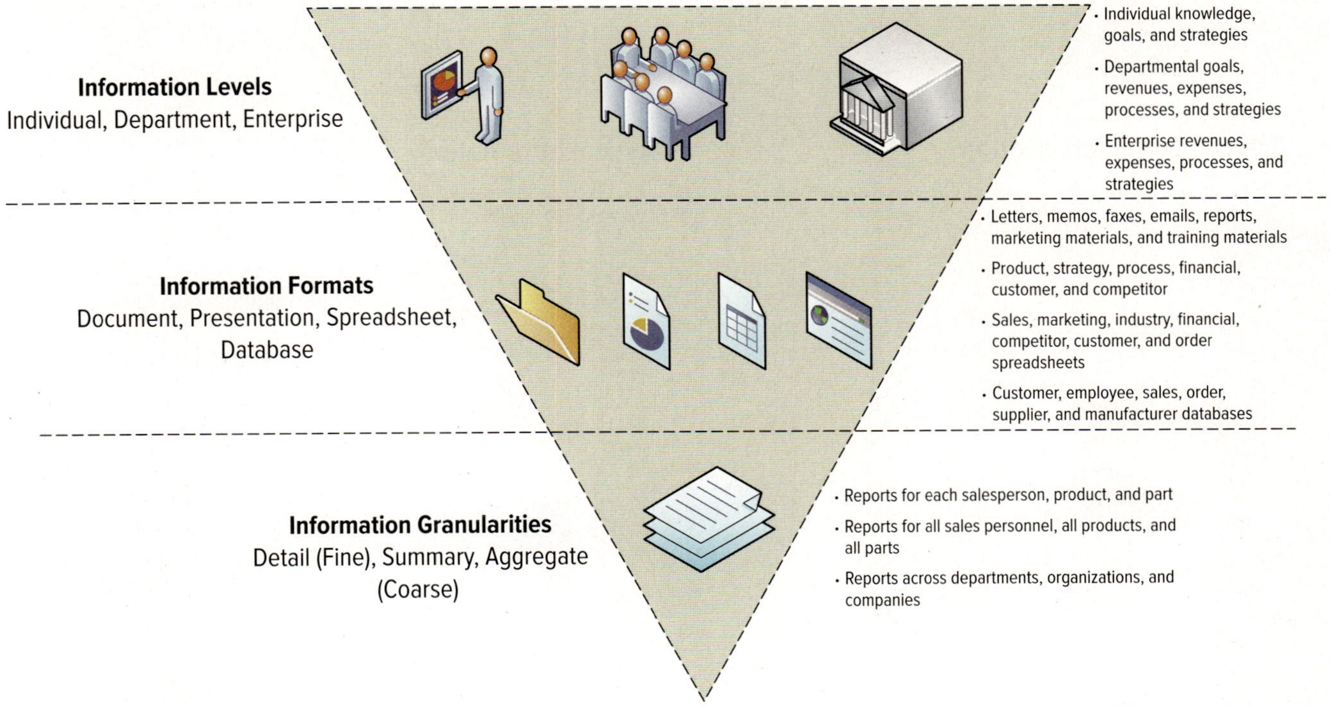

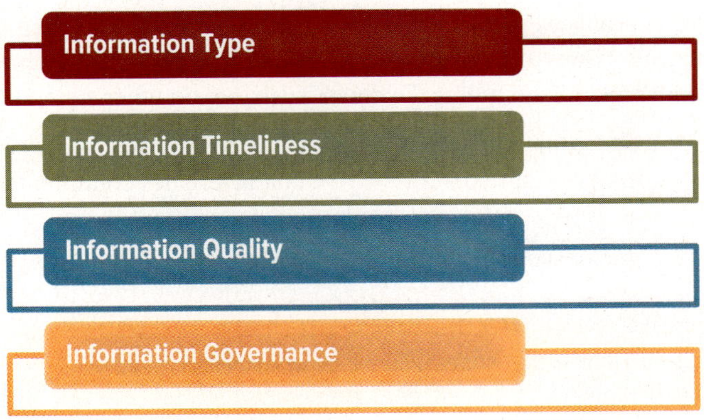

FIGURE 6.2
The Four Primary Traits of the Value of Information

determine how much inventory to carry. Consider Walmart, which handles more than 1 million customer transactions every hour, and Facebook, which keeps track of 400 million active users (along with their photos, friends, and web links). In addition, every time a cash register rings up a sale, a deposit or withdrawal is made from an ATM, or a receipt is given at the gas pump, capturing and storing of the transactional information are required.

Analytical information encompasses all organizational information, and its primary purpose is to support the performing of managerial analysis tasks. Analytical information is useful when making important decisions such as whether the organization should build a new manufacturing plant or hire additional sales personnel. Analytical information makes it possible to do many things that previously were difficult to accomplish, such as spot business trends, prevent diseases, and fight crime. For example, credit card companies crunch through billions of transactional purchase records to identify fraudulent activity. Indicators such as charges in a foreign country or consecutive purchases of gasoline send a red flag highlighting potential fraudulent activity.

Walmart was able to use its massive amount of analytical information to identify many unusual trends, such as a correlation between storms and Pop-Tarts. Yes, Walmart discovered an increase in the demand for Pop-Tarts during the storm season. Armed with the valuable information the retail chain was able to stock up on Pop-Tarts that were ready for purchase when customers arrived. Figure 6.3 displays different types of transactional and analytical information.

Information Timeliness

Timeliness is an aspect of information that depends on the situation. In some firms or industries, information that is a few days or weeks old can be relevant, while in others information that is a few minutes old can be almost worthless. Some organizations, such as 911 response centers, stock traders, and banks, require up-to-the-second information. Other organizations, such as insurance and construction companies, require only daily or even weekly information.

real-time information Immediate, up-to-date information.

real-time system Provides real-time information in response to requests.

information inconsistency Occurs when the same data element has different values.

information integrity issue Occurs when a system produces incorrect, inconsistent, or duplicate data.

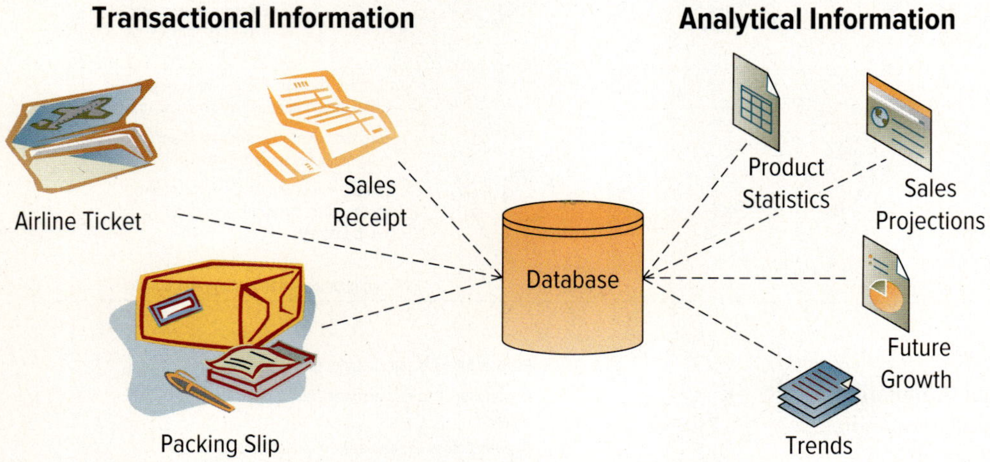

FIGURE 6.3 Transactional versus Analytical Information

Real-time information means immediate, up-to-date information. **Real-time systems** provide real-time information in response to requests. Many organizations use real-time systems to uncover key corporate transactional information. The growing demand for real-time information stems from organizations' need to make faster and more effective decisions, keep smaller inventories, operate more efficiently, and track performance more carefully. Information also needs to be timely in the sense that it meets employees' needs, but no more. If employees can absorb information only on an hourly or daily basis, there is no need to gather real-time information in smaller increments.

Most people request real-time information without understanding one of the biggest pitfalls associated with real-time information—continual change. Imagine the following scenario: Three managers meet at the end of the day to discuss a business problem. Each manager has gathered information at different times during the day to create a picture of the situation. Each manager's picture may be different because of the time differences. Their views on the business problem may not match because the information they are basing their analysis on is continually changing. This approach may not speed up decision making, and it may actually slow it down. Business decision makers must evaluate the timeliness for the information for every decision. Organizations do not want to find themselves using real-time information to make a bad decision faster.

Information Quality

Business decisions are only as good as the quality of the information used to make them. **Information inconsistency** occurs when the same data element has different values. Take for example the amount of work that needs to occur to update a customer who had changed her last name due to marriage. Changing this information in only a few organizational systems will lead to data inconsistencies causing customer 123456 to be associated with two last names. **Information integrity issues** occur when a system produces incorrect, inconsistent, or duplicate data. Data integrity issues can cause managers to consider the system reports invalid and will make decisions based on other sources.

To ensure your systems do not suffer from data integrity issues, review Figure 6.4 for the five characteristics common to

FIGURE 6.4 Five Common Characteristics of High-Quality Information

Characteristic	Questions
Accurate	• Is there an incorrect value in the information? • Example: Is the name spelled correctly? Is the dollar amount recorded properly?
Complete	• Is a value missing from the information? • Example: Is the address complete including street, city, state, and zip code?
Consistent	• Is aggregate or summary information in agreement with detailed information? • Example: Do all total columns equal the true total of the individual item?
Timely	• Is the information current with respect to business needs? • Example: Is information updated weekly, daily, or hourly?
Unique	• Is each transaction and event represented only once in the information? • Example: Are there any duplicate customers?

1. Missing information (no first name)

2. Incomplete information (no street)

5. Inaccurate information (invalid email)

ID	Last Name	First Name	Street	City	State	Zip	Phone	Fax	Email
113	Smith		123 S. Main	Denver	CO	80210	(303) 777-1258	(303) 777-5544	ssmith@aol.com
114	Jones	Jeff	12A	Denver	CO	80224	(303) 666-6868	(303) 666-6868	(303) 666-6868
115	Roberts	Jenny	1244 Colfax	Denver	CO	85231	759-5654	853-6584	jr@msn.com
116	Robert	Jenny	1244 Colfax	Denver	CO	85231	759-5654	853-6584	jr@msn.com

3. Probable duplicate information (similar names, same address, phone number)

4. Potential wrong information (are the phone and fax numbers the same or is this an error?)

6. Incomplete information (missing area codes)

FIGURE 6.5
Example of Low-Quality Information

high-quality information: accuracy, completeness, consistency, timeliness, and uniqueness. Figure 6.5 provides an example of several problems associated with using low-quality information including:

1. *Completeness.* The customer's first name is missing.
2. Another issue with *completeness.* The street address contains only a number and not a street name.
3. *Consistency.* There may be a duplication of information since there is a slight difference between the two customers in the spelling of the last name. Similar street addresses and phone numbers make this likely.
4. *Accuracy.* This may be inaccurate information because the customer's phone and fax numbers are the same. Some customers might have the same number for phone and fax, but the fact that the customer also has this number in the email address field is suspicious.
5. Another issue with *accuracy.* There is inaccurate information because a phone number is located in the email address field.
6. Another issue with *completeness.* The information is incomplete because there is not a valid area code for the phone and fax numbers.

Nestlé uses 550,000 suppliers to sell more than 100,000 products in 200 countries. However, due to poor information, the company was unable to evaluate its business effectively. After some analysis, it found that it had 9 million records of vendors, customers, and materials, half of which were duplicated, obsolete, inaccurate, or incomplete. The analysis discovered that some records abbreviated vendor names while other records spelled out the vendor names. This created multiple accounts for the same customer, making it impossible to determine the true value of Nestlé's customers. Without being able to identify customer profitability, a company runs the risk of alienating its best customers.[1]

show me *the* MONEY

Determining Information Quality Issues

Real People is a magazine geared toward working individuals that provides articles and advice on everything from car maintenance to family planning. *Real People* is currently experiencing problems with its magazine distribution list. More than 30 percent of the magazines mailed are returned because of incorrect address information, and each month it receives numerous calls from angry customers complaining that they have not yet received their magazines. Here is a sample of *Real People*'s customer information. Create a report detailing all of the issues with the information, potential causes of the information issues, and solutions the company can follow to correct the situation.

ID	First Name	Middle Initial	Last Name	Street	City	State	Zip Code
433	M	J	Jones	13 Denver	Denver	CO	87654
434	Margaret	J	Jones	13 First Ave.	Denver	CO	87654
434	Brian	F	Hoover	Lake Ave.	Columbus	OH	87654
435	Nick	H	Schweitzer	65 Apple Lane	San Francisco	OH	65664
436	Richard	A		567 55th St.	New York	CA	98763
437	Alana	B	Smith	121 Tenny Dr.	Buffalo	NY	142234
438	Trevor	D	Darrian	90 Fresrdestil	Dallas	TX	74532

data gap analysis Occurs when a company examines its data to determine if it can meet business expectations, while identifying possible data gaps or where missing data might exist.

data stewardship The management and oversight of an organization's data assets to help provide business users with high-quality data that is easily accessible in a consistent manner.

data steward Responsible for ensuring the policies and procedures are implemented across the organization and acts as a liaison between the MIS department and the business.

data governance Refers to the overall management of the availability, usability, integrity, and security of company data

master data management (MDM) The practice of gathering data and ensuring that it is uniform, accurate, consistent, and complete, including such entities as customers, suppliers, products, sales, employees, and other critical entities that are commonly integrated across organizational systems

Knowing how low-quality information issues typically occur can help a company correct them. Addressing these errors will significantly improve the quality of company information and the value to be extracted from it. The four primary reasons for low-quality information are:

1. Online customers intentionally enter inaccurate information to protect their privacy.
2. Different systems have different information entry standards and formats.
3. Data-entry personnel enter abbreviated information to save time or erroneous information by accident.
4. Third-party and external information contains inconsistencies, inaccuracies, and errors.

Understanding the Costs of Using Low-Quality Information Using the wrong information can lead managers to make erroneous decisions. Erroneous decisions in turn can cost time, money, reputations, and even jobs. Some of the serious business consequences that occur due to using low-quality information to make decisions are:

- Inability to accurately track customers.
- Difficulty identifying the organization's most valuable customers.
- Inability to identify selling opportunities.
- Lost revenue opportunities from marketing to nonexistent customers.
- The cost of sending non-deliverable mail.
- Difficulty tracking revenue because of inaccurate invoices.
- Inability to build strong relationships with customers.

A **data gap analysis** occurs when a company examines its data to determine if it can meet business expectations, while identifying possible data gaps or where missing data might exist.

Understanding the Benefits of Using High-Quality Information High-quality information can significantly improve the chances of making a good decision and directly increase an organization's bottom line. **Data stewardship** is the management and oversight of an organization's data assets to help provide business users with high-quality data that is easily accessible in a consistent manner. A **data steward** is responsible for ensuring the policies and procedures are implemented across the organization and acts as a liaison between the MIS department and the business. One company discovered that even with its large number of golf courses, Phoenix, Arizona, is not a good place to sell golf clubs. An analysis revealed that typical golfers in Phoenix are tourists and conventioneers who usually bring their clubs with them. The analysis further revealed that two of the best places to sell golf clubs in the United States are Rochester, New York, and Detroit, Michigan. Equipped with this valuable information, the company was able to strategically place its stores and launch its marketing campaigns.

High-quality information does not automatically guarantee that every decision made is going to be a good one, because people ultimately make decisions and no one is perfect. However, such information ensures that the basis of the decisions is accurate. The success of the organization depends on appreciating and leveraging the true value of timely and high-quality information.

Information Governance

Information is a vital resource and users need to be educated on what they can and cannot do with it. To ensure a firm manages its information correctly, it will need special policies and procedures establishing rules on how the information is organized, updated, maintained, and accessed. Every firm, large and small, should create an information policy concerning data governance. **Data governance** refers to the overall management of the availability, usability, integrity, and security of company data. **Master data management (MDM)** is the practice of gathering data and ensuring that it is uniform, accurate, consistent, and complete, including such entities as customers, suppliers, products, sales, employees, and other critical entities that are commonly integrated across organizational systems. MDM is commonly included in data governance. A company that supports a data governance program has a defined a policy that specifies who is accountable for various portions or aspects of the data, including its accuracy, accessibility, consistency, timeliness, and completeness. The policy should clearly define the processes concerning how to store, archive, back up, and secure the data. In addition,

data validation Includes the tests and evaluations used to determine compliance with data governance polices to ensure correctness of data.

database Maintains information about various types of objects (inventory), events (transactions), people (employees), and places (warehouses).

database management system (DBMS) Creates, reads, updates, and deletes data in a database while controlling access and security.

query-by-example (QBE) tool Helps users graphically design the answer to a question against a database.

structured query language (SQL) Users write lines of code to answer questions against a database.

data element (or data field) The smallest or basic unit of information.

the company should create a set of procedures identifying accessibility levels for employees. Then, the firm should deploy controls and procedures that enforce government regulations and compliance with mandates such as Sarbanes-Oxley.

It is important to note the difference between data governance and data stewardship. Data governance focuses on enterprise-wide policies and procedures, while data stewardship focuses on the strategic implementation of the policies and procedures. **Data validation** includes the tests and evaluations used to determine compliance with data governance polices to ensure correctness of data. Data validation helps to ensure that every data value is correct and accurate. In Excel you can use data validation to control the type of data or the values that users enter into a cell. For example, you may want to restrict data entry to a certain range of dates, limit choices by using a list, or make sure that only positive whole numbers are entered.

STORING INFORMATION USING A RELATIONAL DATABASE MANAGEMENT SYSTEM LO6.2

The core component of any system, regardless of size, is a database and a database management system. Broadly defined, a **database** maintains information about various types of objects (inventory), events (transactions), people (employees), and places (warehouses). A **database management system (DBMS)** creates, reads, updates, and deletes data in a database while controlling access and security. Managers send requests to the DBMS, and the DBMS performs the actual manipulation of the data in the database. Companies store their information in databases, and managers access these systems to answer operational questions such as how many customers purchased Product A in December or what were the average sales by region. There are two primary tools available for retrieving information from a DBMS. First is a **query-by-example (QBE) tool** that helps users graphically design the answer to a question against a database. Second is a **structured query language (SQL)** that asks users to write lines of code to answer questions against a database. Managers typically interact with QBE tools, and MIS professionals have the skills required to code SQL. Figure 6.6 displays the relationship between a database, a DBMS, and a user. Some of the more popular examples of DBMS include MySQL, Microsoft Access, SQL Server, FileMaker, Oracle, and FoxPro.

A **data element** (or *data field*) is the smallest or basic unit of information. Data elements can include a customer's name, address, email, discount rate, preferred shipping method, product name, quantity ordered, and so on. **Data models** are logical data structures that detail the relationships among data elements using graphics or pictures.

Metadata provides details about data. For example, metadata for an image could include its size, resolution, and date created. Metadata about a text document could contain document length,

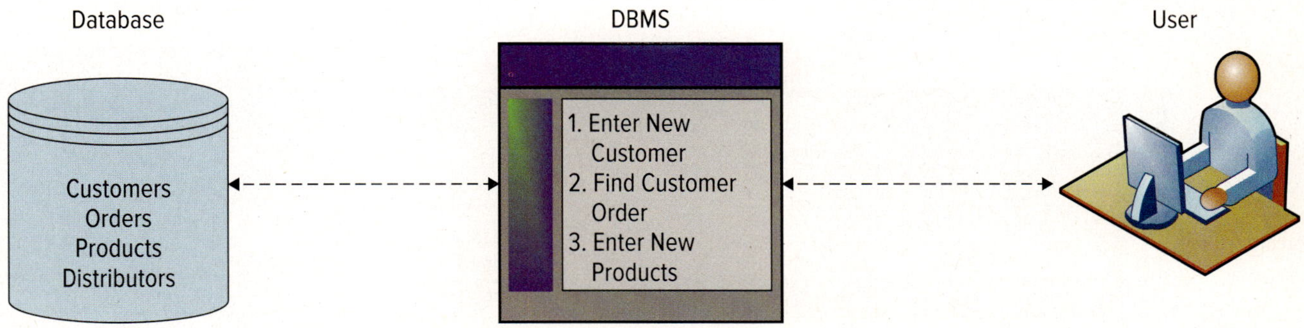

FIGURE 6.6 Relationship of Database, DBMS, and User

data model Logical data structures that detail the relationships among data elements using graphics or pictures.

metadata Details about data.

data dictionary Compiles all of the metadata about the data elements in the data model.

relational database model Stores information in the form of logically related two-dimensional tables.

relational database management system Allows users to create, read, update, and delete data in a relational database.

entity Stores information about a person, place, thing, transaction, or event.

attribute The data elements associated with an entity.

data created, author's name, and summary. Each data element is given a description, such as Customer Name; metadata is provided for the type of data (text, numeric, alphanumeric, date, image, binary value) and descriptions of potential predefined values such as a certain area code; and finally the relationship is defined. A **data dictionary** compiles all of the metadata about the data elements in the data model. Looking at a data model along with reviewing the data dictionary provides tremendous insight into the database's functions, purpose, and business rules.

DBMS use three primary data models for organizing information—hierarchical, network, and the relational database, the most prevalent. A **relational database model** stores information in the form of logically related two-dimensional tables. A **relational database management system** allows users to create, read, update, and delete data in a relational database. Although the hierarchical and network models are important, this text focuses only on the relational database model.

LO6.2 Describe a database, a database management system, and the relational database model.

Storing Data Elements in Entities and Attributes

For flexibility in supporting business operations, managers need to query or search for the answers to business questions such as which artist sold the most albums during a certain month. The relationships in the relational database model help managers extract this information. Figure 6.7 illustrates the primary concepts of the relational database model—entities, attributes, keys, and relationships. An **entity** (also referred to as a table) stores information about a person, place, thing, transaction, or event. The entities, or tables, of interest in Figure 6.7 are *TRACKS, RECORDINGS, MUSICIANS,* and *CATEGORIES.* Notice that each entity is stored in a different two-dimensional table (with rows and columns).

Entities

Foreign keys

Primary keys

TRACKS

TrackNumber	TrackTitle	TrackLength	RecordingID
1	I Won't	3:45	1
2	Begin Again	4:14	1
3	You Got Me	4:00	1
4	Fallin For you	3:35	1
1	I Gotta Feelin	4:49	2
2	Imma Be	4:17	2
3	Boom Boom Pow	4:11	2
4	Meet Me Halfway	4:44	2

RECORDINGS

RecordingID	RecordingTitle	MuscianID	CategoryID
1	Breakthrough	1	1
2	The E.N.D.	2	1
3	Monkey Business	2	1
4	Elephunk	2	1
5	The Fame Monster	3	1
6	Raymond v. Raymond	4	2

Attributes

CATEGORIES

CategoryID	CategoryName
1	Pop
2	R&B
3	Rock
4	Country
5	Blues
6	Classical

Records

MUSICIANS

MusicianID	MusicianName	MusicianPhoto	MusicianNotes
1	Colby Caillat	Colby.jpg	Next concert in Boston 7/1/2011
2	Black Eyed Peas	BYP.bmp	New album due 12/25/2011
3	Lady Gaga	Gaga.tiff	Do not bring young kids to live shows
4	Usher	Usher.bmp	Current album #1 on Billboard

FIGURE 6.7 Primary Concepts of the Relational Database Model

Attributes (also called columns or fields) are the data elements associated with an entity. In Figure 6.7 the attributes for the entity *TRACKS* are *TrackNumber, TrackTitle, TrackLength,* and *RecordingID.* Attributes for the entity *MUSICIANS* are *MusicianID, MusicianName, MusicianPhoto,* and *MusicianNotes.* A **record** is a collection of related data elements (in the *MUSICIANS* table these include "3, Lady Gaga, gag.tiff, Do not bring young kids to live shows"). Each record in an entity occupies one row in its respective table.

Creating Relationships Through Keys

To manage and organize various entities within the relational database model, you use primary keys and foreign keys to create logical relationships. A **primary key** is a field (or group of fields) that uniquely identifies a given record in a table. In the table *RECORDINGS,* the primary key is the field *RecordingID* that uniquely identifies each record in the table. Primary keys are a critical piece of a relational database because they provide a way of distinguishing each record in a table; for instance, imagine you need to find information on a customer named Steve Smith. Simply searching the customer name would not be an ideal way to find the information because there might be 20 customers with the name Steve Smith. This is the reason the relational database model uses primary keys to uniquely identify each record. Using Steve Smith's unique ID allows a manager to search the database to identify all information associated with this customer.

A **foreign key** is a primary key of one table that appears as an attribute in another table and acts to provide a logical relationship between the two tables. For instance, Black Eyed Peas in Figure 6.7 is one of the musicians appearing in the *MUSICIANS* table. Its primary key, *MusicianID,* is "2." Notice that *MusicianID* also appears as an attribute in the *RECORDINGS* table. By matching these attributes, you create a relationship between the *MUSICIANS* and *RECORDINGS* tables that states the Black Eyed Peas *(MusicianID 2)* have several recordings including The E.N.D., Monkey Business, and Elepunk. In essence, *MusicianID* in the *RECORDINGS* table creates a logical relationship (who was the musician that made the recording) to the *MUSICIANS* table. Creating the logical relationship between the tables allows managers to search the data and turn it into useful information.

Coca Cola Relational Database Example

Figure 6.8 illustrates the primary concepts of the relational database model for a sample order of soda from Coca Cola. Figure 6.8 offers an excellent example of how data is stored in a database. For example, the order number is stored in the ORDER table, and each line item is stored in the ORDER LINE table. Entities include CUSTOMER, ORDER, ORDER LINE, PRODUCT, and DISTRIBUTOR. Attributes for CUSTOMER include Customer ID, Customer Name, Contact Name, and Phone. Attributes for PRODUCT include Product ID, Description, and Price. The columns in the table contain the attributes.

record A collection of related data elements.

primary key A field (or group of fields) that uniquely identifies a given record in a table.

foreign key A primary key of one table that appears as an attribute in another table and acts to provide a logical relationship between the two tables.

USING A RELATIONAL DATABASE FOR BUSINESS ADVANTAGES LO6.3

Many business managers are familiar with Excel and other spreadsheet programs they can use to store business data. Although spreadsheets are excellent for supporting some data analysis, they offer limited functionality in terms of security, accessibility, and flexibility and can rarely scale to support business growth. From a business perspective, relational databases offer many advantages over using a text document or a spreadsheet, as displayed in Figure 6.9.

LO6.3 Identify the business advantages of a relational database.

Due Diligence //: That's Not My Mother in the Casket![2]

Information—you simply can't put a value on having the right (or the cost of having the wrong) information. Just look at the mistake made at the Crib Point cemetery in Victoria, Australia, when they were burying Mrs. Ryan, an 85-year-old woman with almost 70 children, grandchildren, and great-grandchildren attending her funeral. The bereaved family of Mrs. Ryan was shocked to lift the lid of her coffin during the funeral to discover another woman lying in her clothes and jewelry. Where was the body of Mrs. Ryan? Mrs. Ryan had been buried earlier that day in the other woman's clothes, jewelry, and plot.

What type of information blunder could possibly occur to allow someone to be buried in the wrong clothes, coffin, and plot? What could the cemetery do to ensure its customers are buried in the correct places? Why is the quality of information important to any business? What issues can occur when a business uses low-quality information to make decisions?

FIGURE 6.8 Potential Relational Database for Coca-Cola Bottling Company of Egypt (TCCBCE)

Order Number: 34562

Coca-Cola Bottling Company of Egypt
Sample Sales Order

Customer: Dave's Sub Shop | Date: 8/6/2008

Quantity	Product	Price	Amount
100	Vanilla Coke	$0.55	$55

Distributor Fee $12.95

Order Total $67.95

CUSTOMER

Customer ID	Customer Name	Contact Name	Phone
23	Dave's Sub Shop	David Logan	(555)333-4545
43	Pizza Palace	Debbie Fernandez	(555)345-5432
765	T's Fun Zone	Tom Repicci	(555)565-6655

ORDER

Order ID	Order Date	Customer ID	Distributor ID	Distributor Fee	Total Due
34561	7/4/2008	23	DEN8001	$22.00	$145.75
34562	8/6/2008	23	DEN8001	$12.95	$67.95
34563	6/5/2008	765	NY9001	$29.50	$249.50

ORDER LINE

Order ID	Line Item	Product ID	Quantity
34561	1	12345AA	75
34561	2	12346BB	50
34561	3	12347CC	100
34562	1	12349EE	100
34563	1	12345AA	100
34563	2	12346BB	100
34563	3	12347CC	50
34563	4	12348DD	50
34563	5	12349EE	100

DISTRIBUTOR

Distributor ID	Distributor Name
DEN8001	Hawkins Shipping
CHI3001	ABC Trucking
NY9001	Van Distributors

PRODUCT

Product ID	Product Description	Price
12345AA	Coca-Cola	$0.55
12346BB	Diet Coke	$0.55
12347CC	Sprite	$0.55
12348DD	Diet Sprite	$0.55
12349EE	Vanilla Coke	$0.55

Increased Flexibility

Databases tend to mirror business structures, and a database needs to handle changes quickly and easily, just as any business needs to be able to do. Equally important, databases need to provide flexibility in allowing each user to access the information in whatever way best suits his or her needs. The distinction between logical and physical views is important in understanding flexible database user views. The **physical view of information** deals with the physical storage of information on a storage device. The **logical view of information** focuses on how individual users logically access information to meet their own particular business needs.

In the database illustration from Figure 6.7, for example, one user could perform a query to determine which recordings had a track length of four minutes or more. At the same time, another user could perform an analysis to determine the distribution of recordings as they relate to the different categories. For example, are there more R&B recordings than rock, or are they evenly distributed? This example demonstrates that while a database has only one physical view, it can easily support multiple logical views that provides for flexibility.

Consider another example—a mail-order business. One user might want a report presented in alphabetical format, in which case last name should appear before first name. Another user, working with a catalog mailing system, would want customer names appearing as first name and then last name. Both are easily achievable, but different logical views of the same physical information.

physical view of information The physical storage of information on a storage device.

logical view of information Shows how individual users logically access information to meet their own particular business needs.

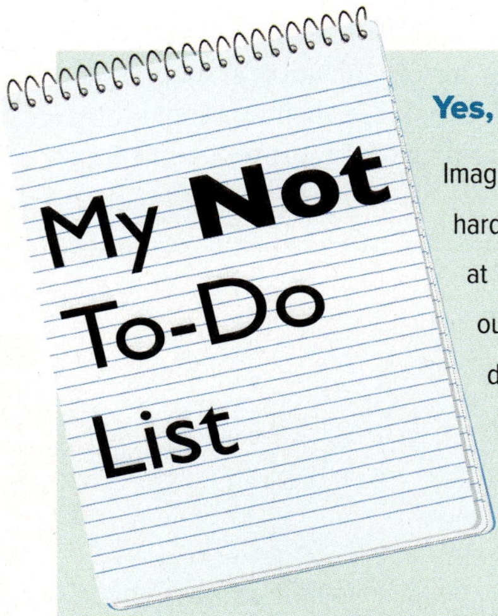

Yes, I Started the Internet[3]

Imagine your favorite co-worker Mary, a hard working employee who is excelling at her job and continuously receives outstanding performance reviews. Suddenly, after two years of hard work, Mary is fired and you are wondering what happened. What will you say when you find out that Mary lied on her résumé about having a master's degree? Will you feel that Mary got what she deserved, or should her outstanding job performance have helped management look past this issue? After all, she is excellent at her job.

Every student should know that if dishonesty is discovered, it is often grounds for termination and possibly legal action. Information integrity is a measure of the quality of information. According to Steven D. Levitt, co-author of *Freakonomics* and a renowned economics professor at the University of Chicago, more than 50 percent of people lie on their résumés. Given such repercussions as Mary's fate, you will want to think twice before ever lying on your résumé. The integrity of the information on your résumé is a direct representation of your personal integrity. How would you handle Mary's situation if you were her manager?

FIGURE 6.9 Business Advantages of a Relational Database

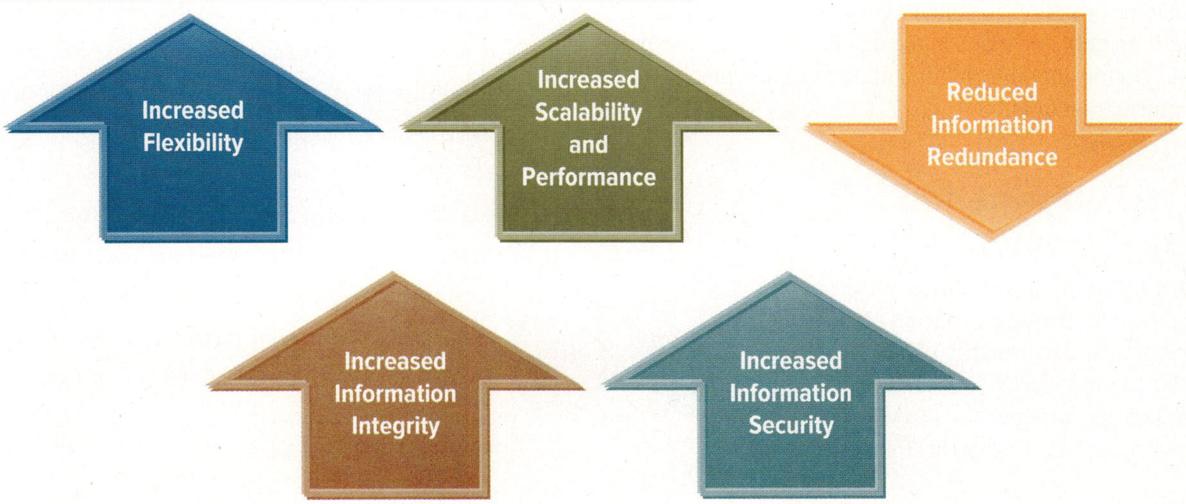

data latency The time it takes for data to be stored or retrieved.

information redundancy The duplication of data, or the storage of the same data in multiple places.

information integrity A measure of the quality of information.

integrity constraint Rules that help ensure the quality of information.

relational integrity constraint Rules that enforce basic and fundamental information-based constraints.

Increased Scalability and Performance

In its first year of operation, the official website of the American Family Immigration History Center, www.ellisisland.org, generated more than 2.5 billion hits. The site offers immigration information about people who entered America through the Port of New York and Ellis Island between 1892 and 1924. The database contains more than 25 million passenger names that are correlated to 3.5 million images of ships' manifests.[4]

The database had to be scalable to handle the massive volumes of information and the large numbers of users expected for the launch of the website. In addition, the database needed to perform quickly under heavy use. **Data latency** is the time it takes for data to be stored or retrieved. Some organizations must be able to support hundreds or thousands of users including employees, partners, customers, and suppliers, who all want to access and share the same information with minimal data latency. Databases today scale to exceptional levels, allowing all types of users and programs to perform information-processing and information-searching tasks.

Reduced Information Redundancy

Information redundancy is the duplication of data, or the storage of the same data in multiple places. Redundant data can cause storage issues along with data integrity issues, making it difficult to determine which values are the most current or most accurate. Employees become confused and frustrated when faced with incorrect information causing disruptions to business processes and procedures. One primary goal of a database is to eliminate information redundancy by recording each piece of information in only one place in the database. This saves disk space, makes performing information updates easier, and improves information quality.

Increased Information Integrity (Quality)

Information integrity is a measure of the quality of information. **Integrity constraints** are rules that help ensure the quality of information. The database design needs to consider integrity constraints. The database and the DBMS ensures that users can never violate these constraints. There are two types of integrity constraints: (1) relational and (2) business critical.

Relational integrity constraints are rules that enforce basic and fundamental information-based constraints. For example, a relational integrity constraint would not allow someone to create an order for a nonexistent customer, provide a markup percentage that was negative, or order zero pounds of raw materials from a supplier. A **business rule** defines how a company performs certain aspects of its business and typically results in either a yes/no or true/false answer. Stating that merchandise returns are allowed within 10 days of purchase is an example of a business rule. **Business-critical integrity constraints** enforce business rules vital to an organization's success and often require more insight and knowledge than relational integrity constraints. Consider a supplier of fresh produce to large

show me *the* MONEY

Excel or Access?

Excel is a great tool with which to perform business analytics. Your friend, John Cross, owns a successful publishing company specializing in Do It Yourself books. John started the business 10 years ago and has slowly grown to 50 employees and $1 million in sales. John has been using Excel to run the majority of his business, tracking book orders, production orders, shipping orders, and billing. John even uses Excel to track employee payroll and vacation dates. To date, Excel has done the job, but as the company continues to grow, the tool is becoming inadequate.

You believe John could benefit from moving from Excel to Access. John is skeptical of the change because Excel has done the job up to now, and his employees are comfortable with the current processes and technology. John has asked you to prepare a presentation explaining the limitations of Excel and the benefits of Access. In a group, prepare the presentation that will help convince John to make the switch.

grocery chains such as Kroger. The supplier might implement a business-critical integrity constraint stating that no product returns are accepted after 15 days past delivery. That would make sense because of the chance of spoilage of the produce. Business-critical integrity constraints tend to mirror the very rules by which an organization achieves success.

The specification and enforcement of integrity constraints produce higher-quality information that will provide better support for business decisions. Organizations that establish specific procedures for developing integrity constraints typically see an increase in accuracy that then increases the use of organizational information by business professionals.

Increased Information Security

Managers must protect information, like any asset, from unauthorized users or misuse. As systems become increasingly complex and highly available over the Internet on many different devices, security becomes an even bigger issue. Databases offer many security features including passwords to provide authentication, access levels to determine who can access the data, and access controls to determine what type of access they have to the information.

For example, customer service representatives might need read-only access to customer order information so they can answer customer order inquiries; they might not have or need the authority to change or delete order information. Managers might require access to employee files, but they should have access only to their own employees' files, not the employee files for the entire company. Various security features of databases can ensure that individuals have only certain types of access to certain types of information.

Identity management is a broad administrative area that deals with identifying individuals in a system (such as a country, a network, or an enterprise) and controlling their access to resources within that system by associating user rights and restrictions with the established identity. Security risks are increasing as more and more databases and DBMS systems are moving to data centers run in the cloud. The biggest risks when using cloud computing are ensuring the security and privacy of the information in the database. Implementing data governance policies and procedures that outline the data management requirements can ensure safe and secure cloud computing.

business rule Defines how a company performs a certain aspect of its business and typically results in either a yes/no or true/false answer.

business-critical integrity constraint Enforces business rules vital to an organization's success and often requires more insight and knowledge than relational integrity constraints.

identity management A broad administrative area that deals with identifying individuals in a system (such as a country, a network, or an enterprise) and controlling their access to resources within that system by associating user rights and restrictions with the established identity.

Due Diligence //:

Sorry, I Didn't Mean to Post Your Social Security Number on the Internet[5]

Programming 101 teaches all students that security is the crucial part of any system. You must secure your data! It appears that some people working for the state of Oklahoma forgot this important lesson when tens of thousands of Oklahoma residents had their sensitive data—including numbers—posted on the Internet for the general public to access. You have probably heard this type of report before, but have you heard that the error went unnoticed for three years? A programmer reported the problem, explaining how he could easily change the page his browser was pointing to and grab the entire database for the state of Oklahoma. Also, because of the programming, malicious users could easily tamper with the database by changing data or adding fictitious data. If you are still thinking that isn't such a big deal, it gets worse. The website also posted the Sexual and Violent Offender Registry. Yes, the Department of Corrections employee data were also available for the general public to review.

© Digital Vision/Getty Images

Why is it important to secure data? What can happen if someone accesses your customer database? What could happen if someone changes the information in your customer database and adds fictitious data? Who should be held responsible for the state of Oklahoma data breech? What are the business risks associated with data security?

content creator The person responsible for creating the original website content.

content editor The person responsible for updating and maintaining website content.

static information Includes fixed data that are not capable of change in the event of a user action.

dynamic information Includes data that change based on user actions.

dynamic catalog An area of a website that stores information about products in a database.

data-driven website An interactive website kept constantly updated and relevant to the needs of its customers using a database.

DRIVING WEBSITES WITH DATA LO6.4

A **content creator** is the person responsible for creating the original website content. A **content editor** is the person responsible for updating and maintaining website content. **Static information** includes fixed data incapable of change in the event of a user action. **Dynamic information** includes data that change based on user actions. For example, static websites supply only information that will not change until the content editor changes the information. Dynamic information changes when a user requests information. A dynamic website changes information based on user requests such as movie ticket availability, airline prices, or restaurant reservations. Dynamic website information is stored in a **dynamic catalog**, or an area of a website that stores information about products in a database.

Websites change for site visitors depending on the type of information they request. Consider, for example, an automobile dealer. The dealer would create a database containing data elements for each car it has available for sale including make, model, color, year, miles per gallon, a photograph, and so on. Website visitors might click on Porsche and then enter their specific requests such as price range or year made. Once the user hits "go" the website automatically provides a custom view of the requested information. The dealer must create, update, and delete automobile information as the inventory changes.

A **data-driven website** is an interactive website kept constantly updated and relevant to the needs of its customers using a database. Data-driven capabilities are especially useful when a firm needs to offer large amounts of information, products, or services. Visitors can become quickly annoyed if they find themselves buried under an avalanche of information when searching a website. A data-driven website can help limit the amount of information displayed to customers based on unique search requirements. Companies even use data-driven websites to make information in their internal databases available to customers and business partners.

There are a number of advantages to using the web to access company databases. First, web browsers are much easier to use than directly accessing the database using a custom-query tool. Second, the web interface requires few or no changes to the database model. Finally, it costs less to add a web interface in front of a DBMS than to redesign and rebuild the system to support changes. Additional data-driven website advantages include:

- Easy to manage content: Website owners can make changes without relying on MIS professionals; users can update a data-driven website with little or no training.
- Easy to store large amounts of data: Data-driven websites can keep large volumes of information organized. Website owners can use templates to implement changes for layouts, navigation, or website structure. This improves website reliability, scalability, and performance.
- Easy to eliminate human errors: Data-driven websites trap data-entry errors, eliminating inconsistencies while ensuring all information is entered correctly.

Zappos credits its success as an online shoe retailer to its vast inventory of nearly 3 million products available through its dynamic data-driven website. The company built its data-driven website catering to a specific niche market: consumers who were tired of finding that their most-desired items were always out of stock at traditional retailers. Zappos' highly flexible, scalable, and secure database helped it rank as the most-available Internet retailer. Figure 6.10 displays Zappos data-driven website illustrating a user querying the database and receiving information that satisfies the user's request.[6]

Companies can gain valuable business knowledge by viewing the data accessed and analyzed from their website. Figure 6.11 displays how running queries or using analytical tools, such as a PivotTable, on the database that is attached to the website can offer insight into the business, such as items browsed, frequent requests, items bought together, and so on.

LO6.4 Explain the business benefits of a data-driven website.

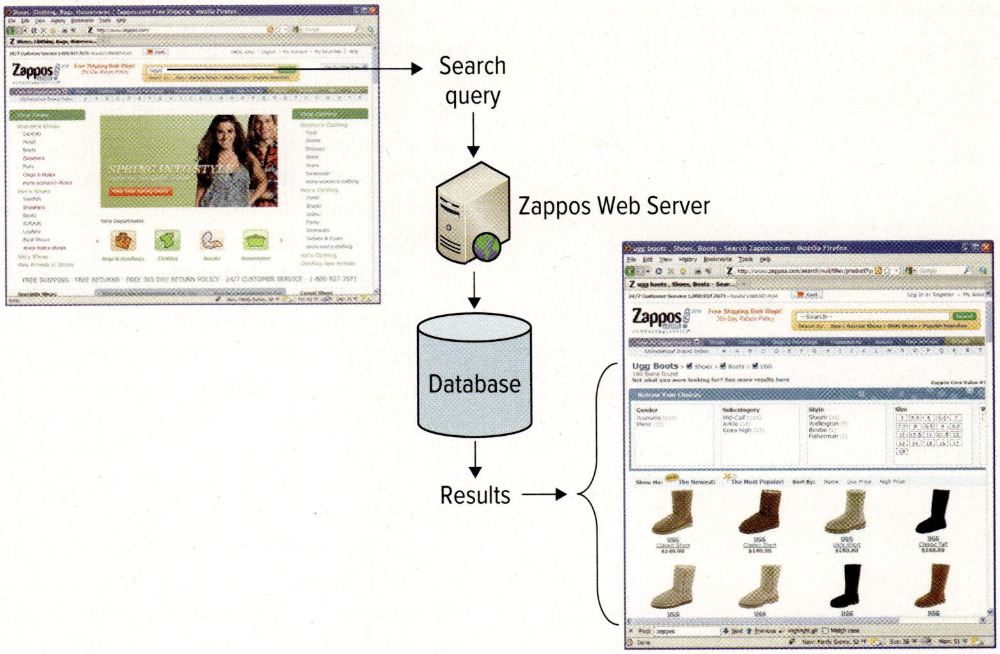

FIGURE 6.10 Zappos.com—A Data-Driven Website

Source: a-b. Zappos.com

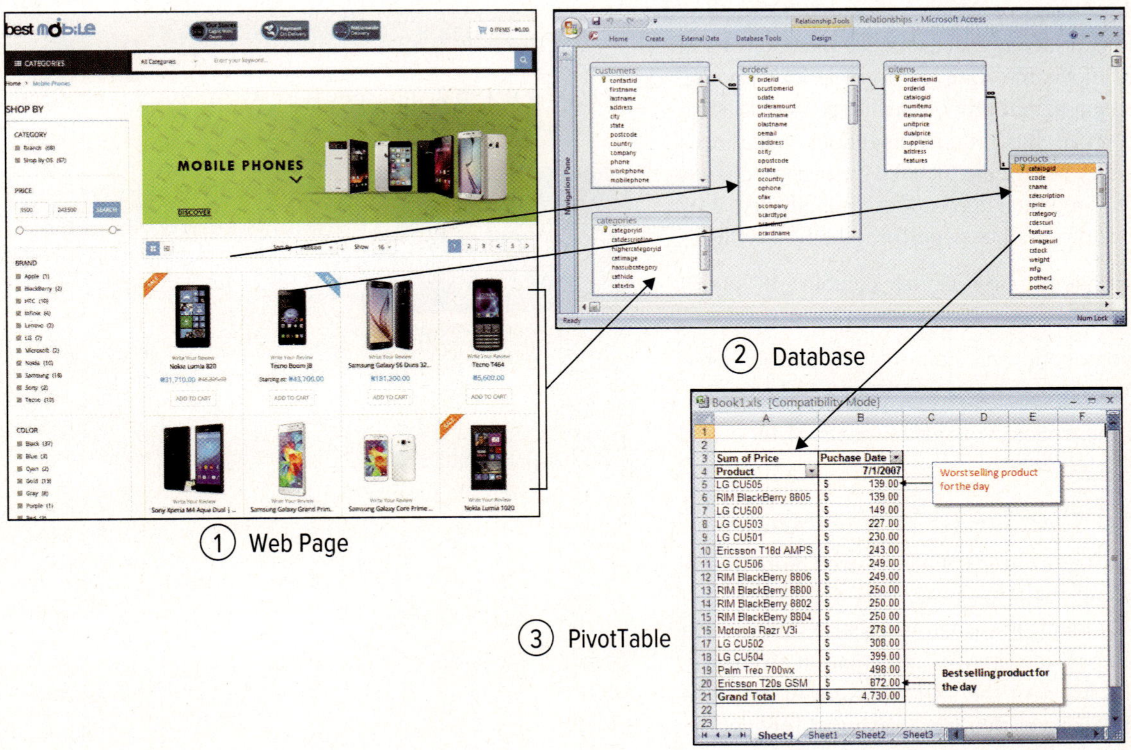

FIGURE 6.11 A data-driven website like BestMobile can provide essential business intelligence

Source: BestMobile.com

{SECTION 6.2} Business Intelligence

LEARNING OUTCOMES

LO6.5 Describe the roles and purposes of data warehouses and data marts in an organization.

LO6.6 Identify the advantages of using business intelligence to support managerial decision making.

LO6.7 Identify the four common characteristics of big data.

LO6.8 Explain data mining and identify the three elements of data mining.

LO6.9 Explain the importance of data analytics and data visualization.

DATA WAREHOUSING LO6.5

Applebee's Neighborhood Grill & Bar posts annual sales in excess of $3.2 billion and is actively using information from its data warehouse to increase sales and cut costs. The company gathers daily information for the previous day's sales into its data warehouse from 1,500 restaurants located in 49 states and seven countries. Understanding regional preferences, such as patrons in Texas preferring steaks more than patrons in New England, allows the company to meet its corporate strategy of being a neighborhood grill appealing to local tastes. The company has found tremendous value in its data warehouse by being able to make business decisions about customers' regional needs. The company also uses data warehouse information to perform the following:

- Base labor budgets on actual number of guests served per hour.
- Develop promotional sale item analysis to help avoid losses from overstocking or understocking inventory.
- Determine theoretical and actual costs of food and the use of ingredients.

History of the Data Warehouse

In the 1990s as organizations began to need more timely information about their business, they found that traditional management information systems were too cumbersome to provide relevant information efficiently and effectively. Most of the systems were in the form of operational databases that were designed for specific business functions, such as accounting, order entry, customer service, and sales, and were not appropriate for business analysis for the reasons shown in Figure 6.12.

During the latter half of the 20th century, the numbers and types of operational databases increased. Many large businesses found themselves with information scattered across multiple systems with different file types (such as spreadsheets, databases, and even word processing files), making it almost impossible for anyone to use the information from multiple sources. Completing reporting requests across operational systems could take days or weeks using antiquated reporting tools that were ineffective for running a business. From this idea, the data warehouse was born as a place where relevant information could be stored and accessed for making strategic queries and reports.

A **repository** is a central location in which data is stored and managed. A **data warehouse** is a logical collection of information—gathered from many different operational databases—that supports business analysis activities and decision-making tasks. The primary purpose of a data warehouse is to combine information, more specifically, strategic information, throughout an organization into a single repository in such a way that the people who need that information can make decisions and undertake business analysis. A key idea within data warehousing is to collect information from multiple systems in a common location that uses a universal querying tool. This allows operational databases to run where they are most efficient for the business, while providing a common location using a familiar format for the strategic or enterprisewide reporting information.

Data warehouses go even a step further by standardizing information. Gender, for instance can be referred to in many ways

FIGURE 6.12 Reasons Business Analysis Is Difficult from Operational Databases.

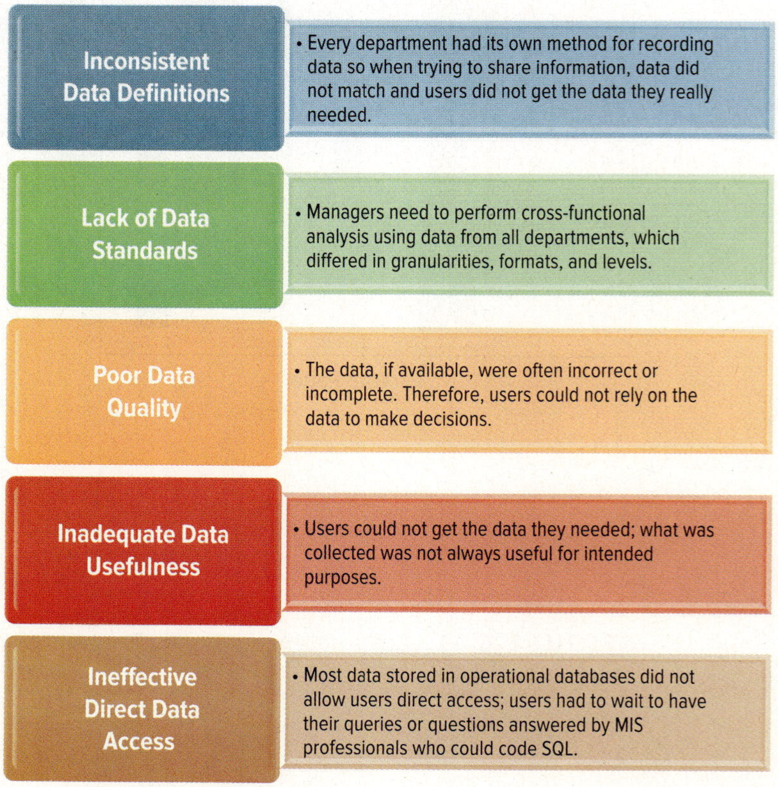

(Male, Female, M/F, 1/0), but it should be standardized on a data warehouse with one common way of referring to each data element that stores gender (M/F). Standardization of data elements allows for greater accuracy, completeness, and consistency and increases the quality of the information in making strategic business decisions. The data warehouse then is simply a tool that enables business users, typically managers, to be more effective in many ways, including:

- Developing customer profiles.
- Identifying new-product opportunities.
- Improving business operations.
- Identifying financial issues.
- Analyzing trends.
- Understanding competitors.
- Understanding product performance. (See Figure 6.13.)

FIGURE 6.13 Data Warehousing Components.

Data Mart

Data aggregation is the collection of data from various sources for the purpose of data processing. One example of a data aggregation is to gather information about particular groups based on specific variables such as age, profession, or income. Businesses collect a tremendous amount of transactional information as part of their routine operations. Marketing, sales, and other departments would like to analyze these data to understand their operations better. Although databases store the details of all transactions (for instance, the sale of a product) and events (hiring a new employee), data warehouses store that same information but in an aggregated form more suited to supporting decision-making tasks. Aggregation, in this instance, can include totals, counts, averages, and the like.

The data warehouse modeled in Figure 6.14 compiles information from internal databases

repository A central location in which data is stored and managed.

data warehouse A logical collection of information, gathered from many different operational databases, that supports business analysis activities and decision-making tasks.

data aggregation The collection of data from various sources for the purpose of data processing.

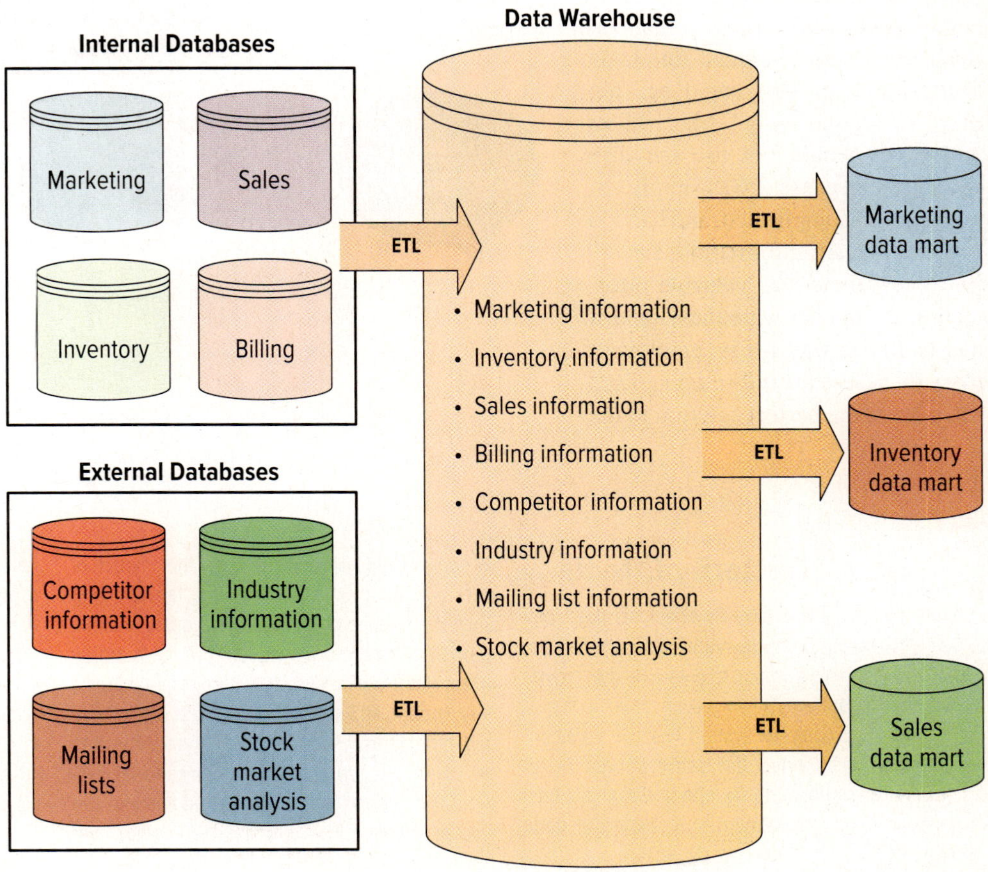

FIGURE 6.14 Model of a Typical Data Warehouse.

extraction, transformation, and loading (ETL) A process that extracts information from internal and external databases, transforms it using a common set of enterprise definitions, and loads it into a data warehouse.

data mart Contains a subset of data warehouse information.

or transactional/operational databases and external databases through **extraction, transformation, and loading (ETL),** which is a process that extracts information from internal and external databases, transforms the information using a common set of enterprise definitions, and loads the information into a data warehouse. The data warehouse then sends subsets of the information to data marts. A **data mart** contains a subset of data warehouse information. To distinguish between data warehouses and data marts, think of data warehouses as having a more organizational focus and data marts as having focused information subsets particular to the needs of a given business unit such as finance or production and operations. Figure 6.14 provides an illustration of a data warehouse and its relationship to internal and external databases, ETL, and data marts.

Lands' End created an organization-wide data warehouse so all its employees could access organizational information. Lands' End soon found out that there could be "too much of a good thing." Many of its employees would not use the data warehouse because it was simply too big, was too complicated, and had too much irrelevant information. Lands' End knew there was valuable information in its data warehouse, and it had to find a way for its employees to easily access the information. Data marts were the perfect solution to the company's information overload problem. Once the employees began using the data marts, they were ecstatic at the wealth of information. Data marts were a huge success for Lands' End.

Information Cleansing (or Scrubbing)

Maintaining quality information in a data warehouse or data mart is extremely important. The Data Warehousing Institute estimates that low-quality information costs U.S. businesses $600 billion annually. That number may seem high, but it is not. If an organization is using a data warehouse or data mart to allocate dollars across advertising strategies, low-quality information will definitely have a negative impact on its ability to make the right decision.

Dirty data is erroneous or flawed data (see Figure 6.15). The complete removal of dirty data from a source is impractical or virtually impossible. According to Gartner Inc., dirty data is

FIGURE 6.15 Dirty Data Problems.

fyi

Butterfly Effects

The butterfly effect, an idea from chaos theory in mathematics, refers to the way a minor event—like the movement of a butterfly's wing—can have a major impact on a complex system like the weather. Dirty data can have the same impact on a business as the butterfly effect. Organizations depend on the movement and sharing of data throughout the organization, so the impact of data quality errors are costly and far-reaching. Such data issues often begin with a tiny mistake in one part of the organization, but the butterfly effect can produce disastrous results, making its way through MIS systems to the data warehouse and other enterprise systems. When dirty data or low-quality data enters organizational systems, a tiny error such as a spelling mistake can lead to revenue loss, process inefficiency, and failure to comply with industry and government regulations. Explain how the following errors can affect an organization:

- A cascading spelling mistake
- Inaccurate customer records
- Incomplete purchasing history
- Inaccurate mailing address
- Duplicate customer numbers for different customers

FIGURE 6.16 Contact Information in Operational Systems.

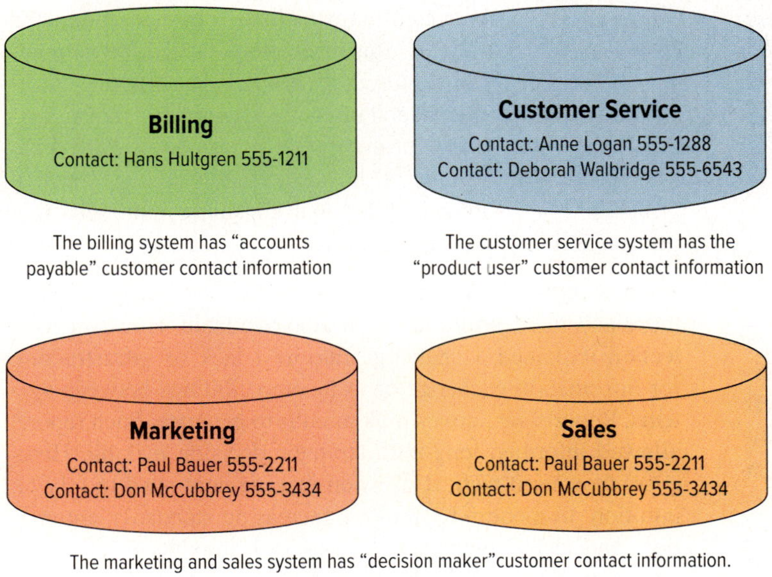

a business problem, not an MIS problem. Over the next two years, more than 25 percent of critical data in Fortune 1000 companies will continue to be flawed; that is, the information will be inaccurate, incomplete, or duplicated.

Obviously, maintaining quality information in a data warehouse or data mart is extremely important. To increase the quality of organizational information and thus the effectiveness of decision making, businesses must formulate a strategy to keep information clean. **Information cleansing or scrubbing** is a process that weeds out and fixes or discards inconsistent, incorrect, or incomplete information.

Specialized software tools exist that use sophisticated procedures to analyze, standardize, correct, match, and consolidate data warehouse information. This step is vitally important because data warehouses often contain information from several databases, some of which can be external to the organization. In a data warehouse, information cleansing occurs first during the ETL process and again once the information is in the data warehouse. Companies can choose information cleansing software from several vendors, including Oracle, SAS, IBM, and Tableau. Ideally, scrubbed information is accurate and consistent.

Looking at customer information highlights why information cleansing is necessary. Customer information exists in several operational systems. In each system, all the details could change—from the customer ID to contact information—depending on the business process the user is performing (see Figure 6.16).

Figure 6.17 displays a customer name entered differently in multiple operational systems. Information cleansing allows an organization to fix these types of inconsistencies and cleans the information in the data warehouse. Figure 6.18 displays the typical events that occur during information cleansing.

information cleansing or scrubbing A process that weeds out and fixes or discards inconsistent, incorrect, or incomplete information.

LO6.5 Describe the roles and purposes of data warehouses and data marts in an organization.

Achieving perfect information is almost impossible. The more complete and accurate an organization wants its information to be, the more it costs (see Figure 6.19). The trade-off for perfect information lies in accuracy versus completeness. Accurate information means it is correct, while complete information means there are no blanks. A birth date of 2/31/10 is an example of complete but inaccurate information (February 31 does not exist). An address containing Denver, Colorado, without a zip code is an example of incomplete information that is accurate. For their information, most organizations determine a percentage high enough to make good decisions at a reasonable cost, such as 85 percent accurate and 65 percent complete.

FIGURE 6.17 Standardizing Customer Name from Operational Systems.

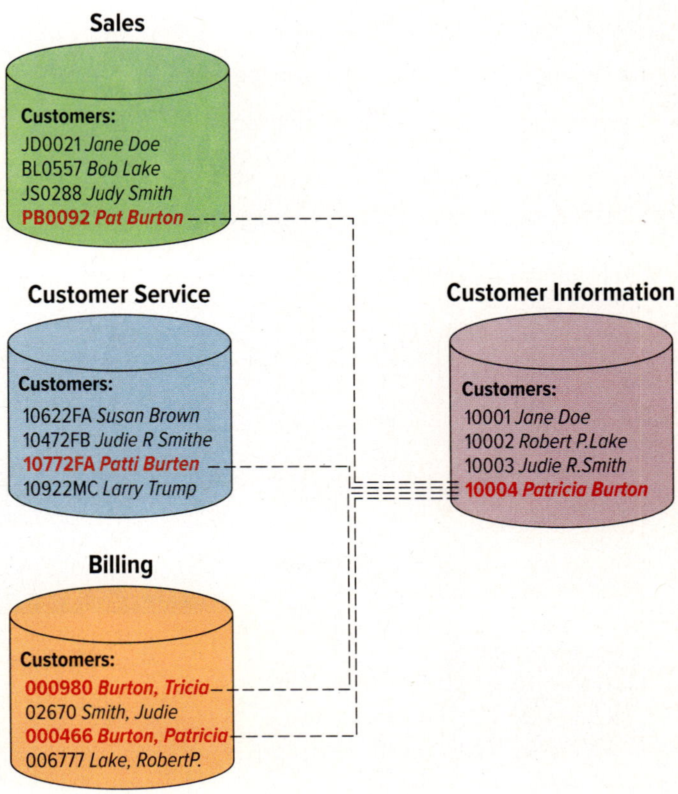

data point An individual item on a graph or a chart.

data broker A business that collects personal information about consumers and sells that information to other organizations.

data lake A storage repository that holds a vast amount of raw data in its original format until the business needs it.

BUSINESS INTELLIGENCE LO6.6

Many organizations today find it next to impossible to understand their own strengths and weaknesses, let alone their biggest competitors', because the enormous volume of organizational data is inaccessible to all but the MIS department. A **data point** is an individual item on a graph or a chart. Organizational data includes far more than simple structured data elements in a database; the set of data also includes unstructured data such as voice mail, customer phone calls, text messages, video clips, along with numerous new forms of data, such as tweets from Twitter.

An early reference to business intelligence occurs in Sun Tzu's book titled *The Art of War.* Sun Tzu claims that to succeed in war, one should have full knowledge of one's own strengths and weaknesses and full knowledge of the enemy's strengths and weaknesses. Lack of either one might result in defeat. A certain school of thought draws parallels between the challenges in business and those of war, specifically:

- Collecting information.
- Discerning patterns and meaning in the information.
- Responding to the resultant information.

Before the start of the information age in the late 20th century, businesses sometimes collected information from non-automated sources. Businesses then lacked the computing resources to properly analyze the information and often made commercial decisions based primarily on intuition. A **data broker** is a business that collects personal information about consumers and sells that information to other organizations.

As businesses started automating more and more systems, more and more information became available. However, collection remained a challenge due to a lack of infrastructure for information exchange or to incompatibilities between systems. Reports sometimes took months to generate. Such reports allowed informed long-term strategic decision making. However, short-term tactical decision making continued to rely on intuition. In modern businesses, increasing standards, automation, and technologies have led to vast amounts of available information. Data warehouse technologies have set up repositories to store this information. Improved ETL has increased the speedy collecting of information. Business intelligence has now become the art of sifting through large amounts of data, extracting information, and turning that information into actionable knowledge.

A **data lake** is a storage repository that holds a vast amount of raw data in its original format until the business needs it. While a traditional data warehouse stores data in files or folders, a data lake uses a flat architecture to store data. Each data element in a data lake is assigned a unique identifier and tagged with a set of extended metadata tags. When a business question arises, the data lake can be queried for all of the relevant data providing a smaller data set that can then be analyzed to help answer the question.

FIGURE 6.18 Information Cleansing Activities.

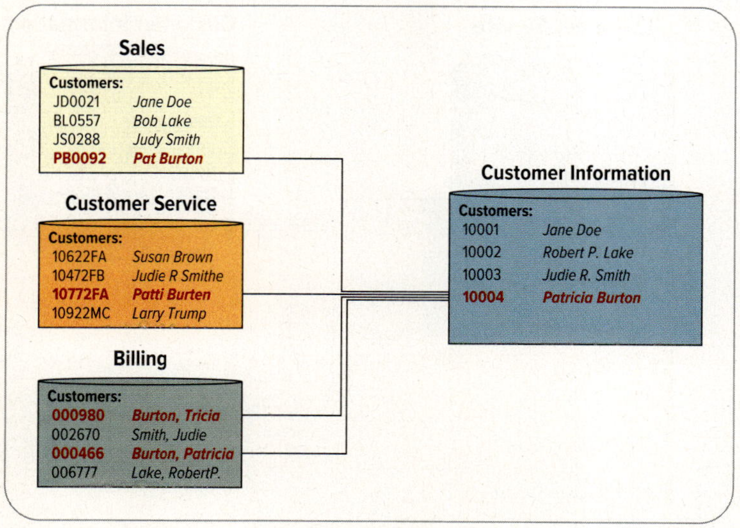

FIGURE 6.19 Accurate and Complete Information.

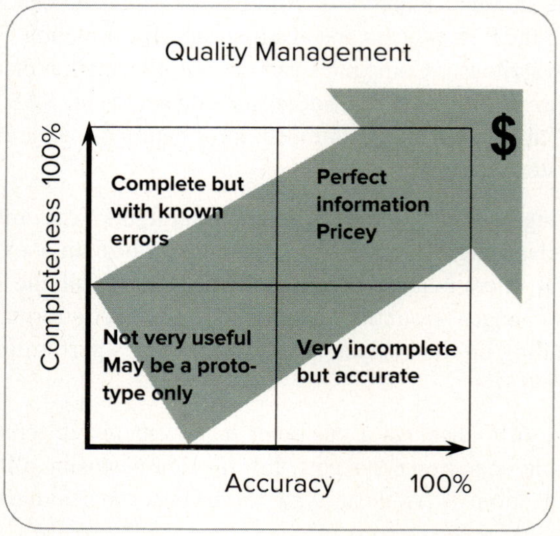

show me *the* MONEY

Clean My Data!

Congratulations! You have just been hired as a consultant for Integrity Information Inc., a start-up business intelligence consulting company. Your first job is to help work with the sales department in securing a new client, The Warehouse. The Warehouse has been operating in the United States for more than a decade, and its primary business is to sell wholesale low-cost products. The Warehouse is interested in hiring Integrity Information Inc. to clean up the data that are stored in its U.S. database. To determine how good your work is, the client would like your analysis of the following spreadsheet. The Warehouse is also interested in expanding globally and wants to purchase several independent wholesale stores located in Australia, Thailand, China, Japan, and the United Kingdom. Before the company moves forward with the venture, it wants to understand what types of data issues it might encounter as it begins to transfer data from each global entity to the data warehouse. Please create a list detailing the potential issues The Warehouse can anticipate encountering as it consolidates the global databases into a single data warehouse.

CUST ID	First Name	Last Name	Address	City	State	Zip	Phone	Last Order Date
233620	Christopher	Lee	12421 W Olympic Blvd	Los Angeles	CA	75080-1100	(972)680-7848	4/18/2014
233621	Bruce	Brandwen	268 W 44th St	New York	PA	10036-3906	(212)471-6077	5/3/2014
233622	Glr	Johnson	4100 E Dry Creek Rd	Littleton	CO	80122-3729	(303)712-5461	5/6/2014
233623	Dave	Owens	466 Commerce Rd	Staunton	VA	24401-4432	(540)851-0362	3/19/2014
233624	John	Coulbourn	124 Action St	Maynard	MA	1754	(978)987-0100	4/24/2014
233629	Dan	Gagliardo	2875 Union Rd	Cheektowaga	NY	14227-1461	(716)558-8191	5/4/2014
23362	Damanceee	Allen	1633 Broadway	New York	NY	10019-6708	(212)708-1576	
233630	Michael	Peretz	235 E 45th St	New York	NY	10017-3305	(212)210-1340	4/30/2014
233631	Jody	Veeder	440 Science Dr	Madison	WI	53711-1064	(608)238-9690 X227	3/27/2014
233632	Michael	Kehrer	3015 SSE Loop 323	Tyler	TX	75701	(903)579-3229	4/28/2014
233633	Erin	Yoon	3500 Carillon Pt	Kirkland	WA	98033-7354	(425)897-7221	3/25/2014
233634	Madeline	Shefferly	4100 E Dry Creek Rd	Littleton	CO	80122-3729	(303)486-3949	3/33/2014
233635	Steven	Conduit	1332 Enterprise Dr	West Chester	PA	19380-5970	(610)692-5900	4/27/2014
233636	Joseph	Kovach	1332 Enterprise Dr	West Chester	PA	19380-5970	(610)692-5900	4/28/2014
233637	Richard	Jordan	1700 N	Philadelphia	PA	19131-4728	(215)581-6770	3/19/2014
233638	Scott	Mikolajczyk	1655 Crofton Blvd	Crofton	MD	21114-1387	(410)729-8155	4/28/2014
233639	Susan	Shragg	1875 Century Park E	Los Angeles	CA	90067-2501	(310)785-0511	4/29/2014
233640	Rob	Ponto	29777 Telegraph Rd	Southfield	MI	48034-1303	(810)204-4724	5/5/2014
233642	Lauren	Butler	1211 Avenue Of The Americas	New York	NY	10036-8701	(212)852-7494	4/22/2014
233643	Christopher	Lee	12421 W Olympic Blvd	Los Angeles	CA	90064-1022	(310)689-2577	3/25/2014
233644	Michelle	Decker	6922 Hollywood Blvd	Hollywood	CA	90028-6117	(323)817-4655	5/8/2014
233647	Natalia	Galeano	1211 Avenue Of The Americas	New York	NY	10036-8701	(646)728-6911	4/23/2014
233648	Bobbie	Orchard	4201 Congress St	Charlotte	NC	28209-4617	(704)557-2444	5/11/2014
233650	Ben	Konfino	1111 Stewart Ave	Bethpage	NY	11714-3533	(516)803-1406	3/19/2014
233651	Lenee	Santana	1050 Techwood Dr NW	Atlanta	GA	30318-KKRR	(404)885-2000	3/22/2014
233652	Lauren	Monks	7700 Wisconsin Ave	Bethesda	MD	20814-3578	(301)771-4772	3/19/2005
233653	Mark	Woolley	10950 Washington Blvd	Culver City	CA	90232-4026	(310)202-2900	4/20/2014

source data Identifies the primary location where data is collected.

data set An organized collection of data.

comparative analysis Compares two or more data sets to identify patterns and trends.

competitive monitoring When a company keeps tabs of its competitor's activities on the web using software that automatically tracks all competitor website activities such as discounts and new products.

FIGURE 6.20 How BI Can Answer Tough Customer Questions.

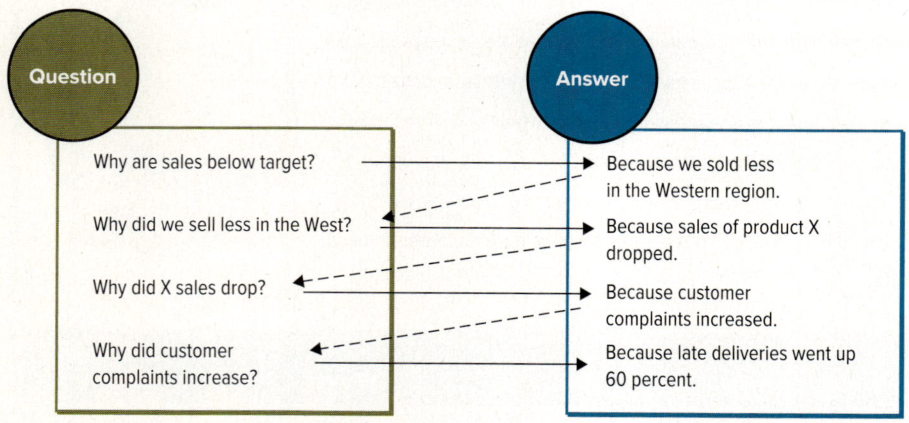

The Problem: Data Rich, Information Poor

An ideal business scenario would be as follows: As a business manager on his way to meet with a client reviews historical customer data, he realizes that the client's ordering volume has substantially decreased. As he drills down into the data, he notices the client had a support issue with a particular product. He quickly calls the support team to find out all of the information and learns that a replacement for the defective part can be shipped in 24 hours. In addition, he learns that the client has visited the website and requested information on a new product line. Armed with all this information, the business manager is prepared for a productive meeting with his client. He now understands the client's needs and issues, and he can address new sales opportunities with confidence.

For many companies the above example is simply a pipe dream. Attempting to gather all of the client information would actually take hours or even days to compile. With so much data available, it is surprisingly hard for managers to get information, such as inventory levels, past order history, or shipping details. **Source data** identifies the primary location where data is collected. Source data can include invoices, spreadsheets, time-sheets, transactions, and electronic sources such as other databases. Managers send their information requests to the MIS department where a dedicated person compiles the various reports. In some situations, responses can take days, by which time the information may be outdated and opportunities lost. Many organizations find themselves in the position of being data rich and information poor. Even in today's electronic world, managers struggle with the challenge of turning their business data into business intelligence.

The Solution: Business Intelligence

Employee decisions are numerous and they include providing service information, offering new products, and supporting frustrated customers. A **data set** is an organized collection of data. A **comparative analysis** can compare two or more data sets to identify patterns and trends. Employees can base their decisions on data sets, experience, or knowledge and preferably a combination of all three. Business intelligence can provide managers with the ability to make better decisions. A few examples of how different industries use business intelligence include:

- **Airlines:** Analyze popular vacation locations with current flight listings.
- **Banking:** Understand customer credit card usage and nonpayment rates.
- **Health care:** Compare the demographics of patients with critical illnesses.
- **Insurance:** Predict claim amounts and medical coverage costs.
- **Law enforcement:** Track crime patterns, locations, and criminal behavior.
- **Marketing:** Analyze customer demographics.
- **Retail:** Predict sales, inventory levels, and distribution.
- **Technology:** Predict hardware failures.

Figure 6.20 displays how organizations using BI can find the cause to many issues and problems simply by asking "Why?" The process starts by analyzing a report such as sales amounts by quarter. Managers will drill down into the report looking for why sales are up or why sales are down. Once they understand why a certain location or product is experiencing an increase in sales, they can share the information in an effort to raise enterprisewide sales. Once they understand the cause for a decrease in sales, they can take effective action to resolve the issue. BI can help managers with **competitive monitoring** where a company keeps tabs of its competitor's activities on the web using software that automatically tracks all competitor website activities such as discounts and new products. Here are a few examples of how managers can use BI to answer tough business questions:

- **Where has the business been?** Historical perspective offers important variables for determining trends and patterns.
- **Where is the business now?** Looking at the current business situation allows managers to take effective action to solve issues before they grow out of control.
- **Where is the business going?** Setting strategic direction is critical for planning and creating solid business strategies.

Ask a simple question—such as who is my best customer or what is my worst-selling product—and you might get as many answers as you have employees. Databases, data warehouses, and data marts can provide a single source of "trusted" data that can answer questions about customers, products, suppliers, production, finances, fraud, and even employees. A **data map** is a technique for establishing a match, or balance, between the source data and the target data warehouse. This technique identifies data shortfalls and recognizes data issues. They can also alert managers to inconsistencies or help determine the cause and effects of enterprisewide business decisions.

All business aspects can benefit from the added insights provided by business intelligence, and you, as a business student, will benefit from understanding how MIS can help you make data-driven decisions. **Data-driven decision management** is an approach to business governance that values decisions that can be backed up with verifiable data. The success of the data-driven approach is reliant upon the quality of the data gathered and the effectiveness of its analysis and interpretation.

In the early days of computing, it usually took a specialist with a strong background in technology to mine data for information because it was necessary for that person to understand how databases and data warehouses worked. Today, business intelligence tools often require very little, if any, support from the MIS department. Business managers can customize dashboards to display the data they want to see and run custom reports on the fly. The changes in how data can be mined and visualized allows business executives who have no technology backgrounds to be able to work with analytics tools and make data-driven decisions.

data map A technique for establishing a match, or balance, between the source data and the target data warehouse.

data-driven decision management An approach to business governance that values decisions that can be backed up with verifiable data.

Data-driven decision management is usually undertaken as a way to gain a competitive advantage. A study from the MIT Center for Digital Business found that organizations driven most by data-based decision making had 4% higher productivity rates and 6% higher profits. However, integrating massive amounts of information from different areas of the business and combining it to derive actionable data in real time can be easier said than done. Errors can creep into data analytics processes at any stage of the endeavor, and serious issues can result when they do.

LO6.6 Identify the advantages of using business intelligence to support managerial decision making.

BUSTED Follow the Data

There is a classic line in the movie *All the President's Men,* which covers the Watergate investigation, where Deep Throat meets with Bob Woodward and coolly advises him to "follow the money." Woodward follows the money, and the Watergate investigation ends with President Nixon's resignation.

If you want to find out what is happening in today's data-filled world, you could probably change those words to "follow the data." IDC reports that the amount of information stored in the digital universe is projected to hit nearly 1.8 zettabytes by 2011, representing a tenfold increase in five years. One of the newest forms of legal requirements emerging from the data explosion is ediscovery, the legal requirements mandating that an organization must archive all forms of software communications, including email, text messages, and multimedia. Yes, the text message you sent four years ago could come back to haunt you.

© Epoxidude/Getty Images

Organizations today have more data than they know what to do with and are frequently overwhelmed with data management. Getting at such data and presenting them in a useful manner for cogent analysis is a tremendous task that haunts managers. What do you think is involved in data management? What is contained in the zettabytes of data stored by organizations? Why would an organization store data? How long should an organization store its data? What are the risks associated with failing to store organizational data?

distributed computing Processes and manages algorithms across many machines in a computing environment.

virtualization Creates multiple "virtual" machines on a single computing device.

THE POWER OF BIG DATA LO6.7

Big data is a collection of large, complex data sets, including structured and unstructured data, which cannot be analyzed using traditional database methods and tools. Big data came into fruition primary due to the last 50 years of technology evolution. Revolutionary technological advances in software, hardware, storage, networking, and computing models have transformed the data landscape, making new opportunities for data collection possible. Big data is one of the latest trends emerging from the convergence of technological factors. For example, cell phones generate tremendous amounts of data and much of it is available for use with analytical applications. Big data includes data sources that include extremely large volumes of data, with high velocity, wide variety, and an understanding of the data veracity. The four common characteristics of big data are detailed in Figure 6.21 and Figure 6.22.

The move to big data combines business with science, research, and government activities. A company can now analyze petabytes of data for patterns, trends, and anomalies gaining insights into data in new and exciting ways. A petabyte of data is equivalent to 20 million four-drawer file cabinets filled with text files or 13 years of HDTV content. Big data requires sophisticated tools to analyze all of the structured and unstructured data from millions of customers, devices, and machine interactions (see Figure 6.23). The two primary computing models that have shaped the collection of big data include distributed computing and vitalization.

Distributed Computing

Distributed computing processes and manages algorithms across many machines in a computing environment (see Figure 6.24). A key component of big data is a distributed computing environment that shares resources ranging from memory to networks to storage. With distributed computing individual computers are networked together across geographical areas and work together to execute a workload or computing processes as if they were one single computing environment. For example, you can distribute a set of programs on the same physical server and use a message service to allow them to communicate and pass information. You can also have a distributed computing environment where many different systems or servers, each with its own computing memory, work together to solve a common problem.

Virtualization

Virtualization is the creation of a virtual (rather than actual) version of computing resources, such as an operating system, a server, a storage device, or network resources (see Figure 6.25). With big data it is now possible to virtualize data so that it can be stored efficiently and cost-effectively. Improvements in network speed and network reliability have removed the physical limitations of being able to manage massive amounts of data at an acceptable pace. The decrease in price of storage and computer memory allow companies to leverage data that would have been inconceivable to collect only 10 years ago.

Analyzing Big Data

With the onset of big data, organizations are collecting more data than ever. Historically, data were housed in functional systems that were not integrated, such as customer service,

FIGURE 6.21 Four Common Characteristics of Big Data.

VARIETY	• Different forms of structured and unstructured data • Data from spreadsheets and databases as well as from email, videos, photos, and PDFs, all of which must be analyzed
VERACITY	• The uncertainty of data, including biases, noise, and abnormalities • Uncertainty or untrustworthiness of data • Data must be meaningful to the problem being analyzed • Must keep data clean and implement processes to keep dirty data from accumulating in systems
VOLUME	• The scale of data • Includes enormous volumes of data generated daily • Massive volume created by machines and networks • Big data tools necessary to analyze zettabytes and brontobytes
VELOCITY	• The analysis of streaming data as it travels around the Internet • Analysis necessary of social media messages spreading globally

FIGURE 6.22 Four V's of Big Data.

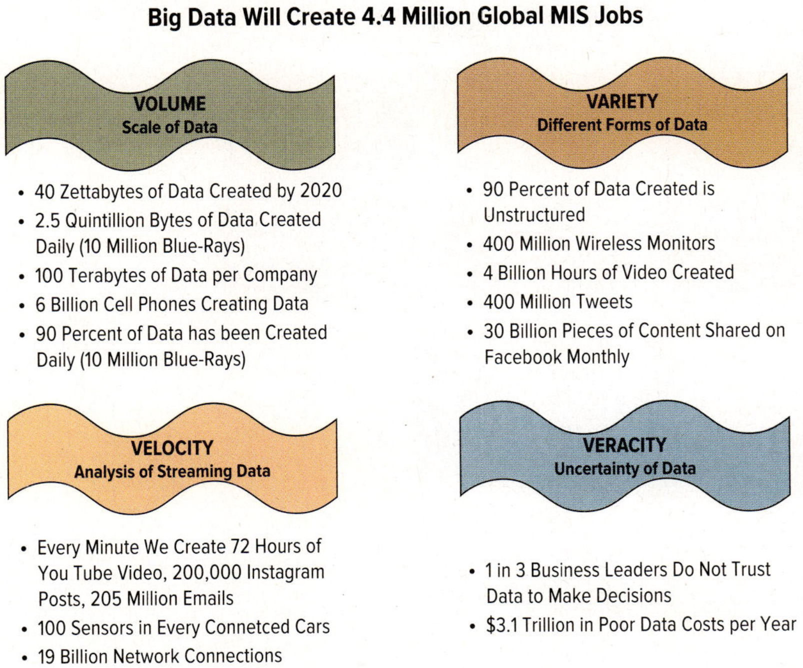

FIGURE 6.23 Structured and Unstructured Data Examples

Structured Data	Unstructured Data
Sensor Data	Satellite Images
Weblog Data	Photographic Data
Financial Data	Video Data
Click-stream Data	Social Media Data
Point of Sale Data	Text Message
Accounting Data	Voice Mail Data

finance, and human resources. Today companies can gather all of the functional data together by the petabyte, but finding a way to analyze the data is incredibly challenging. Figure 6.26 displays the three focus areas business are using to dissect, analyze, and understand organizational data.

LO6.7 Identify the four common characteristics of big data.

FIGURE 6.24 Distributed Computing Environment.

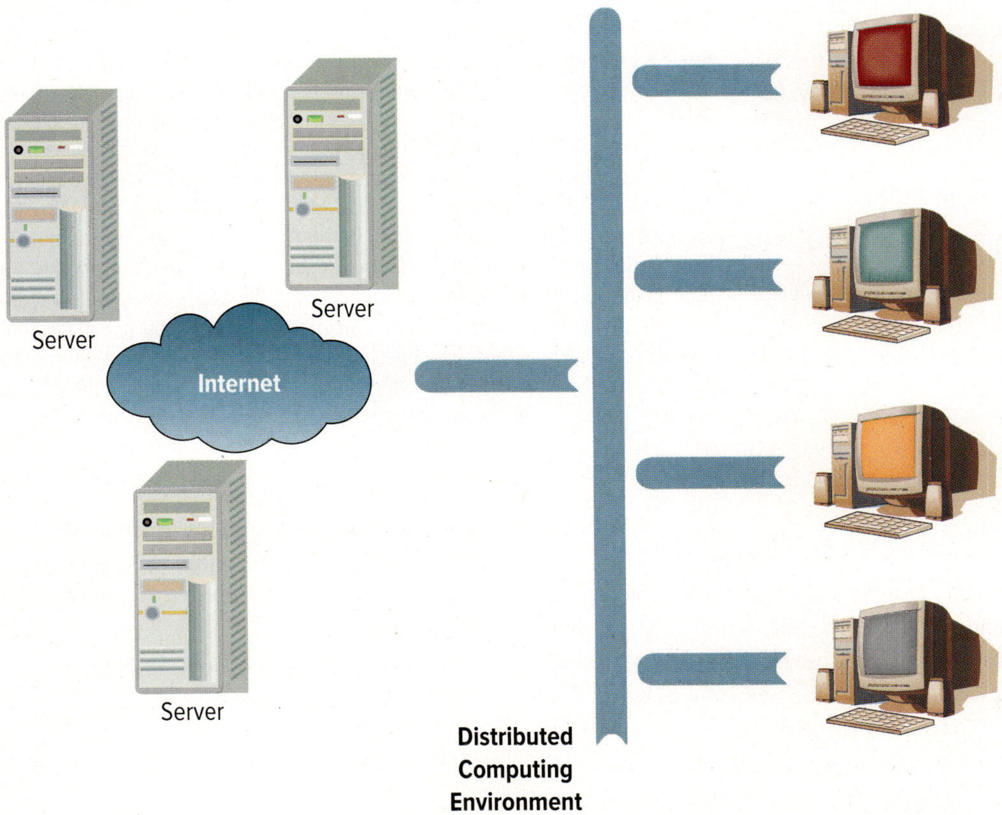

FIGURE 6.25 Virtualization Example.

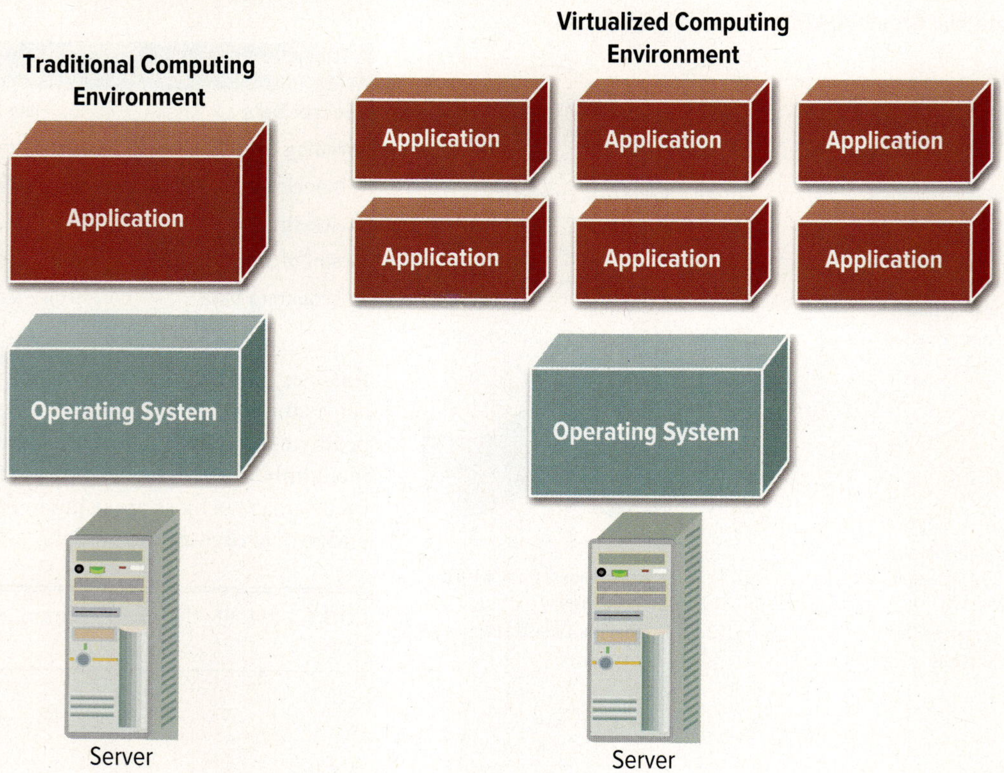

Living the DREAM

2 Trillion Rows of Data Analyzed Daily — No Problem

eBay is the world's largest online marketplace, with 97 million global users selling anything to anyone at a yearly total of $62 billion—more than $2,000 every second. Of course with this many sales, eBay is collecting the equivalent of the Library of Congress worth of data every three days that must be analyzed to run the business successfully. Luckily, eBay discovered Tableau!

Tableau started at Stanford when Chris Stolte, a computer scientist; Pat Hanrahan, an Academy Award–winning professor; and Christian Chabot, a savvy business leader, decided to solve the problem of helping ordinary people understand big data. The three created Tableau, which bridged two computer science disciplines: computer graphics and databases. No more need to write code or understand the relational database keys and categories; users simply drag and drop pictures of what they want to analyze. Tableau has become one of the most successful data visualization tools on the market, winning multiple awards, international expansion, and millions in revenue and spawning multiple new inventions.[7]

Tableau is revolutionizing business analytics, and this is only the beginning. Visit the Tableau website and become familiar with the tool by watching a few of the demos. Once you have a good understanding of the tool, create three questions eBay might be using Tableau to answer, including the analysis of its sales data to find patterns, business insights, and trends.

DATA MINING LO6.8

Reports piled on a manager's desk provide summaries of past business activities and stock market data. Unfortunately, these reports don't offer much insight into why these things are happening or what might happen over the next few months. Data mining to the rescue! **Data mining** is the process of analyzing data to extract information not offered by the raw data alone. Data mining can also begin at a summary information level (coarse granularity) and progress through increasing levels of detail (drilling down) or the reverse (drilling up). Companies use data mining techniques to compile a complete picture of their operations, all within a single view, allowing them to identify trends and improve forecasts. The three elements of data mining include:

1. **Data:** Foundation for data-directed decision making.
2. **Discovery:** Process of identifying new patterns, trends, and insights.
3. **Deployment:** Process of implementing discoveries to drive success.

One retailer discovered that loyalty program customers spent more over time and it strategically invested in specific

data mining The process of analyzing data to extract information not offered by the raw data alone.

data profiling The process of collecting statistics and information about data in an existing source.

data replication The process of sharing information to ensure consistency between multiple data sources.

recommendation engine A data-mining algorithm that analyzes a customer's purchases and actions on a website and then uses the data to recommend complementary products.

estimation analysis Determines values for an unknown continuous variable behavior or estimated future value.

FIGURE 6.26 Business Focus Areas of Big Data.

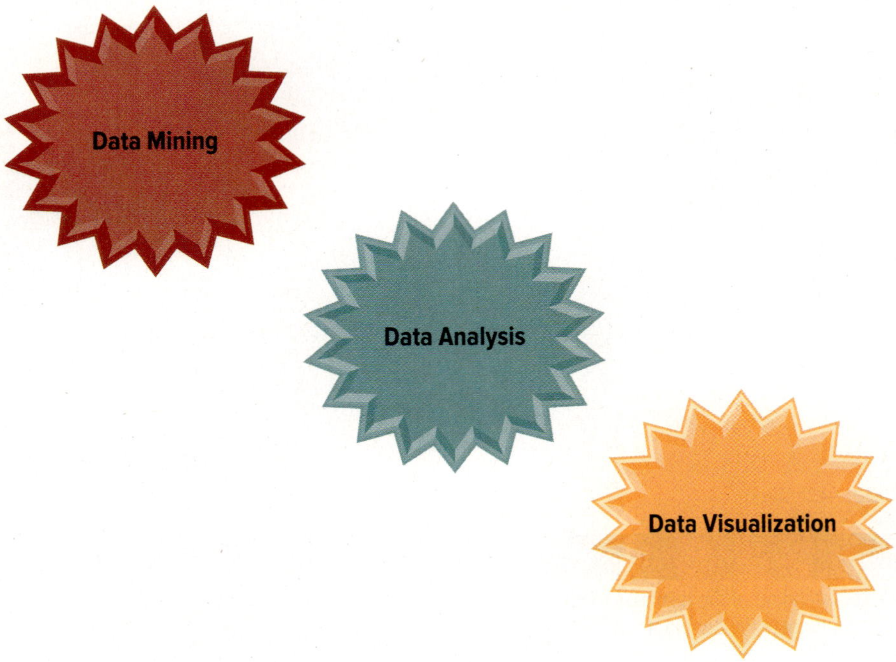

marketing campaigns focusing on these high spenders, thereby maximizing revenue and reducing marketing costs. One manufacturer discovered a sequence of events that preceded accidental releases of toxic chemicals, allowing the factory to remain operational while it prevented dangerous accidents. One insurance company discovered that one of its offices was able to process certain common claim types more quickly than others of comparable size. Armed with this valuable information the company mimicked this office's best practices across its entire organization, improving customer service.

Data Mining Process Model

Data mining is a continuous process or cycle of activity where you continually revisit the problems with new projects. This allows past models to be effectively reused to look for new opportunities in the present and future. Data mining allows users to recycle their work to become more effective and efficient on solving future problems. It is similar to creating a household budget and reusing the same basic budget year after year even though expenses and income change. There are six primary phases in the data-mining process, outlined in Figure 6.27 and detailed in Figure 6.28.

Data Mining Analysis Techniques

Data profiling is the process of collecting statistics and information about data in an existing source. Insights extracted from data profiling can determine how easy or difficult it will be to use existing data for other purposes along with providing metrics on data quality. **Data replication** is the process of sharing information to ensure consistency between multiple data sources. Data mining can determine relationships among such internal factors as price, product positioning, or staff skills, and external factors such as economic indicators, competition, and customer demographics. In addition, it can determine the impact on sales, customer satisfaction, and corporate profits and drill down into summary information to view detailed transactional data. With data mining, a retailer could use point-of-sale records of customer purchases to send targeted promotions based on an individual's purchase history. By mining demographic data from comment or warranty cards, the retailer could develop products and promotions to appeal to specific customer segments.

A **recommendation engine** is a data-mining algorithm that analyzes a customer's purchases and actions on a website and then uses the data to recommend complementary products. Netflix uses a recommendation engine to analyze each customer's film-viewing habits to provide recommendations for other customers with Cinematch, its movie recommendation system. Using Cinematch, Netflix can present customers with a number of additional movies they might want to watch based on the customer's current preferences. Netflix's innovative use of data mining provides its competitive advantage in the movie rental industry. Figure 6.29 displays the common data-mining techniques used to perform advanced analytics such as Netflix's Cinematch.

Estimation Analysis

An **estimation analysis** determines values for an unknown continuous variable behavior or estimated future value. Estimation models predict numeric

affinity grouping analysis Reveals the relationship between variables along with the nature and frequency of the relationships.

outcomes based on historical data. For example, the percentage of high school students that will graduate based on student-teacher ratio or income levels. An estimate is similar to a guess and is one of the least expensive modeling techniques. Many organizations use estimation analysis to determine the overall costs of a project from start to completion or estimates on the profits from introducing a new product line.

Affinity Grouping Analysis **Affinity grouping analysis** reveals the relationship between variables along with the nature and frequency of the relationships. Many people refer to affinity grouping algorithms as association rule generators because they create rules to determine the likelihood of events occurring together at a particular time or following each other in a logical progression. Percentages usually reflect the

FIGURE 6.27 Data Mining Process Model Overview

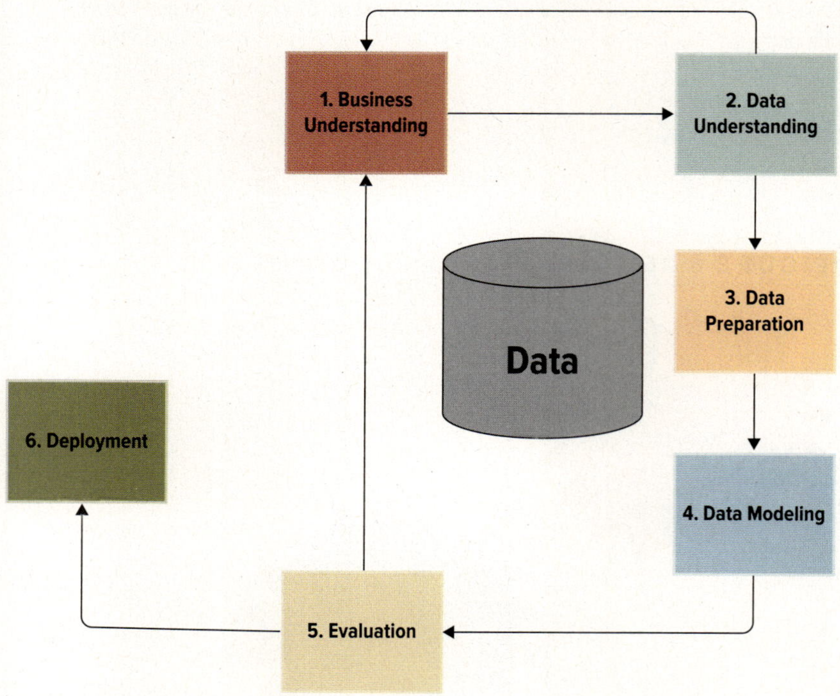

FIGURE 6.28 Data Mining Process Model Activities.

	Phase	Definition	Activities
1	Business Understanding	Gain a clear understanding of the business problem that must be solved and how it impacts the company	• Identify business goals • Situation assessment • Define data-mining goals • Create project plan
2	Data Understanding	Analysis of all current data along with identifying any data quality issues	• Gather data • Describe data • Explore data • Verify data quality
3	Data Preparation	Gather and organize the data in the correct formats and structures for analysis	• Select data • Cleanse data • Integrate data • Format data
4	Data Modeling	Apply mathematical techniques to identify trends and patterns in the data	• Select modeling technique • Design tests • Build models
5	Evaluation	Analyze the trends and patterns to assess the potential for solving the business problem	• Evaluate results • Review process • Determine next steps
6	Deployment	Deploy the discoveries to the organization for work in everyday business	• Plan deployment • Monitor deployment • Analyze results • Review final reports

patterns of these events, for example, "55 percent of the time, events A and B occurred together" or "80 percent of the time that items A and B occurred together, they were followed by item C within three days."

One of the most common forms of association detection analysis is market basket analysis. **Market basket analysis** evaluates such items as websites and checkout scanner information to detect customers' buying behavior and predict future behavior by identifying affinities among customers' choices of products and services (see Figure 6.30). Market basket analysis is frequently used to develop marketing campaigns for cross-selling products and services (especially in banking, insurance, and finance) and for inventory control, shelf-product placement, and other retail and marketing applications.

market basket analysis Evaluates such items as websites and checkout scanner information to detect customers' buying behavior and predict future behavior by identifying affinities among customers' choices of products and services.

cluster analysis A technique used to divide information sets into mutually exclusive groups such that the members of each group are as close together as possible to one another and the different groups are as far apart as possible.

Cluster Analysis **Cluster analysis** is a technique used to divide an information set into mutually exclusive groups such that the members of each group are as close together as possible to one another and the different groups are as far apart as possible. Cluster analysis identifies similarities and differences among data sets allowing similar data sets to be clustered together. A customer database includes attributes such as name and address, demographic information such as gender and age, and financial attributes such as income and revenue spent. A cluster analysis groups similar attributes together to discover segments or clusters, and then examine the attributes

Due Diligence //:

Unethical Data Mining

Mining large amounts of data can create a number of benefits for business, society, and governments, but it can also create a number of ethical questions surrounding an invasion of privacy or misuse of information. Facebook recently came under fire for its data mining practices as it followed 700,000 accounts to determine whether posts with highly emotional content are more contagious. The study concluded that highly emotional texts are contagious, just as with real people. Highly emotional positive posts received multiple positive replies whereas highly emotional negative posts received multiple negative replies. Although the study seems rather innocent, many Facebook users were outraged; they felt the study was an invasion of privacy because the 700,000 accounts had no idea Facebook was mining their posts. As a Facebook user, you willingly consent that Facebook owns every bit and byte of data you post and, once you press submit, Facebook can do whatever it wants with your data. Do you agree or disagree that Facebook has the right to do whatever it wants with the data its 1.5 billion users post on its site?[8]

FIGURE 6.29 Data Mining Techniques.

Estimation Analysis

Determines values for an unknown continuous variable behavior or estimated future value.

Affinity Grouping Analysis

Reveals the relationship between variables along with the nature and frequency of the relationships.

Cluster Analysis

A technique used to divide an information set into mutually exclusive groups such that the members of each group are as close together as possible to one another and the different groups are as far apart as possible.

Classification Analysis

The process of organizing data into categories or groups for its most effective and efficient use.

classfiication analysis The process of organizing data into categories or groups for its most effective and efficient use.

data mining tool Uses a variety of techniques to find patterns and relationships in large volumes of information that predict future behavior and guide decision making.

and values that define the clusters or segments. Marketing managers can drive promotion strategies that target the specific group identified by the cluster analysis (see Figure 6.31).

A great example of using cluster analysis in business is to create target-marketing strategies based on zip codes. Evaluating customer segments by zip code allows a business to assign a level of importance to each segment. Zip codes offer valuable insight into such things as income levels, demographics, lifestyles, and spending habits. With target marketing, a business can decrease its costs while increasing the success rate of the marketing campaign.

Classification Analysis **Classification analysis** is the process of organizing data into categories or groups for its most effective and efficient use. For example, groups of political affiliation and charity donors. The primary goal of a classification analysis is not to explore data to find interesting segments, but to decide the best way to classify records. It is important to note that classification analysis is similar to cluster analysis because it segments data into distinct segments called classes; however, unlike cluster analysis, a classification analysis requires that all classes are defined before the analysis begins. For example, in a classification analysis the analyst defines two classes: (1) a class for customers who default on a loan; (2) a class for customers who did not default on a loan. Cluster analysis is exploratory analysis and classification analysis is much less exploratory and more grouping. (See Figure 6.32.)

Data Mining Modeling Techniques for Predictions

To perform data mining, users need data mining tools. **Data mining tools** use a variety of techniques to find patterns and relationships in large volumes of information that predict future behavior and guide decision making. Data mining uncovers trends and patterns, which analysts use to build models that, when exposed to new information sets, perform a variety of information analysis functions. Data-mining tools for data warehouses help users uncover business intelligence in their data. Data mining uncovers patterns and trends for business analysis such as:

- Analyzing customer buying patterns to predict future marketing and promotion campaigns.
- Building budgets and other financial information.
- Detecting fraud by identifying deceptive spending patterns.
- Finding the best customers who spend the most money.
- Keeping customers from leaving or migrating to competitors.
- Promoting and hiring employees to ensure success for both the company and the individual.

FIGURE 6.30 Market Basket Analysis Example.

© Purestock/Superstock

FIGURE 6.31 Example of Cluster Analysis.

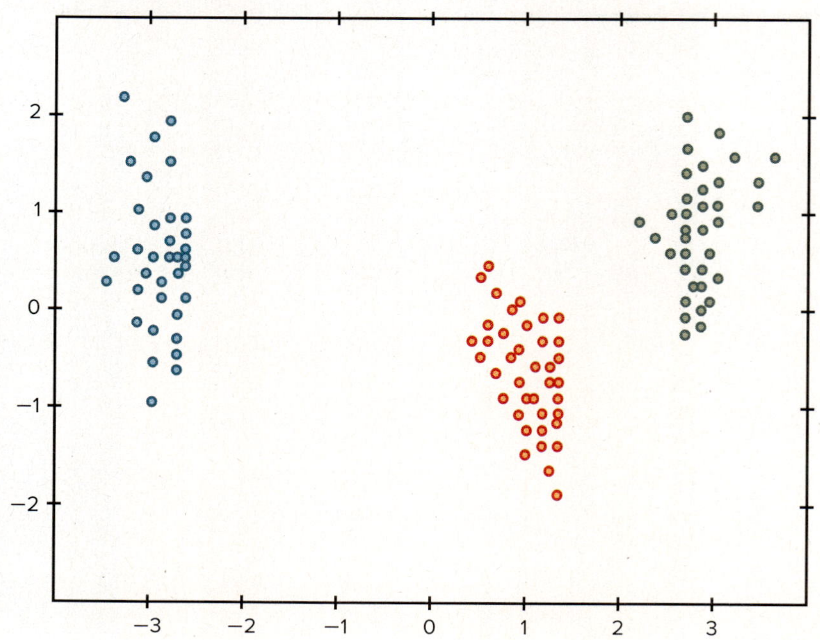

prediction A statement about what will happen or might happen in the future, for example, predicting future sales or employee turnover.

optimization model A statistical process that finds the way to make a design, system, or decision as effective as possible, for example, finding the values of controllable variables that determine maximal productivity or minimal waste.

forecasting model Predictions based on time-series information allowing users to manipulate the time series for forecasting activities.

regression model Includes many techniques for modeling and analyzing several variables when the focus is on the relationship between a dependent variable and one or more independent variables.

FIGURE 6.32 Classification Analysis Example.

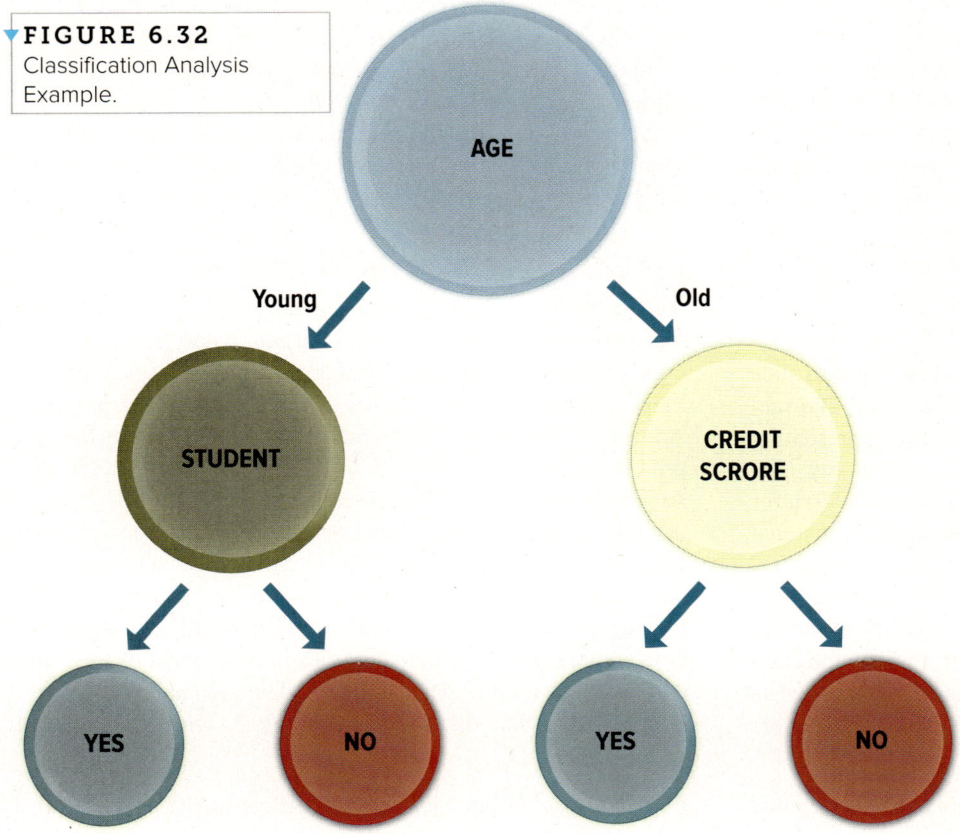

A **prediction** is a statement about what will happen or might happen in the future, for example, predicting future sales or employee turnover. Figure 6.33 displays the three common data-mining techniques for predictions. Please note the primary difference between forecasts and predictions. All forecasts are predictions, but not all predictions are forecasts. For example, when you would use regression to explain the relationship between two variables this is a prediction but not a forecast.

LO6.8 Explain data mining and identify the three elements of data mining.

FIGURE 6.33 Data Mining Modeling Techniques for Predictions.

Prediction Model	Definition	Example
Optimization Model	A statistical process that finds the way to make a design, system, or decision as effective as possible, for example, finding the values of controllable variables that determine maximal productivity or minimal waste.	• Determine which products to produce given a limited amount of ingredients • Choose a combination of projects to maximize overall earnings
Forecasting Model	**Time-series information** is time-stamped information collected at a particular frequency. Forecasts are predictions based on time-series information allowing users to manipulate the time series for forecasting activities.	• Web visits per hour • Sales per month • Customer service calls per day
	time-series information Time-stamped information collected at a particular frequency.	
Regression Model	A statistical process for estimating the relationships among variables. Regression models include many techniques for modeling and analyzing several variables when the focus is on the relationship between a dependent variable and one or more independent variables.	• Predict the winners of a marathon based on gender, height, weight, hours of training • Explain how the quantity of weekly sales of a popular brand of beer depends on its price at a small chain of supermarkets

cube The common term for the representation of multidimensional information.

algorithm Mathematical formulas placed in software that performs an analysis on a data set.

anomaly detection The process of identifying rare or unexpected items or events in a data set that do not conform to other items in the data set.

outlier Data value that is numerically distant from most of the other data points in a set of data.

fast data The application of big data analytics to smaller data sets in near-real or real-time in order to solve a problem or create business value.

DATA ANALYSIS LO6.9

A relational database contains information in a series of two-dimensional tables. With big data information is multidimensional, meaning it contains layers of columns and rows. A dimension is a particular attribute of information. Each layer in big data represents information according to an additional dimension. A **cube** is the common term for the representation of multidimensional information. Figure 6.34 displays a cube (cube *a*) that represents store information (the layers), product information (the rows), and promotion information (the columns).

Once a cube of information is created, users can begin to slice and dice the cube to drill down into the information. The second cube (cube *b*) in Figure 6.34 displays a slice representing promotion II information for all products, at all stores. The third cube (cube *c*) in Figure 6.34 displays only information for promotion III, product B, at store 2. By using multidimensional analysis, users can analyze information in a number of different ways and with any number of different dimensions. For example, users might want to add dimensions of information to a current analysis including product category, region, and even forecasts for actual weather. The true value of big data is its ability to provide multidimensional analysis that allows users to gain insights into their information.

Big data is ideal for off-loading some of the querying against a database. For example, querying a database to obtain an average of sales for product B at store 2 while promotion III is under way might create a considerable processing burden for a database, essentially slowing down the time it takes another person to enter a new sale into the same database. If an organization performs numerous queries against a database (or multiple databases), aggregating that information into big data databases could be beneficial.

Advanced Data Analytics

Algorithms are mathematical formulas placed in software that performs an analysis on a data set. **Analytics** is the science of fact-based decision making. Analytics uses software-based algorithms and statistics to derive meaning from data. Advanced analytics uses data patterns to make forward-looking predictions to explain to the organization where it is headed. **Anomaly detection** is the process of identifying rare or unexpected items or events in a data set that do not conform to other items in the data set. One of the key advantages of performing advanced analytics is to detect anomalies in the data to ensure they are not used in models creating false results. An **outlier** is a data value that is numerically distant from most of the other data points in a set of data. Anomaly detection helps to identify outliers in the data that can cause problems with mathematical modeling.

Fast data is the application of big data analytics to smaller data sets in near-real or real-time in order to solve a problem

FIGURE 6.34 A Cube of Information for Performing a Multidimensional Analysis on Three Different Stores, for Five Different Products, and Four Different Promotions.

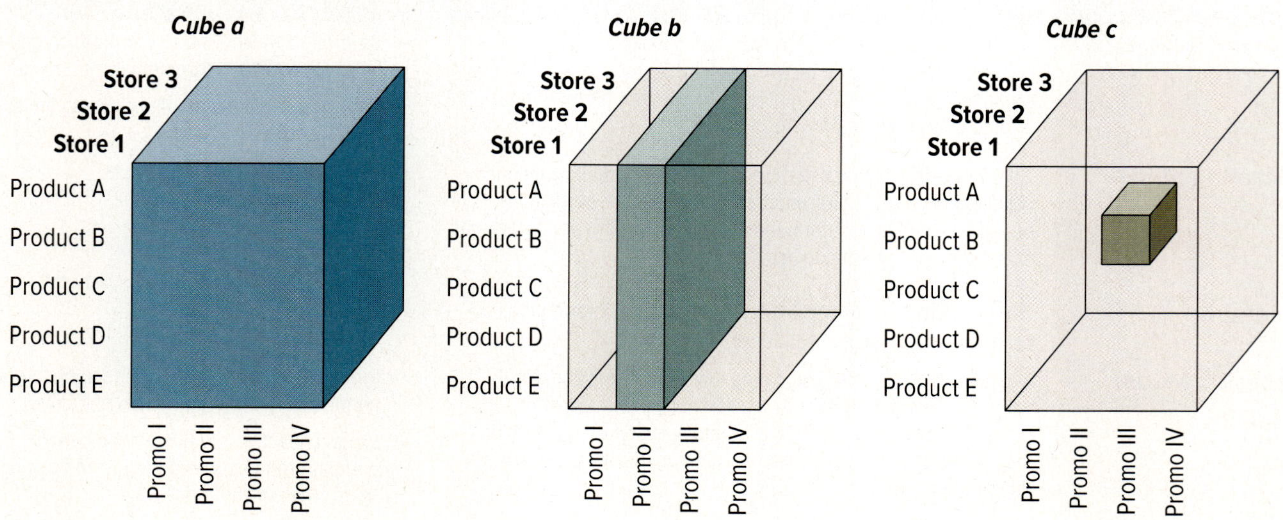

data scientist Extracts knowledge from data by performing statistical analysis, data mining, and advanced analytics on big data to identify trends, market changes, and other relevant information.

infographics (information graphics) Presents the results of data analysis, displaying the patterns, relationships, and trends in a graphical format.

data artist A business analytics specialist who uses visual tools to help people understand complex data.

analysis paralysis Occurs when the user goes into an emotional state of over-analysis (or over-thinking) a situation so that a decision or action is never taken, in effect paralyzing the outcome.

data visualization Describes technologies that allow users to "see" or visualize data to transform information into a business perspective.

or create business value. The term fast data is often associated with business intelligence and the goal is to quickly gather and mine structured and unstructured data so that action can be taken. As the flood of data from sensors, actuators and machine-to-machine (M2M) communication in the Internet of Things (IoT) continues to grow, it has become more important than ever for organizations to identify what data is time-sensitive and should be acted upon right away and what data can sit in a data warehouse or data lake until there is a reason to mine it.

A **data scientist** extracts knowledge from data by performing statistical analysis, data mining, and advanced analytics on big data to identify trends, market changes, and other relevant information. Figure 6.35 displays the techniques a data scientist will use to perform big data advanced analytics.

Data Visualization

Traditional bar graphs and pie charts are boring and at best confusing and at worst misleading. As databases and graphics collide more and more, people are creating infographics, which display information graphically so it can be easily understood. **Infographics (information graphics)** present the results of data analysis, displaying the patterns, relationships, and trends in a graphical format. Infographics are exciting and quickly convey a story users can understand without having to analyze numbers, tables, and boring charts (see Figure 6.36 and Figure 6.37).

A **data artist** is a business analytics specialist who uses visual tools to help people understand complex data. Great data visualizations provide insights into something new about the underlying patterns and relationships. Just think of the periodic table of elements and imagine if you had to look at an Excel spreadsheet showing each element and the associated attributes in a table format. This would be not only difficult to understand but easy to misinterpret. By placing the elements in the visual periodic table, you quickly grasp how the elements relate and the associated hierarchy and data artists are experts at creating a story from the information. Infographics perform the same function for business data as the periodic table does for chemical elements.

Analysis paralysis occurs when the user goes into an emotional state of over-analysis (or over-thinking) a situation so that a decision or action is never taken, in effect paralyzing the outcome. In the time of big data, analysis paralysis is a growing problem. One solution is to use data visualizations to help people make decisions faster. **Data visualization** describes

FIGURE 6.35 Advanced Data Analytics.

Analytics	Description
Behavioral Analysis	Using data about people's behaviors to understand intent and predict future actions.
Correlation Analysis	Determines a statistical relationship between variables, often for the purpose of identifying predictive factors among the variables.
Exploratory Data Analysis	Identifies patterns in data, including outliers, uncovering the underlying structure to understand relationships between the variables.
Pattern Recognition Analysis	The classification or labeling of an identified pattern in the machine learning process.
Social Media Analysis	Analyzes text flowing across the Internet, including unstructured text from blogs and messages.
Speech Analysis	The process of analyzing recorded calls to gather information; brings structure to customer interactions and exposes information buried in customer contact center interactions with an enterprise. Speech analysis is heavily used in the customer service department to help improve processes by identifying angry customers and routing them to the appropriate customer service representative.
Text Analysis	Analyzes unstructured data to find trends and patterns in words and sentences. Text mining a firm's customer support email might identify which customer service representative is best able to handle the question, allowing the system to forward it to the right person.
Web Analysis	Analyzes unstructured data associated with websites to identify consumer behavior and website navigation.

data visualization tools Moves beyond Excel graphs and charts into sophisticated analysis techniques such as pie charts, controls, instruments, maps, time-series graphs, etc.

business intelligence dashboard Tracks corporate metrics such as critical success factors and key performance indicators and include advanced capabilities such as interactive controls, allowing users to manipulate data for analysis.

technologies that allow users to see or visualize data to transform information into a business perspective. Data visualization is a powerful way to simplify complex data sets by placing data in a format that is easily grasped and understood far quicker than the raw data alone. **Data visualization tools** move beyond Excel graphs and charts into sophisticated analysis techniques such as controls, instruments, maps, time-series graphs, and more. Data visualization tools can help uncover correlations and trends in data that would otherwise go unrecognized.

Business intelligence dashboards track corporate metrics such as critical success factors and key performance indicators and include advanced capabilities such as interactive controls, allowing users to manipulate data for analysis. The majority of business intelligence software vendors offer a number of data visualization tools and business intelligence dashboards.

Big data is one of the most promising technology trends occurring today. Of course, notable companies such as Facebook, Google, and Netflix are gaining the most business insights from big data currently, but many smaller markets are entering the scene, including retail, insurance, and health care. Over the next decade, as big data starts to improve your everyday life by providing insights into your social relationships, habits, and careers, you can expect to see the need for data scientists and data artists dramatically increase. ■

LO6.9 Explain the importance of data analytics and data visualization.

FIGURE 6.36 Infographic News Example.

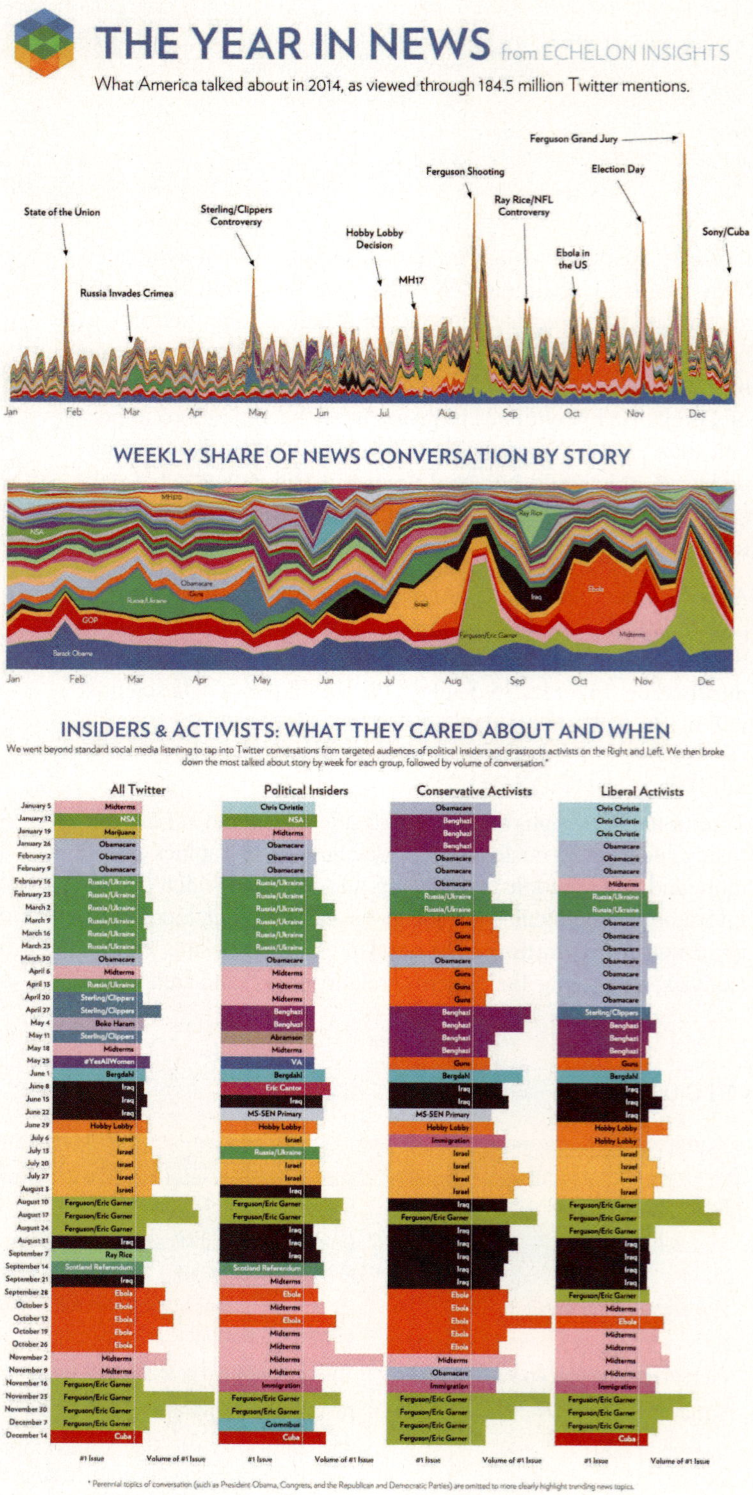

FIGURE 6.37 Infographic Health Example.

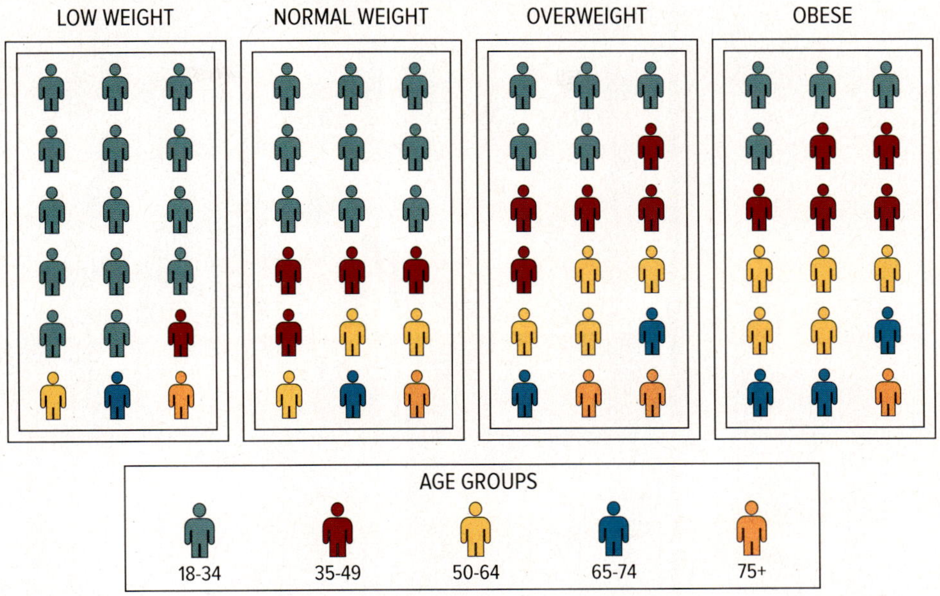

fyi

News Dots

Gone are the days of staring at boring spreadsheets and trying to understand how the data correlate. With innovative data visualization tools, managers can arrange different ways to view the data, providing new forms of pattern recognition not offered by simply looking at numbers. *Slate,* a news publication, developed a new data visualization tool called News Dots, that offers readers a different way of viewing the daily news through trends and patterns. The News Dots tool scans about 500 stories a day from major publications and then tags the content with important keywords such as people, places, companies, and topics. Surprisingly, the majority of daily news overlaps as the people, places, and stories are frequently connected. Using News Dots, you can visualize how the news fits together, almost similar to a giant social network. News Dots uses circles (or dots) to represent the tagged content and arranges them according to size. The more frequently a certain topic is tagged, the larger the dot and its relationship to other dots. The tool is interactive and users simply click a dot to view which stories mention that topic and which other topics it connects to in the network such as a correlation among the U.S. government, Federal Reserve, Senate, bank, and Barack Obama.[9]

How can data visualization help identify trends? What types of business intelligence could you identify if your college used a data visualization tool to analyze student information? What types of business intelligence could you identify if you used a data visualization tool to analyze the industry in which you plan to compete?

© Dimitri Vervitsiotis/Getty Images RF

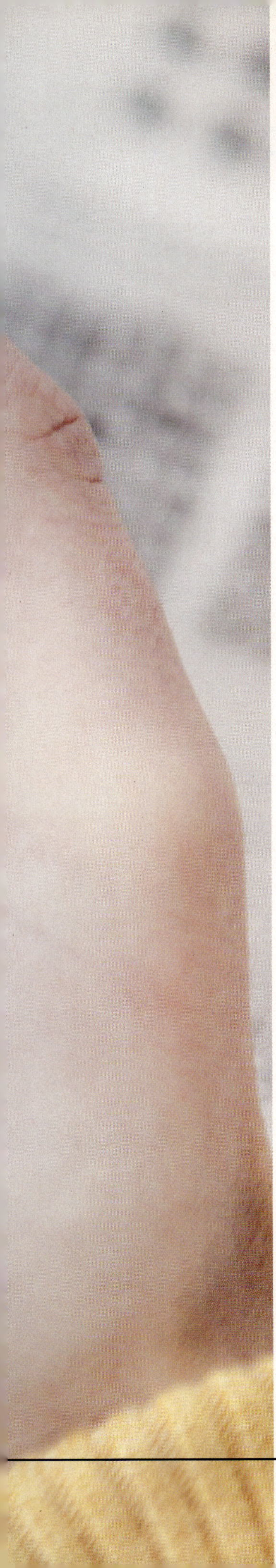

chapter seven

Networks: Mobile Business

what's in IT for me?

The pace of technological change never ceases to amaze as kindergarten classes are now learning PowerPoint and many elementary school children have their own cell phones. What used to take hours to download over a dial-up modem connection can now transfer in a matter of seconds through an invisible, wireless network connection from a computer thousands of miles away. We are living in an increasingly wireless present and hurtling ever faster toward a wireless future. The tipping point of ubiquitous, wireless, handheld, mobile computing is approaching quickly.

As a business student, understanding network infrastructures and wireless

continued on p. 184

CHAPTER OUTLINE

continued from p. 183

technologies allows you to take advantage of mobile workforces. Understanding the benefits and challenges of mobility is a critical skill for business executives, regardless if you are a novice or a seasoned *Fortune* 500 employee. By learning about the various concepts discussed in this chapter, you will develop a better understanding of how business can leverage networking technologies to analyze network types, improve wireless and mobile business processes, and evaluate alternative networking options. ■

{SECTION 7.1} Connectivity: The Business Value of a Networked World

LEARNING OUTCOMES

LO7.1 Explain the five different networking elements creating a connected world.

LO7.2 Identify the benefits and challenges of a connected world.

THE CONNECTED WORLD LO7.1

Computer networks are continuously operating all over the globe supporting our 24/7/365 always on and always connected lifestyles. You are probably using several different networks right now without even realizing it. You might be using a school's network to communicate with teachers, a phone network to communicate with friends, and a cable network to watch TV or listen to the radio. Networks enable telecommunications or the exchange of information (voice, text, data, audio, video). The telecommunication industry has morphed from a government-regulated monopoly to a deregulated market where many suppliers ferociously compete. Competing telecommunication companies offer local and global telephony services, satellite service, mobile radio, cable television, cellular phone services, and Internet access (all of which are detailed in this chapter). Businesses everywhere are increasingly using networks to communicate and collaborate with customers, partners, suppliers, and employees. As a manager, you will face many different communication alternatives, and the focus of this chapter is to provide you with an initial understanding of the different networking elements you will someday need to select (see Figure 7.1).

LO7.1 Explain the five different networking elements creating a connected world.

FIGURE 7.1 Networking Elements Creating a Connected World

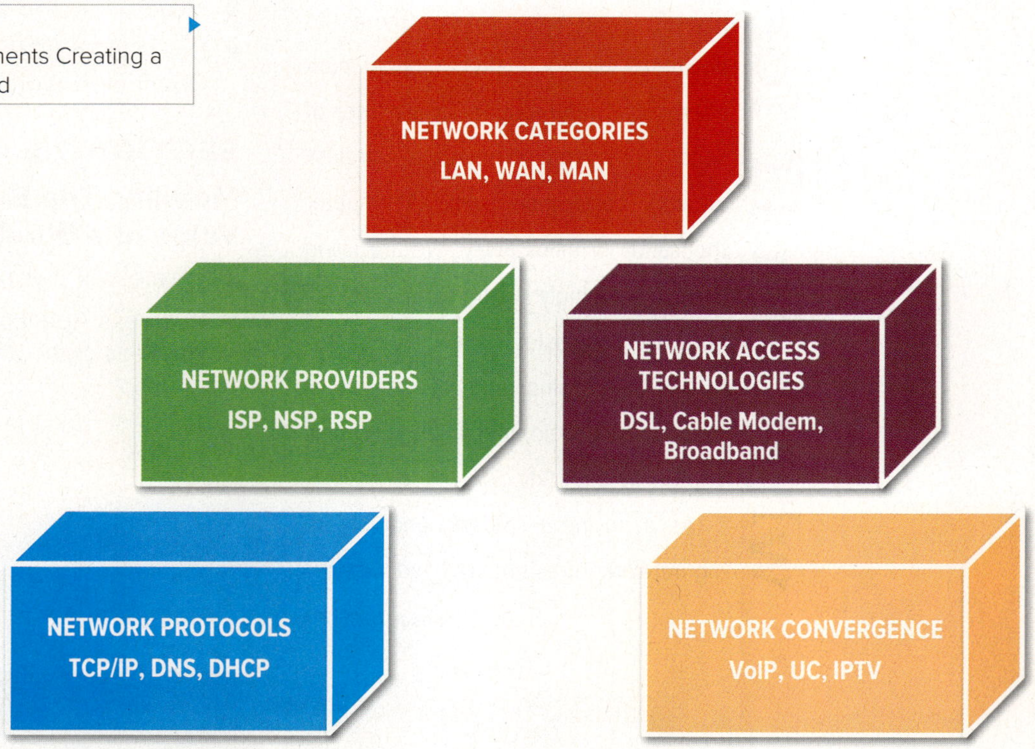

Network Categories

The general idea of a network is to allow multiple devices to communicate at the highest achievable speeds and, very importantly, to reduce the cost of connecting. How a particular network achieves these goals depends in part on how it is physically constructed and connected. Networks are categorized based on geographic span: local area networks, wide area networks, and metropolitan area networks. Today's business networks include a combination of all three.

A **local area network (LAN)** connects a group of computers in close proximity, such as in an office building, school, or home. LANs allow sharing of files, printers, games, and other resources. A LAN also often connects to other LANs, and to wide area networks. A **wide area network (WAN)** spans a large geographic area such as a state, province, or country. Perhaps the best example is the Internet. WANs are essential for carrying out the day-to-day activities of many companies and government organizations, allowing them to transmit and receive information among their employees, customers, suppliers, business partners, and other organizations across cities, regions, and countries and around the world. In networking, **attenuation** represents the loss of a network signal strength measured in decibels (dB) and occurs because the transmissions gradually dissipate in strength over longer distances or because of radio interference or physical obstructions such as walls. A **repeater** receives and repeats a signal to extend its attenuation or range.

WANs often connect multiple smaller networks, such as local area networks or metropolitan area networks. A **metropolitan area network (MAN)** is a large computer network usually spanning a city. Most colleges, universities, and large companies that span a campus use an infrastructure supported by a MAN. Figure 7.2 shows the relationships and a few differences between a LAN, WAN, and MAN. A cloud image often represents the Internet or some large network environment.

While LANs, WANs, and MANs all provide users with an accessible and reliable network infrastructure, they differ in many dimensions; two of the most important are cost and performance. It is easy to establish a network between two computers in the same room or building, but much more difficult if they are in different states or even countries. This means someone looking to build or support a WAN either pays more or gets less performance, or both. Ethernet is the most common connection type for wired networking and is available in speeds from 10 Mbps all the way up to 10,000 Mbps (10 Gbit). The most common wire used for Ethernet networking is Cat5 (Category 5) and the connectors used are RJ45, slightly larger than the RJ11 connectors used by phones, but the same shape.

Network Providers

The largest and most important network, the Internet has evolved into a global information superhighway. Think of it as a network made up of millions of smaller networks, each with the ability to operate independently of, or in harmony with, the others. Keeping the Internet operational is no simple task. No one owns or runs it, but it does have an organized network topology. The Internet is a hierarchical structure linking different levels of service providers, whose millions of devices, LANs, WANs, and MANs supply all the interconnections. At the top of the hierarchy are **national service providers (NSPs)**, private companies that own and maintain the worldwide backbone that supports the Internet. These include Sprint, Verizon, MCI (previously UUNet/WorldCom), AT&T, NTT, Level3, Century Link, and Cable & Wireless Worldwide. Network access points (NAPs) are traffic exchange points in the routing hierarchy of the Internet that connects NSPs. They typically have regional or national coverage and connect to only a few NSPs. Thus, to reach a large portion of the global Internet, a NAP needs to route traffic through one of the NSPs to which it is connected.[1]

One step down in the hierarchy is the regional service provider. **Regional service providers (RSPs)** offer Internet service by connecting to NSPs, but they also can connect directly to each other. Another level down is an Internet service provider (ISP), which specializes in providing management, support, and maintenance to a network. ISPs vary services provided and available bandwidth rates. ISPs link to RSPs and, if they are geographically close, to other ISPs. Some also connect directly to NSPs, thereby sidestepping the hierarchy. Individuals and companies use local ISPs to connect to the Internet, and large companies tend to connect directly using an RSP. Major ISPs in the United States include AOL, AT&T, Comcast, Earthlink, and NetZero. The further up the hierarchy, the faster the connections and the greater the bandwidth. The backbone shown in Figure 7.3 is greatly simplified, but it illustrates the concept that basic global interconnections are provided by the NSPs, RSPs and ISPs.[2]

local area network (LAN) Connects a group of computers in proximity, such as in an office building, school, or home.

wide area network (WAN) Spans a large geographic area such as a state, province, or country.

attenuation Represents the loss of a network signal strength measured in decibels (dB) and occurs because the transmissions gradually dissipate in strength over longer distances or because of radio interference or physical obstructions such as walls.

repeater Receives and repeats a signal to extend its attenuation or range.

metropolitan area network (MAN) A large computer network usually spanning a city.

national service providers (NSPs) Private companies that own and maintain the worldwide backbone that supports the Internet.

regional service providers (RSPs) Offer Internet service by connecting to NSPs, but they also can connect directly to each other

FIGURE 7.2 Network Categories: LAN, WAN, and MAN

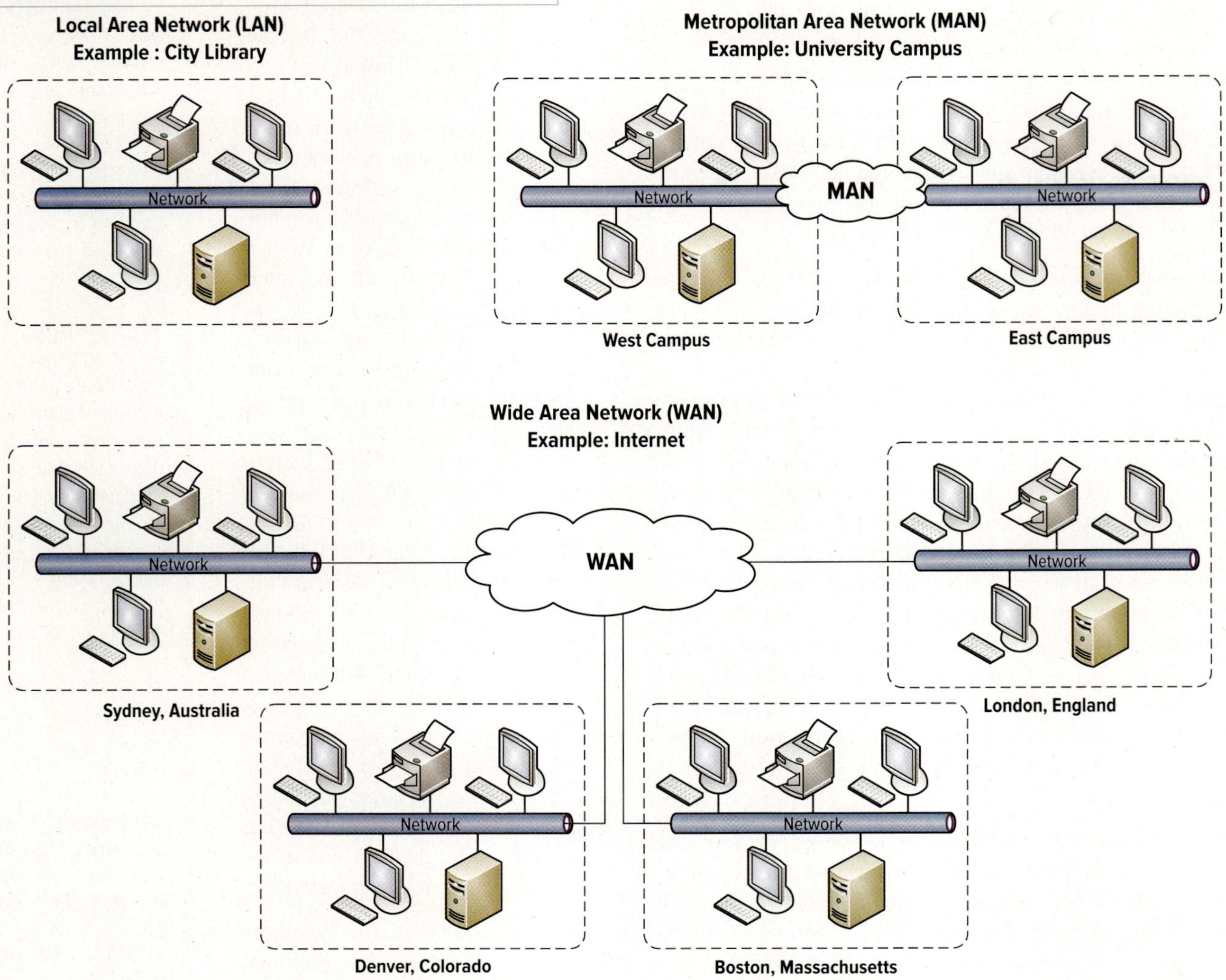

FIGURE 7.3 Internet Topology

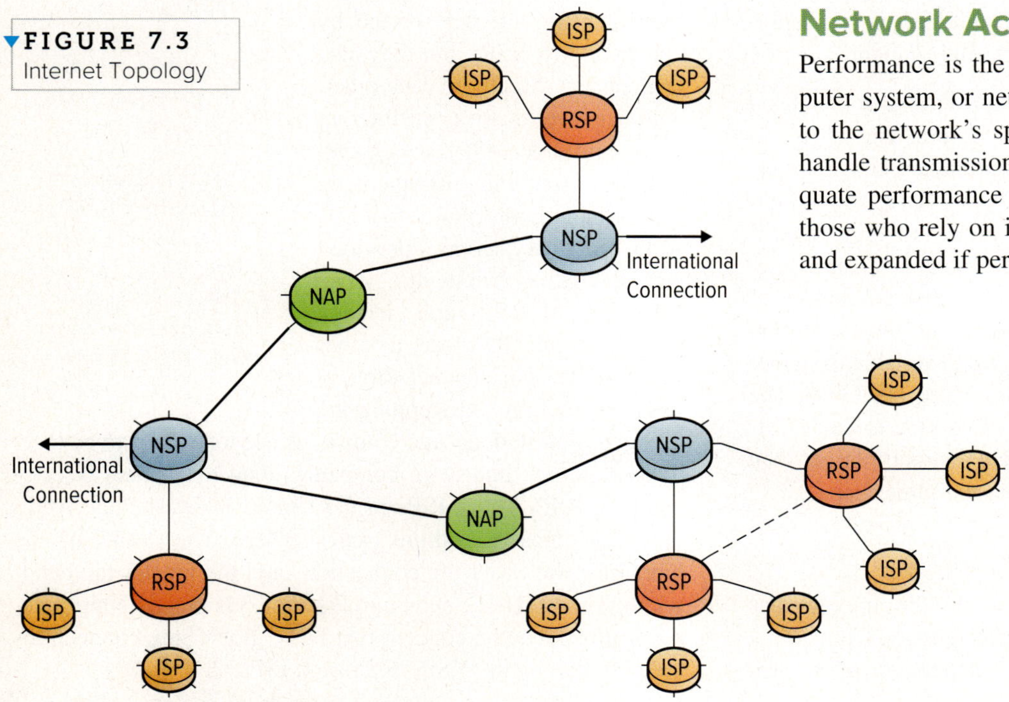

Network Access Technologies

Performance is the ultimate goal of any computer, computer system, or network. Performance is directly related to the network's speed of data transfer and capacity to handle transmission. A network that does not offer adequate performance simply will not get the job done for those who rely on it. Luckily, networks can be upgraded and expanded if performance is inadequate.

We measure network performance in terms of **bandwidth**, the maximum amount of data that can pass from one point to another in a unit of time. Bandwidth is similar to water traveling through a hose. If the hose is large, water can flow through it quickly. Data differs from a hose in that it must travel great distances, especially on a WAN, and not all areas of the network have the same bandwidth. A network essentially has many different hoses of unequal

Bandwidth	Abbreviation	Bits per Second (bps)	Example
Kilobits	Kbps	1 Kbps = 1,000 bps	Traditional modem = 56 Kbps
Megabits	Mbps	1 Mbps = 1,000 Kbps	Traditional Ethernet = 10 Mbps Fast Ethernet = 100 Mbps
Gigabits	Gbps	1 Gbps = 1,000 Mbps	Gigabit Ethernet = 1,000 Mbps

FIGURE 7.4 Bandwidth Speeds

capacity connected together, which will restrict the flow of data when one is smaller than the others. Therefore, the speed of transmission of a network is determined by the speed of its smallest bandwidth.

A **bit** (short for binary digit) is the smallest element of data and has a value of either 0 or 1. Bandwidth is measured in terms of **bit rate** (or data rate), the number of bits transferred or received per unit of time. Figure 7.4 represents bandwidth speeds in terms of bit rates. Bandwidth is typically given in bits per second (abbreviated as bps) and bytes per second (abbreviated as Bps). It is important to note that these two terms are not interchangeable.

A **modem** is a device that enables a computer to transmit and receive data. A connection with a traditional telephone line and a modem, which most residential users had in the 1990s, is called dial-up access. Today, many users in underdeveloped countries and in rural areas in developed countries still use dial-up. It has two drawbacks. First, it is slow, providing a maximum rate of 56 Kbps. (At 56 Kbps, it takes eight minutes to download a three-minute song and more than a day to download a two-hour movie.) Second, dial-up modem access ties up the telephone line so the user cannot receive and make phone calls while online. The good news is this is not as big an issue as it once was as many people have cell phones and no longer require using the telephone line for making phone calls.[3]

Once the most common connection method worldwide, dialup is quickly being replaced by broadband. **Broadband** is a high-speed Internet connection that is always connected. High-speed in this case refers to any bandwidth greater than 2 Mbps. Not long ago, broadband speeds were available only at a premium price to support large companies' high-traffic networks. Today, inexpensive access is available for home use and small companies.

The two most prevalent types of broadband access are digital subscriber lines and high-speed Internet cable connections. **Digital subscriber line (DSL)** provides high-speed digital data transmission over standard telephone lines using broadband modem technology, allowing both Internet and telephone services to work over the same phone lines. Consumers typically obtain DSL Internet access from the same company that provides their wired local telephone access, such as AT&T or Century Link. Thus, a customer's telephone provider is also its ISP, and the telephone line carries both data and telephone signals using a DSL modem. DSL Internet services are used primarily in homes and small businesses.

DSL has two major advantages over dial-up. First, it can transmit and receive data much faster—in the 1 to 2 Mbps range for downloading and 128 Kbps to 1 Mbps for uploading. (Most high-speed connections are designed to download faster than they upload, because most users download more—including viewing web pages—than they upload.) The second major advantage is that because they have an "always on" connection to their ISP, users can simultaneously talk on the phone and access the Internet. DSL's disadvantages are that it works over a limited physical distance and remains unavailable in many areas where the local telephone infrastructure does not support DSL technology.[4]

While dial-up and DSL use local telephone infrastructure, **high-speed Internet cable connections** provide Internet access using a cable television company's infrastructure and a special cable modem. A **cable modem (or broadband modem)** is a type of digital modem used with high-speed cable Internet service. Cable modems connect a home computer (or network of home computers) to residential cable TV service, while DSL modems connect to residential public telephone service. The ISP typically supplies the cable and DSL modems. Cisco Systems is one of the largest companies producing computer networking products and services, including the Linksys brand of networking components. Typically, broadband or high-speed Internet service has an average transfer rate 10 times faster than conventional dial-up service. **Telecommuting (virtual workforce)** allows users to work from remote locations, such as home or a hotel, using high-speed Internet to access business applications and data.

bandwidth The maximum amount of data that can pass from one point to another in a unit of time.

bit The smallest element of data and has a value of either 0 or 1.

bit rate The number of bits transferred or received per unit of time.

modem A device that enables a computer to transmit and receive data.

broadband A high-speed Internet connection that is always connected.

digital subscriber line (DSL) Provides high-speed digital data transmission over standard telephone lines using broadband modem technology allowing both Internet and telephone services to work over the same phone lines.

high-speed Internet cable connection Provides Internet access using a cable television company's infrastructure and a special cable modem.

cable modem (or broadband modem) A type of digital modem used with high-speed cable Internet service.

telecommuting (virtual workforce) Allows users to work from remote locations such as a home or hotel, using high-speed Internet to access business applications and data.

broadband over power line (BPL) Technology makes possible high-speed Internet access over ordinary residential electrical lines and offers an alternative to DSL or high-speed cable modems.

packet A single unit of binary data routed through a network.

standard packet format Includes a packet header, packet body containing the original message, and packet footer.

packet header Lists the destination (for example, in IP packets the destination is the IP address) along with the length of the message data.

packet footer Represents the end of the packet or transmission end.

Unlike DSL, high-speed Internet cable is a shared service, which means everyone in a certain radius, such as a neighborhood, shares the available bandwidth. Therefore, if several users are simultaneously downloading a video file, the actual transfer rate for each will be significantly lower than if only one person were doing so. On average, the available bandwidth using cable can range from 512 Kbps to 50 Mbps for downloading and 786 Kbps for uploading.[5]

Another alternative to DSL or high-speed Internet cable is dedicated communications lines leased from AT&T or another provider. The most common are T1 lines, a type of data connection able to transmit a digital signal at 1.544 Mpbs. Although this speed might not seem impressive, and T1 lines are more expensive than DSL or cable, they offer far greater reliability because each is composed of 24 channels, creating 24 separate connections through one line. If a company has three separate plants that experience a high volume of data traffic, it might make sense to lease lines for reliability of service.[6]

A company must match its needs with Internet access methods. If it always needs high bandwidth access to communicate with customers, partners, or suppliers, a T1 line may be the most cost-effective method. Figure 7.5 provides an overview of the main methods for Internet access. The bandwidths in the figure represent average speeds; actual speeds vary depending upon the service provider and other factors such as the type of cabling and speed of the computer.[7]

Broadband over power line (BPL) technology makes possible high-speed Internet access over ordinary residential electrical lines and offers an alternative to DSL or high-speed cable modems. BPL works by transmitting data over electrical lines using signaling frequencies higher than the electrical (or voice in the case of DSL) signals. BPL allows computer data to be sent back and forth across the network with no disruption to power output in the home. Many homeowners are surprised to learn that their electrical system can serve as a home network running speeds between 1 and 3 Mbps with full Internet access. Unfortunately, limitations such as interference and availability have affected BPL's popularity.

Network Protocols

A **packet** is a single unit of binary data routed through a network. Packets directly impact network performance and reliability by subdividing an electronic message into smaller, more manageable packets. **Standard packet formats** include a packet header, packet body containing the original message, and packet footer. The **packet header** lists the destination (for example, in IP packets the destination is the IP address) along with the length of the message data. The **packet footer** represents the end of the packet or transmission end. The packet header and packet footer contain error-checking information to ensure the entire message is sent and received. The receiving device reassembles the individual packets into the original by stripping off the headers and footers and then piecing together the packets in the correct sequence. **Traceroute** is a utility application that monitors the network path of packet data sent to a remote computer. Traceroute programs send a series of test messages over the network (using the name or IP address) until the last message finally reaches its destination. When finished, traceroute displays the path from the initial computer to the

Access Technology	Description	Bandwidth	Comments
Dial-up	On-demand access using a modem and regular telephone line.	Up to 56 Kbps	Cheap but slow compared with other technologies.
DSL	Always-on connection. Special modem needed.	Download: 1 Mbps to 2 Mbps Upload: 128 Kbps to 1 Mbps	Makes use of the existing local telephone infrastructure.
Cable	Always-on connection. Special cable modem and cable line required.	Download: 512 Kbps to 50 Mbps Upload: 786 Kbps	It is a shared resource with other users in the area.
T1	Leased lines for high bandwidth.	1.544 Mbps	More expensive than dial-up, DSL, or cable.

FIGURE 7.5
Types of Internet Access

destination computer. A **proxy** is software that prevents direct communication between a sending and receiving computer and is used to monitor packets for security reasons.

A **protocol** is a standard that specifies the format of data as well as the rules to be followed during transmission. Computers using the same protocol can communicate easily, providing accessibility, scalability, and connectability between networks. **File transfer protocol (FTP)** is a simple network protocol that allows the transfer of files between two computers on the Internet. To transfer files with FTP, the FTP client program initiates a connection to a remote computer running FTP "server" software. After completing the connection the client can choose to send and/or receive files electronically. Network access technologies use a standard Internet protocol called **transmission control protocol/Internet protocol (TCP/IP)**, which provides the technical foundation for the public Internet as well as for large numbers of private networks. One of the primary reasons for developing TCP/IP was to allow diverse or differing networks to connect and communicate with each other, essentially allowing LANs, WANs, and MANs to grow with each new connection. An **IP address** is a unique number that identifies where computers are located on the network. IP addresses appear in the form of xxx.xxx.xxx.xxx, though each grouping can be as short as a single digit.

TCP (the TCP part of TCP/IP) verifies the correct delivery of data because data can become corrupt when traveling over a network. TCP ensures the size of the data packet is the same throughout its transmission and can even retransmit data until delivered correctly. IP (the IP part of TCP/IP) verifies the data are sent to the correct IP address, numbers represented by four strings of numbers ranging from 0 to 255 separated by periods. For example, the IP address of www.apple.com is 97.17.237.15.

Here is another way to understand TCP/IP. Consider a letter that needs to go from the University of Denver to Apple's headquarters in Cupertino, California. TCP makes sure the envelope is delivered and does not get lost along the way. IP acts as the sending and receiving labels, telling the letter carrier where to deliver the envelope and whom it was from. The Postal Service mainly uses street addresses and zip codes to get letters to their destinations, which is really what IP does with its addressing method. Figure 7.6 illustrates this example. However, unlike the Postal Service, which allows multiple people to share the same physical address, each device using an IP address to connect to the Internet must have a unique address or else it could not detect which individual device a request should be sent to.

One of the most valuable characteristics of TCP/IP is how scalable its protocols have proven to be as the Internet has grown from a small network with just a few machines to a huge internetwork with millions of devices. While some changes have been required periodically to support this growth, the core of TCP/IP is the same as it was more than 25 years ago.[8] **Dynamic host configuration protocol (DHCP)** allows dynamic IP address allocation so users do not have to have a preconfigured IP address to use the network. DHCP allows a computer to access and locate information about a computer on the server, enabling users to locate and renew their IP address. ISPs usually use DHCP to allow customers to join the Internet with minimum effort. DHCP assigns unique IP addresses to devices, then releases and renews these addresses as devices leave and return to the network.

If there is one flaw in TCP/IP, it is the complexity of IP addresses. This is why we use a **domain name system (DNS)** to convert IP addresses into *domains,* or identifying labels that use a variety of recognizable naming conventions. Therefore, instead of trying to remember 97.17.237.15, users can simply specify a domain name to access a computer or website, such as www.apple.com. Figure 7.7 lists the most common Internet domains.[10]

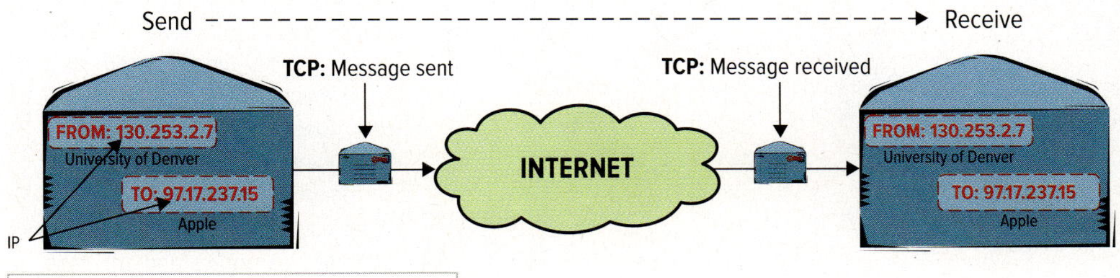

FIGURE 7.6 Example of TCP/IP

traceroute A utility application that monitors the network path of packet data sent to a remote computer.

proxy Software that prevents direct communication between a sending and receiving computer and is used to monitor packets for security reasons.

protocol A standard that specifies the format of data as well as the rules to be followed during transmission.

file transfer protocol (FTP) A simple network protocol that allows the transfer of files between two computers on the Internet.

transmission control protocol/Internet protocol (TCP/IP) Provides the technical foundation for the public Internet as well as for large numbers of private networks.

IP address A unique number that identifies where computers are located on the network.

dynamic host configuration protocol (DHCP) Allows dynamic IP address allocation so users do not have to have a preconfigured IP address to use the network.

domain name system (DNS) Converts IP address into domains, or identifying labels that use a variety of recognizable naming conventions.

network convergence The efficient coexistence of telephone, video, and data communication within a single network, offering convenience and flexibility not possible with separate infrastructures.

FIGURE 7.7 Internet Domains

Domain Name	Use
.biz	Reserved for businesses
.com	Reserved for commercial organizations and businesses
.edu	Reserved for accredited postsecondary institutions
.gov	Reserved for U.S. government agencies
.info	Open to any person or entity, but intended for information providers
.mil	Reserved for U.S. military
.net	Open to any person or entity
.org	Reserved for nonprofit organizations

The list of domain names is expected to expand in the coming years to include entities such as .pro (for accountants, lawyers, and physicians), .aero (for the air-transport industry), and .museum (for museums). The creation of an .xxx domain was recently approved for pornographic content. Countries also have domain names such as .au (Australia), .fr (France), and .sp (Spain).

Websites with heavy traffic often have several computers working together to share the load of requests. This offers load balancing and fault tolerance, so when requests are made to a popular site such as www.facebook.com, they will not overload a single computer and the site does not go down if one computer fails. A single computer can also have several host names—for instance, if a company is hosting several websites on a single server, much as an ISP works with hosting.

Domain names are essentially rented, with renewable rights, from a domain name registrar, such as godaddy.com. Some registrars only register domain names, while others provide hosting services for a fee. ICANN (Internet Corporation for Assigning Names and Numbers) is a nonprofit governance and standards organization that certifies all domain name registrars throughout the world. With the certification, each registrar is authorized to register domain names, such as .com, .edu, or .org.[11]

Network Convergence

In part due to the explosive use of the Internet and connectivity of TCP/IP, there is a convergence of network devices, applications, and services. Consumers, companies, educational institutions, and government agencies extensively engage in texting, web surfing, videoconference applications, online gaming, and ebusiness. **Network convergence** is the efficient coexistence of telephone, video, and data communication within a single network, offering convenience and flexibility not possible with separate infrastructures. Almost any type of information can be

BUSTED Never Run with Your iPod[9]

Jennifer Goebel, a 27-year-old female, was disqualified from her first place spot in the Lakefront Marathon in Milwaukee after race officials spotted her using an iPod. Officials nullified Goebel's first place time of 3:02:50 because of a controversial 2007 rule put into place banning headphones or portable music devices by U.S. Track and Field (USTAF), the governing body for running events. Race officials only decided to take action after viewing online photos of Goebel using her iPod during the last part of the race. The interesting part of this story—Goeble posted the photos herself on her website. USTAF claims the ban is required because music could give some runners a competitive advantage, as well as safety concerns when runners can't hear race announcements.

© JGI/Jamie Grill/Getty Images RF

Do you agree with the USTAF's decision to disqualify Jennifer Goebel? How could an iPod give a runner a competitive advantage? With so many wireless devices entering the market, it is almost impossible to keep up with the surrounding laws. Do you think Goebel was aware of the headphone ban? In your state, what are the rules for using wireless devices while driving? Do you agree with these rules? How does a business keep up with the numerous, ever-changing rules surrounding wireless devices? What could happen to a company that fails to understand the laws surrounding wireless devices?

converted into digital form and exchanged over a network. Network convergence then allows the weaving together of voice, data, and video. The benefits of network convergence allow for multiple services, multiple devices, but one network, one vendor, and one bill, as suggested by Figure 7.8.

One of the challenges associated with network convergence is using the many different tools efficiently and productively. Knowing which communication channel—PC, text message, videoconference—to use with each business participant can be a challenge. **Unified communications (UC)** is the integration of communication channels into a single service. UC integrates communication channels allowing participants to communicate using the method that is most convenient for them. UC merges instant messaging, videoconferencing, email, voice mail, and VoIP. This can decrease the communication costs for a business while enhancing the way individuals communicate and collaborate.

One area experiencing huge growth in network convergence is the use of the Internet for voice transmission. **Voice over IP (VoIP)** uses IP technology to transmit telephone calls. For the first time in more than 100 years, VoIP is providing an opportunity to bring about significant change in the way people communicate using the telephone. VoIP service providers—specialists as well as traditional telephone and cable companies and some ISPs—allow users to call anyone with a telephone number, whether local, long distance, cellular, or international.

FIGURE 7.8 The Benefits of Network Convergence

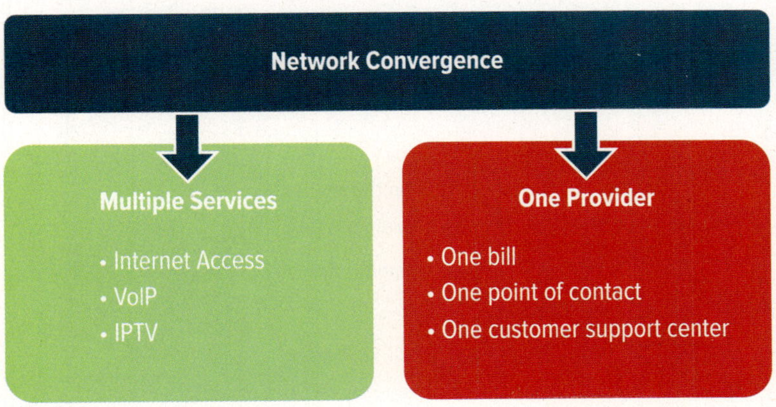

Two ways to use VoIP for telephone calls are through a web interface that allows users to make calls from their computer and through a phone attached to a VoIP adapter that links directly to the Internet through a broadband modem. Figure 7.9 illustrates these two ways along with the use of VoIP-enabled phones, bypassing the need for an adapter.

VoIP services include fixed-price unlimited local and long-distance calling plans (at least within the United States and Canada), plus a range of interesting features, such as:

- The ability to have more than one phone number, including numbers with different area codes.
- Integrating email and voice mail so users can listen to their voice mail using their computer.
- The ability to receive personal or business calls via computer, no matter where the user is physically located.[12]

The biggest benefit of VoIP is its low cost. Because it relies on the Internet connection, however, service can be affected if the bandwidth is not appropriate or Internet access is not available.

Skype is a perfect example of IP applied to telephone use. Unlike typical VoIP systems that use a client and server infrastructure, Skype uses a peer-to-peer network. **Peer-to-peer network (P2P)** is a computer network that relies on the computing power and bandwidth of the participants in the network rather than a centralized server. Skype's user directory is distributed among the users in its network, allowing scalability without a complex and expensive centralized infrastructure. Peer-to-peer networks became an overnight sensation years ago through a service called Napster that distributed digital music illegally. Skype has found a way to use this resource to provide value to its users.[13]

As the popularity of VoIP grows, governments are becoming more interested in regulating it as they do

unified communications (UC) The integration of communication channels into a single service.

voice over IP (VoIP) Uses IP technology to transmit telephone calls.

peer-to-peer (P2P) network A computer network that relies on the computing power and bandwidth of the participants in the network rather than a centralized server.

FIGURE 7.9 VoIP Connectivity

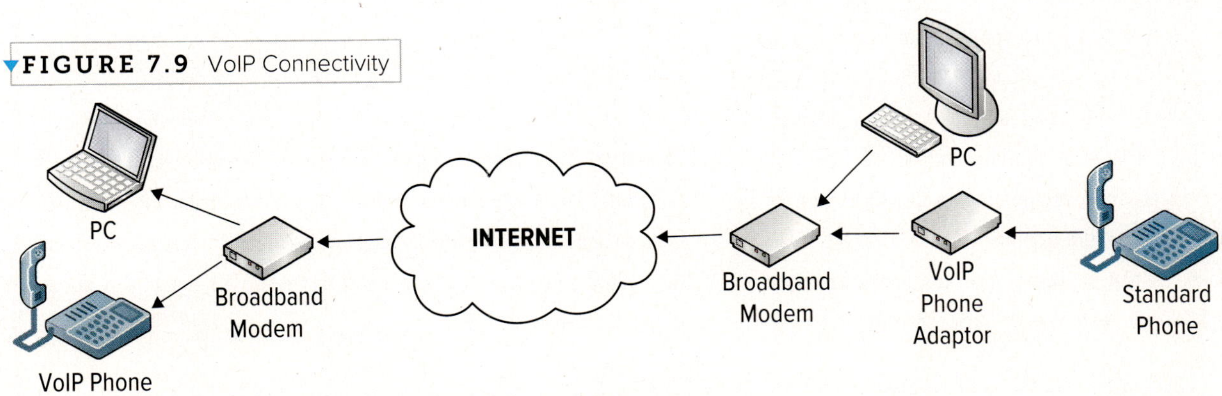

Internet protocol TV (IPTV) Distributes digital video content using IP across the Internet and private IP networks.

traditional telephone services. In the United States, the Federal Communications Commission requires compliance among VoIP service providers comparable to those for traditional telephone providers such as support for local number portability, services for the disabled, and law enforcement for surveillance, along with regulatory and other fees.

An exciting and new convergence is occurring in the area of television with **Internet Protocol TV (IPTV)**, which distributes digital video content using IP across the Internet and private IP networks. Comcast provides an example of a private IP network that also acts as a cable TV provider. Traditional television sends all program signals simultaneously to the television, allowing the user to select the program by selecting a channel. With IPTV, the user selects a channel and the service provider sends only that single program to the television. Like cable TV, IPTV uses a box that acts like a modem to send and receive the content (see Figure 7.10). A few IPTV features include:

- Support of multiple devices: PCs and televisions can access IPTV services.
- Interactivity with users: Interactive applications and programs are supported by IPTV's two-way communication path.
- Low bandwidth: IPTV conserves bandwidth because the provider sends only a single channel.
- Personalization: Users can choose not only what they want to watch, but also when they want to watch it.[14]

FIGURE 7.10
IPTV Components

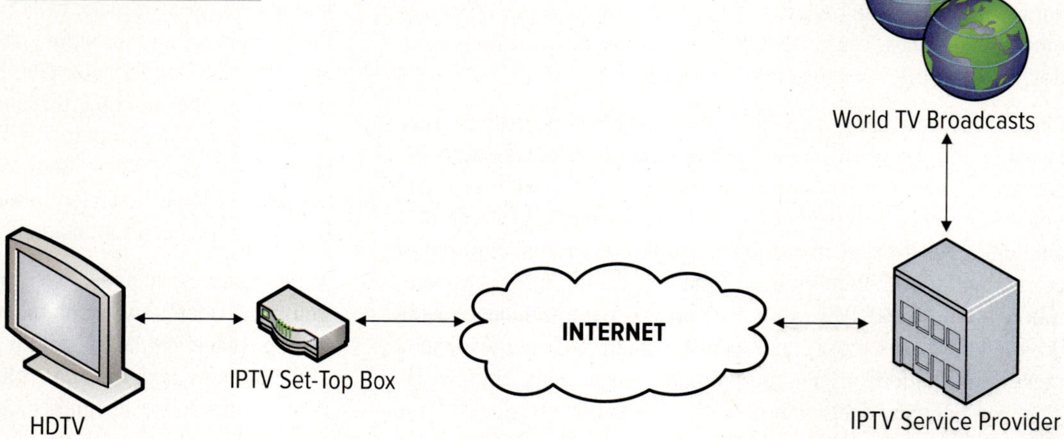

show me *the* MONEY

Net Neutrality

Net neutrality—the great debate has been raging for some time now, with the battle lines clearly drawn. *Net neutrality* is about ensuring that everyone has equal access to the Internet. It is the founding principle that all consumers should be able to use the Internet and be free to access its resources without any form of discrimination.

On one side of the debate are the ISPs, such as Comcast, that are building the Internet infrastructure and want to charge customers relative to their use, namely, the amount of bandwidth they consume. The ISPs argue that more and more users accessing bandwidth-intense resources provided by the likes of YouTube and Netflix place huge demands on their networks. They want Internet access to move from a flat-rate pricing structure to a metered service.

On the other hand, content providers, such as Google, support the counterargument that if ISPs move toward metered schemes, this may limit the usage of many resources on the Internet such as iTunes and Netflix. A metered service may also stifle the innovative opportunities the open Internet provides.

The U.S. Court of Appeals for the District of Columbia Circuit struck down the Federal Communications Commission's net neutrality rules, which would have required Internet service providers to treat all Web traffic equally. The ruling will allow ISPs to charge companies such as Netflix and Amazon fees for faster content delivery.

Do you agree that the government should control the Internet? Should website owners be legally forced to receive or transmit information from competitors or other websites they find objectionable? Provide examples of when net neutrality might be good for a business and when net neutrality might be bad for a business. Overall, is net neutrality good or bad for business?[15]

BENEFITS AND CHALLENGES OF A CONNECTED WORLD LO7.2

Before networks, transferring data between computers was time-consuming and labor-intensive. People had to physically copy data from machine to machine using a disk.

LO7.2 Identify the benefits and challenges of a connected world.

Resource sharing makes all applications, equipment (such as a high-volume printer), and data available to anyone on the network, without regard to the physical location of the resource or the user. Sharing physical resources also supports a sustainable MIS infrastructure, allowing companies to be agile, efficient, and responsible at the same time. Cloud computing (see Chapter 5) and virtualization consolidate information as well as systems that enhance the use of shared resources. By using shared resources, cloud computing and virtualization allow for collective computing power, storage, and software, in an on-demand basis.

Perhaps even more important than sharing physical resources is sharing data. Most companies, regardless of size, depend not just on their customer records, inventories, accounts receivable, financial statements, and tax information, but also on their ability to share these, especially with operations in remote locations. Networking with a LAN, WAN, or MAN allows employees to share data quickly and easily and to use applications such as databases and collaboration tools that rely on sharing. By sharing data, networks have made business processes more efficient. For example, as soon as an order is placed, anyone in the company who needs to view it—whether in marketing, purchasing, manufacturing, shipping, or billing—can do so.

Intranets and extranets let firms share their corporate information securely. An **intranet** is a restricted network that relies on Internet technologies to provide an Internet-like environment

intranet A restricted network that relies on Internet technologies to provide an Internet-like environment within the company for information sharing, communications, collaboration, web publishing, and the support of business process.

fyi Music in the Clouds[16]

Years ago, if you wanted to save music to your computer you were required to have an enormous hard drive, which was rather expensive. Today, you can listen to music in the cloud. Of course we do not mean real clouds, but the term cloud is now used as a metaphor for the Internet. Most songs exist somewhere in the "cloud," and websites like YouTube, Pandora, or HypeMachine are all services allowing you to listen to streaming music without saving a single song to your own device. Wherever those elusive songs actually live—somewhere in the cloud—you can play, collect, and share them without downloading a single thing. Five sites you can use to access music in the cloud include:

- **Fizy:** A Turkish site compiles audio from around the net into a database from which you can create your own playlists.
- **Muziic:** Developed by high school student David Nelson with help from his dad. This upstart accesses the songs on YouTube via an iTunes interface.
- **Songza:** Songza wraps the music of Imeem and YouTube in a sweet, simple web interface.
- **Spotify:** A P2P streaming architecture lets users in supported countries create collections from a massive in-house music archive.
- **Twones:** Twones allows you to download software for playback and tracks user activity on multiple online service and offline players through a single web interface.

The world of online music is a dream come true for most music lovers because you can listen to any song your heart desires with a quick Google search. What role do copyright laws play in the world of online music? If you were to start an online music business, what types of technologies would you use? Where is the future of online music headed? What are the risks associated with the online music business? If you were just starting a band, where would you post your music to gain the most exposure? What would be the risks of posting your band's music online?

© ML Harris/Getty Images

extranet An extension of an intranet that is only available to authorized outsiders, such as customers, partners, and suppliers.

virtual private network (VPN) Companies can establish direct private network links among themselves or create private, secure Internet access, in effect a "private tunnel" within the Internet.

within the company for information sharing, communications, collaboration, web publishing, and the support of business processes, as suggested in Figure 7.11. This network is protected by security measures such as passwords, encryption, and firewalls, and thus only authorized users can access it. Intranets provide a central location for all kinds of company-related information such as benefits, schedules, strategic directions, and employee directories.[17]

An **extranet** is an extension of an intranet that is available only to authorized outsiders, such as customers, partners, and suppliers. Having a common area where these parties can share information with employees about, for instance, order and invoice processing can be a major competitive advantage in product development, cost control, marketing, distribution, and supplier relations. Companies can establish direct private network links among themselves or create private, secure Internet access, in effect a "private tunnel" within the Internet, called a **virtual private network (VPN)**. Figure 7.12 illustrates using a VPN to connect to a corporate server.

Extranets enable customers, suppliers, consultants, subcontractors, business prospects, and others to access selected intranet websites and other company network resources that allow the sharing of information. Consultants and contractors can facilitate the design of new products or services. Suppliers can ensure that the raw materials necessary for the company to function are in stock and can be delivered in a timely fashion. Customers can access ordering and payment functions and check order status. The extranet links the company to the outside world in a way that improves its operations.

Extranets provide business value in several ways. First, by relying on web browsers they make customer and supplier access to company resources easy and fast. Second, they enable a company to customize interactive web-enabled services for the intended audience, to build and strengthen strategic relationships with customers and suppliers. Finally, extranets can allow and improve collaboration with customers and other business partners.

Networks have created a diverse, yet globally connected world. By eliminating time and distance, networks make it possible to communicate in ways not previously imaginable. Even though networks provide many business advantages, they also create increased challenges in (1) security and (2) social, ethical, and political issues.

Security

Networks are a tempting target for mischief and fraud. A company first has to ensure proper identification of users and authorization of network access. Outside suppliers might be allowed to access production plans via the company's extranet, for example, but they must not be able to see other information such as financial records. The company should also preserve the integrity of its data; only qualified users should be allowed to change and update data, and only well-specified data.

FIGURE 7.11 Intranet Uses

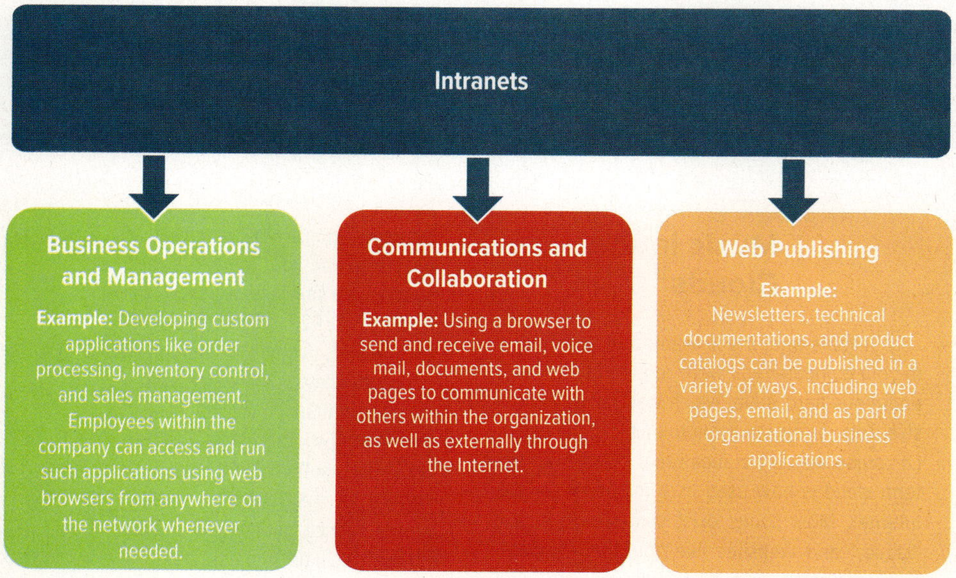

FIGURE 7.12 Using a VPN

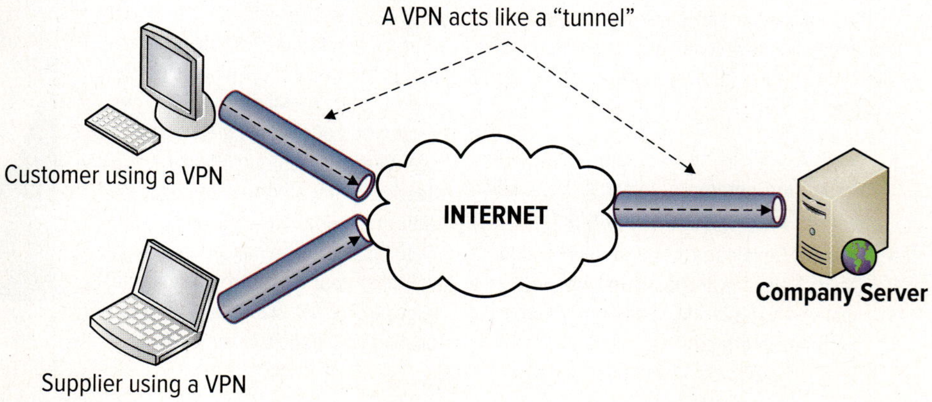

Security problems intensify on the Internet where companies need to guard against fraud, invalid purchases, and misappropriation of credit card information.

Two methods for encrypting network traffic on the web are secure sockets layer and secure hypertext transfer protocol. **Secure sockets layer (SSL)** is a standard security technology for establishing an encrypted link between a web server and a browser, ensuring that all data passed between them remain private. Millions of websites use SSL to protect their online transactions with their customers.

To create an SSL connection, a web server requires an **SSL Certificate**, an electronic document that confirms the identity of a website or server and verifies that a public key belongs to a trustworthy individual or company. (Public key is described in Chapter 4.) Typically, an SSL Certificate will contain a domain name, the company name and address, and the expiration date of the certificate and other details. Verisign is the leading Internet Certification Authority that issues SSL Certificates. When a browser connects to a secure site, it retrieves the site's SSL Certificate, makes sure it has not expired, and confirms a Certification Authority has issued it. If the certificate fails on any one of these validation measures, the browser will display a warning to the end user that the site is not secure. If a website is using SSL, a lock icon appears in the lower right-hand corner of the user's web browser.

Secure hypertext transfer protocol (SHTTP or HTTPS) is a combination of HTTP and SSL to provide encryption and secure identification of an Internet server. HTTPS protects against interception of communications, transferring credit card information safely and securely with special encryption techniques. When a user enters a web address using *https://* the browser will encrypt the message. However, the server receiving the message must be configured to receive HTTPS messages.

secure sockets layer (SSL) A standard security technology for establishing an encrypted link between a web server and a browser, ensuring that all data passed between them remains private.

SSL Certificate An electronic document that confirms the identity of a website or server and verifies that a public key belongs to a trustworthy individual or company.

secure hypertext transfer protocol (SHTTP or HTTPS) A combination of HTTP and SSL to provide encryption and secure identification of an Internet server.

My Not To-Do List

Should Airlines Allow Cellphones on Flights?[18]

The Federal Communications Commission has proposed allowing passengers to use their mobile wireless devices, including cell phones, while flying above 10,000 feet. Cell phones on airplanes would not be using the traditional cellular networks because they are not designed to operate at 35,000 feet. Rather, calls would be batched and bounced down to the ground through a satellite or specialized air-to-ground cellular system, forcing airlines to charge much more per minute than standard carrier rates.

Supporters say that cell phone use does not interfere with aviation safety and that on foreign airlines where it is permitted, passengers' calls tend to be short and unobtrusive.

Critics argue that allowing voice calls in flight would compromise flight attendants' ability to maintain order in an emergency, increase cabin noise and tension among passengers, and add unacceptable risk to aviation security. They also point out that a majority of the traveling public want the cell phone ban maintained. Do you agree or disagree with the use of cell phones on airlines?

Due Diligence //:

Teddy the Guardian

Two London-based entrepreneurs are building an Internet of huggable things for sick children to make any hospital visit more like a trip to Disneyland. Teddy The Guardian captures heart rate, temperatures, and blood-oxygen levels when a child grabs it by the paw to give it a cuddle. All measurements are sent wirelessly to nurses and parents, mobile devices. The new cute, cuddly teddy bear is packed full of sensors designed to track children's vital signs and help quickly find out potential issues. Teddy The Guardian takes from 5 to 7 seconds to record measurements and is programmed to run five times per hour. Future versions of Teddy The Guardian will be interactive, using machine learning to find out the child's favorite song or bedtime story and then play the related content for a more soothing hospital visit. Big pharmaceutical companies in the United States have already placed over $500,000 in orders and plan to donate the bears to hospitals and clinics.

This is clearly a brilliant idea, and soon we will see Teddy The Guardian in many local hospitals and clinics. Can you identify any additional markets where Teddy The Guardian should focus? Can you think of any ethical issues related to huggable things? Can you think of any security issues related to huggable things?

digital divide A worldwide gap giving advantage to those with access to technology.

personal area network (PAN) Provide communication over a short distance that is intended for use with devices that are owned and operated by a single user.

bluetooth Wireless PAN technology that transmits signals over short distances between cell phones, computers, and other devices.

wireless LAN (WLAN) A local area network that uses radio signals to transmit and receive data over distances of a few hundred feet.

In summary, each company needs to create a network security policy that specifies aspects of data integrity availability and confidentiality or privacy as well as accountability and authorization. With a variety of security methods, such as SSL and SHTTP, a company can protect its most important asset, its data.

Social, Ethical, and Political Issues

Only a small fraction of the world's population has access to the Internet, and some people who have had access in the past have lost it due to changes in their circumstances such as unemployment or poverty. Providing network access to those who want or need it helps to level the playing field and removes the **digital divide**, a worldwide gap giving advantage to those with access to technology. Organizations trying to bridge the divide include the Boston Digital Bridge Foundation, which concentrates on local schoolchildren and their parents, helping to make them knowledgeable about computers, programs, and the Internet. Other organizations provide inexpensive laptops and Internet access in low-income areas in developing countries.[19]

Another social issue with networking occurs with newsgroups or blogs where like-minded people can exchange messages. If the topics are technical in nature or sports related such as cycling, few issues arise. Problems can begin when social media feature topics people can be sensitive about, such as politics, religion, or sex, or when someone posts an offensive message to someone else. Different countries have different and even conflicting laws about Internet use, but because the Internet knows no physical boundaries, communication is hard to regulate, even if anyone could. Some people believe network operators should be responsible for the content they carry, just as newspapers and magazines are. Operators, however, feel that like the post office or phone companies, they cannot be expected to police what users say. If they censored messages, how would they avoid violating users' rights to free speech?

Many employers read and censor employee emails and limit employee access to distracting entertainment such as YouTube and social networks such as Facebook. Spending company time "playing" is not a good use of resources, they believe.

Social issues can even affect the government and its use of networks to snoop on citizens. The FBI has installed a system at many ISPs to scan all incoming and outgoing email for nuggets of interest. The system was originally called Carnivore but bad publicity caused it to be renamed DCS1000. While the name is much more generic, its goal is the same—locate information on illegal activities by spying on millions of people. A common conception associated with networking technologies is "Big Brother is watching!" People are wary of how much information is available on the Internet and how easily it can fall into the wrong hands.[20]

{SECTION 7.2} Mobility: The Business Value of a Wireless World

LEARNING OUTCOMES

LO7.3 Describe the different wireless network categories.

LO7.4 Explain the different wireless network business applications.

WIRELESS NETWORKS LO7.3

As far back as 1896, Italian inventor Guglielmo Marconi demonstrated a wireless telegraph, and in 1927, the first radiotelephone system began operating between the United States and Great Britain. Automobile-based mobile telephones were offered in 1947. In 1964, the first communications satellite, Telstar, was launched, and soon after, satellite-relayed telephone service and television broadcasts became available. Wireless networks have exploded since then, and newer technologies are now maturing that allow companies and home users alike to take advantage of both wired and wireless networks.[21]

Before delving into a discussion of wireless networks, we should distinguish between mobile and wireless, terms that are often used synonymously but actually have different meanings. *Mobile* means the technology can travel with the user, for instance, users can download software, email messages, and web pages onto a laptop or other mobile device for portable reading or reference. Information collected while on the road can be synchronized with a PC or company server. *Wireless,* on the other hand, refers to any type of operation accomplished without the use of a hard-wired connection. There are many environments in which the network devices are wireless but not mobile, such as wireless home or office networks with stationary PCs and printers. Some forms of mobility do not require a wireless connection; for instance, a worker can use a wired laptop at home, shut down the laptop, drive to work, and attach the laptop to the company's wired network.

In many networked environments today, users are both wireless and mobile; for example, a mobile user commuting to work on a train can maintain a VoIP call and multiple TCP/IP connections at the same time. Figure 7.13 categorizes wireless networks by type.

LO7.3 Describe the different wireless network categories.

FIGURE 7.13 Wireless Communication Network Categories

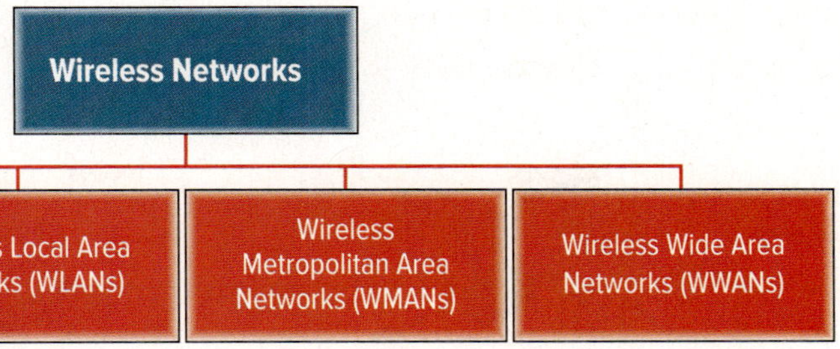

Personal Area Networks

A **personal area network (PAN)** provides communication for devices owned by a single user that work over a short distance. PANs are used to transfer files, including email, calendar appointments, digital photos, and music. A PAN can provide communication between a wireless headset and a cell phone or between a computer and a wireless mouse or keyboard. Personal area networks generally cover a range of less than 10 meters (about 30 feet). **Bluetooth** is a wireless PAN technology that transmits signals over short distances among cell phones, computers, and other devices. The name is borrowed from Harald Bluetooth, a king in Denmark more than 1,000 years ago. Bluetooth eliminates the need for wires, docking stations, or cradles, as well as all the special attachments that typically accompany personal computing devices. Bluetooth operates at speeds up to 1 Mbps within a range of 33 feet or less. Devices that are Bluetooth-enabled communicate directly with each other in pairs, like a handshake. Up to eight can be paired simultaneously. And Bluetooth is not just for technology devices. An array of Bluetooth-equipped appliances, such as a television set, a stove, and a thermostat, can be controlled from a cell phone—all from a remote location.[22]

Wireless LANs

A **wireless LAN (WLAN)** is a local area network that uses radio signals to transmit and receive data over distances of a few hundred feet. An **access point (AP)** is the computer or network device that serves as an interface between devices and the network. Each computer initially connects to the access point and then to other computers on the network. A **wireless access point (WAP)** enables devices to connect to a wireless network to communicate with each other. WAPs with **multiple-in/multiple-out (MIMO) technology** have multiple transmitters and receivers, allowing them to send and receive greater amounts of data than traditional networking devices. **Wireless fidelity (Wi-Fi)** is a means by which portable devices can connect wirelessly to a local area network, using access points that send and receive data via radio waves. Wi-Fi has a maximum range of about 1,000 feet in open areas such as a city park and 250 to 400 feet in closed areas such as an office building. **Wi-Fi infrastructure** includes the inner workings of a Wi-Fi service or utility, including the signal transmitters, towers, or poles, along with additional equipment required to send out a Wi-Fi signal. Most WLANs use a Wi-Fi infrastructure in which a wireless device, often a laptop, communicates through an access point or base station by means of, for instance, wireless fidelity.

Areas around access points where users can connect to the Internet are often called hotspots. **Hotspots** are designated locations where Wi-Fi access points are publicly available. Hotspots are found in places such as restaurants, airports, and hotels—places where business professionals tend to gather. Hotspots are extremely valuable for those business professionals who travel extensively and need access to business applications. By positioning hotspots at strategic locations throughout a building, campus, or city, network administrators can keep Wi-Fi users continuously connected to a network or the Internet, no matter where they roam.[23]

In a Wi-Fi network, the user's laptop or other Wi-Fi-enabled device has a wireless adapter that translates data into a radio signal and transmits it to the wireless access point. The wireless access point, which consists of a transmitter with an antenna that is often built into the hardware, receives the signal and decodes it. The access point then sends the information to the Internet over a wired broadband connection, as illustrated in Figure 7.14. When receiving data, the wireless access point takes the information from the Internet, translates it into a radio signal, and sends it to the computer's wireless adapter. If too many people try to use the Wi-Fi network at one time, they can experience interference or dropped connections. Most laptop computers come with built-in wireless transmitters and software to enable computers to automatically discover the existence of a Wi-Fi network.

Wi-Fi operates at considerably higher frequencies than cell phones use, which allows greater bandwidth. The bandwidths associated with Wi-Fi are separated according to several wireless networking standards, known as 802.11, for carrying out

access point (AP) The computer or network device that serves as an interface between devices and the network.

wireless access point (WAP) Enables devices to connect to a wireless network to communicate with each other.

multiple-in/multiple-out (MIMO) technology Multiple transmitters and receivers allow sending and receiving greater amounts of data than traditional networking devices.

wireless fidelity (Wi-Fi) A means by which portable devices can connect wirelessly to a local area network, using access points that send and receive data via radio waves.

Wi-Fi infrastructure Includes the inner workings of a Wi-Fi service or utility, including the signal transmitters, towers, or poles, along with additional equipment required to send a Wi-Fi signal.

hotspot Designated locations where Wi-Fi access points are publicly available.

Institute of Electrical and Electronics Engineers (IEEE) An organization that researches and institutes electrical standards for communication and other technologies.

IEEE 802.11n (or Wireless-N) The newest standard for wireless networking.

wireless MAN (WMAN) A metropolitan area network that uses radio signals to transmit and receive data.

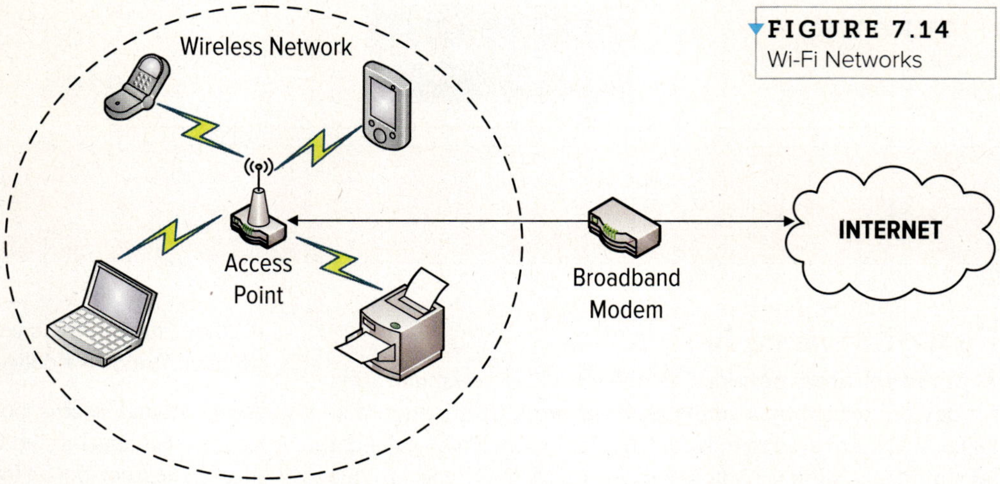

FIGURE 7.14
Wi-Fi Networks

wireless local area network communication. The **Institute of Electrical and Electronics Engineers (IEEE)** researches and institutes electrical standards for communication and other technologies. **IEEE 802.11n (or Wireless-N)** is the newest standard for wireless networking. Compared with earlier standards such as 802.11b, Wireless-N offers faster speeds, more flexibility, and greater range. The organization denotes different versions of the standard—for example, Wireless-G and Wireless-N—by a lowercase letter at the end of this number. Figure 7.15 outlines the bandwidths associated with a few of these standards.[24]

An increasing number of digital devices, including most laptops, netbooks, tablets such as the iPad, and even printers are incorporating Wi-Fi technology into their design. Cell phones are incorporating Wi-Fi so they can automatically switch from the cell network to a faster Wi-Fi network where available for data communications. BlackBerrys and iPhones can connect to an access point for data communications such as email and web browsing, but not for voice unless they use the services of Skype or another VoIP.

Wireless MANs

A **wireless MAN (WMAN)** is a metropolitan area network that uses radio signals to transmit and receive data. WMAN technologies have not been highly successful to date, mainly

Wi-Fi Standard	Bandwidth
802.11a	54 Mbps
802.11b	11 Mbps
802.11g	54 Mbps
802.11n	140 Mbps

FIGURE 7.15
Wi-Fi Standards and Bandwidths

show me *the* MONEY

Wireless Networks and Streetlamps[27]

Researchers at Harvard University and BBN Technologies have designed CitySense, a wireless network capable of reporting real-time sensor data across the entire city of Cambridge, Massachusetts. CitySense is unique because it solves a constraint on previous wireless networks—battery life. The network mounts each node on a municipal streetlamp, where it draws power from city electricity. Researchers installed 100 sensors on streetlamps throughout Cambridge using a grant from the National Science Foundation. Each node will include an embedded PC running the Linux OS, an 802.11 Wi-Fi interface, and weather sensors.

One of the challenges in the design was how the network would allow remote nodes to communicate with the central server at Harvard and BBN. CitySense will do that by letting each node form a mesh with its neighbors, exchanging data through multiple-hop links. This strategy allows a node to download software or upload sensor data to a distant server hub using a small radio with only a one-kilometer range.

You are responsible for deploying a CitySense network around your city. What goals would you have for the system besides monitoring urban weather and pollution? What other benefits could a CitySense network provide? How could local businesses and citizens benefit from the network? What legal and ethical concerns should you understand before deploying the network? What can you do to protect your network and your city from these issues?

because they are not widely available, at least in the United States. One with the potential for success is **Worldwide Interoperability for Microwave Access (WiMAX)**, a communications technology aimed at providing high-speed wireless data over metropolitan area networks. In many respects, WiMAX operates like Wi-Fi, only over greater distances and with higher bandwidths. A WiMAX tower serves as an access point and can connect to the Internet or another tower. A single tower can provide up to 3,000 square miles of coverage, so only a few are needed to cover an entire city. WiMAX can support data communications at a rate of 70 Mbps. In New York City, for example, one or two WiMAX access points around the city might meet the heavy demand more cheaply than hundreds of Wi-Fi access points. WiMAX can also cover remote or rural areas where cabling is limited or nonexistent, and where it is too expensive or physically difficult to install wires for the relatively few users.[25]

WiMAX can provide both line-of-sight and non-line-of-sight service. A non-line-of-sight service uses a small antenna on a mobile device that connects to a WiMAX tower less than six miles away where transmissions are disrupted by physical obstructions. This form of service is similar to Wi-Fi but has much broader coverage area and higher bandwidths. A line-of-sight option offers a fixed antenna that points at the WiMAX tower from a rooftop or pole. This option is much faster than non-line-of-sight service, and the distance between the WiMAX tower and antenna can be as great as 30 miles. Figure 7.16 illustrates the WiMAX infrastructure.[26]

Some cellular companies are evaluating WiMAX as a means of increasing bandwidth for a variety of data-intensive applications such as those used by smartphones. Sprint Nextel and Clearwire are building a nationwide WiMAX network in the United States. WiMAX-capable gaming devices, laptops, cameras, and even cell phones are being manufactured by companies including Intel, Motorola, Nokia, and Samsung.[28]

Worldwide Interoperability for Microwave Access (WiMAX) A communications technology aimed at providing high-speed wireless data over metropolitan area networks.

wireless WAN (WWAN) A wide area network that uses radio signals to transmit and receive data.

FIGURE 7.16
WiMAX Infrastructure

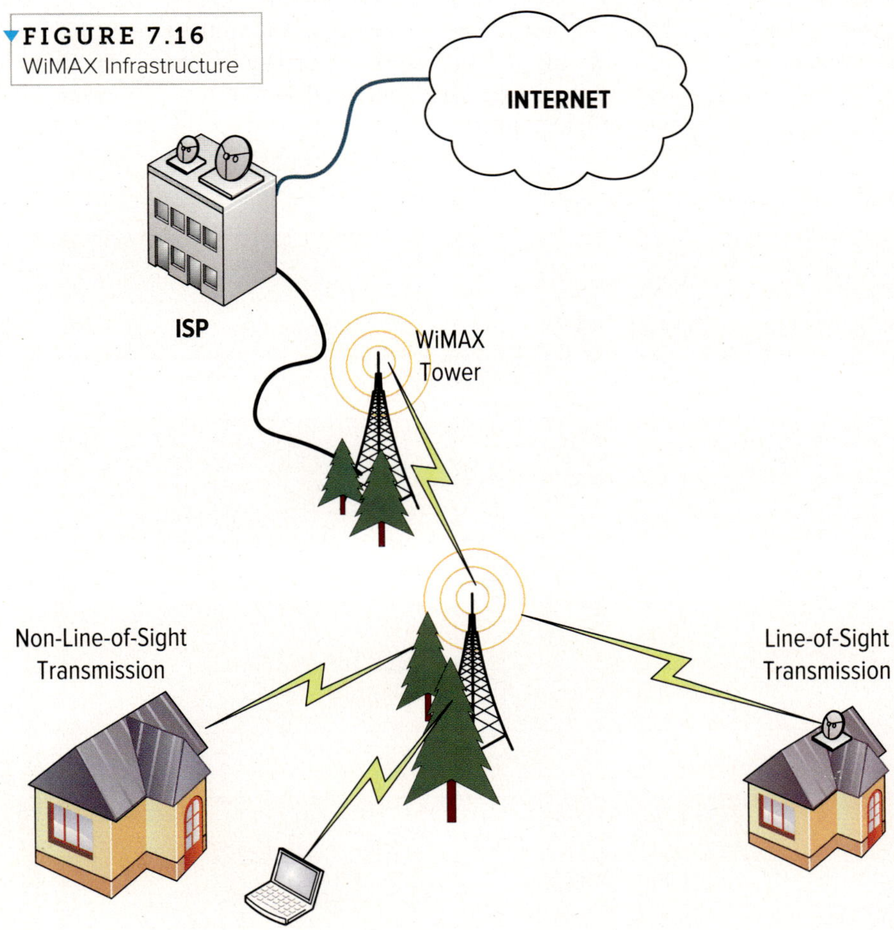

Wireless WAN—Cellular Communication System

A **wireless WAN (WWAN)** is a wide area network that uses radio signals to transmit and receive data. WWAN technologies can be divided into two categories: cellular communication systems and satellite communication systems.

Although mobile communications have been around for generations, including the walkie-talkies of the 1940s and mobile radiophones of the 1950s, it was not until 1983 that cellular telephony became available commercially. A cell phone is a device for voice and data, communicating wirelessly through a collection of stationary ground-based sites called base stations, each of which is linked to its nearest neighbor stations. Base station coverage areas are about 10 square miles and are called cells, as Figure 7.17 illustrates.[29]

The first cell phone was demonstrated in 1973 by Motorola (it weighed almost 2 pounds), but it took 10 years for the technology to become commercially available. The Motorola DynaTAC, marketed in 1983, weighed one pound and cost about $4,000. Cellular technology has come a long way since then.[30]

Cellular systems were originally designed to provide voice services to mobile customers and thus were designed to interconnect cells to the public telephone network. Increasingly, they provide data services and Internet connectivity. There are more cell phones than landline phones in many countries today, and it is no longer uncommon for cell phones to be the only phones people have.

smartphones Offer more advanced computing ability and connectivity than basic cell phones.

3G A service that brings wireless broadband to mobile phones.

streaming A method of sending audio and video files over the Internet in such a way that the user can view the file while it is being transferred.

Voice over LTE (VoLTE) Allows mobile voice calls to be made over broadband networks, creating–under the right network conditions–clearer audio and fewer dropped calls.

FIGURE 7.17
Cell Phone Communication System Overview

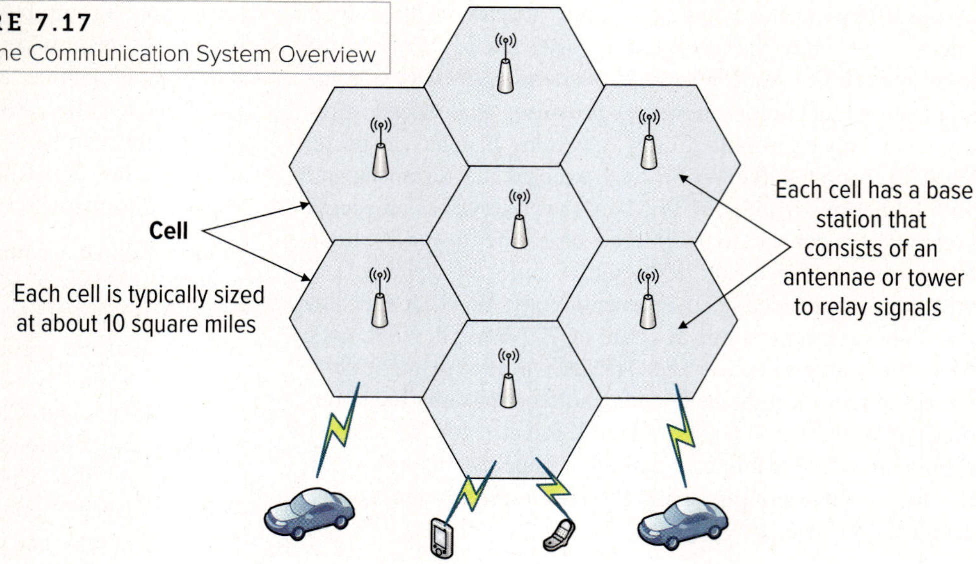

Cell phones have morphed into **smartphones** that offer more advanced computing ability and connectivity than basic cell phones. They allow for web browsing, emailing, listening to music, watching video, computing, keeping track of contacts, sending text messages, and taking and sending photos. The Apple iPhone and RIM BlackBerry are examples of smartphones.

Cell phones and smartphones, or mobile phones as they are collectively called, need a provider to offer services, much as computer users need an ISP to connect to the Internet. The most popular mobile phone providers in the United States are AT&T, Sprint, T-Mobile, and Verizon. They offer different cell phones, features, coverage areas, and services. One of the services is third-generation, or **3G**, services that bring wireless broadband to mobile phones. Figure 7.18 lists the cell phone generations. The 3G networks let users surf web pages, enjoy streaming music, watch video-on-demand programming, download and play 3-D games, and participate in social media and teleconferencing. **Streaming** is a method of sending audio and video files over the Internet in such a way that the user can view the file while it is being transferred. Streaming is not limited to cellular usage; all wireless and even wired networks can take advantage of this method. The most obvious advantage is speed, a direct benefit for mobile and wireless devices since they are still not as fast as their wired counterparts. **Voice over LTE (VoLTE)** allows mobile voice calls to be made over broadband networks, creating—under the right network conditions—clearer audio and fewer dropped calls. One easy way to think of VoLTE is as, essentially, a VoIP call on your mobile phone. The functionality is still the same, but the data transfers in a faster and more efficient manner.[31]

FIGURE 7.18 Cell Phone Generations

Generation	Description	Speed
1G	The original analog cell phone network.	Speed = 9.6 Kbps
2G – 2.5G	Digital cell phone service.	Speed = 10 Kbps–144 Kbps
3G – 3.5G	Broadband Internet services over cellular network.	Speed = 144 Kbps–11 Mbps
4G	Very high-speed access, anywhere, anytime, to anything digital—audio, video, text.	Speed = 2–300 Mbps

Wireless WAN - Satellite Communication System

The other wireless WAN technology is a satellite communication system. A **satellite** is a space station that orbits the Earth receiving and transmitting signals from Earth-based stations over a wide area. When satellite systems first came into consideration in the 1990s, the goal was to provide wireless voice and data coverage for the entire planet, without the need for mobile phones to roam between many different provider networks. But by the time satellite networks were ready for commercial use, they had already been overtaken by cellular systems.

The devices used for satellite communication range from handheld units to mobile base stations to fixed satellite dish receivers. The peak data transmission speeds range from 2.4 Kbps to 2 Mbps. For the everyday mobile professional, satellite communication may not provide a compelling benefit, but for people requiring voice and data access from remote locations or guaranteed coverage in nonremote locations, satellite technology is a viable solution.

Conventional communication satellites move in stationary orbits approximately 22,000 miles above Earth. A newer satellite medium, the low-orbit satellite, travels much closer to Earth and is able to pick up signals from weak transmitters. Low-orbit satellites also consume less power and cost less to launch than conventional satellites. With satellite networks, businesspeople almost anywhere in the world have access to full communication capabilities, including voice, videoconferencing, and Internet access. Figure 7.19 briefly illustrates the satellite communication system.[33]

satellite A space station that orbits the Earth receiving and transmitting signals from Earth-based stations over a wide area.

wired equivalent privacy (WEP) An encryption algorithm designed to protect wireless transmission data.

FIGURE 7.19 Satellite Communication System

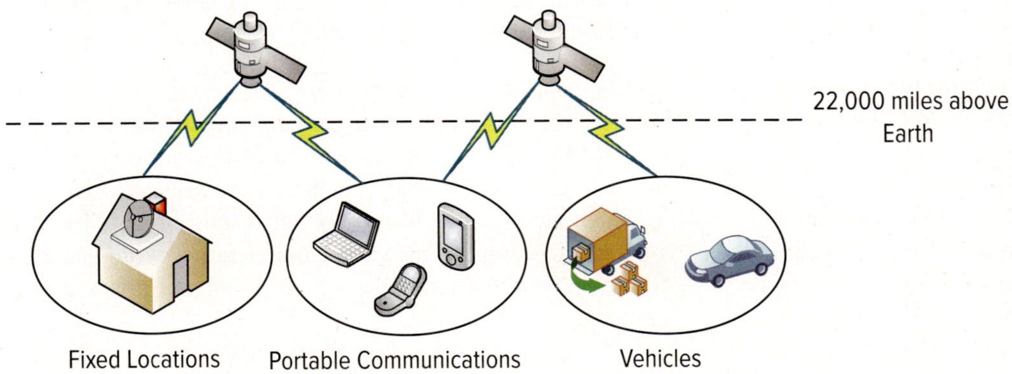

Protecting Wireless Connections

Network intrusions can occur if access codes or passwords are stored on a device that is lost or stolen. However, anytime a wireless network connects to a wired one, the wireless network can serve as a conduit for a hacker to gain entry into an otherwise secure wired network. This risk is especially high if the wireless network is not sufficiently secured in its own right.

Before the emergence of the Internet, hackers generally had to be physically present within the corporate complex to gain access to a wired network. The thousands, if not millions, of access points enabled by the Internet now allow hackers to work from a distance. This threat has spawned a variety of security techniques, from firewalls to VPNs to SSL and HTTPS.

Several techniques can secure wireless networks from unauthorized access whether used separately or in combination. One method is authenticating Wi-Fi access points. Because Wi-Fi communications are broadcast, anyone within listening distance can intercept communications. Every time someone uses an unsecured website via a public Wi-Fi access point, his or her logon name and password are sent over the open airwaves with a high risk that someone might eavesdrop or capture logon names, passwords, credit card numbers, and other vital information. **Wired equivalent privacy (WEP)** is an encryption

Living the DREAM

Saving the World One Phone at a Time

The mobile phone is helping to fight poverty and increase world economic development. It can dramatically improve living standards for people living on a few dollars a day by helping them find work, providing information about crop prices, or calling for medical help. By using mobile phones to find the best local marketplace prices for sardines, a group of poor fishermen in Kerala, India, increased their profits by an average of 8 percent. The fishermen were able to call ahead to a port to identify a buyer. In Muruguru, Kenya, Grace Wachira runs a small knitting company. Before using a mobile phone, she would walk hours to the nearest town to buy her supplies or meet customers. Using her mobile phone, she can now call for her supplies to be delivered and to communicate with her customers.

What type of mobile phones are these people buying? What other uses can a mobile phone provide for people living in poor, rural regions? How can people in rural areas turn owning a mobile phone into a small-scale business?[32]

Wi-Fi protected access (WPA) A wireless security protocol to protect Wi-Fi networks.

war chalking The practice of tagging pavement with codes displaying where Wi-Fi access is available.

war driving Deliberately searching for Wi-Fi signals from a vehicle.

IT consumerization The blending of personal and business use of technology devices and applications.

mobile device management(MDM) Remotely controls smartphones and tablets, ensuring data security.

algorithm designed to protect wireless transmission data. If you are using a Wi-Fi connection, WEP encrypts the data by using a key that converts the data to a nonhuman readable form. The purpose of WEP was to provide wireless networks with the equivalent level of security as wired networks. Unfortunately, the technology behind WEP has been demonstrated to be relatively insecure compared to newer protocols such as WPA. WLANs that use Wi-Fi have a built-in security mechanism called **Wi-Fi protected access (WPA)**, a wireless security protocol to protect Wi-Fi networks. It is an improvement on the original Wi-Fi security standard, wired equivalent privacy (WEP), and provides more sophisticated data encryption and user authentication. Anyone who wants to use an access point must know the WPA encryption key to access the Wi-Fi connection.

War chalking is the practice of tagging pavement with codes displaying where Wi-Fi access is available. The codes for war chalking tell other users the kind of access available, the speed of the network, and if the network is secured. **War driving** is deliberately searching for Wi-Fi signals while driving by in a vehicle. Many individuals who participate in war driving simply map where Wi-Fi networks are available. Other individuals have a more malicious intent and use war driving to hack or break into these networks. War driving has been a controversial practice since its inception and has raised the awareness of the importance of wireless network security.

Managing Mobile Devices

IT consumerization is the blending of personal and business use of technology devices and applications. Today's workforce grew up with the Internet and its members do not differentiate between corporate and personal technology. Employees want to use the same technology they have at home in the office. This blending of personal and business technology is having a significant impact on corporate MIS departments, which traditionally choose all of the technology for the organization. Today, MIS departments must determine how to protect their networks and manage technology that they did not authorize or recommend. Two ways an MIS department can manage IT consumerization is through mobile device management and mobile application management.

Mobile device management (MDM) remotely controls smartphones and tablets, ensuring data security. MIS departments implement MDM by requiring passcodes on organizational smartphones to ensure data encryption and, in the event of a lost smartphone, that all data on the device can be deleted remotely. MDM tools can also enforce policies, track inventory, and perform real-time monitoring and reporting. One problem with MDM is that the full-device approach can be too heavy-handed in an era when employees, not their employers, own their smartphones and tablets. Users may wonder, "If I only use my phone to check email at night, why do I have to enter my work password every time I want to use the phone?" or "If I lose my phone, why does my IT department want to wipe pictures of my dog remotely?"

Mobile application management administers and delivers applications to corporate and personal smartphones and tablets. MAM software assists with software delivery, licensing, and maintenance and can limit how sensitive data can be shared among apps. An important feature of MAM is that it provides corporate network administrators with the ability to wipe corporate mobile apps from an end user's device remotely.

fyi

Sports Sensors

A sensor is a device that detects or measures a physical property such as heat, light, sound, or motion and records, indicates, or otherwise reacts to it in a particular way. With wireless apps and sensors, a number of new, high-tech tools for amateurs provide coach-quality feedback to athletes of all levels, including:

- **Tennis (Sony):** Sony recently created a tennis-tracking device and app that will let users collect the kind of game-play data that used to be available only to professionals.
- **Golf (Swingbyte):** The ultralight sensor clips to the club and monitors speed, acceleration, arc, and other statistics.
- **Hockey (Fwd Powershot):** The ultralight sensor fits into the handle end of the stick and measures swing speed, angle, and acceleration.
- **Basketball (94Fifty Smart Sensor):** Embedded in a standard ball, the sensor tracks shot speed, arc, and backspin plus dribble speed and force.
- **Baseball (Zepp):** Stuck to the knob of the bat, the sensor tracks the speed and plane of a swing and the angle of impact.[34]

In a group, create a product that takes advantage of sensors, including what the sensor would measure and how it would deliver the feedback to the user.

BUSINESS APPLICATIONS OF WIRELESS NETWORKS LO7.4

Companies of all types and sizes have relied on wireless technology for years. Shipping and trucking companies developed some of the earliest wireless applications to help track vehicles and valuable cargo, optimize the logistics of their global operations, perfect their delivery capabilities, and reduce theft and damage. Government agencies such as the National Aeronautics and Space Administration and the Department of Defense have relied on satellite technologies for decades to track the movement of troops, weaponry, and military assets; to receive and broadcast data; and to communicate over great distances.

Wireless technologies have also aided the creation of new applications. Some build upon and improve existing capabilities. UPS, for example, is combining several types of wireless network technologies from Bluetooth to WWANs and deploying scanners and wearable data-collection terminals to automate and standardize package management and tracking across all its delivery centers. Figure 7.20 displays the three business applications taking advantage of wireless technologies.

LO7.4 Explain the different wireless network business applications.

Radio-Frequency Identification (RFID)

Radio-frequency identification (RFID) uses electronic tags and labels to identify objects wirelessly over short distances. It holds the promise of replacing existing identification technologies such as the bar code. RFID wirelessly exchanges information between a tagged object and a reader/writer. An **RFID tag** is an electronic identification device that is made up of a chip and antenna. An **RFID reader (RFID interrogator)** is a transmitter/receiver that reads the contents of RFID tags in the area. A RFID system is comprised of one or more RFID tags, one or more RFID readers, two or more antennas (one on the tag and one on each reader), RFID application software, and a computer system or server, as Figure 7.21 illustrates. Tags, often smaller than a grain of rice, can be applied to books or clothing items as part of an adhesive bar-code label, or included in items such as ID cards or packing labels. Readers can be stand-alone devices, such as for self-checkout in a grocery store, integrated with a mobile device for portable use, or built in as in printers. The reader sends a wireless request that is received by all tags in the area that have been programmed to listen to wireless signals. Tags receive the signal via their antennas and respond by transmitting their stored data. The tag can hold many types of data, including a product number, installation instructions, and history of activity (such as the date the item was shipped). The reader receives a signal from the tag using its antenna, interprets the information sent, and transfers the data to the associated computer system or server.

FIGURE 7.20 Wireless Business Applications

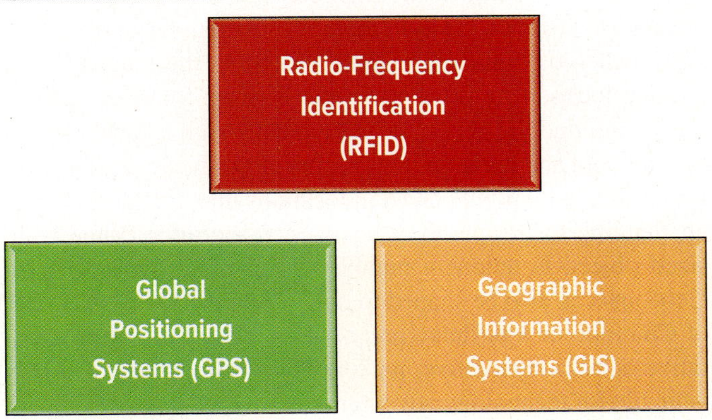

Passive RFID tags do not have a power source, whereas **active RFID tags** have their own transmitter and a power source (typically a battery). The power source runs the microchip's circuitry and broadcasts a signal to the reader (similar to the way a cell phone transmits signals to a base station). Passive RFID tags draw power from the RFID reader, which sends out electromagnetic waves that induce a current in the tag's antenna. **Semi-passive RFID tags** use a battery to run the microchip's circuitry, but communicate by drawing power from the RFID reader. **Asset tracking** occurs when a company places active or semi-passive RFID tags on expensive products or assets to gather data on the items' location with little or no manual intervention. Asset tracking allows a company to focus on its supply chain, reduce theft, identify the last known user of assets, and automate maintenance routines. Active and semi-passive tags are useful for tracking high-value goods that need to be scanned over long ranges, such as railway cars on a track. The cost of active and semi-passive RFID tags is significant; hence, low-cost items typically use passive RFID tags.

radio-frequency identification (RFID) Uses electronic tags and labels to identify objects wirelessly over short distances.

RFID tag An electronic identification device that is made up of a chip and antenna.

RFID reader (RFID interrogator) A transmitter/receiver that reads the contents of RFID tags in the area.

passive RFID tags Do not have a power source.

active RFID tags Have their own transmitter and a power source (typically a battery).

semi-passive RFID tags Include a battery to run the microchip's circuitry, but communicate by drawing power from the RFID reader.

asset tracking Occurs when a company places active or semi-passive RFID tags on expensive products or assets to gather data on the items' location with little or no manual intervention.

RFID accelerometer A device that measures the acceleration (the rate of change of velocity) of an item and is used to track truck speeds or taxicab speeds.

chipless RFID tags Use plastic or conductive polymers instead of silicon-based microchips, allowing them to be washed or exposed to water without damaging the chip.

global positioning system (GPS) A satellite-based navigation system providing extremely accurate position, time, and speed information.

automatic vehicle location (AVL) Uses GPS tracking to track vehicles.

latitude Represents a north/south measurement of position.

longitude Represents an east/west measurement of position.

geocache A GPS technology adventure game that posts on the Internet the longitude and latitude location of an item for users to find.

geocoin A round coin-sized object that is uniquely numbered and hidden in geocache.

estimated time of arrival (ETA) The time of day of an expected arrival at a certain destination; typically used for navigation applications.

FIGURE 7.21 Elements of an RFID system

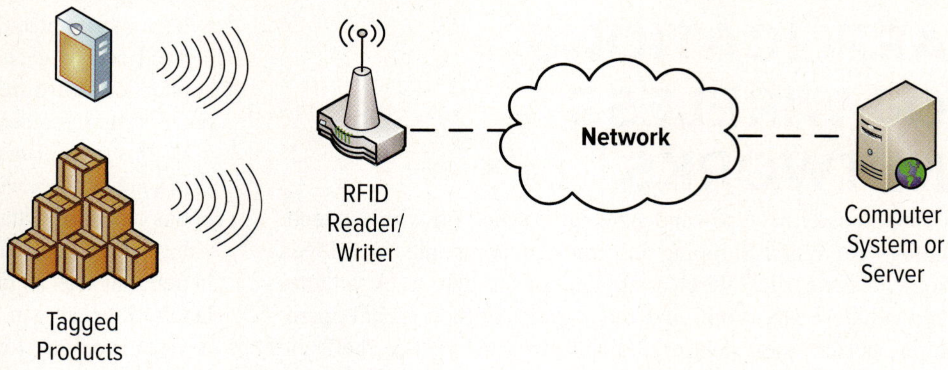

The **RFID accelerometer** is a device that measures the acceleration (the rate of change of velocity) of an item and is used to track truck speeds or taxi cab speeds. **Chipless RFID tags** use plastic or conductive polymers instead of silicon-based microchips, allowing them to be washed or exposed to water without damaging the chip. Examples of the innovative uses of RFID include:

- RFID chips injected under the skin of animals using a syringe can help ranchers meet regulations, track wild animals for ecological studies, and return lost pets to their owners.
- Retail stores use RFID to track and monitor inventory. Hospitals and pharmaceutical companies meet government regulations and standards with RFID. Even local libraries are using RFID to control theft and speed up the checkout process.
- Car manufacturers install RFID antitheft systems. Toll roads use RFID to collect payments from passing cars.
- Hospitals track patients', doctors', and nurses' locations to facilitate emergency situations and ensure safety. RFID also tracks equipment location to ensure quick response times during an emergency.
- American Express and MasterCard use RFID for automatic payments.
- Walmart and other large retailers use RFID to maintain inventory, stop shoplifting, and speed customer checkout processes.[35]

Global Positioning System (GPS)

A **global positioning system (GPS)** is a satellite-based navigation system providing extremely accurate position, time, and speed information. The U.S. Department of Defense developed the technology in the early 1970s and later made it available to the public. GPS uses 24 global satellites that orbit Earth, sending signals to a receiver that can communicate with three or four satellites at a time. A GPS receiver can be a separate unit connected to a mobile device using cable or wireless technology such as Bluetooth, or it can be included in devices such as mobile phones or vehicle navigation systems. **Automatic vehicle location (AVL)** uses GPS tracking to track vehicles. AVL systems use a GPS receiver in the vehicle that links to a control center. Garmin is one of the more popular manufacturers of GPS tracking systems, offering vehicle tracking, phone and laptop integration, and hiker navigation for water and air.

The satellites broadcast signals constantly, while the receiver measures the time it takes for the signals to reach it. This measurement, which uses the speed of the signal to determine the distance, is taken from three distinct satellites to provide precise location information. The time measurements depend on high-powered clocks on each satellite and must be precise, because an error of one-thousandth of a second can result in a location variation of more than 200 miles. GPS can produce very accurate results, typically within 5 to 50 feet of the actual location (military versions have higher accuracy). GPS also provides latitude, longitude, and elevation information. **Latitude** represents a north/south measurement of position. **Longitude** represents an east/west measurement of position. **Geocache** is a GPS technology adventure game that posts the longitude and latitude location for an item on the Internet for users to find. GPS users find the geocache and typically sign a guest book or take an item and leave an item for the next adventure players to find. Caches are often placed in locations that are interesting or challenging for people to discover. A **geocoin**, a round coin-sized object, is uniquely numbered and hidden in geocache. Geocoins can also be shaped to match a theme such as the state of Colorado or a birthday party hat. Geocoins are often decorative or commemorative, making them collectible and highly valuable for technology adventures.

estimated time enroute (ETE) The time remaining before reaching a destination using the present speed; typically used for navigation applications.

geographic information system (GIS) Stores, views, and analyzes geographic data, creating multidimensional charts or maps.

cartography The science and art of making an illustrated map or chart.

edge matching (warping, rubber sheeting) Occurs when paper maps are laid edge to edge, and items that run across maps but do not match are reconfigured to match.

GIS map automation Links business assets to a centralized system where they can be tracked and monitored over time.

spatial data (geospatial data or geographic information) Identifies the geographic location of features and boundaries on Earth, such as natural or constructed features, oceans, and more.

GPS applications are in every kind of company vehicle these days—from police cars to bulldozers, from dump trucks to mayoral limousines. Emergency response systems use GPS to track each of their vehicles and so dispatch those closest to the scene of an accident. If a vehicle is missing, its GPS locator can help locate it. **Estimated time of arrival (ETA)** is the time of day of an expected arrival at a certain destination and is typically used for navigation applications. **Estimated time enroute (ETE)** is the time remaining before reaching a destination using the present speed and is typically used for navigation applications.

Geographic Information Systems (GIS)

GPS provides the foundation for geographic information systems. A **geographic information system (GIS)** stores, views, and analyzes geographic data creating, multidimensional charts or maps. For example, GIs are monitoring global warming by measuring the speed of glaciers melting in Canada, Greenland, and Antarctica. **Cartography** is the science and art of making an illustrated map or chart. GIS allows users to interpret, analyze, and visualize data in different ways that reveal patterns and trends in the form of reports, charts, and maps. **Edge matching (warping, rubber sheeting)** occurs when paper maps are laid edge to edge and items that run across maps but do not match are reconfigured to match. Edge matching is a critical component of creating a GIS database because map misalignments occur frequently for many reasons, including survey error and cartographic errors. **GIS map automation** links business assets to a centralized system where they can be tracked and monitored over time.

Spatial data (geospatial data or geographic information) identifies the geographic location of features and boundaries on Earth, such as natural or constructed features, oceans, and more. Spatial data can be mapped and is stored as coordinates and topology. A GIS accesses, manipulates, and analyzes spatial data. **Geocoding** in spatial databases is a

Living the DREAM

Wi-Fi For Fishes

Not too long ago, the Seattle Aquarium decided it needed to take a deep dive into its network infrastructure and deploy wireless across its facilities. Now, a year and half in, the aquarium has found Wi-Fi to be a tool that not only lets it serve visitors in unique ways but enriches the exchanges possible between staff members and the community, says Pam Lamon, the aquarium's web and social media coordinator. For instance, there are long stretches when Umi, the aquarium's 40-pound giant Pacific octopus, doesn't move at all. Now, staff members armed with tablets can roam around the exhibit showing visitors videos of Umi feeding while they field questions.

Wireless even lets the aquarium interact with people who can't visit in person. For instance, during a recent Google + Hangout on Air, a young boy from an East Coast school asked an aquarium diver how many fish were swimming in the tank with her. The diver, wearing a wetsuit and a face-mask with a microphone and speaker, began pointing out fish. "One, two, three, four, five, six, seven," she counted off, before giving up and telling him there were 500, give or take a few. "It's a little bit hard to know for sure because they just don't hold still while we count them," she joked.

The Seattle Aquarium is far from alone among businesses and organizations that are tapping into wireless to expand or improve services. As wireless has morphed from a pleasant perk to a necessity for employees and clients across industries, many businesses are finding they can no longer make do without wireless or with limited Wi-Fi services. Today, not only is there incentive to find better solutions, but companies have access to more sophisticated equipment to help them pinpoint network problems. From next-generation access points to cloud-based management systems, wireless tools can provide expanded capabilities, are easy to manage, and are available in a range of prices.[36]

In a group, choose a business in your area that could benefit from wireless technology, such as the Seattle Aquarium, and create a plan detailing the additional services it could offer its customers.

geocoding A coding process that takes a digital map feature and assigns it an attribute that serves as a unique ID (tract number, node number) or classification (soil type, zoning category).

location-based services (LBS) Applications that use location information to provide a service.

coding process that assigns a digital map feature to an attribute that serves as a unique ID (tract number, node number) or classification (soil type, zoning category). GIS professionals are certified in geocoding practices to ensure industry standards are met when classifying spatial data.

Companies that deal in transportation combine GISs with database and GPS technology. Airlines and shipping companies can plot routes with up-to-the-second information about the location of all their transport vehicles. Hospitals can locate their medical staff with GIS and sensors that pick up transmissions from ID badges. Automobiles have GPSs linked to GIS maps that display the car's location and driving directions on a dashboard screen. GM offers the OnStar system, which sends a continuous stream of information to the OnStar center about the car's exact location.

Some mobile phone providers combine GPS and GIS capabilities so they can locate users within a geographical area about the size of a tennis court to assist emergency services such as 911. Farmers can use GIS to map and analyze fields, telling them where to apply the proper amounts of seed, fertilizer, and herbicides.

A GIS can find the closest gas station or bank or determine the best way to get to a particular location. But it is also good at finding patterns, such as finding the most feasible location to hold a conference according to where the majority of a company's customers live and work. GIS can present this information in a visually effective way.

Some common GIS uses include:

- Finding what is nearby. Given a specific location, the GIS finds sources within a defined radius. These might be entertainment venues, medical facilities, restaurants, or gas stations. Users can also use GIS to locate vendors that sell a specific item they want and get the results as a map of the surrounding area or an address.
- Routing information. Once users have an idea where they want to go, GIS can provide directions to get there using either a map or step-by-step instructions. Routing information can be especially helpful when combined with search services.
- Sending information alerts. Users may want to be notified when information relevant to them becomes available near their location. A commuter might want to know that a section of the highway has traffic congestion, or a shopper might want to be notified when a favorite store is having a sale on a certain item.
- Mapping densities. GIS can map population and event densities based on a standard area unit, such as square miles, making it easy to see distributions and concentrations. Police can map crime incidents to determine where additional patrolling is required, and stores can map customer orders to identify ideal delivery routes.
- Mapping quantities. Users can map quantities to find out where the most or least of a feature may be. For example, someone interested in opening a specialty coffee shop can determine how many others are already in the area, and city planners can determine where to build more parks.[37]

A GIS can provide information and insight to both mobile users and people at fixed locations. Google Earth combines satellite imagery, geographic data, and Google's search capabilities to create a virtual globe that users can download to a computer or mobile device. Not only does this provide useful business benefits, but it also allows for many educational opportunities. Instead of just talking about the Grand Canyon, an instructor can use Google Earth to view that region.

BUSTED Snapping a Theftie

Has your smart phone ever been stolen? If so, you are not alone; more than 3 million Americans' phones were stolen in 2013, which is twice the number in 2012, according to a Consumer Reports survey. Of course, every good entrepreneur can spot an opportunity, and a new antitheft app is one step ahead of criminals who are targeting smart phones.

Lookout is among the latest additions to the growing antitheft industry, and the app features some smart ways of helping you get one step ahead of thieves. A smart phone's front-facing camera is often regarded as merely a portal to endless selfie photographs. But Lookout puts the camera to good use by capturing a photo of you—or of any would-be thief—when someone inputs your phone's password incorrectly three times. That photo, or theftie, is instantly emailed to the phone's owner, along with the device's approximate location. The antitheft app is free to download, but this handy photo feature is not available on iPhones due to Apple restrictions and comes with an annual charge of $30.[39]

Lookout's team has been adding new features to the app's alerts, based on the methods thieves use to steal phones undetected. The app also will send emails to its owner if anyone attempts to remove the phone's SIM card, enables Airplane mode, or turns off the device. From that point, the owner can choose to lock or wipe the phone remotely.

Do you agree that antitheft apps are smart business? Are any ethical issues involved in taking thefties? How would you feel if company security policy required you to install Lookout on your cell phone? If you could add a new feature to Lookout, how would it work and what would it do to deter smart phone theft?

GPS and GIS both utilize **location-based services (LBS)**, applications that use location information to provide a service. LBS is designed to give mobile users instant access to personalized local content and range from 911 applications to buddy finders ("Let me know when my friend is within 1,000 feet") to games (treasure hunts) to location-based advertising ("Visit the Starbucks on the corner and get $1.00 off a latte"). Many LBS applications complement GPS and GIS, such as:

- Emergency services
- Field service management
- Find-it services
- Mapping
- Navigation
- Tracking assets
- Traffic information
- Vehicle location
- Weather information
- Wireless advertising[38]

Just as Facebook and Twitter helped fuel the Web 2.0 revolution, applications such as Foursquare, Gowalla, and Loopt are bringing attention to LBS. Each application is a mobile phone service that helps social media users find their friends' location. Facebook and Twitter have added location-based services to complement their applications.

© Entienou/Getty Images RF

coming up

Organizations use various types of information systems to help run their daily operations. These primarily transactional systems concentrate on the management and flow of low-level data items for basic business processes such as purchasing and order delivery. The data are often rolled up and summarized into higher-level decision support systems to help firms understand what is happening in their organizations and how best to respond. To achieve seamless and efficient handling of data and informed decision making, organizations must ensure that their enterprise systems are tightly integrated, providing an end-to-end view of operations.

This module introduces various types of enterprise information systems and their role in helping firms reach their strategic goals, including supply chain management, customer relationship management, and enterprise resource planning. Organizations that can correlate and summarize enterprisewide information are prepared to meet their strategic business goals and outperform their competitors.

This module then dives into how enterprise systems can be built to support global businesses, the challenges in that process, and how well things turn out if systems are built according to good design principles, sound management practices, and flexibility to support ever-changing business needs. Making this happen requires not only extensive planning, but also well-honed people skills. ■

ENTERPRISE MIS

© Alija/Getty Images RF

chapter EIGHT

enterprise applications: business communications

What's in IT for me?

This chapter introduces high-profile strategic initiatives an organization can undertake to help it gain competitive advantages and business efficiencies—supply chain management, customer relationship management, and enterprise resource planning. At the simplest level, organizations implement enterprise systems to gain efficiency in business processes, effectiveness in supply chains, and an overall understanding of customer needs and behaviors. Successful organizations recognize the competitive advantage of maintaining healthy relationships with employees, customers, suppliers, and partners. Doing so has a direct and positive effect on revenue and greatly adds to a company's profitability.

continued on p. 212

CHAPTER OUTLINE

integration Allows separate systems to communicate directly with each other, eliminating the need for manual entry into multiple systems.

eintegration The use of the Internet to provide customers with the ability to gain personalized information by querying corporate databases and their information sources.

application integration The integration of a company's existing management information systems to each other.

data integration The integration of data from multiple sources, which provides a unified view of all data.

continued from p. 210

You, as a business student, must understand the critical relationship your business will have with its employees, customers, suppliers, and partners. You must also understand how to analyze your organizational data to ensure you are not just meeting but exceeding expectations. Enterprises are technologically empowered as never before to reach their goals of integrating, analyzing, and making intelligent business decisions. ■

{SECTION 8.1} Supply Chain Management

LEARNING OUTCOMES

LO8.1 Explain integrations and the role they play in connecting a corporation.

LO8.2 Describe supply chain management along with its associated benefits and challenges.

LO8.3 Identify the three technologies that are reinventing the supply chain.

BUILDING A CONNECTED CORPORATION THROUGH INTEGRATIONS LO8.1

Until the 1990s, each department in the United Kingdom's Ministry of Defense and Army headquarters had its own information system, and each system had its own database. Sharing information was difficult, requiring employees to manually input the same information into different systems multiple times. Often, management could not even compile the information it needed to answer questions, solve problems, and make decisions.

To combat this challenge the ministry integrated its systems, or built connections among its many databases. These connections or **integrations** allow separate systems to communicate directly with each other, eliminating the need for manual entry into multiple systems. Building integrations allows the sharing of information across databases along with dramatically increasing its quality. The army can now generate reports detailing its state of readiness and other essential intelligence, tasks that were nearly impossible before the integrations. **Eintegration** is the use of the Internet to provide customers with the ability to gain personalized information by querying corporate databases and their information sources. **Application integration** is the integration of a company's existing management information systems. **Data integration** is the integration of data from multiple sources, which provides a unified view of all data.

Two common methods are used for integrating databases. The first is to create forward and backward integrations that link processes (and their underlying databases) in the value chain. A **forward integration** takes information entered into a given system and sends it automatically to all downstream systems and processes. A **backward integration** takes information entered into a given system and sends it automatically to all upstream systems and processes. Figure 8.1 demonstrates how this method works across the systems or processes of sales, order entry, order fulfillment, and billing. In the order entry system, for example, an employee can update the customer's information. Via the integrations, that information is sent upstream to the sales system and downstream to the order fulfillment and billing systems. Ideally, an organization wants to build both forward and backward integrations, which provide the flexibility to create, update, and delete information in any of the systems. However, integrations are expensive and difficult to build and maintain, causing most organizations to invest in forward integrations only.

The second integration method builds a central repository for a particular type of information. Figure 8.2 provides an example of customer information integrated using this method across four different systems in an organization. Users can create, update, and delete customer information only in the central customer database. As users perform these tasks, integrations automatically send the new and/or updated customer information to the other systems. The other systems limit users to read-only access of the customer information stored in them. Both integration methods do not entirely eliminate information redundancy, but they do ensure information consistency among multiple systems.

LO8.1 Explain integrations and the role they play in connecting a corporation.

FIGURE 8.1 A Forward and Backward Customer Information Integration Example

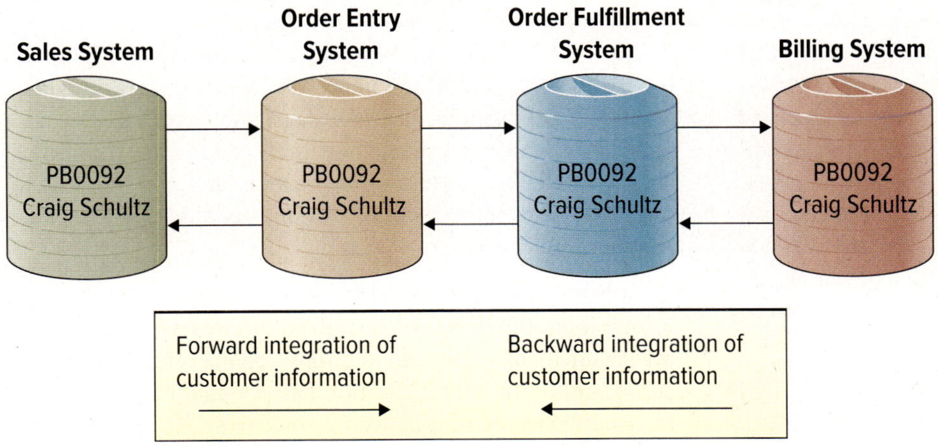

Integration Tools

Enterprise systems provide enterprisewide support and data access for a firm's operations and business processes. These systems can manage customer information across the enterprise, letting you view everything your customer has experienced from sales to support. Enterprise systems are often available as a generic, but highly customizable, group of programs for business functions such as accounting, manufacturing, and marketing. Generally, the development tools for customization are complex programming tools that require specialist capabilities.

Enterprise application integration (EAI) connects the plans, methods, and tools aimed at integrating separate enterprise systems. A legacy system is a current or existing system that will become the base for upgrading or integrating with a new system. EAI reviews how legacy systems fit into the new shape of the firm's business processes and devises ways to efficiently reuse what already exists while adding new systems and data.

Integrations are achieved using **middleware**—several different types of software that sit between and provide connectivity for two or more software applications. Middleware translates information between disparate systems. **Enterprise application integration (EAI) middleware** takes a new approach to middleware by packaging commonly used applications together, reducing the time needed to integrate applications from multiple vendors. The remainder of this chapter covers the three enterprise systems most organizations use to integrate their disparate departments and separate operational systems: supply chain management (SCM), customer relationship management (CRM), and enterprise resource planning (ERP) (see Figure 8.3). Figure 8.4 displays the data points where these applications integrate and illustrates the underlying premise of architecture infrastructure design.

Companies run on interdependent applications, such as SCM, CRM, and ERP. If one application performs poorly, the entire

FIGURE 8.2 Integrating Customer Information among Databases

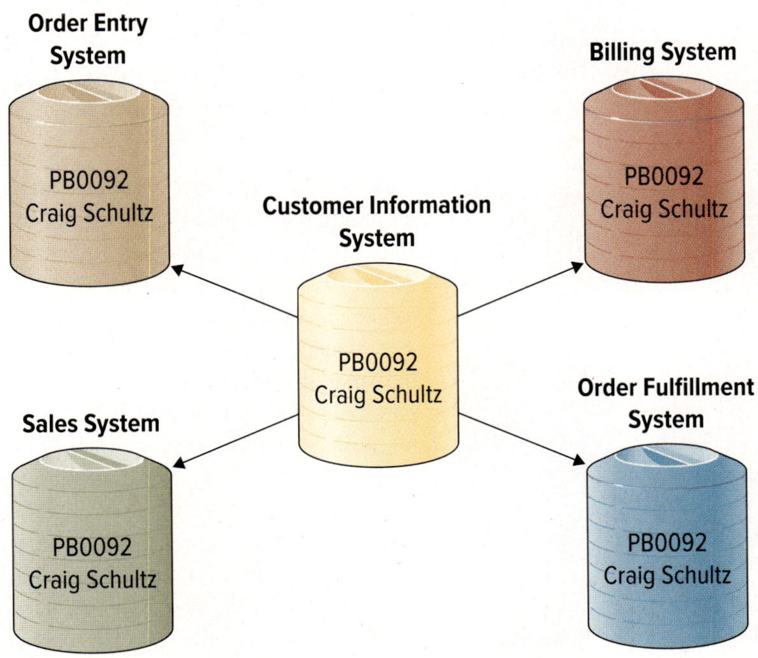

forward integration Takes information entered into a given system and sends it automatically to all downstream systems and processes.

backward integration Takes information entered into a given system and sends it automatically to all upstream systems and processes.

enterprise system Provides enterprisewide support and data access for a firm's operations and business processes.

enterprise application integration (EAI) Connects the plans, methods, and tools aimed at integrating separate enterprise systems.

middleware Several different types of software that sit between and provide connectivity for two or more software applications.

enterprise application integration (EAI) middleware Takes a new approach to middleware by packaging commonly used applications together, reducing the time needed to integrate applications from multiple vendors.

supply chain All parties involved, directly or indirectly, in obtaining raw materials or a product.

supply chain management (SCM) The management of information flows between and among activities in a supply chain to maximize total supply chain effectiveness and corporate profitability.

customer value delivery system is affected. For example, no matter how great a company is at CRM, if its SCM system does not work and the customer never receives the finished product, the company will lose that customer. The world-class enterprises of tomorrow must be built on the foundation of world-class applications implemented today.

SUPPLY CHAIN MANAGEMENT LO8.2

The average company spends nearly half of every dollar it earns on suppliers and raw materials to manufacture products. It is not uncommon to hear of critical success factors focusing on getting the right products, to the right place, at the right time, at the right cost. For this reason, tools that can help a company source raw materials, manufacture products, and deliver finished goods to retailers and customers are in high demand. A **supply chain** consists of all parties involved, directly or indirectly, in obtaining raw materials or a product. Figure 8.5 highlights the five basic supply chain activities a company undertakes to manufacture and distribute products. To automate and enable sophisticated decision making in these critical areas, companies are turning to systems that provide demand forecasting, inventory control, and information flows between suppliers and customers.

Supply chain management (SCM) is the management of information flows between and among activities in a supply chain to maximize total supply chain effectiveness and corporate profitability. In the past, manufacturing efforts focused primarily on quality improvement efforts within the company; today these efforts reach across the entire supply chain, including customers, customers' customers, suppliers, and suppliers' suppliers. Today's supply chain is an intricate network of business partners linked through communication channels and relationships. Supply chain management systems manage and enhance these relationships with the primary goal of creating a fast, efficient, and low-cost network of business relationships that take products from concept to market. SCM systems create the integrations or tight process and information linkages between all participants in the supply chain. Supply chain management performs three main business processes (see Figure 8.6):

1. Materials flow from suppliers and their upstream suppliers at all levels.
2. Materials are transformed into semifinished and finished products—the organization's own production processes.
3. Products are distributed to customers and their downstream customers at all levels.

Consider a customer purchasing a mountain bike from a dealer. Dozens of steps are required to complete this transaction from beginning to end. The customer places an order with the dealer. The dealer purchases the bike from the manufacturer. The manufacturer purchases the raw materials required to make the bike such as aluminum, rubber tires, brakes, accessories, and packaging from different suppliers. The raw materials are stored in the manufacturer's warehouse until a production order requires the bike to be built, at which time the finished product is sent

FIGURE 8.3 The Three Primary Enterprise Systems

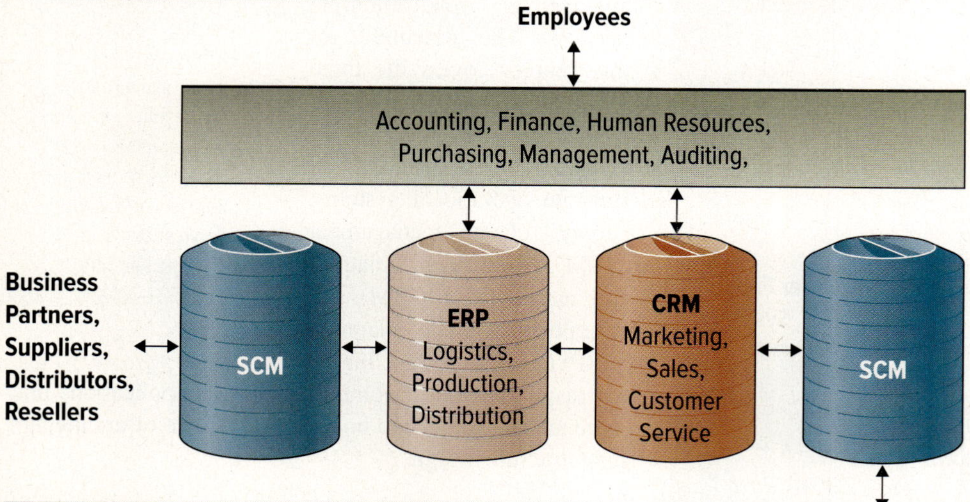

FIGURE 8.4 Integrations between SCM, CRM, and ERP Applications.

FIGURE 8.5 The Five Basic Supply Chain Activities

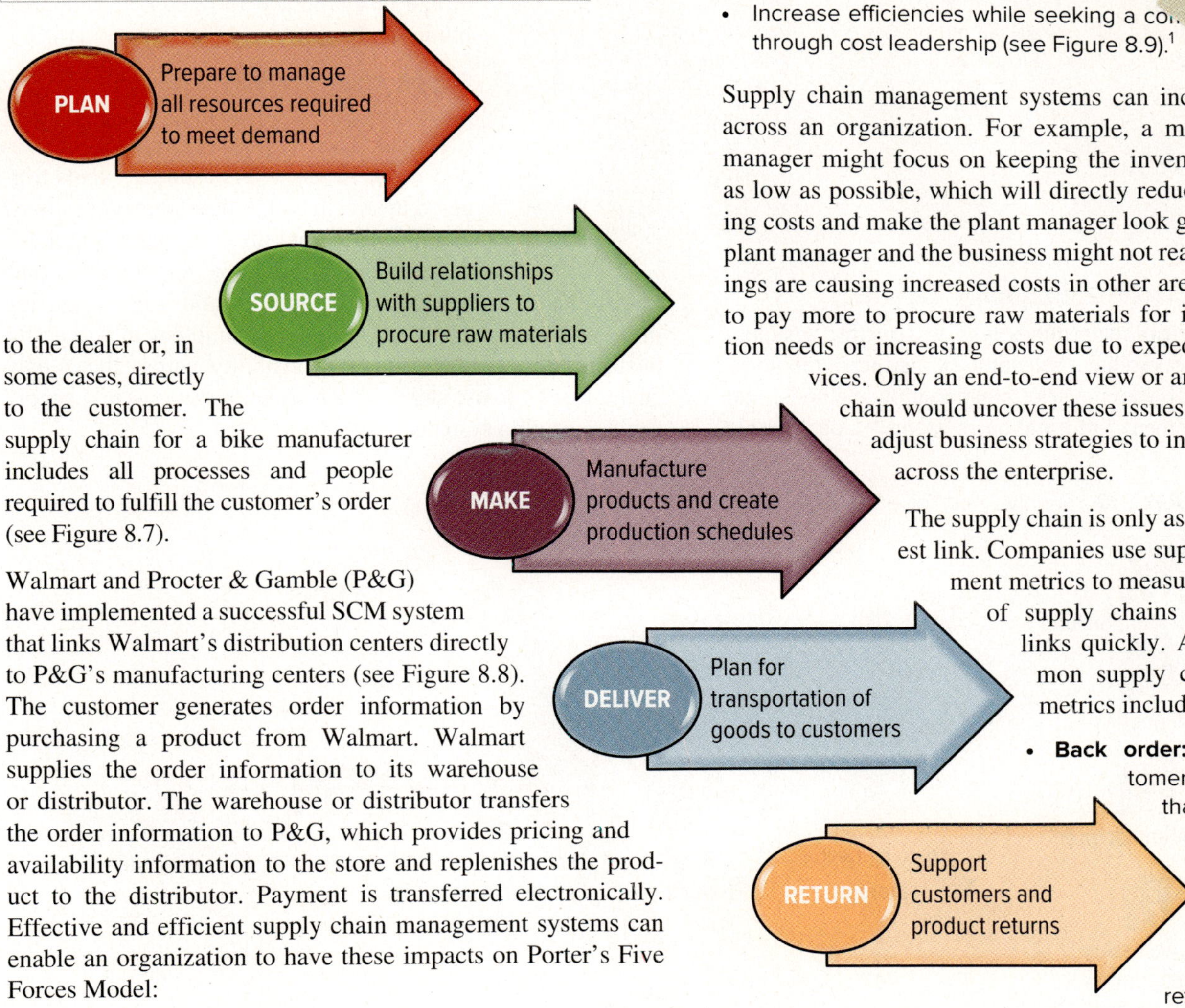

to the dealer or, in some cases, directly to the customer. The supply chain for a bike manufacturer includes all processes and people required to fulfill the customer's order (see Figure 8.7).

Walmart and Procter & Gamble (P&G) have implemented a successful SCM system that links Walmart's distribution centers directly to P&G's manufacturing centers (see Figure 8.8). The customer generates order information by purchasing a product from Walmart. Walmart supplies the order information to its warehouse or distributor. The warehouse or distributor transfers the order information to P&G, which provides pricing and availability information to the store and replenishes the product to the distributor. Payment is transferred electronically. Effective and efficient supply chain management systems can enable an organization to have these impacts on Porter's Five Forces Model:

- Decrease the power of its buyers. Increase its supplier power.
- Increase buyers' switching costs to reduce the threat of substitute products or services.
- Create entry barriers to reduce the threat
- Increase efficiencies while seeking a co… through cost leadership (see Figure 8.9).[1]

Supply chain management systems can increase pro… across an organization. For example, a manufacturing p… manager might focus on keeping the inventory of Product A as low as possible, which will directly reduce the manufacturing costs and make the plant manager look great. However, the plant manager and the business might not realize that these savings are causing increased costs in other areas, such as having to pay more to procure raw materials for immediate production needs or increasing costs due to expedited shipping services. Only an end-to-end view or an integrated supply chain would uncover these issues, allowing a firm to adjust business strategies to increase profitability across the enterprise.

The supply chain is only as strong as its weakest link. Companies use supply chain management metrics to measure the performance of supply chains to identify weak links quickly. A few of the common supply chain management metrics include:

- **Back order:** An unfilled customer order for a product that is out of stock.
- **Inventory cycle time:** The time it takes to manufacture a product and deliver it to the retailer.
- **Customer order cycle time:** The agreed upon time between the purchase of a product and the delivery of the product.
- **Inventory turnover:** The frequency of inventory replacement.

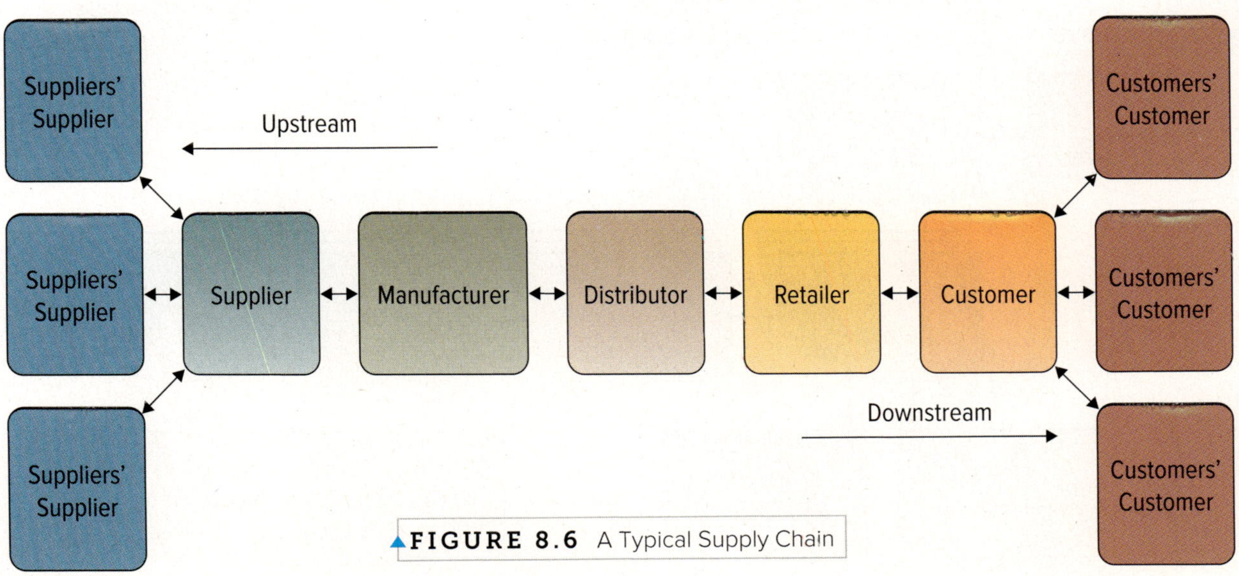

FIGURE 8.6 A Typical Supply Chain

upply chain design Determines how to structure a supply chain including the product, selection of partners, the location and capacity of warehouses, transportation methods, and supporting management information systems.

supply chain visibility The ability to view all areas up and down the supply chain in real time.

supply chain planning system Uses advanced mathematical algorithms to improve the flow and efficiency of the supply chain while reducing inventory.

Visibility into the Supply Chain

Supply chain design determines how to structure a supply chain including the product, selection of partners, the location and capacity of warehouses, transportation methods, and supporting management information systems. Considerable evidence shows that this type of supply chain design results in superior supply chain capabilities and profits.

Supply chain visibility is the ability to view all areas up and down the supply chain in real time. To react to demand, an organization needs to know all customer events triggered upstream and downstream and so must their suppliers and their suppliers' suppliers. Without this information, supply chain participants are blind to the supply and demand needs occurring in the marketplace, a factor required to implement successful business strategies. To improve visibility across the supply chain, firms can use supply chain planning systems and supply chain execution systems.

FIGURE 8.7 Supply Chain for a Bike Manufacturer

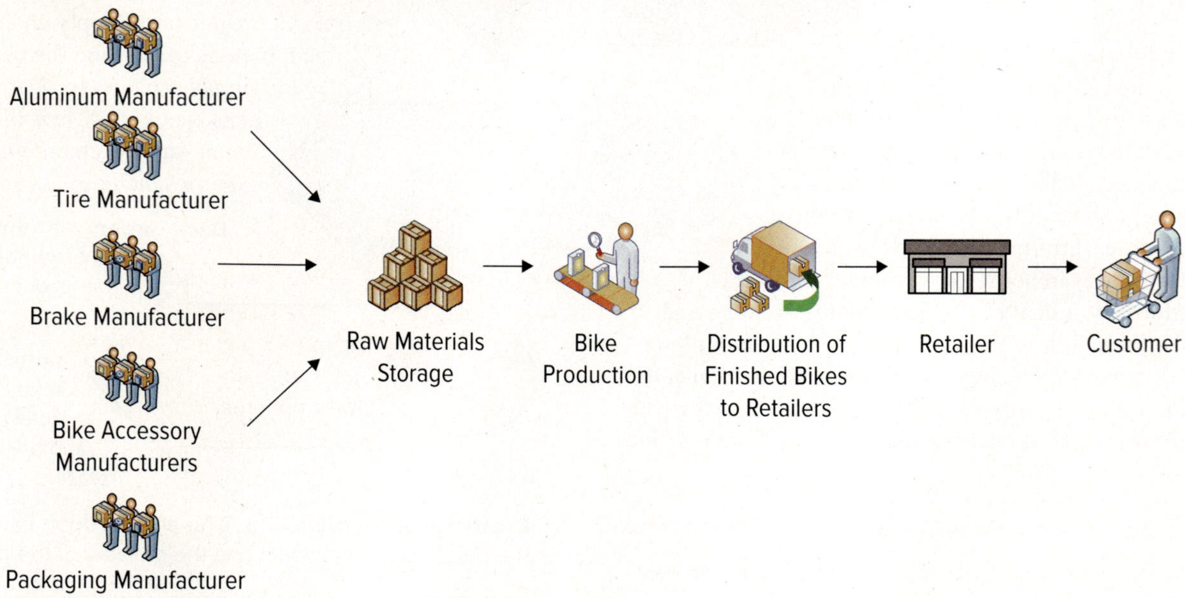

FIGURE 8.8 Supply Chain for a Product Purchased from Walmart

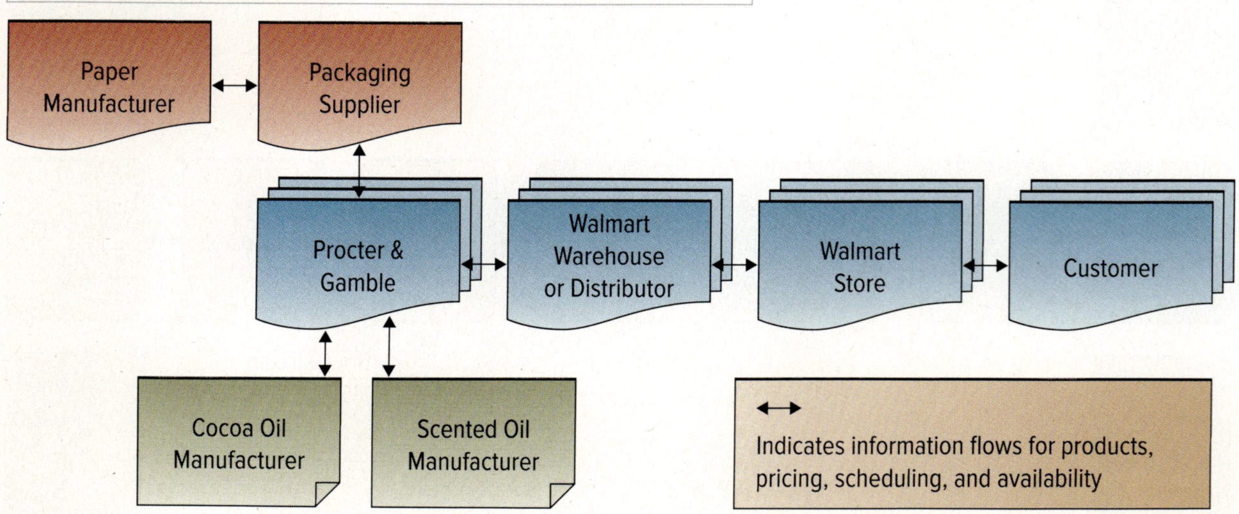

Supply chain planning systems use advanced mathematical algorithms to improve the flow and efficiency of the supply chain while reducing inventory. To yield accurate results, however, supply chain planning systems require information inputs that are correct and up to date regarding customers, orders, sales, manufacturing, and distribution capabilities.

Ideally, the supply chain consists of multiple firms that function as efficiently and effectively as a single firm, with full information visibility. **Supply chain execution systems** ensure supply chain cohesion by automating the different activities of the supply chain. For example, a supply chain execution system might electronically route orders from a manufacturer to a supplier using **electronic data interchange (EDI)**, a standard format for the electronic exchange of information between supply chain participants. Figure 8.10 details how supply chain planning and supply chain execution systems interact with the supply chain.

A good example of inventory issues that occur when a company does not have a clear vision of its entire supply chain is the bullwhip effect. The **bullwhip effect** occurs when distorted product-demand information ripples from one partner to the next throughout the supply chain. The misinformation regarding a slight rise in demand for a product could cause different members in the supply chain to stockpile inventory. These changes ripple throughout the supply chain, magnifying the issue and creating excess inventory and costs for all. For example, if a car dealership is having a hard time moving a particular brand of car, it might offer significant discounts to try to move the inventory. Without this critical information, the car manufacturer might see a rise in demand for this particular brand of car and increase production orders, not realizing that the dealerships are actually challenged with selling the inventory. Today, integrated supply chains provide managers with the visibility to see their suppliers' and customers' supply chains, ensuring that supply always meets demand.

supply chain execution system Ensures supply chain cohesion by automating the different activities of the supply chain.

electronic data interchange (EDI) A standard format for the electronic exchange of information between supply chain participants.

bullwhip effect Occurs when distorted product-demand information ripples from one partner to the next throughout the supply chain.

FIGURE 8.9 Effective and Efficient Supply Chain Management's Effect on Porter's Five Forces

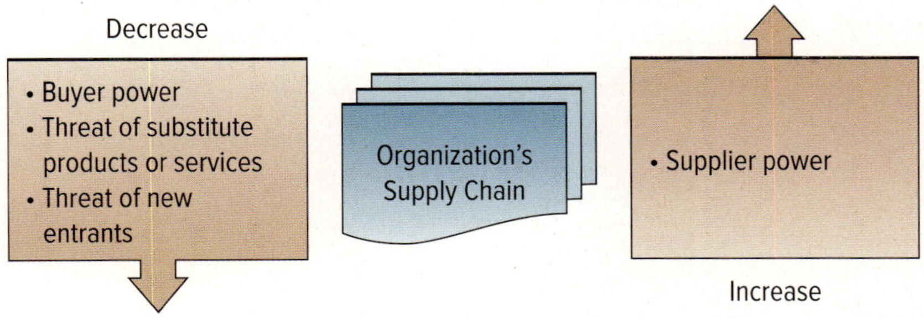

LO8.2 Describe supply chain management along with its associated benefits and challenges.

FIGURE 8.10 Supply Chain Planning's and Supply Chain Execution's Roles in the Supply Chain

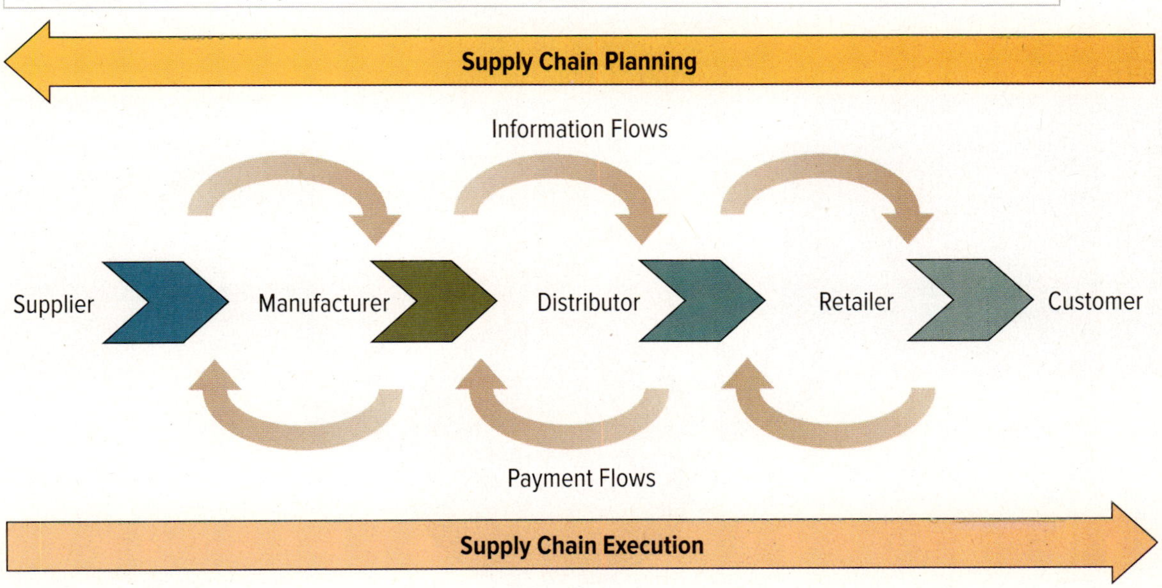

TECHNOLOGIES REINVENTING THE SUPPLY CHAIN LO8.3

LO8.3 Identify the three technologies that are reinventing the supply chain.

Optimizing the supply chain is a critical business process for any successful organization. Just think of the complexity of Walmart's supply chain and the billions of products being sent around the world guaranteeing every shelf is fully stocked. The three components of supply chain management on which companies focus to find efficiencies include procurement, logistics, and materials management (see Figure 8.11).

Procurement is the purchasing of goods and services to meet the needs of the supply chain. The procurement process is a key supply chain strategy because the capability to purchase input materials at the right price is directly correlated to the company's ability to operate. Without the right inputs, the company simply can't create cost-effective outputs. For example, if McDonald's could not procure potatoes or had to purchase potatoes at an outrageous price, it would be unable to create and sell its famous french fries. In fact, procuring the right size potatoes that can produce the famous long french fries is challenging in some countries where locally grown potatoes are too small. Procurement can help a company answer the following questions:

- What quantity of raw materials should we purchase to minimize spoilage?
- How can we guarantee that our raw materials meet production needs?
- At what price can we purchase materials to guarantee profitability?
- Can purchasing all products from a single vendor provide additional discounts?

Logistics includes the processes that control the distribution, maintenance, and replacement of materials and personnel to support the supply chain. Recall from the value chain analysis in Chapter 1 that the primary value activities for an organization include inbound and outbound logistics. *Inbound logistics* acquires raw materials and resources and distributes them to manufacturing as required. *Outbound logistics* distributes goods and services to customers. Logistics controls processes inside a company (warehouse logistics) and outside a company (transport logistics) and focuses on the physical execution part of the supply chain. Logistics includes the increasingly complex management of processes, information, and communication to take a product from cradle to grave. **Cradle-to-grave** provides logistics support throughout the entire system or life of the product. Logistics can help a company answer the following questions:

- What is the quickest way to deliver products to our customers?
- What is the optimal way to place items in the warehouse for picking and packing?

FIGURE 8.11
The Three Business Areas of Supply Chain Management

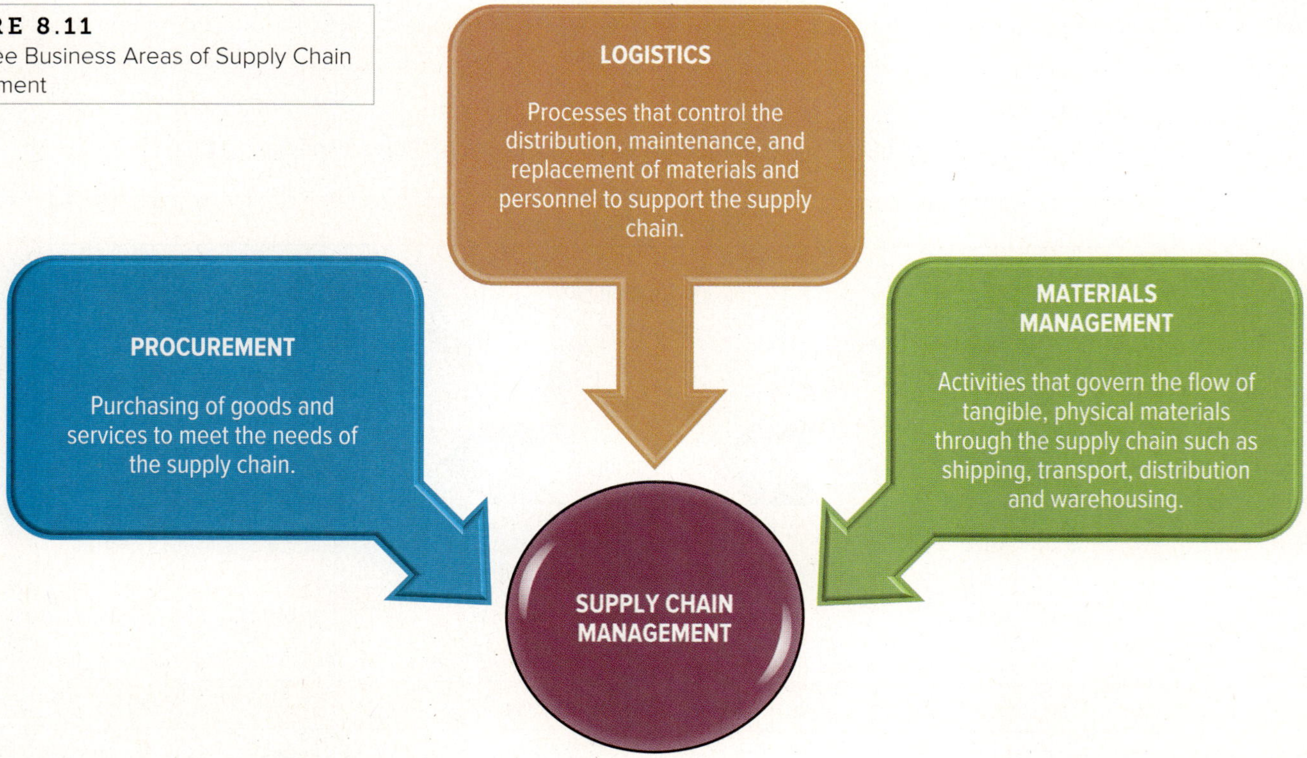

procurement The purchasing of goods and services to meet the needs of the supply chain.

logistics Includes the processes that control the distribution, maintenance, and replacement of materials and personnel to support the supply chain.

cradle-to-grave Provides logistics support throughout the entire system or life of the product.

materials management Includes activities that govern the flow of tangible, physical materials through the supply chain such as shipping, transport, distribution, and warehousing.

3D printing Builds—layer by layer in an additive process—a three-dimensional solid object from a digital model.

- What is the optimal path to an item in the warehouse?
- What path should the vehicles follow when delivering the goods?
- What areas or regions are the trucks covering?

Materials management includes activities that govern the flow of tangible, physical materials through the supply chain such as shipping, transport, distribution, and warehousing. In materials management, you focus on quality and quantity of materials as well as on how you will plan, acquire, use, and dispose of such materials. It can include the handling of liquids, fuel, produce, and plants and a number of other potentially hazardous items. Materials management focuses on handling all materials safely, efficiently, and in compliance with regulatory requirements and disposal requirements. Materials management can help a company answer the following concerns:

- What are our current inventory levels?
- What items are running low in the warehouse?
- What items are at risk of spoiling in the warehouse?
- How do we dispose of spoiled items?
- What laws need to be followed for storing hazardous materials?
- Which items must be refrigerated when being stored and transported?
- What are the requirements to store or transport fragile items?

As with all other areas of business, disruptive technologies are continuously being deployed to help businesses find competitive advantages in each component of the supply chain, as outlined in Figure 8.12.

3D Printing Supports Procurement

The process of **3D printing** (additive manufacturing) builds—layer by layer in an additive process—a three-dimensional solid object from a digital model. The additive manufacturing process of 3D printing is profoundly different from traditional manufacturing processes. The *Financial Times* and other sources are stating that 3D printing has the potential to be vastly more disruptive to business than the Internet. That is a bold statement!

FIGURE 8.12 Disruptive Business Technologies

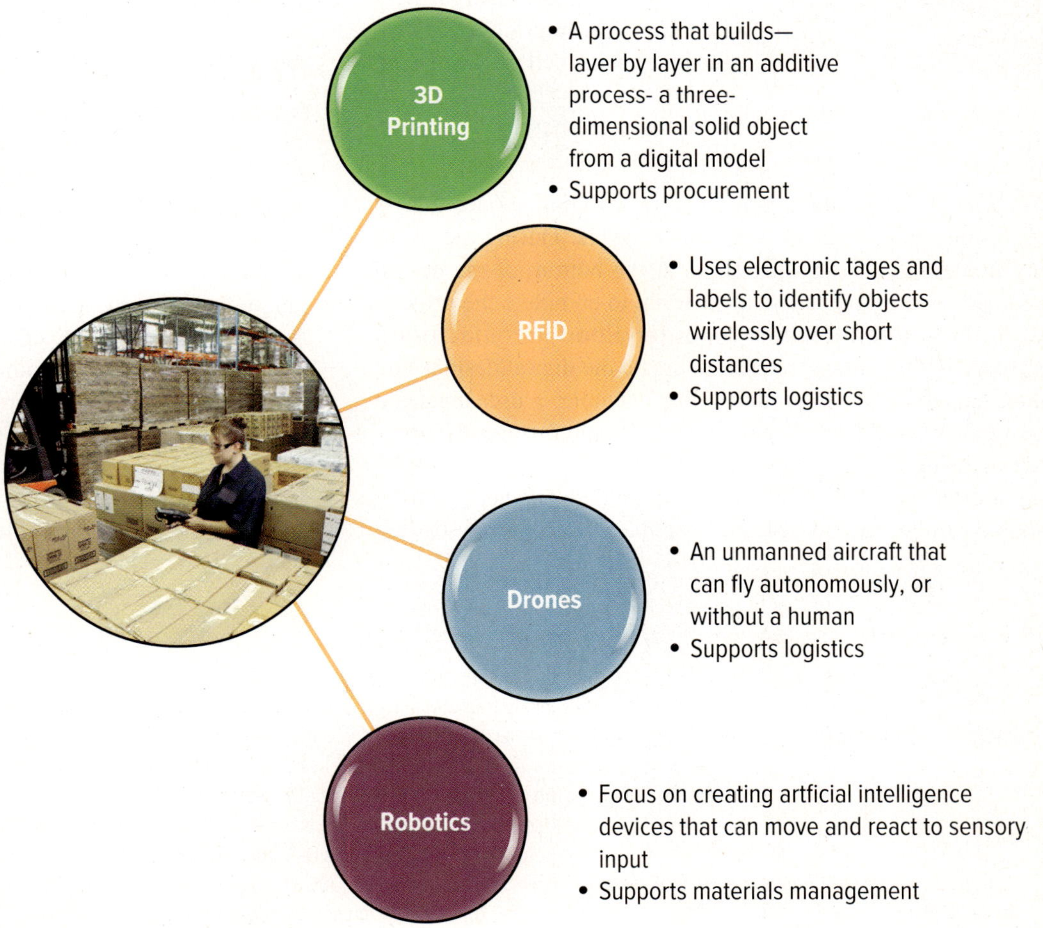

© Shannon Faulk/DreamPictures/Getty Images

computer-aided design/computer-aided manufacturing (CAD/CAM) Systems are used to create the digital designs and then manufacture the products.

maker movement A cultural trend that places value on an individual's ability to be a creator of things as well as a consumer of things.

makerspace A community center that provides technology, manufacturing equipment, and educational opportunities to the public that would otherwise be inaccessible or unaffordable.

The reason people are betting on 3D printing to disrupt business is that it brings production closer to users, thus eliminating steps in the supply chain similar to disintermediation by the Internet. Three-dimensional printing also promotes mass customization, small production batches, and reduction in inventory. Traditionally, the costs associated with 3D printing made it accessible only to large corporations. Now with inexpensive printers, scanners, and applications, the technology is accessible to small and midsized businesses and home users. With the advances in 3D printing, the need to procure materials will become far easier because businesses can simply print the parts and components required for the production process. There is no doubt about it—3D printing will affect production process and supply chains and cause business disruption. These printers are creating auto parts, cell phone covers, jewelry, toys, bicycles, and manufacturing prototypes for testing purposes.

To print a 3D product, users create a digital model that is sliced into thin cross-sections called layers. During the printing process, the 3D printer starts at the bottom of the design and adds successive layers of material to complete the project. **Computer-aided design/computer-aided manufacturing (CAD/CAM)** systems are used to create the digital designs and then manufacture the products. For example, a user creates a design with a CAD application and then manufactures the product by using CAM systems. Before 3D printers existed, creating a prototype was time-consuming and expensive, requiring skilled craftsmen and specific machinery. Instead of sending modeling instructions to a production company, advances in 3D printing allow users to create prototypes and products on demand from their desks. Shipping required parts from around the world could become obsolete because the spare parts can now be 3D printed on demand. This could have a major impact on how businesses large and small operate and interact on a global scale in the future.

The **maker movement** is a cultural trend that places value on an individual's ability to be a creator of things as well as a consumer of things. In this culture, individuals who create things are called "makers." The movement is growing rapidly and is expected to be economically disruptive; as ordinary people become more self-sufficient, they will be able to make their own products instead of procuring brand-name products from retail stores. Makers come from all walks of life, with diverse skill sets and interests. The thing they have in common is creativity, an interest in design, and access to tools and raw materials that make production possible. The growth of the maker movement is often attributed to the rise of community **makerspaces**, a community center that provides technology, manufacturing equipment, and educational opportunities to the public that would otherwise be inaccessible or unaffordable. Although the majority of makers are hobbyists, entrepreneurs and small manufacturers are also taking advantage of the classes and tools available in makerspaces.

RFID Supports Logistics

A television commercial shows a man in a uniform quietly moving through a family home. The man replaces the empty cereal box with a full one just before a hungry child opens the cabinet; he then opens a new sack of dog food as the hungry bulldog eyes him warily, and, finally, hands a full bottle of shampoo to the man in the shower whose bottle had just run out. The next wave in supply chain management will be home-based supply chain fulfillment. Walgreens is differentiating itself from other national chains by marketing itself as the family's just-in-time supplier. Consumers today are becoming incredibly comfortable with the idea of going online to purchase products when they want, how they want, and at the price they want. Walgreens is developing custom websites for each household, which allow families to order

Living the DREAM

3D Printing for Poverty

Thirty-three-year-old Kodjo Afate Grikou wanted to help his community in West Africa to print necessities that they can't source locally, such as kitchen utensils for cooking. The structure of the 3D printer he had in mind uses very little in terms of new parts because it is mostly made up of ewaste and scrap metal. Before building this printer, he set up his project on the European social funding website, ulule. The project received more than $10,000, despite the printer costing only $1,000, mostly through purchasing new parts that he couldn't find locally. Grikou hopes that his innovation will inspire teenagers and young people in his community to attend school and gain an education so they can make further life-changing developments that will benefit not only their lives but also others around them. In a group, brainstorm ways 3D printing can help rural communities fight poverty.

electronically and then at their convenience go to the store to pick up their goods at a special self-service counter or the drive-through window. Walgreens is making a promise that goes beyond low prices and customer service and extends right into the home.

Radio-frequency identification (RFID) uses electronic tags and labels to identify objects wirelessly over short distances. It holds the promise of replacing existing identification technologies such as the bar code. RFID tags are evolving, too, and the advances will provide more granular information to enterprise software. Today's tags can store an electronic product code. In time, tags could hold more information, making them portable mini-databases. **RFID's Electronic Product Code (RFID EPC)** promotes serialization or the ability to track individual items by using the unique serial number associated with each RFID tag. Although a bar code might identify a product such as a bottle of salad dressing, an RFID EPC tag can identify each specific bottle and allow item-level tracking to determine whether the product has passed its expiration date. Businesses can tell automatically where all its items are in the supply chain just by gathering the data from the RFID chips. The possibilities of RFID are endless, and one area it is affecting is logistics. RFID tags for applications such as highway toll collection and container tracking remain in continuous use for several years. Like regular electronic components, the tags are adhered to rigid substrates and packaged in plastic enclosures. In contrast, tags on shipping cartons are used for a much shorter time and are then destroyed. Disposable tags are adhered to printed, flexible labels pasted onto the carton, and these smart labels contain an RFID chip and antenna on the back. A thermal printer/encoder prints alphanumeric and bar code data on the labels while encoding the chip at the same time. Figures 8.13 and 8.14 display how an RFID system works in the supply chain.

radio-frequency identification (RFID) Uses electronic tags and labels to identify objects wirelessly over short distances.

RFID's electronic product code (RFID EPC) Promotes serialization or the ability to track individual items by using the unique serial number associated with each RFID tag.

drone An unmanned aircraft that can fly autonomously, or without a human.

robotics Focuses on creating artificial intelligence devices that can move and react to sensory input.

Drones Support Logistics

A **drone** is an unmanned aircraft that can fly autonomously, or without a human. Amazon.com is piloting drone aircraft for package deliveries. Amazon is now working on small drones that could someday deliver customers' packages in half an hour or less. UPS and FedEx have also been experimenting with their own versions of flying parcel carriers. Drones are already here and use GPS to help coordinate the logistics of package delivery. The problems with drones include FAA approval and the advanced ability to detect and avoid objects. GPS coordinates can easily enable the drone to find the appropriate package delivery location, but objects not included in the GPS, such as cars, dogs, and children, will need to be detected and avoided.

FedEx founder Fred Smith stated that his drones are up and running in the lab; all he requires to move his fleet of drones from the lab to production is approval from regulators. "We have all this stuff working in the lab right now, we don't need to reinvent the wheel," remarks Smith. "We need a set of rules from the FAA. It's just a matter of getting the laws in place so companies can begin building to those specifications and doing some real field testing."[2]

FIGURE 8.13 RFID Components

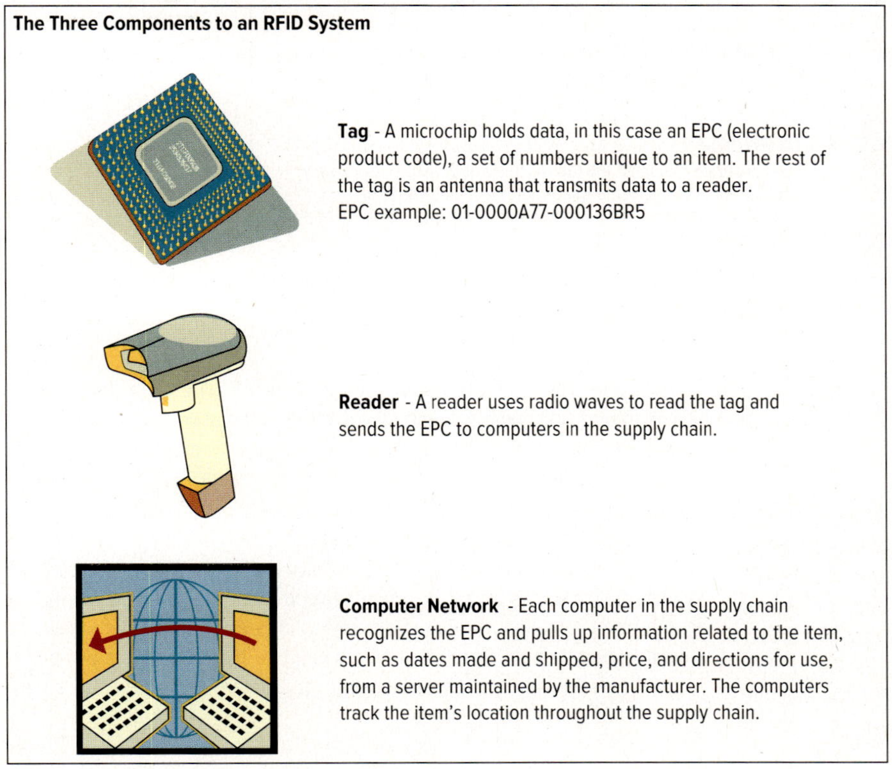

Robotics Supports Materials Management

Robotics focuses on creating artificial intelligence devices that can move and react to sensory input. The term *robot* was coined by Czech playwright Karl Capek in his play *R.U.R.* (*Rossum's Universal Robots*), which opened in Prague in 1921. Robota is the Czech word for "forced labor." The term *robotics* was introduced by writer Isaac Asimov; in his science fiction book *I, Robot,* published in 1950, he presented three laws of robotics:

1. A robot may not injure a human being, or, through inaction, allow a human being to come to harm.
2. A robot must obey the orders given it by human beings except where such orders would conflict with the First Law.
3. A robot must protect its own existence as long as such protection does not conflict with the First or Second Law.[4]

You can find robots in factories performing high-precision tasks, in homes vacuuming the floor and the pool, and in dangerous situations such as cleaning toxic wastes or defusing bombs. Amazon alone has more than 10,000 robots in its warehouses, picking, packing, and managing materials to fulfill customer orders. The robots are made by Kiva Systems, a company Amazon bought for $775 million in 2012. Kiva pitches its robots—which can cost between a few million dollars and as much as roughly $20 million—as simplifying and reducing costs via materials management. The robots are tied into a complex grid that optimizes item placement in the warehouse and allows the robots to pick the

FIGURE 8.14 RFID in the Supply Chain

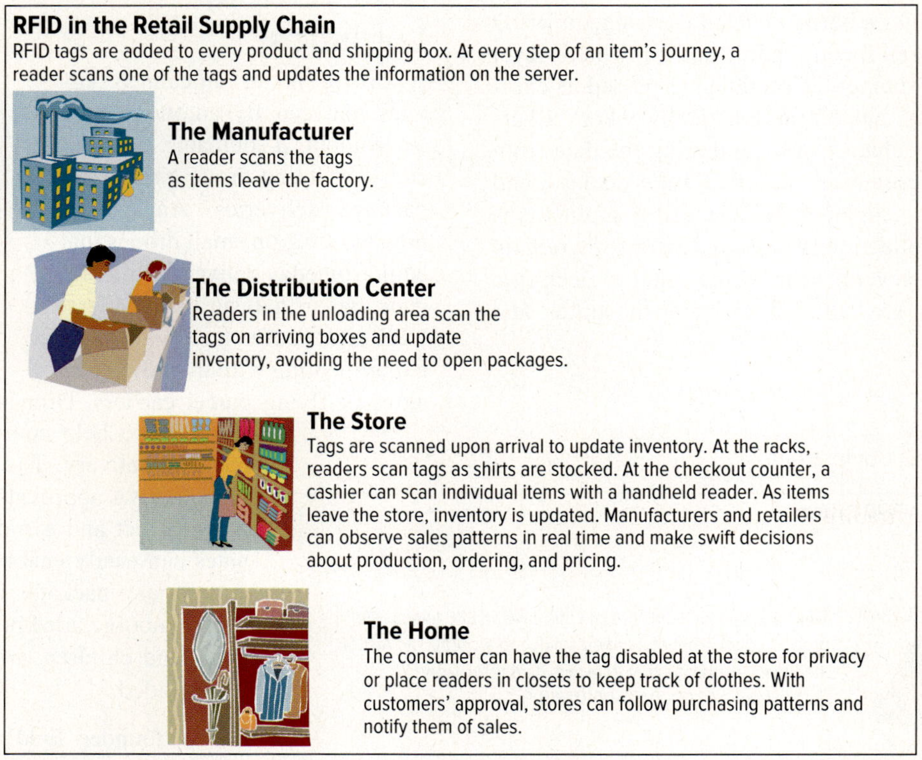

Due Diligence //:

3D Printing Weapons

In 1976, the big movie studios sued Sony for releasing the first VCR because it advertised it as "a way of recording feature-length movies from TV to VHS tape for watching and taking over to friends' houses." Over the next eight years Universal Studios, along with other powerful media groups, fought Sony over creating the device because it could allow users to violate copyright laws. The courts went back and forth for years attempting to determine whether Sony would be held liable for creating a device that enabled users to break copyright laws. In 1984, the U.S. Supreme Court ruled in favor of Sony: "If a device is capable of sustaining a substantial non-infringing use, then it is lawful to make and sell that device. That is, if the device is merely capable of doing something legit, it is legal to make no matter how it is used in practice."

Just think of cars, knives, guns, and computers as they are all used to break the law, and nobody would be allowed to produce them if they were held responsible for how people used them. Do you agree that if you make a tool and sell it to someone who goes on to break the law, you should be held responsible? Do you agree that 3D printers will be used to infringe copyright, trademark, and patent protections? If so, should 3D printers be illegal?

Due Diligence //:

Robots Took My Job[3]

Kiva's little orange robots are becoming the latest craze and a truly fascinating innovation in warehouse management. Kiva's robots are replacing conveyor belts and carousels at the order fulfillment warehouses of retailers such as Zappos, Staples, and Diapers.com.

According to the Kiva site, the Kiva Mobile Fulfillment System (Kiva MFS) uses a breakthrough parallel processing approach to order fulfillment with a unique material handling system that simultaneously improves productivity, speed, accuracy, and flexibility. Every distribution center (DC) strives to attain flexible, efficient order fulfillment but struggles with the limitations of current tools. Traditional automation and sortation systems such as conveyors, tilt tray sorters, sliding shoe sorters, horizontal and vertical carousels, and other automated material handling systems simply tinker with Henry Ford's serial assembly line concept. Kiva Systems has created an innovative order fulfillment system that eliminates the constraints of existing warehouse automation and puts the supplier back in control.

In distribution centers, warehouses, and manufacturing plants equipped with the Kiva MFS, operators stand still while the products come to them. Pallets, cases, and orders are stored on inventory pods that are picked up and moved by a fleet of mobile robotic drive units. As a result, any product can go to any operator at any time to fill any order.

One of Kiva's biggest customers, Zappos, was acquired by Amazon. Why would this information be important to Kiva? What impact could Amazon have on Kiva's business? What impact could Kiva have on Amazon's business? What other types of businesses could use Kiva to improve distribution productivity? How would your warehouse employees react if you told them you were looking at implementing Kiva robots?

© Beth Hall/Bloomberg via Getty Images

inventory items and bring them to the workers for packing. Watching an order fulfillment center equipped with Kiva robots is amazing; the operators stand still while the products come to them. Inventory pods store the products that are carried and transferred by a small army of little orange robots, eliminating the need for traditional systems such as conveyors and sorters. Though assessing the costs and benefits of robots versus human labor can be difficult, Kiva boasts that a packer working with its robots can fulfill three to four times as many orders per hour. Zappos, Staples, and Amazon are just a few of the companies taking advantage of the latest innovation in warehouse management by replacing traditional order fulfillment technologies such as conveyor belts with Kiva's little orange robots.

The Extended Supply Chain

As the supply chain management market matures, it is becoming even more sophisticated and incorporating additional functionality such as marketing, customer service, and even product development to its extended supply chain. Advanced

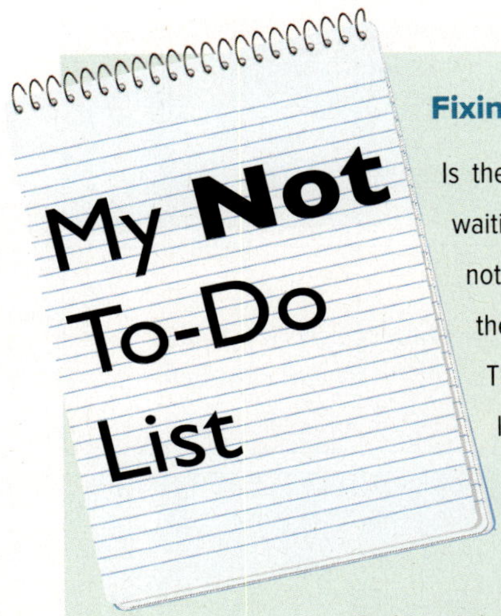

Fixing the Post Office[5]

Is there anything more frustrating than waiting in line at the Post Office? Well, not only are those lines frustrating, they are also becoming unprofitable. The United States Postal Service is looking at a $15 billion loss, one of the greatest catastrophes in its history.

What is killing the Post Office? Perhaps it is Stamps.com, a website that allows you to customize and print your own stamps 24 hours a day. Getting married? You can place a photo of the happy couple right on the stamp for the invitations. Starting a business? You can place your business logo on your stamps. Stamps.com even keeps track of all of a customer's postal spending using client codes, and it can recommend optimal delivery methods. Plus, Stamps.com gives you postage discounts you can't even get at the Post Office or with a postage meter.

What new products are stealing business from the Post Office? How could the Post Office create new products and services to help grow its business? How could the Post Office use cost, quality, delivery, flexibility, and service to revamp its operations management processes?

communications tools, easy-to-use decision support systems, and building trust among participants when sharing information are all making the home-based supply chain possible. A few of the fastest-growing extensions for supply chain management are included in Figure 8.15.

FIGURE 8.15 Extending the Supply Chain

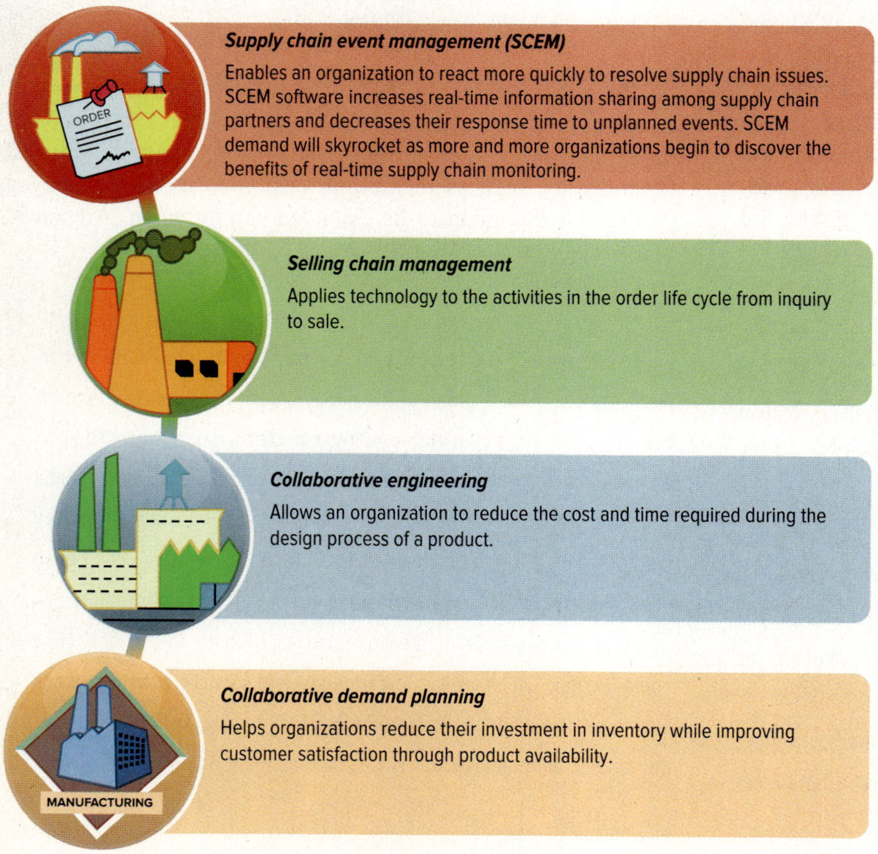

{SECTION 8.2}

Customer Relationship Management and Enterprise Resource Planning

LEARNING OUTCOMES

LO8.4 Describe customer relationship management along with its associated benefits and challenges.

LO8.5 Describe enterprise resource planning along with its associated benefits and challenges.

LO8.6 Discuss the current technologies organizations are integrating in enterprise resource planning systems.

CUSTOMER RELATIONSHIP MANAGEMENT LO8.4

Today, most competitors are simply a mouse-click away. This intense marketplace has forced organizations to switch from being sales focused to being customer focused. **Customer relationship management (CRM)** involves managing all aspects of a customer's relationship with an organization to increase customer loyalty and retention and an organization's profitability. CRM allows an organization to gain insights into customers' shopping and buying behaviors in order to develop and implement enterprisewide strategies. The key players in CRM initiatives are outlined in Figure 8.16. CRM strategic goals include:

- Identify sales opportunities.
- Classify low-value customers and create marketing promotions to increase consumer spending.
- Classify high-value customers and create marketing promotions to increase consumer loyalty.
- Analyze marketing promotions by product, market segment, and sales region.
- Identify customer relationship issues along with strategies for quick resolution.

customer relationship management (CRM) A means of managing all aspects of a customer's relationship with an organization to increase customer loyalty and retention and an organization's profitability.

FIGURE 8.16 Customer Relationship Management Key Players

Lead: A person or company that is unknown to your business.

Account: An existing business relationship exists and can include customers, prospects, partners, and competitors.

Contact: Specific individual representing the account.

Sales Opportunity: An opportunity exists for a potential sale of goods or services related to an account or contact.

The complicated piece of the CRM puzzle is identifying customers and the many communication channels they use to contact companies including call centers, web access, email, sales representatives, faxes, and cell phones. A single customer may access an organization multiple times through many different channels (see Figure 8.17). CRM systems can help to collect all of the points of customer contact along with sales and financial information to provide a complete view of each customer (see Figure 8.18.) CRM systems track every communication between the customer and the organization and provide access to cohesive customer information for all business areas from accounting to order fulfillment. Understanding all customer communications allows the organization to communicate effectively with each customer. It gives the organization a detailed understanding of each customer's products and services record regardless of the customer's preferred communication channel. For example, a customer service representative can easily view detailed account information and history through a CRM system when providing information to a customer such as expected delivery dates, complementary product information, and customer payment and billing information.

Companies that understand individual customer needs are best positioned to achieve success. Of course, building successful customer relationships is not a new business practice; however, implementing CRM systems allows a company to operate more efficiently and effectively in the area of supporting

FIGURE 8.17 Customer Contact Points

FIGURE 8.18 Customer Relationship Management Overview

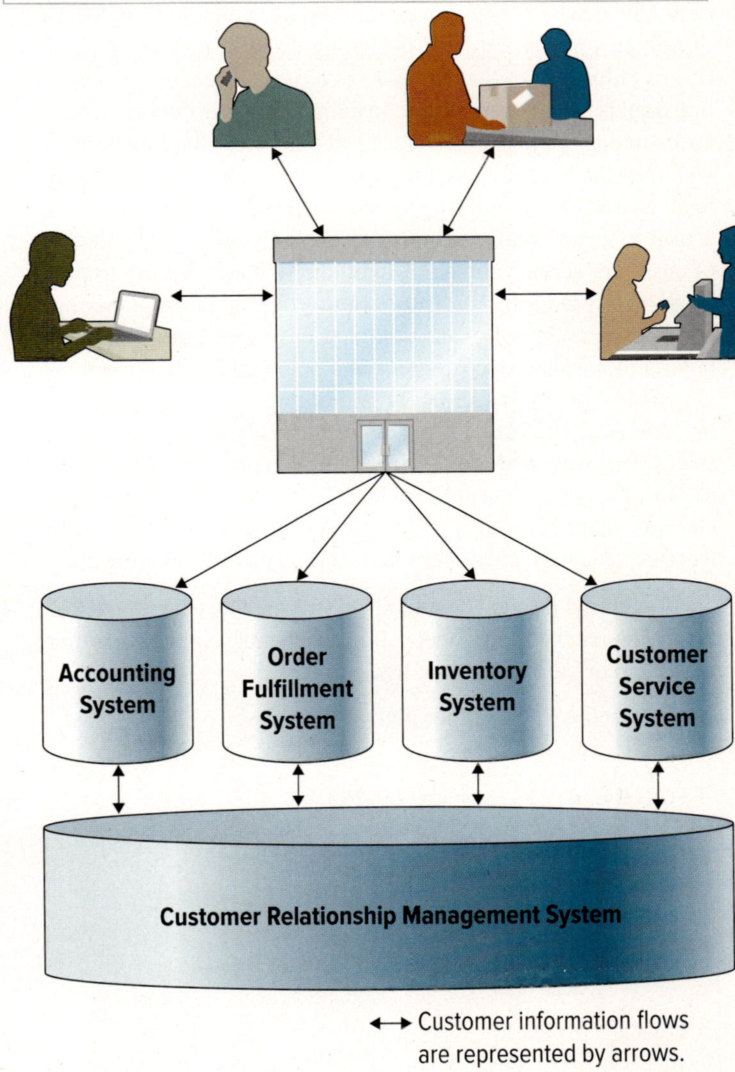

fyi Ruby Receptionists

Great businesses are driven by exceptional customer experiences and interactions. Ruby is a company operating from Portland, Oregon, that has a team of smart and cheerful virtual receptionists that you can hire to carry out all your customer interactions—remotely. Ruby aims to deliver the perfect mix of friendliness, charm, can-do attitude, and professionalism to all its clients' customer calls. Best of all, customers believe the Ruby receptionists are working right in your office, not in Portland, Oregon. Ruby promises to bring back the lost art of human interaction by delighting each and every customer who calls.

Explain the importance of customer service for customer relationship management. Do you agree that a company can improve customer service by hiring Ruby Receptionists? If you owned a small business, would you be comfortable hiring Ruby Receptionists?

customer analytics Involves gathering, classifying, comparing, and studying customer data to identify buying trends, at-risk customers, and potential future opportunities.

sales analytics Involves gathering, classifying, comparing, and studying company sales data to analyze product cycles, sales pipelines, and competitive intelligence.

CRM reporting technologies Help organizations identify their customers across other applications.

CRM analysis technologies Help organizations segment their customers into categories such as best and worst customers.

CRM predicting technologies Help organizations predict customer behavior, such as which customers are at risk of leaving.

customer needs. CRM moves far beyond technology by identifying customer needs and designing specific marketing campaigns tailored to each. This enables a firm to treat customers as individuals, gaining important insights into their buying preferences and shopping behaviors. Firms that treat their customers well reap the rewards and generally see higher profits and highly loyal customers. Identifying the most valuable customers allows a firm to ensure that these customers receive the highest levels of customer service and are offered the first opportunity to purchase new products. **Customer analytics** involves gathering, classifying, comparing, and studying customer data to identify buying trends, at-risk customers, and potential future opportunities. **Sales analytics** involves gathering, classifying, comparing, and studying company sales data to analyze product cycles, sales pipelines, and competitive intelligence. Software with advanced analytics capabilities helps you attract and retain loyal and profitable customers and gives you the insight you need to increase revenues, customer satisfaction, and customer loyalty.

Firms can find their most valuable customers by using the RFM formula—recency, frequency, and monetary value. In other words, an organization must track:

- How *recently* a customer purchased items.
- How *frequently* a customer purchases items.
- The *monetary* value of each customer purchase.

After gathering this initial CRM information, the firm can analyze it to identify patterns and create marketing campaigns and sales promotions for different customer segments. For example, if a customer buys only at the height of the season, the firm should send a special offer during the off-season. If a certain customer segment purchases shoes but never accessories, the firm can offer discounted accessories with the purchase of a new pair of shoes. If the firm determines that its top 20 percent of customers are responsible for 80 percent of the revenue, it can focus on ensuring these customers are always satisfied and receive the highest levels of customer service.

There are three phases of CRM: (1) reporting, (2) analyzing, and (3) predicting. **CRM reporting technologies** help organizations identify their customers across other applications. **CRM analysis technologies** help organizations segment their customers into categories such as best and worst customers. **CRM predicting technologies** help organizations predict customer behavior, such as which customers are at risk of leaving. Figure 8.19 highlights a few of the important questions an organization can answer in these areas by using CRM technologies.

FIGURE 8.19 Evolution of CRM

REPORTING
Customer Identification: Asking What Happened

- What is the total revenue by customer?
- How many units did we make?
- What were total sales by product?
- How many customers do we have?
- What are the current inventory levels?

ANALYZING
Customer Segmentation: Asking Why It Happened

- Why did sales not meet forecasts?
- Why was production so low?
- Why did we not sell as many units as previous years?
- Who are our customers?
- Why was revenue so high?
- Why are inventory levels low?

PREDICTING
Customer Prediction: Asking What Will Happen

- What customers are at risk of leaving?
- Which products will our customers buy?
- Who are the best customers for a marketing campaign?
- How do we reach our customers?
- What will sales be this year?
- How much inventory do we need to preorder?

The Power of the Customer

A standard rule of business states that the customer is always right. Although most businesses use this as their motto, they do not actually mean it. Ebusiness firms, however, must adhere to this rule as the power of the customer grows exponentially in the information age. Various websites and videos on YouTube reveal the power of the individual consumer (see Figure 8.20). A decade ago if you had a complaint against a company, you could make a phone call or write a letter. Now you can contact hundreds or thousands of people around the globe and voice your complaint or anger with a

FIGURE 8.20
Sites like DoNotBuyDodge.com and JetBlueHostage.com demonstrate the power of the consumer in the digital age

a. Source: dontbuydodgechryslervehicles.com; **b. Source:** JetBlue.com

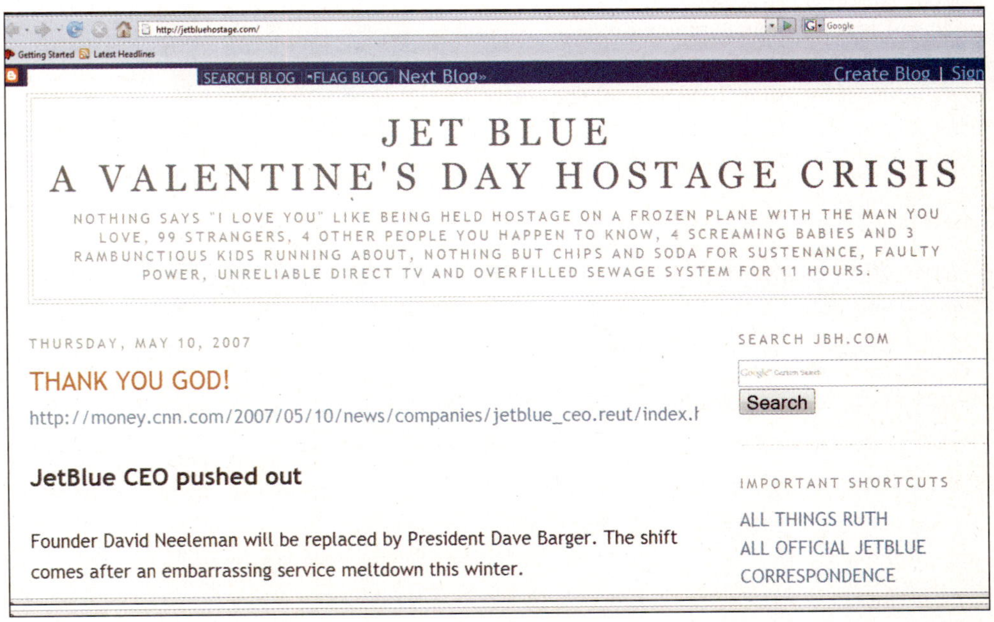

operational CRM Supports traditional transactional processing for day-to-day front-office operations or systems that deal directly with the customers.

analytical CRM Supports back-office operations and strategic analysis and includes all systems that do not deal directly with the customers.

company or product. You—the customer—can now take your power directly to millions of people, and companies have to listen.

Measuring CRM Success Using CRM metrics to track and monitor performance is a best practice for many companies. Figure 8.21 displays a few common CRM metrics a manager can use to track the success of the system. Just remember that you only want to track between five and seven of the hundreds of CRM metrics available.

Operational and Analytical CRM

The two primary components of a CRM strategy are operational CRM and analytical CRM. **Operational CRM** supports traditional transactional processing for day-to-day front-office operations or systems that deal directly with the customers. **Analytical CRM** supports back-office operations and strategic analysis and includes all systems that do not deal directly with the customers. Figure 8.22 provides an overview of the two.

Figure 8.23 shows the different technologies marketing, sales, and customer service departments can use to perform operational CRM.

Marketing and Operational CRM

Companies are no longer trying to sell one product to as many customers as possible; instead, they are trying to sell one customer as many products as possible. Marketing departments switch to this new way of doing business by using CRM technologies that allow them to gather and analyze customer information to tailor successful marketing campaigns. In fact, a marketing campaign's success is directly proportional to the organization's ability to gather and analyze the right customer information. The three primary operational CRM technologies a marketing department can implement to increase customer satisfaction are:

1. List generator.
2. Campaign management.
3. Cross-selling and up-selling.

show me the MONEY

Nice Emotions

New emotion-detection software called Perform, created by Nice Systems, helps firms improve customer service by identifying callers who are displeased or upset. Perform determines a baseline of emotion and can detect emotional issues during the first few seconds of a call; any variation from the baseline activates an alert. When an elderly person who was highly distressed over medical costs hung up during a phone call to the insurance company, Perform identified the customer's frustration and automatically emailed a supervisor. The supervisor was able to review a recording of the conversation and immediately called the customer back suggesting ways to lower the costs.

How do you think emotion-detection software will affect customer relationships? What other departments or business processes could benefit from its use? Create a new product that uses emotion-detection software. What business problem would your product solve and who would be your primary customers?

FIGURE 8.21 CRM Metrics

Sales Metrics	Customer Service Metrics	Marketing Metrics
Number of prospective customers	Cases closed same day	Number of marketing campaigns
Number of new customers	Number of cases handled by agent	New customer retention rates
Number of retained customers	Number of service calls	Number of responses by marketing campaign
Number of open leads	Average number of service requests by type	Number of purchases by marketing campaign
Number of sales calls	Average time to resolution	Revenue generated by marketing campaign
Number of sales calls per lead	Average number of service calls per day	Cost per interaction by marketing campaign
Amount of new revenue	Percentage compliance with service-level agreement	Number of new customers acquired by marketing campaign
Amount of recurring revenue	Percentage of service renewals	Customer retention rate
Number of proposals given	Customer satisfaction level	Number of new leads by product

FIGURE 8.22 Operational CRM and Analytical CRM

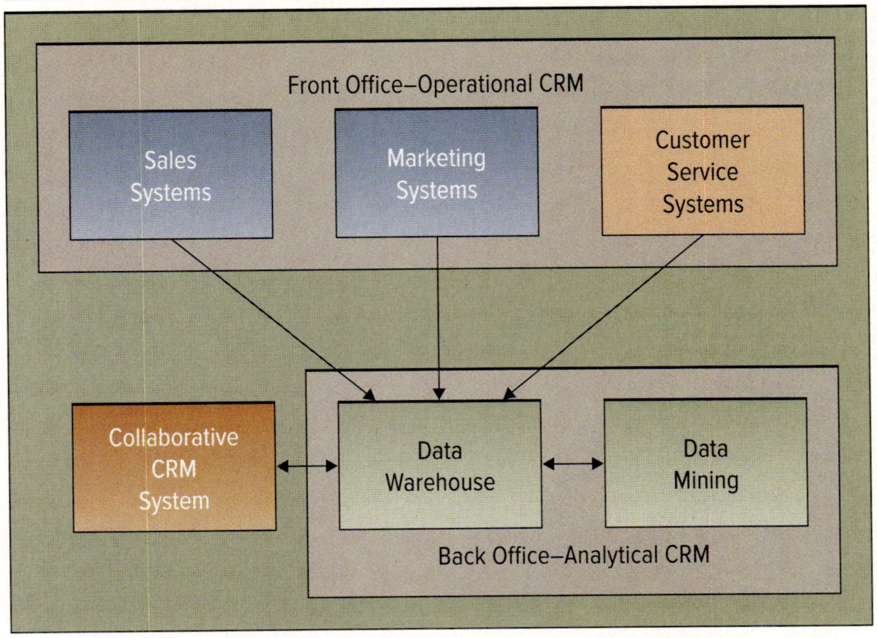

list generator Compiles customer information from a variety of sources and segments it for different marketing campaigns.

campaign management system Guides users through marketing campaigns by performing such tasks as campaign definition, planning, scheduling, segmentation, and success analysis.

cross-selling Selling additional products or services to an existing customer.

FIGURE 8.23 Operational CRM Technologies

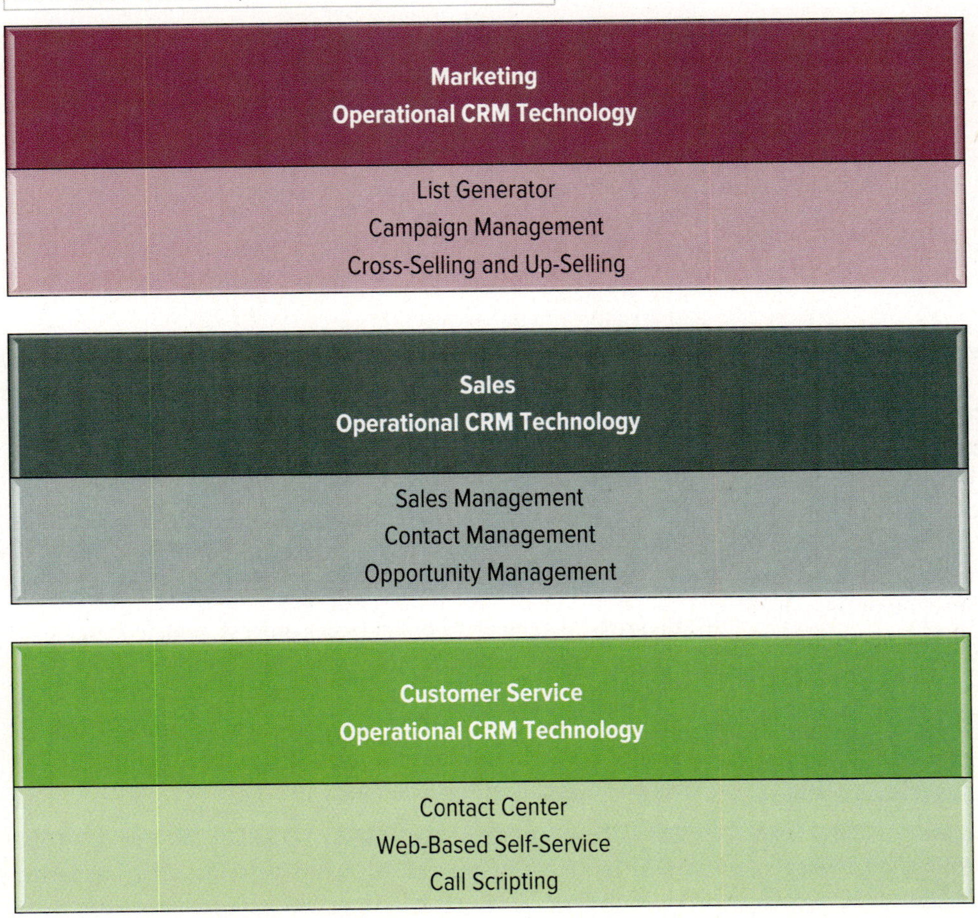

List Generator

List generators compile customer information from a variety of sources and segment it for different marketing campaigns. These sources include website visits, questionnaires, surveys, marketing mailers, and so on. After compiling the customer list, it can be filtered based on criteria such as household income, gender, education level, political facilitation, age, or other factors. List generators provide the marketing department with valuable information on the type of customer it must target to find success for a marketing campaign.

Campaign Management

Campaign management systems guide users through marketing campaigns by performing such tasks as campaign definition, planning, scheduling, segmentation, and success analysis. These advanced systems can even calculate the profitability and track the results for each marketing campaign.

Cross-Selling and Up-Selling

Two key sales strategies a marketing campaign can deploy are cross-selling and up-selling. **Cross-selling** is selling additional products or services to an existing customer. For example, if

up-selling Increasing the value of the sale.

customer service and support (CSS) A part of operational CRM that automates service requests, complaints, product returns, and information requests.

sales force automation (SFA) Automatically tracks all the steps in the sales process.

BUSTED I'm Stuck in London and I've Been Robbed—Help Me![6]

There are so many people using Facebook that people can quickly become overwhelmed with friend requests. Without knowing who your friends are, it is easy to find yourself a victim of a scam. Internet impostors are perfecting the technique of impersonating friends on social networking sites like Facebook with lucrative results and suckering individuals out of thousands of dollars. Emotional email pleas sent by imposters, such as "I'm stuck in London and I've been robbed, help me," have become so effective that the FBI has issued warnings to consumers about social networking sites. "Fraudsters continue to hijack accounts on social networking sites and spread malicious software by using various techniques," the FBI stated after logging 3,200 complaints about such incidents within a week.

© John Slater/Getty Images

When Barry Schwartz logged on to Twitter, he had 20 messages waiting for him, all with the unwelcome news: someone was impersonating his company on Twitter. Schwartz runs RustyBrick, a 15-employee, $2 million website development company. The impostor had set up a profile using a slight variation of the company's name and started following Schwartz's 4,000 customer contacts with a message similar to spam: "Hey guys, you have to get this new Twitter Success Guide—it's priceless." A devastated Schwartz stated, "The last thing I want is to have people thinking that I'm following them and I'm selling a Twitter Success Guide."

Internet impostors impersonate organizations as well as individuals. What could happen to an organization whose customers are contacted by an impostor asking for money or selling a product? What happens when the relationship with a customer turns sour? What type of power does a disgruntled customer or employee have against a company? Why is it more important than ever to build strong relationships with your customers, employees, partners, and suppliers?

you were to purchase Tim Burton's movie *Alice in Wonderland* on Amazon, you would also be asked if you want to purchase the movie's soundtrack or the original book. Amazon is taking advantage of cross-selling by offering customers goods across its book, movie, and music product lines. **Up-selling** is increasing the value of the sale. McDonald's performs upselling by asking customers whether they would like to super-size their meals for an extra cost. CRM systems offer marketing departments all kinds of information about customers and products, which can help identify up-selling and cross-selling opportunities to increase revenues.

Sales and Operational CRM

Sales departments were the first to begin developing CRM systems. They had two primary motivations to track customer sales information electronically. First, sales representatives were struggling with the overwhelming amount of customer account information they were required to maintain and track. Second, managers found themselves hindered because much of their vital customer and sales information remained in the heads of their sales representatives, even if the sales representative left the company. Finding a way to track customer information became a critical success factor for many sales departments. **Customer service and support (CSS)** is a part of operational CRM that automates service requests, complaints, product returns, and information requests.

Figure 8.24 depicts the typical sales process, which begins with an opportunity and ends with billing the customer for the sale. Leads and potential customers are the lifeblood of all sales organizations, whether they sell computers, clothing, consulting, or cars. How leads are handled can make the difference between revenue growth and decline.

Sales force automation (SFA) automatically tracks all the steps in the sales process. SFA products focus on increasing customer satisfaction, building customer relationships, and

sales management CRM system Automates each phase of the sales process, helping individual sales representatives coordinate and organize all their accounts.

contact management CRM system Maintains customer contact information and identifies prospective customers for future sales, using tools such as organizational charts, detailed customer notes, and supplemental sales information.

opportunity management CRM system Targets sales opportunities by finding new customers or companies for future sales.

contact center or call center Where customer service representatives answer customer inquiries and solve problems, usually by email, chat, or phone.

improving product sales. The three primary operational CRM technologies a sales department can adopt are:

1. Sales management CRM systems.
2. Contact management CRM systems.
3. Opportunity management CRM systems.

Sales Management CRM Systems

Sales management CRM systems automate each phase of the sales process, helping individual sales representatives coordinate and organize all their accounts. Features include calendars, reminders for important tasks, multimedia presentations, and document generation. These systems can even provide an analysis of the sales cycle and calculate how each individual sales representative is performing during the sales process.

Contact Management CRM Systems

A **contact management CRM system** maintains customer contact information and identifies prospective customers for future sales, using tools such as organizational charts, detailed customer notes, and supplemental sales information. For example, a contact management system can take an incoming telephone number and automatically display the person's name along with a comprehensive history including all communications with the company. This allows the sales representative to personalize the phone conversation and ask such things as, "How is your new laptop working, Sue?" or "How was your family vacation to Colorado?" The customer feels valued since the sales associate knows her name and even remembers details of their last conversation.

FIGURE 8.24 A Typical Sales Process

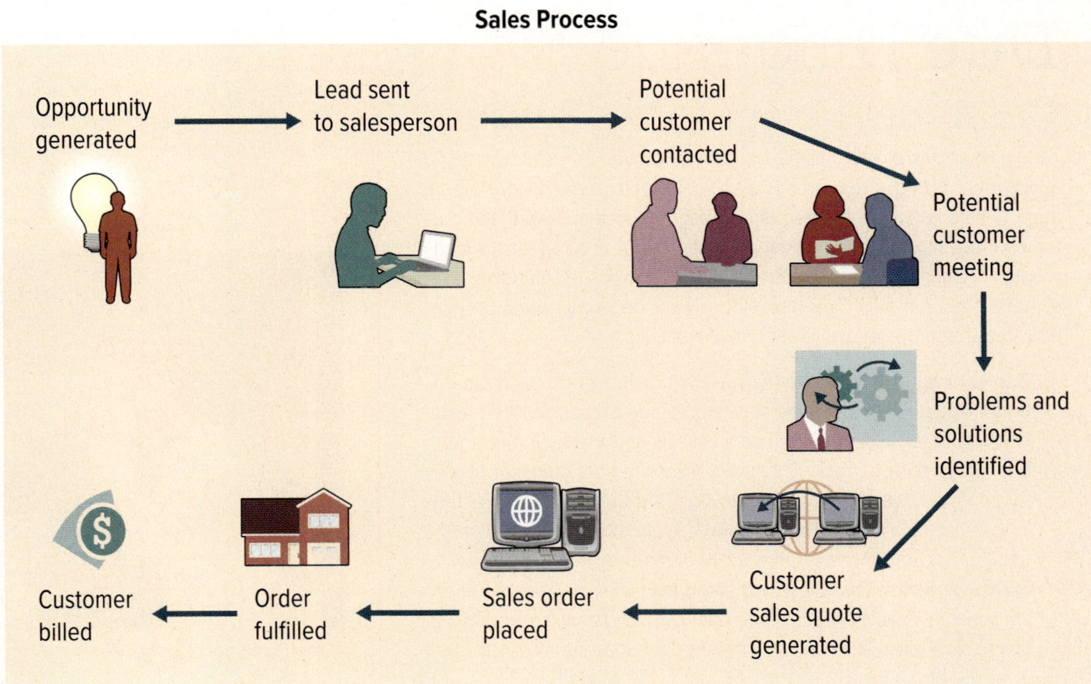

Opportunity Management CRM Systems

Opportunity management CRM systems target sales opportunities by finding new customers or companies for future sales. They determine potential customers and competitors and define selling efforts including budgets and schedules. Advanced systems can even calculate the probability of a sale, which can save sales representatives significant time and money when qualifying new customers. The primary difference between contact management and opportunity management is that contact management deals with existing customers and opportunity management with new or potential customers.

Customer Service and Operational CRM

Most companies recognize the importance of building strong customer relationships during the marketing and sales efforts, but they must continue this effort by building strong post-sale relationships also. A primary reason firms lose customers is due to negative customer service experiences. Providing

web-based self-service system Allows customers to use the web to find answers to their questions or solutions to their problems.

click-to-talk Allows customers to click on a button and talk with a representative via the Internet.

outstanding customer service is challenging, and many CRM technologies can assist organizations with this important activity. The three primary ones are:

1. Contact center.
2. Web-based self-service.
3. Call scripting.

Contact Center

A **contact center** or **call center** is where customer service representatives answer customer inquiries and solve problems, usually by email, chat, or phone. It is one of the best assets a customer-driven organization can have because maintaining a high level of customer support is critical to obtaining and retaining customers. Figure 8.25 highlights a few of the services contact center systems offer.

Contact centers also track customer communication histories along with problem resolutions—information critical for providing a comprehensive customer view to the service representative. Representatives who can quickly comprehend the customer's concerns provide tremendous value to the customer and to the company. Nothing makes frustrated customers happier than not having to explain their problems all over again to yet another customer service representative.

Web-Based Self-Service

Web-based self-service systems allow customers to use the web to find answers to their questions or solutions to their problems. FedEx uses web-based self-service systems to let customers electronically track packages without having to talk to a customer service representative. Another feature of web-based self-service is **click-to-talk** functions, which allow customers to click on a button and talk with a representative via the Internet. Powerful customer-driven features such as these add value to any organization by providing customers with real-time information that helps resolve their concerns.

FIGURE 8.25 Common Services Provided by Contact Centers

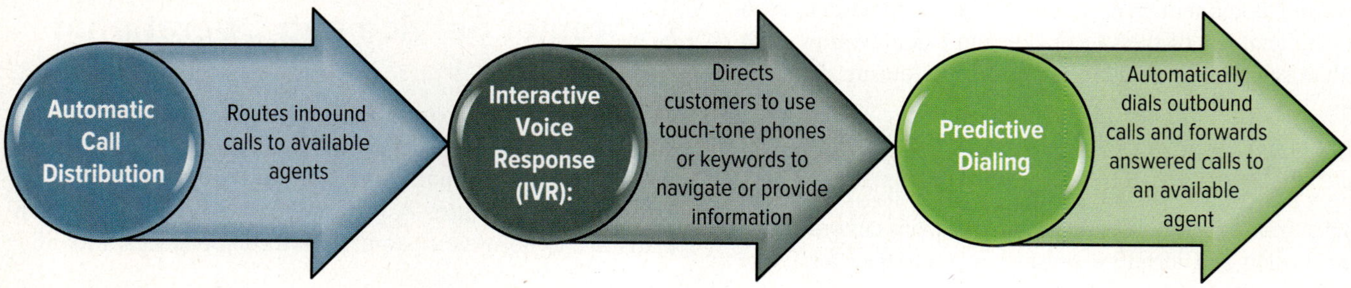

Due Diligence //:

Customer Power to the Rescue[7]

Today, when one of your customers is unhappy, you don't have to worry about them telling a few friends and family; you have to worry about them telling everyone on the planet. Disgruntled employees and customers have many channels they can use to fight back against a faulty product or unethical company. Free or low-cost websites empower consumers to tell not only their friends, but also the world, about the way they have been treated. Here are a few examples:

- **Bad experience with Blue Marble Biking:** Tourist on biking tour is bitten by a dog and requires stitches. Company is barred from hotel because of incident; in turn, it bars the tourist from any further tours.
- **Best Buy receipt check:** Shopper declines to show register receipt for purchase to door guard at Lakewood Best Buy, which is voluntary. Employees attempt to seize cart, stand in shopper's path, and park a truck behind shopper's car to prevent departure.
- **Enterprise Rent-A-Car is a failing enterprise:** Enterprise Rent-A-Car did not honor reservations, did not have cars ready as stated, rented cars with nearly empty tanks, and charged higher prices to corporate account holders.

The Internet is raising the stakes for customer service. With the ability to create a website dedicated to a particular issue, a disgruntled customer can have nearly the same reach as a manufacturer.

The Internet is making it more difficult for companies to ignore their customers' complaints. Search the web for the most outrageous story of a disgruntled customer.

© Image Source/Corbis RF

Call Scripting

Companies that market and sell highly technical products have a difficult time finding competent customer service representatives. **Call scripting systems** gather product details and issue resolution information that can be automatically generated into a script for the representative to read to the customer. These systems even provide questions the representative can ask the customer to troubleshoot the problem and find a resolution. This feature not only helps reps answer difficult questions quickly but also presents a uniform response so customers don't receive different answers.

Analytical CRM

Analytical CRM provides information about customers and products that was once impossible to locate, such as which type of marketing and sales campaign to launch and which customers to target and when. Unlike operational CRM, which automates call centers and sales forces with the aim of enhancing customer service, analytical CRM works by using business intelligence to identify patterns in product sales and customer behaviors. **Uplift modeling** is a form of predictive analytics for marketing campaigns that attempts to identify target markets or people who could be convinced to buy products. The "uplift" refers to the increased sales that can follow after this form of analytical CRM analysis. Analytical CRM provides priceless customer information, supports important business decisions, and plays a vital role in your organization's success.

Analytical CRM tools can slice and dice vast amounts of information to create custom views of customers, products, and market segments, highlighting opportunities for cross-selling and up-selling. Analytical CRM provides **customer segmentation**, which divides a market into categories that share similar attributes such as age, location, gender, habits, and so on. By segmenting customers into groups, it becomes easier to create targeted marketing and sales campaigns, ensuring that you are not wasting resources marketing products to the wrong customers. **Website personalization** occurs when a website has stored enough data about a person's likes and dislikes to fashion offers more likely to appeal to that person. Many marketers use CRM to personalize customer communications and decide which customers are worth pursuing. Here are a few examples of the information insights analytical CRM can help an organization gain.

- **Find new profitable customers:** Analytical CRM could highlight that the most profitable market segment consists of women between 35 and 45 years old who drive SUVs and live within 30 miles of the city limits. The firm could then find a way to locate these customers for mailings and other opportunities.
- **Exceed customer expectations:** Analytical CRM helps a firm move past the typical "Dear Mr. Smith" greeting by personalizing communications. For example, if the firm knows the customer's favorite brand and size of shoe it can notify the customer that a pair of size 12 Nike cross trainers are available for him to try on the next time he visits the store.
- **Discover the activities the firm performs the best:** Analytical CRM can determine what an organization does better than its

show me the MONEY

Straight Jacket Customer Service

You might not want to put the fact that you won the Straightjacket Award on your résumé unless you worked for Rackspace, a Texas company that specializes in hosting websites. At Rackspace, the coveted Straightjacket Award is won by the employee who best delivers "fanatical customer support," one of the firm's critical success factors. The company motivates its customer service representatives by dividing them into teams, each responsible for its own profitability. The company then measures such things as customer turnover, up-selling, cross-selling, and referrals. The team with the highest scores wins the Straightjacket Award and each member receives a 20 percent bonus.

Assume your professor has hired you as the employee relationship manager for your class. What type of award would you create to help increase class participation? What type of award would you create to help increase the overall average on exams? What type of award would you create to help increase student collaboration? Be sure to name your awards and describe their details. Also, what type of metrics would you create to measure your awards? How could a CRM system help you implement your awards?

call scripting system Gathers product details and issue resolution information that can be automatically generated into a script for the representative to read to the customer.

uplift modeling A form of predictive analytics for marketing campaigns that attempts to identify target markets or people who could be convinced to buy products.

customer segementation Divides a market into categories that share similar attributes such as age, location, gender, habits, and so on.

website personalization Occurs when a website has stored enough data about a person's likes and dislikes to fashion offers more likely to appeal to that person.

supplier relationship management (SRM) Focuses on keeping suppliers satisfied by evaluating and categorizing suppliers for different projects.

partner relationship management (PRM) Discovers optimal sales channels by selecting the right partners and identifying mutual customers.

employee relationship management (ERM) Provides web-based self-service tools that streamline and automate the human resource department.

enterprise resource planning (ERP) Integrates all departments and functions throughout an organization into a single MIS system (or integrated set of MIS systems) so employees can make decisions by viewing enterprisewide information about all business operations.

competitors. If a restaurant caters more lunches to midsized companies than its competition does, it can purchase a specialized mailing targeting these customers for future mailings.

- **Eliminate competition:** Analytical CRM can determine sales trends allowing the company to provide customers with special deals outsmarting its competition. A sports store might identify its best customers for outdoor apparel and invite them to a private sale right before the competition runs its sale.
- **Care about customers:** Analytical CRM can determine what customers want and need, so a firm can contact them with an invitation to a private sale, reminder that a product needs a tune-up, or send them a personalized letter along with a discount coupon to help spark a renewed relationship.

The Future of CRM

Organizations are discovering a wave of other key business areas where it is beneficial to build strong relationships beyond customers. These include supplier relationship management (SRM), partner relationship management (PRM), and employee relationship management (ERM) as outlined in Figure 8.26.

Supplier relationship management (SRM) focuses on keeping suppliers satisfied by evaluating and categorizing suppliers for different projects. SRM applications help companies analyze suppliers based on a number of key variables including prices, inventory availability, and business focus or strategies. It can then determine the best supplier to collaborate with and develop strong relationships with to streamline processes, outsource services, and provide products the firm could not offer alone.

Partner relationship management (PRM) discovers optimal sales channels by selecting the right partners and identifying mutual customers. A PRM system offers real-time sales channel information about such things as inventory availability, pricing strategies, and shipping information, allowing a company to expand its market by offering specialized products and services.

Employee relationship management (ERM) provides web-based self-service tools that streamline and automate the human resource department. Employees are the backbone of an enterprise and the communication channel to customers, partners, and suppliers. Their relationship with the company is far more complex and long-lasting than the relationship with customers; thus many enterprises are turning to ERM systems to help retain key employees.

LO8.4 Describe customer relationship management along with its associated benefits and challenges.

ENTERPRISE RESOURCE PLANNING LO8.5

Today's business leaders need significant amounts of information to be readily accessible with real-time views into their businesses so that decisions can be made when they need to be, without the added time of tracking data and generating reports.

FIGURE 8.26 Extending Customer Relationship Management

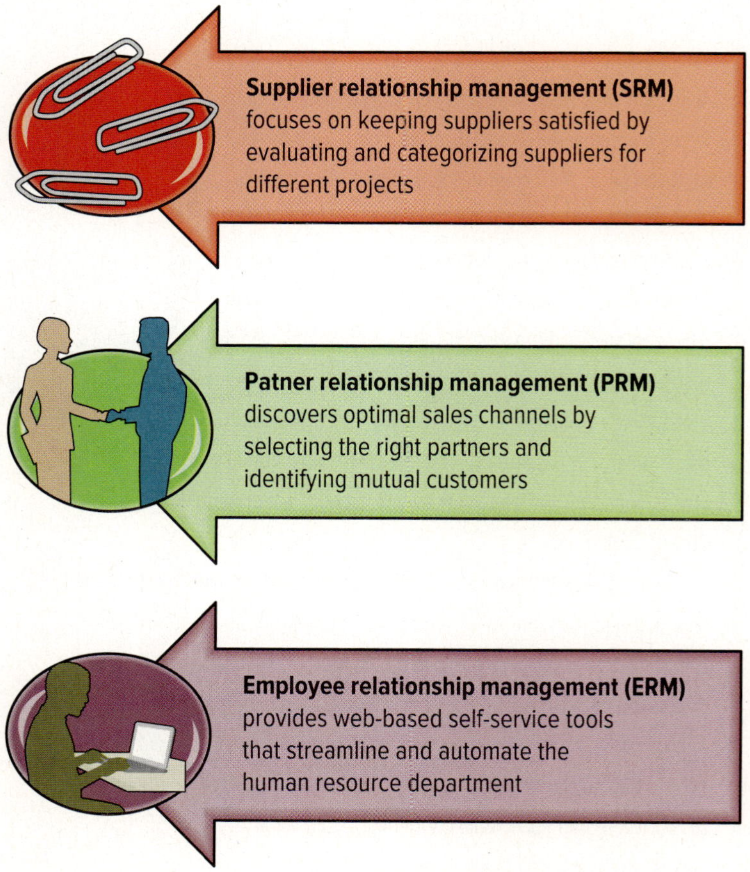

Enterprise resource planning (ERP) integrates all departments and functions throughout an organization into a single system (or integrated set of MIS systems) so that employees can make decisions by viewing enterprisewide information on all business operations. To truly understand the complexity of ERP systems you must think about the many different functional business areas and their associated business processes as well as cross-functional business processes such as supply chain management and customer relationship management and beyond. At its most basic level, ERP software integrates these various business functions into one complete system to streamline business processes and information across the entire organization. Essentially, ERP helps employees do their jobs more efficiently by breaking down barriers between business units.

Many organizations fail to maintain consistency across business operations. If a single department, such as sales, decides to implement a new system without considering the other departments, inconsistencies can occur throughout the company. Not all systems are built to talk to each other and share data, and if sales suddenly implements a new system that marketing and accounting cannot use or is inconsistent in the way it handles information, the company's operations become siloed. Figure 8.27 displays sample data from a sales database, and Figure 8.28 displays samples from an accounting database. Notice the differences in data formats, numbers, and identifiers. Correlating this data would be difficult, and the inconsistencies would cause numerous reporting errors from an enterprisewide perspective.

common data repository Allows every department of a company to store and retrieve information in real-time allowing information to be more reliable and accessible.

module software design Divides the system into a set of functional units (named modules) that can be used independently or combined with other modules for increased business flexibility.

FIGURE 8.27 Sales Information Sample

	A	B	C	D	E	F	G
1	OrderDate	ProductName	Quantity	Unit Price	Unit Cost	Customer ID	SalesRep ID
2	Monday, January 04, 2015	Mozzarella cheese	41.5	$ 24.15	$ 15.35	AC45	EX-107
3	Monday, January 04, 2015	Romaine lettuce	90.65	$ 15.06	$ 14.04	AC45	EX-109
4	Tuesday, January 05, 2015	Red onions	27.15	$ 12.08	$ 10.32	AC67	EX-104
5	Wednesday, January 06, 2015	Romaine lettuce	67.25	$ 15.16	$ 10.54	AC96	EX-109
6	Thursday, January 07, 2015	Black olives	79.26	$ 12.18	$ 9.56	AC44	EX-104
7	Thursday, January 07, 2015	Romaine lettuce	46.52	$ 15.24	$ 11.54	AC32	EX-104
8	Thursday, January 07, 2015	Romaine lettuce	52.5	$ 15.26	$ 11.12	AC84	EX-109
9	Friday, January 08, 2015	Red onions	39.5	$ 12.55	$ 9.54	AC103	EX-104
10	Saturday, January 09, 2015	Romaine lettuce	66.5	$ 15.98	$ 9.56	AC4	EX-104
11	Sunday, January 10, 2015	Romaine lettuce	58.26	$ 15.87	$ 9.50	AC174	EX-104
12	Sunday, January 10, 2015	Pineapple	40.15	$ 33.54	$ 22.12	AC45	EX-104
13	Monday, January 11, 2015	Pineapple	71.56	$ 33.56	$ 22.05	AC4	EX-104
14	Thursday, January 14, 2015	Romaine lettuce	18.25	$ 15.00	$ 10.25	AC174	EX-104
15	Thursday, January 14, 2015	Romaine lettuce	28.15	$ 15.26	$ 10.54	AC44	EX-107
16	Friday, January 15, 2015	Pepperoni	33.5	$ 15.24	$ 10.25	AC96	EX-109
17	Friday, January 15, 2015	Parmesan cheese	14.26	$ 8.05	$ 4.00	AC96	EX-104
18	Saturday, January 16, 2015	Parmesan cheese	72.15	$ 8.50	$ 4.00	AC103	EX-109
19	Monday, January 18, 2015	Parmesan cheese	41.5	$ 24.15	$ 15.35	AC45	EX-107
20	Monday, January 18, 2015	Romaine lettuce	90.65	$ 15.06	$ 14.04	AC45	EX-109
21	Wednesday, January 20, 2015	Tomatoes	27.15	$ 12.08	$ 10.32	AC67	EX-104
22	Thursday, January 21, 2015	Peppers	67.25	$ 15.16	$ 10.54	AC96	EX-109
23	Thursday, January 21, 2015	Mozzarella cheese	79.26	$ 12.18	$ 9.56	AC44	EX-104
24	Saturday, January 23, 2015	Black olives	46.52	$ 15.24	$ 11.54	AC32	EX-104
25	Sunday, January 24, 2015	Mozzarella cheese	52.5	$ 15.26	$ 11.12	AC84	EX-109
26	Tuesday, January 26, 2015	Romaine lettuce	39.5	$ 12.55	$ 9.54	AC103	EX-104
27	Wednesday, January 27, 2015	Parmesan cheese	66.5	$ 15.98	$ 9.56	AC4	EX-104
28	Thursday, January 28, 2015	Peppers	58.26	$ 15.87	$ 9.50	AC174	EX-104
29	Thursday, January 28, 2015	Mozzarella cheese	40.15	$ 33.54	$ 22.12	AC45	EX-104
30	Friday, January 29, 2015	Tomatoes	71.56	$ 33.56	$ 22.05	AC4	EX-104
31	Friday, January 29, 2015	Peppers	18.25	$ 15.00	$ 10.25	AC174	EX-104

FIGURE 8.28 Accounting Information Sample

	A	B	C	D	E	F	G	H	I	J
1	OrderDate	ProductName	Quantity	Unit Price	Total Sales	Unit Cost	Total Cost	Profit	Customer	SalesRep
2	04-Jan-15	Mozzarella cheese	41	24	984	18	738	246	The Station	Debbie Fernandez
3	04-Jan-15	Romaine lettuce	90	15	1,350	14	1,260	90	The Station	Roberta Cross
4	05-Jan-15	Red onions	27	12	324	8	216	108	Bert's Bistro	Loraine Schultz
5	06-Jan-15	Romaine lettuce	67	15	1,005	14	938	67	Smoke House	Roberta Cross
6	07-Jan-15	Black olives	79	12	948	6	474	474	Flagstaff House	Loraine Schultz
7	07-Jan-15	Romaine lettuce	46	15	690	14	644	46	Two Bitts	Loraine Schultz
8	07-Jan-15	Romaine lettuce	52	15	780	14	728	52	Pierce Arrow	Roberta Cross
9	08-Jan-15	Red onions	39	12	468	8	312	156	Mamm'a Pasta Palace	Loraine Schultz
10	09-Jan-15	Romaine lettuce	66	15	990	14	924	66	The Dandelion	Loraine Schultz
11	10-Jan-15	Romaine lettuce	58	15	870	14	812	58	Carmens	Loraine Schultz
12	10-Jan-15	Pineapple	40	33	1,320	28	1,120	200	The Station	Loraine Schultz
13	11-Jan-15	Pineapple	71	33	2,343	28	1,988	355	The Dandelion	Loraine Schultz
14	14-Jan-15	Romaine lettuce	18	15	270	14	252	18	Carmens	Loraine Schultz
15	14-Jan-15	Romaine lettuce	28	15	420	14	392	28	Flagstaff House	Debbie Fernandez
16	15-Jan-15	Pepperoni	33	53	1,749	35	1,155	594	Smoke House	Roberta Cross
17	15-Jan-15	Parmesan cheese	14	8	112	4	56	56	Smoke House	Loraine Schultz
18	16-Jan-15	Parmesan cheese	72	8	576	4	288	288	Mamm'a Pasta Palace	Roberta Cross
19	18-Jan-15	Parmesan cheese	10	8	80	4	40	40	Mamm'a Pasta Palace	Loraine Schultz
20	18-Jan-15	Romaine lettuce	42	15	630	14	588	42	Smoke House	Roberta Cross
21	20-Jan-15	Tomatoes	48	9	432	7	336	96	Two Bitts	Loraine Schultz
22	21-Jan-15	Peppers	29	21	609	12	348	261	The Dandelion	Roberta Cross
23	21-Jan-15	Mozzarella cheese	10	24	240	18	180	60	Mamm'a Pasta Palace	Debbie Fernandez
24	23-Jan-15	Black olives	98	12	1,176	6	588	588	Two Bitts	Roberta Cross
25	24-Jan-15	Mozzarella cheese	45	24	1,080	18	810	270	Carmens	Loraine Schultz
26	26-Jan-15	Romaine lettuce	58	15	870	14	812	58	Two Bitts	Loraine Schultz
27	27-Jan-15	Parmesan cheese	66	8	528	4	264	264	Flagstaff House	Loraine Schultz
28	28-Jan-15	Peppers	85	21	1,785	12	1,020	765	Pierce Arrow	Loraine Schultz
29	28-Jan-15	Mozzarella cheese	12	24	288	18	216	72	The Dandelion	Debbie Fernandez
30	29-Jan-15	Tomatoes	40	9	360	7	280	80	Pierce Arrow	Roberta Cross

The two key components of an ERP system help to resolve these issues and include a common data repository and modular software design. A **common data repository** allows every department of a company to store and retrieve information in real-time allowing information to be more reliable and accessible. **Module software design** divides the system into a set of functional units (named modules) that can be used independently or combined with other modules for increased business flexibility. Module software design allows customers to mix-and-match modules so they purchase only the required modules. If a company wants to implement the system slowly it can begin with just one module, such as accounting, and then incorporate additional modules such as purchasing and scheduling.

ERP systems share data supporting business processes within and across departments. In practice, this means that employees in different divisions—for example, accounting and sales—can rely on the same information for their specific needs. ERP software also offers some degree of synchronized reporting and automation. Instead of forcing

FIGURE 8.29 Enterprise Resource Planning System Overview

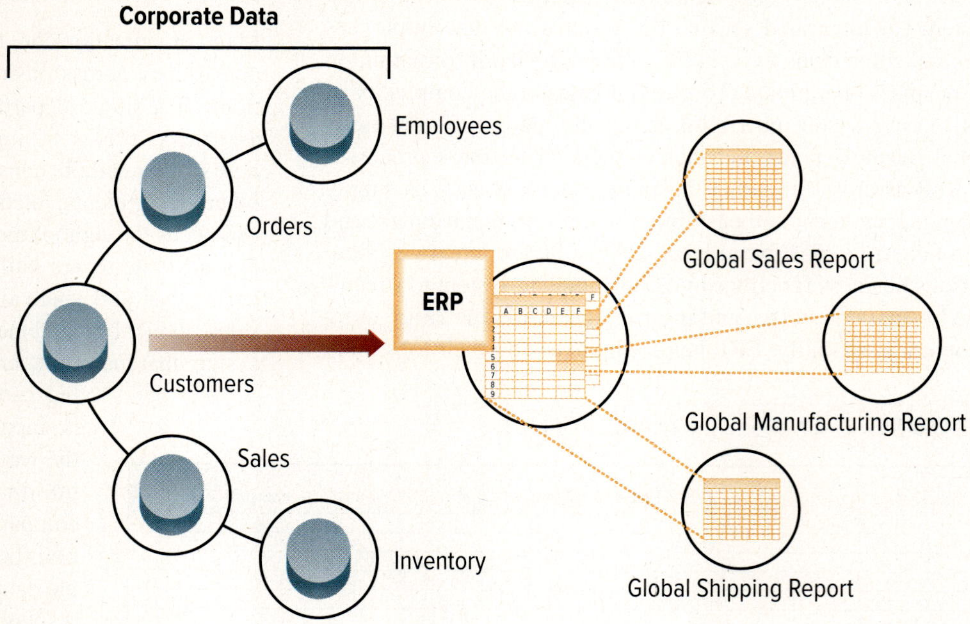

employees to maintain separate databases and spreadsheets that have to be manually merged to generate reports, some ERP solutions allow staff to pull reports from one system. For instance, with sales orders automatically flowing into the financial system without any manual re-keying, the order management department can process orders more quickly and accurately, and the finance department can close the books faster. Other common ERP features include a portal or dashboard to enable employees to quickly understand the business's performance on key metrics.

Figure 8.29 shows how an ERP system takes data from across the enterprise, consolidates and correlates it, and generates enterprise-wide organizational reports. Original ERP implementations promised to capture all information onto one true "enterprise" system, with the ability to touch all the business processes within the organization. Unfortunately, ERP solutions have fallen short of these promises, and typical implementations have penetrated only 15 to 20 percent of the organization. The issue ERP intends to solve is that knowledge within a majority of organizations currently resides in silos that are maintained by a select few, without the ability to be shared across the organization, causing inconsistency across business operations.

The heart of an ERP system is a central database that collects information from and feeds information into all the ERP system's individual application components (called modules), supporting diverse business functions such as accounting, manufacturing, marketing, and human resources. When a user enters or updates information in one module, it is immediately and automatically updated throughout the entire system, as illustrated in Figure 8.30.

FIGURE 8.30 ERP Integration Data Flow

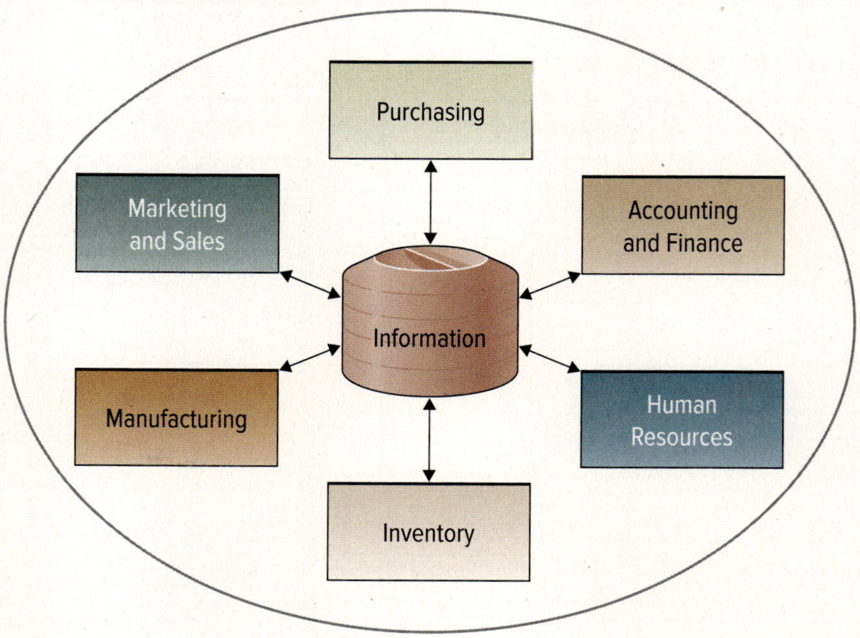

ERP automates business processes such as order fulfillment—taking an order from a customer, shipping the purchase, and then billing for it. With an ERP system, when a customer service representative takes an order from a customer, he or she has all the information necessary to complete the order (the customer's credit rating and order history, the company's inventory levels, and the delivery schedule). Everyone else in the company sees the same information and has access to the database that holds the customer's new order. When one department finishes with the order, it is automatically routed via the ERP system to the next department. To find out where the order is at any point, a user need only log in to the ERP system and track it down, as illustrated in Figure 8.31.

In most organizations, information has traditionally been isolated within specific departments, whether on an individual database, in a file cabinet, or on an employee's PC. ERP enables

FIGURE 8.31 ERP Process Flow

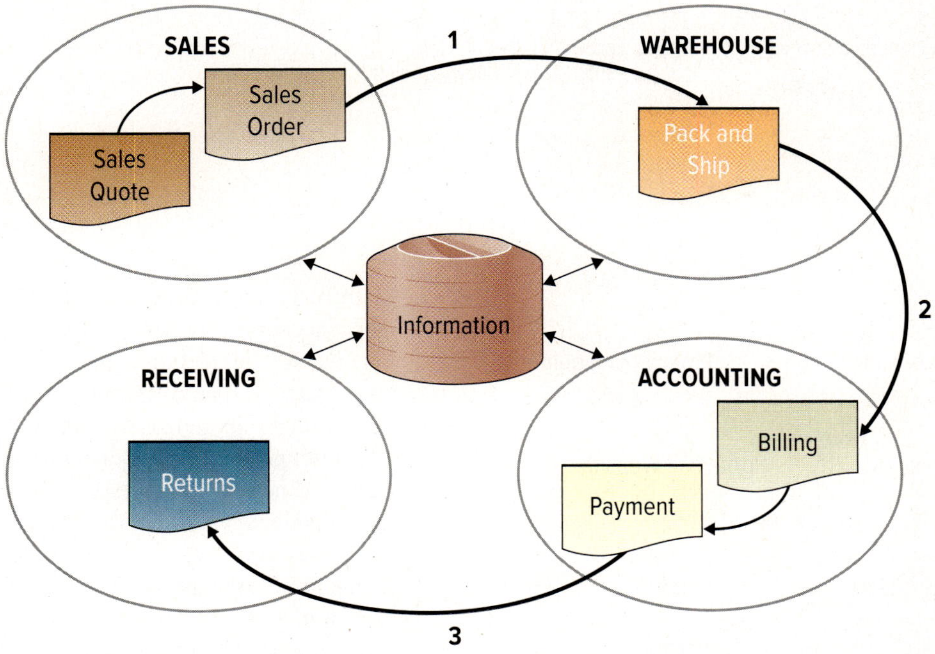

Applications such as SCM, CRM, and ERP are the backbone of ebusiness. Integration of these applications is the key to success for many companies. Integration allows the unlocking of information to make it available to any user, anywhere, anytime.

Most organizations today have no choice but to piece their SCM, CRM, and ERP applications together since no one vendor can respond to every organizational need; hence, customers purchase applications from multiple vendors. As a result, organizations face the challenge of integrating their systems. For example, a single organization might choose its CRM components from Siebel, SCM components from i2, and financial components and HR management components from Oracle. Figure 8.34 displays the general audience and purpose for each of these applications that have to be integrated.

employees across the organization to share information across a single, centralized database. With extended portal capabilities, an organization can also involve its suppliers and customers to participate in the workflow process, allowing ERP to penetrate the entire value chain, and help the organization achieve greater operational efficiency (see Figure 8.32).

The Benefits of ERP

Originally, ERP solutions were developed to deliver automation across multiple units of an organization, to help facilitate the manufacturing process and address issues such as raw materials, inventory, order entry, and distribution. However, ERP was unable to extend to other functional areas of the company such as sales, marketing, and shipping. It could not tie in any CRM capabilities that would allow organizations to capture customer-specific information, nor did it work with websites or portals used for customer service or order fulfillment. Call center or quality assurance staff could not tap into the ERP solution, nor could ERP handle document management, such as cataloging contracts and purchase orders.

ERP has grown over the years to become part of the extended enterprise. From its beginning as a tool for materials planning, it has extended to warehousing, distribution, and order entry. With its next evolution, ERP expands to the front office including CRM. Now administrative, sales, marketing, and human resources staff can share a tool that is truly enterprisewide. To compete on a functional level today, companies must adopt an enterprisewide approach to ERP that utilizes the Internet and connects to every facet of the value chain. Figure 8.33 shows how ERP has grown to accommodate the needs of the entire organization.

The current generation of ERP, ERP-II is composed of two primary components—core and extended. **Core ERP components** are the traditional components included in most ERP systems and primarily focus on internal operations. **Extended ERP components** are the extra components that meet organizational needs not covered by the core components and primarily focus on external operations. Figure 8.35 provides an example of an ERP system with its core and extended components.

Core ERP Components

The three most common core ERP components focusing on internal operations are:

1. Accounting and finance.
2. Production and materials management.
3. Human resources.

Accounting and Finance ERP Components

Deeley Harley-Davidson Canada (DHDC), the exclusive Canadian distributor of Harley-Davidson motorcycles, has improved inventory, turnaround time, margins, and customer satisfaction—all with the implementation of a financial ERP system. The system has opened up the power of information to the company and is helping it make strategic decisions when it still has the time to change things. The ERP system provides the company with ways to manage inventory, turnaround time, and warehouse space more effectively.

Accounting and finance ERP components manage accounting data and financial processes within the enterprise

core ERP component The traditional components included in most ERP systems and primarily focus on internal operations.

extended ERP component The extra components that meet organizational needs not covered by the core components and primarily focus on external operations.

accounting and finance ERP component Manages accounting data and financial processes within the enterprise with functions such as general ledger, accounts payable, accounts receivable, budgeting, and asset management.

production and materials management ERP component Handles production planning and execution tasks such as demand forecasting, production scheduling, job cost accounting, and quality control.

FIGURE 8.32 The Organization before and after ERP

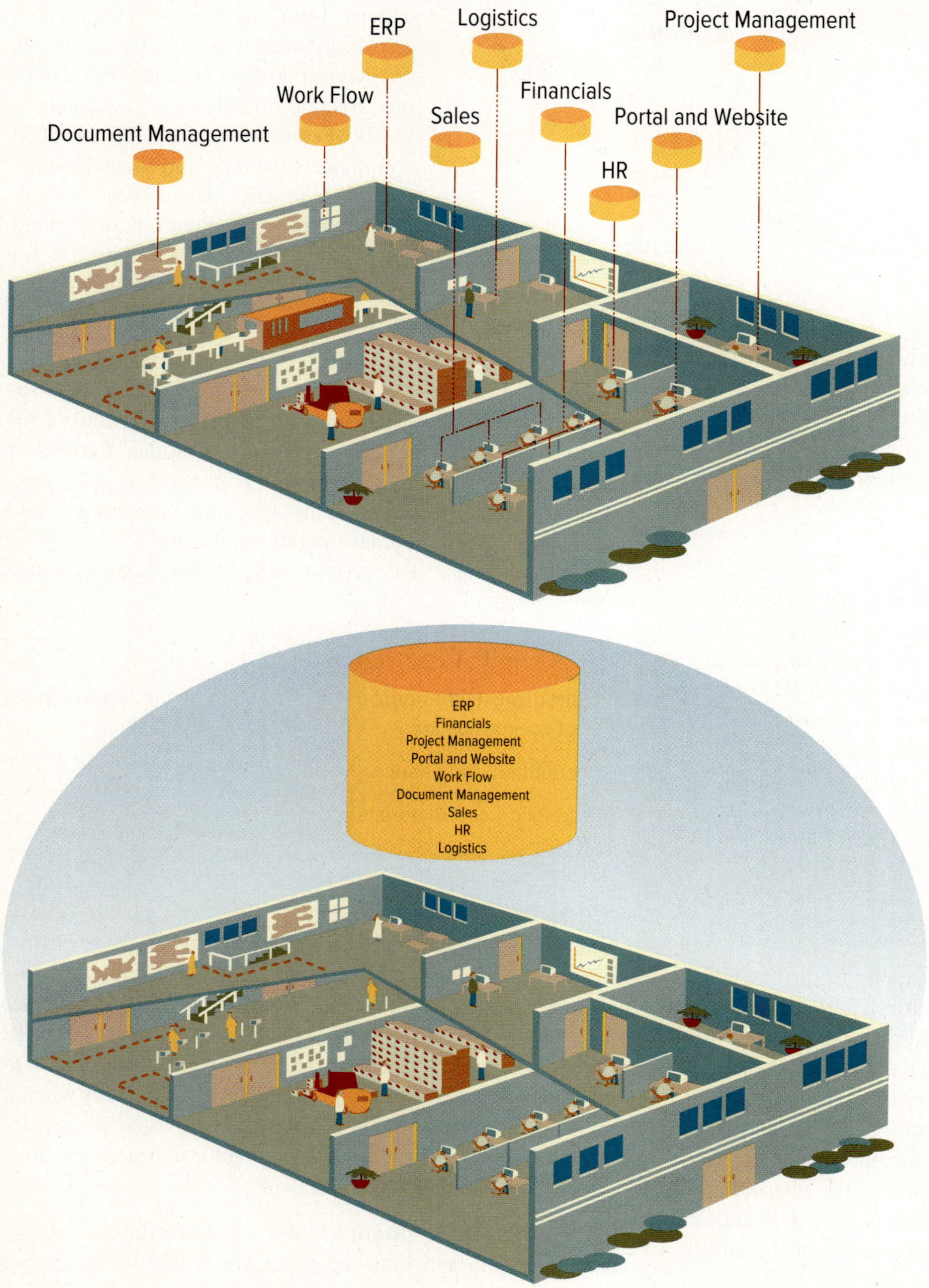

with functions such as general ledger, accounts payable, accounts receivable, budgeting, and asset management. One of the most useful features included in an ERP accounting/finance component is its credit-management feature. Most organizations manage their relationships with customers by setting credit limits, or a limit on how much a customer can owe at any one time. The company then monitors the credit limit whenever the customer places a new order or sends in a payment. ERP financial systems help to correlate customer orders with customer account balances determining credit availability. Another great feature is the ability to perform product profitability analysis. ERP financial components are the backbone behind product profitability analysis and allow companies to perform all types of advanced profitability modeling techniques.

Production and Materials Management ERP

Production and materials management ERP components handle production planning and execution tasks such as demand forecasting, production scheduling, job cost accounting, and quality control. Demand forecasting helps determine production schedules and materials purchasing. A company that makes its own product prepares a detailed production schedule, and a company that buys products for resale develops a materials requirement plan. Companies typically produce multiple products, each of which has many different parts. Production lines, consisting of

FIGURE 8.33 The Evolution of ERP

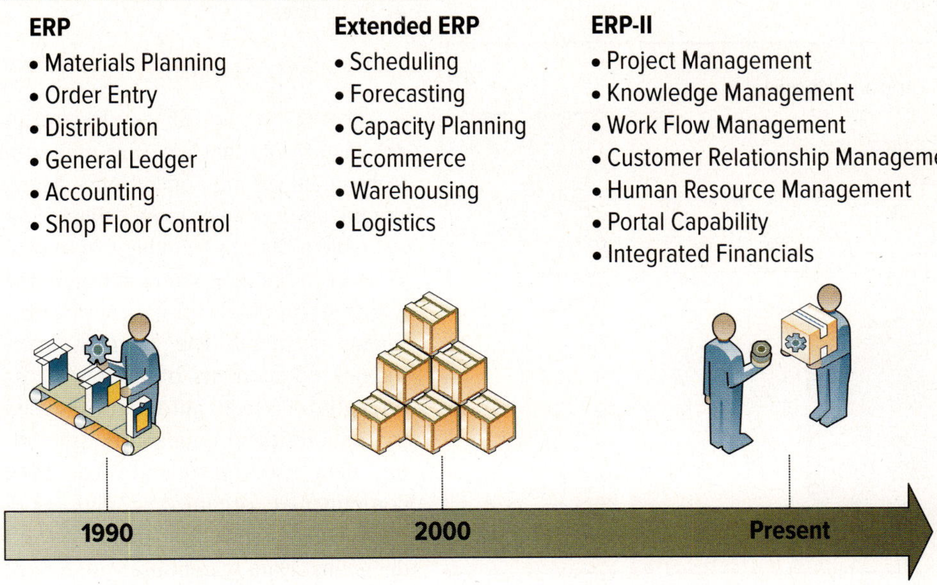

FIGURE 8.34 Primary Users and Business Benefits of Strategic Initiatives

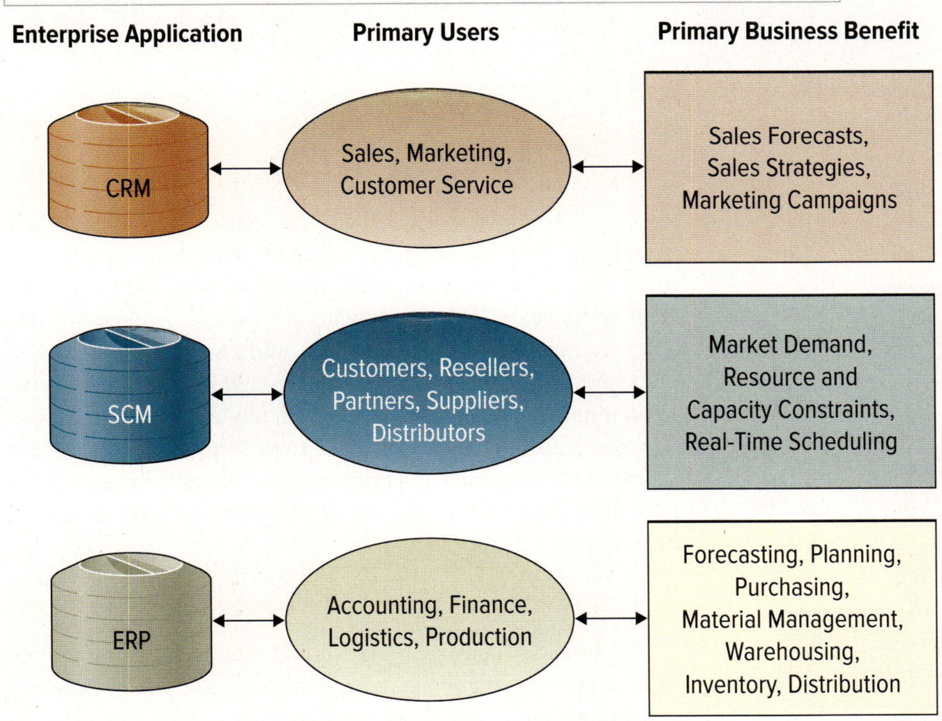

machines and employees, build the different types of products. The company must then define sales forecasting for each product to determine production schedules and materials purchasing. Figure 8.36 displays the typical ERP production planning process. The process begins with forecasting sales in order to plan operations. A detailed production schedule is developed if the product is produced and a materials requirement plan is completed if the product is purchased.

Grupo Farmanova Intermed, located in Costa Rica, is a pharmaceutical marketing and distribution company that markets nearly 2,500 products to approximately 500 customers in Central and South America. The company identified a need for software that could unify product logistics management in a single country. It decided to deploy PeopleSoft financial and distribution ERP components allowing the company to improve customer data management, increase confidence among internal and external users, and coordinate the logistics of inventory. With the software the company enhanced its capabilities for handling, distributing, and marketing its pharmaceuticals.

human resources ERP component Tracks employee information including payroll, benefits, compensation, and performance assessment and ensures compliance with all laws.

Human Resources ERP Components

Human resources ERP components track employee information including payroll, benefits, compensation, and performance assessment and ensure compliance with all laws. Human resources components even offer features that allow the organization to perform detailed analysis on its employees to determine such things as the identification of individuals who are likely to leave the company unless additional compensation or benefits are provided. These components can also identify which employees are using which resources, such as online training and long-distance telephone services. They can also help determine whether the most talented people are working for those business units with the highest priority—or where they would have the greatest impact on profit.

Extended ERP Components

Extended ERP components meet the organizational needs not covered by the core components and primarily focus on external operations. Many are Internet-enabled and require interaction with customers, suppliers, and business partners outside

FIGURE 8.35
Core ERP Components and Extended ERP Components

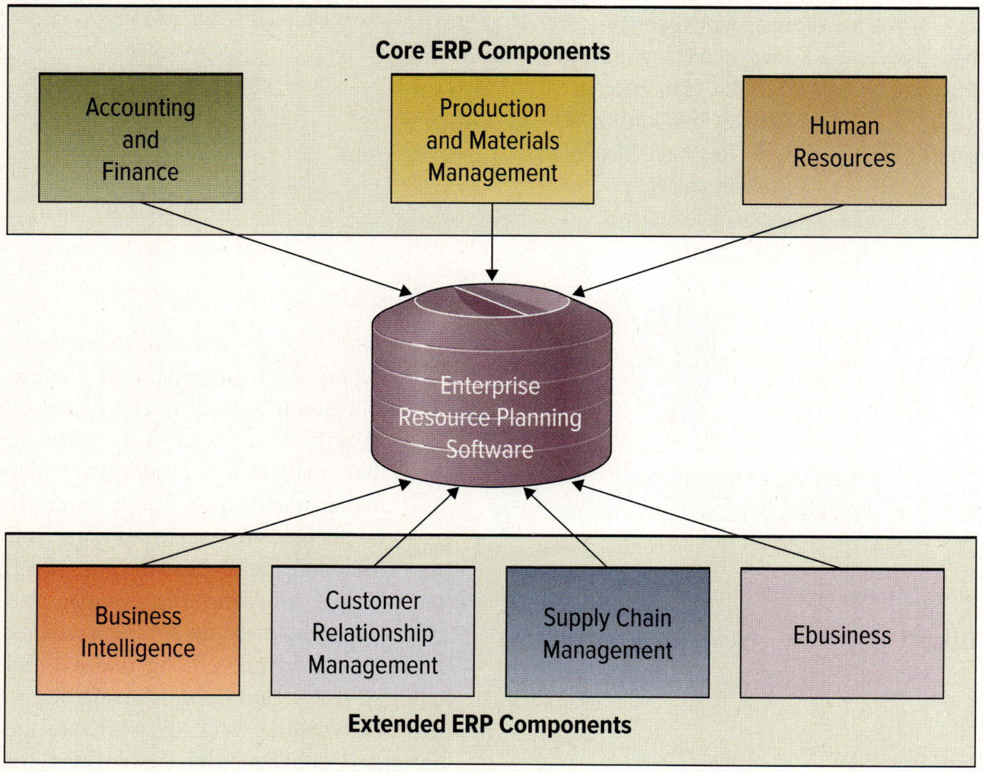

FIGURE 8.36 The Production Planning Process

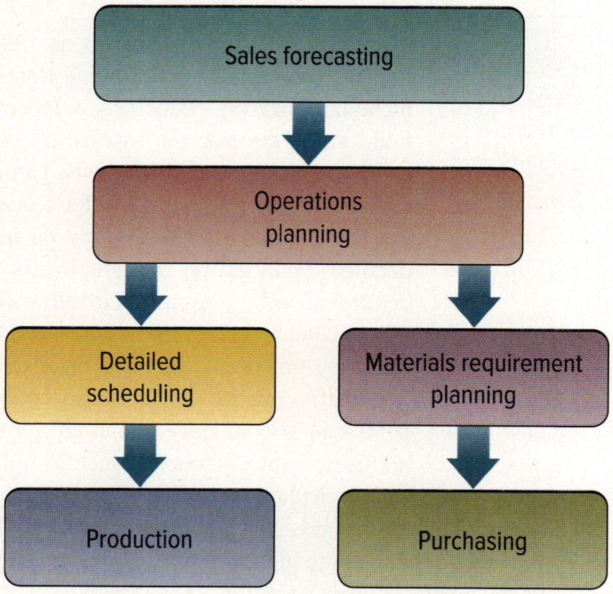

the organization. The four most common extended ERP components are:

1. Business intelligence.
2. Customer relationship management.
3. Supply chain management.
4. Ebusiness.

Business Intelligence ERP Components ERP systems offer powerful tools that measure and control organizational operations. Many organizations have found that these valuable tools can be enhanced to provide even greater value through the addition of powerful business intelligence systems. The business intelligence components of ERP systems typically collect information used throughout the organization (including data used in many other ERP components), organize it, and apply analytical tools to assist managers with decisions. Data warehouses are one of the most popular extensions to ERP systems, with over two-thirds of U.S. manufacturers adopting or planning such systems.

Customer Relationship Management ERP Components ERP vendors are expanding their functionality to provide services formerly supplied by customer relationship management (CRM) vendors such as Siebel. CRM components provide an integrated view of customer data and interactions allowing organizations to work more effectively with customers and be more responsive to their needs. CRM components typically include contact centers, sales force automation, and marketing functions. These improve the customer experience while identifying a company's most (and least) valuable customers for better allocation of resources.

Supply Chain Management ERP Components ERP vendors are expanding their systems to include SCM functions that manage the information flows between and among supply chain stages, maximizing total supply chain effectiveness and profitability. SCM components allow a firm to monitor and control all stages in the supply chain from the acquisition of raw materials to the receipt of finished goods by customers.

Ebusiness ERP Components The original focus of ERP systems was the internal organization. In other words, ERP systems are not fundamentally ready for the external world of ebusiness. The newest and most exciting extended ERP components are the ebusiness components. Two of the primary features of ebusiness components are elogistics and eprocurement. **Elogistics** manages the transportation and storage of goods. **Eprocurement** is the business-to-business (B2B) online purchase and sale of supplies and services. A common mistake many businesses make is jumping into online business without properly integrating the entire organization on the ERP system. One large toy manufacturer announced less than a week before Christmas that it would be unable to fulfill any of its online orders. The company had all the toys in the warehouse, but it could not organize the basic order processing function to get the toys delivered to consumers on time.

Ebusiness and ERP complement each other by allowing companies to establish a web presence and fulfill orders expeditiously. A common mistake made by many businesses is deploying a web presence before the integration of back-office systems or an ERP system. For example, one large toy manufacturer announced less than a week before Christmas that it would be unable to fulfill any of its web orders. The company had all the toys in the warehouse, but it could not organize the basic order processing function to get the toys delivered to the consumers on time.

Customers and suppliers are now demanding access to ERP information including order status, inventory levels, and invoice reconciliation. Plus, the customers and partners want all this information in a simplified format available through a website. This is a difficult task to accomplish because most ERP systems are full of technical jargon, which is why employee training is one of the hidden costs associated with ERP implementations. Removing the jargon to

elogistics Manages the transportation and storage of goods.

eprocurement The business-to-business (B2B) online purchase and sale of supplies and services.

show me *the* MONEY

Classic Cars

Classic Cars Inc. operates high-end automotive dealerships that offer luxury cars along with luxury service. The company is proud of its extensive inventory, top-of-the-line mechanics, and especially its exceptional service, which even includes a cappuccino bar at each dealership.

The company currently has 40 sales representatives at four locations. Each location maintains its own computer systems, and all sales representatives have their own contact management systems. This splintered approach to operations causes numerous problems, including customer communication issues, pricing strategy issues, and inventory control issues. A few examples include:

- A customer shopping at one dealership can go to another dealership and receive a different price quote for the same car.
- Sales representatives are frequently stealing each other's customers and commissions.
- Sales representatives frequently send their customers to other dealerships to see specific cars and when the customer arrives, the car is not on the lot.
- Marketing campaigns are not designed to target specific customers; they are typically generic, such as 10 percent off a new car.
- If a sales representative quits, all of his or her customer information is lost.

You are working for Customer One, a small consulting company that specializes in enterprisewide strategies. The owner of Classic Cars Inc., Tom Felders, has hired you to help him formulate a strategy to put his company back on track. Develop a proposal for Tom, detailing how an ERP system can alleviate the company's issues and create new opportunities.

software customization Modifies software to meet specific user or business requirements.

balanced scorecard A management system, as well as a measurement system, that a firm uses to translate business strategies into executable tasks.

accommodate untrained customers and partners is one of the more difficult tasks when web-enabling an ERP system. To accommodate the growing needs of the ebusiness world, ERP vendors need to build two new channels of access into the ERP system information—one channel for customers (B2C) and one channel for businesses, suppliers, and partners (B2B).

Measuring ERP Success

There is no guarantee of success for an ERP system. It is difficult to measure the success of an ERP system because one system can span an entire organization, including thousands of employees across the globe. ERPs focus on how a corporation operates internally, and optimizing these operations takes significant time and energy.

Two of the primary forces driving ERP failure include software customization and ERP costs. **Software customization** modifies existing software according to the business's or user's requirements. Since ERP systems must fit business processes, many enterprises choose to customize their ERP systems to ensure that they meet business and user needs. Figure 8.37 displays the different forms of software customization a business will undertake to ensure the success of an ERP implementation. Heavy customization leads to complex code that must be continuously maintained and upgraded. It should be noted that customizing an ERP system is costly and complex and should only be done when there is a specific business advantage. According to Meta Group, it takes the average company 8 to 18 months to see any benefits from an ERP system. The primary risk for an ERP implementation includes the associated costs displayed in Figure 8.38.

One of the best methods of measuring ERP success is the balanced scorecard, created by Dr. Robert Kaplan and Dr. David Norton, both from the Harvard Business School. The **balanced scorecard** is a management system, as well as a measurement system, that a firm uses to translate business strategies into executable tasks. It provides feedback for both internal and external business processes, allowing continuous improvement. Kaplan and Norton describe the balanced scorecard as follows: "The balanced scorecard retains traditional financial measures. But financial measures tell the story of past events, an adequate story for industrial age companies for which investments in long-term capabilities and customer relationships were not critical for success. These financial measures are inadequate, however, for guiding and evaluating the journey that information age companies must make to create future value through investment in customers, suppliers, employees, processes, technology, and innovation."[8] The balanced scorecard uses four perspectives to monitor an organization:

1. The learning and growth perspective.
2. The internal business process perspective.
3. The customer perspective.
4. The financial perspective (see Figure 8.39).

LO8.5 Describe enterprise resource planning along with its associated benefits and challenges.

FIGURE 8.37 Software Customization Examples

	Software Customization
Business Processes or Workflows	Software can be customized to support the needs of business process work-flows unique to each business or department.
Code Modifications	The most expensive customization occurs when application code is changed and should only be done if the code changes provide specific competitive advantages.
Integrations	Data integration is key for business process support that spans functional areas and legacy systems.
Reports, Documents, Forms	Customization to reports, documents, and forms can consist of simple layout or design changes or complex logic programming rules for specific business requirements.
User-Interface Changes	An ERP system can be customized to ensure that each user has the most efficient and effective view of the application.

FIGURE 8.38 ERP Costs

	ERP Costs
Software Costs	Purchasing the software can cost millions of dollars for a large enterprise.
Consulting Fees	Hiring external experts to help implement the system correctly can cost millions of dollars.
Process Rework	Redefine processes to ensure that the company is using the most efficient and effective processes.
Customization	If the software package does not meet all of the company's needs, customizing the software may be required.
Integration	Ensuring that all software products, including disparate systems not part of the ERP system, are working together or are integrated.
Testing	Testing that all functionality works correctly along with testing all integrations.
Training	Training all new users and creating the training user manuals.
Data Warehouse Integration and Data Conversions	Moving data from an old system into the new ERP system.

on-premise system Includes a server at a physical location using an internal network for internal access and firewalls for remote users' access.

legacy system An old system that is fast approaching or beyond the end of its useful life within an organization.

cloud computing Stores, manages, and processes data and applications over the Internet rather than on a personal computer or server.

FIGURE 8.39
The Four Primary Perspectives of the Balanced Scorecard

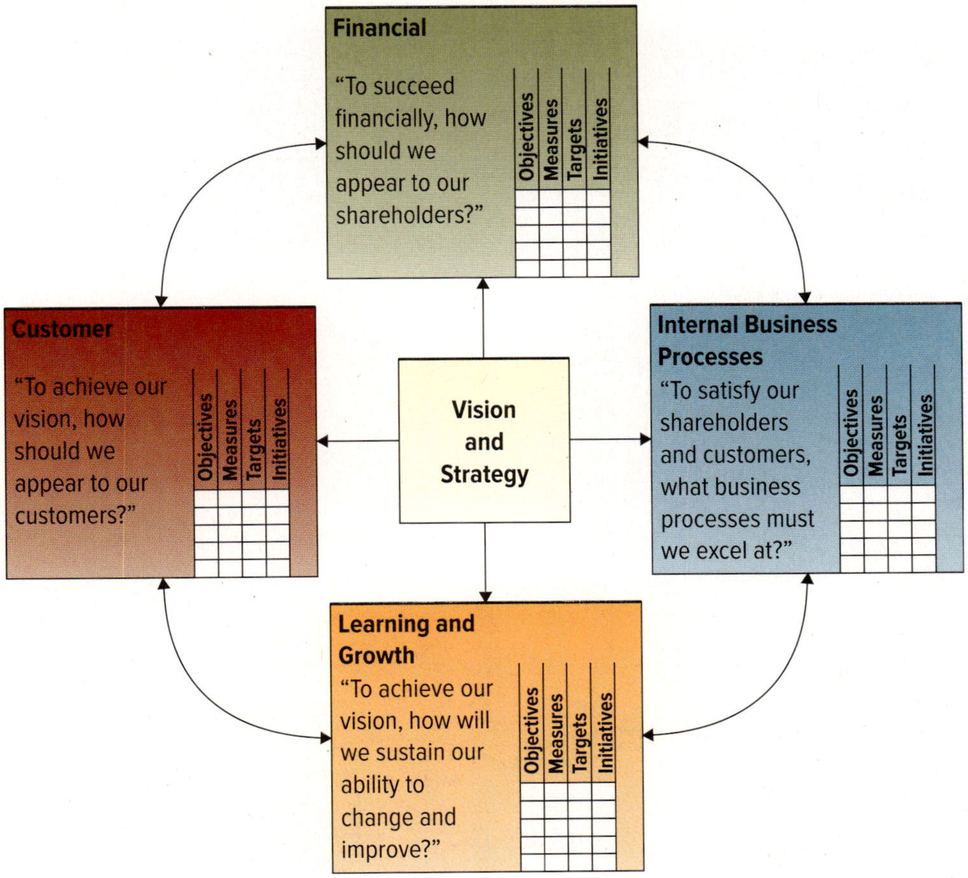

ORGANIZATIONAL INTEGRATION WITH ERP LO8.6

The goal of ERP is to integrate all of the organizational systems into one fully functioning, high-performance system that is capable of meeting all business needs and user requirements. Traditional ERP systems were typically accessed from a computer on the customers' premises or office. Tomorrow's ERP systems will enhance the ability of organizations to apply context to decision making and adapt more easily to changing events. ERP systems in the future will focus on usability, ubiquity, accessibility, and mobility drawing many advantages including:

- Drive cost efficiencies.
- Faster time to market.
- Better enable mobile workforce.
- Better leverage data to provide insights.
- New product development.

Of course, ERP of the future will have many challenges including data management, source record management, and coordinating integrations and support activities. Figure 8.40 displays the three primary ERP implementation choices driving the next generation of business operations.

On-Premise ERP

Until a decade ago, virtually all ERP systems were installed on-premise. **On-premise systems** include a server at a physical location using an internal network for internal access and firewalls for remote users' access. Remote users had to access the ERP system through a firewall, which protected the system against unauthorized access. These systems are known as on-premise systems, and they are still in wide use today. The ERP, SCM, and CRM systems that run on-premise are referred to as legacy systems. **Legacy system** is an old system that is fast approaching or beyond the end of its useful life with in an organization.

Cloud ERP

The cloud has changed the legacy model of ERP implementation. According to the National Institute of Standards and Technology (NIST) **cloud computing** stores, manages, and processes data and applications over the Internet rather than on a personal computer or server. Cloud computing offers new ways to store, access, process, and analyze information and connect people and resources from any location in the world an Internet connection is available. As shown in Figure 8.41, users connect to the cloud from their personal computers or portable devices by using a client, such as a web browser. To these individual users, the cloud appears as their personal application, device, or document. It is like storing all of your software and documents in the cloud, and all you need is a device to access

Software as a Service (SaaS) Delivers applications over the cloud using a pay-per-use revenue model.

hybrid ERP Splits the ERP functions between an on-premises ERP system and one or more functions handled as Software as a Service (SaaS) in the cloud.

FIGURE 8.40 ERP Implementation Choices

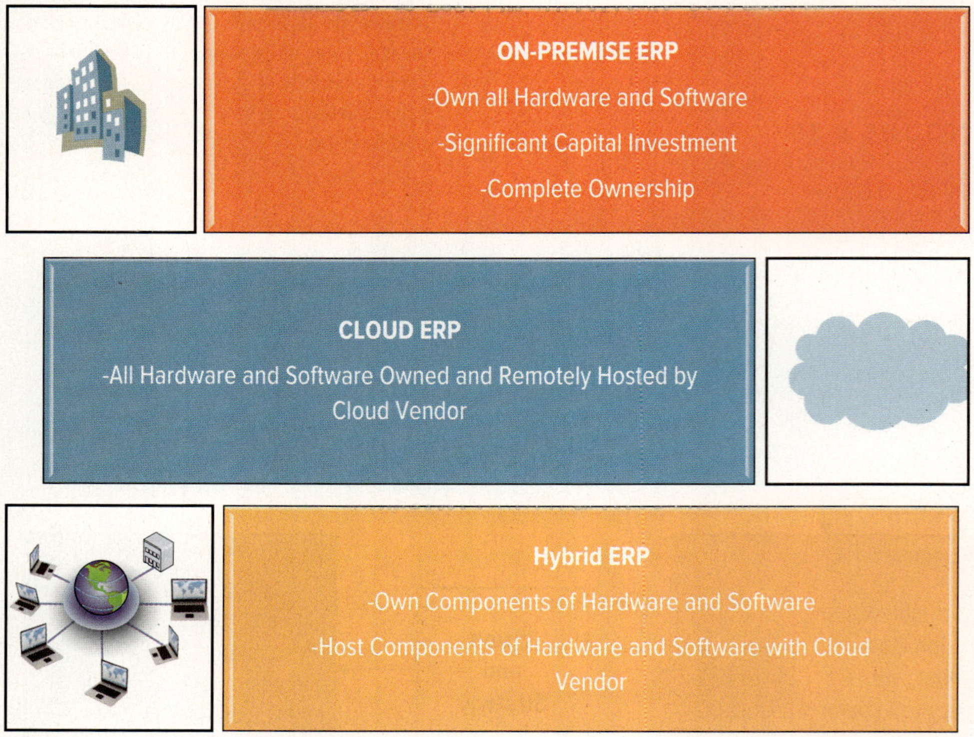

the cloud. No more hard drives, software, or processing power—that is all located in the cloud, transparent to the users. Users are not physically bound to a single computer or network; they can access their programs and documents from wherever they are, whenever they need to. Just think of having your hard drive located in the sky and you can access your information and programs using any device from wherever you are. The best part is that even if your machine crashes, is lost, or is stolen, the information hosted in the cloud is safe and always available.

FIGURE 8.41 Cloud Computing Example.

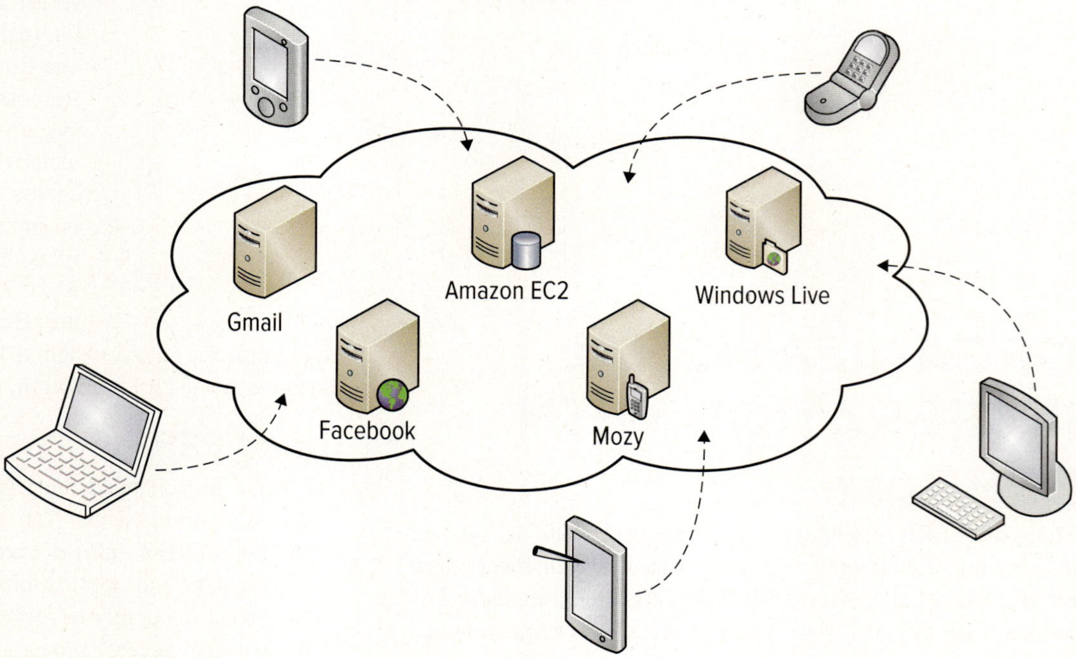

Software as a Service (SaaS) delivers applications over the cloud using a pay-per-use revenue model. Before its introduction, companies often spent huge amounts of money implementing and customizing specialized applications to satisfy their business requirements. Many of these applications were difficult to implement, expensive to maintain, and challenging to use. Usability was one of the biggest drivers for creating interest in and success for cloud computing service providers. SaaS ERP uses the cloud platform to enable organizations not only to unite around business processes, but also to gather cloud data across supplier networks and supply chains to drive greater efficiency in manufacturing projects. The move to SaaS ERP is attracting many small and midsized businesses that simply cannot afford the costs associated with a traditional large ERP implementation.

SaaS offers a number of advantages; the most obvious is tremendous cost savings. The software is priced on a per-use basis with no up-front costs, so companies get the immediate benefit of reducing capital expenditures. They also get the added benefits of scalability and flexibility to test new software on a rental basis. Figure 8.42 displays the many advantages of SaaS implementations.

Cloud ERP has been slow to take off across business because many people were initially uncomfortable with placing sensitive data in the cloud. As the tremendous cost-saving advantages associated with cloud applications and SaaS become more apparent, the reservations against cloud ERP are dissipating.

Large organizations tend to have difficulty adjusting to cloud solutions simply because they want greater levels of control over their enterprise applications. Smaller, less complex organizations that lack sophisticated MIS departments are more likely to gravitate toward the cloud because it is easy for them to change business processes to fit the software. SaaS ERP can provide a company with the flexibility of on-premise software and the added benefits of a vendor maintaining and housing the applications off the premises. The biggest concerns for organizations interested in cloud ERP solutions is data security and potential vendor outages causing business downtime. Without an on-premises MIS department, the organization is truly at the mercy of the vendor during any system outage, and for critical organizational systems like ERP, this could be an unacceptable risk.

Hybrid ERP

It is conventional wisdom that a diversified stock portfolio is a very effective hedge against investment risk. For the same reason, companies that are not comfortable with the risk and/or loss of control associated with moving wholesale into ERP cloud computing, but still want to explore this evolving infrastructure, might find a hybrid ERP approach to be the perfect answer. By "hybrid ERP approach," we mean mostly on site, but with some carefully selected hosted applications.

Building an all-encompassing ERP system traditionally ended in expensive failures. Nike, K-Mart, and Hershey all lost over $100 million in failed ERP implementations. Based on the need to avoid expensive failures along with the emergence of cloud computing, enterprises can now adopt hybrid ERP architectures. The idea behind **hybrid ERP** is to split the ERP functions between an on-premises ERP system and one or more functions handled as Software as a Service (SaaS) in the cloud. Typically the on-premise legacy application operates at the corporate headquarters, whereas cloud-based specific applications support business needs such as mobility and web-based functionality. It is also becoming increasingly popular. In fact many analysts are predicting that hybrid ERP will become a mainstay in the ERP market in the next few years.

Often a hybrid ERP system is implemented when the legacy system becomes very large and costly to customize, maintain, and upgrade or when mergers and acquisitions leave an organization with multiple ERP solutions that it is unable to consolidate to a single ERP system. Hybrid ERP architectures also support organizations with multiple operations based in multiple geographic locations. The following scenarios are common in organizations that use hybrid architectures of ERP:

- A business with a very specific local focus—single-site or multisite within a single country or region.
- A business with operations geared strongly toward a specific industry that doesn't feature strongly at corporate headquarters.

FIGURE 8.42 Advantages of SaaS Implementations

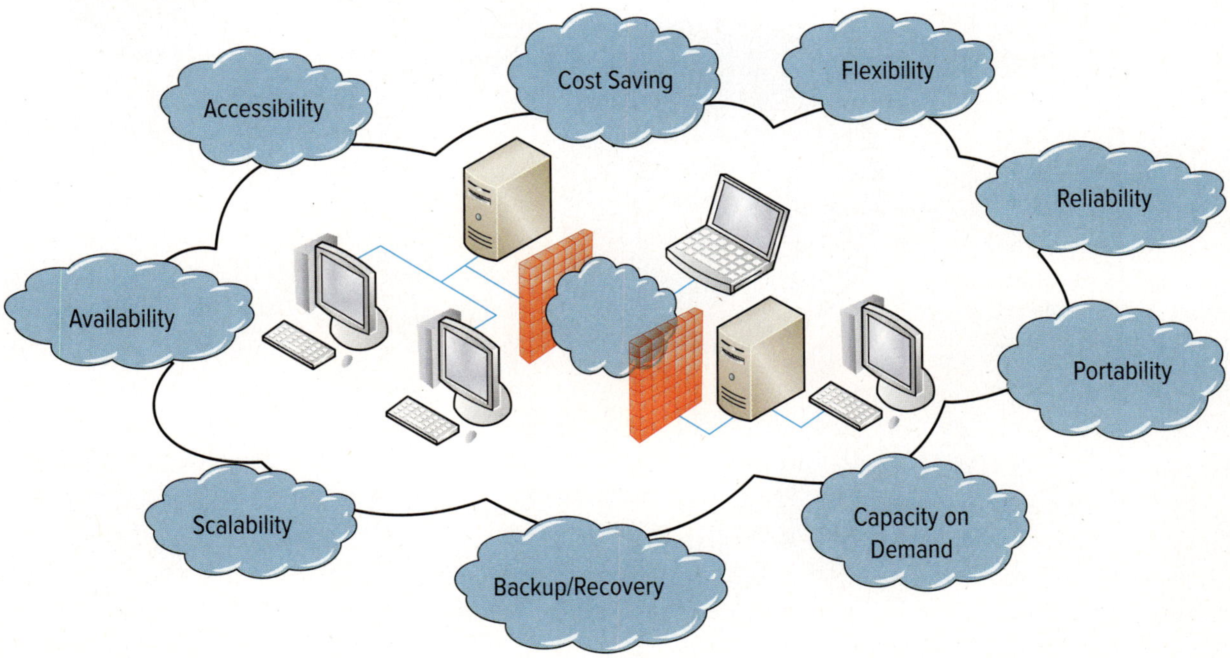

- A newly acquired operation with a mismatch of multiple outdated, unsupported ERPs.
- A small subsidiary with no formal ERP in place.

Managing the data across the enterprise is one of the biggest concerns for organizations deploying hybrid ERP architectures. It is critical for the business to have absolutely no duplication of effort between the two ERP systems. Consistency is required for any hybrid application to ensure that there is always a single source of information for accounting, financials, customer service, production, and other business areas. Hundreds of ERP vendors offer best-of-breed ERP applications or vertical market solutions to meet the unique requirements of specific industries such as manufacturing, distribution, retail, and others. Figure 8.43 displays an overview of ERP vendors by business size. Figure 8.44 displays the important factors driving the future of ERP.

LO8.6 Discuss the current technologies organizations are integrating in enterprise resource planning systems.

FIGURE 8.43 ERP Vendors by Tier

ERP VENDORS BY TIER		
	Enterprise Size	**ERP Vendor**
Tier I	Large Enterprise	• SAP • Oracle • Microsoft
Tier II	Midsize Business	• Infor • Lawson • Epicor • Sage
Tier III	Small Business	• Exact Globe • Syspro • NetSuite • Consona

FIGURE 8.44 Organizational Integration of ERP

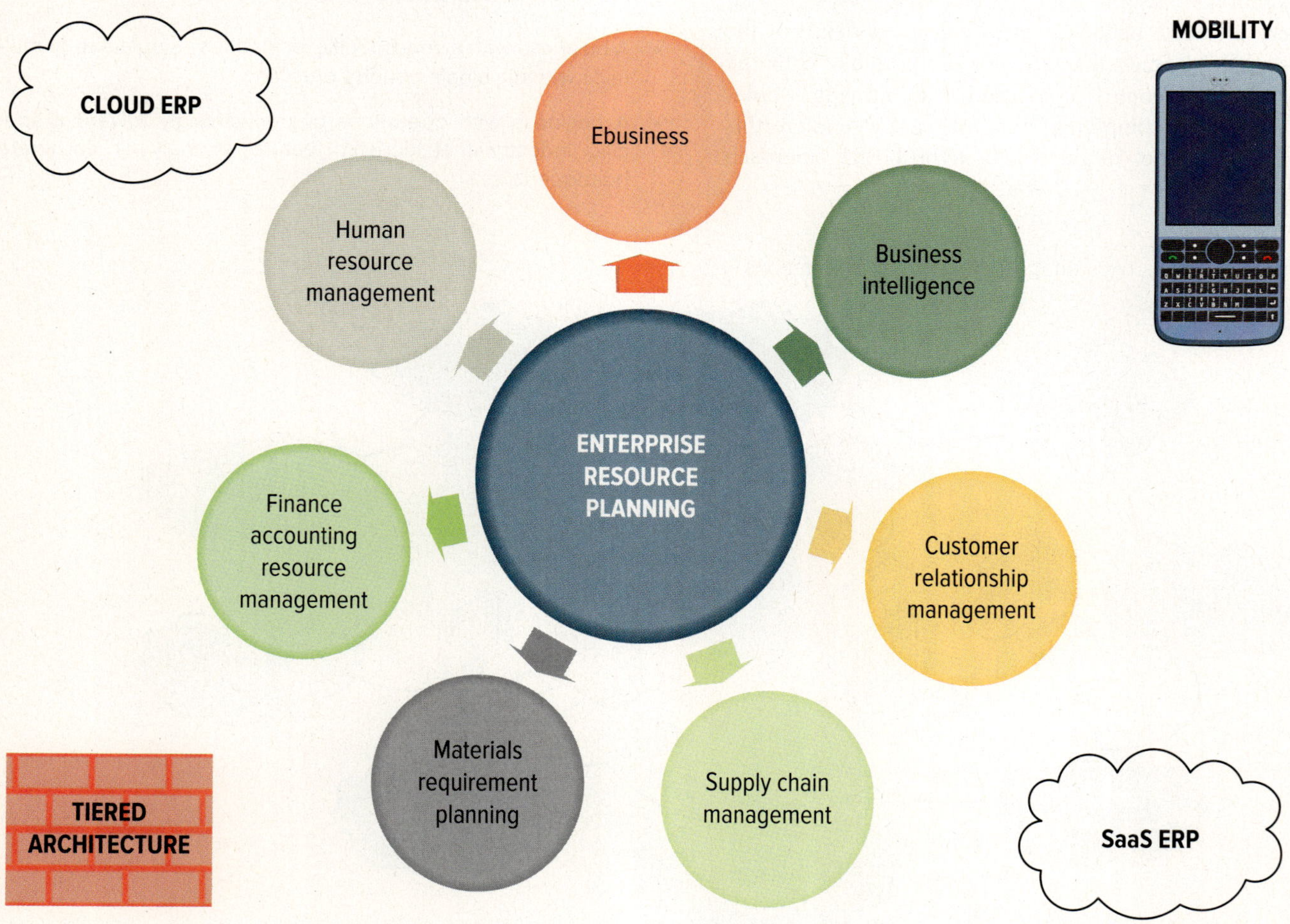

fyi Bean Integration

At Flavors, a premium coffee shop, customers receive more than just a great cup of coffee—they receive exposure to music, art, literature, and town events. Flavors' calendar for programs gives customers a quick view into this corner of the world—from live music and art displays to volunteering or a coffee tasting. Flavors offers the following:

- Music center: Information is available for all live music events occurring in the area. The store also hosts an open microphone two nights a week for local musicians.
- Art gallery: A space in the store is filled with great pieces from local artists.
- Book clubs: Customers can meet to discuss current and classic literature.
- Coffee sampler: Customers can sample coffees from around the world with the experts.
- Community events: Weekly meetings are held, where customers can find ways to become more involved in their community.
- Brewing courses: The finer details of the brewing, grinding, and blending equipment for sale in Flavors stores—from the traditional press to a digital espresso machine—are taught. There is also a trouble-shooting guide developed by brewing specialists.

Flavors' sales are great and profits are soaring; however, current operations need an overhaul. The owners of Flavors, J. P. Field and Marla Lily, built the business piece by piece over the past 12 years. The following offers a quick look at current operations.

- Flavors does not receive any information on how many of its customers attend live music events. Musicians typically maintain a fan email listing and CD sales records for the event; however, this information is not always provided to the store.
- Book club events are booked and run through the local bookstore, Pages Up. Pages Up runs a tab during the book club and provides Flavors with a check at the end of each month for all book club events. Flavors has no access to book club customer information or sales information.
- The artist gallery is run by several local artists who pay Flavors a small commission on each sale. Flavors has no input into the art contained in the store or information on customers who purchase art.
- Coffee sampler events are run through Flavors' primary operations.
- Community event information is open to all members of the community. Each event is run by a separate organization, which provides monthly event feedback to Flavors in a variety of formats from Word to Access files.
- Brewing and machine resource courses are run by the equipment manufacturer, and all customer and sales information is provided to Flavors in a Word document at the end of each year.

You have been hired as an integration expert by Flavors. The owners want to revamp the way the company operates so it can take advantage of marketing and sales opportunities across its many different lines of business, such as offering customers who attend book club events discounts on art and brewing and machine resource courses. They also want to gain a better understanding of how the different events affect sales. For example, should they have more open microphone nights or more book clubs? Currently, they have no way to tell which events result in higher sales. Create an integration strategy so Flavors can take advantage of CRM, SCM, and ERP across the company.

© Ingram Publishing/Superstock RF

© Paul Taylor/Getty Images

chapter nine

systems development and project management: corporate responsibility

What's in IT for me?

This chapter provides an overview of how organizations build information systems. As a business student, you need to understand this process because information systems are the underlying foundations of company operations. Your understanding of the principles of building information systems will make you a more valuable employee. You will be able to identify trouble spots early and make suggestions during the design process that will result in a better information systems project—one that satisfies both you and your business.

Building an information system is like constructing a house. You could sit back

continued on p. 250

legacy system An old system that is fast approaching or beyond the end of its useful life within an organization.

conversion The process of transferring information from a legacy system to a new system.

software customization Modifies software to meet specific user or business requirements.

off-the-shelf application software Supports general business processes and does not require any specific software customization to meet the organization's needs.

continued from p. 249

and let the developers do all the design work, construction, and testing and hope the finished product will satisfy your needs. However, participating in the process helps to guarantee that your needs are not only heard, but also met. It is good business practice to have direct user input steering the development of the finished product. Your knowledge of the systems development process will allow you to participate and ensure you are building flexible enterprise architectures that support not only current business needs, but also future ones. ■

{SECTION 9.1} Developing Enterprise Applications

LEARNING OUTCOMES

LO9.1 Describe the seven phases of the systems development life cycle.

LO9.2 Summarize the different software development methodologies.

LO9.3 Explain why a company would implement a service-oriented architecture.

THE SYSTEMS DEVELOPMENT LIFE CYCLE (SDLC) LO9.1

The multimillion-dollar Nike SCM system failure is legendary as Nike CEO Philip Knight famously stated, "This is what we get for our $400 million?" Nike partnered with i2 to implement an SCM system that never came to fruition. i2 blamed the failed implementation on the fact that Nike failed to use the vendor's implementation methodology and templates. Nike blamed the failure on faulty software.[1]

It is difficult to get an organization to work if its systems do not work. In the information age, software success, or failure, can lead directly to business success, or failure. Companies rely on software to drive business operations and ensure work flows throughout the company. As more and more companies rely on software to operate, so do the business-related consequences of software successes and failures.

The potential advantages of successful software implementations provide firms with significant incentives to manage software development risks. However, an alarmingly high number of software development projects come in late or over budget, and successful projects tend to maintain fewer features and functions than originally specified. Understanding the basics of software development, or the systems development life cycle, will help organizations avoid potential software development pitfalls and ensure that software development efforts are successful.

Before jumping into software development, it is important to understand a few key terms. A **legacy system** is an old system that is fast approaching or beyond the end of its useful life within an organization. **Conversion** is the process of transferring information from a legacy system to a new system. **Software customization** modifies software to meet specific user or business requirements. **Off-the-shelf application software** supports general business processes and does not require any specific software customization to meet the organization's needs.

The **systems development life cycle (SDLC)** is the overall process for developing information systems, from planning and analysis through implementation and maintenance. The SDLC is the foundation for all systems development methods, and hundreds of different activities are associated with each phase. These activities typically include determining budgets, gathering system requirements, and writing detailed user documentation.

The SDLC begins with a business need, proceeds to an assessment of the functions a system must have to satisfy the need, and ends when the benefits of the system no longer outweigh its maintenance costs. This is why it is referred to as a life cycle. The SDLC is comprised of seven distinct phases: planning, analysis, design, development, testing, implementation, and maintenance (see Figure 9.1).

LO9.1 Describe the seven phases of the systems development life cycle.

Phase 1: Planning

The **planning phase** establishes a high-level plan of the intended project and determines project goals. Planning is the first and most critical phase of any systems development effort, regardless of whether the effort is to develop a system that allows customers to order products online, determine

FIGURE 9.1
The SDLC and Its Associated Activities

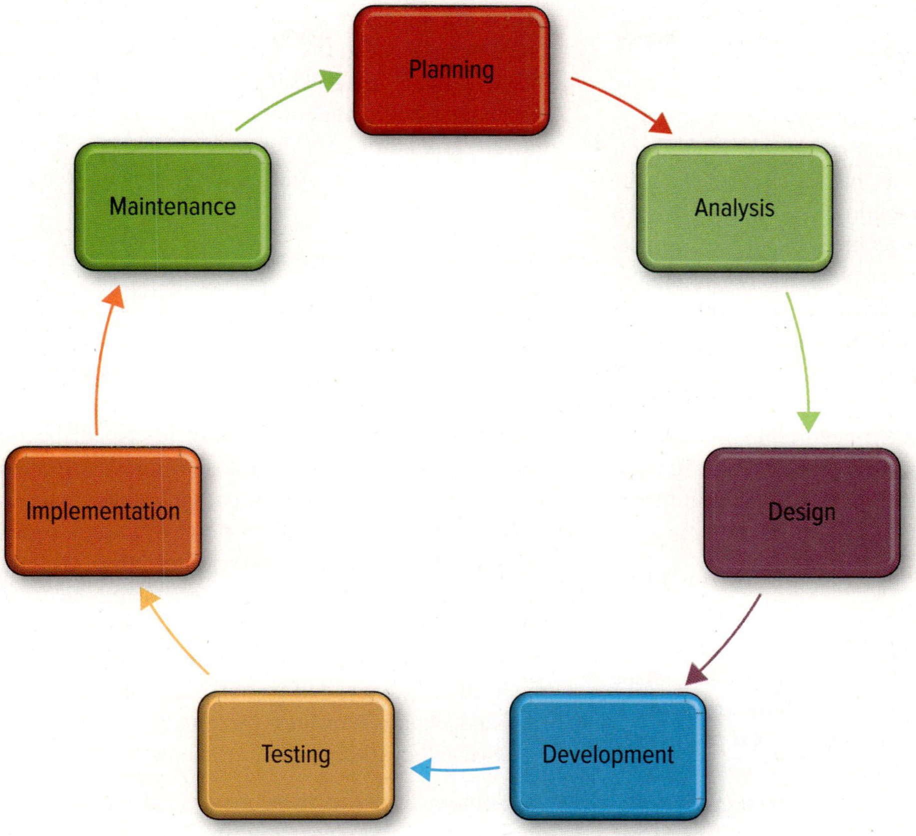

Phase	Associated Activity
Planning	■ Brainstorm issues and identify opportunities for the organization
	■ Prioritize and choose projects for development
	■ Set the project scope
	■ Develop the project plan
Analysis	■ Gather the business requirement for the system
	■ Define any constraints associated with the system
Design	■ Design the technical architecture required to support the system
	■ Design the system models
Development	■ Build the technical architecture
	■ Build the database
	■ Build the applications
Testing	■ Write the test conditions
	■ Perform system testing
Implementation	■ Write detailed user documentation
	■ Provide training for the system users
Maintenance	■ Build a help desk to support the system users
	■ Provide an environment to support system changes

systems development life cycle (SDLC) The overall process for developing information systems, from planning and analysis through implementation and maintenance.

planning phase Establishes a high-level plan of the intended project and determines project goals.

change agent A person or event that is the catalyst for implementing major changes for a system to meet business changes.

brainstorming A technique for generating ideas by encouraging participants to offer as many ideas as possible in a short period of time without any analysis until all the ideas have been exhausted.

project Temporary activity a company undertakes to create a unique product, service, or result.

project management The application of knowledge, skills, tools, and techniques to project activities to meet project requirements.

project manager An individual who is an expert in project planning and management, defines and develops the project plan, and tracks the plan to ensure the project is completed on time and on budget.

project scope Describes the business needs and the justification, requirements, and current boundaries for the project.

project plan A formal, approved document that manages and controls project execution.

analysis phase The firm analyzes its end-user business requirements and refines project goals into defined functions and operations of the intended system.

business requirement The specific business requests the system must meet to be successful.

the best logistical structure for warehouses around the world, or develop a strategic information alliance with another organization. Organizations must carefully plan the activities (and determine why they are necessary) to be successful. A **change agent** is a person or event that is the catalyst for implementing major changes for a system to meet business changes. **Brainstorming** is a technique for generating ideas by encouraging participants to offer as many ideas as possible in a short period without any analysis until all the ideas have been exhausted. Many times, new business opportunities are found as the result of a brainstorming session.

The Project Management Institute (PMI) develops procedures and concepts necessary to support the profession of project management (www.pmi.org). PMI defines a **project** as a temporary activity a company undertakes to create a unique product, service, or result. **Project management** is the application of knowledge, skills, tools, and techniques to project activities to meet project requirements. A **project manager** is an individual who is an expert in project planning and management, defines and develops the project plan, and tracks the plan to ensure the project is completed on time and on budget. The project manager is the person responsible for executing the entire project and defining the project scope that links the project to the organization's overall business goals. The **project scope** describes the business need (the problem the project will solve) and the justification, requirements, and current boundaries for the project. The **project plan** is a formal, approved document that manages and controls the entire project.

Phase 2: Analysis

In the **analysis phase** the firm analyzes its end-user business requirements and refines project goals into defined functions and operations of the intended system. **Business requirements** are the specific business requests the system must meet to be successful, so the analysis phase is critical because business requirements drive the entire systems development effort. A sample business requirement might state, "The CRM system must track all customer inquiries by product, region, and sales representative." The business requirement will state what the system must accomplish to be considered successful. If a system does not meet the business requirements, it will be deemed a failed project. For this reason, the organization must spend as much time, energy, and resources as necessary to gather accurate and detailed business requirements. (Figure 9.2 displays ways to gather business requirements.)

Requirements management is the process of managing changes to the business requirements throughout the project. Projects are typically dynamic in nature, and change should be expected and anticipated for successful project completion. A **requirements definition document** prioritizes all of the business requirements by order of importance to the company. **Sign-off** is the users' actual signatures indicating they approve all of the business requirements.

fyi

Have You Met Ted? If Not, You Need To![2]

You'll remember this day because it is the day you were introduced to Ted (www.ted.com). Ted, a small nonprofit started in 1984, is devoted to Ideas Worth Spreading, an annual conference focused around three worlds: Technology, Entertainment, and Design. Ted brings together the world's most fascinating thinkers and doers, who are challenged to give the talk of their lives in 18 minutes. Each talk is videotaped and posted to the Ted website including such famous speakers as:

- Chris Anderson: editor of Wired and author of *Technology's Long Tail.*
- Tim Berners-Lee: inventor of the World Wide Web.
- Jeff Bezos: founder of Amazon.com.
- Richard Branson: founder of Virgin.
- Bill Clinton: former President of the United States.
- Peter Diamandis: runs the X Prize Foundation.
- Sergey Brin and Larry Page: co-founders of Google.
- Malcolm Gladwell: author of *Blink* and *The Tipping Point.*
- Bill Gates: founder of Microsoft.
- Seth Godin: marketing guru.
- Steven Levitt: *Freakanomics* author.

How can you use Ted to find innovation in the business environment?

FIGURE 9.2 Methods for Gathering Business Requirements

Methods for Gathering Business Requirements
Perform a **joint application development (JAD)** session where employees meet, sometimes for several days, to define or review the business requirements for the system.
Interview individuals to determine current operations and current issues.
Compile questionnaires to survey employees to discover issues.
Make observations to determine how current operations are performed.
Review business documents to discover reports, policies, and how information is used throughout the organization.

Once a business analyst takes a detailed look at how an organization performs its work and its processes, the analyst can recommend ways to improve these processes to make them more efficient and effective. **Process modeling** involves graphically representing the processes that capture, manipulate, store, and distribute information between a system and its environment. One of the most common diagrams used in process modeling is the data flow diagram. A **data flow diagram (DFD)** illustrates the movement of information between external entities and the processes and data stores within the system (see Figure 9.3). Process models and data flow diagrams establish the specifications of the system. **Computer-aided software engineering (CASE)** tools are software suites that automate systems analysis, design, and development. Process models and data flow diagrams can provide the basis for the automatic generation of the system if they are developed using a CASE tool.

FIGURE 9.3 Sample Data Flow Diagram

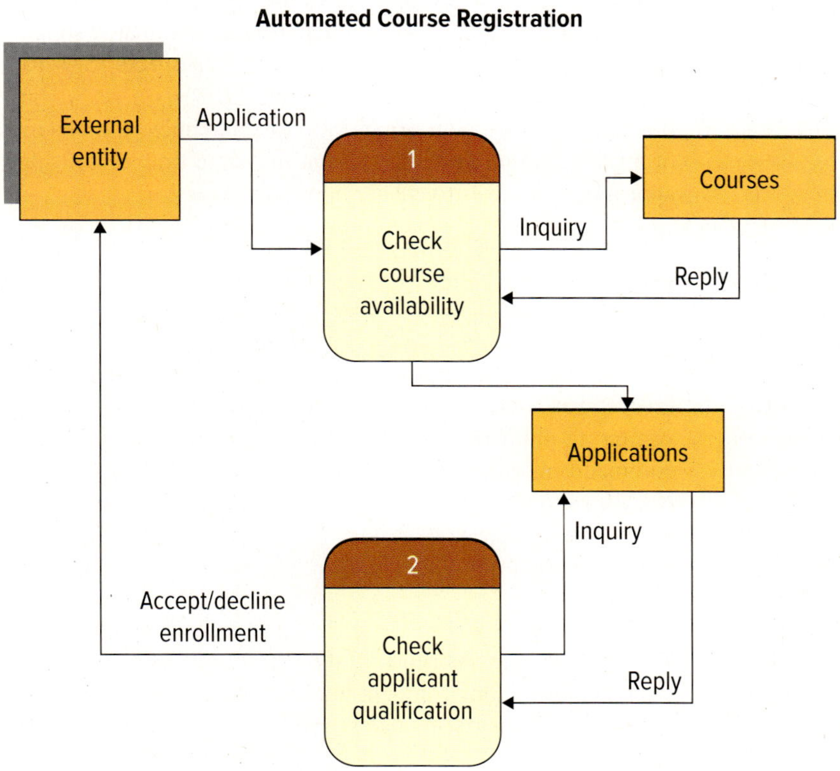

Phase 3: Design

The **design phase** establishes descriptions of the desired features and operations of the system, including screen layouts, business rules, process diagrams, pseudo code, and other documentation. During the analysis phase, end users and MIS specialists work together to gather the detailed business requirements for the proposed project from a logical point of view. That is, during analysis, business requirements are documented without respect to technology or the technical infrastructure that will support the system. Moving into the design phase turns the project focus to the physical or technical point of view, defining the technical architecture that will support the system, including data models, screen designs, report layouts, and database models (see Figure 9.4).

The graphical user interface (GUI) is the interface to an information system. GUI screen design is the ability to model the information system screens for an entire system by using icons, buttons, menus, and submenus. Data models represent a formal way to express data relationships to a database

joint application development (JAD) A session where employees meet, sometimes for several days, to define or review the business requirements for the system.

requirements management The process of managing changes to the business requirements throughout the project.

requirements definition document Prioritizes all of the business requirements by order of importance to the company.

sign-off Users' actual signatures, indicating they approve all of the business requirements.

data flow diagram Illustrates the movement of information between external entities and the processes and data stores within the system.

computer-aided software engineering (CASE) Software tools provide automated support for the development of the system.

design phase Establishes descriptions of the desired features and operations of the system including screen layouts, business rules, process diagrams, pseudo code, and other documentation.

development phase Takes all the detailed design documents from the design phase and transforms them into the actual system.

software engineering A disciplined approach for constructing information systems through the use of common methods, techniques, or tools.

computer-aided software engineering (CASE) Software tools provide automated support for the development of the system.

control objects for information and related technologies (COBIT) A set of best practices that helps an organization to maximize the benefits of an information system, while at the same time establishing appropriate controls to ensure minimum errors.

scripting language A programming method that provides for interactive modules to a website.

object-oriented language Languages group data and corresponding processes into objects.

fourth-generation languages (4GL) Programming languages that look similar to human languages.

FIGURE 9.4 Sample Technical Architecture

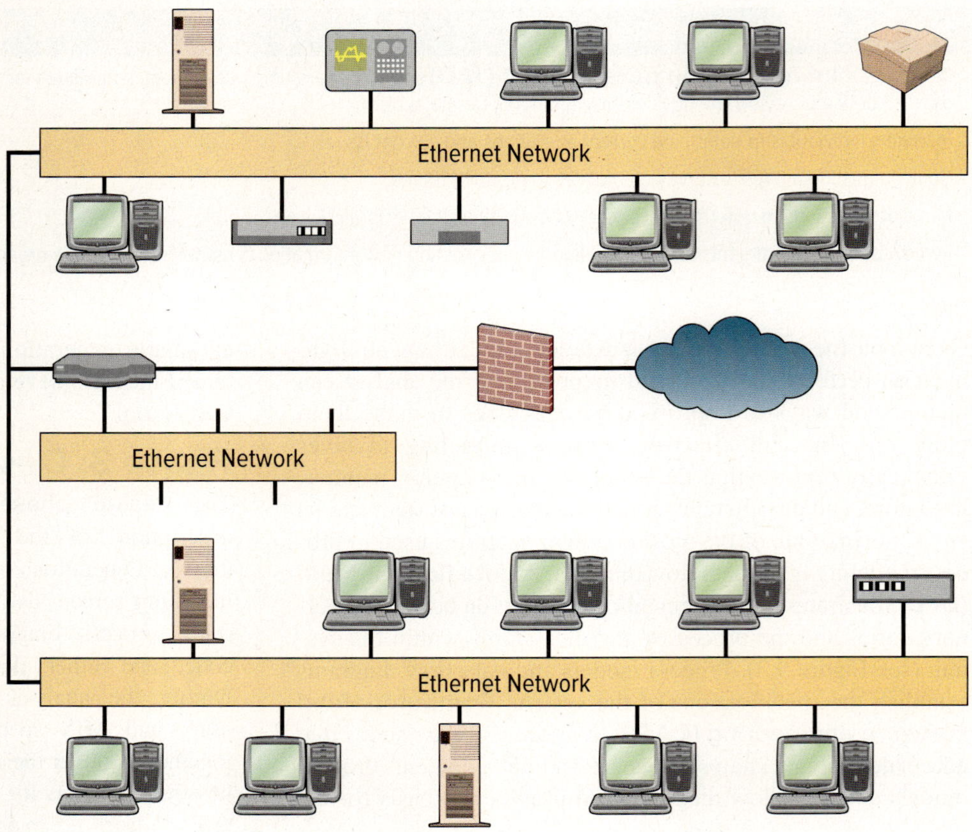

management system (DBMS). Entity relationship diagrams document the relationships between entities in a database environment (see Figure 9.5).

Phase 4: Development

The **development phase** takes all the detailed design documents from the design phase and transforms them into the actual system. In this phase, the project transitions from preliminary designs to actual physical implementation. During development, the company purchases and implements the equipment necessary to support the architecture. **Software engineering** is a disciplined approach for constructing information systems through the use of common methods, techniques, or tools. Software engineers use **computer-aided software engineering (CASE)** tools, which provide automated support for the development of the system. **Control objects for information and related technology (COBIT)** is a set of best practices that helps an organization to maximize the benefits of an information system, while at the same time establishing appropriate controls to ensure minimum errors.

During development, the team defines the programming language it will use to build the system. A **scripting language** is a programming method that provides for interactive modules to a website. **Object-oriented languages** group data and corresponding processes into objects. **Fourth-generation languages (4GL)** are programming languages that look similar to human languages. For example, a typical 4GL command might state, "FIND ALL RECORDS WHERE NAME IS "SMITH"." Programming languages are displayed in Figure 9.6.

Phase 5: Testing

The **testing phase** brings all the project pieces together into a special testing environment to eliminate errors and bugs and verify that the system meets all the business requirements

testing phase Brings all the project pieces together into a special testing environment to eliminate errors and bugs and verify that the system meets all the business requirements defined in the analysis phase.

bugs Defects in the code of an information system.

test condition Details the steps the system must perform along with the expected result of each step.

FIGURE 9.5 Sample Entity Relationship Diagram

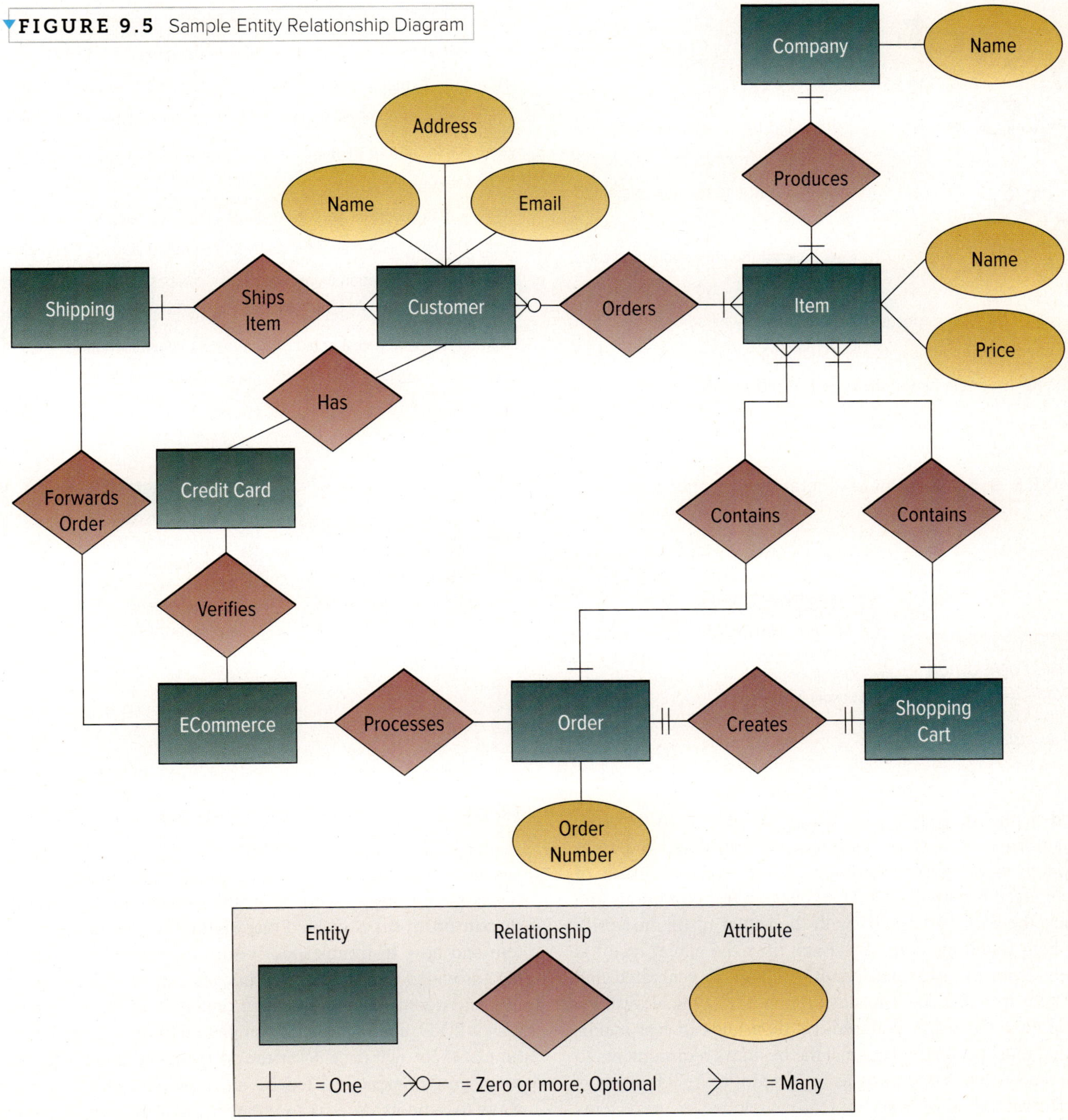

implementation phase The organization places the system into production so users can begin to perform actual business operations with it.

user documentation Highlights how to use the system and how to troubleshoot issues or problems.

online training Runs over the Internet or on a CD or DVD, and employees complete the training on their own time at their own pace.

workshop training Held in a classroom environment and led by an instructor.

help desk A group of people who respond to users' questions.

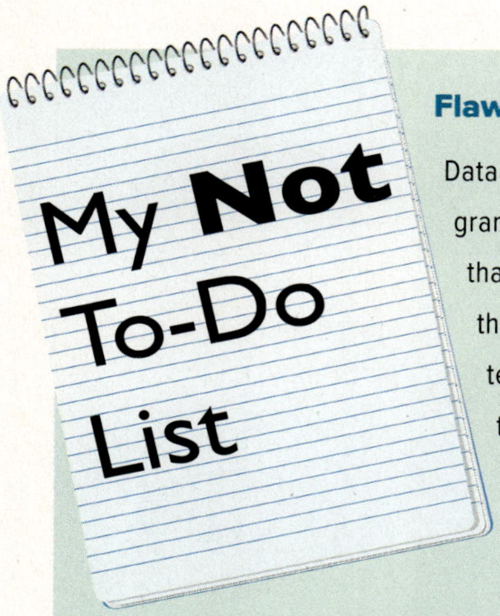

Flawed Development

Data must be secure! A computer programming course would teach you that security is a critical component that must be included in every system. Apparently, the employees that developed the new system for the state of Oklahoma were out sick during this important class. The new system mistakenly posted confidential data, including Social Security numbers, for thousands of Oklahoma residents on the state's website. The really unfortunate part of this systems blunder is that the error went unnoticed for more than three years. A programmer found the error when he realized that by changing his web browser he could redirect his page to the entire database for the state of Oklahoma. To make matters even worse, due to development issues, a hacker could have easily changed all the data in the database or added false data to elements such as the state's Sexual and Violent Offender Registry.

Why is it important to secure data? What can happen if someone accesses your customer database? What could happen if someone changes the information in your customer database and adds fictitious data? What phases in the systems development life cycle should have found these errors? How could these errors go unnoticed for over three years? Who should be held responsible for the system issues?

FIGURE 9.6 Overview of Programming Languages

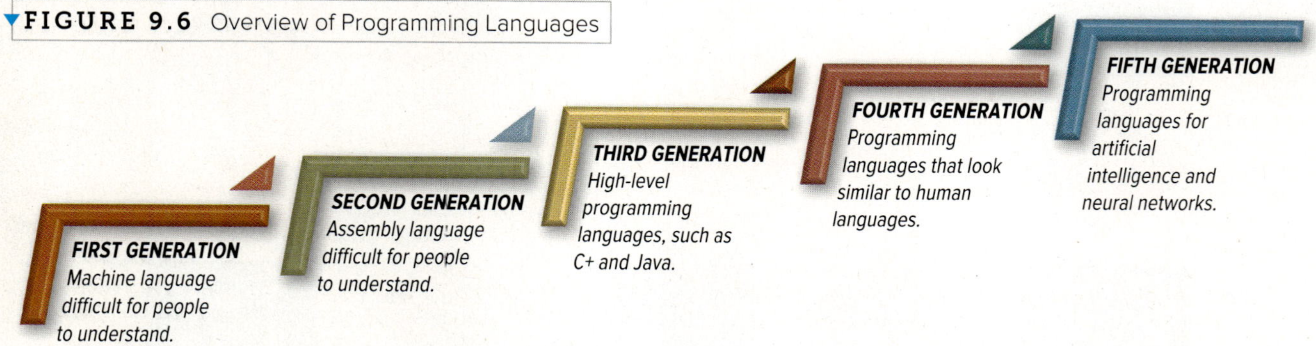

defined in the analysis phase. **Bugs** are defects in the code of an information system. **Test conditions** detail the steps the system must perform along with the expected result of each step (see Figure 9.7). Testers execute test conditions and compare the expected results with the actual results to verify the system functions correctly. Each time the actual result is different from the expected result, a "bug" is generated and the system must be fixed in development. A typical systems development effort has hundreds or thousands of test conditions that must be verified against the business requirements to ensure the system is operating as expected. Figure 9.8 displays the different types of tests typically included in a systems development effort.

Phase 6: Implementation

In the **implementation phase**, the organization places the system into production so users can begin to perform actual business operations with it. In this phase, the detailed **user documentation** is created that highlights how to use the system and how to troubleshoot issues or problems. Training is also provided for the system users and can take place online or in a classroom. **Online training** runs over the Internet or on a CD or DVD, and employees complete the training on their own time at their own pace. **Workshop training** is held in a classroom environment and led by an instructor. One of the best ways to support users is to create a **help desk** or a group of people who respond to users' questions. Figure 9.9 displays the

fyi Reducing Ambiguity in Business Requirements

The number one reason projects fail is because of bad business requirements. Business requirements are considered "bad" because of ambiguity or insufficient involvement of end users during analysis and design. A requirement is unambiguous if it has the same interpretation for all parties. Different interpretations by different participants will usually result in unmet expectations. Here is an example of an ambiguous requirement and an example of an unambiguous requirement:

- **Ambiguous requirement:** The financial report must show profits in local and U.S. currencies.
- **Unambiguous requirement:** The financial report must show profits in local and U.S. currencies using the exchange rate printed in *The Wall Street Journal* for the last business day of the period being reported.

Ambiguity is impossible to prevent completely because it is introduced into requirements in natural ways. For example:

- Requirements can contain technical implications that are obvious to the IT developers but not to the customers.
- Requirements can contain business implications that are obvious to the customer but not to the IT developers.
- Requirements may contain everyday words whose meanings are "obvious" to everyone, yet different for everyone.
- Requirements are reflections of detailed explanations that may have included multiple events, multiple perspectives, verbal rephrasing, emotion, iterative refinement, selective emphasis, and body language—none of which are captured in the written statements.

© DCPhoto/Alamy RF

You have been hired to build an employee payroll system for a new coffee shop. Review the following business requirements, and highlight any potential issues.

- All employees must have a unique employee ID.
- The system must track employee hours worked based on the employee's last name.
- Employees must be scheduled to work a minimum of eight hours per day.
- Employee payroll is calculated by multiplying the employee's hours worked by $7.25.
- Managers must be scheduled to work morning shifts.
- Employees cannot be scheduled to work more than eight hours per day.
- Servers cannot be scheduled to work morning, afternoon, or evening shifts.
- The system must allow managers to change and delete employees from the system.

FIGURE 9.7 Sample Test Conditions

Test Condition Number	Date Tested	Tested	Test Condition	Expected Result	Actual Result	Pass/Fail
1	1/1/09	Emily Hickman	Click system Start button	Main menu appears	Same as expected result	Pass
2	1/1/09	Emily Hickman	Click Logon button in main menu	Logon screen appears asking for user name and password	Same as expected result	Pass
3	1/1/09	Emily Hickman	Type Emily Hickman in the user name field	Emily Hickman appears in the user name field	Same as expected result	Pass
4	1/1/09	Emily Hickman	Type Zahara 123 in the password field	XXXXXXXXX appears in the password field	Same as expected result	Pass
5	1/1/09	Emily Hickman	Click OK button	User logon request is sent to database and user name and password are verified	Same as expected result	Pass
6	1/1/09	Emily Hickman	Click Start	User name and password are accepted and the system main menu appears	Screen appeared stating logon failed and user name and password were incorrect	Fail

maintenance phase The organization performs changes, corrections, additions, and upgrades to ensure the system continues to meet its business goals.

corrective maintenance Makes system changes to repair design flaws, coding errors, or implementation issues.

preventive maintenance Makes system changes to reduce the chance of future system failure.

FIGURE 9.8 Different Forms of System Testing

FIGURE 9.9 System Implementation Methods

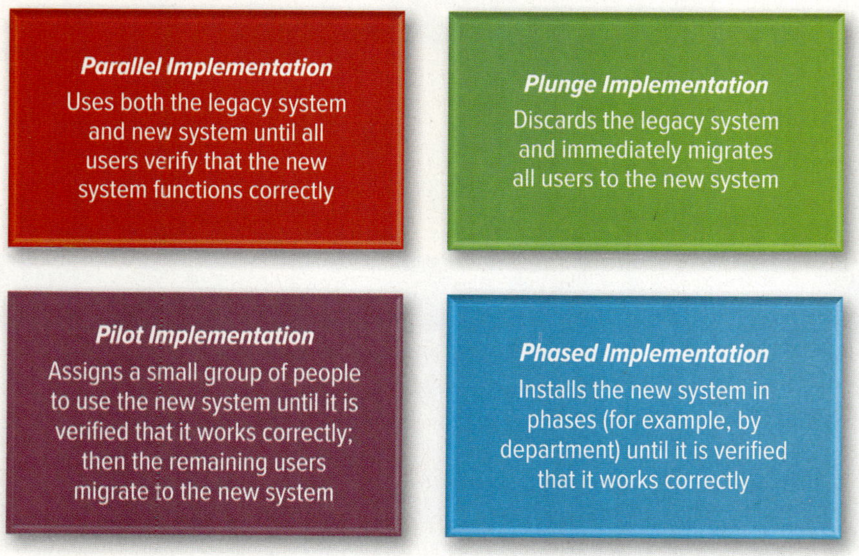

different implementation methods an organization can choose to ensure success.

Phase 7: Maintenance

Maintaining the system is the final sequential phase of any systems development effort. In the **maintenance phase**, the organization performs changes, corrections, additions, and upgrades to ensure the system continues to meet business goals. This phase continues for the life of the system because the system must change as the business evolves and its needs change, which means conducting constant monitoring, supporting the new system with frequent minor changes (for

methodology A set of policies, procedures, standards, processes, practices, tools, techniques, and tasks that people apply to technical and management challenges.

waterfall methodology A sequence of phases in which the output of each phase becomes the input for the next.

prototyping A modern design approach where the designers and system users use an iterative approach to building the system.

FIGURE 9.10 Examples of System Reports

Report	Examples
Internal report	Presents data that are distributed inside the organization and intended for employees within an organization. Internal reports typically support day-to-day operations monitoring that supports managerial decision making.
Detailed internal report	Presents information with little or no filtering or restrictions of the data.
Summary internal report	Organizes and categorizes data for managerial perusal. A report that summarizes total sales by product for each month is an example of a summary internal report. The data for a summary report are typically categorized and summarized to indicate trends and potential problems.
Exception reporting	Highlights situations occurring outside of the normal operating range for a condition or standard. These internal reports include only exceptions and might highlight accounts that are unpaid or delinquent or identify items that are low in stock.
Information system control report	Ensures the reliability of information, consisting of policies and their physical implementation, access restrictions, or record keeping of actions and transactions.
Information systems audit report	Assesses a company's information system to determine necessary changes and to help ensure the information systems' availability, confidentiality, and integrity.
Post-implementation report	Presents a formal report or audit of a project after it is up and running.

example, new reports or information capturing), and reviewing the system to be sure it is moving the organization toward its strategic goals. **Corrective maintenance** makes system changes to repair design flaws, coding errors, or implementation issues. **Preventive maintenance** makes system changes to reduce the chance of future system failure. During the maintenance phase, the system will generate reports to help users and MIS specialists ensure it is functioning correctly (see Figure 9.10).

SOFTWARE DEVELOPMENT METHODOLOGIES LO9.2

Today, systems are so large and complex that teams of architects, analysts, developers, testers, and users must work together to create the millions of lines of custom-written code that drive enterprises. For this reason, developers have created a number of different systems development life cycle methodologies. A **methodology** is a set of policies, procedures, standards, processes, practices, tools, techniques, and tasks that people apply to technical and management challenges. Firms use a methodology to manage the deployment of technology with work plans, requirements documents, and test plans, for instance. A formal methodology can include coding standards, code libraries, development practices, and much more.

The oldest and the best known is the **waterfall methodology**, a sequence of phases in which the output of each phase becomes the input for the next (see Figure 9.11). In the SDLC, this means the steps are performed one at a time, in order, from planning through implementation and maintenance. The traditional waterfall method no longer serves most of today's development efforts, however; it is inflexible and expensive, and it requires rigid adherence to the sequence of steps. Its success rate is only about 1 in 10. Figure 9.12 explains some issues related to the waterfall methodology.

Today's business environment is fierce. The desire and need to outsmart and outplay competitors desire and need remain intense. Given this drive for success, leaders push internal development teams and external vendors to deliver agreed-upon systems faster and cheaper so they can realize benefits as early as possible. Even so, systems remain large and complex. The traditional waterfall methodology no longer serves as an adequate systems development methodology in most cases. Because this development environment is the norm and not the exception anymore, development teams use a new breed of alternative development methods to achieve their business objectives.

Prototyping is a modern design approach where the designers and system users use an iterative approach to building the

discovery prototyping Builds a small-scale representation or working model of the system to ensure it meets the user and business requirements.

iterative development Consists of a series of tiny projects.

agile methodology Aims for customer satisfaction through early and continuous delivery of useful software components developed by an iterative process using the bare minimum requirements.

FIGURE 9.11 The Traditional Waterfall Methodology

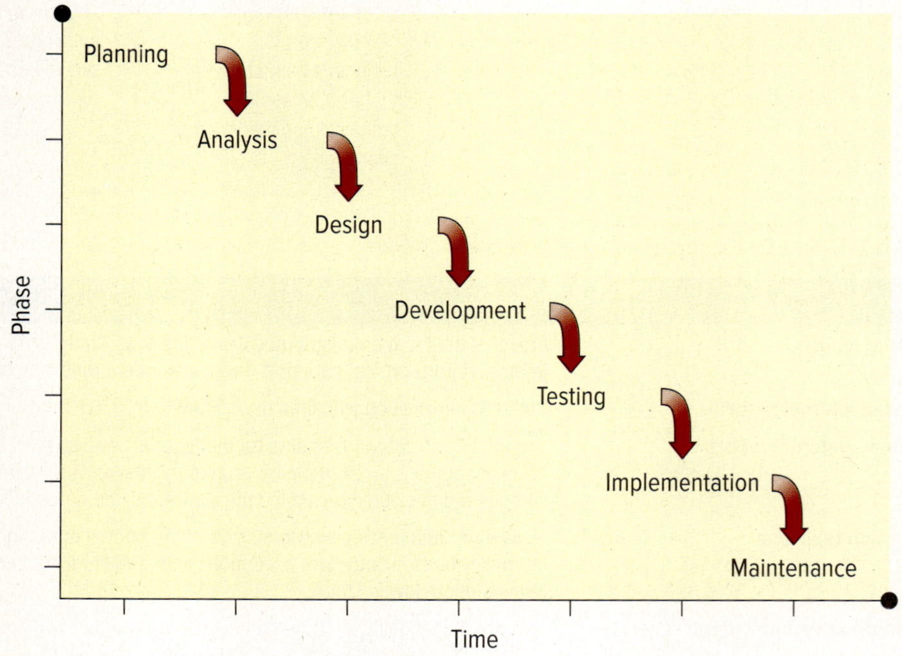

system. **Discovery prototyping** builds a small-scale representation or working model of the system to ensure it meets the user and business requirements. The advantages of prototyping include:

- Prototyping encourages user participation.
- Prototypes evolve through iteration, which better supports change.
- Prototypes have a physical quality allowing users to see, touch, and experience the system as it is developed.
- Prototypes tend to detect errors earlier.
- Prototyping accelerates the phases of the SDLC, helping to ensure success.

Agile Software Development Methodologies

It is common knowledge that the smaller the project, the greater the success rate. The iterative development style is the ultimate in small projects. Basically, **iterative development** consists of a series of tiny projects. It has become the foundation of multiple agile methodologies. Figure 9.13 displays an iterative approach.

An **agile methodology** aims for customer satisfaction through early and continuous delivery of useful software components developed by an iterative process using the bare minimum requirements. Agile methodology is what it sounds like: fast and efficient, with lower costs and fewer features. Using agile methods helps refine feasibility and supports the process for getting rapid feedback as functionality is introduced. Developers can adjust as they move along and better clarify unclear requirements.

show me *the* MONEY

Planning for the Unexpected

Unexpected situations happen all the time, and the more you plan for them the better prepared you'll be when developing software. Your employees will get into accidents, contract viruses and diseases, and experience other life issues. All of these scenarios lead to unplanned absenteeism, which can throw your project plan into a tailspin. What can happen to a project when a key employee suddenly quits or is forced to go on short-term disability? When reviewing all the different SDLC methodologies, which one offers the greatest flexibility for unplanned employee downtime? If you could choose when your employee was absent, which phase in the SDLC would be the safest for your project to still continue and achieve success? What can you do to ensure that you are preparing for unplanned absenteeism on your project plan?

One key to delivering a successful product or system is to deliver value to users as soon as possible—give them something they want and like early to create buy-in, generate enthusiasm, and, ultimately, reduce scope. Using agile methodologies helps maintain accountability and helps to establish a barometer for the satisfaction of end users. It does no good to accomplish something on time and on budget if it does not satisfy the end user. The primary forms of agile methodologies include:

- Rapid prototyping or rapid application development methodology.
- Extreme programming methodology.
- Rational unified process (RUP) methodology.
- Scrum methodology.

It is important not to get hung up on the names of the methodologies—some are proprietary brand names; others are generally accepted names. It is more important to know how these alternative methodologies are used in today's business environment and the benefits they can deliver.

Rapid Application Development (RAD) Methodology

In response to the faster pace of business, rapid application development has become a popular route for accelerating systems development. **Rapid application development (RAD) methodology (also called rapid prototyping)** emphasizes extensive user involvement in the rapid and evolutionary construction of working prototypes of a system, to accelerate the

rapid application development (RAD) methodology (also called rapid prototyping) Emphasizes extensive user involvement in the rapid and evolutionary construction of working prototypes of a system, to accelerate the systems development process.

FIGURE 9.12 Disadvantages of the Waterfall Methodology

	Issues Related to the Waterfall Methodology
The business problem	Any flaws in accurately defining and articulating the business problem in terms of what the business users actually require flow onward to the next phase.
The plan	Managing costs, resources, and time constraints is difficult in the waterfall sequence. What happens to the schedule if a programmer quits? How will a schedule delay in a specific phase impact the total cost of the project? Unexpected contingencies may sabotage the plan.
The solution	The waterfall methodology is problematic in that it assumes users can specify all business requirements in advance. Defining the appropriate IT infrastructure that is flexible, scalable, and reliable is a challenge. The final IT infrastructure solution must meet not only current but also future needs in terms of time, cost, feasibility, and flexibility. Vision is inevitably limited at the head of the waterfall.

FIGURE 9.13 The Iterative Approach

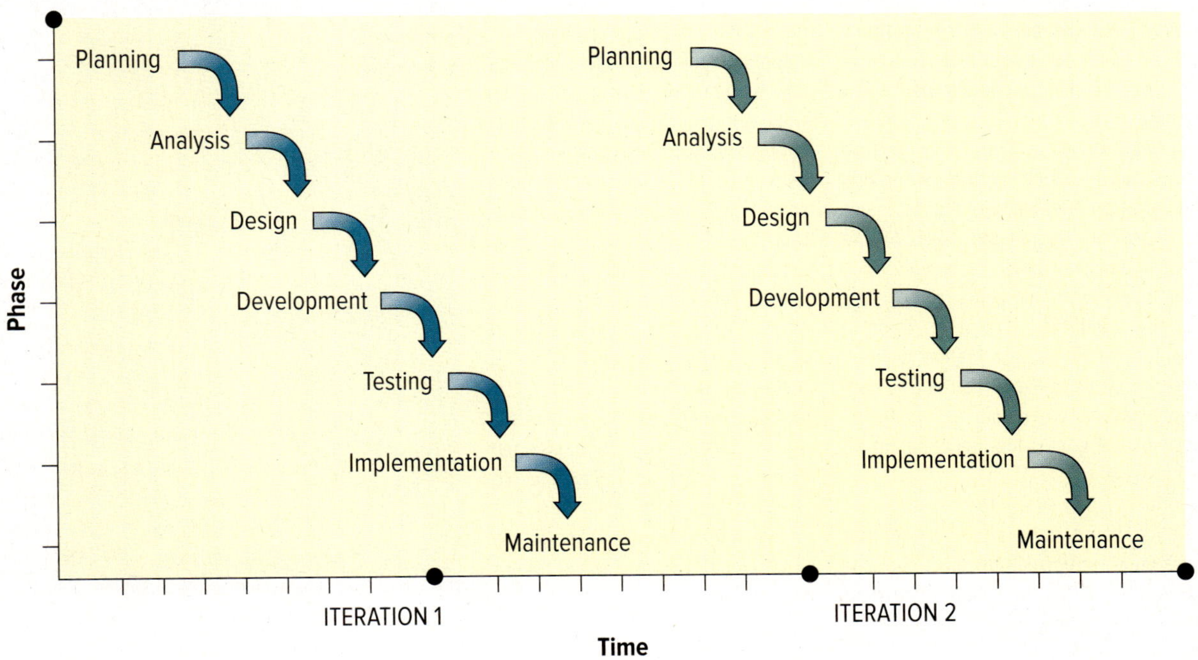

extreme programming (XP) methodology Breaks a project into four phases, and developers cannot continue to the next phase until the previous phase is complete.

systems development process. Figure 9.14 displays the fundamentals of RAD.

Extreme Programming Methodology

Extreme programming (XP) methodology, like other agile methods, breaks a project into four phases, and developers cannot continue to the next phase until the previous phase is complete. The delivery strategy supporting XP is that the quicker the feedback the more improved the results. XP has four basic phases: planning, designing, coding, and testing. Planning can include user interviews, meetings, and small releases. During design, functionality is not added until it is required or needed. During coding, the developers work together soliciting continuous feedback from users, eliminating the communication gap that generally exists between developers and customers. During testing, the test requirements are generated before any code is developed. Extreme programming saves time and produces successful projects by continuously reviewing and revamping needed and unneeded requirements.

Customer satisfaction is the primary reason XP finds success as developers quickly respond to changing business requirements, even late in the life cycle. XP encourages managers, customers, and developers to work together as a team to ensure the delivery of high-quality systems. XP is similar to a puzzle; there are many small pieces and individually the pieces make no sense, but when they are pieced together they can create a new system.

FIGURE 9.14 Fundamentals of RAD

Fundamentals of RAD
Focus initially on creating a prototype that looks and acts like the desired system.
Actively involve system users in the analysis, design, and development phases.
Accelerate collecting the business requirements through an interactive and iterative construction approach.

BUSTED Faking Your Own Death[5]

Facing insurmountable troubles, some people turn to faking their own death to escape legal issues and even the Marines. Here are a few examples:

- Marcus Schrenker, a Wall Street investor whose company was under investigation for fraud, disappeared while flying his plane over Alabama. Schrenker's plane was found in a swamp, and the last anyone heard from Schrenker was a distressed radio call—until he was discovered in a campground a few weeks later.
- A Colorado man returning from a hike reported that his friend, Lance Hering, had been injured on the hike, and rescue teams were dispatched to find the hiker. All the rescuers found was blood, a water bottle, and Hering's shoes. Two years later, Hering was arrested with his father at an airport in Washington state. Hering, a Marine, claimed he faked his death to avoid returning to Iraq, where he feared other soldiers would kill him because of something incriminating he had witnessed.
- One Florida woman, Alison Matera, informed her friends, family, and church choir that she was entering hospice because she was dying of cancer. Matera's plan unraveled when she appeared at her own funeral service, claiming to be her own long-lost identical twin sister. Police were called, and Matera admitted faking both her cancer and death.

Unexpected situations happen all the time, and the more you plan for them the better prepared you'll be when developing software. Hopefully, your employees are not faking their own deaths, but they will get into accidents, have babies, contract viruses and diseases, and face other life issues. All of these scenarios lead to unplanned absenteeism, which can throw your project plan into a tailspin. What can happen to a project when a key employee suddenly quits or is forced to go on short-term disability? When reviewing all of the different SDLC methodologies, which one offers the greatest flexibility for unplanned employee downtime? If you could choose when your employee was absent, during which phase in the SDLC would it be the safest if your project were to still continue and achieve success? What can you do to ensure you are preparing for unplanned absenteeism on your project plan?

Rational Unified Process (RUP) Methodology

The **rational unified process (RUP) methodology**, owned by IBM, provides a framework for breaking down the development of software into four "gates." Each gate consists of executable iterations of the software in development. A project stays in a gate waiting for the stakeholder's analysis, and then it either moves to the next gate or is cancelled. The gates include:[3]

- **Gate one: inception.** This phase ensures all stakeholders have a shared understanding of the proposed system and what it will do.
- **Gate two: elaboration.** This phase expands on the agreed-upon details of the system, including the ability to provide an architecture to support and build it.
- **Gate three: construction.** This phase includes building and developing the product.
- **Gate four: transition.** Primary questions answered in this phase address ownership of the system and training of key personnel.[4]

Because RUP is an iterative methodology, the user can reject the product and force the developers to go back to gate one. RUP helps developers avoid reinventing the wheel and focuses on rapidly adding or removing reusable chunks of processes addressing common problems.

Scrum Methodology

Another agile methodology, **scrum methodology**, uses small teams to produce small pieces of software using a series of "sprints," or 30-day intervals, to achieve an appointed goal. In rugby, a scrum is a team pack and everyone in the pack works together to move the ball down the field. In scrum methodology, each day ends or begins with a stand-up meeting to monitor and control the development effort.

LO9.2 Summarize the different software development methodologies.

DEVELOPING A SERVICE-ORIENTED ARCHITECTURE LO9.3

One of the latest trends in systems development is creating a service-oriented architecture. **Service-oriented architecture (SOA)** is a business-driven enterprise architecture that supports integrating a business as linked, repeatable activities, tasks, or services. SOA ensures that MIS systems can adapt quickly, easily, and economically to support rapidly changing business needs. SOA promotes a scalable and flexible enterprise architecture that can implement new or reuse existing MIS components, creating connections among disparate applications and systems. It is important to understand that SOA is not a concrete architecture; it is thought that leads to a concrete architecture. It might be described as a style, paradigm, concept, perspective, philosophy, or representation. That is, SOA is an approach, a way of thinking, a value system that leads to decisions that design a concrete architecture allowing enterprises to plug in new services or upgrade existing services in a granular approach. Figure 9.15 discusses the problems that can be addressed by implementing SOA. Figure 9.16 displays the three key technical concepts of SOA.

Service

Service-oriented architecture begins with a service—an SOA **service** being simply a business task, such as checking a potential customer's credit rating when opening a new account. It is important to stress that this is part of a business process. Services are like software products; however, when describing SOA, do not think about software or MIS. Think about what a company does on a day-to-day basis and break up those business processes into repeatable business tasks or components.

SOA works with services that are not just software or hardware but, rather, business tasks. It is a pattern for developing a more flexible kind of software application that can promote loose coupling among software components while reusing existing investments in technology in new, more valuable ways across the organization. SOA is based on standards that enable interoperability, business agility, and innovation to generate more business value for those who use these principles.

SOA helps companies become more agile by aligning business needs and the IT capabilities that support these needs. Business drives requirements for IT; SOA enables the IT environment to respond to these requirements effectively and efficiently. SOA is about helping companies apply reusability and flexibility that can lower cost (of development, integration, and maintenance), increase revenue, and obtain sustainable competitive advantage through technology.

It is very important to note that SOA is an evolution. Although its results are revolutionary, it builds on many technologies used in the marketplace, such as web services, transactional

rational unified process (RUP) methodology Provides a framework for breaking down the development of software into four "gates."

scrum methodology Uses small teams to produce small pieces of software using a series of "sprints," or 30-day intervals, to achieve an appointed goal.

service-oriented architecture (SOA) A business-driven enterprise architecture that supports integrating a business as linked, repeatable activities, tasks, or services.

service Tasks that customers will buy to satisfy a want or need.

FIGURE 9.15 Business Issues and SOA Solutions

Service-Oriented Architecture Solutions	
• Agents unable to see policy coverage information remotely • Calls/faxes used to get information from other divisions • Clinical patient information stored on paper • Complex access to supplier design drawings	Integrate information to make it more accessible to employees.
• High cost of handling customer calls • Reconciliation of invoice deductions and rebates • Hours on hold to determine patient insurance eligibility • High turnover leading to excessive hiring and training costs	Understand how business processes interact to manage administrative costs better.
• Decreasing customer loyalty due to incorrect invoices • Customers placed on hold to check order status • Inability to update policy endorsements quickly • Poor service levels	Improve customer retention and deliver new products and services through reuse of current investments.
• Time wasted reconciling separate databases • Manual processes such as handling trade allocations • Inability to detect quality flaws early in cycle • High percentage of scrap and rework	Improve people productivity with better business integration and connectivity.

technologies, information-driven principles, loose coupling, components, and object-oriented design. The beauty of SOA is that these technologies exist together in SOA through standards, well-defined interfaces, and organizational commitments to reuse key services instead of reinventing the wheel. SOA is not just about technology, but about how technology and business link themselves for a common goal of business flexibility.

FIGURE 9.16 SOA Concepts

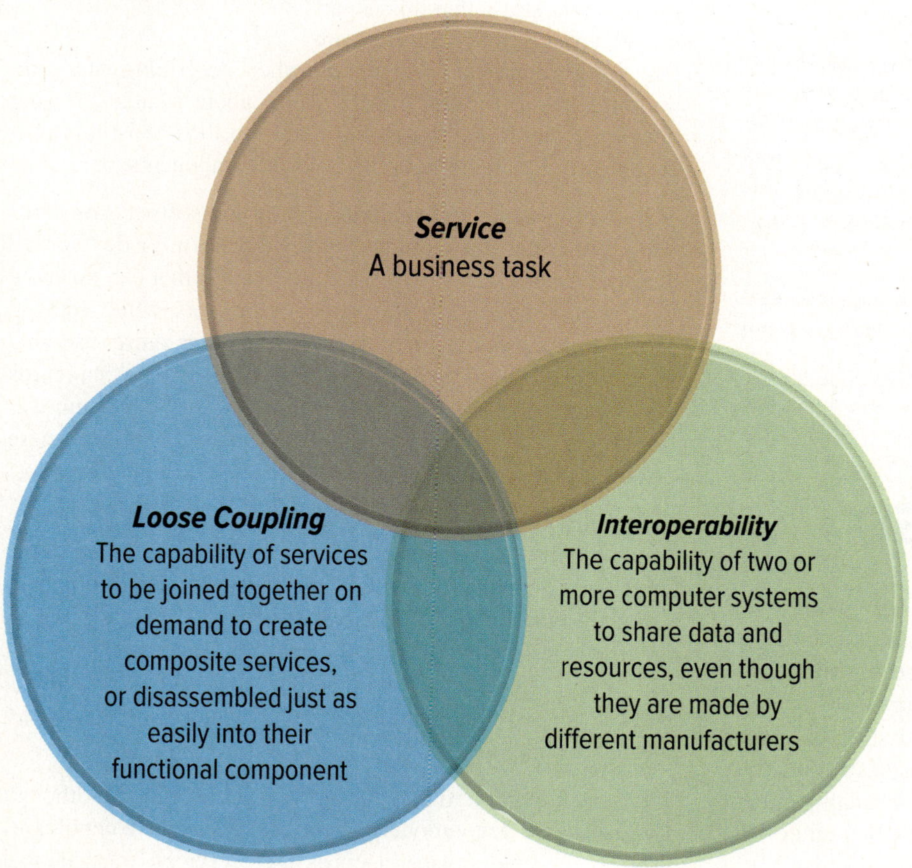

Interoperability

As defined earlier, **interoperability** is the capability of two or more computer systems to share data and resources, even though they are made by different manufacturers. Businesses today use a variety of systems that have resulted in diverse operating environments. This diversity has inundated businesses with the lack of interoperability. With SOA, a business can create solutions that draw on functionality from these existing, previously isolated systems that are portable, interoperable, or both, regardless of the environment in which they exist.

A **web service** is an open-standards way of supporting interoperability. Web services are application programming interfaces (API) that can be accessed over a network, such as the Internet, and executed on a remote system hosting the requested services. SOA is a style of architecture that enables the creation of applications that are built by combining loosely coupled and interoperable services. In SOA, since the basic unit of communication is a message rather than an operation, web services are usually loosely coupled. Although SOA can exist without web services, the best-practice implementation of SOA for flexibility always involves web services.

Technically, web services are based on **Extensible Markup Language (XML)**, a markup language for documents, containing structured information. The technical specifics of XML's capabilities go beyond the scope of this book, but for our purposes, they support things such as ebusiness transactions, mathematical equations, and a thousand other kinds of structured data. XML is a common data representation that can be used as the medium of exchange between programs that are written in different programming languages and execute different kinds of machine instructions. In simple terms, think about XML as the official translator for structured information. Structured information is both the content (word, picture, and so on) and the role it plays. XML is the basis for all web service technologies and the key to interoperability; every web service specification is based on XML.

Loose Coupling

Part of the value of SOA is that it is built on the premise of loose coupling of services. **Loose coupling** is the capability of services to be joined on demand to create composite services or disassembled just as easily into their functional components. Loose coupling is a way of ensuring that the technical details such as language, platform, and so on are decoupled from the service. For example, look at currency conversion. Today all banks have multiple currency converters, all with different rate refreshes at different times. By creating a common service, conversion of currency, that is loosely coupled to all banking functions that require conversion, the rates, times, and samplings can be averaged to ensure floating the treasury in the most effective manner possible. Another example is common customer identification. Most businesses lack a common customer ID and, therefore, have no way to determine who the customers are and what they buy for what reason. Creating a common customer ID that is independent of applications and databases allows loosely coupling the service, customer ID, to data and applications without the application or database ever knowing who it is or where it is.

The difference between traditional, tightly bound interactions and loosely coupled services is that, before the transaction occurs, the functional pieces (services) operating within the SOA are dormant and disconnected. When the business process initiates, these services momentarily interact with each other. They do so for just long enough to execute their piece of the overall process, and then they go back to their dormant state, with no long-standing connection to the other services with which they just interacted.

The next time the same service is called, it could be as part of a different business process with different calling and destination services. A great way to understand this is through the analogy of the telephone system. At the dawn of widespread phone usage, operators had to plug in a wire physically to create a semi-permanent connection between two parties. Callers were "tightly bound" to each other. Today you pick up your cell phone and put it to your ear, and there's no dial tone—it's disconnected. You enter a number, push "Talk," and only then does the process initiate, establishing a loosely coupled connection just long enough for your conversation. Then when the conversation is over, your cell phone goes back to dormant mode until a new connection is made with another party. As a result, supporting a million cell phone subscribers does not require the cell phone service provider to support a million live connections; it requires supporting only the number of simultaneous conversations at any given time. It allows for a much more flexible and dynamic exchange.

interoperability The capability of two or more computer systems to share data and resources, even though they are made by different manufacturers.

web service An open-standards way of supporting interoperability.

extensible markup language (XML) A markup language for documents, containing structured information.

loose coupling The capability of services to be joined on demand to create composite services or disassembled just as easily into their functional components.

LO9.3 Explain why a company would implement a service-oriented architecture.

show me the MONEY

Scratch

Scratch is a visual programming language that is perfect for anyone learning to code. Scratch creates programs by connecting blocks of code by using a drag-and-drop GUI so users do not have to type programming languages. Users can simply select colored blocks of code that, when joined, create a script or a set of computer instructions that can make objects such as people and animals move and speak. Users can create interactive stories, games, and animations with the click of a button.

Scratch is a free project created by the Lifelong Kindergarten Group at the MIT Media Lab and currently has more than 8 million users. The goal of Scratch is to help young people learn to think creatively, reason systematically, and work collaboratively—essential skills for life in the 21st century.

In a group, visit the Scratch website at http://scratch.mit.edu/. What type of system development methodology is Scratch using? What skills can young people learn from creating Scratch programs?

tangible benefits Easy to quantify and typically measured to determine the success or failure of a project.

intangible benefits Difficult to quantify or measure.

feasibility The measure of the tangible and intangible benefits of an information system.

{SECTION 9.2} Project Management

LEARNING OUTCOMES

LO9.4 Explain project management and identify the primary reasons projects fail.

LO9.5 Identify the primary project planning diagrams.

LO9.6 Identify the three different types of outsourcing along with their benefits and challenges.

USING PROJECT MANAGEMENT TO DELIVER SUCCESSFUL PROJECTS LO9.4

No one would think of building an office complex by turning loose 100 different construction teams to build 100 different rooms with no single blueprint or agreed-upon vision of the completed structure. Yet this is precisely the situation in which many large organizations find themselves when managing information technology projects. Organizations routinely overschedule their resources (human and otherwise), develop redundant projects, and damage profitability by investing in nonstrategic efforts that do not contribute to the organization's bottom line. Business leaders face a rapidly moving and unforgiving global marketplace that will force them to use every possible tool to sustain competitiveness; project management is one of those tools. For this reason, business personnel must anticipate being involved in some form of project management during their career. Figure 9.17 displays a few examples of the different types of projects organizations encounter.

Tangible benefits are easy to quantify and typically measured to determine the success or failure of a project. **Intangible benefits** are difficult to quantify or measure (see Figure 9.18 for examples). One of the most difficult decisions managers make is identifying the projects in which to invest time, energy, and resources. An organization must choose what it wants to do—justifying it, defining it, and listing expected results—and how to do it, including project budget, schedule, and analysis of project risks. **Feasibility** is the measure of the tangible and intangible benefits of an information system. Figure 9.19 displays several types of feasibility studies business analysts can use to determine the projects that best fit business goals.

With today's volatile economic environment, many businesses are being forced to do more with less. Businesses today must respond quickly to a rapidly changing business environment by continually innovating goods and services. Effective

FIGURE 9.17 Types of Organizational Projects

a. © Ingram Publishing; b. © ColorBlind Images/Blend Images LLC; c-d. © Royalty-Free/Corbis; e. © webphotographeer/Getty Images

FIGURE 9.18 Examples of Tangible and Intangible Benefits

FIGURE 9.19 Types of Feasibility Studies

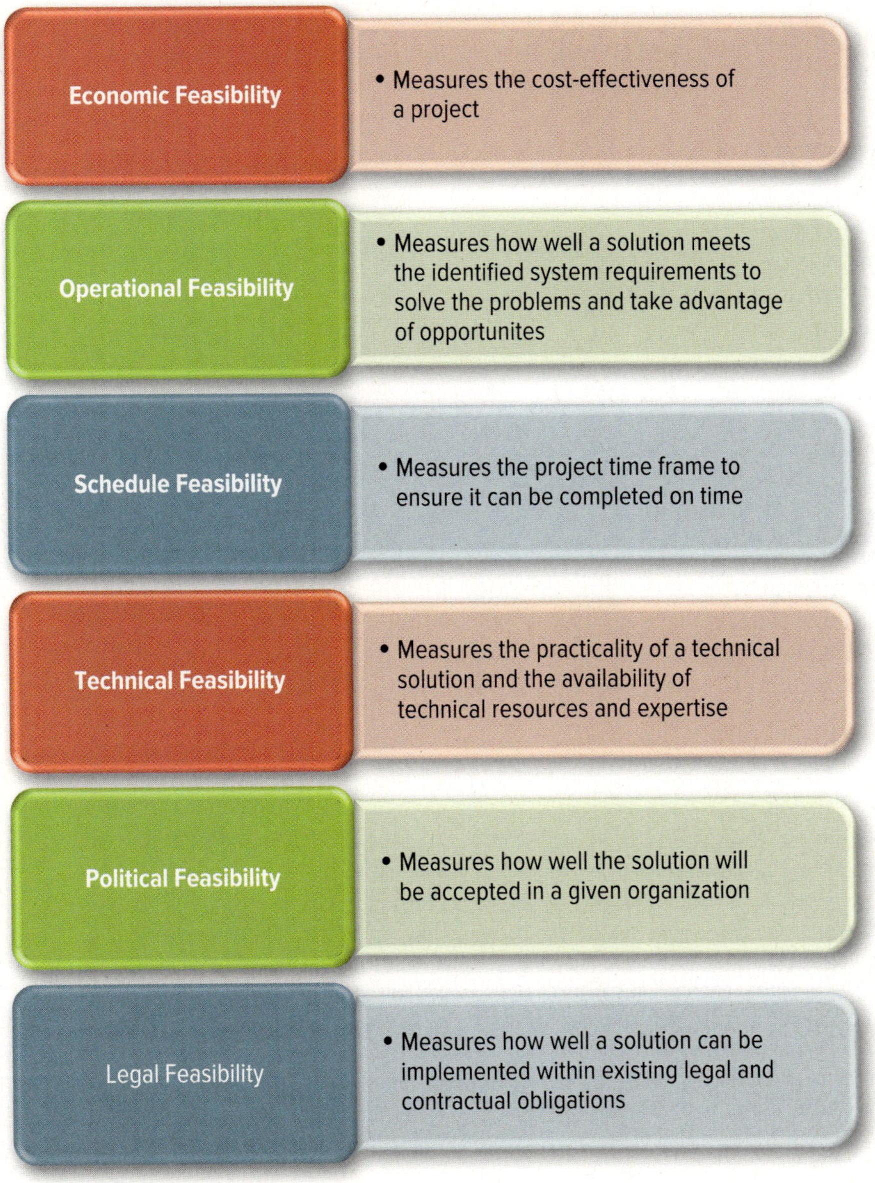

project management provides a controlled way to respond to changing market conditions, to foster global communications, and to provide key metrics to enable managerial decision making. Developing projects within budget and on time is challenging, and with the help of solid project management skills, managers can avoid the primary reasons projects fail, including:

- Unclear or missing business requirements.
- Skipped SDLC phases.
- Changing technology.
- The cost of finding errors.
- Balance of the triple constraints.

LO9.3 Explain project management and identify the primary reasons projects fail.

Unclear or Missing Business Requirements

The most common reason systems fail is because the business requirements are either missing or incorrectly gathered during the analysis phase. The business requirements drive the entire system. If they are not accurate or complete, the system will not be successful.

Skipped Phases

The first thing individuals tend to do when a project falls behind schedule is to start skipping phases in the SDLC. For example, if a project is three weeks behind in the development phase, the project manager might decide to cut testing from six weeks to three weeks. Obviously, it is impossible to perform all the testing in half the time. Failing to test the system will lead to unfound errors, and chances are high that the system will fail. It is critical that an organization perform all phases in the SDLC during every project. Skipping any of the phases is sure to lead to system failure.

FIGURE 9.20 The Cost of Fixing Errors

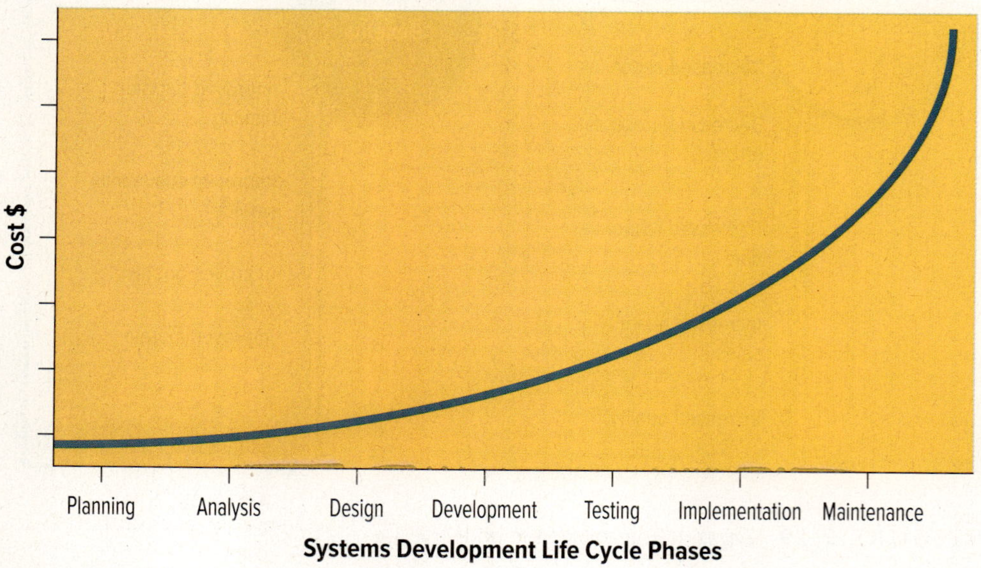

Changing Technology

Many real-world projects have hundreds of business requirements, take years to complete, and cost millions of dollars. As Moore's Law states, technology changes at an incredibly fast pace; therefore, it is possible that an entire project plan will need to be revised in the middle of a project as a result of a change in technology. Technology changes so fast that it is almost impossible to deliver an information system without feeling the pain of updates.

The Cost of Finding Errors in the SDLC

It is important to discuss the relationship between the SDLC and the cost for the organization to fix errors. An error found during the analysis and design phase is relatively inexpensive to fix. All that is typically required is a change to a Word document. However, exactly the same error found during the testing or implementation phase is going to cost the organization an enormous amount to fix because it has to change the actual system. Figure 9.20 displays how the cost to fix an error grows exponentially the later the error is found in the SDLC.

Balance of the Triple Constraint

Figure 9.21 displays the relationships among the three primary and interdependent variables in any project—time, cost, and scope. All projects are limited in some way by these three constraints. The Project Management Institute calls the framework for evaluating these competing demands *the triple constraint.*

FIGURE 9.21 The Triple Constraint: Changing One Changes All

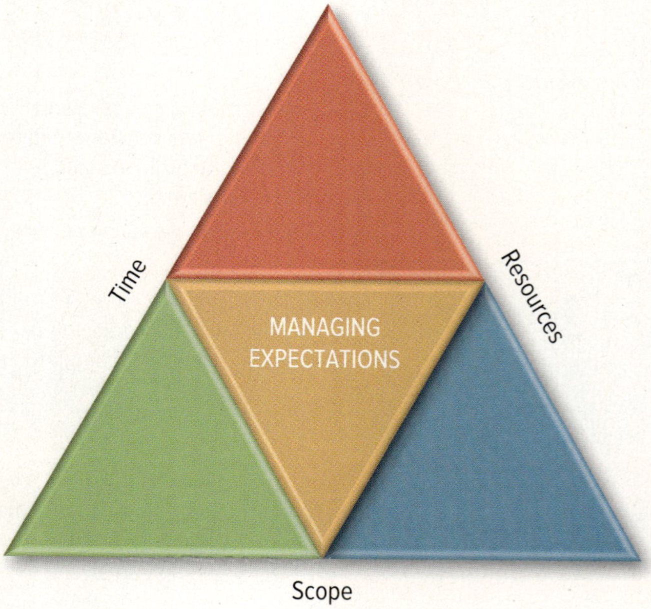

fyi Sharepoint

Life is good when you can complete all your projects by the due date and under budget. Life is not good when you miss your deadlines, exceed your budget, and fail to meet the business requirements. One tool that can help ensure that your life always stays good is Microsoft SharePoint. With SharePoint, you can connect with employees enterprisewide to collaborate, share ideas, and reinvent the way work flows. Whether working as a team or an individual, SharePoint helps you organize information, people, and projects. SharePoint can make any manager's life easier by organizing teamwork around common milestones. You can make sure that work is completed by assigning people tasks that can be tracked and prioritized. You can keep an eye on important details with real-time summaries of your projects that warns you about delays and keeps next steps and milestones on your radar. Explain why using a project management/collaboration tool such as SharePoint can help ensure that you never fail as a manager. Be sure to explain any project management terms such as deliverables, dependencies, and milestones.

FIGURE 9.22 *PMBOK* Elements of Project Management

Tool	Description
Communication plan	Defines the how, what, when, and who regarding the flow of project information to stakeholders and is key for managing expectations.
Executive sponsor	The person or group who provides the financial resources for the project.
Project assumption	Factors considered to be true, real, or certain without proof or demonstration. Examples include hours in a workweek or time of year the work will be performed.
Project constraint	Specific factors that can limit options, including budget, delivery dates, available skilled resources, and organizational policies.
Project deliverable	Any measurable, tangible, verifiable outcome, result, or item that is produced to complete a project or part of a project. Examples of project deliverables include design documents, testing scripts, and requirements documents.
Project management office (PMO)	An internal department that oversees all organizational projects. This group must formalize and professionalize project management expertise and leadership. One of the primary initiatives of the PMO is to educate the organization on techniques and procedures necessary to run successful projects.
Project milestone	Represents key dates when a certain group of activities must be performed. For example, completing the planning phase might be a project milestone. If a project milestone is missed, then chances are the project is experiencing problems.
Project objectives	Quantifiable criteria that must be met for the project to be considered a success.
Project requirements document	Defines the specifications for product/output of the project and is key for managing expectations, controlling scope, and completing other planning efforts.
Project scope statement	Links the project to the organization's overall business goals. It describes the business need (the problem the project will solve) and the justification, requirements, and current boundaries for the project. It defines the work that must be completed to deliver the product with the specified features and functions, and it includes constraints, assumptions, and requirements—all components necessary for developing accurate cost estimates.
Project stakeholder	Individuals and organizations actively involved in the project or whose interests might be affected as a result of project execution or project completion.
Responsibility matrix	Defines all project roles and indicates what responsibilities are associated with each role.
Status report	Periodic reviews of actual performance versus expected performance.

The relationship among these variables is such that if any one changes, at least one other is likely to be affected. For example, moving up a project's finish date could mean either increasing costs to hire more staff or decreasing the scope to eliminate features or functions. Increasing a project's scope to include additional customer requests could extend the project's time to completion or increase the project's cost—or both—to accommodate the changes. Project quality is affected by the project manager's ability to balance these competing demands. High-quality projects deliver the agreed upon product or service on time and on budget. Project management is the science of making intelligent trade-offs between time, cost, and scope. Benjamin Franklin's timeless advice—by *failing* to prepare, you prepare to *fail*—applies to many of today's software development projects.

The Project Management Institute created the *Project Management Body of Knowledge (PMBOK)* for the education and certification of project managers. Figure 9.22 summarizes the key elements of project planning according to *PMBOK*.

LO9.4 Explain project management and identify the primary reasons projects fail.

PRIMARY PROJECT PLANNING DIAGRAMS LO9.5

Project planning is the process of detailed planning that generates answers to common operational questions such as why are we doing this project or what is the project going to accomplish for the business? Some of the key questions project planning can help answer include:

- How are deliverables being produced?
- What activities or tasks need to be accomplished to produce the deliverables?
- Who is responsible for performing the tasks?
- What resources are required to perform the tasks?
- When will the tasks be performed?
- How long will it take to perform each task?
- Are any tasks dependent upon other tasks being completed before they can begin?
- How much does each task cost?

kill switch A trigger that enables a project manager to close the project before completion.

PERT (Program Evaluation and Review Technique) chart A graphical network model that depicts a project's tasks and the relationships between them.

dependency A logical relationship that exists between the project tasks, or between a project task and a milestone.

critical path Estimates the shortest path through the project ensuring all critical tasks are completed from start to finish.

Gantt chart A simple bar chart that lists project tasks vertically against the project's time frame, listed horizontally.

- What skills and experience are required to perform each task?
- How is the performance of the task being measured including quality?
- How are issues being tracked?
- How is change being addressed?
- How is communication occurring and when?
- What risks are associated with each task?

The project objectives are among the most important areas to define because they are essentially the major elements of the project. When an organization achieves the project objectives, it has accomplished the major goals of the project and the project scope is satisfied. Project objectives must include metrics so that the project's success can be measured. The metrics can include cost, schedule, and quality metrics. Figure 9.23 lists the SMART criteria—useful reminders about how to ensure the project has created understandable and measurable objectives.

The project plan is a formal, approved document that manages and controls project execution. The project plan should include a description of the project scope, a list of activities, a schedule, time estimates, cost estimates, risk factors, resources, assignments, and responsibilities. In addition to these basic components, most project professionals also include contingency plans, review and communications strategies, and a **kill switch**—a trigger that enables a project manager to close the project before completion.

A good project plan should include estimates for revenue and strategic necessities. It also should include measurement and reporting methods and details as to how top leadership will engage in the project. It also informs stakeholders of the benefits of the project and justifies the investment, commitment, and risk of the project as it relates to the overall mission of the organization.

Managers need to continuously monitor projects to measure their success. If a project is failing, the manager must cancel the project and save the company any further project costs. Canceling a project is not necessarily a failure as much as it is successful resource management as it frees resources that can be used on other projects that are more valuable to the firm.

The most important part of the plan is communication. The project manager must communicate the plan to every member of the project team and to any key stakeholders and executives.

FIGURE 9.23 SMART Criteria for Successful Objective Creation

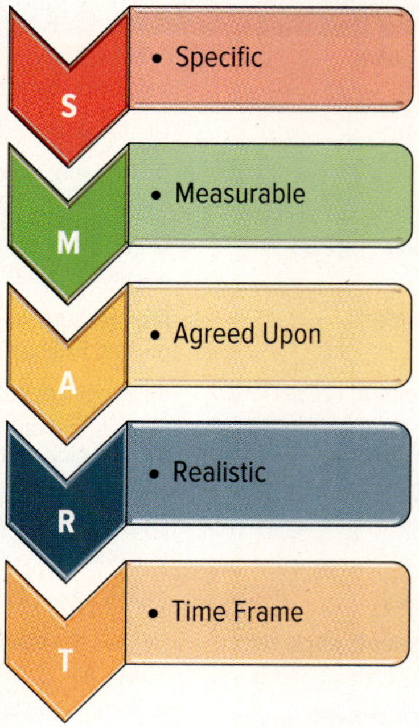

The project plan must also include any project assumptions and be detailed enough to guide the execution of the project. A key to achieving project success is earning consensus and buy-in from all key stakeholders. By including key stakeholders in project plan development, the project manager allows them to have ownership of the plan. This often translates to greater commitment, which in turn results in enhanced motivation and productivity. The two primary diagrams most frequently used in project planning are PERT and Gantt charts.

A **PERT (Program Evaluation and Review Technique) chart** is a graphical network model that depicts a project's tasks and the relationships between them. A **dependency** is a logical relationship that exists between the project tasks, or between a project task and a milestone. PERT charts define dependency between project tasks before those tasks are scheduled (see Figure 9.24). The boxes in Figure 9.24 represent project tasks, and the project manager can adjust the contents of the boxes to display various project attributes such as schedule and actual start and finish times. The arrows indicate that a task depends on the start or the completion of a different task. The **critical path** estimates the shortest path through the project ensuring all critical tasks are completed from start to finish. The red line in Figure 9.24 displays the critical path for the project.

A **Gantt chart** is a simple bar chart that lists project tasks vertically against the project's time frame, listed horizontally. A Gantt chart works well for representing the project schedule. It also shows actual progress of tasks against the planned duration. Figure 9.25 displays a software development project using a Gantt chart.

LO9.5 Identify the primary project planning diagrams.

FIGURE 9.24 PERT Chart Example

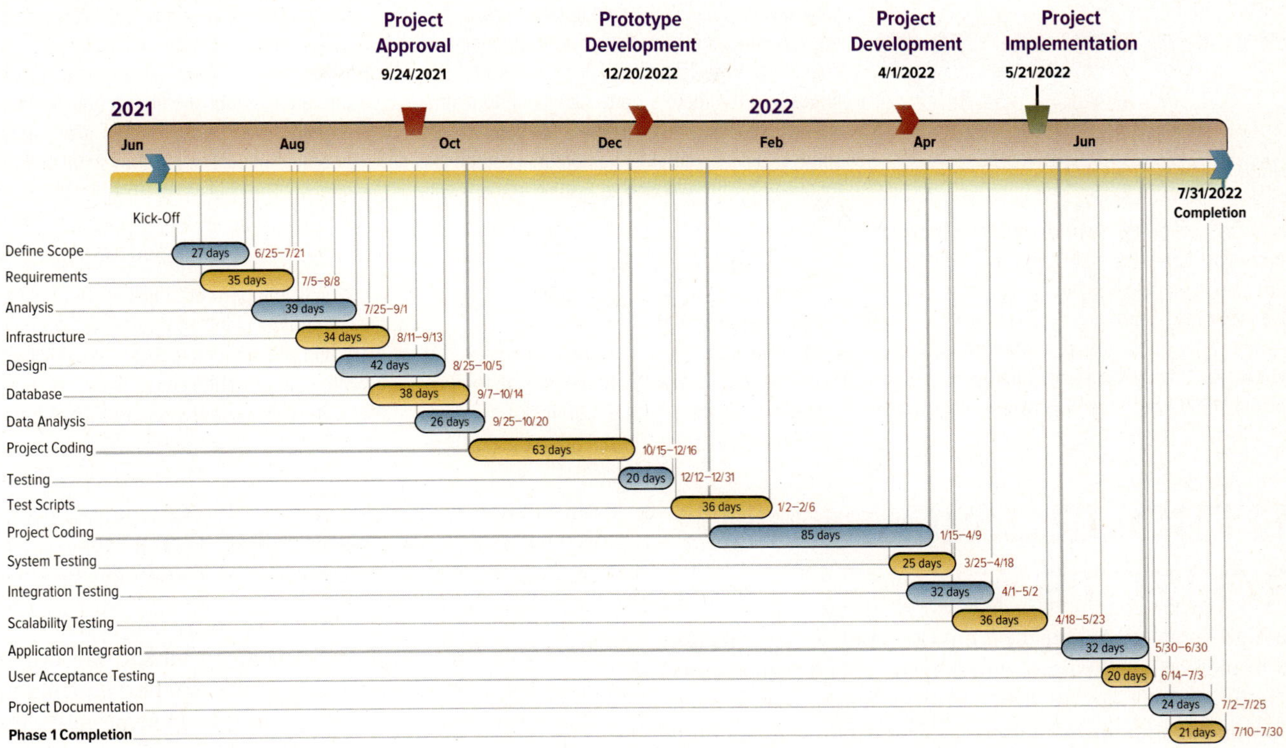

FIGURE 9.25 Microsoft Project, a Gantt Chart Example

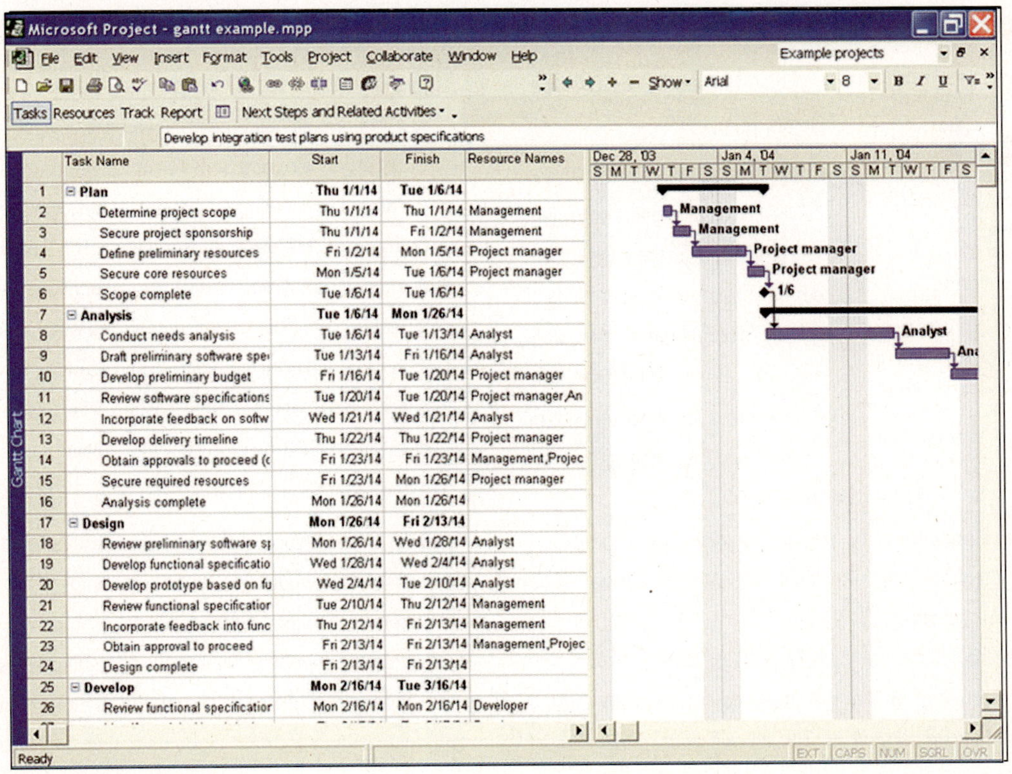

Source: Microsoft Office 2016

Living the DREAM

CharityFocus.org[6]

Don't ask what the world needs. Ask what makes you come alive, and go do it. Because what the world needs is people who have come alive.—Howard Thurman

This is the quote found at the bottom of the website for CharityFocus.org. CharityFocus, created in 1999, partners volunteers with small nonprofit organizations to build custom web solutions. CharityFocus is completely run by volunteers, and the services of its volunteers are absolutely free. The nonprofit believes that it is impossible to create a better world without inner change resulting from selfless service. In the spirit of selfless service, volunteers created the following on the website to inspire and cultivate change:

- **DailyGood:** Email service that delivers a little bit of good news to thousands of people all over the world.
- **KarmaTube:** Site that uses the power of video to document multiple acts of compassion, generosity, and selflessness.
- **Conversations:** Site (Conversations.org) that hosts in-depth interviews of everyday heroes and a broad spectrum of artists.
- **HelpOthers:** A kindness portal based on the smile, a universally recognized symbol. People smile because they are happy and people smile because they want to become happy. The purpose of HelpOthers.org is to bring more of those smiles in the world through small acts of kindness.

Why is it important to give back to communities around the globe and share systems development and project management skills? Would you volunteer for CharityFocus? What are the risks associated with volunteering for CharityFocus?

OUTSOURCING PROJECTS LO9.6

In the high-speed global business environment, an organization needs to increase profits, grow market share, and reduce costs. Two basic options are available to organizations wishing to develop and maintain their information systems—in-sourcing or outsourcing.

In-sourcing (in-house development) uses the professional expertise within an organization to develop and maintain its information technology systems. In-sourcing has been instrumental in creating a viable supply of IT professionals and in creating a better quality workforce combining both technical and business skills.

Outsourcing is an arrangement by which one organization provides a service or services for another organization that chooses not to perform them in-house. In some cases, the entire MIS department is outsourced, including planning and business analysis as well as the design, development, and maintenance of equipment and projects. Outsourcing can range from a large contract under which an organization such as IBM manages all

My Not To-Do List

Honestly, It Cost $7,500 for a Steak Dinner[7]

The next time one of your employees submits an expense report, you might want to think twice: there are a number of websites offering all kinds of phony documentation that individuals can use to help cheat on their taxes, expense reports, or even spouses. Here are a few you should be aware of:

- **Customreceipts.com:** This site prints fake ATM receipts for those individuals who want to casually let other people see their massive bank balance.
- **Alibi Network:** Creates custom tailored excuses, such as a call claiming to be an "emergency" so that the employee can leave that boring meeting or dreadful company picnic. The site will even write and send false invitations for business events or telephone an unfaithful partner "confirming" that their beloved will be caught up in a meeting.
- **CorruptedFiles.com**: Sells corrupted files guaranteed not to open on a Mac or PC, allowing employees to miss that deadline.
- **Restaurant Maloney & Porcelli's:** This innovative, yet perhaps unethical, restaurant started the "expense a steak" tool that works by entering the bill for the dinner and automatically creates a fake, work-related receipt ranging from cab rides to office supply stores. For example, enter a meal costing $149.37 and the program generates a $135.73 receipt from the "Office Supply Hut" and a $13.64 receipt from "The Panini Experience."

Does the existence of services like these affect how you will run your business? What would you do to an employee who was using one of these services? What would happen to a company's budget if it believed the fraudulent expenses were required to be paid by the business? How can a company fight back against these types of fraudulent activities without wasting enormous amounts of time and energy?

MIS services for another company, to hiring contractors and temporary staff on an individual basis. Common reasons companies outsource include:

- Core competencies. Many companies have recently begun to consider outsourcing as a way to acquire best-practices and the business process expertise of highly skilled technology resources for a low cost. Technology is advancing at such an accelerated rate that companies often lack the technical resources required to keep current.
- Financial savings. It is far cheaper to hire people in China and India than pay the required salaries for similar labor in the United States.
- Rapid growth. Firms must get their products to market quickly and still be able to react to market changes. By taking advantage of outsourcing, an organization can acquire the resources required to speed up operations or scale to new demand levels.
- The Internet and globalization. The pervasive nature of the Internet has made more people comfortable with outsourcing abroad as India, China, and the United States become virtual neighbors.

Outsourcing MIS enables organizations to keep up with market and technology advances—with less strain on human and financial resources and more assurance that the IT infrastructure will keep pace with evolving business priorities (see Figure 9.26). The three forms of outsourcing options available for a project are:

1. **Onshore outsourcing**—engaging another company within the same country for services.
2. **Nearshore outsourcing**—contracting an outsourcing arrangement with a company in a nearby country. Often this country will share a border with the native country.
3. **Offshore outsourcing**—using organizations from developing countries to write code and develop systems. In offshore outsourcing the country is geographically far away.

Since the mid-1990s, major U.S. companies have been sending significant portions of their software development work offshore—primarily to vendors in India, but also to vendors in China, eastern Europe (including Russia), Ireland, Israel, and the Philippines. The big selling point for offshore outsourcing is inexpensive but good work. The overseas counterpart to an American programmer who earns as much as $63,000 per year is paid as little as $5,000 per year (see Figure 9.27). Developing countries in Asia and South Africa offer some outsourcing services but are challenged by language difference, inadequate telecommunication equipment, and regulatory obstacles. India is the largest offshore marketplace because it promotes English along with a technologically advanced population. Infosys, NIIT, Mahindra Satyam, Tata Consultancy Services, and Wipro are among the biggest Indian outsourcing service providers, each of which has a large presence in the United States.[8]

LO9.6 Identify the three different types of outsourcing along with their benefits and challenges.

Outsourcing Benefits

The many benefits associated with outsourcing include:

- Increased quality and efficiency of business processes.
- Reduced operating expenses for head count and exposure to risk for large capital investments.

in-sourcing (in-house development) Uses the professional expertise within an organization to develop and maintain its information technology systems.

outsourcing An arrangement by which one organization provides a service or services for another organization that chooses not to perform them in-house.

onshore outsourcing Engaging another company within the same country for services.

nearshore outsourcing Contracting an outsourcing arrangement with a company in a nearby country.

offshore outsourcing Using organizations from developing countries to write code and develop systems.

FIGURE 9.26 Outsourcing Models

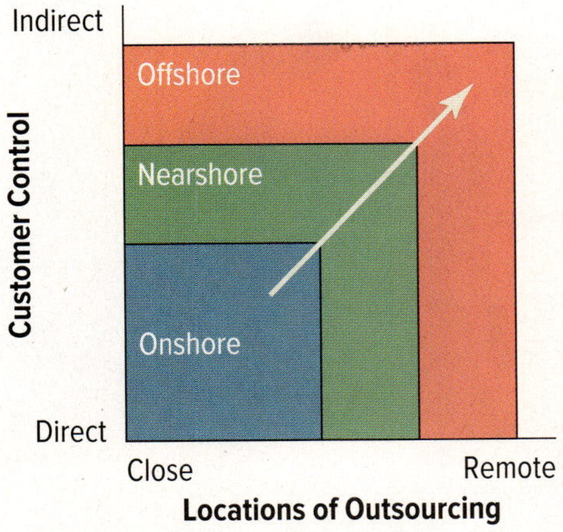

FIGURE 9.27 Typical Salary Ranges for Computer Programmers

Country	Salary Range Per Year
China	$5,000–$9,000
India	6,000–10,000
Philippines	6,500–11,000
Russia	7,000–13,000
Ireland	21,000–28,000
Canada	25,000–50,000
United States	60,000–90,000

Source: From Edward Yourdon, Death March, 2nd edition, © 2004. Reproduced by permission of Pearson Education, Inc., Upper Saddle River, New Jersey.

- Access to outsourcing service provider's expertise, economies of scale, best practices, and advanced technologies.
- Increased flexibility for faster response to market changes and less time to market for new products or services.

Outsourcing Challenges

Outsourcing comes with several challenges. These arguments are valid and should be considered when a company is thinking about outsourcing. Many challenges can be avoided with proper research. The challenges include:

- Length of contract. Most companies look at outsourcing as a long-term solution with a time period of several years. Training and transferring resources around the globe is difficult and expensive, hence most companies pursuing offshore outsourcing contract for multiple years of service. A few of the challenges facing the length of the contract include:

1. It can be difficult to break the contract.
2. Forecasting business needs for the next several years is challenging and the contract might not meet future business needs.
3. Re-creating an internal MIS department if the outsource provider fails is costly and challenging.

- Threat to competitive advantage. Many businesses view MIS as a competitive advantage and view outsourcing as a threat because the outsourcer could share the company's trade secrets.
- Loss of confidentiality. Information on pricing, products, sales, and customers can be a competitive asset and often critical for business success. Outsourcing could place confidential information in the wrong hands. Although confidentiality clauses contained in the contracts are supposed to protect the company, the potential risk and costs of a breach must be analyzed.

Every type of organization in business today relies on software to operate and solve complex problems or create exciting opportunities. Software built correctly can support nimble organizations and transform with them as they and their businesses transform. Software that effectively meets employee needs will help an organization become more productive and enhance decision making. Software that does not meet employee needs might have a damaging effect on productivity and can even cause a business to fail. Employee involvement in software development, along with the right implementation, is critical to the success of an organization.

Due Diligence //:

DUI in a Golf Cart[9]

Swedish police stopped Bill Murray and charged him with drunk driving when he attempted to drive his golf cart from Café Opera, an upscale restaurant in the center of town, back to his hotel. A golf cart only goes about three miles per hour, and it seems odd that you can be issued a DUI for driving one. However, different countries have different laws. A few other cultural blunders you want to avoid include:

- Several managers of an American company realized the brand name of the cooking oil they were marketing in a Latin American country translated into Spanish as "Jackass Oil."
- American Motors was excited to market its new car, the Matador, which was based on the image of courage and strength. However, in Puerto Rico the name Matador equates to "killer," and consumers were not willing to drive a Killer car on the country's hazardous roads.
- A new cologne advertisement pictured an idyllic scene with a man and his dog. It failed in Islamic countries because dogs are considered unclean.
- One popular Procter & Gamble European soap commercial featured a woman bathing and her husband entering the bathroom and smiling. P&G decided that the commercial did so well they would air it in Japan. The problem? The Japanese considered this ad an invasion of privacy, inappropriate behavior, and in very poor taste.
- One American refused to accept an offer of a cup of coffee from a Saudi businessman. Such a rejection is considered very rude, and the entire deal was ended.
- A golf ball manufacturing company packaged golf balls in packs of four for convenient purchase in Japan. Unfortunately, pronunciation of the word "four" in Japanese sounds like the word "death," and items packaged in fours are unpopular.

Companies that are expanding globally are looking for opportunities, not problems. Yet local laws and procedures that come into play when setting up shop abroad—everything from hiring and firing to tax filings—can be a minefield. What types of culture, language, and legal issues should a company expect to encounter when dealing with an outsourcing company? What can a company do to mitigate these risks?

© Image Source/Getty Images RF

show me *the* MONEY

Death March

Edward Yourdon's book *Death March* describes the complete software developer's guide to surviving "mission impossible" projects. MIS projects are challenging, and project managers are expected to achieve the impossible by pulling off a successful project even when pitted against impossible challenges. In *Death March,* infamous software developer Edward Yourdon presents his project classification displayed here. Yourdon measures projects based on the level of pain and chances for success.

- **Mission Impossible Project:** This project has a great chance of success and your hard work will pay off as you find happiness and joy in the work. For example, this is the type of project where you work all day and night for a year and become the project hero as you complete the mission impossible and reap a giant promotion as your reward.
- **Ugly Project:** This project has a high chance of success but is very painful and offers little happiness. For example, you work day and night to install a new accounting system and although successful, you hate accounting and dislike the company and its products.
- **Kamikaze Project:** This is a project that has little chance of success but you are so passionate about the content that you find great happiness working on the project. For example, you are asked to build a website to support a cancer foundation, a cause near to your heart, but the company is nonprofit and doesn't have any funds to help buy the software you need to get everything working. You patch the system together and implement many manual work-arounds just to keep the system functioning.
- **Suicide Project:** This project has no chance of success and offers you nothing but pain. This is the equivalent of your worst nightmare project. Word of caution, avoid suicide projects![12]

Analyze your school and work projects and find a project that would fit in each box. What could you have done differently on your suicide project to ensure its success? What can you do to avoid being placed on a suicide project? Given the choice, which type of project would you choose to work on and why?

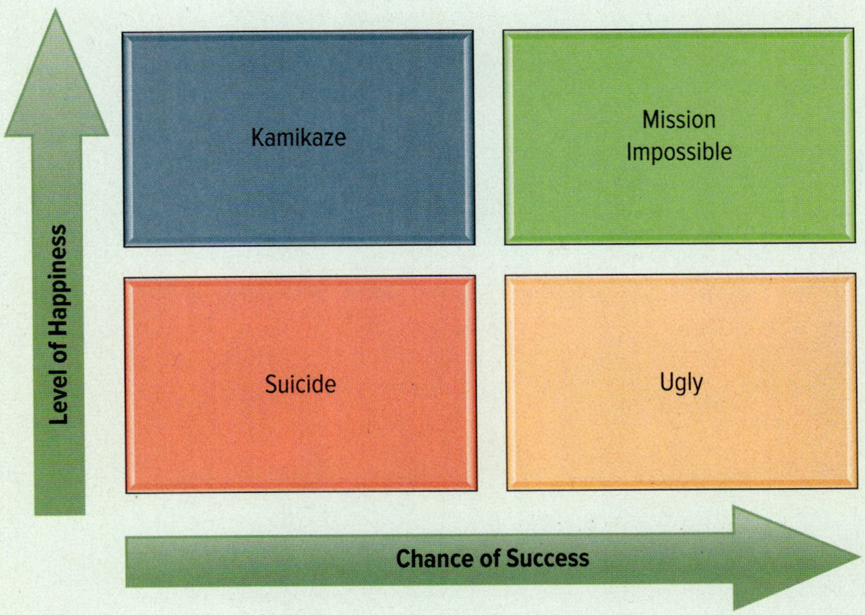

Glossary

3D printing Builds—layer by layer in an additive process—a three-dimensional solid object from a digital model.

3G A service that brings wireless broadband to mobile phones.

A

acceptable use policy (AUP) A policy that a user must agree to follow to be provided access to corporate email, information systems, and the Internet.

access point (AP) The computer or network device that serves as an interface between devices and the network.

accessibility Refers to the varying levels that define what a user can access, view, or perform when operating a system.

accounting and finance ERP component Manages accounting data and financial processes within the enterprise with functions such as general ledger, accounts payable, accounts receivable, budgeting, and asset management.

active RFID tags Have their own transmitter and a power source (typically a battery).

administrator access Unrestricted access to the entire system.

advanced encryption standard (AES) Introduced by the National Institute of Standards and Technology (NIST), AES is an encryption standard designed to keep government information secure.

adware Software, while purporting to serve some useful function and often fulfilling that function, also allows Internet advertisers to display advertisements without the consent of the computer user.

adwords Keywords that advertisers choose to pay for and appear as sponsored links on the Google results pages.

affinity grouping analysis Reveals the relationship between variables along with the nature and frequency of the relationships.

agile methodology Aims for customer satisfaction through early and continuous delivery of useful software components developed by an iterative process using the bare minimum requirements.

agile MIS infrastructure Includes the hardware, software, and telecommunications equipment that, when combined, provides the underlying foundation to support the organization's goals.

algorithm Mathematical formulas placed in software that performs an analysis on a data set.

analysis paralysis Occurs when the user goes into an emotional state of over-analysis (or over-thinking) a situation so that a decision or action is never taken, in effect paralyzing the outcome.

analysis phase The firm analyzes its end-user business requirements and refines project goals into defined functions and operations of the intended system.

analytical CRM Supports back-office operations and strategic analysis and includes all systems that do not deal directly with the customers.

analytical information Encompasses all organizational information, and its primary purpose is to support the performing of managerial analysis or semistructured decisions.

analytics The science of fact-based decision making.

anomaly detection The process of identifying rare or unexpected items or events in a data set that do not conform to other items in the data set.

anti-spam policy Simply states that email users will not send unsolicited emails (or spam).

antivirus software Scans and searches hard drives to prevent, detect, and remove known viruses, adware, and spyware.

applet A program that runs within another application such as a website.

application integration The integration of a company's existing management information systems to each other.

application programming interface (API) A set of routines, protocols, and tools for building software applications.

artificial intelligence (AI) Simulates human thinking and behavior such as the ability to reason and learn.

As-Is process model Represents the current state of the operation that has been mapped, without any specific improvements or changes to existing processes.

asset tracking Occurs when a company places active or semi-passive RFID tags on expensive products or assets to gather data on the items' location with little or no manual intervention.

asynchronous communication Communication such as email in which the message and the response do not occur at the same time.

attenuation Represents the loss of a network signal strength measured in decibels (dB) and occurs because the transmissions gradually dissipate in strength over longer distances or because of radio interference or physical obstructions such as walls.

attribute The data elements associated with an entity.

augmented reality The viewing of the physical world with computer-generated layers of information added to it.

authentication A method for confirming users' identities.

authorization The process of providing a user with permission including access levels and abilities such as file access, hours of access, and amount of allocated storage space.

automatic vehicle location (AVL) Uses GPS tracking to track vehicles.

automation Involves computerizing manual tasks making them more efficient and effective and dramatically lowering operational costs.

availability Refers to the time frames when the system is operational.

B

backup An exact copy of a system's information.

backward integration Takes information entered into a given system and sends it automatically to all upstream systems and processes.

balanced scorecard A management system, as well as a measurement system, that a firm uses to translate business strategies into executable tasks.

bandwidth The maximum amount of data that can pass from one point to another in a unit of time.

behavioral analytics Uses data about people's behaviors to understand intent and predict future actions.

benchmark Baseline values the system seeks to attain.

benchmarking A process of continuously measuring system results, comparing those results to optimal system performance (benchmark values), and identifying steps and procedures to improve system performance.

best practices The most successful solutions or problem-solving methods that have been developed by a specific organization or industry.

big data A collection of large, complex data sets, including structured and unstructured data, which cannot be analyzed using traditional database methods and tools.

Big Data as a Service (BDaaS) Offers a cloud-based Big Data service to help organizations analyze massive amounts of data to solve business dilemmas.

biometrics The identification of a user based on a physical characteristic, such as a fingerprint, iris, face, voice, or handwriting.

bit The smallest element of data and has a value of either 0 or 1.

bit rate The number of bits transferred or received per unit of time.

blog, or web log An online journal that allows users to post their own comments, graphics, and video.

bluetooth Wireless PAN technology that transmits signals over short distances between cell phones, computers, and other devices.

bottleneck Occurs when resources reach full capacity and cannot handle any additional demands; they limit throughput and impede operations.

BPMN activity Used to control the flow of a process.

BPMN event Anything that happens during the course of a business process.

BPMN flows Display the path in which the process flows.

brainstorming A technique for generating ideas by encouraging participants to offer as many ideas as possible in a short period of time without any analysis until all the ideas have been exhausted.

bring your own device (BYOD) policy Allows employees to use their personal mobile devices and computers to access enterprise data and applications.

broadband A high-speed Internet connection that is always connected.

broadband over power line (BPL) Technology makes possible high-speed Internet access over ordinary residential electrical lines and offers an alternative to DSL or high-speed cable modems.

bugs Defects in the code of an information system.

bullwhip effect Occurs when distorted product-demand information ripples from one partner to the next throughout the supply chain.

business continuity planning (BCP) Details how a company recovers and restores critical business operations and systems after a disaster or extended disruption.

business impact analysis A process that identifies all critical business functions and the effect that a specific disaster may have upon them.

business intelligence (BI) Information collected from multiple sources such as suppliers, customers, competitors, partners, and industries that analyze patterns, trends, and relationships for strategic decision making.

business intelligence dashboard Tracks corporate metrics such as critical success factors and key performance indicators and include advanced capabilities such as interactive controls, allowing users to manipulate data for analysis.

business model A plan that details how a company creates, delivers, and generates revenues.

business process Standardized set of activities that accomplish a specific task.

business process improvement Attempts to understand and measure the current process and make performance improvements accordingly.

business process model A graphic description of a process, showing the sequence of process tasks, which is developed for a specific purpose and from a selected viewpoint.

business process model and notation (BPMN) A graphical notation that depicts the steps in a business process.

business process modeling (or mapping) The activity of creating a detailed flowchart or process map of a work process that shows its inputs, tasks, and activities in a structured sequence.

business process patent A patent that protects a specific set of procedures for conducting a particular business activity.

business process reengineering (BPR) The analysis and redesign of workflow within and between enterprises.

business requirement The specific business requests the system must meet to be successful.

business rule Defines how a company performs a certain aspect of its business and typically results in either a yes/no or true/false answer.

business strategy A leadership plan that achieves a specific set of goals or objectives such as increasing sales, decreasing costs, entering new markets, or developing new products or services.

business-critical integrity constraint Enforces business rules vital to an organization's success and often requires more insight and knowledge than relational integrity constraints.

business-facing process Invisible to the external customer but essential to the effective management of the business; they include goal setting, day-to-day planning, giving performance feedback and rewards, and allocating resources.

business-to-business (B2B) Applies to businesses buying from and selling to each other over the Internet.

business-to-consumer (B2C) Applies to any business that sells its products or services directly to consumers online.

buyer power The ability of buyers to affect the price they must pay for an item.

C

cable modem (or broadband modem) A type of digital modem used with high-speed cable Internet service.

call scripting system Gathers product details and issue resolution information that can be automatically generated into a script for the representative to read to the customer.

campaign management system Guides users through marketing campaigns by performing such tasks as campaign definition, planning, scheduling, segmentation, and success analysis.

capacity Represents the maximum throughput a system can deliver; for example, the capacity of a hard drive represents the size or volume.

capacity planning Determines future environmental infrastructure requirements to ensure high-quality system performance.

carbon emissions Includes the carbon dioxide and carbon monoxide in the atmosphere, produced by business processes and systems.

cartography The science and art of making an illustrated map or chart.

certificate authority A trusted third party, such as VeriSign, that validates user identities by means of digital certificates.

change agent A person or event that is the catalyst for implementing major changes for a system to meet business changes.

chief automation officer Determines if a person or business process can be replaced by a robot or software.

chief data officer Responsible for determining the types of information the enterprise will capture, retain, analyze, and share.

chief information officer (CIO) Responsible for (1) overseeing all uses of MIS and (2) ensuring that MIS strategically aligns with business goals and objectives.

chief intellectual property officer Manage and defend intellectual property, copyrights, and patents.

chief knowledge officer (CKO) Responsible for collecting, maintaining, and distributing company knowledge.

chief privacy officer (CPO) Responsible for ensuring the ethical and legal use of information within a company.

chief security officer (CSO) Responsible for ensuring the security of MIS systems and developing strategies and MIS safeguards against attacks from hackers and viruses.

chief technology officer (CTO) Responsible for ensuring the throughput, speed, accuracy, availability, and reliability of an organization's information technology.

chief user experience officer Create the optimal relationship between user and technology.

Child Online Protection Act (COPA) A law that protects minors from accessing inappropriate material on the Internet.

chipless RFID tags Use plastic or conductive polymers instead of silicon-based microchips, allowing them to be washed or exposed to water without damaging the chip.

classfiication analysis The process of organizing data into categories or groups for its most effective and efficient use.

clean computing A subset of sustainable MIS, refers to the environmentally responsible use, manufacture, and disposal of technology products and computer equipment.

click-fraud The abuse of pay-per-click, pay-per-call, and pay-per-conversion revenue models by repeatedly clicking on a link to increase charges or costs for the advertiser.

click-to-talk Allows customers to click on a button and talk with a representative via the Internet.

clickstream data Exact pattern of a consumer's navigation through a site.

client A computer designed to request information from a server.

closed source Any proprietary software licensed under exclusive legal right of the copyright holder.

cloud bursting When a company uses its own computing infrastructure for normal usage and accesses the cloud when it needs to scale for high/peak load requirements, ensuring a sudden spike in usage does not result in poor performance or system crashes.

cloud computing Stores, manages, and processes data and applications over the Internet rather than on a personal computer or server.

cloud fabric The software that makes the benefits of cloud computing possible, such as multi-tenancy.

cloud fabric controller An individual who monitors and provisions cloud resources similar to a server administrator at an individual company.

cluster analysis A technique used to divide information sets into mutually exclusive groups such that the members of each group are as close together as possible to one another and the different groups are as far apart as possible.

cold site A separate facility that does not have any computer equipment but is a place where employees can move after a disaster.

collaboration system A set of tools that supports the work of teams or groups by facilitating the sharing and flow of information.

collective intelligence Collaborating and tapping into the core knowledge of all employees, partners, and customers.

common data repository Allows every department of a company to store and retrieve information in real-time allowing information to be more reliable and accessible.

community cloud Serves a specific community with common business models, security requirements, and compliance considerations.

comparative analysis Compares two or more data sets to identify patterns and trends.

competitive advantage A feature of a product or service on which customers place a greater value than on similar offerings from competitors.

competitive click-fraud A computer crime where a competitor or disgruntled employee increases a company's search advertising costs by repeatedly clicking on the advertiser's link.

competitive intelligence The process of gathering information about the competitive environment, including competitors' plans, activities, and products, to improve a company's ability to succeed.

competitive monitoring When a company keeps tabs of its competitor's activities on the web using software that automatically tracks all competitor website activities such as discounts and new products.

computer-aided software engineering (CASE) Software tools provide automated support for the development of the system.

computer-aided design/computer-aided manufacturing (CAD/CAM) Systems are used to create the digital designs and then manufacture the products.

confidentiality The assurance that messages and information remain available only to those authorized to view them.

consumer-to-business (C2B) Applies to any consumer who sells a product or service to a business on the Internet.

consumer-to-consumer (C2C) Applies to customers offering goods and services to each other on the Internet.

contact center or call center Where customer service representatives answer customer inquiries and solve problems, usually by email, chat, or phone.

contact management CRM system Maintains customer contact information and identifies prospective customers for future sales, using tools such as organizational charts, detailed customer notes, and supplemental sales information.

content creator The person responsible for creating the original website content.

content editor The person responsible for updating and maintaining website content.

content filtering Occurs when organizations use software that filters content, such as emails, to prevent the accidental or malicious transmission of unauthorized information.

content management system (CMS) Helps companies manage the creation, storage, editing, and publication of their website content.

control objects for information and related technologies (COBIT) A set of best practices that helps an organization to maximize the benefits of an information system, while at the same time establishing appropriate controls to ensure minimum errors.

conversion The process of transferring information from a legacy system to a new system.

copyright The legal protection afforded an expression of an idea, such as a song, book, or video game.

core ERP component The traditional components included in most ERP systems and primarily focus on internal operations.

core process Business processes, such as manufacturing goods, selling products, and providing service that make up the primary activities in a value chain.

corporate social responsibility Companies' acknowledged responsibility to society.

corrective maintenance Makes system changes to repair design flaws, coding errors, or implementation issues.

counterfeit software Software that is manufactured to look like the real thing and sold as such.

cradle-to-grave Provides logistics support throughout the entire system or life of the product.

critical path Estimates the shortest path through the project ensuring all critical tasks are completed from start to finish.

critical success factors (CSFs) Crucial steps companies perform to achieve their goals and objectives and implement their strategies.

CRM analysis technologies Help organizations segment their customers into categories such as best and worst customers.

CRM predicting technologies Help organizations predict customer behavior, such as which customers are at risk of leaving.

CRM reporting technologies Help organizations identify their customers across other applications.

cross-selling Selling additional products or services to an existing customer.

crowdfunding Sources capital for a project by raising many small amounts from a large number of individuals, typically via the Internet.

crowdsourcing Refers to the wisdom of the crowd.

cryptography The science that studies encryption, which is the hiding of messages so that only the sender and receiver can read them.

cube The common term for the representation of multidimensional information.

customer analytics Involves gathering, classifying, comparing, and studying customer data to identify buying trends, at-risk customers, and potential future opportunities.

customer relationship management (CRM) A means of managing all aspects of a customer's relationship with an organization to increase customer loyalty and retention and an organization's profitability.

customer segementation Divides a market into categories that share similar attributes such as age, location, gender, habits, and so on.

customer service and support (CSS) A part of operational CRM that automates service requests, complaints, product returns, and information requests.

customer-facing process Results in a product or service that is received by an organization's external customer.

cyberbulling Threats, negative remarks, or defamatory comments transmitted via the Internet or posted on a website.

cybermediation Refers to the creation of new kinds of intermediaries that simply could not have existed before the advent of ebusiness.

cyberterrorism The use of computer and networking technologies against persons or property to intimidate or coerce governments, individuals, or any segment of society to attain political, religious, or ideological goals.

cybervandalism The electronic defacing of an existing website.

cyberwar An organized attempt by a country's military to disrupt or destroy information and communication systems for another country.

cycle time The time required to process an order.

D

data Raw facts that describe the characteristics of an event or object.

data aggregation The collection of data from various sources for the purpose of data processing.

Data as a Service (DaaS) Facilitates the accessibility of business-critical data in a timely, secure, and affordable manner.

data artist A business analytics specialist who uses visual tools to help people understand complex data.

data broker A business that collects personal information about consumers and sells that information to other organizations.

data center A facility used to house management information systems and associated components, such as telecommunications and storage systems.

data dictionary Compiles all of the metadata about the data elements in the data model.

data element (or data field) The smallest or basic unit of information.

data flow diagram Illustrates the movement of information between external entities and the processes and data stores within the system.

data gap analysis Occurs when a company examines its data to determine if it can meet business expectations, while identifying possible data gaps or where missing data might exist.

data governance Refers to the overall management of the availability, usability, integrity, and security of company data

data integration The integration of data from multiple sources, which provides a unified view of all data.

data lake A storage repository that holds a vast amount of raw data in its original format until the business needs it.

data mart Contains a subset of data warehouse information.

data mining The process of analyzing data to extract information not offered by the raw data alone.

data mining tool Uses a variety of techniques to find patterns and relationships in large volumes of information that predict future behavior and guide decision making.

data model Logical data structures that detail the relationships among data elements using graphics or pictures.

data point An individual item on a graph or a chart.

data profiling The process of collecting statistics and information about data in an existing source.

data replication The process of sharing information to ensure consistency between multiple data sources.

data scientist Extracts knowledge from data by performing statistical analysis, data mining, and advanced analytics on big data to identify trends, market changes, and other relevant information.

data steward Responsible for ensuring the policies and procedures are implemented across the organization and acts as a liaison between the MIS department and the business.

data stewardship The management and oversight of an organization's data assets to help provide business users with high-quality data that is easily accessible in a consistent manner.

data set An organized collection of data.

data validation Includes the tests and evaluations used to determine compliance with data governance polices to ensure correctness of data.

data latency The time it takes for data to be stored or retrieved.

data map A technique for establishing a match, or balance, between the source data and the target data warehouse.

data visualization Describes technologies that allow users to "see" or visualize data to transform information into a business perspective.

data visualization tools Moves beyond Excel graphs and charts into sophisticated analysis techniques such as pie charts, controls, instruments, maps, time-series graphs, etc.

data warehouse A logical collection of information, gathered from many different operational databases, that supports business analysis activities and decision-making tasks.

data-driven decision management An approach to business governance that values decisions that can be backed up with verifiable data.

database Maintains information about various types of objects (inventory), events (transactions), people (employees), and places (warehouses).

database management system (DBMS) Creates, reads, updates, and deletes data in a database while controlling access and security.

data-driven website An interactive website kept constantly updated and relevant to the needs of its customers using a database.

decision support system (DSS) Model information using OLAP, which provides assistance in evaluating and choosing among different courses of action.

decrypt Decodes information and is the opposite of encrypted.

dependency A logical relationship that exists between the project tasks, or between a project task and a milestone.

design phase Establishes descriptions of the desired features and operations of the system including screen layouts, business rules, process diagrams, pseudo code, and other documentation.

destructive agents Malicious agents designed by spammers and other Internet attackers to farm email addresses off websites or deposit spyware on machines.

development phase Takes all the detailed design documents from the design phase and transforms them into the actual system.

digital certificate A data file that identifies individuals or organizations online and is comparable to a digital signature.

digital Darwinism Implies that organizations that cannot adapt to the new demands placed on them for surviving in the information age are doomed to extinction.

digital dashboard Tracks KPIs and CSFs by compiling information from multiple sources and tailoring it to meet user needs.

digital divide A worldwide gap giving advantage to those with access to technology.

digital rights management A technological solution that allows publishers to control their digital media to discourage, limit, or prevent illegal copying and distribution.

disaster recovery as a service (DRaaS) Offers backup services that use cloud resources to protect applications and data from disruption caused by disaster.

digital subscriber line (DSL) Provides high-speed digital data transmission over standard telephone lines using broadband modem technology allowing both Internet and telephone services to work over the same phone lines.

disaster recovery cost curve Charts (1) the cost to the company of the unavailability of information and technology and (2) the cost to the company of recovering from a disaster over time.

disaster recovery plan A detailed process for recovering information or a system in the event of a catastrophic disaster.

discovery prototyping Builds a small-scale representation or working model of the system to ensure it meets the user and business requirements.

disintermediation Occurs when a business sells direct to the customer online and cuts out the intermediary.

disruptive technology A new way of doing things that initially does not meet the needs of existing customers.

distributed computing Processes and manages algorithms across many machines in a computing environment.

domain name hosting (web hosting) A service that allows the owner of a domain name to maintain a simple website and provide email capacity.

domain name system (DNS) Converts IP address into domains, or identifying labels that use a variety of recognizable naming conventions.

dot-com The original term for a company operating on the Internet.

downtime Refers to a period of time when a system is unavailable.

drive-by hacking A computer attack where an attacker accesses a wireless computer network, intercepts data, uses network services, and/or sends attack instructions without entering the office or organization that owns the network.

drone An unmanned aircraft that can fly autonomously, or without a human.

dumpster diving Looking through people's trash, another way hackers obtain information.

dynamic catalog An area of a website that stores information about products in a database.

dynamic host configuration protocol (DHCP) Allows dynamic IP address allocation so users do not have to have a preconfigured IP address to use the network.

dynamic information Includes data that change based on user actions.

dynamic report A report that changes automatically during creation.

dynamic process A continuously changing process that provides business solutions to ever-changing business operations.

dynamic scaling Means that the MIS infrastructure can be automatically scaled up or down based on needed requirements.

E

ebusiness Includes ecommerce along with all activities related to internal and external business operations such as servicing customer accounts, collaborating with partners, and exchanging real-time information.

ebusiness model A plan that details how a company creates, delivers, and generates revenues on the Internet.

ecommerce The buying and selling of goods and services over the Internet.

edge matching (warping, rubber sheeting) Occurs when paper maps are laid edge to edge, and items that run across maps but do not match are reconfigured to match.

ediscovery (or electronic discovery) Refers to the ability of a company to identify, search, gather, seize, or export digital information in responding to a litigation, audit, investigation, or information inquiry.

effectiveness MIS metrics Measure the impact MIS has on business processes and activities including customer satisfaction and customer conversion rates.

efficiency MIS metrics Measure the performance of MIS itself such as throughput, transaction speed, and system availability.

egovernment Involves the use of strategies and technologies to transform government(s) by improving the delivery of services and enhancing the quality of interaction between the citizen-consumer within all branches of government.

eintegration The use of the Internet to provide customers with the ability to gain personalized information by querying corporate databases and their information sources.

electronic data interchange (EDI) A standard format for the electronic exchange of information between supply chain participants.

elogistics Manages the transportation and storage of goods.

email privacy policy Details the extent to which email messages may be read by others.

emergency A sudden, unexpected event requiring immediate action due to potential threat to health and safety, the environment, or property.

emergency notification service An infrastructure built for notifying people in the event of an emergency.

emergency preparedness Ensures a company is ready to respond to an emergency in an organized, timely, and effective manner.

employee monitoring policy States explicitly how, when, and where the company monitors its employees.

employee relationship management (ERM) Provides web-based self-service tools that streamline and automate the human resource department.

encryption Scrambles information into an alternative form that requires a key or password to decrypt.

energy consumption The amount of energy consumed by business processes and systems.

enterprise application integration (EAI) Connects the plans, methods, and tools aimed at integrating separate enterprise systems.

enterprise application integration (EAI) middleware Takes a new approach to middleware by packaging commonly used applications together, reducing the time needed to integrate applications from multiple vendors.

enterprise architect A person grounded in technology, fluent in business, and able to provide the important bridge between MIS and the business.

enterprise resource planning (ERP) Integrates all departments and functions throughout an organization into a single MIS system (or integrated set of MIS systems) so employees can make decisions by viewing enterprisewide information about all business operations.

enterprise system Provides enterprisewide support and data access for a firm's operations and business processes.

entity Stores information about a person, place, thing, transaction, or event.

entry barrier A feature of a product or service that customers have come to expect and entering competitors must offer the same for survival.

epolicies Policies and procedures that address information management along with the ethical use of computers and the Internet in the business environment.

eprocurement The business-to-business (B2B) online purchase and sale of supplies and services.

eshop (estore or etailer) An online version of a retail store where customers can shop at any hour.

estimated time enroute (ETE) The time remaining before reaching a destination using the present speed; typically used for navigation applications.

estimated time of arrival (ETA) The time of day of an expected arrival at a certain destination; typically used for navigation applications.

estimation analysis Determines values for an unknown continuous variable behavior or estimated future value.

ethical computer use policy Contains general principles to guide computer user behavior.

ethics The principles and standards that guide our behavior toward other people.

ewaste Refers to discarded, obsolete, or broken electronic devices.

executive information system (EIS) A specialized DSS that supports senior-level executives and unstructured, long-term, nonroutine decisions requiring judgment, evaluation, and insight.

expert system Computerized advisory programs that imitate the reasoning processes of experts in solving difficult problems.

explicit knowledge Consists of anything that can be documented, archived, and codified, often with the help of MIS.

extended ERP component The extra components that meet organizational needs not covered by the core components and primarily focus on external operations.

extensible markup language (XML) A markup language for documents, containing structured information.

extraction, transformation, and loading (ETL) A process that extracts information from internal and external databases, transforms it using a common set of enterprise definitions, and loads it into a data warehouse.

extranet An extension of an intranet that is only available to authorized outsiders, such as customers, partners, and suppliers.

extreme programming (XP) methodology Breaks a project into four phases, and developers cannot continue to the next phase until the previous phase is complete.

F

fact The confirmation or validation of an event or object.

failback Occurs when the primary machine recovers and resumes operations, taking over from the secondary server.

failover A specific type of fault tolerance, occurs when a redundant storage server offers an exact replica of the real-time data, and if the primary server crashes the users are automatically directed to the secondary server or backup server.

fair information practices A general term for a set of standards governing the collection and use of personal data and addressing issues of privacy and accuracy.

fast data The application of big data analytics to smaller data sets in near-real or real-time in order to solve a problem or create business value.

fault tolerance A general concept that a system has the ability to respond to unexpected failures or system crashes as the backup system immediately and automatically takes over with no loss of service.

feasibility The measure of the tangible and intangible benefits of an information system.

feedback Information that returns to its original transmitter (input, transform, or output) and modifies the transmitter's actions.

file transfer protocol (FTP) A simple network protocol that allows the transfer of files between two computers on the Internet.

firewall Hardware and/or software that guard a private network by analyzing incoming and outgoing information for the correct markings.

first-mover advantage An advantage that occurs when a company can significantly increase its market share by being first to market with a competitive advantage.

folksonomy Similar to taxonomy except that crowdsourcing determines the tags or keyword-based classification system.

forecasting model Predictions based on time-series information allowing users to manipulate the time series for forecasting activities.

foreign key A primary key of one table that appears as an attribute in another table and acts to provide a logical relationship between the two tables.

forward integration Takes information entered into a given system and sends it automatically to all downstream systems and processes.

fourth-generation languages (4GL) Programming languages that look similar to human languages.

fuzzy logic A mathematical method of handling imprecise or subjective information.

G

Gantt chart A simple bar chart that lists project tasks vertically against the project's time frame, listed horizontally.

genetic algorithm An artificial intelligence system that mimics the evolutionary, survival-of-the-fittest process to generate increasingly better solutions to a problem.

geocache A GPS technology adventure game that posts on the Internet the longitude and latitude location of an item for users to find.

geocoding A coding process that takes a digital map feature and assigns it an attribute that serves as a unique ID (tract number, node number) or classification (soil type, zoning category).

geocoin A round coin-sized object that is uniquely numbered and hidden in geocache.

geographic information system (GIS) Stores, views, and analyzes geographic data, creating multidimensional charts or maps.

GIS map automation Links business assets to a centralized system where they can be tracked and monitored over time.

global positioning system (GPS) A satellite-based navigation system providing extremely accurate position, time, and speed information.

goods Material items or products that customers will buy to satisfy a want or need. Clothing, groceries, cell phones, and cars are all examples of goods that people buy to fulfill their needs.

granularity Refers to the level of detail in the model or the decision-making process.

green personal computer (green PC) Built using environment-friendly materials and designed to save energy.

grid computing A collection of computers, often geographically dispersed, that are coordinated to solve a common problem.

H

hackers Experts in technology who use their knowledge to break into computers and computer networks, either for profit or motivated by the challenge.

hardware Consists of the physical devices associated with a computer system.

hashtag A keyword or phrase used to identify a topic and is preceded by a hash or pound sign (#).

help desk A group of people who respond to users' questions.

high availability Occurs when a system is continuously operational at all times.

high-speed Internet cable connection Provides Internet access using a cable television company's infrastructure and a special cable modem.

horizontal privilege escalation Attackers grant themselves the same access levels they already have but assume the identity of another user.

hot site A separate and fully equipped facility where the company can move immediately after a disaster and resume business.

hotspot Designated locations where Wi-Fi access points are publicly available.

human resources ERP component Tracks employee information including payroll, benefits, compensation, and performance assessment and ensures compliance with all laws.

human-generated data Data that humans, in interaction with computers, generate.

hybrid cloud Includes two or more private, public, or community clouds, but each cloud remains separate and is only linked by technology that enables data and application portability.

hybrid ERP Splits the ERP functions between an on-premises ERP system and one or more functions handled as Software as a Service (SaaS) in the cloud.

hypertext markup language (HTML) Links documents allowing users to move from one to another simply by clicking on a hot spot or link.

hypertext transport protocol (HTTP) The Internet protocol web browsers use to request and display web pages using universal resource locators.

I

identity theft The forging of someone's identity for the purpose of fraud.

identity management A broad administrative area that deals with identifying individuals in a system (such as a country, a network, or an enterprise) and controlling their access to resources within that system by associating user rights and restrictions with the established identity.

IEEE 802.11n (or Wireless-N) The newest standard for wireless networking.

implementation phase The organization places the system into production so users can begin to perform actual business operations with it.

incident Unplanned interruption of a service.

incident management The process responsible for managing how incidents are identified and corrected.

incident record Contains all of the details of an incident.

infographics (information graphics) Presents the results of data analysis, displaying the patterns, relationships, and trends in a graphical format.

information Data converted into a meaningful and useful context.

information age The present time, during which infinite quantities of facts are widely available to anyone who can use a computer.

information architecture The set of ideas about how all information in a given context should be organized.

information cleansing or scrubbing A process that weeds out and fixes or discards inconsistent, incorrect, or incomplete information.

information ethics Govern the ethical and moral issues arising from the development and use of information technologies, as well as the creation, collection, duplication, distribution, and processing of information itself (with or without the aid of computer technologies).

information granularity The extent of detail within the information (fine and detailed or coarse and abstract).

information inconsistency Occurs when the same data element has different values.

information integrity A measure of the quality of information.

information integrity issue Occurs when a system produces incorrect, inconsistent, or duplicate data.

information MIS infrastructure Identifies where and how important information, such as customer records, is maintained and secured.

information privacy policy Contains general principles regarding information privacy.

information reach Measures the number of people a firm can communicate with all over the world.

information redundancy The duplication of data, or the storage of the same data in multiple places.

information richness Refers to the depth and breadth of details contained in a piece of textual, graphic, audio, or video information.

information secrecy The category of computer security that addresses the protection of data from unauthorized disclosure and confirmation of data source authenticity.

information security A broad term encompassing the protection of information from accidental or intentional misuse by persons inside or outside an organization.

information security plan Details how an organization will implement the information security policies.

information security policies Identify the rules required to maintain information security, such as requiring users to log off before leaving for lunch or meetings, never sharing passwords with anyone, and changing passwords every 30 days.

Infrastructure as a Service (IaaS) The delivery of computer hardware capability, including the use of servers, networking, and storage, as a service.

insiders Legitimate users who purposely or accidentally misuse their access to the environment and cause some kind of business-affecting incident.

in-sourcing (in-house development) Uses the professional expertise within an organization to develop and maintain its information technology systems.

instant messaging (sometimes called IM or IMing) A service that enables "instant" or real-time communication between people.

Institute of Electrical and Electronics Engineers (IEEE) An organization that researches and institutes electrical standards for communication and other technologies.

intangible benefits Difficult to quantify or measure.

integration Allows separate systems to communicate directly with each other, eliminating the need for manual entry into multiple systems.

integrity constraint Rules that help ensure the quality of information.

intellectual property Intangible creative work that is embodied in physical form and includes copyrights, trademarks, and patents.

intelligent agent A special-purpose knowledge-based information system that accomplishes specific tasks on behalf of its users.

intelligent system Various commercial applications of artificial intelligence.

interactivity Measures advertising effectiveness by counting visitor interactions with the target ad, including time spent viewing the ad, number of pages viewed, and number of repeat visits to the advertisement.

intermediaries Agents, software, or businesses that provide a trading infrastructure to bring buyers and sellers together.

Internet A massive network that connects computers all over the world and allows them to communicate with one another.

Internet censorship Government attempts to control Internet traffic, thus preventing some material from being viewed by a country's citizens.

Internet of Things A world where interconnected, Internet-enabled devices or "things" can collect and share data without human intervention.

Internet protocol TV (IPTV) Distributes digital video content using IP across the Internet and private IP networks.

Internet service provider (ISP) A company that provides access to the Internet for a monthly fee.

Internet use policy Contains general principles to guide the proper use of the Internet.

interoperability The capability of two or more computer systems to share data and resources, even though they are made by different manufacturers.

intranet A restricted network that relies on Internet technologies to provide an Internet-like environment within the company for information sharing, communications, collaboration, web publishing, and the support of business process.

intrusion detection software (IDS) Features full-time monitoring tools that search for patterns in network traffic to identify intruders.

IP address A unique number that identifies where computers are located on the network.

IT consumerization The blending of personal and business use of technology devices and applications.

iterative development Consists of a series of tiny projects.

J

joint application development (JAD) A session where employees meet, sometimes for several days, to define or review the business requirements for the system.

K

key performance indicators (KPIs) Quantifiable metrics a company uses to evaluate progress towards critical success factors.

kill switch A trigger that enables a project manager to close the project before completion.

knowledge Skills, experience, and expertise coupled with information and intelligence that creates a person's intellectual resources.

knowledge management (KM) Involves capturing, classifying, evaluating, retrieving, and sharing information assets in a way that provides context for effective decisions and actions.

knowledge management system (KMS) Supports the capturing, organization, and dissemination of knowledge (i.e., know-how) throughout an organization.

knowledge worker Individuals valued for their ability to interpret and analyze information.

L

latitude Represents a north/south measurement of position.

legacy system An old system that is fast approaching or beyond the end of its useful life within an organization.

list generator Compiles customer information from a variety of sources and segments it for different marketing campaigns.

local area network (LAN) Connects a group of computers in proximity, such as in an office building, school, or home.

location-based services (LBS) Applications that use location information to provide a service.

logical view of information Shows how individual users logically access information to meet their own particular business needs.

longitude Represents an east/west measurement of position.

long tail Referring to the tail of a typical sales curve.

loose coupling The capability of services to be joined on demand to create composite services or disassembled just as easily into their functional components.

logistics Includes the processes that control the distribution, maintenance, and replacement of materials and personnel to support the supply chain.

loyalty program A program to reward customers based on spending.

M

machine to machine (M2M) Devices that connect directly to other devices.

machine-generated data Data created by a machine without human intervention.

mail bomb Sends a massive amount of email to a specific person or system that can cause that user's server to stop functioning.

maintainability (or flexibility) Refers to how quickly a system can transform to support environmental changes.

maintenance phase The organization performs changes, corrections, additions, and upgrades to ensure the system continues to meet its business goals.

maker movement A cultural trend that places value on an individual's ability to be a creator of things as well as a consumer of things.

makerspace A community center that provides technology, manufacturing equipment, and educational opportunities to the public that would otherwise be inaccessible or unaffordable.

management information systems A business function, like accounting and human resources, which moves information about people, products, and processes across the company to facilitate decision making and problem solving.

managerial business processes Semidynamic, semiroutine, monthly business processes such as resource allocation, sales strategy, or manufacturing process improvements.

managerial level Employees are continuously evaluating company operations to hone the firm's abilities to identify, adapt to, and leverage change.

market basket analysis Evaluates such items as websites and checkout scanner information to detect customers' buying behavior and predict future behavior by identifying affinities among customers' choices of products and services.

market share The proportion of the market that a firm captures.

mashup A website or web application that uses content from more than one source to create a completely new product or service.

mashup editor WYSIWYGs or What You See Is What You Get tools.

mass customization The ability of an organization to tailor its products or services to the customers' specifications.

master data management (MDM) The practice of gathering data and ensuring that it is uniform, accurate, consistent, and complete, including such entities as customers, suppliers, products, sales, employees, and other critical entities that are commonly integrated across organizational systems

materials management Includes activities that govern the flow of tangible, physical materials through the supply chain such as shipping, transport, distribution, and warehousing.

metadata Details about data.

methodology A set of policies, procedures, standards, processes, practices, tools, techniques, and tasks that people apply to technical and management challenges.

metrics Measurements that evaluate results to determine whether a project is meeting its goals.

metropolitan area network (MAN) A large computer network usually spanning a city.

microblogging The practice of sending brief posts (140 to 200 characters) to a personal blog, either publicly or to a private group of subscribers who can read the posts as IMs or as text messages.

middleware Several different types of software that sit between and provide connectivity for two or more software applications.

MIS infrastructure Includes the plans for how a firm will build, deploy, use, and share its data, processes, and MIS assets.

MIS skills gap The difference between existing MIS workplace knowledge and the knowledge required to fulfill the business goals and strategies.

mobile device management(MDM) Remotely controls smartphones and tablets, ensuring data security.

mobile business (or mbusiness, mcommerce) The ability to purchase goods and services through a wireless Internet-enabled device.

model A simplified representation or abstraction of reality.

modem A device that enables a computer to transmit and receive data.

Moore's Law Refers to the computer chip performance per dollar doubling every 18 months.

module software design Divides the system into a set of functional units (named modules) that can be used independently or combined with other modules for increased business flexibility.

multiple-in/multiple-out (MIMO) technology Multiple transmitters and receivers allow sending and receiving greater amounts of data than traditional networking devices.

multi-tenancy A single instance of a system serves multiple customers.

multifactor authentication Requires more than two means of authentication such as what the user knows (password),

mutation The process within a genetic algorithm of randomly trying combinations and evaluating the success (or failure) of the outcome.

N

national service providers (NSPs) Private companies that own and maintain the worldwide backbone that supports the Internet.

native advertising An online marketing concept in which the advertiser attempts to gain attention by providing content in the context of the user's experience in terms of its content, format, style, or placement.

nearshore outsourcing Contracting an outsourcing arrangement with a company in a nearby country.

network A communications system created by linking two or more devices and establishing a standard methodology in which they can communicate.

network convergence The efficient coexistence of telephone, video, and data communication within a single network, offering convenience and flexibility not possible with separate infrastructures.

network effect Describes how products in a network increase in value to users as the number of users increases.

network virtualization Combines networks by splitting the available bandwidth into independent channels that can be assigned in real time to a specific device.

neural network A category of AI that attempts to emulate the way the human brain works.

nonrepudiation A contractual stipulation to ensure that ebusiness participants do not deny (repudiate) their online actions.

O

object-oriented language Languages group data and corresponding processes into objects.

offshore outsourcing Using organizations from developing countries to write code and develop systems.

on-premise system Includes a server at a physical location using an internal network for internal access and firewalls for remote users' access.

off-the-shelf application software Supports general business processes and does not require any specific software customization to meet the organization's needs.

online analytical processing (OLAP) The manipulation of information to create business intelligence in support of strategic decision making.

online training Runs over the Internet or on a CD or DVD, and employees complete the training on their own time at their own pace.

online transaction processing (OLTP) The capturing of transaction and event information using technology to (1) process the information according to defined business rules, (2) store the information, and (3) update existing information to reflect the new information.

onshore outsourcing Engaging another company within the same country for services.

open source Refers to any software whose source code is made available free for any third party to review and modify.

open system Consists of nonproprietary hardware and software based on publicly known standards that allows third parties to create add-on products to plug into or interoperate with the system.

operational business processes Static, routine, daily business processes such as stocking inventory, checking out customers, or daily opening and closing processes.

operational CRM Supports traditional transactional processing for day-to-day front-office operations or systems that deal directly with the customers.

operational level Employees develop, control, and maintain core business activities required to run the day-to-day operations.

opportunity management CRM system Targets sales opportunities by finding new customers or companies for future sales.

opt in A user can opt in to receive emails by choosing to allow permissions to incoming emails.

opt out Customer specifically chooses to deny permission of receiving emails.

optimization model A statistical process that finds the way to make a design, system, or decision as effective as possible, for example, finding the values of controllable variables that determine maximal productivity or minimal waste.

outlier Data value that is numerically distant from most of the other data points in a set of data.

outsourcing An arrangement by which one organization provides a service or services for another organization that chooses not to perform them in-house.

P

packet A single unit of binary data routed through a network.

packet footer Represents the end of the packet or transmission end.

packet header Lists the destination (for example, in IP packets the destination is the IP address) along with the length of the message data.

paradigm shift Occurs when a new radical form of business enters the market that reshapes the way companies and organizations behave.

partner relationship management (PRM) Discovers optimal sales channels by selecting the right partners and identifying mutual customers.

passive RFID tags Do not have a power source.

password String of alphanumeric characters used to authenticate a user and provide access to a system.

patent An exclusive right to make, use, and sell an invention granted by a government to the inventor.

pay-per-call Generates revenue each time users click on a link that takes them directly to an online agent waiting for a call.

pay-per-click Generates revenue each time a user clicks on a link to a retailer's website.

pay-per-conversion Generates revenue each time a website visitor is converted to a customer.

peer-to-peer (P2P) network A computer network that relies on the computing power and bandwidth of the participants in the network rather than a centralized server.

performance Measures how quickly a system performs a process or transaction.

personal area network (PAN) Provide communication over a short distance that is intended for use with devices that are owned and operated by a single user.

personalization Occurs when a company knows enough about a customer's likes and dislikes that it can fashion offers more likely to appeal to that person, say by tailoring its website to individuals or groups based on profile information, demographics, or prior transactions.

PERT (Program Evaluation and Review Technique) chart A graphical network model that depicts a project's tasks and the relationships between them.

pharming Reroutes requests for legitimate websites to false websites.

pharming attack Uses a zombie farm, often by an organized crime association, to launch a massive phishing attack.

phishing A technique to gain personal information for the purpose of identity theft, usually by means of fraudulent emails that look as though they came from legitimate sources.

phishing expedition A masquerading attack that combines spam with spoofing.

physical security Tangible protection such as alarms, guards, fireproof doors, fences, and vaults.

physical view of information The physical storage of information on a storage device.

pirated software The unauthorized use, duplication, distribution, or sale of copyrighted software.

planning phase Establishes a high-level plan of the intended project and determines project goals.

Platform as a Service (PaaS) Supports the deployment of entire systems including hardware, networking, and applications using a pay-per-use revenue model.

podcasting Converts an audio broadcast to a digital music player.

portability Refers to the ability of an application to operate on different devices or software platforms, such as different operating systems.

Porter's three generic strategies Generic business strategies that are neither organization nor industry specific and can be applied to any business, product, or service.

Porter's Five Forces Model A model for analyzing the competitive forces within the environment in which a company operates, to assess the potential for profitability in an industry.

prediction A statement about what will happen or might happen in the future, for example, predicting future sales or employee turnover.

predictive analytics Extracts information from data and uses it to predict future trends and identify behavioral patterns.

preventive maintenance Makes system changes to reduce the chance of future system failure.

pretexting A form of social engineering in which one individual lies to obtain confidential data about another individual.

primary key A field (or group of fields) that uniquely identifies a given record in a table.

primary value activities Found at the bottom of the value chain, these include business processes that acquire raw materials and manufacture, deliver, market, sell, and provide after-sales services.

privacy The right to be left alone when you want to be, to have control over your personal possessions, and not to be observed without your consent.

private cloud Serves only one customer or organization and can be located on the customers' premises or off the customer's premises.

privilege escalation A network intrusion attack that takes advantage of programming errors or design flaws to grant the attacker elevated access to the network and its associated data and applications.

procurement The purchasing of goods and services to meet the needs of the supply chain.

product differentiation An advantage that occurs when a company develops unique differences in its products with the intent to influence demand.

production The process where a business takes raw materials and processes them or converts them into a finished product for its goods or services.

production and materials management ERP component Handles production planning and execution tasks such as demand forecasting, production scheduling, job cost accounting, and quality control.

productivity The rate at which goods and services are produced based upon total output given total inputs.

project Temporary activity a company undertakes to create a unique product, service, or result.

project management The application of knowledge, skills, tools, and techniques to project activities to meet project requirements.

project manager An individual who is an expert in project planning and management, defines and develops the project plan, and tracks the plan to ensure the project is completed on time and on budget.

project plan A formal, approved document that manages and controls project execution.

project scope Describes the business needs and the justification, requirements, and current boundaries for the project.

protocol A standard that specifies the format of data as well as the rules to be followed during transmission.

prototyping A modern design approach where the designers and system users use an iterative approach to building the system.

proxy Software that prevents direct communication between a sending and receiving computer and is used to monitor packets for security reasons.

public cloud Promotes massive, global, industrywide applications offered to the general public.

public key encryption (PKE) Uses two keys: a public key that everyone can have and a private key for only the recipient.

Q

query-by-example (QBE) tool Helps users graphically design the answer to a question against a database.

R

radio-frequency identification (RFID) Uses electronic tags and labels to identify objects wirelessly over short distances.

ransomware A form of malicious software that infects your computer and asks for money. Simplelocker is a new ransomware program that encrypts your personal files and demands payment for the files' decryption keys.

rapid application development (RAD) methodology (also called rapid prototyping) Emphasizes extensive user involvement in the rapid and evolutionary construction of working prototypes of a system, to accelerate the systems development process.

rational unified process (RUP) methodology Provides a framework for breaking down the development of software into four "gates."

real simple syndication (RSS) A web format used to publish frequently updated works, such as blogs, news headlines, audio, and video in a standardized format.

real-time communication Occurs when a system updates information at the same rate it receives it.

real-time information Immediate, up-to-date information.

real-time system Provides real-time information in response to requests.

recommendation engine A data-mining algorithm that analyzes a customer's purchases and actions on a website and then uses the data to recommend complementary products.

record A collection of related data elements.

recovery The ability to get a system up and running in the event of a system crash or failure that includes restoring the information backup.

redundancy Occurs when a task or activity is unnecessarily repeated.

regression model Includes many techniques for modeling and analyzing several variables when the focus is on the relationship between a dependent variable and one or more independent variables.

regional service providers (RSPs) Offer Internet service by connecting to NSPs, but they also can connect directly to each other.

reintermediation Steps are added to the value chain as new players find ways to add value to the business process.

relational database management system Allows users to create, read, update, and delete data in a relational database.

relational database model Stores information in the form of logically related two-dimensional tables.

relational integrity constraint Rules that enforce basic and fundamental information-based constraints.

report A document containing data organized in a table, matrix, or graphical format allowing users to easily comprehend and understand information.

repository A central location in which data is stored and managed.

reliability (or accuracy) Ensures a system is functioning correctly and providing accurate information.

repeater Receives and repeats a signal to extend its attenuation or range.

reputation system Where buyers post feedback on sellers.

requirements definition document Prioritizes all of the business requirements by order of importance to the company.

requirements management The process of managing changes to the business requirements throughout the project.

return on investment (ROI) Indicates the earning power of a project.

RFID accelerometer A device that measures the acceleration (the rate of change of velocity) of an item and is used to track truck speeds or taxicab speeds.

RFID's electronic product code (RFID EPC) Promotes serialization or the ability to track individual items by using the unique serial number associated with each RFID tag.

RFID reader (RFID interrogator) A transmitter/receiver that reads the contents of RFID tags in the area.

RFID tag An electronic identification device that is made up of a chip and antenna.

rivalry among existing competitors One of Porter's five forces; high when competition is fierce in a market and low when competitors are more complacent.

robotics Focuses on creating artificial intelligence devices that can move and react to sensory input.

S

sales analytics Involves gathering, classifying, comparing, and studying company sales data to analyze product cycles, sales pipelines, and competitive intelligence.

sales force automation (SFA) Automatically tracks all the steps in the sales process.

sales management CRM system Automates each phase of the sales process, helping individual sales representatives coordinate and organize all their accounts.

satellite A space station that orbits the Earth receiving and transmitting signals from Earth-based stations over a wide area.

scalability Describes how well a system can scale up or adapt to the increased demands of growth.

scripting language A programming method that provides for interactive modules to a website.

scrum methodology Uses small teams to produce small pieces of software using a series of "sprints," or 30-day intervals, to achieve an appointed goal.

search engine Website software that finds other pages based on keyword matching.

search engine optimization (SEO) Combines art along with science to determine how to make URLs more attractive to search engines, resulting in higher search engine ranking.

search engine ranking Evaluates variables that search engines use to determine where a URL appears on the list of search results.

secure hypertext transfer protocol (SHTTP or HTTPS) A combination of HTTP and SSL to provide encryption and secure identification of an Internet server.

secure sockets layer (SSL) A standard security technology for establishing an encrypted link between a web server and a browser, ensuring that all data passed between them remains private.

selfie A self-photograph placed on a social media website.

semantic web A component of Web 3.0 that describes things in a way that computers can understand.

semi-passive RFID tags Include a battery to run the microchip's circuitry, but communicate by drawing power from the RFID reader.

semistructured decision Occurs in situations in which a few established processes help to evaluate potential solutions, but not enough to lead to a definite recommended decision.

server A computer dedicated to providing information in response to requests.

server virtualization Combines the physical resources, such as servers, processors, and operating systems, from the applications.

service-oriented architecture (SOA) A business-driven enterprise architecture that supports integrating a business as linked, repeatable activities, tasks, or services.

serviceability How quickly a third party or vendor can change a system to ensure it meets user needs and the terms of any contracts, including agreed levels of reliability, maintainability or availability.

service Tasks that customers will buy to satisfy a want or need.

shopping bot Software that will search several retailer websites and provide a comparison of each retailer's offerings including price and availability.

sign-off Users' actual signatures, indicating they approve all of the business requirements.

single-factor authentication The traditional security process, which requires a username and password.

single-tenancy Each customer or tenant must purchase and maintain an individual system.

smart card A device about the size of a credit card, containing embedded technologies that can store information and small amounts of software to perform some limited processing.

smart grid Delivers electricity using two-way digital technology.

snapshot A view of data at a particular moment in time.

smartphones Offer more advanced computing ability and connectivity than basic cell phones.

social bookmarking Allows users to share, organize, search, and manage bookmarks.

social engineering Hackers use their social skills to trick people into revealing access credentials or other valuable information.

social graphs Represent the interconnection of relationships in a social network.

social media Refers to websites that rely on user participation and user-contributed content.

social media manager A person within the organization who is trusted to monitor, contribute, filter, and guide the social media presence of a company, individual, product, or brand.

social media monitoring The process of monitoring and responding to what is being said about a company, individual, product, or brand.

social media policy Outlines the corporate guidelines or principles governing employee online communications.

social network An application that connects people by matching profile information.

social networking The practice of expanding your business and/or social contacts by constructing a personal network.

social networking analysis (SNA) Maps group contacts identifying who knows each other and who works together.

social tagging Describes the collaborative activity of marking shared online content with keywords or tags as a way to organize it for future navigation, filtering, or search.

software The set of instructions the hardware executes to carry out specific tasks.

Software as a Service (SaaS) Delivers applications over the cloud using a pay-per-use revenue model.

software customization Modifies software to meet specific user or business requirements.

software engineering A disciplined approach for constructing information systems through the use of common methods, techniques, or tools.

source code Contains instructions written by a programmer specifying the actions to be performed by computer software.

source data Identifies the primary location where data is collected.

source document Describes the original transaction record along with details such as its date, purpose, and amount spent and includes cash receipts, canceled checks, invoices, customer refunds, employee time sheet, etc.

spam Unsolicited email.

spatial data (geospatial data or geographic information) Identifies the geographic location of features and boundaries on Earth, such as natural or constructed features, oceans, and more.

spear phishing A phishing expedition in which the emails are carefully designed to target a particular person or organization.

spyware A special class of adware that collects data about the user and transmits it over the Internet without the user's knowledge or permission.

SSL Certificate An electronic document that confirms the identity of a website or server and verifies that a public key belongs to a trustworthy individual or company.

stakeholder A person or group that has an interest or concern in an organization.

standard packet format Includes a packet header, packet body containing the original message, and packet footer.

static information Includes fixed data that are not capable of change in the event of a user action.

static process A systematic approach in an attempt to improve business effectiveness and efficiency.

static report A report created once based on data that does not change.

storage virtualization Combines multiple network storage devices so they appear to be a single storage device.

strategic business processes Dynamic, nonroutine, long-term business processes such as financial planning, expansion strategies, and stakeholder interactions.

strategic level Managers develop overall business strategies, goals, and objectives as part of the company's strategic plan.

streaming A method of sending audio and video files over the Internet in such a way that the user can view the file while it is being transferred.

streamlining Improves business process efficiencies simplifying or eliminating unnecessary steps.

structured data Data that has a defined length, type, and format and includes numbers, dates, or strings such as Customer Address.

structured decision Involves situations where established processes offer potential solutions.

structured query language (SQL) Users write lines of code to answer questions against a database.

supplier power One of Porter's five forces; measures the suppliers' ability to influence the prices they charge for supplies (including materials, labor, and services).

supplier relationship management (SRM) Focuses on keeping suppliers satisfied by evaluating and categorizing suppliers for different projects.

supply chain All parties involved, directly or indirectly, in obtaining raw materials or a product.

supply chain design Determines how to structure a supply chain including the product, selection of partners, the location and capacity of warehouses, transportation methods, and supporting management information systems.

supply chain execution system Ensures supply chain cohesion by automating the different activities of the supply chain.

supply chain management (SCM) The management of information flows between and among activities in a supply chain to maximize total supply chain effectiveness and corporate profitability.

supply chain planning system Uses advanced mathematical algorithms to improve the flow and efficiency of the supply chain while reducing inventory.

supply chain visibility The ability to view all areas up and down the supply chain in real time.

support value activities Found along the top of the value chain and includes business processes, such as firm infrastructure, human resource management, technology development, and procurement, that support the primary value activities.

sustainable MIS disposal Refers to the safe disposal of MIS assets at the end of their life cycle.

sustainable MIS infrastructure Identifies ways that a company can grow in terms of computing resources while simultaneously becoming less dependent on hardware and energy consumption.

sustainable, or "green," MIS Describes the production, management, use, and disposal of technology in a way that minimizes damage to the environment.

sustaining technology Produces an improved product customers are eager to buy, such as a faster car or larger hard drive.

swim lane Layout arranges the steps of a business process into a set of rows depicting the various elements.

SWOT analysis Evaluates an organization's strengths, weaknesses, opportunities, and threats to identify significant influences that work for or against business strategies.

switching costs Costs that make customers reluctant to switch to another product or service.

synchronous communication Communications that occur at the same time such as IM or chat.

system virtualization The ability to present the resources of a single computer as if it is a collection of separate computers ("virtual machines"), each with its own virtual CPUs, network interfaces, storage, and operating system.

system A collection of parts that link to achieve a common purpose.

systems development life cycle (SDLC) The overall process for developing information systems, from planning and analysis through implementation and maintenance.

systems thinking A way of monitoring the entire system by viewing multiple inputs being processed or transformed to produce outputs while continuously gathering feedback on each part.

T

tacit knowledge The knowledge contained in people's heads.

tag Specific keywords or phrases incorporated into website content for means of classification or taxonomy.

tangible benefits Easy to quantify and typically measured to determine the success or failure of a project.

taxonomy The scientific classification of organisms into groups based on similarities of structure or origin.

technology failure Occurs when the ability of a company to operate is impaired because of a hardware, software, or data outage.

technology recovery strategies Focus specifically on prioritizing the order for restoring hardware, software, and data across the organization that best meets business recovery requirements.

teergrubing Anti-spamming approach where the receiving computer launches a return attack against the spammer, sending email messages back to the computer that originated the suspected spam.

telecommuting (virtual workforce) Allows users to work from remote locations such as a home or hotel, using high-speed Internet to access business applications and data.

test condition Details the steps the system must perform along with the expected result of each step.

testing phase Brings all the project pieces together into a special testing environment to eliminate errors and bugs and verify that the system meets all the business requirements defined in the analysis phase.

threat An act or object that poses a danger to assets.

threat of new entrants One of Porter's five forces, high when it is easy for new competitors to enter a market and low when there are significant entry barriers to joining a market.

threat of substitute products or services One of Porter's five forces, high when there are many alternatives to a product or service and low when there are few alternatives from which to choose.

time bombs Computer viruses that wait for a specific date before executing instructions.

time-series information Time-stamped information collected at a particular frequency.

To-Be process model Shows the results of applying change improvement opportunities to the current (As-Is) process model.

tokens Small electronic devices that change user passwords automatically.

traceroute A utility application that monitors the network path of packet data sent to a remote computer.

transaction processing system (TPS) The basic business system that serves the operational level (analysts) and assists in making structured decisions.

transactional information Encompasses all of the information contained within a single business process or unit of work, and its primary purpose is to support the performing of daily operational or structured decisions.

transmission control protocol/Internet protocol (TCP/IP) Provides the technical foundation for the public Internet as well as for large numbers of private networks.

two-factor authentication Requires the user to provide two means of authentication, what the user knows (password) and what the user has (security token).

typosquatting A problem that occurs when someone registers purposely misspelled variations of well-known domain names.

U

unavailable When a system is not operating or cannot be used.

unified communications (UC) The integration of communication channels into a single service.

universal resource locator (URL) The address of a file or resource on the web such as www.apple.com.

unstructured data Data that is not defined and does not follow a specified format and is typically free-form text such as emails, Twitter tweets, and text messages.

unstructured decision Occurs in situations in which no procedures or rules exist to guide decision makers toward the correct choice.

up-selling Increasing the value of the sale.

upcycle Reuses or refurbishes ewaste and creates a new product.

uplift modeling A form of predictive analytics for marketing campaigns that attempts to identify target markets or people who could be convinced to buy products.

usability The degree to which a system is easy to learn and efficient and satisfying to use.

user-contributed content (also referred to as user-generated content) Content created and updated by many users for many users.

user documentation Highlights how to use the system and how to troubleshoot issues or problems.

utility computing Offers a pay-per-use revenue model similar to a metered service such as gas or electricity.

V

value chain analysis Views a firm as a series of business processes that each add value to the product or service.

variable A data characteristic that stands for a value that changes or varies over time.

vertical privilege escalation Attackers grant themselves a higher access level such as administrator, allowing the attacker to perform illegal actions such as running unauthorized code or deleting data.

videoconference Allows people at two or more locations to interact via two-way video and audio transmissions simultaneously as well as share documents, data, computer displays, and whiteboards.

virtual private network (VPN) Companies can establish direct private network links among themselves or create private, secure Internet access, in effect a "private tunnel" within the Internet.

virtual reality A computer-simulated environment that can be a simulation of the real world or an imaginary world.

virtualization Creates multiple "virtual" machines on a single computing device.

vishing (or voice phishing) A phone scam that attempts to defraud people by asking them to call a bogus telephone number to "confirm" their account information.

visualization Produces graphical displays of patterns and complex relationships in large amounts of data.

Voice over LTE (VoLTE) Allows mobile voice calls to be made over broadband networks, creating—under the right network conditions—clearer audio and fewer dropped calls.

virus Software written with malicious intent to cause annoyance or damage.

voice over IP (VoIP) Uses IP technology to transmit telephone calls.

voiceprint A set of measurable characteristics of a human voice that uniquely identifies an individual.

vulnerability A system weakness that can be exploited by a threat; for example, a password that is never changed or a system left on while an employee goes to lunch.

W

war chalking The practice of tagging pavement with codes displaying where Wi-Fi access is available.

war driving Deliberately searching for Wi-Fi signals from a vehicle.

warm site A separate facility with computer equipment that requires installation and configuration.

waterfall methodology A sequence of phases in which the output of each phase becomes the input for the next.

Web 1.0 (or Business 1.0) Refers to the World Wide Web during its first few years of operation between 1991 and 2003.

Web 2.0 (or Business 2.0) The next generation of Internet use—a more mature, distinctive communications platform characterized by new qualities such as collaboration, sharing, and free.

web accessibility Means that people with disabilities—including visual, auditory, physical, speech, cognitive, and neurological disabilities—can use the web.

web accessibility initiative (WAI) Brings together people from industry, disability organizations, government, and research labs from around the world to develop guidelines and resources to help make the web accessible to people with disabilities, including auditory, cognitive, neurological, physical, speech, and visual disabilities.

web browser Allows users to access the WWW.

web service An open-standards way of supporting interoperability.

web conferencing (webinar) Blends videoconferencing with document-sharing and allows the user to deliver a presentation over the web to a group of geographically dispersed participants.

web-based self-service system Allows customers to use the web to find answers to their questions or solutions to their problems.

website bookmark A locally stored URL or the address of a file or Internet page saved as a shortcut.

website name stealing The theft of a website's name that occurs when someone, posing as a site's administrator, changes the ownership of the domain name assigned to the website to another website owner.

website personalization Occurs when a website has stored enough data about a person's likes and dislikes to fashion offers more likely to appeal to that person.

wide area network (WAN) Spans a large geographic area such as a state, province, or country.

wired equivalent privacy (WEP) An encryption algorithm designed to protect wireless transmission data.

Wi-Fi infrastructure Includes the inner workings of a Wi-Fi service or utility, including the signal transmitters, towers, or poles, along with additional equipment required to send a Wi-Fi signal.

wiki A type of collaborative web page that allows users to add, remove, and change content, which can be easily organized and reorganized as required.

wireless access point (WAP) Enables devices to connect to a wireless network to communicate with each other.

Wi-Fi protected access (WPA) A wireless security protocol to protect Wi-Fi networks.

wireless fidelity (Wi-Fi) A means by which portable devices can connect wirelessly to a local area network, using access points that send and receive data via radio waves.

wireless LAN (WLAN) A local area network that uses radio signals to transmit and receive data over distances of a few hundred feet.

wireless MAN (WMAN) A metropolitan area network that uses radio signals to transmit and receive data.

wireless WAN (WWAN) A wide area network that uses radio signals to transmit and receive data.

workflow Includes the tasks, activities, and responsibilities required to execute each step in a business process.

workflow control systems Monitor processes to ensure tasks, activities, and responsibilities are executed as specified.

workplace MIS monitoring Tracks people's activities by such measures as number of keystrokes, error rate, and number of transactions processed.

workshop training Held in a classroom environment and led by an instructor.

World Wide Web (WWW) Provides access to Internet information through documents including text, graphics, audio, and video files that use a special formatting language called HTML.

Worldwide Interoperability for Microwave Access (WiMAX) A communications technology aimed at providing high-speed wireless data over metropolitan area networks.

worm Spreads itself not only from file to file but also from computer to computer.

Z

zombie A program that secretly takes over another computer for the purpose of launching attacks on other computers.

zombie farm A group of computers on which a hacker has planted zombie programs.

notes

CHAPTER 1

1. Interesting Facts, www.interestingfacts.o'g, accessed June 2016.
2. http://www.intel.com/content/www/us/en/internet-of-things/industrysolutions. html, accessed May 2014; Michael Chui, Markus Löffler, and Roger Roberts, "The Internet of Things," Mckinsey Quarterly, March 2010, http://www.mckinsey.com/insights/high_tech_ telecoms_internet/the_internet_of_things; Stefan Ferber, "How the Internet of Things Changes Everything," Harvard Business Review, May 2013.
3. Thomas L. Friedman, *The World Is Flat* (New York: Farrar, Straus & Giroux, 2005); Thomas Friedman, "The World Is Flat," www.thomaslfriedman.com, accessed June 2010; Thomas L. Friedman, "The Opinion Pages," *The New York Times,* topics.nytimes.com/top/opinion/editorialsandoped/oped/columnists/thomaslfriedman, accessed June 2012.
4. www.sochi2014.com/en/medal-standings, accessed January 2014
5. http://www.intel.com/content/www/us/en/internet-of-things/industrysolutions.html, accessed May 2014; Michael Chui, Markus Löffler,and Roger Roberts, "The Internet of Things," Mckinsey Quarterly,March 2010, http://www.mckinsey.com/insights/high_tech_telecoms_internet/the_internet_of_things; Stefan Ferber, "How theInternet of Things Changes Everything," Harvard Business Review,May 2013.
6. www.idc.com, accessed January 2016
7. Ina Fried, "Apple Earnings Top Estimates," *CNET News,* October 11, 2005, http://news.cnet.com/Appleearnings-topestimates/2100-1041_3-5893289.html?tag5lia;rcol, accessed July 2012.
8. Frederic Paul, "Smart Social Networking for Your Small Business," www.forbes.com/2009/06/05/social-networkinginterop-entrepreneurs-technology-bmighty.html, accessed July 2012.
9. Michael E. Porter, "The Five Competitive Forces That Shape Strategy," The Harvard Business Review Book Series, *Harvard Business Review,* January 2008; Michael E. Porter, "Competitive Strategy: Techniques for Analyzing Industries and Competitors," *Harvard Business Review,* January 2002; Michael E. Porter, *On Competition,* The Harvard Business Review Book Series (Boston: Harvard Business School Publishing, 1985); Harvard Institute for Strategy and Competitiveness, http://www.isc.hbs.edu/, accessed June 2012.
10. Michael E. Porter, "The Five Competitive Forces That Shape Strategy," The Harvard Business Review Book Series, *Harvard Business Review,* January 2008; Michael E. Porter, "Competitive Strategy: Techniques for Analyzing Industries and Competitors," *Harvard Business Review,* January 2002; Michael E. Porter, *On Competition,* The Harvard Business Review Book Series (Boston: Harvard Business School Publishing, 1985); Harvard Institute for Strategy and Competitiveness, http://www.isc.hbs.edu/, accessed June 2012.
11. Michael E. Porter, "The Five Competitive Forces That Shape Strategy," The Harvard Business Review Book Series, *Harvard Business Review,* January 2008; Michael E. Porter, "Competitive Strategy: Techniques for Analyzing Industries and Competitors," *Harvard Business Review,* January 2002; Michael E. Porter, *On Competition,* The Harvard Business Review Book Series (Boston: Harvard Business School Publishing, 1985); Harvard Institute for Strategy and Competitiveness, http://www.isc.hbs.edu/, accessed June 2012.
12. Michael E. Porter, "The Five Competitive Forces That Shape Strategy," The Harvard Business Review Book Series, *Harvard Business Review,* January 2008; Michael E. Porter, "Competitive Strategy: Techniques for Analyzing Industries and Competitors," *Harvard Business Review,* January 2002; Michael E. Porter, *On Competition,* The Harvard Business Review Book Series (Boston: Harvard Business School Publishing, 1985); Harvard Institute for Strategy and Competitiveness, http://www.isc.hbs.edu/, accessed June 2012.
13. Michael E. Porter, "The Five Competitive Forces That Shape Strategy," The Harvard Business Review Book Series, *Harvard Business Review,* January 2008; Michael E. Porter, "Competitive Strategy: Techniques for Analyzing Industries and Competitors," *Harvard Business Review,* January 2002; Michael E. Porter, *On Competition,* The Harvard Business Review Book Series (Boston: Harvard Business School Publishing, 1985); Harvard Institute for Strategy and Competitiveness, http://www.isc.hbs.edu/, accessed June 2012.
14. Michael E. Porter, "The Five Competitive Forces That Shape Strategy," The Harvard Business Review Book Series, *Harvard Business Review,* January 2008; Michael E. Porter, "Competitive Strategy: Techniques for Analyzing Industries and Competitors," *Harvard Business Review,* January 2002; Michael E. Porter, *On Competition,* The Harvard Business Review Book Series (Boston: Harvard Business School Publishing, 1985); Harvard Institute for Strategy and Competitiveness, http://www.isc.hbs.edu/, accessed June 2012.
15. Michael E. Porter, "The Five Competitive Forces That Shape Strategy," The Harvard Business Review Book Series, *Harvard Business Review,* January 2008; Michael E. Porter, "Competitive Strategy: Techniques for Analyzing Industries and Competitors," *Harvard Business Review,* January 2002; Michael E. Porter, *On Competition,* The Harvard Business Review Book Series (Boston: Harvard Business School Publishing, 1985); Harvard Institute for Strategy and Competitiveness, http://www.isc.hbs.edu/, accessed June 2012.
16. Michael E. Porter, "The Five Competitive Forces That Shape Strategy," The Harvard Business Review Book Series, *Harvard Business Review,* January 2008; Michael E. Porter, "Competitive Strategy: Techniques for Analyzing Industries and Competitors," *Harvard Business Review,* January 2002; Michael E. Porter, *On Competition,* The Harvard Business Review Book Series (Boston: Harvard Business School Publishing, 1985); Harvard Institute for Strategy and Competitiveness, http://www.isc.hbs.edu/, accessed June 2012.
17. Michael E. Porter, "The Five Competitive Forces That Shape Strategy," The Harvard Business Review Book Series, *Harvard Business Review,* January 2008; Michael E. Porter, "Competitive Strategy: Techniques for Analyzing Industries and Competitors," *Harvard Business Review,* January 2002; Michael E. Porter, *On Competition,* The Harvard Business Review Book Series (Boston: Harvard Business School Publishing, 1985); Harvard Institute for Strategy and Competitiveness, http://www.isc.hbs.edu/, accessed June 2012.
18. "One Laptop per Child," http://laptop.org/en/, accessed June 2011.
19. Porter, "The Five Competitive Forces That Shape Strategy"; Porter, "Competitive Strategy"; Porter, *On Competition;* Harvard Institute for Strategy and Competitiveness, http://www.isc.

20. Robert Lenzer, "Bernie Madoff's $50 Billion Ponzi Scheme," *Forbes,* December, 12, 2008, www.forbes.com/2008/12/12/madoff-ponzi-hedge-pf-ii-in_rl_1212croesus_inl.html.

CHAPTER 2

1. Tom Davenport, "Tom Davenport: Back to Decision-Making Basics,"BusinessWeek, March 11, 2008
2. Ken Blanchard, "Effectiveness vs. Efficiency," *Wachovia Small Business,* www.wachovia.com, accessed October 2012.
3. Srivaths, "The Best Advice I Ever Got," Fortune, October 25, 2012. http://fortune.com/2012/10/25/the-best-advice-i-ever-got/
4. "What Is Systems Thinking," *SearchCIO.com,* http://searchcio.tech.
5. "French Trader in Scandal Ordered Behind Bars," *MSNBC,* February 8, 2008, www.msnbc.msn.com/id/23065812/.
6. www.collegehunkshaulingjunk.com/, accessed July 2012.
7. Sharon Begley, "Software au Natural"; Neil McManus, "Robots at Your Service"; Santa Fe Institute, www.dis.anl.gov/abms/, accessed June 24, 2007; Michael A. Arbib (Ed.), *The Handbook of Brain Theory and Neural Networks* (MIT Press,mitpress.mit.edu, 1995); L. Biacino and G. Gerla, "Fuzzy Logic, Continuity and Effectiveness," Archive for Mathematical Logic.
8. Caroline Winter, "Fitbit for Testosterone Junkies: Health-TrackingGadgets Reach the Molecular Level," BusinessWeek, June 6, 2014. http://www.businessweek.com/articles/2014-06-06/fitbit-fortestosterone-junkies-health-tracking-gadgets-reach-the-molecular-level.
9. Rachel King, "Soon That Nearby Worker Might Be a Robot," *Bloomberg Businessweek,* June 1, 2010, www.businessweek.com/technology/content/jun2010/tc2010061_798891.htm.
10. ToddBishop,'Microsoftpatentslong-distancevirtualhandshakes,hugs', December 26, 2012, GeekWire, http://www.geekwire.com/2012/microsoft-patents-longdistance-virtual-handshakes-hugs/.
11. Business Process Reengineering Six Sigma, www.sixsigma.com; Michael Hammer, *Beyond Reengineering: How the Process Centered Organization Is Changing Our Work and Our Lives* (New York: HarperCollins Publishers, 1996); Richard Chang, *Process Reengineering in Action: A Practical Guide to Achieving Breakthrough Results* (Quality Improvement Series) (New Jersey: Pfeiffer, John Wiley & Sons, Inc., 1996);H. James Harrington, *Business Process Improvement Workbook: Documentation, Analysis, Design, and Management of Business Process Improvement* (New York: McGraw-Hill, 1997).
12. Sharon Begley, "Software au Natural"; Neil McManus, "Robots at Your Service"; Santa Fe Institute, www.dis.anl.gov/abms/, accessed June 24, 2007; Michael A. Arbib (Ed.), The Handbook of Brain Theory and Neural Networks (MIT Press, mitpress.mit.edu, 1995); L. Biacino and G. Gerla, "Fuzzy Logic, Continuity and Effectiveness," Archive for Mathematical Logic.
13. Object Management Group Business Process Model and Notation, www.bpmn.org.
14. "Business Process Reengineering Six Sigma," www.isixsigma.com/me/bpr/, accessed May 10, 2010. Michael Hammer, BeyondReengineering: How the Process-Centered Organization Is ChangingOur Work and Our Lives (New York: HarperCollins Publishers, 1996);Richard Chang, Process Reengineering in Action: A Practical Guideto Achieving Breakthrough Results, Quality Improvement Series (SanFrancisco: Pfeiffer, 1996).
15. "Business Process Reengineering Six Sigma," www.isixsigma.com/me/bpr/, accessed May 10, 2010. Michael Hammer, BeyondReengineering: How the Process-Centered Organization Is Changing Our Work and Our Lives (New York: HarperCollins Publishers, 1996);Richard Chang, Process Reengineering in Action: A Practical Guideto Achieving Breakthrough Results, Quality Improvement Series (SanFrancisco: Pfeiffer, 1996).
16. "Business Process Reengineering Six Sigma," www.isixsigma.com/me/bpr/, accessed May 10, 2010. Michael Hammer, BeyondReengineering: How the Process-Centered Organization Is ChangingOur Work and Our Lives (New York: HarperCollins Publishers, 1996);Richard Chang, Process Reengineering in Action: A Practical Guideto Achieving Breakthrough Results, Quality Improvement Series (SanFrancisco: Pfeiffer, 1996).
17. "Reply All? World's Worst Email Blunders," http://news.sky.com/home/article/1272091, accessed July 2012.
18. Business Process Reengineering Six Sigma, www.sixsigma.com; Hammer, *Beyond Reengineering;* Chang, "Process Reengineering in Action"; Harrington, *Business Process Improvement Workbook.*
19. Steven Robbins, "Tips for Mastering E-Mail Overload," HarvardBusiness School, October 25, 2009, http://hbswk.hbs.edu/archive/4438.html.
20. "Business Process Reengineering Six Sigma," www.isixsigma.com/me/bpr/, accessed May 10, 2010. Michael Hammer, BeyondReengineering: How the Process-Centered Organization Is ChangingOur Work and Our Lives (New York: HarperCollins Publishers, 1996);Richard Chang, Process Reengineering in Action: A Practical Guideto Achieving Breakthrough Results, Quality Improvement Series (SanFrancisco: Pfeiffer, 1996).
21. "Business Process Reengineering Six Sigma," www.isixsigma.com/me/bpr/, accessed May 10, 2010. Michael Hammer, BeyondReengineering: How the Process-Centered Organization Is ChangingOur Work and Our Lives (New York: HarperCollins Publishers, 1996);Richard Chang, Process Reengineering in Action: A Practical Guideto Achieving Breakthrough Results, Quality Improvement Series (SanFrancisco: Pfeiffer, 1996).

CHAPTER 3

1. "Polaroid Files for Bankruptcy Protection," www.dpreview.com/news/0110/01101201polaroidch11.asp, accessed July 2013.
2. Clayton Christensen, *The Innovator's Dilemma* (Boston: Harvard Business School, 1997).
3. Clayton Christensen, *The Innovator's Dilemma* (Boston: Harvard Business School, 1997).
4. info.cern.ch, accessed March 1, 2013.
5. Brier Dudley, "Changes in Technology Almost Too Fast to Follow," *The Seattle Times,* October 13, 2005.
6. Max Chafkin, "Good Domain Names Grow Scarce," *Inc.*, July 1, 2009, http://www.inc.com/magazine/20090701/good-domain-names-grow-scarce.html.
7. Chris Anderson, "The Long Tail: Why the Future of Business Is Selling Less of More," www.longtail.com/2006.
8. "Disintermediation," *TechTarget,* http://whatis.techtarget.com/definition/0,,sid9_gci211962,00.html, accessed April 2013.
9. "Reintermediation," www.pcmag.com; www.pcmag.com/encyclopedia_term/0,2542,t=reintermediation&i=50364,00.asp, accessed April 2013.
10. Erin Kim, "From eBay Store to a $24 million Business, http://www.inc.com/erin-kim/applicant-of-the-week-nasty-gal.html," Inc. Magazine,April 2012, http://www.inc.com/erin-kim/applicant-of-the-weeknasty-gal.html.

11. "The Complete Web 2.0 Directory," www.go2web20.net/, accessed June 24, 2007; "Web 2.0 for CIOs," www.cio.com/article/16807; www.emarketer.com, accessed January 2013.
12. Tim O'Reilly, "What Is Web 2.0: Design Patterns and Business Modelsfor the Next Generation of Software," www.oreillynet.com/pub/a/oreilly/tim/news/2005/09/30/what-is-web-20.html, accessed June 25,2007; "Web 2.0 for CIOs."
13. www.craigslist.org/about/, accessed July 2013.
14. Ibid
15. "The Complete Web 2.0 Directory"; "Web 2.0 for CIOs"; www.emarketer.com.
16. Joel Holland, "Risk It When You Are Young," *Entrepreneur Magazine,* July 2010,http://www.entrepreneur.com/magazine/entrepreneur/2010/july/207174.htm.
17. Tony Bradley, "Firefox 3.6 Becomes Number Two Browser as IE6 Declines," www.pcworld.com, September 1, 2010, http://www.pcworld.com/businesscenter/article/204698, accessed April 2013.
18. Kit Eaton, "Is Facebook Becoming the Whole World's Social Network?" *Fast Company,* April 7, 2010, www.fastcompany.com/1609312/facebook-global-expansionsocial-networking-privacy-world-phone-book-users.
19. Daniel Pink, "Folksonomy," *The New York Times,* December 11, 2005, www.nytimes.com/2005/12/11/magazine/11ideas1-21.html.
20. Daniel Nations, "What Is Social Bookmarking,"About.com: Web Trends, http://webtrends.about.com/od/socialbookmarking101/p/aboutsocialtags.htm, accessed April 2013.
21. www.eurpac.com/, *Artist2Market,* accessed July 2013.
22. "Banana Code Connects Consumers and Farm," *DoleOrganic.com,* http://www.dole.com/NutritionInstituteLanding/NI_Articles/NI_DoleDiet/NI_DoleDiet_Detail/tabid/1058/Default.aspx?contentid56328, accessed April 2013.
23. "Kiva—Loans that Change Lives," www.kiva.org, accessed April 10,2015.
24. Gary Matuszak, "Enterprise 2.0: Fad or Future," *KPMG International,* www.kpmg.com/Global/en/. . ./Enterprise. . ./Enterprise-2-Fad-or-Future.pdf, accessed April 2013.
25. Tim Berners-Lee, "Semantic Web Road Map," October 14, 1998, www.w3.org/DesignIssues/Semantic.html, accessed April 2013.

CHAPTER 4

1. Michael Schrage, "Build the Business Case," *CIO Magazine,* www.cio.com/article/31780/Build_the_Business_Case_Extracting_Value_from_the_Customer, March 15, 2003.
2. Richard Mason, "Four Ethical Issues of the Information Age," *Management Information Systems Quarterly* 10, no. 1 (March 1986), http://www.misq.org/archivist/vol/no10/issue1/vol10no1mason.html, accessed April 2013.
3. http://www.ftc.gov/ogc/coppa1.htm, accessed April 2013
4. Richard Mason, "Four Ethical Issues of the Information Age," *Management Information Systems Quarterly* 10, no. 1 (March 1986), http://www.misq.org/archivist/vol/no10/issue1/vol10no1mason.html, accessed April 2013.
5. Jon Perlow, "New in Labs: Stop Sending Mail You Later Regret," http://gmailblog.blogspot.com/2008/10/new-inlabs-stop-sending-mail-you-later.html, accessed June 2013.
6. Dave Lee, "Google to face data watchdogs over 'right to be forgotten'," BBCNews.com, April 2014, http://www.bbc.com/news/technology-28458194.
7. www.consumer.ftc.gov/features/feature-0014-identity-theft, accessed April 2014.
8. Daniel Schorn, "Whose Life Is It Anyways?" *CBS News,* http://www.cbsnews.com/stories/2005/10/28/60minutes/main990617.shtml, accessed February 2009.
9. Thomas Claburn, "Web 2.0. Internet Too Dangerous for Normal People," *InformationWeek,* April 1, 2009, http://www.informationweek.com/news/internet/web2.0/showArticle.jhtml?articleID=216402352&queryText=web%202.0%20security%20concerns.
10. Daniel Schorn, "Whose Life Is It Anyways?" *CBS News,* http://www.cbsnews.com/stories/2005/10/28/60minutes/main990617.shtml, accessed February 2009.
11. Thomas Claburn, "Web 2.0. Internet Too Dangerous for NormalPeople," *InformationWeek,* April 1, 2009, http://www.informationweek.com/news/internet/web2.0/showArticle.jhtml?articleID=216402352&queryText=web%202.0%20security%20concerns.
12. Newcastle University, "Improving Password Protection with Easy to Remember Drawings," *ScienceDaily,* November 1, 2007, www.sciencedaily.com-/releases/2007/10/071030091438.htm, accessed April 2013.
13. Thomas Claburn, "Web 2.0. Internet Too Dangerous for Normal People," *InformationWeek,* April 1, 2009, www.informationweek.com/news/internet/web2.0/showArticle.jhtml?articleID=216402352&queryText=web%202.0%20security%20concerns.
14. Kim Zetter, "Lifelock's CEO Identity Stolen 13 Times," Wired, May 28, 2010, http://www.wired.com/threatlevel/2010/05/lifelock-identity-theft.
15. Newcastle University, "Improving Password Protection with Easy to Remember Drawings," *ScienceDaily,* November 1, 2010.
16. Paige Baltzan, email received May 21, 2010.

CHAPTER 5

1. "The New Student Excuse?" www.insidehighered.com/news/2009/06/05/corrupted, accessed June 5, 2009.
2. TechTarget.com, http://events.techtarget.com/html/topic-disaster_recovery.html, accessed May 2014.
3. "The Great 1906 San Francisco Earthquake," *USGS,* http://earthquake.usgs.gov/regional/nca/1906/18april/index.php, accessed July 2013.
4. TechTarget.com, http://events.techtarget.com/html/topic-disaster_recovery.html, accessed May 2014.
5. Doug Johnson, "When Zombies Attack," http://magazine.ufl.edu/2011/05/when-zombies-attack/, accessed June 2012.
6. http://www.livescience.com/41967-world-e-waste-to-grow-33-percent-2017.html, http://www.entrepreneur.com/article/226675, accessed March 2014.
7. "Moore's Law," www.intel.com/technology/mooreslaw, accessed April 2013; Electronics TakeBack Coalition, "Facts and Figures on E-Waste and Recycling," www.electronicstakeback.com, accessed April 2012; "EPA Report to Congress on Server and Data Center Energy Efficiency," www.energystar.gov/ia/partners/prod_development/downloads/EPA_Report_Exec_Summary_Final.pdf, accessed January 2012.
8. EPA.gov, "eCycle Cell Phones," http://www.epa.gov/osw/partnerships/plugin/cellphone/, accessed June 2012.
9. "Moore's Law," www.intel.com/technology/mooreslaw, accessed April 2, 2010; Electronics TakeBack Coalition, "Facts and Figures on E-Waste and Recycling," www.

electronicstakeback.com, accessed April 3, 2010; "EPA Report to Congress on Server and Data Center Energy Efficiency," www.energystar.gov/ia/partners/prod_development/downloads/EPA_Report_Exec_Summary_Final.pdf, accessed January 23, 2008.

10. "Switch on the Benefits of Grid Computing," h20338.www2.hp.com/enterprise/downloads/7_Benefits%20of%20grid%20computing.pdf, accessed April 2, 2010; "Talking to the Grid," www.technologyreview.com/energy/23706/, accessed April 3, 2010; "Tech Update: What'sAll the Smart Grid Buzz About?" www.fieldtechnologiesonline.com/download.mvc/Whats-All-The-Smart-Grid-Buzz-About-0001, accessed April 3, 2010.
11. www.nature.org/greenliving/carboncalculator/, accessed May 2014.
12. "Switch on the Benefits of Grid Computing,"h20338.www2.hp.com/enterprise/downloads/7_Benefits%20of%20grid%20computing.pdf, accessed April 2010; "Talking to the Grid," www.technologyreview.com/energy/23706/, accessed April 2010;"Tech Update: What's All the Smart Grid Buzz About?" www.fieldtechnologiesonline.com/download.mvc/Whats-All-The-Smart-Grid-Buzz-About-0001, accessed April 2012.
13. "VMware-History of Virtualization," www.virtualizationworks.com/Virtualization-History.asp, accessed January 2013.
14. Nic Cubrilovic, "The Anatomy of the Twitter Attack," *TechCrunch,* http://techcrunch.com/2009/07/19/theanatomy-of-the-twitter-attack/, accessed June 2012.
15. Rich Miller, "Google Data Center FAQ," www.datacenteknowledge.com/archives/2008/03/27/google-datacenter-faq/, accessed April 2013.

CHAPTER 6

1. Mitch Betts, "Unexpected Insights," *ComputerWorld,* April 14, 2013, www.computerworld.com, accessed September 2012.
2. *BBC News,* "Grieving Relatives Find Stranger In Mum's Casket," www.bbcnews.com, accessed June 2012.
3. Steven D. Levitt and Stephen J. Dubner, "Freakonomics, The Hidden Side of Everything," http://www.freakonomics.com/, accessed July 2012.
4. Ericka Chickowski, "Goldman Sachs Sued for Illegal DatabaseAccess," Darkreading.com, May 11, 2010, http://www.darkreading.com/database_security/security/attacks/show Article.jhtml?articleID5 224701564&cid 5 nl_DR_DAILY_2010-05-12_htm.
5. Ericka Chickowski, "Goldman Sachs Sued for Illegal DatabaseAccess," Darkreading.com, May 11, 2010, http://www.darkreading.com/database_security/security/attacks/show Article.jhtml?articleID5 224701564&cid 5 nl_DR_DAILY_2010-05-12_htm.
6. www.zappos.com, accessed April 2013.
7. www.tableau.com, accessed March 2014.
8. Mary Schlangenstein, "Facebook Manipulated User Feeds," *Bloomberg Businessweek,* June 29, 2012, http://www.bloomberg.com/news/2014-06-29/facebook-allowed-researchers-to-influence-users-in-2012-study.html, accessed April 2014.
9. "Data, Data Everywhere," *The Economist,* www.economist.com/specialreports/displayStory.cfm?story_id 5 15557443.

CHAPTER 7

1. "Top 23 U.S. ISPs by Subscriber: Q3 2010," *ISP Planet,* www.isp-planet.com/research/rankings/usa.html.
2. "Top 23 U.S. ISPs by Subscriber: Q3 2010," ISP Planet, www.isp-planet.com/research/rankings/usa.html.
3. "Bandwidth Meter Online Speed Test," *CNET Reviews,* http://reviews.cnet.com/internet-speed-test/, accessed June 2012; "Broadband Technology Overview," www.corning.com/docs/opticalfiber/wp6321.pdf, accessed February 2011
4. "Bandwidth Meter Online Speed Test," *CNET Reviews,* http://reviews.cnet.com/internet-speed-test/, accessed June 2012; "Broadband Technology Overview," www.corning.com/docs/opticalfiber/wp6321.pdf, accessed February 2011
5. "Top 23 U.S. ISPs by Subscriber: Q3 2010," *ISP Planet,* www.isp-planet.com/research/rankings/usa.html.
6. "Bandwidth Meter Online Speed Test," *CNET Reviews,* http://reviews.cnet.com/internet-speed-test/, accessed June 2012; "Broadband Technology Overview," www.corning.com/docs/opticalfiber/wp6321.pdf, accessed February 2011
7. "Bandwidth Meter Online Speed Test," *CNET Reviews,* http://reviews.cnet.com/internet-speed-test/, accessed June 2012; "Broadband Technology Overview," www.corning.com/docs/opticalfiber/wp6321.pdf, accessed February 2011
8. Chris Matyszczyk, "Marathon Winner Disqualified for Wearing iPod," *CNET News,* October 11, 2009, http://news.cnet.com/8301-17852_3-10372586-71.html; Tom Held, "Second Lakefront Marathon Winner Disqualified for iPod Use," http://www.jsonline.com/blogs/lifestyle/63668622.html, accessed June 2012.
9. www.savetheinternet.com, accessed May 2012.
10. www.godaddy.com, accessed May 2012.
11. "IP Telephony/Voice over IP (VoIP): An Introduction," *Cisco,* www.cisco.com/en/US/tech/tk652/tk701/tsd_technology_support_protocol_home.html, accessed April 2012; "VoIP Business Solutions," www.vocalocity.com, accessed January 2012.
12. "IP Telephony/Voice over IP (VoIP): An Introduction," *Cisco,* www.cisco.com/en/US/tech/tk652/tk701/tsd_technology_support_protocol_home.html, accessed April 2012; "VoIP Business Solutions," www.vocalocity.com, accessed January 2012.
13. "IP Telephony/Voice over IP (VoIP): An Introduction," *Cisco,* www.cisco.com/en/US/tech/tk652/tk701/tsd_technology_support_protocol_home.html, accessed April 2012; "VoIP Business Solutions," www.vocalocity.com, accessed January 2012.
14. Chris Silva and Benjamin Gray, "Key Wireless Trends That Will Shape Enterprise Mobility in 2008," www.forrester.com, accessed February 2012.
15. Alina Selyukh and David Ingram, "U.S. appeals court strikes down FCC net neutrality rules," *Reuters,* February 2014, http://www.reuters.com/article/2014/01/14/us-usa-court-netneutrality-idUSBREA0D11420140114.
16. Andrew McAfee, "What Every CEO Needs to Know About the Cloud,: *Harvard Business Review,* November 2011
17. Damian Joseph, "The GPS Revolution," *Bloomberg Businessweek,* May 27, 2009, www.businessweek.com/innovate/content/may2009/id20090526_735316.htm.
18. Aaron Cooper, "FCC to consider allowing cell phone calls on flights," CNN.com, November 2014, http://www.cnn.com/2013/11/21/travel/fcc-cell-phones-flights/.
19. The Liberty Coalition, "Carnivore—DCS 1000," July 27, 2006, www.libertycoalition.net/node/247.
20. "A Science Odyssey," *PBS,* www.pbs.org/wgbh/aso/databank/entries/btmarc.html.
21. "Rip Curl Turns to Skype for Global Communications," www.voipinbusiness.co.uk/rip_curl_turns_to_skype_for_gl.asp, July 7, 2006, accessed January 21, 2008; "Navigating the Mobility

Wave," www.busmanagement.com, accessed February 2012; "Sprint Plans Launch of Commercial WiMAX Service in Q2 2008," www.intomobile.com, accessed February 2012 Deepak Pareek, WiMAX: Taking Wireless to the MAX (Boca Raton, FL:CRC Press, 2006), pp. 150–93;wimax.com, accessed February 2012.

22. "Rip Curl Turns to Skype for Global Communications," www.voipinbusiness.co.uk/rip_curl_turns_to_skype_for_gl.asp, July 7, 2006, accessed January 21, 2008; "Navigating the Mobility Wave," www.busmanagement.com, accessed February 2012; "Sprint Plans Launch of Commercial WiMAX Service in Q2 2008," www.intomobile.com, accessed February 2012 Deepak Pareek, WiMAX: Taking Wireless to the MAX (Boca Raton, FL:CRC Press, 2006), pp. 150–93; wimax.com, accessed February 2012.

23. "Rip Curl Turns to Skype for Global Communications," www.voipinbusiness.co.uk/rip_curl_turns_to_skype_for_gl.asp, July 7, 2006, accessed January 21, 2008; "Navigating the Mobility Wave," www.busmanagement.com, accessed February 2012; "Sprint Plans Launch of Commercial WiMAX Service in Q2 2008," www.intomobile.com, accessed February 2012 Deepak Pareek, WiMAX: Taking Wireless to the MAX (Boca Raton, FL:CRC Press, 2006), pp. 150–93; wimax.com, accessed February 2012.

24. "Rip Curl Turns to Skype for Global Communications," www.voipinbusiness.co.uk/rip_curl_turns_to_skype_for_gl.asp, July 7, 2006, accessed January 21, 2008; "Navigating the Mobility Wave," www.busmanagement.com, accessed February 2012; "Sprint Plans Launch of Commercial WiMAX Service in Q2 2008," www.intomobile.com, accessed February 2012; Deepak Pareek, *WiMAX: Taking Wireless to the MAX* (Boca Raton, FL: CRC Press, 2006), pp. 150–93;wimax.com, accessed February 2012.

25. "Rip Curl Turns to Skype for Global Communications," www.voipinbusiness.co.uk/rip_curl_turns_to_skype_for_gl.asp, July 7, 2006, accessed January 21, 2008; "Navigating the Mobility Wave," www.busmanagement.com, accessed February 2012; "Sprint Plans Launch of Commercial WiMAX Service in Q2 2008," www.intomobile.com, accessed February 2012 Deepak Pareek, WiMAX: Taking Wireless to the MAX (Boca Raton, FL:CRC Press, 2006), pp. 150–93; wimax.com, accessed February 2012.

26. "Rip Curl Turns to Skype for Global Communications," www.voipinbusiness.co.uk/rip_curl_turns_to_skype_for_gl.asp, July 7, 2006, accessed January 21, 2008; "Navigating the Mobility Wave," www.busmanagement.com, accessed February 2012; "Sprint Plans Launch of Commercial WiMAX Service in Q2 2008," www.intomobile.com, accessed February 2012 Deepak Pareek, WiMAX: Taking Wireless to the MAX (Boca Raton, FL:CRC Press, 2006), pp. 150–93; wimax.com, accessed February 2012.

27. "Rip Curl Turns to Skype for Global Communications," www.voipinbusiness.co.uk/rip_curl_turns_to_skype_for_gl.asp, July 7, 2006, accessed January 21, 2008; "Navigating the Mobility Wave," www.busmanagement.com, accessed February 2012; "Sprint Plans Launch of Commercial WiMAX Service in Q2 2008," www.intomobile.com, accessed February 2012; Deepak Pareek, WiMAX: Taking Wireless to the MAX (Boca Raton, FL: CRC Press, 2006), pp. 150–93; wimax.com, accessed February 2012.

28. Melissa Delaney, "How Businesses Make the Most of Wireless-Networks," August 2013. http://www.biztechmagazine.com/article/2013/08/how-businesses-make-most-wireless-networks.

29. "Rip Curl Turns to Skype for Global Communications," www.voipinbusiness.co.uk/rip_curl_turns_to_skype_for_gl.asp, July 7, 2006, accessed January 21, 2008; "Navigating the Mobility Wave," www.busmanagement.com, accessed February 2012; "Sprint Plans Launch of Commercial WiMAX Service in Q2 2008," www.intomobile.com, accessed February 2012 Deepak Pareek, WiMAX: Taking Wireless to the MAX (Boca Raton, FL:CRC Press, 2006), pp. 150–93; wimax.com, accessed February 2012.

30. "Rip Curl Turns to Skype for Global Communications," www.voipinbusiness.co.uk/rip_curl_turns_to_skype_for_gl.asp, July 7, 2006, accessed January 21, 2008; "Navigating the Mobility Wave," www.busmanagement.com, accessed February 2012; "Sprint Plans Launch of Commercial WiMAX Service in Q2 2008," www.intomobile.com, accessed February 2012 Deepak Pareek, WiMAX: Taking Wireless to the MAX (Boca Raton, FL:CRC Press, 2006), pp. 150–93; wimax.com, accessed February 2012.

31. "Rip Curl Turns to Skype for Global Communications," www.voipinbusiness.co.uk/rip_curl_turns_to_skype_for_gl.asp, July 7, 2006, accessed January 21, 2008; "Navigating the Mobility Wave," www.busmanagement.com, accessed February 2012; "Sprint Plans Launch of Commercial WiMAX Service in Q2 2008," www.intomobile.com, accessed February 2012; Deepak Pareek, *WiMAX: Taking Wireless to the MAX* (Boca Raton, FL: CRC Press, 2006), pp. 150–93;wimax.com, accessed February 2012.

32. V. C. Gungor and F. C. Lambert, "A Survey on Communication Networks for Electric System Automation, Computer Networks," *International Journal of Computer and Telecommunications Networking, May 15, 2006, pp. 877–97.*

33. "Rip Curl Turns to Skype for Global Communications," www.voipinbusiness.co.uk/rip_curl_turns_to_skype_for_gl.asp, July 7, 2006, accessed January 21, 2008; "Navigating the Mobility Wave," www.busmanagement.com, accessed February 2012; "Sprint Plans Launch of Commercial WiMAX Service in Q2 2008," www.intomobile.com, accessed February 2012 Deepak Pareek, WiMAX: Taking Wireless to the MAX (Boca Raton, FL:CRC Press, 2006), pp. 150–93; wimax.com, accessed February 2012.

34. Stephan Ferris, "This High-Tech Tennis Racket Comes With a Built-In Digital Coach," *Bloomberg Businessweek,* June 2014. http://www.businessweek.com/articles/2014-06-05/babolat-tennis-rackets-sensors-measure-swing-speed-strength.

35. Michael Dortch, "Winning RFID Strategies for 2008," *Benchmark Report,* December 31, 2007.

36. Melissa Delaney, "How Businesses Make the Most of Wireless Networks," August 2013. http://www.biztechmagazine.com/article/2013/08/how-businesses-make-most-wireless-networks.

37. Natasha Lomas, "Location Based Services to Boom in 2008," *Bloomberg Businessweek,* February 11, 2008, www.businessweek.com/globalbiz/content/feb2008/gb20080211_420894.htm.

38. Natasha Lomas, "Location Based Services to Boom in 2008," Bloomberg Businessweek, February 11, 2008, www.businessweek.com/globalbiz/content/feb2008/gb20080211_420894.htm.

39. Natasha Lomas, "Location Based Services to Boom in 2008," *Bloomberg Businessweek,* February 11, 2008, http://www.businessweek.com/globalbiz/content/feb2008/gb20080211_420894.htm.

CHAPTER 8

1. Michael E. Porter, "The Five Competitive Forces That Shape Strategy," The Harvard Business Review Book Series, *Harvard Business Review,* January 2008; Michael E. Porter, "Competitive Strategy: Techniques for Analyzing Industries and Competitors," *Harvard Business Review,* January 2002; Michael E. Porter, *On Competition,* The Harvard Business Review Book

Series (Harvard Business Press, 1985); Harvard Institute for Strategy and Competitiveness, www.isc.hbs.edu/, accessed June 2010.

2. "Ups Researching Its Own Delivery Drones To Compete With Amazon's Prime Air" by Ben Popper, The Verge, December 03, 2013. http://www.theverge.com/2013/12/3/5169878/ups-is-researching-its-own-delivery-drones-to-compete-with-amazons?source=email_rt_mc_body&app=n
3. "Kiva—Loans That Change Lives," www.kiva.org, accessed April 2013.
4. Link for reference: https://www.technologyreview.com/s/527336/do-we-need-asimovs-laws/
5. "Post Office Losses Reach $4.7B for Year," *CBS News,* August 5, 2009, http://www.cbsnews.com/stories/2009/08/05/national/main5216012.shtml.
6. Rachel King, "Saving Face Online," *BusinessWeek,* www.businessweek.com/magazine/, accessed June 2010.
7. Timothy Keiningham and Lerzan Aksoy, "When Customer Loyalty Is a Bad Thing," *Bloomberg Businessweek,* May 8, 2009.
8. The Balanced Scorecard, www.balancedscorecard.org, accessed February 2010.

CHAPTER 9

1. "Four Steps to Getting Things on Track," *Bloomberg Businessweek,* July 7, 2010, www.businessweek.com/idg/2010-07-07/project-management-4-steps-to-getting-things-on-track.html.
2. www.ted.com, accessed June 2012.
3. CIO Magazine, June 1, 2006; "The Project Manager in the IT Industry," www.standishgroup.com; G. McGraw, "Making Essential Software Work," *EETimes,* September 2010; "Overcoming Software Development Problems," www.samspublishing.com, accessed October 2012; Agile Alliance Manifesto, www.agile.com, accessed November 2012; IBM Rational Unified Process, http://www-01.ibm.com/software/awdtools/rup/, accessed January 2013.
4. Ibid.
5. Jose Martinez, "Lesson in Fraud: NYU Employee Submitted $409K in Fake Expenses Using Receipts from Garbage," *Daily News,* December 23, 2009.
6. CharityFocus.org, www.charityfocus.org/new/, accessed June 2012.
7. Jose Martinez, "Lesson in Fraud: NYU Employee Submitted $409K in Fake Expenses Using Receipts from Garbage," *Daily News,* December 23, 2009.
8. "Overcoming Software Development Problems," www.samspublishing.com, accessed October 2012
9. Karl Ritter, "Bill Murray Faces DUI after Golf-Cart Escapade in Sweden," *The Seattle Times,* August 22, 2007, http://seattletimes.nwsource.com/html/entertainment/2003848077_webmurray22.html.

index

A

B

C

D

E

F

G

H

I

J

K

L

M

Q

R

S

T

U

V

W

X

Y

Z